ESSENTIAL
SCANDINAVIA

1st Edition

**Where to Stay and Eat
for All Budgets**

**Must-See Sights
and Local Secrets**

Ratings You Can Trust

Fodor's Travel Publications   New York, Toronto, London, Sydney, Auckland
www.fodors.com

FODOR'S ESSENTIAL SCANDINAVIA

Editors: Kelly Kealy, Laura Kidder, Molly Moker

Editorial Contributors: Lindsay Bennett, Robert Brenner, Linda Coffman, Ralph Grizzle, Rob Hincks, Kay Xander Mellish, Laura Stadler-Jensen, Audrey Tempelsman, Sarah Lookofsky

Production Editor: Jennifer DePrima

Maps & Illustrations: David Lindroth, *cartographers*; Bob Blake, Rebecca Baer, *map editors*; William Wu, *information graphics*

Design: Fabrizio La Rocca, *creative director*; Guido Caroti, Siobhan O'Hare, *art directors*; Tina Malaney, Chie Ushio, Ann McBride, Jessica Walsh, *designers*; Melanie Marin, *senior picture editor*

Cover Photo (Church in Sogn of Fjordane, Norway): Simon Matthews/iStockphoto. (Viking ship, Oslo, Norway): Kim Hart/fototeca9x12. (Road sign): Povi E. Petersen/Shutterstock. (Vodka): Mikael Damkier/Shutterstock. (Stockholm): Mikael Damkier/iStockphoto. (Chair): Knoll. (Finnish sauna): Bojan Tezak/iStockphoto. (Mittens): Erik W. Kolstad/Shutterstock. (Puffin): Fred Didier/iStockphoto.

Production Manager: Angela L. McLean

COPYRIGHT

1st Edition

ISBN 978-1-4000-0883-4

ISSN 1943-0078

SPECIAL SALES

This book is available at special discounts for bulk purchases for sales promotions or premiums. Special editions, including personalized covers, excerpts of existing books, and corporate imprints, can be created in large quantities for special needs. For more information, write to Special Markets/Premium Sales, 1745 Broadway, MD 6-2, New York, New York 10019, or e-mail specialmarkets@randomhouse.com.

AN IMPORTANT TIP & AN INVITATION

Although all prices, opening times, and other details in this book are based on information supplied to us at press time, changes occur all the time in the travel world, and Fodor's cannot accept responsibility for facts that become outdated or for inadvertent errors or omissions. So **always confirm information when it matters,** especially if you're making a detour to visit a specific place. Your experiences—positive and negative— matter to us. If we have missed or misstated something, **please write to us.** We follow up on all suggestions. Contact the Essential Scandinavia editor at editors@fodors.com or c/o Fodor's at 1745 Broadway, New York, NY 10019.

PRINTED IN THE UNITED STATES OF AMERICA

10 9 8 7 6 5 4 3 2 1

Be a Fodor's Correspondent

Your opinion matters. It matters to us. It matters to your fellow Fodor's travelers, too. And we'd like to hear it. In fact, we need to hear it.

When you share your experiences and opinions, you become an active member of the Fodor's community. That means we'll not only use your feedback to make our books better, but we'll publish your names and comments whenever possible. Throughout our guides, look for "Word of Mouth," excerpts of your unvarnished feedback.

Here's how you can help improve Fodor's for all of us.

Tell us when we're right. We rely on local writers to give you an insider's perspective. But our writers and staff editors—who are the best in the business—depend on you. Your positive feedback is a vote to renew our recommendations for the next edition.

Tell us when we're wrong. We're proud that we update most of our guides every year. But we're not perfect. Things change. Hotels cut services. Museums change hours. Charming cafés lose charm. If our writer didn't quite capture the essence of a place, tell us how you'd do it differently. If any of our descriptions are inaccurate or inadequate, we'll incorporate your changes in the next edition and will correct factual errors at fodors.com immediately.

Tell us what to include. You probably have had fantastic travel experiences that aren't yet in Fodor's. Why not share them with a community of like-minded travelers? Maybe you chanced upon a beach or bistro or B&B that you don't want to keep to yourself. Tell us why we should include it. And share your discoveries and experiences with everyone directly at fodors.com. Your input may lead us to add a new listing or highlight a place we cover with a "Highly Recommended" star or with our highest rating, "Fodor's Choice."

Give us your opinion instantly at our feedback center at www.fodors.com/feedback. You may also e-mail editors@fodors.com with the subject line "Essential Scandinavia Editor." Or send your nominations, comments, and complaints by mail to Essential Scandinavia Editor, Fodor's, 1745 Broadway, New York, NY 10019.

You and travelers like you are the heart of the Fodor's community. Make our community richer by sharing your experiences. Be a Fodor's correspondent.

Happy Traveling!

Tim Jarrell, Publisher

CONTENTS

MAPS

WHAT'S
WHERE

1 **Denmark.** The Kingdom of Denmark dapples the Baltic Sea in an archipelago of some 450 islands and the arc of one peninsula. For almost 600 years Copenhagen (pop. 1.5 million) has been the seat of this kingdom. Coziness is a Danish trait, and you'll find lots of it in Copenhagen's canals, cafés, and narrow streets. But don't let the low-slung skyline fool you: downtown Copenhagen is a sophisticated cultural hub. North of Copenhagen, which is on the island of Zealand, are royal castles, ritzy beach towns, and top-notch museums. Funen, the smaller of the country's two main islands, is the birthplace of Hans Christian Andersen and its coastline and gardens are the inspiration for fairy tales. Jutland is Denmark's western peninsula, and its hub is Billund, home to Legoland. In North Jutland you'll find the city of Aalborg, full of vitality. At the country's northernmost point stands Skagen, a luminous, dune-covered place that attracts artists and those seeking the sea.

2 **Norway.** Norway, roughly 400,000 square km (155,000 square mi), is about the same size as California. Western Norway is the fabled land of the fjords, and storybook Bergen is known as the region's fjord capital. Less mountainous eastern Norway is where you'll find the country's real capital, Oslo, a friendly and manageable city. Kristiansand is to Oslo's south in the Sørlandet region, known for its long, unspoiled stretches of beach. Halfway between Oslo and Bergen lies Hardangervidda (Hardanger Plateau), Norway's largest national park. Head to nearby Geilo for skiing, or farther north to chilly yet charming Trondheim. From here, a thin expanse of land stretches up to the Nordkapp (North Cape), where you can take in the Midnight Sun and one of the world's wildest landscapes.

3 **Sweden.** Stockholm's 14 small islands contain its bustling, skyscraper-lined boulevards and twisting medieval streets. South of the capital city, in the densely forested Småland province, you'll find fine crystal glassware by Kosta, Boda, and Orrefors. Continue south to Skåne province for lush farmland, coastal headlands, golden beaches, and historic castles. Sweden's second-largest city, Göteborg, was a Viking port in the 11th century, and today is Scandinavia's busiest shipping city and a cultural hub. North of Göteborg, the Bohuslän region has a rocky coastline dotted with attractive fishing

villages; head south for prime beach time along the Swedish Riviera. Dalarna, the central region of Sweden, is the focal point of most of the country's myth, symbolism, and tradition.

4 **Finland.** Finland is a provocative blend of past and present, urban and natural. In Helsinki, the country's capital and largest city, enjoy innovative, clean-lined design in everything from clothing to kitchenware and a burgeoning Modern Finnish cuisine. Yet the heart of its mobile phone- and coffee-loving people lies in the serenity of cottages beside its roughly 200,000 lakes, to which most of its 5 million citizens retreat to fish and enjoy their beloved saunas each summer. Lapland, north of the Arctic Circle, is Europe's largest wilderness and home to Santa Claus, cross-country and downhill skiing and, in winter, the brilliant Northern Lights.

QUINTESSENTIAL SCANDINAVIA

Beer & Aquavit

Aquavit is a Scandinavian liquor of about 40% alcohol by volume. Its name comes from aqua vitae (Latin for "water of life"). Like other liquors made in Scandinavia, it is distilled from potatoes or grains and is flavored with herbs such as caraway seeds, cumin, dill, fennel, or coriander. Aquavit, or akvavit, is an acquired taste. It's usually drunk as a shot, or as the Danes say, a "snaps," during meals—especially during the appetizer course—along with a chaser of beer.

There's a renewed interest in the Danish national drink: beer (or øl in Danish). Danes are rarely short of an excuse for a beer celebration, and Christmas and Easter are no exceptions, when both Carlsberg and Tuborg breweries release special holiday beers. Microbreweries have popped up all over the country, and even in Copenhagen, where Carlsberg

beer was founded in the early 19th century, loyalty for that stalwart is wavering in favor of newer flavors and brands. Independent microbreweries in Copenhagen alone include Nørrebro Bryghus, Vesterbro Bryghys, Bryggeriet Apollo, and Færgekroen (in Tivoli). Denmark now has more breweries per capita than any other European country.

Design

If there's one word associated with Sweden around the world, it is *design*. Even the most unobservant of visitors can't fail to notice a design sensibility that seems to pervade every corner of the nation; from the airport you land in to the furnishings in your hotel room to the table setting in the restaurant, most things Swedish have an air of the simply fabulous. Focused product design started early in Sweden with the graceful curves of the Viking ships. The 20th-century Swedish

utilitarian vision of society cemented the nation's aesthetic approach. As Sweden prospered, and as more homes were built, Swedish designers made objects in which functionality was blended with a guarded, well-planned modern aesthetic. The rest of Sweden quickly followed suit, and the Swedish consumer was bombarded with practical but seductive objects, from Ericsson phones and Electrolux refrigerators to SAAB cars and affordable IKEA practicality. Design also encompasses many facets of Danish life, like lighting, electronics, and everyday household items. The Danish-design aesthetic itself is simple and inventive, marked by clean lines. Even the local grocery store will impress you with "Made in Denmark" kitchen items that somehow look so much better than the fare sold back home.

Saunas

An authentic Finnish sauna is an obligatory experience, and not hard to find: there are 1.6 million saunas in this country of just over 5 million people. The traditional Finnish sauna—which involves relaxing on wooden benches, pouring water onto hot coals, and swatting your neighbor's back with birch branches—is an integral part of cabin life and now city life. Almost every hotel has at least one free sauna available, usually at standard times in the morning or evening for men and women to use separately. Larger hotels offer private saunas in the higher-class rooms and suites. Public saunas (swimsuits required) are becoming increasingly popular, even in winter, when sauna goers jump into the water through a large hole in the ice (called *avantouinti*). Public swimming pools are also equipped with saunas that can be used at no extra charge. For information, contact the Finnish Sauna Society.

GREAT ITINERARIES

SAND, SURF & SHIPS, SCANDINAVIA-STYLE

Scandinavia is defined by water. Glaciers, rivers, and sea tides determine the geography; oceans shape the history and culture. Tiny Denmark, for example, would probably not exist as a country today, except for the way it sticks up like a cork in the bottleneck entrance to the Baltic Sea. Its shape makes it strategically important for such major shipping and trading countries as England, which has both attacked and defended the country over trading issues during the past 400 years. What better way, then, to see the land of the Vikings than by water?

Denmark
3 days. Fly to Copenhagen. Explore the city and its waterways: Nyhavn's tall ships and myriad restaurants; Christianshavn, with its encircling moat and canals reflecting colorful old buildings; and the canal-ringed palace of Christiansborg, where you can visit the Danish Parliament and the royal reception rooms. Enjoy the twinkling lights and happy atmosphere of Tivoli from mid-April through mid-September and its frostier but less-crowded attributes several weeks before Christmas. Take a harbor cruise, passing *Den Lille Havfrue* (*The Little Mermaid*), perched on her rock. Sun on the beaches north of town or sail the Øresund—maybe even all the way around Sjælland. You'll love the castle of Frederiksborg, set in its lake a little less than an hour north of Copenhagen, and the Karen Blixen Museum at Rungstedlund. Continue by air to Stockholm.

Sweden
6 days. Beautiful Stockholm is made up of 14 islands surrounded by sparkling water, clean enough for fishing and swimming even in the city center. You can take ferries all around town and out into the enchanting archipelago, with its 24,000 islands. Don't miss the picturesque Old Town; the museum for the salvaged 17th-century warship *Vasa*; or Skansen, the world's oldest open-air museum.

From Stockholm, take the train across Sweden to Göteborg, where you can explore the west-coast beaches warmed by the Gulf Stream. Be sure to try sea fishing or windsurfing. Take a ferry to Oslo.

Norway
5 days. In Oslo, visit the Viking Ship and Kon-Tiki museums and the fabulous Vigeland sculpture park. The Bergen Railway will carry you across the roof of Norway in 6½ dramatic hours. If you can spare an extra day, stop in Myrdal for a side trip on the Flåm Railway and a cruise on a fjord before continuing to Bergen. Here you can explore Bryggen, a collection of reconstructed houses dating from the Hansa period in the 14th century, the famous fish market, and the funicular. View the magnificent, ever-changing Norwegian coastline aboard a Coastal Express ship to Trondheim, where you can fly to Oslo or Copenhagen, then home.

Gotland & Örland

Alternate days. If you already know Stockholm, consider visiting the beautiful islands of Gotland and Örland. Gotland is the largest island in the Baltic, with peaceful little towns and fishing villages, and a striking capital, Visby, with a medieval flavor and a well-preserved city wall dating from the 14th and 15th centuries. "Medieval Week" in early August is celebrated with mummers, knights, tournaments, and lots of other special attractions. Ferries sail from Stockholm and several other Swedish ports.

Örland is a farther-away destination, and will involve renting a car (the bus takes a long time, and a taxi to here would be prohibitively expensive). Alternately, if you head there right from Gotland, a ferry sometimes runs between Visby (on Gotland) and Oskarshamn (near Kalmar, right across the channel from Örland), though you'd still need to rent a car to

get to Kalmar. However you get there, cross from Kalmar to Örland on the E22 road across the bridge and explore Sweden's smallest province. Not to be missed is Borgholms Slott, the largest castle ruin in Northern Europe.

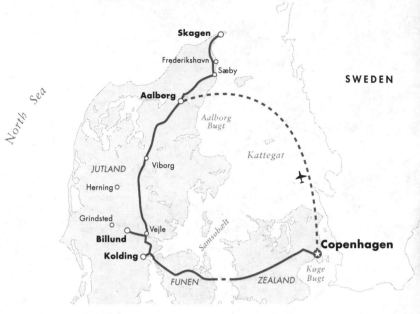

DENMARK CLASSIC

Day 1

Start off an ideal weeklong itinerary of Denmark in magical Copenhagen. The city is safe, walkable, historic, and pretty. You can get oriented by traipsing around on your own or taking a guided walking or bus tour. Make time to people-watch in the Tivoli Gardens.

Day 2

Today, continue to explore Copenhagen. Feel like royalty at Christiansborg Slot, where you can don slippers and tour the Royal Reception Chambers (be sure to check the complicated opening hours before making a visit). Or go antiestablishment and head out to Christiania, a fascinating anarchists' commune in Christianshavn. In the evening, indulge in Danish cuisine at one of Copenhagen's cutting-edge restaurants, such as the Paul, Restaurant Herman, or Kong Hans Kælder.

Day 3

On your third day, head to the Jutland region at the top of the country: take an hour-long flight to Aalborg, and then drive or take the train to Skagen (pronounced Skane). Here you find immense skies, fantastic sunsets, and a lovely, seaside ambience that has been attracting savvy travelers for years. Spend the rest of the day exploring the town, whether it's ambling along the pebble beaches or ducking into the Skagen Museum, which shows broad impressionist canvases from talented 19th-century Danish artists.

Day 4

Take the morning and early afternoon to finish soaking up Skagen. You could meander around on a bike or see the famous Danish artists Michael and Anna Ancher's House, which includes Anna's studio. Head back to Aalborg late in the day via car or train. The nightlife scene is pretty good here, if you decide to stay overnight; otherwise, have a bite to eat, and then fly, drive or take the train to Billund, home of Legoland.

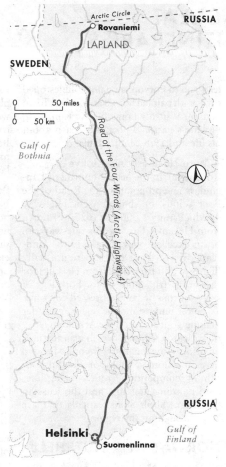

Day 5

Today, it's all about toys: you're off to Legoland. The whimsical display of meticulous miniature cities and villages from around the world is a must-see, even if you aren't traveling with children. Take a train back to Copenhagen this evening to catch your flight home tomorrow.

Alternative. If you'd rather have a taste of the Danish rural countryside, head south by train to Kolding instead of Legoland. This town has a little of everything, including a wonderful modern art museum, good shopping, and country inns. The train ride back to Copenhagen from here is a little over two hours, and allows you a chance to see the countryside before you get back to the big city.

FINLAND GREAT ITINERARY

Days 1–3

A definite first-day experience in Helsinki should be Havis Amanda, the iconic girl-and-dolphins fountain that was sculpted by Ville Vallgren and completed in 1908. Don't miss Finlandiatalo, the concert hall designed by Finland's greatest architect, Alvar Aalto; the Temppeliaukio Kirkko, hollowed out from rock with only its dome showing; or the magnificent sculpture commemorating the composer Jean Sibelius. The Gallen-Kallela Estate is a studio-castle in the National Romantic style built on a rocky peninsula. It was designed by the artist Akseli Gallen-Kallela for his paintings, drawings, sculpture, textiles, and furniture. Fine china and pottery are displayed at the Hackman Factory Shop Arabia, and you can see fine textiles being made at the Marimekko factory. Most of all, make sure you leave

plenty of time over these first few days to relax with a coffee by the waterfront, taking in the city's beautiful, Russian-influenced architecture.

Days 4 & 5

From Helsinki take a ferry to Suomenlinna, a former island fortress from 1748. You can easily while away an afternoon threading in and out of the remains of the fortress and the beautiful lilacs that blanket the island seasonally. If trains or cobblestones are your thing, ride the historical museum rails (summer Saturdays only) in old cars from the 1950s and '60s; they will

GREAT ITINERARIES

lead you to Porvoo, a quaint cobblestoned town with painted houses and an Old Town Square. Visit the home of J.L. Runeberg, Finland's national poet, and learn about his life and 19th-century Finland.

A More Northerly Alternative

Rovaniemi, in the heart of northern Lapland, is an end point for the Road of the Four Winds, or, simply, Arctic Highway 4, which runs 1,000 km (625 mi) north from Helsinki. Driving this one-way can be an excellent way to take in the landscape, if you have time; there are daily flights to and from here from Helsinki for the return trip south or for both legs of your journey if you're pressed for time. To better understand the region, consider making your first stop the Arktikum (Arctic Research Center), which also features an informative museum. If you're headed here in summer, look for the salmon-fishing competition, reindeer herding, gold panning, logging, and the Russian Orthodox Skolt Sámi festivals that are held throughout the region.

NORWAY IN A NUTSHELL

The famous Norway in a Nutshell tour was devised by Norwegian State Railways ⊕*www.nsb.no*, or NSB, in the 1960s, and has since become the most popular way to see Norway, both for independent travelers and for those taking part in a guided trip. Tickets can be purchased through myriad agencies, including NSB's own tour company, **Fjord Tours AS** ⊕*www. norwaynutshell.com*, and tourist information offices throughout the country.

Essentially a highlights tour, you can complete the trip in one whirlwind day, but we suggest taking a more leisurely six-day tour. You can start from either Oslo or Bergen and do a one-way or round-trip tour. Below we've outlined the most popular route, one-way from Oslo to Bergen.

Days 1 & 2: Oslo

Norway's capital makes a good starting point since most flights to Norway arrive here. Spend your first two days exploring the city. Take it easy on the first day by exploring the downtown area—meander on Karl Johans Gate, see Akershus Castle and the Kvadraturen, and walk through Vigelands (Frogner) Park. On your second day, head out to Bygdøy and visit the area's museums.

Day 3: Oslo to Flåm

On your third day, start early and take the Bergen train line to Flåm. Note that when you reach Myrdal, you have to transfer to the Flåm railway. The five-hour trip across Norway's interior between Oslo and Bergen passes over the Hardangervidda plateau and is considered one of the most spectacular train rides in the world. It only gets better on the Flåm railway, which winds between towering mountains and immense fjords, passing cascading waterfalls and tiny villages. The trip from Myrdal to Flåm covers 20 km (12 mi) and takes 53 minutes. You should reach Flåm by late afternoon, giving you enough time to relax in an outdoor café, do a little souvenir shopping, and perhaps see the Flåmsbanemuseet, or Flåm Railway Museum, which gives you a look at how the Flåm railway was engineered.

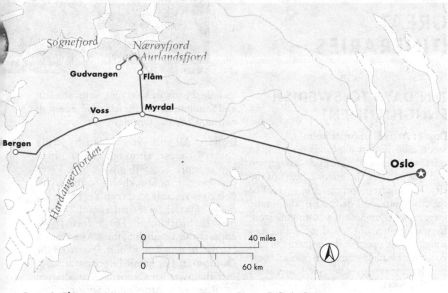

Day 4: Flåm to Voss

This leg of your journey begins with a boat trip from Flåm through Aurlandsfjord and into the Nærøyfjord, the narrowest fjord in Europe. Both inlets are part of the larger Sognefjord, one of Norway's most famous fjords and, at 204 km (127 mi), its longest. The ride lasts two hours and ends at Gudvangen, at which point you board a bus for the one-hour trip to Voss up the Nærøyfjord Valley and along the old Stalheimskleivane Road with its dramatic hairpin bends. If you can, try to book your stay at the 18th-century Stalheim Hotel, 36 km (22 mi) outside Voss.

Days 5 & 6: Bergen

From Voss, the train to Bergen takes one hour. When you get to Bergen, check into your hotel and head to Bryggen for dinner. Here along Bergen's wharf are some of the city's oldest and best-preserved buildings. Spend your sixth day exploring Bergen. If you have time, visit Troldhaugen, which was composer Edvard Grieg's house for 22 years; it's a half-day trip from Bergen's center.

GREAT ITINERARIES

TEN DAYS TO SWEDISH ENLIGHTENMENT

Day 1: Arrival in Stockholm

Stockholm is best explored on foot, so start with a walk around downtown and Gamla Stan, the historic heart of the city. In the afternoon, take in several of the city's museums or head to the serene greenery of Djurgården, a 20-minute walk from the center of town. Fine dining and a night at the opera will complete the day. For a more budget-conscious option, some people-watching over beers in Stureplan is just the ticket.

Logistics. The best way to get downtown from the airport is by the express train, Arlanda Express. Stockholm's metro and bus networks are excellent; tickets are available for single rides, 10 rides, or unlimited travel for 24 or 72 hours. Better still is the Stockholm Card (Stockholmskortet) with 24 or 48 hours of unlimited travel and free entry to more than 60 museums included in the price.

Days 2–5: Royalty, Antiquity & the Archipelago

Don't miss Skansen, Stockholm's fantastic open-air museum, and Drottningholms Slott, home to Sweden's royal family and one of the most delightful palaces in Europe. Also of interest is the view from the top of Stadshuset, the city hall. Spend the afternoon strolling through Sigtuna, Sweden's oldest town, or Uppsala, the site of one of Europe's oldest universities.

At least one afternoon—or a few days, if you have the time—should be spent exploring the archipelago; to do this you can rent a small boat (strong arms required), charter a boat (well in advance), or hop on a ferry between islands (our favorite spots include the towns Vaxholm, Saltsjobaden, and Sandhamn, and the islands Fjäderholmarna, Utö, and Grinda).

Logistics: All this ground can be easily covered by car, although the archipelago is more accessible by water. Ferry transport from Stockholm to the archipelago is reliable and regular. There are many boat charter and rental companies in Stockholm. For information, contact the Swedish Sailing Association (⇨ *Boating in Stockholm Sports & the Outdoors*). For small-boat rental, contact the Swedish Canoeing Association (⇨ *Boating in Stockholm Sports & the Outdoors*). There are many daily trains between Stockholm and Uppsala (the journey is less than an hour). Drottningholms Slott can be reached by ferry from Stockholm's center.

Days 6–8: Driving Dalarna

Pick up a rental car in Stockholm and head northwest to Dalarna. The goal is to circle Lake Siljan. If you have a few days, there are plenty of fun stops along the way (and you can visit Uppsala, if you haven't yet, outside of Stockholm). Some highlights include a visit to a Dala horse factory in Nusnäs; a swim at Sollerön; and a lakeside picnic in front of the beautiful Leksand Kyrka. Be sure to make a detour to see the Carl Larsson Gården, a short drive southeast of Tällberg on Route 80, in the village of Sundborn.

Logistics: Driving time between Stockholm and the Dalarna region is about three hours. Both Avis and Europcar have one-way drop-off facilities at Dala Airport if you decide to skip the drive back to Stockholm and fly directly out of Dala Airport.

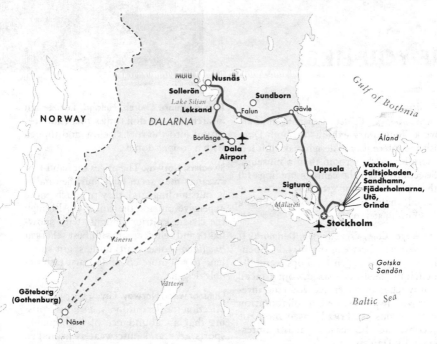

Days 9 & 10: Fresh Seafood & Beaches in Göteborg

Fly from Stockholm or from Dala Airport to Göteborg. This is your official welcome to the west coast. Spend the day exploring the city's dock district, the cultural Vasastan neighborhood, and the rejuvenated Haga and Linné areas. Be sure to sample the local fish at one of the city's fantastic restaurants.

The next day, get out of town. Try Näset, a wonderful beach 7 mi southwest of town, taking Bus 19 (which leaves every 20 minutes from 7 AM to 8 PM daily). A dip in the Atlantic will gear you up for an afternoon of museum-hopping back in town; be sure to check out Röhsska Museet and Konstmuseet.

Logistics: Göteborg's tram system is a cheap and fun way to get around. A Göteborg Pass includes unlimited public transport, plus entry to many museums around town. If you are traveling on foot, keep an eye out for trams, which can appear unexpectedly.

TIPS

Speed limits and alcohol levels are strictly enforced by Swedish police.

Many museums are closed on Mondays and are busy in the afternoons with school visits.

Water is plentiful and clean in Sweden. Always carry your bathing suit in case you want to take a dip.

Sweden's constitution upholds the right to roam. Do as the Swedes do and explore any beach, field, forest, lake, or river that strikes your fancy.

Off season and away from major cities, many attractions keep limited hours. Check in advance to be certain.

IF YOU LIKE

Design

Dansk Design Center, Copenhagen, Denmark. Temporary exhibits on both Danish and international design make this feel more like a showroom than a museum. Selections from the center's holdings fill the semipermanent ground-floor space. (Think chairs by Arne Jacobsen and Bang & Olufsen stereos.)

The Royal Café, Copenhagen, Denmark. If the setting—between the Royal Copenhagen and Georg Jensen shops—and the delicious sushi-ish–sized, open-faced sandwiches don't entice you, the interior will. It was created in collaboration with legends like Fritz Hansen and Arne Jacobsen to showcase what is quintessentially Danish.

Museet for Moderne Kunst, Denmark. The building recalls a ship, which is appropriate to the location on the coast 20 km (12 mi) southwest of Copenhagen. Come for the modern sculpture—particularly the works by Danish artists.

Trapholt Museum for Moderne Kunst, Kolding, Denmark. The country's largest modern-art museum has 20th-century Danish paintings, a renowned Danish furniture collection, and a large ceramics collection.

Design District, Helsinki. The artist- and designer-owned shops of this shopping district—and their personable proprietors—beckon.

Fiskars Village, Finland. Consider a day-trip to a picturesque medieval town where you can peruse design exhibits and the personal shops of artisans-in-residence such as glass-blowers, jewelry makers, and blacksmiths.

Temple Square Church, Finland. For design in architecture, don't miss this church—carved into the rocks below and topped with a copper dome.

Sweaters, Norway. The prices for hand-knit sweaters may seem high, but the quality is outstanding and they're much more expensive outside the country. Although the classic knitting designs, with snowflakes and reindeer, are still best sellers at *husfliden* (home-craft) outlets, gift stores tend to sell more contemporary, fashionable designs.

Outdoor wear, Norway. Given Norwegians' affection for the outdoors, it's not surprising that an abundance of high-quality sports gear and outerwear is available. Good buys include Helly Hansen rain gear, insulated boots, and the *supertrøye,* a gossamer-thin insulated undershirt.

Crafts, Norway. Look for embroidered cloth; pewter and wrought-iron candlesticks; candles; glass; and wood bowls, spoons, and platters made of birch roots, decorated with rosemaling. Other, more offbeat, items include *ostehøvler* (cheese slicers) and *kransekakeformer,* graduated forms for making almond ring cakes.

Stadshuset, Stockholm. Ragnar Östberg's ornately designed yet functional 1923 town-hall building has become an unofficial symbol of Stockholm. A trip to the top of the tower is rewarded by a breathtaking panorama of the city.

The Kingdom of Glass, Sweden. A 113-km (70-mi) stretch of densely forested land is home to Sweden's world-famous glass industry. Visitors here can enjoy superb glass and crystal design and experience glassblowing first-hand before picking up some original examples to take home.

History

Nationalmuseet, Copenhagen. For the historian in you rather than the linguist, immerse yourself in the Viking exhibits labeled in English; one exhibit shows how the Vikings could navigate their ships across vast oceans at a time when most people believed the world was flat.

Vikingeskibshallen, Denmark. Take the hour-long train ride north of Copenhagen to the Vikingeskibshallen (Viking Ship Museum) in Roskilde, where five ships found in the Roskilde Fjord and dating from around AD 1000 have been restored.

Viking Royalty, Denmark. Rent a car or take a train and stay overnight in Vejle, on the large peninsula of Jylland; then head for Jelling, where two Viking kings—Gorm the Old and his son, Harald Bluetooth—reigned. They left two large burial mounds and two runic stones, dating from around AD 950.

Nobel History, Oslo. Head to the Rådhuset (City Hall) to see the place where the Nobel Peace Prize is awarded every December. To really appreciate the experience, though, consider a stop first at the Nobels Fredssenter (Nobel Peace Center) for some high-tech, interactive exhibits.

Vikings, Norway. For the authoritative Viking run-down in Oslo, go straight to Vikingskiphuset (Viking Ship Museum), which has the finest single collection of excavated and preserved Viking ships, once used as tombs for nobles.

Iron age, Gotland, Sweden. If you take the ferry out to the island of Gotland, southeast of Stockholm, you'll be rewarded not just with natural beauty but with the opportunity to walk among deserted Iron Age homesteads and trading places. Head to the Länsmuseet på Gotland, the local museum, for more on this and other illustrious periods in Gotland's history.

Drottningholms Slott, West of Stockholm. This delightful confection is full of insights into how mid-18th-century royalty lived. Today's royal family moved here from Stockholm, so if you see the curtains twitching, it's probably them observing how 21st-century subjects live.

Frederiksborg Slot, Denmark. One of the few of Denmark's Castles you can truly say is beautiful contains the National History Museum. In addition to portraits and historical paintings, the museum also has an activity area where kids can dress up as historical figures.

Kronborg Slot, Denmark. This gloomy, chilly pile was the inspiration for Elsinore Castle in Shakespeare's *Hamlet*. It's complete with cannon-studded bastions, an enormous dining hall, and, of course, dungeons.

Russian Influence, Finland. From the double-headed eagle of the Czarina's Stone to a regal statue of Czar Alexander II, Helsinki is dotted with picturesque reminders of its near-century under Russian rule.

Finland's Castle, Finland. The storied past of the magnificent Suomenlinna (Finland's Castle), including its 40-year construction and two major battles, breathes within the fortress' parks, gardens, and museums.

Turku Castle, Finland. Built partially in the 13th century and partially in the 16th, Turun Linna (Turku Castle) is a larger-than-life testament to the historical importance of Finland's original capital.

IF YOU LIKE

The Outdoors

The Island of Møn, south of Copenhagen. Hunt for fossils on the craggy beach while enjoying the salt air, the beech forests, and the chalk white cliffs. Duck into the GeoCenter Møns Klint, a small natural history museum, and have your fossil finds identified.

The Lakes District of Jutland, Denmark. From the town of Silkeborg, take one of the excursion boats or the world's last coal-fired paddle steamer, *Hjejlen*, which departs in summer (mid-June through August) from the harbor.

Plage Robinson, Denmark. Just west of Tangier, this much-visited beach offers sun and sand, the Grottes d'Hercules where mythology has Hercules resting up after separating Africa from Europe, and a lively café and restaurant scene.

Hiking in Jotunheimen or Rondane national parks, Norway. The jagged peaks of Jotunheimen and the rounded mountains of Rondane offer countless wonderful hiking opportunities for all skill levels.

Fishing inland and off the coast, Norway. Some 200 species of saltwater fish live and breed along the coast, particularly cod, pollack, and the smeltlike capelin. Near Geilo and Lillehammer are rivers and lakes well stocked with salmon, trout, Arctic char, pike, grayling, whitefish, and perch.

Orienteering, Norway. One of Norway's most popular mass-participation sports is based on running or hiking over territory with a map and compass to find control points marked on a map. Special cards can be purchased at sports shops, which you can then punch at control points found during an orienteering season.

Skiing in the birthplace of the sport, Norway. Norway's ski slopes are the stuff of legend. If you're brave enough to visit Norway in winter, you'll definitely want to plan a trip to Lillehammer, Geilo, Rondane, or Hallingdal.

Island Hopping, Archipelago, Stockholm. Beauty and sheer relaxation don't come any better than this. Whether you hitch a ride or charter your own boat, exploring the 25,000 islands of Stockholm's archipelago is among the greatest Swedish adventures.

Kayaking, Sweden. Gotland, Sweden's rugged, cliff-faced holiday island is the perfect place for sea kayaking. Views of the island from the water beat those of the water from the island—and nothing beats a Gotland sunset from a bobbing boat of your own.

Wilderness expeditions, Finland. Take a photo safari to capture the unrivaled landscape, canoe down the clear waters filled with salmon and trout, forage for mushrooms in the forest, or pick cloudberries and lingonberries in the bogs.

Ice fishing, Finland. The fish-rich waters of the Baltic archipelago and innumerable inland lakes and streams assure you will never run out of places to go fishing. The waters of the Ålands are especially rich with pike, whitefish, salmon, and perch, and ice fishing makes this a year-round sport.

Adventures in Lapland, Finland. Opportunities to explore the forests and moors, rapids and waterfalls, mountains and gorges of Finland's Lapland abound. Intrepid explorers can probe the deepest areas of the national forests on skis or by snowmobile.

ABOUT THIS BOOK

Our Ratings

Sometimes you find terrific travel experiences and sometimes they just find you. But usually the burden is on you to select the right combination of experiences. That's where our ratings come in.

As travelers we've all discovered a place so wonderful that its worthiness is obvious. And sometimes that place is so unique that superlatives don't do it justice: you just have to be there to know. These sights, properties, and experiences get our highest rating, **Fodor's Choice**, indicated by orange stars throughout this book.

Black stars highlight sights and properties we deem **Highly Recommended**, places that our writers, editors, and readers praise again and again for consistency and excellence.

By default, there's another category: any place we include in this book is by definition worth your time, unless we say otherwise. And we will.

Disagree with any of our choices? Care to nominate a place or suggest that we rate one more highly? Visit our feedback center at www.fodors.com/feedback.

Budget Well

Hotel and restaurant price categories from ¢ to $$$$ are defined in the opening pages of each chapter. For attractions, we always give standard adult admission fees; reductions are usually available for children, students, and senior citizens. Want to pay with plastic? **AE, D, DC, MC, V** following restaurant and hotel listings indicate whether American Express, Discover, Diner's Club, MasterCard, and Visa are accepted.

Restaurants

Unless we state otherwise, restaurants are open for lunch and dinner daily. We mention dress only when there's a specific requirement and reservations only when they're essential or not accepted—it's always best to book ahead.

Hotels

Hotels have private bath, phone, TV, and air-conditioning and operate on the European Plan (aka EP, meaning without meals), unless we specify that they use the Continental Plan (CP, with a continental breakfast), Breakfast Plan (BP, with a full breakfast), or Modified American Plan (MAP, with breakfast and dinner) or are all-inclusive (including all meals and most activities). We always

list facilities but not whether you'll be charged an extra fee to use them, so when pricing accommodations, find out what's included.

Many Listings

- ★ Fodor's Choice
- ★ Highly recommended
- ⊠ Physical address
- ✢ Directions
- ⌕ Mailing address
- ☎ Telephone
- 🖶 Fax
- ⊕ On the Web
- ✉ E-mail
- 🖃 Admission fee
- ☉ Open/closed times
- Ⓜ Metro stations
- ▤ Credit cards

Hotels & Restaurants

- 🏨 Hotel
- 🛏 Number of rooms
- ⌂ Facilities
- ¶⊙¶ Meal plans
- ✕ Restaurant
- ⌨ Reservations
- ⤜ Smoking
- 🍷 BYOB
- ✕🏨 Hotel with restaurant that warrants a visit

Outdoors

- ⛳ Golf
- ⛺ Camping

Other

- ☺ Family-friendly
- ⇨ See also
- ⊠ Branch address
- ⌦ Take note

Cruising in Scandinavia

WORD OF MOUTH

"We sailed from Bergen to Kirkenes in late July. It never did get dark, just a very long twilight. By October, say, the days would be quite short. Some ports—Ålesund, for example—were visited for several hours. Others, only minutes. It's a wonderful, scenic voyage, so free of hassles."

—USNR

purchases; and you may be asked to show officials what you've bought. If your cruise is a transatlantic crossing, U.S. Customs clears ships sailing into arrival ports. After showing your passport to immigration officials, you must collect your luggage from the dock, then stand in line to pass through the inspection point. This can take up to an hour.

ALLOWANCES   You're always allowed to bring goods of a certain value back home without having to pay any duty or import tax. But there's a limit on the amount of tobacco and liquor you can bring back duty-free. The values of so-called "duty-free" goods are included in these amounts. When you shop abroad, save all your receipts, as customs inspectors may ask to see them as well as the items you purchased. If the total value of your goods is more than the duty-free limit, you'll have to pay a tax (most often a flat percentage) on the value of everything beyond that limit. For U.S. citizens who have been in Europe for at least 48 hours, the duty-free exemption is $800. But the duty-free exemption includes only 200 cigarettes, 100 cigars, and 1 liter of alcohol (this includes wine); above these limits, you have to pay duties, even if you didn't spend more than the $800 limit.

SENDING
PACKAGES
HOME   Although you probably won't want to spend your time looking for a post office, you can send packages home duty-free, with a limit of one parcel per addressee per day (except alcohol or tobacco products or perfume worth more than $5). You can mail up to $200 worth of goods to yourself, or $100 worth of goods to a friend or relative; label the package "personal use" or "unsolicited gift" (depending on which is the case) and attach a list of the contents and their retail value. If the package contains your used personal belongings, mark it "personal goods returned" to avoid paying duty on your laundry. You do not need to declare items that were sent home on your declaration forms for U.S. Customs.

CRUISE LINES

Seated in an airplane after a week of enjoying an exceptionally nice cruise, I overheard the couple behind me discussing their "dreadful" cruise vacation. What a surprise when they mentioned the ship's name. It was the one I'd just spent a glorious week on. I never missed a meal. They hated the food. My cabin was comfortable and cheery, if not large. Their identical accommodations resembled a "cave." One size definitely does not fit all in cruising. What's appealing to one passenger may be unacceptable to another. Ultimately, most cruise complaints arise from passengers whose expectations were not met. The couple I eavesdropped on were on the wrong cruise line and ship for them.

I enjoy cruises. Some have suited me more than others, but I've never sailed on a cruise that was completely without merit. Make no mistake about it: cruise lines have distinct personalities, but not all luxury or mainstream cruise lines are alike, although they will share many basic similarities. The cruise industry is a fluid one—that means that when new features are introduced, they may not be found on all ships, even those within the same cruise line. For instance, you won't find an ice-skating rink on any but the biggest Royal Caribbean ships. However, most cruise lines attempt to standardize the overall experience throughout their fleets, which is why you'll find a waterslide on every Carnival ship (though at this writing, Carnival has no Scandinavian ports of call).

Just as trends and fashion evolve over time, cruise lines embrace the ebb and flow of change. To keep pace with today's lifestyles, some cruise lines strive to include something that will appeal to everyone on their ships. Others focus on narrower elements and are more traditional. Today's passengers have higher expectations and they sail on ships that are far superior to their predecessors. And they often do so at a much lower comparable fare than in the past.

So which cruise line is best? Only you can determine which is best for you. You won't find ratings by Fodor's—either quality stars or value scores. Why? Think of those people seated behind me on the airplane. Ratings are personal and heavily weighted to the reviewer's opinion. Your responsibility is to select the right cruise for you—no one knows your expectations better than you do yourself. It's your time, money, and vacation that's at stake. No matter how knowledgeable your travel agent is, how sincere your friends are, or what any expert can tell you, you are the only one who really knows what you like. The short wait for a table might not bother you because you would prefer a casual atmosphere with open seating; however, some people want the security of a set time at an assigned table served by a waiter who gets to know their preferences. You know what you are willing to trade off in order to get what you want.

MAINSTREAM CRUISE LINES

The mainstream lines are the ones most often associated with modern cruising. They offer the advantage of something for everyone and nearly every available sports facility imaginable. Some ships even have ice-skating rinks, 18-hole miniature golf courses, bowling alleys, and rock-climbing walls.

Generally speaking, the mainstream lines have two basic ship sizes—large cruise ships and mega-ships—in their fleets. These vessels have plentiful outdoor deck space, and many have a wraparound outdoor promenade deck that allows you to stroll or jog the ship's perimeter. In the newest vessels, traditional meets trendy. You'll find atrium lobbies and expansive sun- and sports decks, picture windows instead of portholes, and cabins that open onto private verandas. For all their resort-style innovations, they still feature cruise-ship classics—afternoon tea, complimentary room service, and lavish pampering. The smallest ships carry 1,000 passengers or fewer, while the largest accommodate more than 3,000 passengers and are filled with diversions.

These ships tend to be big and boxy. Picture windows are standard equipment, and cabins in the top categories have private verandas. From their casinos and discos to their fitness centers, everything is bigger and more extravagant than on other ships. You'll pay for many extras on the mainstream ships, from drinks at the bar, to that cup of cappuccino, to spa treatments, to a game of bowling, to dinner in a specialty restaurant. You may want to rethink a cruise aboard one of these ships if you want a little downtime, since you'll be joined by 1,500 to 3,000 fellow passengers.

PREMIUM CRUISE LINES

Premium cruise lines have a lot in common with the mainstream cruise lines, but with a little more of everything. The atmosphere is more refined, surroundings more gracious, and service more polished and attentive. There are still activities like pool games, although they aren't quite the high jinks typical of mainstream ships. In addition to traditional cruise activities, onboard lectures are common. Production shows are somewhat more sophisticated than on mainstream lines.

Ships tend to be newer midsize to large vessels that carry fewer passengers than mainstream ships and have a more spacious feel. Decor is usually more glamorous and subtle, with toned-down colors and extensive original art. Staterooms range from inside cabins for three or four to outside cabins with or without balconies to suites with numerous amenities, including butlers on some lines.

Most premium ships offer traditional assigned seatings for dinner. High marks are afforded the quality cuisine and presentation. Many ships have upscale bistros or specialty restaurants, which usually require reservations and command an additional charge. Although premium lines usually have as many extra charges as mainstream lines, the overall quality of what you receive is higher.

LUXURY CRUISE LINES

Comprising only 5% of the market, the exclusive luxury cruise lines, such as Crystal, Cunard, Regent Seven Seas, Seabourn, and Silversea offer high staff-to-guest ratios for personal service, superior cuisine in a single seating (except Crystal, with two assigned seatings, and Cunard, with dual-class dining assignments), and a highly inclusive product with few onboard charges. These small and midsize ships offer much more space per passenger than you will find on the mainstream lines' vessels. Lines differ in what they emphasize, with some touting luxurious accommodations and entertainment and others focusing on exotic destinations and onboard enrichment.

If you consider travel a necessity rather than a luxury and frequent posh resorts, then you will appreciate the extra attention and the higher level of comfort that luxury cruise lines offer. Itineraries on these ships often include the marquee ports, but luxury ships also visit some of the more uncommon destinations. With an intimate size, the smaller luxury ships can visit such ports as Marbella, Spain, and Korçula, Croatia.

EUROPEAN CRUISE LINES

With more similarities to American-owned cruise lines than differences, these European-owned-and-operated cruise lines compare favorably to the mainstream cruise lines of a decade ago. Although some lines have embarked upon shipbuilding programs that rival the most ambitious in the cruise industry, most European fleets consist of older, yet well-maintained vessels. These cruises cater to Europeans—announcements may be broadcast in as many as five languages—and Americans are generally in the minority. English is widely spoken by the crew, however.

RIVER CRUISES

Riverboats and barges present an entirely different perspective on European cruising. Smaller than even the smallest ocean cruise ships, they offer a convenient alternative to bus tours—you only unpack once—while navigating the rivers and canals to reach legendary inland cities. Just as on cruise ships, accommodations and meals are included. Some shore excursions might be part of the package as well.

OTHER CRUISE LINES

A few small cruise lines sail through Europe and offer boutique to nearly bed-and-breakfast experiences. Most of these niche vessels accommodate 200 or fewer passengers, and their focus is on soft adventure. They have itineraries that usually leave plenty of time for exploring and other activities on- or offshore. Many of these cruises schedule casual enrichment talks that often continue on decks, at meals, and during trips ashore.

AZAMARA CRUISES

In something of a surprise move, parent company Royal Caribbean International announced the formation of an all-new, deluxe cruise line in 2007. Two vessels originally slated for service in the Celebrity Cruises fleet, which were built for now-defunct Renaissance Cruises and acquired with the purchase of Spanish cruise line Pullmantur, are the basis for the new line, Azamura Cruises. Designed to offer exotic destination–driven itineraries, Azamara Cruises are set to present a more intimate onboard experience, while allowing access to the less-traveled ports of call experienced travelers want to visit.

One distinguishing aspect of Azamara is a wide range of enrichment programs to accompany the destination-rich itineraries. Popular enrichment programs include guest speakers and experts on a wide variety of topics, including destinations, technology, cultural explorations, art, music, and design. Lectures might include how to get the best photos from your digital camera or the proper way to pair wine and food, as taught by resident sommeliers. An onboard "excursion expert" can not only help you select shore excursions based on your personal interests, but also will serve as a destination guide, offering information about the culture and history of each port of call. Entertainment, on the other hand, leans toward cabaret-size production shows and variety entertainers in the main lounge. Diverse musical offerings throughout the ships range from upbeat dance bands to intimate piano bar entertainers.

Expect all the classic dinner favorites but with an upscale twist, such as gulf shrimp with cognac and garlic, or a filet mignon with black truffle sauce. Each ship offers two specialty restaurants: the Mediterranean-influenced Aqualina and the stylish steak and seafood restaurant Prime C.

Guests in suites receive two nights of complimentary dining in the two specialty restaurants, while guests in staterooms receive one. Daily in-cabin afternoon tea service and delivery of canapés is available to all passengers who want them.

Azamara is designed to appeal to discerning travelers, primarily American couples of any age who appreciate a high level of service in a non-structured atmosphere. The ships are not family-oriented and do not have facilities or programs for children.

All evenings are designated resort casual; there are no scheduled formal nights. However, passengers who choose to wear formal attire are welcome to do so.

Gratuities are automatically charged to onboard accounts at the daily rate of $12.25 per person, which covers all service personnel, including restaurant and stateroom staffs. Amounts may be adjusted according to the level of service received. A standard 15% is added to beverage charges.

Contact *Azamara Cruises, 1050 Caribbean Way, Miami, FL 33132-2096 877/ 222-2526 or 877/999-9553 www.azamaracruises.com.*

CELEBRITY CRUISES

Celebrity Cruises has based its reputation on sleek ships and superior food. Style and layout vary from ship to ship, lending each a unique personality. In terms of size and amenities, Celebrity's vessels rival almost any in cruising, but with a level of refinement rare on bigger ships. In less than a decade, Celebrity won the admiration of its passengers and its competitors—who have copied its nouvelle cuisine and cigar clubs and hired its personnel (a true compliment). Celebrity rose above typical mass-market cruise cuisine by hiring chef Michel Roux as a consultant. While Roux is no longer affiliated with the line, his legacy remains. Menus are creative; both familiar and exotic dishes have been customized to appeal to American palates. All food is prepared from scratch, using only fresh produce and herbs, aged beef, and fresh fish—even the ice cream on board is homemade. Entertainment choices range from Broadway-style productions, captivating shows, and lively discos to Monte Carlo–style casinos and specialty lounges. Multimillion-dollar art collections grace the entire fleet, which merged with Royal Caribbean International in 1997.

Celebrity attracts everyone from older couples to honeymooners. Summertime children's programs are as good as those on any cruise line. Service is friendly and first-class, rapid and accurate in the dining rooms. Waiters, stewards, and bartenders are enthusiastic, take pride in their work, and try to please.

Tip your cabin steward/butlers $3.50 per day; chief housekeeper 50¢ per day; dining-room waiter $3.50 per day; assistant waiter $2 per day; and restaurant manager 75¢ per day, for a total of $10.25 per person, per day. Passengers may adjust the amount based on the level of service experienced. A 15% service charge is added to all beverage checks. For children under 12, or the third or fourth person in the stateroom, half the above amount is recommended. Gratuities are typically handed out on the last night of the cruise, but they may be charged to your shipboard account as well.

Contact ☐ *Celebrity Cruises, 1050 Caribbean Way, Miami, FL 33132-2096* ☎ *305/539–6000 or 800/437–3111* 🖶 *800/437–5111* ⊕ *www.celebritycruises.com.*

COSTA CRUISES

The Genoa-based Costa Crociere, parent company of Costa Cruises, had been in the shipping business for more than 100 years and in the passenger business for almost 50 years when it was bought by Airtours and Carnival Cruises in 1997; Carnival gained sole ownership of the line in 2000, but the ships retain their original flavor. Costa's Italian-inspired vessels bring the Mediterranean vitality of *La Dolce Vita*. The ships are a combination of classic and modern design. A new vessel-building program has brought Costa ships into the 21st century with innovative, large-ship designs that reflect their Italian heritage and style without overlooking the amenities expected by modern cruisers. Festive shipboard activities include some of Italy's favorite pastimes, such as games of boccie and a wacky toga party, yet there is also a nod to the traditional cruise-ship entertainment expected by North Americans. Supercharged social staffs work overtime to get everyone in the mood and encourage everyone to be a part of the action.

Passengers tend to be a little older—the average age is 54—and have an interest in all things Italian. You don't find a lot of first-time cruisers on Costa ships.

Suggested tipping guidelines are as follows: cabin steward, $3 per day; waiter, $3 per day; busboy, $1.50 per day; maître d' and head waiter, $1 per day. A 15% gratuity is added to beverage bills (including mineral water in the dining room). Gratuities are charged to your shipboard account for convenience but may be adjusted based on the level of service experienced.

Contact ☐ *Costa Cruises, 200 S. Park Rd., Suite 200, Hollywood, FL 33021-8541* ☎ *954/266–5600 or 800/462–6782* 🖶 *954/266–2100* ⊕ *www.costacruises.com.*

CRYSTAL CRUISES

Crystal's two midsize ships stand out for their modern design, amenities, and spaciousness. Built to deliver the first-rate service and amenities expected from a luxury line, these vessels have many of the onboard facilities of a big ship. Crystal ships have long set standards for pampering—one reason these vessels often spend several days at sea rather than in port. White-glove service, stellar cuisine, and tasteful, understated surroundings create a comfortable cocoon for passengers. Large spas offer innovative therapies, body wraps, and exotic, Asian-inspired treatments by Steiner Leisure. Feng shui principles were scrupulously adhered to in their creation, so the spa areas are havens of serenity. To the typical litany of cruise-ship diversions, Crystal adds enrichment opportunities that include destination-oriented lectures and talks by scholars, political figures, and diplomats; hands-on classes in music and art; and deluxe theme cruises that emphasize such topics as food and wine or the fine arts.

The food alone is a good enough reason to book a Crystal cruise. Dining in the main restaurants is an event starring Continental-inspired cuisine served by European-trained waiters. Off-menu item requests are honored when possible, and special dietary considerations are handled with ease. Casual poolside dining from the grills is offered on some evenings in a relaxed, no-reservations-required option. While two assigned dining room seatings are advertised as an advantage that offers "flexibility," the reality is that open-seating is the true mark of choice and the most preferred option at this level of luxury cruising. If you haven't done so in advance, on embarkation day you can reserve a table to dine one night in each specialty restaurant, but don't dawdle until the last minute. Most passengers hurry to request reservations during the time allotted and if you wait, you may find a line has developed—one of the few lines you'll encounter on board—and all the choice dining times are already booked.

Crystal's target clientele is affluent and older but still active. On select cruises highly trained and experienced youth counselors are brought in to oversee activities for kids and teens, but this is not a particularly family-friendly cruise line. Baby food, high chairs, and booster seats are available upon request.

Staff are well trained, friendly, highly motivated, and thoroughly professional. However, Crystal's fares do not include tips, so the crew can be noticeably solicitous of gratuities. Suggested tipping guidelines are as follows: stewardess, $4 per passenger, per day (single travelers, $5 per day); senior waiter, $4 per passenger, per day; waiter, $3 per passenger, per day; butler (Penthouse Decks), $4 per passenger, per day. For specialty restaurants, $6 per person, per dinner is suggested. Gratuities for the maître d', headwaiter, assistant stewardess, and room service personnel are at your discretion. A 15% gratuity for bar drinks and wines is automatically added to bar checks. The suggested gratuity for Crystal Spa & Salon services is also 15%. Gratuities may be prepaid or charged to your shipboard account.

Contact ⌐ *Crystal Cruises, 2049 Century Park E, Suite 1400, Los Angeles, CA 90067* ☎ *310/785–9300 or 888/799–4625* 🖷 *310/785–9201* ⊕ *www.crystal cruises.com.*

CUNARD LINE

One of the world's most distinguished names in ocean travel since 1840, Cunard Line's history of deluxe transatlantic crossings and worldwide cruising is legendary for comfortable accommodations, excellent cuisine, and personal service. Though the line is now owned by Carnival, its high-end ships still carry on with a decidedly British sensibility.

Entertainment has a decidedly English flavor, with nightly production shows or cabaret-style performances and even plays starring Great Britain's Royal Academy of Dramatic Arts alumni. An authentic pub adds to the British ambience, while a wide variety of musical styles can be found for dancing and listening in other bars and lounges. Cunard's fine enrichment programs are presented by expert guest lecturers in their fields. Classes vary by cruise and include a wide assortment of topics taught by top designers, master chefs, and artists. Even seamanship and navigation courses are offered to novice mariners. You can pre-plan your activities prior to departure by consulting the syllabus of courses available online at Cunard Line's Web site.

In the tradition of multiple-class ocean liners, dining room assignments are made according to the accommodation category booked. The line's ships also have highly regarded specialty restaurants with menus by acclaimed chefs Daniel Boulud and Todd English. Discerning, well-traveled American and British couples from their late-30s to retirees are attracted by Cunard's traditional style and the notion of a cruise aboard an ocean liner. Although resort-casual clothing prevails throughout the day, Cunard vessels are ocean liners at heart and, as expected, are dressier than most cruise ships at night. Although most crew members are international rather than British, service is formal and sophisticated.

Suggested gratuities of $13 per person per day (for Grill Restaurant accommodations) or $11 per person per day (all other accommodations) are automatically charged to shipboard accounts for distribution to stewards and waiter staff. A 15% gratuity is added to beverage tabs for bar service. At passengers' discretion, gratuities for special services may be presented directly to individual crew members.

Contact ⓓ *Cunard Line, 24303 Town Center Dr., Valencia, CA 91355* ☎ *661/753–1000 or 800/728–6273* ⊕ *www.cunard.com.*

FRED. OLSEN CRUISES

Family-owned Fred. Olsen Cruise Lines proudly boasts a Norwegian heritage of seamanship and a fleet of small ships that offer an intimate cruising experience. While the fleet doesn't consist of new vessels, all were well constructed originally and have been refitted since 2001. Two sister ships from the defunct luxury Royal Viking Line, *Royal Viking Star* and *Royal Viking Sky,* have reunited under the Fred. Olsen house flag and now sail as *Black Watch* and *Boudicca.* And while the line is destination-focused—itineraries are seldom repeated within any cruise season—itinerary planning is versatile.

Shipboard ambience is friendly, relaxed, and unabashedly British. As Fred. Olsen Cruise Lines expands, the line takes pride in maintaining the consistency their passengers prefer and expect, both on board and ashore. Activities and entertainment are traditional cruise-ship fare with a laid-back tempo, though on a much smaller scale than you find on the typical American mega-ship. Ballroom dancers outnumber the late-night disco set, and shows are more cabaret than Vegas. Particular favorites with most passengers are theme nights and the crew show. Cruises range from four-night "mini-breaks" to lengthier 7- to 78-night sailings. British pounds are used for all transactions on board.

Well-traveled, mature British passengers who enjoy the time-honored shipboard environment with a formal style make up the majority on board Fred. Olsen sailings. However, it's not unusual to find several generations of families all cruising together during summer months and school holiday breaks, when children's activity programs are offered to please grandparents who wish to spend quality time with their extended families.

Recommended gratuities are £2 passenger per day for your cabin steward and the same amount for your dining room waiter.

Contact ✉ *Fred. Olsen House, White House Rd., Ipswich, England* ☏ *01473/742–424* ⊕ *www.fredolsencruises.com.*

HOLLAND AMERICA LINE

. Founded in 1873, Holland America Line (HAL) is one of the oldest names in cruising. Steeped in the traditions of the transatlantic crossing, its cruises are classic, conservative affairs renowned for their grace and gentility. Service is taken seriously: the line maintains a school in Indonesia to train staff members. Food is very good by cruise-ship standards, and presentations on Rosenthal china are creative. In response to the challenge presented by its competitors, Holland America has introduced a lighter side to its menus, including many pastas and "heart-healthy" dishes. Holland America passengers tend to be older and less active than those traveling on the ships of its parent line, Carnival; however, despite an infusion of younger adults and families on board, they remain refined without being stuffy or stodgy. As its ships attract a more youthful clientele, Holland America has taken steps to shed its "old folks" image, now offering trendier cuisine, a culinary arts center, and an expanded "Club Hal" children's program. Still, these are not party cruises, and Holland America has managed to preserve the refined and relaxing qualities that have always been its hallmark, even on sailings that cater more to younger passengers and families.

In late 2003 HAL initiated the "Signature of Excellence" program to raise product and service standards throughout the fleet; upgrades to all ships were complete by the end of 2006 and add significantly to the onboard experience. Pillow-top mattresses, 250-thread-count cotton bed linens, Egyptian-cotton towels, magnifying makeup mirrors, waffle and terry robes, fresh fruit baskets, flat-screen televisions, and DVD players are features of all accommodations. In addition, all suites have duvets on beds, fully stocked minibars, personalized stationery, and access to the exclusive Neptune Lounge where beverages, breakfast pastries, afternoon snacks, and evening canapés are available. Dining is enhanced by the reservations-only Pinnacle Grill on every ship, one-on-one service in the main dining rooms, and table-side beverage service in the Lido casual dining room. The spas have tranquil relaxation areas

1

and trendy thermal suites furnished with heated tile chaises. Explorations Café, powered by *The New York Times,* combines a coffee bar, a computer center, and cozy library-reading room complete with tabletop versions of the *Times'* infamous crossword puzzles.

Gratuities of $10 per passenger, per day are automatically added to onboard accounts to be distributed to stewards and waitstaff. Passengers may adjust the amount based on the level of service experienced. Tips for room service delivery and spa and salon services are at passengers' discretion. A 15% gratuity is added to bar service tabs.

Contact Holland America Line, 300 Elliott Ave. W, Seattle, WA 98119 206/ 281-3535 or 800/577-1728 206/281-7110 www.hollandamerica.com.

HURTIGRUTEN

Originally intended as a communications and travel link between the villages on Norway's western coast, Hurtigruten (formerly known in the U.S. as Norwegian Coastal Voyage) provides an up-close look at the fascinatingly intricate fjords, mountains, and villages that not too long ago were isolated and difficult to navigate. Sailing with comfortable cruise ships that still do double-duty transferring cargo and the occasional village-to-village passenger, the Hurtigruten itineraries are often described as "the world's most beautiful voyage," as they provide access to some of the most stunning scenery and the unique cultures of Norway, many of them above the Arctic Circle.

Eleven Hurtigruten ships are committed year-round to Norwegian coastal itineraries, known in Norway as "Hurtigruten," the word from which the cruise line's name is derived. Options include six-night northbound, five-night southbound, or 11-night round-trip sailings, calling at 34 ports in each one-way segment. During the summer, the Millennium, Contemporary, and Mid-Generation ships follow this route; in the winter, *Nordnorge* and *Nordkapp* reposition, joining the company's newest ship, *MS Fram,* in the southern hemisphere to sail Antarctic and Chilean Fjord itineraries, replaced in Norway by *Lofoten* and *Nordstjernen.* The *Polar Star* and *Nordstjernen* make summer voyages to Spitsbergen, an island midway between Norway and the North Pole. The *MS Fram* makes summer expeditions to Greenland as well as a 67-day longitudinal world cruise in the fall.

Americans are usually in the minority on these sailings. Travelers who find this kind of cruising attractive are usually sophisticated yet unpretentious individuals who can be comfortable in an internationally diverse group. They tend to be independent folks who are comfortable controlling their vacation experiences and are perfectly content enjoying spectacular scenery and visiting picturesque communities, mostly on their own.

There is a "no tipping required" policy, and the mostly Norwegian crew does not expect gratuities. If you want to tip a crew member for exceptional service, however, it is at your discretion.

Contact ✉ *405 Park Ave., Suite 904, New York, NY* ☎ *800/323-7436* ⊕ *www. hurtigruten.us.*

LINDBLAD EXPEDITIONS

Founded by Sven-Olof Lindblad in 1979, Lindblad Expeditions has earned a reputation for creating eye-opening expeditions to out-of-the-way places, always emphasizing responsible tourism. Operating a fleet of small expedition ships that nose into ports where large cruise ships cannot go, the company prides itself on providing adventurous travelers with original and authentic experiences. Important components to all of Lindblad's cruises, the company's onboard expedition leaders and naturalists (all experts in their field), have a passion for helping travelers uncover—and interpret—the mysteries of nature and history.

Lindblad Expeditions' underlying mission is to introduce "curious and intrepid travelers" to the "international capitals of wildness." The far-flung reaches of Alaska, Antarctica, Baja, Central America, and Galapagos serve up what the company calls "the most fascinating, unspoiled, and life-enhancing destinations on the planet." That's not to say that Lindblad ignores traditional destinations, because its ships also sail in the British Isles, the Mediterranean, and the Baltic—even in the Caribbean—but the emphasis is always on active exploration and learning.

Of the more popular learning opportunities are Photo Expeditions, developed in collaboration with Lindblad's partner, the National Geographic Society. Photo Expeditions offer passengers opportunities to shoot in some of earth's most engaging destinations with some of the world's greatest photographers.

Lindblad offers active vacations, and if there were icons for the cruise line, they might well be the kayak and the Zodiac (an inflatable tender useful for tendering or excursions). All ships offer opportunities to launch from small ships to even smaller vessels for exploration of the marine world. Shore excursions are included in the cruise fare. Lindblad's cruises, in fact, are nearly all-inclusive. About the only thing you'll need to dip into your wallet for is alcohol.

The award-winning expedition company also has been recognized for its efforts toward sustainable tourism initiatives. Recipient of the 2007 Global Tourism Business Award, Lindblad Expeditions supports such programs as the protection of the Galapagos National Park and Marine Reserve, raising more than $3.5 million to fund conservation of the region.

Lindblad considers its passengers to be active, engaged explorers, and indeed the cruise line appeals to inquisitive minds who enjoy exploring—and learning about—the planet. Lindblad's passengers—who tend to be aged 55-plus—are likely to be fit for the many activities that the cruise line offers, including hiking, snorkeling, and kayaking. Recommended gratuities for the ship's crew is $10 per day per passenger.

Contact ✉ *96 Morton St., New York, NY* ☎ *800/397-3348* ⊕ *www.expeditions.com.*

MSC CRUISES

1

With several seasons of Caribbean sailing behind them, MSC Cruises has outgrown its "newcomer" status in the region. More widely known as one of the world's largest cargo shipping companies, parent company Mediterranean Shipping Company has operated cruises with an eclectic fleet since the late 1980s but expanded their cruising reach by introducing graceful, medium-size ships in the Caribbean. Prices are toward the low end of the mainstream premium category.

Some MSC Cruises itineraries adopt activities that appeal to American passengers without abandoning those preferred by Europeans—prepare for announcements in Italian as well as in English. In addition to guest lecturers, computer classes, and cooking lessons featured in the onboard enrichment program, a popular option is Italian language classes. Nightly shows accentuate MSC Cruises' Mediterranean heritage—there might be a flamenco show in the main showroom and live music for listening and dancing in the smaller lounges. Dinner on MSC ships is a traditional seven-course event centered on authentic Italian fare. Menus list Mediterranean regional specialties and classic favorites prepared from scratch the old-fashioned way. In a nod to American tastes, broiled chicken breast, grilled salmon, and Caesar salad are always available in addition to the regular dinner menu.

Suggested amounts for gratuities covering services onboard are approximately $8 to $12 per passenger per day. MSC Cruises advises that the amount of a gratuity should naturally reflect the quality of services received. Gratuities are incorporated into all bar purchases.

Contact MSC Cruises, 6750 N. Andrews Ave., Fort Lauderdale, FL 33309 954/772–6262 or 800/666–9333 ⊕ www.msccruises.com.

NORWEGIAN CRUISE LINE

Norwegian Cruise Line (NCL) was established in 1966, when one of Norway's oldest and most respected shipping companies, Oslo-based Klosters Rederi A/S, acquired the *Sunward* and repositioned the ship from Europe to the then-obscure Port of Miami. With the formation of a company called Norwegian Caribbean Lines, the cruise industry as we know it today was born. NCL launched an entirely new concept with its regularly scheduled cruises on a single-class ship, with an informal kind of luxury. No longer simply a means of transportation, the ship became a destination unto itself, offering guests an affordable alternative to land-based resorts. The *Sunward*'s popularity prompted other cruise lines to build ships to accommodate the burgeoning market, eventually turning Miami into the world's number one port of embarkation. NCL led the way with its fleet of sleek new ships. In another bold move, NCL purchased the former *France* in 1979 and rebuilt the grand ocean liner in Bremerhaven, Germany, for casual cruising. Rechristened *Norway,* she assumed the honored position as flagship of the fleet and was retired from service in 2003. The late 1980s brought new ships and a new corporate name when Norwegian Caribbean Lines became Norwegian

Cruise Line in 1987. NCL continued its expansion by acquiring other cruise lines, stretching and refurbishing older ships, and building new mega-ships, including the line's newest, two 2,400-berth "Freestyle Cruising" ships, *Norwegian Pearl* and *Norwegian Gem*. The line is now expanding its roster of European itineraries.

Freestyle Cruising created a sensation in the industry when Asian shipping giant Star Cruises acquired NCL early in 2000—the new owners were confounded that Americans meekly conformed to rigid dining schedules and dress codes. All that changed with NCL's introduction of a host of flexible dining options that allow passengers to choose open seating in the main dining rooms or dine in any of a number of à la carte and specialty restaurants at any time and with whom they please. While the Freestyle Cruising concept now applies to the entire NCL fleet, you'll still see fewer options on some of the smaller, older ships. The line has even loosened the dress code to resort casual at all times and relaxed the disembarkation process by inviting passengers to relax in their cabins until it's time to leave the ship (instead of gathering in a lounge to wait for their numbers to be called). Noted for top-quality, high-energy entertainment and emphasis on fitness facilities and programs, NCL combines action and activities in a casual, free-flowing atmosphere. For children and teens, each NCL vessel offers "Kid's Crew" program of supervised entertainment for young cruisers ages 2 through 17. An abundance of family-friendly staterooms interconnect in most categories, enabling families of nearly any size to find suitable accommodations. NCL's passenger list usually includes a wide range of ages, including families and couples, mostly from the United States and Canada.

NCL applies a service charge to passengers' shipboard accounts: $10 per passenger, per day for those 13 and older and $5 per day for children ages 3–12. A 15% gratuity is added to bar tabs and spa bills.

Contact ☐ *Norwegian Cruise Line, 7665 Corporate Center Dr., Miami, FL 33126* ☎ *305/ 436–4000 or 800/327–7030* ⊕ *www.ncl.com.*

OCEANIA CRUISES

This distinctive cruise line was founded by Frank Del Rio and Joe Watters, cruise industry veterans with the know-how to satisfy inquisitive passengers with interesting ports of call and upscale touches for fares much lower than you would expect. Oceania Cruises set sail in 2003 to carve a unique, almost "boutique" niche in the cruise industry by obtaining midsize "R-class" ships that made up the now-defunct Renaissance Cruises fleet.

Intimate and cozy public spaces reflect the importance of socializing on Oceania ships. Evening entertainment leans toward light cabaret, solo artists, music for dancing, and conversation with fellow passengers; however, you'll find lively karaoke sessions on the schedule as well. The sophisticated adult atmosphere is enhanced on sea days by a combo performing jazz or easy-listening melodies poolside. Several top cruise-industry chefs were lured away from other cruise lines to insure that the artistry of world-renowned, master chef Jacques Pépin, who crafted five-star menus for Oceania, is properly carried out. The results are sure to please the most discriminating palate. Oceania serves some of the best food at sea, particularly impressive for a cruise line that charges far less than luxury rates. Intimate specialty restaurants require reservations, but there is no additional charge for the Italian restaurant or the steak house. While small, the spa, salon, and well-equipped fitness center are adequate for the number of passengers on board.

Varied, destination-rich itineraries are an important characteristic of Oceania Cruises, and most sailings are in the 10- to 12-night range, which means more interesting, less-visited ports. Before arrival in ports of call, lectures are presented on the historical background, culture, and traditions of the islands. Oceania Cruises appeal to singles and couples from their late-30s to well-traveled retirees, who have the time for—and prefer—longer cruises. Most passengers are attracted to the casually sophisticated atmosphere, creative cuisine, and European service. Oceania Cruises are adult-oriented and not a good choice for families, particularly those traveling with infants and toddlers. No dedicated children's facilities are available; however, teenagers with sophisticated tastes (and who don't mind the absence of a video arcade) would enjoy the emphasis on intriguing ports of call.

For convenience, $11.50 per person, per day is added to onboard accounts for distribution to stewards and waitstaff and an additional $3.50 per person, per day is added for suite occupants where butler service is provided. Passengers may adjust the amount based on the level of service experienced. Bar bills add an automatic 18% to all beverage tabs for bartenders and servers.

Contact 🖉 *Oceania Cruises, 8300 NW 33rd St., Suite 308, Miami, FL 33122* ☎ *305/ 514–2300 or 800/531–5658* ⊕ *www.oceaniacruises.com.*

P&O CRUISES

P&O Cruises (originally the Peninsular & Oriental Steam Navigation Company), boasts an illustrious history in passenger shipping since 1837. While the company's suggestion that they invented cruising may not be entirely accurate, P&O is assuredly a pioneer of modern cruising. Having set aside such throwbacks as passenger classes, the company acquired Princess Cruises in 1974. P&O then purchased Sitmar Cruises and merged it with Princess in 1988, and the passenger-cruise business—known as P&O Princess—was spun off in 2000.

P&O Cruises remains Britain's leading cruise line, sailing the UK's largest and most modern fleet. The ships are equipped with every modern facility you could think of, from swimming pools to stylish restaurants, spas, bars, casinos, theaters, and showrooms. An abundance of balcony and outside cabins ensures that a view to the sea is never far away. P&O ships, with accommodation from inside cabins to lavish suites, cater to a wide cross section of budgets and tastes.

To offer passengers a variety of choices, P&O has adapted their fleet to match their preferences. While most of the fleet caters to families as well as couples and singles of all ages, *Arcadia* and *Artemis* are adults-only ships.

Count on fellow passengers to be predominantly British singles, couples, and families, although you may find Scandinavians, Americans, and Australians aboard for some sailings. *Arcadia* and *Artemis* are all-adult ships, and passengers must be 18 or older to sail aboard them.

The recommended gratuity is £3.75 (or its equivalent) per passenger (age 12 and older) per day.

Contact **P&O Cruises.** ✉ *Richmond House, Terminus Terrace, Southampton, UK* ☎ *0845/678–00–14* ⊕ *www.pocruises.com.*

PRINCESS CRUISES

Rising from modest beginnings in 1965, when it began offering cruises to Mexico with a single ship, Princess has become one of the world's most well-known cruise lines. Its fleet sails to more destinations each year than any other major line. Princess was catapulted to stardom in 1977, when its flagship became the setting for *The Love Boat* television series, which introduced millions of viewers to the still-new concept of a seagoing vacation. The name and famous "seawitch" logo have remained synonymous with cruising ever since. While the recent addition of three medium-size vessels to the fleet offers a welcome smaller-ship choice, Princess more often follows the "big is better" trend when designing new ships. Even so, the line doesn't sacrifice quality for quantity when it comes to building beautiful vessels. Decor and materials are top-notch, and service, especially in the dining rooms, is of a high standard. In short, Princess is refined without being pretentious.

All Princess ships feature the line's innovative "Personal Choice Cruising" program, an individualized, unstructured style of cruising that gives passengers choice and flexibility in customizing their cruise experience—multiple dining locations, flexible entertainment, and affordable private balconies are all highlights. For traditionalists, one dining room is reserved for two assigned dinner seatings. Alternative restaurants are a staple throughout the fleet, but vary by ship class. Enrichment programs featuring guest lecturers and opportunities to learn new skills or crafts are welcome additions to a roster of adult activities, which still includes staples such as bingo and art auctions. You can even earn PADI scuba diving certification in just one week by participating in the "Open Water Diver" program during select sailings.

Princess passengers' average age is 45, and you see a mix of younger and older couples on board. For young passengers aged three to 17, each Princess vessel has a playroom, teen center, and programs of supervised activities designed for different age-specific groups. The ships are some of the most accessible at sea, and passengers with disabilities can select from staterooms in a variety of categories that are tailored for their special needs.

Princess suggests tipping $10 per person, per day. Gratuities are automatically added to onboard accounts, which passengers can adjust at the purser's desk; 15% is added to bar bills.

Contact *Princess Cruises, 24305 Town Center Dr., Santa Clarita, CA 91355-4999* 661/753-0000 or 800/774-6237 www.princess.com.

REGENT SEVEN SEAS CRUISES

Regent Seven Seas Cruises (RSSC) is part of Carlson Hospitality Worldwide, one of the world's major hotel-and-travel companies. The cruise line was formed in December 1994 with the merger of the one-ship Diamond Cruises and Seven Seas Cruises lines. From these modest beginnings, RSSC has grown into a major luxury player in the cruise industry, adopting the "Regent" label in early 2006. With the launch of the *Seven Seas Mariner* in March 2001, RSSC introduced the world's first all-suite, all-balcony cruise ship. *Seven Seas Voyager,* a second 700-passenger all-suite, all-balcony ship followed in April 2003. Subtle improvements throughout the fleet are ongoing, such as computer service with Wi-Fi capability for your own laptop and cell phone access, even when you are at sea. At this writing, other impending improvements included new bedding with down comforters and Egyptian cotton linens, Regent-branded bath amenities, flat-screen televisions, DVD players, and new clocks for all accommodations. Top suites will also feature iPod music systems and Bose speakers.

The line's spacious ocean-view staterooms have the industry's highest percentage of private balconies; you'll always find open seating at dinner; tips are included in the fare and no additional tipping is expected. With an emphasis on Continental and regional cuisines, dining room menus may appear to be the usual beef Wellington and Maine lobster, but in the hands of Regent Seven Seas chefs the results are outstanding. Specialty dining varies by ship within the fleet, but casual, Mediterranean-inspired bistro dinners are offered in the venues that serve as daytime casual Lido buffet restaurants. Regent has introduced an all-inclusive beverage policy that offers not only soft drinks and bottled water but also cocktails and select wines at all bars and restaurants throughout the ships. Activities are oriented toward onboard enrichment programs, socializing, and exploring the destinations on the itinerary. Spa and salon services are provided by the high-end Carita of Paris. Avoid disappointment by prearranging your preferred spa appointments and specialty restaurant reservations through the line's Web site. While RSSC's vessels are adult-oriented and do not have dedicated children's facilities, a "Club Mariner" youth program for children is offered on selected sailings. Although passengers tend to be older and affluent, they are quite active. Regent Seven Seas Cruises manages to provide a high level of personal service and sense of intimacy on small-to-midsize ships, which have the stability of larger vessels.

Contact *Regent Seven Seas Cruises, 1000 Corporate Dr., Suite 500, Fort Lauderdale, FL 33334* 954/776-6123 or 877/505-5370 954/772-3763 www.rssc.com.

ROYAL CARIBBEAN INTERNATIONAL

Imagine if the Mall of America were sent to sea. That's a fair approximation of what the mega-ships of Royal Caribbean International (RCI) are all about. These large-to-giant vessels are indoor-outdoor wonders, with every conceivable activity in a resortlike atmosphere, including atrium lobbies, shopping arcades, large spas, expansive sundecks, and rock-climbing walls. Several ships have such elaborate facilities as 18-hole miniature-golf courses, ice-skating rinks, and in-line skating tracks. Freedom-class ships, RCI's latest additions, and presently the world's largest cruise ships, even have the first surf parks at sea. These mammoth ships are quickly overshadowing the smaller vessels in Royal Caribbean's fleet, although RCI regularly rejuvenates older vessels, adding new facilities to mirror the latest trends, including plush new bedding that has been installed fleetwide. Happily, passengers now have five generations of mega-ships to choose from, including the prototype, the *Sovereign of the Seas,* which was completely rejuvenated in late 2004.

The centerpiece of Royal Caribbean mega-ships is the multideck atrium, a hallmark that has been duplicated by many other cruise lines. The brilliance of this design is that all the major public rooms radiate from this central point, so you can learn your way around these huge ships within minutes of boarding. Ships in the Vision series (*Legend, Splendour, Enchantment, Grandeur,* and *Rhapsody of the Seas*) are especially bright and airy, with sea views almost anywhere you happen to be. The main problem with RCI's otherwise well-conceived vessels is that, when booked to over 100% capacity, there are too many people on board, making for an exasperating experience during embarkation, when tendering, and at disembarkation. However, waiting in lines and other small annoyances aside, Royal Caribbean is one of the best-run and most popular cruise lines.

Although the line competes directly with Carnival and NCL for passengers—active couples and singles in their 30s to 50s, as well as a large family contingent—there are distinct differences of ambience and energy. Royal Caribbean is a bit more sophisticated and subdued than the competition, even while delivering a good time on a grand scale.

Royal Caribbean suggests the following tips per passenger: stateroom attendant, $3.50 a day; dining-room waiter, $3.50 a day; assistant waiter, $2 a day. Gratuities for headwaiters and other service personnel are at your discretion. A 15% gratuity is automatically added to beverage and bar bills. All gratuities may be charged to your onboard account.

Contact ☞ *Royal Caribbean International, 1050 Caribbean Way, Miami, FL 33132* ☎ *305/539-6000 or 800/327-6700* ⊕ *www.royalcaribbean.com.*

SAGA CRUISES

Saga Holidays, the UK-based tour company founded in 1951 and designed to offer vacation packages to mature travelers, started its cruise program in 1975 with charter sailings. After building a 20-year reputation for comfortable cruise travel, Saga purchased its first ship in

1996, the venerable *Sagafjord,* and renamed it *Saga Rose.* Following the success of *Saga Rose,* her former sister ship *Vistafjord* was acquired in 2004 and sails as *Saga Ruby.* Itineraries brim with longer sailings to far-flung corners of the globe, making Saga voyages destination oriented.

Classic cruisers in every sense of the word, Saga's passengers are travelers who expect inspiring itineraries coupled with traditional onboard amenities and comfortable surroundings. In the style of Saga Holidays' land-based tours, Saga Cruises takes care of the details that discerning passengers don't wish to leave to chance—from providing insurance and arranging visas to placing fruit and water in every cabin.

Activities and entertainment range from dance lessons to presentations of West End–style productions, from computer software lessons to lectures on wide-ranging topics. Wine-tasting, deck game competitions, classical concerts, and even bingo are found on the daily programs. Both ships have card rooms, but you won't find casinos.

With numerous accommodations designed for solo cruisers, Saga Cruises are particularly friendly for senior singles. Especially convenient on lengthy sailings, each ship features complimentary self-service launderettes and ironing facilities.

Saga Cruises are exclusively for passengers age 50 and older; the minimum age for traveling companions is 40. The overwhelming majority of passengers are from Great Britain, with a sprinkling of North Americans in the mix.

Gratuities are included in the fare, and additional tipping is not expected.

Contact ✉ *The Saga Building, Folkstone, Kent, UK* ☎ *1303/771–111* ⊕ *www. sagacruises.com.*

SEABOURN CRUISE LINE

Ultraluxury pioneer Seabourn was founded on the principle that dedication to personal service in elegant surroundings would appeal to sophisticated, independent-minded passengers whose lifestyles demand the best. Its fleet of three nearly identical, all-suite ships is known simply as the "Yachts of Seabourn." Following extensive makeovers in early 2006, they belie their age. The "yachts" remain favorites with people who can take care of themselves but would rather do so aboard a ship that caters to their individual preferences. Dining and evening socializing are generally more stimulating to Seabourn passengers than splashy song-and-dance reviews; however, proportionately scaled production and cabaret shows are presented in the main showroom and smaller lounge. The library stocks not only books but also movies for those who prefer to watch them in the privacy of their suites (popcorn will naturally be delivered with a call to room service). Complimentary "Massage Moments" on deck are mini-previews of the relaxing treatments available in the spa, which offers a variety of massages, body wraps, and facials.

Saving Money on Your Cruise Fare

You can save on your cruise fare in several ways. Obviously, you should shop around. Some travel agents will discount cruise prices, though this is becoming a thing of the past. One thing never changes—do not ever, under any circumstances, pay brochure rate. You can do better, often as much as half off published fares. These are a few simple strategies you can follow:

■ Book early: Cruise lines discount their cruises if you book early, particularly during the annual "Wave" season between January and March.

■ Cruise during the off-season: If you take a cruise during the early spring (especially March and April) or late fall (after mid-October) you'll often find specials.

■ Book late: Sometimes you can book a last-minute cruise at substantial savings if the ship hasn't filled all its cabins.

■ Choose accommodations with care: Cabins are usually standardized and location determines the fare. Selecting a lower category can result in savings while giving up nothing in terms of cabin size and features.

■ Book a "guarantee": You won't be able to select your own cabin because the cruise line will assign you one in the category you book, but a "guarantee" fare can be substantially lower than a regular fare.

■ Cruise with friends and family: Book a minimum number of cabins, and your group can generally receive a special discounted fare.

■ Reveal your age and affiliations: Fare savings may be available for seniors and members of certain organizations, as well as cruise line stockholders.

■ Cruise often: Frequent cruisers usually get discounts from their preferred cruise lines.

These sleek 10,000-ton ships are celebrated for extraordinary levels of personalized service, suites of 277 square feet or more—40% with balconies—and exceptional cuisine designed by famed chef-restaurateur Charlie Palmer. Casual dining alternatives have been introduced, including "Tastings @ 2," serving innovative cuisine in multiple courses nightly in the Veranda Café, where outdoor tables enhance the romantic atmosphere and a second—even more laid back—"Sky Grill" dinner with sizzling steaks and seafood is sometimes offered in the open-air Sky Bar. While both require reservations; happily, there is no additional charge for either. All drinks, including wine and alcohol, are complimentary throughout the voyage, and tipping is neither required nor expected. Shore excursions often include privileged access to historic and cultural sites during hours when they are not open to the public.

Seabourn's yachtlike vessels appeal to affluent couples of all ages who enjoy destination-intense itineraries, a subdued atmosphere, and exclusive service. Passengers tend to be 50-plus and retired couples who are accustomed to evening formality. The ships are adult-oriented with no children's programs or facilities. Additionally, Seabourn does not allow children less than one year of age.

CLOSE UP

Past Passengers—An Exclusive Group

1

Your cruise is over—pat yourself on the back. Your plans and preparation for an out-of-the-ordinary trip have paid off, and you'll now have lasting memories of a great vacation. Before you even have a chance to fill your scrapbook, the cruise line wants you to consider doing it all over again. And why not? You're a seasoned sailor, so take advantage of your experience. To entice you back on a future cruise, you may find you're automatically a member of an exclusive club—Latitudes (Norwegian Cruise Line), Mariner Society (Holland America Line), Captain's Circle (Princess Cruises), Venetian Society (Silversea Cruises)—to name but a few. Members receive the cruise line's magazine for past passengers, exclusive offers, shipboard perks such as a repeaters' party hosted by the captain, and even members-only cruises.

Contact ✆ *Seabourn Cruise Line, 6100 Blue Lagoon Dr., Suite 400, Miami, FL 33126* ☎ *305/463–3000 or 800/929–9391* 🖷 *305/463–3010* ⊕ *www.seabourn.com.*

SILVERSEA CRUISES

High-quality features and personalization are Silversea maxims. Silversea ships have full-size showrooms, domed dining rooms, and a selection of bars and shops, yet all accommodations are spacious outside suites, most with private verandas. Silversea ships have large swimming pools in expansive Lidos—the space- and crew-to-passenger ratios are among the best at sea in the luxury small-ship category. Although their ships schedule more activities than other comparably sized luxury vessels, you can either take part or opt instead for a good book and any number of quiet spots to read or snooze in the shade. South Pacific–inspired Mandara Spa offers numerous treatments, including exotic massages, facials, and body wraps. A plus is that appointments for spa treatments and salon services, as well as shore excursion bookings, can be made online from 60 days until 48 hours prior to sailing.

European-style service is personal—exacting and hospitable, yet discreet. A major selling point is the nearly all-inclusive nature of Silversea voyages, which include gratuities and all beverages. Silversea is so all-inclusive that you'll find your room key/charge card is seldom used for anything but opening your suite door. Perhaps more compelling is the line's flair for originality. The pasta chef's daily special is a passenger favorite, as is the galley brunch, held just once each cruise, when the galley is transformed into a buffet restaurant. Dishes from Silversea's chefs are complemented by those of La Collection du Monde, created by the cruise line's culinary partner Relais & Châteaux. Menus include both hot and cold appetizers, at least four entrée selections, a vegetarian alternative, and "Cruiselite" cuisine that is low in cholesterol, sodium, and fat. Special off-menu orders are prepared whenever possible as long as the ingredients are onboard. In the event that they aren't, you may find after a day in port that a trip to the market was made in order to fulfill your request.

Silversea Cruises appeal to sophisticated, affluent couples who enjoy the country clublike atmosphere, exquisite cuisine, and polished service. Adult-oriented, these ships have no dedicated children's facilities, and Silversea does not allow children less than one year of age and may limit the number of children under three on any particular cruise. Tipping is not required or expected.

Contact ⌂ *Silversea Cruises, 110 E. Broward Blvd., Fort Lauderdale, FL 33301* ☏ *954/ 522–4477 or 800/722–9955* ⊕ *www.silversea.com.*

COMING ASHORE

By Lindsay Bennett and Ralph Grizzle

The number of ships doing Baltic itineraries continues to expand; while traditionally cruises in this region tended to be on the longer side, there are now an increasing number of one-week cruises in these northern waters during the summer. Whatever the length of your time at sea, the first step will undoubtedly be getting off the boat; what follows is a quick reference for pier location information in the most common Scandinavian ports of call.

DENMARK

ÅRHUS

Cruise ships dock at Pier 2, a 10-minute walk to the city center. If your ship calls during the summer, you may arrive in time for one of Århus' many festivals.

COPENHAGEN

The city's cruise port is one of the best in Europe. Although it's 10 minutes from the downtown core, it's within walking distance of the Little Mermaid and the attractions of the seafront. Taxis wait outside the cruise terminal. The on-site Copenhagen Cruise Information Center is run by the city tourist office and there is a selection of shops housed in the renovated old wharf warehouses selling typical souvenirs. There is a dedicated cruise lounge at Magasin at Kongens Nytorv in the city center where you can wait for transfers, leave purchases for later collection, or have a rest during your trip.

FINLAND

HELSINKI

Ships dock at one of two terminals in the South Harbor. From Katajanokka Terminal, local Bus 13 or Tram T4 will take you to Helsinki city center, but this is also reachable on foot. Larger ships dock at the city commercial port in the West Harbor, which is 15 minutes by car from the downtown area. The shuttle service provided by the ship is the most cost-effective way of getting into town. The terminal is also served by Bus 15. Taxis wait at the terminal entrance to take visitors downtown.

Drinking & Gambling Ages

Many underage passengers have learned to their chagrin that the rules that apply on land are also adhered to at sea. On most mainstream cruise ships you must be 21 in order to imbibe alcoholic beverages. There are exceptions—for instance, on cruises departing from countries where the legal drinking age is typically lower than 21. By and large, if you haven't achieved the magic age of 21, your shipboard charge card will be coded as booze-free, and bartenders won't risk their jobs to sell you alcohol.

Gambling is a bit looser, and 18-year olds can try their luck on cruise lines such as Carnival, Celebrity, Holland America, Silversea, Norwegian, and Royal Caribbean; most other cruise lines adhere to the age-21 minimum. Casinos are trickier to patrol than bars, though, and minors who look "old enough" may get away with dropping a few coins in an out-of-the-way slot machine before being spotted on a hidden security camera. If you hit a big jackpot, you may have a lot of explaining to do to your parents.

NORWAY

ÅLESUND

Ålesund is at the entrance to the world-famous Geirangerfjord. Turrets, spires, and medieval ornaments rise above the skyline of the colorful town and its charming architecture. Cruise ships dock at the cruise terminal at Stornespiren/Prestebrygga, less than a five-minute walk from the city center.

BERGEN

Cruise ships dock at Skoltegrunnskaien and Jekteviken/Dokkeskjærskaien. Both are within a 15-minute walk to the city center, and shuttle buses are available from Jekteviken/Dokkeskjærskaien. From Skoltegrunnskaien, buses stop near the docks. The trip to the city center costs NKr 12. Once in the city center nearly all of the attractions are within walking distance.

HAMMERFEST

Ships dock either at a pier that is within walking distance of the town center or at Fugienes, about a mile away. Be prepared to pay about NKr 84 (US$15) for taxi transfer from Fugienes to the town center. Rather than tie up at Fugienes, ships sometimes anchor and tender passengers ashore to the dock in the town center. There is no terminal in the port area and only limited facilities, but the town center is only a few steps away and has everything you might need.

HONNINGSVÅG

Northern Norway's largest port welcomes about 100 cruise ships annually during the summer season. Ships dock at one of five piers, all within walking distance of the city center. The piers themselves have no services, but within 100 meters are shops, museums, tourist information, post office, banks, restaurants, and an ice bar.

OSLO

Cruise ships navigate beautiful Oslofjord en route to Oslo and dock in the compact city center. Many of Oslo's attractions can be explored on foot from the docks, but Olso has a good subway system, as well as plentiful buses and taxis.

TROMSØ

Cruise ships dock either in the city center at Prostneset or 4 km (2.5 mi) north of the city center at Breivika. Step off the ship in Prostneset, and you're in the city center, but there are no facilities at either pier.

TRONDHEIM

Cruise ships dock at one of two piers. Both of these are within easy walking distance of the city center. There are no facilities at the piers, but you'll find everything you need—from banks to tourist offices—in the city.

SWEDEN

GÖTEBORG (GOTHENBURG)

Cruise ships dock in the inner harbor of the vast port. There are no passenger facilities at the docking site. It's a 1-km (½-mi) walk to the downtown area but only a couple of minutes by taxi.

STOCKHOLM

Most vessels dock at various quays in the heart of the Gamla Stan (Old Town). How far you have to walk to the attractions depends on at which quay you are moored. This is one port where you'll want to be out on deck as the ship arrives and the city comes within camera distance. If all berths are full (eight of them) there is a mooring buoy in the harbor, and passengers will be tendered ashore. You can reach everything in the city (museums, shops, restaurants, and cafés) from the quays on foot.

Alternatively, some vessels dock at Nynasham outside the city. It is a 15-minute walk from the port at Nynasham to the railway station for the one-hour journey into central Stockholm. A one-day travel card covers this journey and all other public transport trips within the city. SL (Stockholm Transport) runs a modern and reliable public transit system. Tickets are valid for one hour from validation and cost SKr 20–SKr 26 per journey within Zone 1 (central Stockholm). A one-day card is SKr 90.

VISBY

Vessels dock in the town port; from here, it is a 5- to 10-minute walk into the center of town. The port has only the most basic facilities, but shops and restaurants are on hand in town.

Denmark

WORD OF MOUTH

"We walk up the pier and notice one of the buildings Hans Christian Andersen lived in for a time. We take the obligatory photo of me in front of it and move on to the next store for a scrumptious warm waffle with ice cream and strawberry sauce on top—something I will have at least once a day for the rest of the time I am here!"

—Escargot

"Copenhagen is *very* well laid out for cyclists—you can even bring your bike on the metro, as long as you buy an extra ticket for it. Remember also that Copenhagen proper is fairly small so biking around is quite easy (and it's what many of the locals do)."

—Erin464

Updated
by Sarah
Lookofsy,
Laura Stadler-
Jensen, Audrey
Templesman,
and Kay
Xander Mellish

THE KINGDOM OF DENMARK DAPPLES the Baltic Sea in an archipelago of some 450 islands and the crescent of one peninsula. Measuring 43,069 square km (17,028 square mi) and with a population of 5.5 million, it is the geographical link between Scandinavia and Europe. Half-timber villages and tidy agriculture rub shoulders with provincial towns and a handful of cities, where pedestrians set the pace, not traffic. Mothers safely park baby carriages outside bakeries while outdoor cafés fill with cappuccino-sippers, and lanky Danes pedal to work in lanes thick with bicycle traffic.

The Danes' lifestyle is certainly enviable, not yet the pressure-cooked life of some other Western countries. Long one of the world's most liberal nations, Denmark has a highly developed social-welfare system. Hefty taxes are the subject of grumbles and jokes, but Danes are proud of their state-funded medical and educational systems and high standard of living.

The history of this little country stretches back 250,000 years, when Jutland was inhabited by nomadic hunters, but it wasn't until AD 500 that a tribe from Sweden, called the Danes, migrated south and christened the land Denmark. The Viking expansion that followed was based on the country's strategic position in the north. Intrepid navies navigated to Europe and Canada, invading and often pillaging, until, under King Knud (Canute) the Great (995–1035), they captured England by 1018.

After the British conquest, Viking supremacy declined as feudal Europe learned to defend itself. Under the leadership of Valdemar IV (1340–75), Sweden, Norway, Iceland, Greenland, and the Faroe Islands became a part of Denmark. Sweden broke away by the mid-15th century and battled Denmark for much of the next several hundred years, whereas Norway remained under Danish rule until 1814, and Iceland until 1943. Greenland and the Faroe Islands are still self-governing Danish provinces.

Denmark prospered again in the 16th century, thanks to the Sound Dues, a levy charged to ships crossing the Øresund. Under King Christian IV, a construction boom crowned the land with what remain architectural gems today, but his fantasy spires and castles, compounded with the Thirty Years' War in the 17th century, led to state bankruptcy.

By the 18th century, absolute monarchy had given way to representative democracy, and culture flourished. Then—in a fatal mistake—Denmark refused to surrender its navy to the English during the Napoleonic Wars. Lord Nelson famously turned his blind eye to the destruction and bombed Copenhagen to bits. The defeated King Frederik VI handed Norway to Sweden. Denmark's days of glory were over.

Though Denmark was unaligned during World War II, the Nazis invaded in 1940. The small but strong resistance movement that was active throughout the war years is greatly celebrated. After the war, Denmark focused inward, refining its welfare system and concentrating on its main industries of agriculture, shipping, and financial and technical services. It's an outspoken member of the European Union (EU), championing environmental responsibility and supporting development in emerging economies.

The best way to discover more of Denmark is to strike up a conversation with an affable and hospitable Dane. *Hyggelig* defies definition but comes close to meaning a cozy and charming hospitality. The ultimate *hygge* for Danes constitutes gathering indoors during the cold and dark months, lighting candles, eating sweets, and talking into the night.

2

ORIENTATION AND PLANNING

GETTING ORIENTED

Denmark is divided into three regions: the two major islands of Zealand and Funen and the peninsula of Jutland. To the east, Zealand is Denmark's largest and most populated island, with Copenhagen as its focal point. Denmark's second-largest island, Funen, is a pastoral, undulating land of farms and beach villages, with Odense as its one major town. To the west, the relatively vast Jutland connects Denmark to the European continent; here you find the towns of Århus and Aalborg.

Copenhagen. Copenhagen fidgets with its modern identity as both a Scandinavian–European link and cozy capital. The center of Danish politics, culture, and finance, it copes through balance and a sense of humor with a taste for the absurd. Stroll the streets and you'll pass classic architecture painted in candy colors and businessmen clad in jeans and T-shirts.

Zealand. The countryside surrounding Copenhagen in the rest of Zealand is not to be missed. Less than an hour from the city, fields and half-timber cottages checker the land. Roskilde, to the east, has a 12th-century cathedral, and in the north, the Kronborg Castle of *Hamlet* fame crowns Helsingør. Beaches, some chic, some deserted, are powdered with fine white sand.

Funen. Funen rightly earned its storybook reputation by making cuteness a local passion. The city of Odense, Hans Christian Andersen's birthplace, is cobbled with crooked old streets and Lilliputian cottages.

Jutland Jutland's landscape is the most severe, with Ice Age–chiseled fjords and hills, sheepishly called mountains by the Danes. In the cities of Århus and Aalborg, you can find museums and nightlife rivaling Copenhagen's.

PLANNING

WHEN TO GO

Summertime—when the lingering sun of June, July, and August brings out the best in the climate and the Danes—is the best time to visit. In July most Danes flee to their summer homes or go abroad. If you do go in winter, the weeks preceding Christmas are a prime time to explore Tivoli. Although the experience is radically different from the flower-

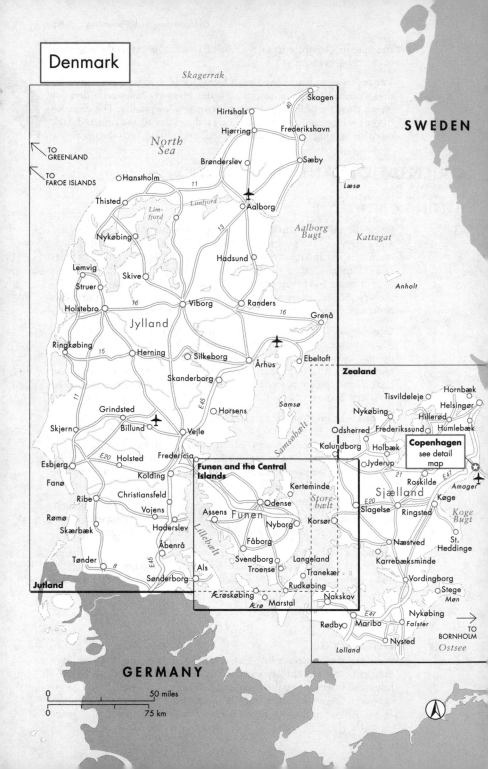

TOP REASONS TO GO

■ Learn the secret of happiness. Study after study has, in recent years, proclaimed Danes to be the world's happiest people. What's the secret behind such record-breaking contentment? Perhaps it's the free health care and education or the six weeks of vacation annually. Or it might just be a hedonistic Viking approach to life that involves consuming extraordinary quantities of candy and beer.

■ Bask in the late-day sun. At the height of summer, when daylight extends beyond the 17th hour, Danes make the most of it by sitting outdoors with blankets, snacks, and good friends. Even after the sun has set, darkness never entirely envelops the land, so these get-togethers often continue into the wee hours.

■ Immerse yourself in design. Although several Danish design classics might seem better suited for a James Bond movie set than a domestic interior, many of these signature designs are subtly incorporated into everyday life. Pay attention to your surroundings: it's quite possible that the local restaurant's cutlery or that comfortable chair in the hotel lobby are included in museum collections worldwide.

■ Take a leasurely stroll. Rain or shine, boots and umbrellas or sunglasses, Denmark is a lovely place to take in on foot. Roam the narrow cobblestone streets, harbor fronts, and neatly trimmed parks and gardens, noticing signature sights along the way. Denmark is very flat, so no steep climbs await you.

2

filled summertime park, the winter park has a charm all its own: shops with Christmas gifts and decorations, stalls serving mulled wine, seasonal displays, and thousands of bulbs to light up the darkness.

CLIMATE

Mainland Denmark and its surrounding islands have a cool maritime climate with mild to warm summers and cold (but not frigid) winters. Late summer and early fall is the rainiest season, but even then, precipitation is rarely heavy. Winter is dark and misty, but it's a great time to visit museums, libraries, and the countless atmospheric meeting places in which the Danes take refuge.

The following are average daily maximum and minimum temperatures for Copenhagen.

Jan.	28°F	-2°C	May	46°F	8°C	Sept.	52°F	11°C
	36°F	2°C		61°F	16°C		64°F	18°C
Feb.	27°F	-3°C	June	64°F	11°C	Oct.	45°F	7°C
	36°F	2°C		66°F	19°C		54°F	12°C
Mar.	30°F	-1°C	July	57°F	14°C	Nov.	37°F	3°C
	41°F	5°C		72°F	22°C		45°F	7°C
Apr.	37°F	3°C	Aug.	57°F	14°C	Dec.	34°F	1°C
	52°F	11°C		70°F	21°C		39°F	4°C

BUSINESS HOURS

Banks are open 9:30 to 4 most weekdays (though many have hours until 5:30 or 6 on Thursday). Shops are open from 9:30 or 10 to 5 or 6 weekdays, Saturday from 9 to 5, and are closed on Sunday. Monday is the most common day for museums to go dark. Major holidays include: New Years Eve and Day, Holy (Maundy) Thursday, Good Friday, Easter Sunday and Monday, Ascension (40 days after Easter), Whitsun/Pentecost (Sunday and Monday 10 days after Ascension), Constitution Day (June 5), Midsummer Eve and Day (late June), Christmas Eve and Day, and Boxing Day (day after Christmas).

GETTING HERE AND AROUND

AIR TRAVEL

Kastrup International Airport (CPH), 10 km (6 mi) from the center of Copenhagen, is the hub of Scandinavian and international air travel in Denmark. Jutland has regional hubs in Aalborg (AAL), Århus (AAR), and Billund (BLL), which handle mainly domestic and some European traffic. SAS, the main carrier, flies to the capital from several North American cities. Continental Airlines offer a direct flight to Copenhagen from New York. Delta flies nonstop daily between Atlanta and Copenhagen. Icelandair and Finnair have connecting flights to Copenhagen via Reykjavík and Helsinki, respectively.

From New York, flights to Copenhagen take 7 hours, 40 minutes. From Chicago, they take 9 hours, 30 minutes. From Seattle and Los Angeles the flight time is about 10 hours, 55 minutes. Flight times within the country are all less than 1 hour.

Contacts Continental Airlines (⊕ *www.continental.com*). **Delta** (⊕ *www.delta. com*). **Finnair** (⊕ *www.finnair.fi*). **Icelandair** (⊕ *www.icelandair.com*). **SAS Scandinavian Airlines** (⊕ *www.flysas.com*).

BOAT TRAVEL

Although more people are driving or taking buses and trains over new bridges spanning the waters, ferries are still a good way to explore Denmark and Scandinavia, especially if you have a rail pass. The Eurail Scandinavia Pass, for travel anywhere within Scandinavia (Denmark, Sweden, Norway, and Finland), is valid on some ferry crossings.

DFDS Seaways sails from Harwich in the United Kingdom to Esbjerg (20 hours) on Jutland's west coast. DFDS also sails to Oslo from Copenhagen. Fjord Line is as another company with service between Denmark and Norway. Scandlines connects Denmark with Sweden, and Germany.

CAR FERRIES   Vehicle-bearing hydrofoils operate between Jutland's Ebeltoft or Århus to Odden on Zealand; the trip takes about 1 hour. You can also take the slower (2 hours, 40 minutes), but less expensive, car ferry from Århus to Kalundborg on Zealand. From there, Route 23 leads to Copenhagen. Make reservations for the ferry in advance through Mols-Linien. (*Note:* During the busy summer months, passengers without reservations for their vehicles can wait hours.) The Helsingør/Helsingborg vehicle and passenger ferry (Scandlines) takes only 20 minutes.

Contacts **DFDS Seaways** (⊕ *www.dfds.com*). **Fjord Lines** (⊕ *www.fjordline.com*). **Mols-Linien** (⊕ *www.molslinien.dk*). **Scandlines** (⊕ *www.scandlines.dk*).

BUS TRAVEL

Private bus operators and Danish State Railways (DSB) have collaborated to create an online travel planner called *Rejseplanen,* which consolidates schedule and route information for the country's trains and buses.

Eurolines links the principal Danish cities to major European cities. Säfflebussen offers routes to Sweden. Domestic companies include Thinggaard Express, Hurtigbussen, and Gråhundbus. Abildskou offers service from Copenhagen to several major cities. Bus tickets are usually sold online or on board the buses immediately before departure.

Contacts **Rejseplanen** (⊕ *www.rejseplanen.dk*). **Abildskou** (☎ *70/21–08–88* ⊕ *www.abildskou.dk*). **Eurolines** (☎ *70/10–00–30* ⊕ *www.eurolines.com*). **Hurtigbussen** (☎ *36/13–14–15* ⊕ *www.hurtigbussen.dk*). **Gråhundbus** (☎ *44/68–44–00* ⊕ *www.graahundbus.dk*). **Säfflebussen** (☎ *33/23–54–20* ⊕ *www.safflebussen.se*). **Thinggaard Express** (☎ *98/11–66–00* ⊕ *www.ekspresbus.dk*).

CAR TRAVEL

The only part of Denmark that's connected to the European continent is Jutland, via the E45 highway from Germany. The E20 highway then leads to Funen and Zealand. The Storebæltsbro Bridge connects Funen and Zealand via the E20 highway; the E20 then continues east, over the Lillebæltsbro Bridge, to Copenhagen. You can reach many of the smaller islands via toll bridges.

Øresundsbroen, the monumental bridge that connects Denmark with Sweden, was inaugurated in 2000. The drive that takes you across it from Copenhagen to Malmö takes approximately 45 minutes.

Rental rates in Copenhagen begin at DKr 550 a day and DKr 2,220 a week. This doesn't include an additional per-kilometer fee and any insurance you purchase; there's also a 25% tax on car rentals. The good news? Most companies have special weekend offers.

All passengers must wear seat belts, and cars must have low beams on at all times. It's illegal to talk on the phone while driving. Drive on the right and give way to traffic—*especially to bicyclists*—on the right. A red-and-white YIELD sign or a line of white triangles across the road means you must yield to traffic on the road you are entering. Don't turn right on red unless there is a green arrow indicating that it's allowed.

Speed limits are 50 kph (30 mph) in built-up areas; 100 kph (60 mph) on highways; and 80 kph (50 mph) on other roads. Speeding and, especially, drinking and driving are punished severely, even if no damage is caused. The consumption of one or two beers might lead to a violation, and motorists traveling across the Øresund Bridge must remember that Sweden has an even lower legal limit for blood-alcohol levels. Foreigners must pay all fines on the spot.

GASOLINE Gas costs about DKr 10 per liter (¼ gallon). Stations are mostly self-service and open from 6 or 7 AM to 9 PM or later.

PARKING   You can usually park on the right side of the road, though not on main roads and highways. Signs reading PARKERING/STANDSNING FORBUNT mean no parking or stopping. In town, parking disks are used where there are no automated ticket-vending machines. Get disks from gas stations, post offices, police stations, or tourist offices, and set them to show your time of arrival. For most downtown parking you must buy a ticket from an automatic vending machine and display it on the dash. Parking costs about DKr 10 or more per hour. Parking is generally free on Sundays and public holidays.

TRAIN TRAVEL

Trains within Europe are well connected to Denmark, with Copenhagen serving as the main hub; however, it's often not much cheaper than flying, especially if you make your arrangements from the United States. The DSB and a few private companies cover the country with a dense network of service, supplemented by buses in remote areas. Hourly InterCity trains connect the main towns in Jutland and Funen with Copenhagen and Zealand; faster InterCityLyn trains run on the most important stretches.

You can reserve seats (for an extra DKr 20) on most longer-distance routes. When traveling on InterCity and InterCityLyn, reservations are a good idea as some trains often sell out. Buy tickets online in advance or at stations. Call Arriva for train travel in central and western Jutland, or the DSB Travel Office for the rest of the country.

Contacts Arriva (☎ *70/27–74–82* ⊕ *www.arriva.dk*). **DSB Travel Office** (☎ *70/ 13–14–15* ⊕ *www.dsb.dk*).

RESTAURANTS

Traditional Danish fare relies on provisions native to the region: grains, potatoes, pork, beef, and fish. Most meals begin with *sild,* pickled herring of various flavors, served on *rugbrød,* a very dark and dense rye-based bread. This bread also provides the basis for the most common Danish lunch: *smørrebrød*—open-face sandwiches piled high with various meats, vegetables, and condiments. For dinner, try *flæskesteg,* pork roast with a crispy rind, which is commonly served with *rødkål,* stewed red cabbage, and potatoes.

Denmark's major cities have a good selection of restaurants serving both traditional Danish and international cuisines. Danes start the workday early, which means they generally eat lunch at noon and consume their evening meal on the early side. Make your dinner reservations for no later than 9 PM. Bars and cafés stay open later, and most offer at least light fare.

HOTELS

All hotels listed have private bath unless otherwise noted. Many Danes prefer a shower to a bath, so if you particularly want a bath, ask for it— and be prepared to pay more. Older hotels may have rooms described as "double," which in fact have one double bed plus one foldout sofa big enough for two people.

2

Two things about hotels usually surprise North Americans: the size of Scandinavian beds and the size of Scandinavian breakfasts. Scandinavian double beds are often about 60 inches wide or slightly less, close in size to the U.S. queen size. King-size beds (72 inches wide) are difficult to find and, if available, require special reservations.

APARTMENT AND VILLA RENTALS

Each year many Danes rent out their summer homes in the countryside and along the coast. Travel during the shoulder seasons when, typically, a simple house accommodating four people costs from DKr 1,000 weekly; it can be up to 10 times that in summer. You should book well in advance. A group of Danes who regularly rent out their holiday houses have formed the Association of Danish Holiday House Letters (ADHHL). DanCenter and Feriepartner Danmark also offer vacation rentals. Homes for You lists fully furnished homes and apartments in Copenhagen.

Local Agents DanCenter (☎ 70/13–00–00 in Copenhagen ⊕ www.dancenter. com). **Feriehusudlejernes Brancheforeningen (ADHHL)** (☎ 96/30–22–44 ⊕ www.fbnet.dk). **Feriepartner Danmark** (☎ 47/74–63–34 in Liseleje ⊕ www. feriepartner.com). **Homes for You** (☎ 33/33–08–05 ⊕ www.hay4you.dk).

BED AND BREAKFASTS

Contact Dansk Bed & Breakfast to order their B&B catalog for the whole of Denmark. Odense Tourist Bureau maintains its own list for the Funen and the Central Islands region.

Reservation Services Dansk Bed & Breakfast (☎ 39/61–04–05 ⊕ www. bedandbreakfast.dk). **Odense Tourist Bureau** (☎ 66/12–75–20 ⊕ www. bed-breakfast-fyn.dk).

FARM AND HOME STAYS

A farm vacation is perhaps the best way to experience the Danish countryside, sharing meals with your host family and perhaps helping with the chores. Bed-and-breakfast packages are about DKr 250. Half and full board, with additional meals, can also often be arranged. Contact Dansk Landboturisme for details.

If you aren't necessarily looking for a pastoral experience but would still like to get an insider's view of Danish society, consider a homestay. Meet the Danes helps travelers find accommodation in Danish homes. The informative local hosts can give you invaluable tips regarding sightseeing, shopping, dining, and nightlife.

Contacts Dansk Landboturisme (Farm Holidays ☎ 86/37–39–00 ⊕ www.bond egaardsferie.dk). **Meet the Danes** (☎ 23/28–43–47 ⊕ www.meetthedanes.dk).

HOSTELS

Youth hostels in Denmark are open to everyone regardless of age. If you have an International Youth Hostels Association card (it costs DKr 160 to obtain in Denmark), the rate is DKr 100–DKr 475 during peak season for a single bed; DKr 275–DKr 800 per person for a private room with toilet and/or shower. Without the card, there's a surcharge of about DKr 30 per person. Prices don't include breakfast.

Hostels fill up quickly in summer, so make your reservations early. Bring your own linens or sleep sheet, although these can usually be rented at the hostel. Sleeping bags aren't allowed.

Contacts Danhostel Danmarks Vandrerhjem (☎ *33/31–36–12* ⊕ *www.danhostel. com*). **Hostelling International—USA** (⊕ *www.hihostels.com*).

KROER

The old stagecoach *kroer* (inns) scattered throughout Denmark can be cheap yet charming alternatives to standard hotels. You can cut your costs by contacting Danske Kroer & Hoteller to invest in Inn Cheques, valid at 83 participating inns and hotels throughout the country. Each check costs about DKr 750 per couple and entitles you to an overnight stay in a double room including breakfast. Family checks for three (DKr 900) and four (DKr 1050) are also available. Please note, the organization also includes a few chain hotels bereft of the charm you might be expecting. Also, some of the participating establishments tack on a surcharge in addition to the Inn Cheque.

Contact Danske Kroer & Hoteller (☎ *75/64–87–00* ⊕ *www.krohotel.dk*).

WHAT IT COSTS IN DANISH KRONER				
¢	$	$$	$$$	$$$$
COPENHAGEN				
Restaurants	under 100	100–200	200–300	300–400	over 400
Hotels	under 1,000	1,000–1,500	1,500–2,000	2,000–2,500	over 2,500
ELSEWHERE				
Restaurants	under 100	100–150	150–200	200–250	over 250
Hotels	under 1,000	1,000–1,250	1,250–1,500	1,500–1,750	over 1,750

Restaurant prices are based on the median main course price at dinner. Hotel prices are for two people in a standard double room in high season.

ESSENTIALS

ELECTRICITY The electrical current in Denmark is 220 volts, 50 cycles alternating current (AC). Outlets take the Continental plugs, with two round plugs. To use your North American blow-dryer, say, you'll need both a converter and an adapter.

EMERGENCIES The general 24-hour emergency number throughout Denmark is 112. For auto emergencies, contact your rental agency or Falck, the emergency road service. The American embassy is in Copenhagen.

Contacts Falck (☎ *70/33–33–11* ⊕ *www.falck.dk*). **General Emergency Number** (☎ *112*). **U.S. Embassy** (✉ *Dag Hammarskjølds Allé 24, Østerbro, Copenhagen* ☎ *33/41–71–00* ⊕ *www.usembassy.dk*).

ENTRY REQUIREMENTS U.S. citizens need only a valid passport for stays of up to three months.

LANGUAGE Danish is a difficult tongue for foreigners. Danes are good linguists, however, and almost everyone, except perhaps elderly people in rural areas, speaks English. In Sønderjylland, the southern region of Jutland, most people speak or understand German.

Difficult-to-pronounce Danish characters include the "ø," pronounced a bit like a very short "er," similar to the French "eu"; "æ," which sounds like the "a" in "ape" but with a glottal stop, or the "a" in "cat," depending on the region; and the "å" (also written "aa"), which sounds like "or." The important thing about these characters isn't that you pronounce them correctly—foreigners usually can't—but that you know to look for them in the phone book at the very end. Mr. Søren Åstrup, for example, will be found after "Z"; Æ and Ø follow.

MONEY
MATTERS

Currency and Exchange. The monetary unit in Denmark is the krone (DKr), divided into 100 øre. Even though Denmark hasn't adopted the euro, the Danish krone is firmly bound to it at about DKr 7.5 to 1€, with only minimal fluctuations in exchange rates.

At this writing, the krone stood at 5.03 to the U.S. dollar and 7.46 to the euro. ATMs are located around most towns and cities. Look for the red signs for KONTANTEN/DANKORT AUTOMAT. Many, but not all, machines are open 24 hours. Check with your bank about daily withdrawal limits before you go.

Pricing. Denmark's economy is stable, and inflation remains reasonably low. On the other hand, the Danish cost of living is quite high. In some areas prices are comparable to European capitals; prices for certain goods and services may be higher. As in all of Scandinavia, alcoholic beverages and tobacco products are very expensive due to heavy taxation.

Sample Prices. Cup of coffee, DKr 20–DKr 30; bottle of beer, DKr 30–DKr 35; soda, DKr 20–DKr 25; ham sandwich, DKr 35–DKr 45; 1½-km (1-mi) taxi ride, about DKr 57.

Taxes. All hotel, restaurant, and departure taxes and VAT (what the Danes call *moms*) are automatically included in prices. VAT is 25%.

Tipping. It has long been held that the egalitarian Danes don't expect to be tipped. That said, most people do tip, and those who receive tips appreciate them. Service is included in hotel bills. Many tourist restaurants have started adding a gratuity to bills; always check to see if it's been included. If not, a token tip is the rule of thumb. The same holds true for taxis—if a trip costs DKr 58, most people will give the driver DKr 60. If the driver is extremely friendly or helpful, tip more at your own discretion. Hotel porters expect about DKr 5 per bag.

PHONES

The country code for Denmark is 45. Dial the eight-digit number for calls anywhere within the country. To call abroad, dial 00, then the country code (e.g.,1 for the United States and Canada), the area code, and the number. For national directory assistance, dial 118; for an international operator, dial 113; for a directory-assisted international call, dial 115. Most operators speak English.

Local phones accept 1-, 2-, 5-, 10-, and 20-kroner coins. Pick up the receiver, dial the number, always including the area code, and wait until the party answers; then deposit the coins. You have roughly a minute per krone; on some phones you can make another call on the same payment if your time has not run out. When it does, you will hear a beep and your call will be disconnected unless you deposit another coin. Coin-operated phones are becoming increasingly rare; it's less frustrating and less expensive to buy a local phone card from a kiosk or a post office.

Denmark, like most European countries, has a different cellular-phone switching system from the one used in North America. Newer phones can handle both technologies; check with the dealer where you purchased your phone to see if it can work on the European system. Fixed-rate Danish SIM cards can be purchased at most kiosks and inserted into your phone. If all else fails, several companies rent cellular phones.

VISITOR INFO   **Contacts Danmarks Turistråd** (*Danish Tourist Board* ☎ *32/88–99–00, 212/ 885–9700 in New York* ⊕ *www.visitdenmark.com*). **Scandinavian Tourist Board** (⊕ *www.goscandinavia.com*).

COPENHAGEN

Copenhagen—København in Danish—has no glittering skylines and hardly any of the high-stress bustle common to most capitals. Throngs of bicycles glide along in ample bike lanes at a pace that's utterly human. The early-morning air in the pedestrian streets of the city's core is redolent of freshly baked bread and soap-scrubbed storefronts. If there's such a thing as a cozy city, this is it.

The town was a fishing colony until 1157, when Valdemar the Great gave it to Bishop Absalon, who built a castle on what is now the parliament, Christiansborg. It grew as a center on the Baltic trade route and became known as *købmændenes havn* (merchants' harbor) and eventually København. In the 15th century it became the royal residence and the capital of Norway and Sweden. From 1596 to 1648, Christian IV, a Renaissance king obsessed with fine architecture, began a building boom that crowned the city with towers and castles, many of which still stand. They're almost all that remain of the city's 800-year history; much of Copenhagen was destroyed by two major fires in the 18th century and by British bombing during the Napoleonic Wars.

Despite a tumultuous history, Copenhagen survives as the liveliest Scandinavian capital. With its backdrop of copper towers and crooked rooftops, the venerable city is soothed by one of the highest standards of living in the world and spangled by the lights and gardens of Tivoli.

GETTING HERE AND AROUND
AIR TRAVEL   Copenhagen Airport is 10 km (6 mi) southeast of downtown in Kastrup. The 20-minute taxi ride downtown costs DKr 190–DKr 250, depending on route and time of day. The city's sleek and affordable subterranean train system takes about 14 minutes to zip passengers into Copenhagen's main train station. Buy a ticket (DKr 28.50) upstairs in the airport train station at Terminal 3. Trains depart every 4 minutes

CUTTING COSTS

As expensive as it is, Denmark is in many ways less pricey than the rest of Scandinavia. That said, read on for ways you can save money on a trip here.

AIR TRAVEL

SAS Visit Scandinavia/Europe Air Pass cost between $72 and $204, depending on routing and destination, and are valid for destinations within Denmark, Norway, Sweden, and Finland. They're sold only to non-Europeans. You must buy the coupons in conjunction with transatlantic flights, and you can use them year-round for a maximum of three months.

Contact Scandinavian Airlines (☎ 800/221–2350 ⊕ www.flysas. com).

GROUND TRANSPORTATION

Eurail Denmark and Eurail Scandinavia passes also get you discounts on private train lines, ferries, and select museums. Eurail is only available for non-Europeans and can be bought online in advance of your trip. A Eurail Denmark Pass is available for three or seven days of travel within a month ($99 and $149). Eurail Scandinavia Pass affords 4 to 10 days of travel within 60 days ($369–$569). All prices are for second-class travel.

Rail Pass Contacts DER Travel Services (☎ 800/782–2424 ⊕ www.der.com). **Eurail** (⊕ www. eurail.com). **Nordic Saga Tours** (☎ 800/840–6449 ⊕ www.nordic saga.com). **Passage Tours** (☎ 800/431–1511 ⊕ www.passage tours.com). **Rail Europe** (☎ 888/ 382–7245 ⊕ www.raileurope. com). **ScanAm World Tours** (☎ 800/545–2204 ⊕ www.scandina viantravel.com).

HOTELS

Ask a travel agent about discounts, including summer hotel checks for Best Western and Scandic. Most countries also offer summer bargains for foreign tourists; winter bargains can be even greater.

Look for hotels that include breakfast and discounted weekend rates. Although it's wise to reserve two months in advance, last-minute (i.e., same-day) rooms booked at a tourist office can lead to savings of up to 50%.

Scandinavian countries offer Hotel and Inn Checques, or prepaid vouchers, for everything from luxe hotels to country cottages. These vouchers, which you can buy from travel agents or online from Danske Kroer & Hoteller or ProSkandinavia, are sold individually and in packets and offer savings of up to 50%. Breakfast is usually included when using them. Be sure to mention that you'll be paying with these vouchers when you reserve.

Contact Danske Kroer & Hoteller (☎ 75/64–87–00 ⊕ www.krohotel. dk). **ProSkandinavia** (☎ +47 22/ 41–13–12 in Norway).

during the day and every 15 minutes during night hours. Trains also travel from the airport directly to Malmö, Sweden (DKr 60), leaving every 20 minutes and taking 20 minutes in transit. Trains run from 5 AM to midnight. On Thursday, Friday, and Saturday, trains run all night. Note that a free airport bus connects the international terminal with the domestic terminal.

CAR TRAVEL   All major international car-rental agencies are represented in Copenhagen; most are at Copenhagen Airport or near Vesterport Station. The E20 highway, via bridges, connects Jutland with Funen, and goes on to Copenhagen. Farther north, from Århus (in Jutland) you can get direct auto-catamaran service to Kalundborg (on Zealand). From there, Route 23 leads to Roskilde, about 72 km (45 mi) east. Take Route 21 east and follow the signs to Copenhagen, another 40 km (25 mi).

The trip over the Øresund Bridge to Malmö, Sweden takes about 45 minutes, and the steep bridge toll stands at DKr 260 per car.

If you're only planning to sightsee in central Copenhagen, however, a car won't be convenient. Parking spaces are at a premium and, when available, are expensive. A maze of one-way streets and bicycle lanes make it even more complicated. If you're going to drive, choose a small car that's easy to parallel park and bring a lot of small change to feed the meters.

Car Rental Avis (✉ *Kampmannsg. 1, Vesterbro* ☎ *70/24–77–07* ⊕ *www.avis.dk*). **Hertz** (✉ *Ved Vesterport 3, Vesterbro* ☎ *33/17–90–20* ⊕ *www.hertzdk.dk*).

PUBLIC   Copenhagen's Hovedbanegården (Central Station) is the hub of the DSB
TRANSPORT   rail network and is connected to most major cities in Europe. Intercity trains run regularly (usually every hour) from 6 AM to midnight for principal towns in Funen and Jutland. Other major stations include Vesterport (in Vesterbro), Nørreport (in Nørrebro), and Østerport in (Østerbro). You can make reservations at most stations, online, and through travel agents.

Most trains and buses operate from 5 AM (Sunday 6 AM) to midnight. After that, night buses run every half hour from 1 AM to 4:30 AM from the main bus station at Rådhus Pladsen to most areas of the city and surroundings.

Trains and buses operate on the same ticket system and divide Copenhagen and surrounding areas into three zones. Unlimited travel within two zones (inner city area) for one hour costs DKr 20 for an adult. A discount *klippe kort* (clip card), good for 10 rides, costs DKr 125 for two zones. The card must be stamped in the automatic ticket machines on buses or at stations. (If you don't stamp your clip card, you can be fined up to DKr 600.) Cards can be stamped multiple times for multiple passengers and/or longer rides.

Buses have a Danish information line with an automatic answering menu that's not very helpful, but try pressing the number 1 on your phone and wait for a human to pick up. The info line operates daily 7 AM–9:30 PM. You might do better by asking a bus driver or stopping by the Movia Buses main office (open weekdays 10–5:30 PM) on the Rådhus Pladsen, where the helpful staff speaks English.

The harbor buses are small ferries that travel up and down the canal, with stops at the Royal Library's Black Diamond, Knippelsbro, Nyhavn, the Opera, Holmen, and Nordre Toldbod. The boats are a great way to get around the city while enjoying lovely vistas along the way. The harbor buses run regularly from 7 AM to 11 PM (10 AM to 11 PM on weekends). Standard bus fares and tickets apply.

The Metro system runs regularly from 5 AM to midnight, and all night on weekends. There are currently two Metro lines in operation. Both run from the suburb of Vanløse; one runs to western Amager, while the other continues eastward toward the airport. The major Metro hubs in central Copenhagen are Nøreport Station and Kongens Nytorv. The Metro is a good option for trips to Frederiksberg, Christianshavn, Amager Strandpark, and the airport. Stations are marked with a dark-red Metro logo. They link the northern suburb of Vanløse to the airport and Western Amager.

> ## SIGHTSEEING SAVINGS
>
> The CPHCard offers unlimited travel on buses, harbor buses and Metro and suburban trains (S-trains), as well as admission to some 60 museums and sights throughout the Copenhagen area. You can choose between a 24- and a 72-hour card (DKr 199 or DKr 429). The card also gets you discounts on things like car rental and Scandlines' crossing of the Sound (Øresund) between Sweden and Denmark. Buy the cards at bus and train stations, tourist offices, hotels, and online. They're worthwhile if you're planning a nonstop, intense sightseeing tour.

Contacts Bus information (☎ *36/13–14–15* ⊕ *www.moviatrafik.dk*). **DSB Information** (☎ *70/13–14–15* ⊕ *www.dsb.dk*). **Metro information** (☎ *70/15–16–15* ⊕ *www.m.dk*). **S-train information** (☎ *70/13–14–15* ⊕ *www.rejseplan.dk*).

TAXI TRAVEL The shiny computer-metered Mercedes and Volvo cabs aren't cheap. The base charge is DKr 24–DKr 40, plus DKr 11.50–DKr 15.80 per kilometer, depending on the time of day. A cab is available when it displays the sign FRI (free); you can hail cabs, pick them up in front of the main train station or at taxi stands, or call for one. Outside the city center, always call for a cab, as your attempts to hail one will be in vain. Please note that calling a cab is more expensive than hailing one.

Contacts Amager Øbro Taxi (☎ *32/51–51–51*). **Koøbenhavns Taxa** (☎ *35/35–35–35*).

ESSENTIALS

Currency Exchange The Change Group (✉ *Vimmelskaftet 47, Downtown* ☎ *33/93–04–18*). **Den Danske Bank** (✉ *Copenhagen Airport, Kastrup* ☎ *32/46–02–80* ⊕ *www.danskebank.dk*). **Forex** (✉ *Banegårdspladsen 7, main train station, Vesterbro* ☎ *33/11–22–20* ⊕ *www.forex-valutaveksling.dk*).

Emergencies Police, fire, and ambulance (☎ *112*).

Hospital Rigshospitalet (✉ *Blegdamsvej 9, Østerbro* ☎ *35/45–35–45*).

24-Hour Pharmacy Steno Apotek (✉ *Vesterbrog. 6C, Vesterbro* ☎ *33/14–82–66* ⊕ *www.apoteket.dk*).

VISITOR INFO   **Wonderful Copenhagen** (✉ *Vesterbrog. 4C, Vesterbro* ☎ *70/22–24–42* ⊕ *www. visitcopenhagen.com*).

EXPLORING COPENHAGEN

Be it sea or canal, water surrounds Copenhagen. A network of bridges and drawbridges connects the two main islands—Zealand and Amager—on which Copenhagen is built. The seafaring atmosphere is indelible, especially around the districts of Nyhavn and Christianshavn.

Copenhagen is small, with most sights within 2½ square km (1 square mi) at its center. Sightseeing, especially downtown, is best done on foot at an unhurried pace. Or follow the example of the Danes and rent a bike. That said, excellent bus and train systems can come to the rescue of weary legs.

With just one day in Copenhagen, start at Kongens Nytorv and Nyhavn and head up the pedestrian street of Strøget in the direction of Rådhuspladsen. You can detour to see the exteriors of Christiansborg, Børsen, Rundetårn, and Rosenborg Slot along the way. If you're not up for a walk, one of the guided canal tours will give you a good sense of the city. In summer or around Christmas time, round off your day with a relaxed stroll and nightcap in Tivoli. With additional days in Copenhagen, plan to spend time inside one or more of the following: Rosenborg Slot, Ny Carlsberg Glyptotek, Nationalmuseet, Statens Museum for Kunst, and Kastellet. Alternatively, make your way toward one of the surrounding neighborhoods: Christianshavn for small café-lined canals; Christiania for hippie culture past and present; or Nørrebro and Vesterbro for a mixture of ethnic shops and trendy youth culture. Noteworthy side trips for longer stays include the expansive park of Dyrehaven in Charlottenlund, the Lilliputian village of Dragør, the historic castle in Hillerød, the Louisiana modern art museum in Humlebæk, Hamlet's castle in Helsingør, and the Viking Ship Museum in Roskilde.

Some Copenhagen sights, especially churches, keep short hours, particularly in fall and winter. It's a good idea to call ahead or check with the tourist offices to confirm opening times.

CENTRUM: ON AND AROUND STRØGET

Centrum (central Copenhagen, aka downtown and city center) is packed with shops, restaurants, and businesses, as well as the crowning architectural achievements of Christian IV. The current boundaries of the city center roughly match the fortified borders under the reign of Christian IV (1588–1648), when the city was separated from its surroundings with fortified walls and moats. Access to the Copenhagen was limited to four gates: Vesterport (near the current City Hall), Nørreport (near Nørreport Station, Østerport (near Kastellet), and Amagerport, which separated Christianshavn from Amager. Many of Copenhagen's parks, lakes, and fortresses that you will inevitably pass when touring the city were part of this elaborate defense system.

Centrum is cut by the city's pedestrian spine, called Strøget (pronounced *Stroy*-et), Europe's longest pedestrian shopping street. It's actually a series of five streets: Frederiksberggade, Nygade, Vimmelskaftet, Amagertorv, and Østergade. By mid-morning, particularly on Saturday, it's congested with people, baby strollers, and motionless-until-paid mimes.

2

GETTING AROUND
Strøget is 1.8 km long (approximately 1 mi). Plan to explore it and its side streets and grand squares on foot. A hurried walk (20 minutes or so) will take you from Kongens Nytorv in the east to Rådhuspladsen and Tivoli, which border Vesterbro in the west. But to fully experience the area, consider spending a few hours or even a full day for shopping, café visits, and taking in notable sights.

Strøget is also a good starting point from which to explore other parts of the city. A half-day detour from Kongens Nytorv, at the eastern end of the strip, takes you through Nyhavn, Amalienborg Castle, the Marble Church, the Resistance Museum, Kastellet and the Little Mermaid. From Amagertorv, also on the eastern part of Strøget, you can take another manageable walk to check out the sights around Chritiansborg and Børsen before crossing Knippelsbro Bridge to relax in a Christianshavn Café or, for a longer walk, continuing on to Christiania.

Walking north from Amagertorv, Købmagergade takes you in the direction of Kongens Have, Rosenborg Slot, and Statens Museum for Kunst, the National Gallery, and farther north and northeast toward the neighborhoods of Nørrebro and Østerbro. From the westernmost hub of Rådhuspladsen, Tivoli, Glyptoteket, Danish Design Center, and the neighborhood of Vesterbro are all within walking distance.

Shops along Strøget tend to keep longer hours than those elsewhere; from 10 to 7 on weekdays and 10 to 5 on Saturday. Most stores are closed on Sunday. Strøget is good for major stores, posh boutiques, porcelain shops, and street performances. If you prefer unique, non-chain shops, head to the colloquially named Strædet (composed of Kompagnistræde and Læderstræde), one block south, which runs parallel to the main drag from the area just south of Rådhuspladsen to Højbro Plads and Amagertorv. This quieter strip has cafés, design stores, and antiques dealers.

TOP ATTRACTIONS
6   **Christiansborg Slot.** Surrounded by canals on three sides, the massive granite Christiansborg Castle is where the queen officially receives guests.
Fodor'sChoice From 1441 until the fire of 1795, it was used as the royal residence.
★ Even though the first two castles on the site were burned, Christiansborg remains an impressive neobaroque and neoclassical compound. Free tours of the **Folketinget** (*Parliament House* ☎*33/37–55–00* ⊕*www. folketinget.dk*) are given weekdays from July until mid-September. English-language tours begin at 2. Additional tours are offered on Sunday. At the **Kongelige Repræsantationlokaler** (*Royal Reception Chambers* ☎*33/92–64–92*), you're asked to don slippers to protect the floors. Admission is DKr 65; entry is via guided tour only. Tours are given daily May through September. English-language tours are at 11, 1,

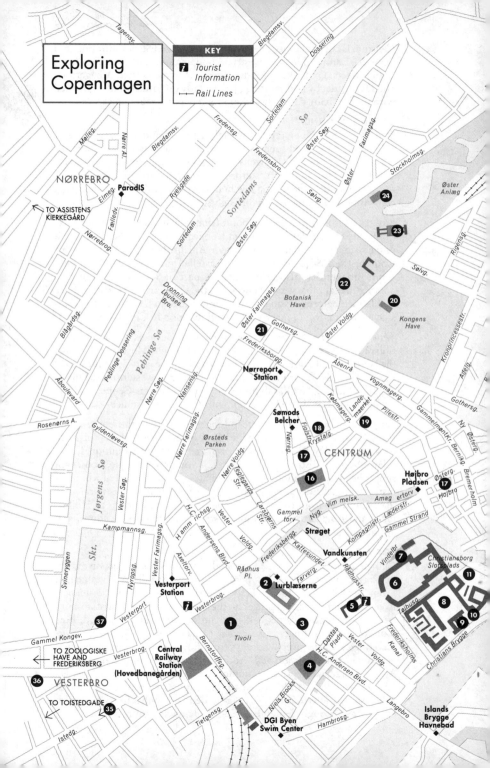

Exploring Copenhagen

KEY

🛈 Tourist Information

⊢━ Rail Lines

NØRREBRO

ParadIS

TO ASSISTENS
KIERKEGÅRD

Tagensv.
Blegdamsv.
Dossering
Sortedam
Sø
Øster Søg.
Øster Farimagsg.
Stockholmsg.
Øster Anlæg

24

23

22

Botanisk Have

20

Kongens Have

Sølvg.
Rigensg.

21

Frederiksborg.

Nørreport Station

Åbenrå

Vognmagerg.

Gammelmel
Kr. Bernikg.
Ny Østerg.
Gothersg.

Sømods Belcher

18

Landemærket

19

Pilestr.

17

CENTRUM

16

Højbro Pladsen

17

Østerg.
Højbro
Bremerholm

Vim melsk.   Amagertorv
Nyg.   Læderstr.
Strøget   Kompagnistr.   Gammel Strand

Vandkunsten

7

Christiansborg Slotsplads

6

11

5 🛈

8

9

10

Vesterport Station 🛈

Vesterbrog.

1

Tivoli

2 Lurblæserne

3

Rådhus Pl.

Central Railway Station (Hovedbanegården)

4

H.C. Andersen Blvd.

37

Gammel Kongev.

TO ZOOLOGISKE HAVE AND FREDERIKSBERG

36 VESTERBRO

TO TOISTEDGADE

35

DGI Byen Swim Center

Islands Brygge Havnebad

Jørgens Sø
Peblinge Sø
Sortedams Sø

Dronning Louises Bro

Ørsteds Parken

ORGANIZED TOURS

There are many ways to take in the city. The tourist office monitors all tours and has brochures on the various operators and trips. Most tours run through the summer into September.

BY BIKE

More Danes bike to work than they do drive. Bikes are well suited to Copenhagen's flat terrain, rentals are readily available, and most roads have bike lanes. Rentals cost DKr 75–DKr 300 a day, with a deposit of DKr 500–DKr 1,000. You may also be lucky enough to find a free city bike chained up at racks in various spots around town, including Nørreport and Nyhavn. Just insert a DKr 20 coin; you'll get it back upon returning the bike.

City Safari (⊠ *Dansk Arkitektur Center Strandg. 27B, Christianshavn* ☎ *33/23–94–90* ⊕ *www. citysafari.dk*) bike tours run three hours. They offer a tour of historic sites as well as a Copenhagen by Night trip. The guides not only point out main attractions and provide helpful travel information, but also give some insight into the daily routines of the Danes. Theme tours are also available.

BY BOAT

Canal Tours (☎ *32/96–30–00* ⊕ *www.canaltours.dk*) offers a Harbor and Canal Tour (one hour) that leaves from Gammel Strand and Nyhavn every half hour in summer (heated and roofed boats are in service throughout most of the winter). The company also organizes lunch and dinner cruises. Just south of the embarkation point for Canal Tours City and Harbor Tour is **Netto Boats** (☎ *32/54–41–02* ⊕ *www. havnerundfart.dk*), which offers hour-long tours for about half the price of its competitors.

BY BUS

The Grand Tour of Copenhagen (2½ hours) offered by **Copenhagen Coach Service/Paaske Bus** (☎ *32/66–00–00* ⊕ *www.sightseeing.dk*) includes Rosenborg Castle, Tivoli, the Glyptotek, the Danish Parliament, the Stock Exchange, the Danish Royal Theater, Nyhavn, Amalienborg Castle, and the Little Mermaid. The City Tour (1½ hours) is more general. The one-hour Open Top Tours are given on double-deckers that allow you to embark and disembark along the route all day with one ticket.

WALKING TOURS

Copenhagen Walking Tours (☎ *40/81–12–17* ⊕ *www.copenhagen-walkingtours.dk*) has five two-hour English-language tours. In addition to tours related to culture and city history, they offer a Hans Christian Andersen–theme walk and a tour of Jewish Copenhagen.

and 3. From October through April, there are tours every day at 3 PM except Monday. The **Højesteret** (*Supreme Court* ⊠ *Prins Joørgens Gård, Copenhagen K, Centrum*) was built on the site of the city's first fortress. The guards at the entrance are knowledgeable and friendly; ask them about the court's complicated opening hours. While the castle was being rebuilt around 1900, the national museum excavated the **ruins of Bishop Absalon's castle** (☎ *33/92–64–92*) beneath it. The resulting dark, subterranean maze contains fascinating models and architectural relics. The ruins are open daily 10–4, and admission is DKr 40. ⌧*Slotsholmen (area around Christiansborg, bordered by Boorsgade, Vindebrogade, and Frederiksholms Kanal) Centrum.*

⑨ Kongelige Bibliotek (*Royal Library*). If you like grand architecture and great views, you really should visit the majestic Royal Library. Among its more than 2 million volumes are accounts of Viking journeys to America and Greenland and original manuscripts by Hans Christian Andersen and Karen Blixen (Isak Dinesen). Peer through the glass opening in the door to the old, ornate reading room, which is open only to readers.

The library's massive new glass-and-granite addition, called the Black Diamond, looms between the main building and the waterfront. The Black Diamond hosts temporary historical exhibits that often feature books, manuscripts, and artifacts culled from the library's extensive holdings. The National Museum of Photography, also housed in the Black Diamond, contains temporary exhibitions with handouts and wall texts in English.

Escalators that lift you from sea level to the main study areas provide spectacular views of both the harbor and an impressive ceiling mural by the Danish artist Per Kirkeby. The park that lies between the library and the parliament is a lovely place for a stroll or a pensive rest. ⌧*Søren Kierkegaards Pl. 1, Centrum* ☎*33/47–47–47* ⊕*www. kb.dk* ⌧*Library free; temporary exhibits DKr 40* ☉*Museum weekdays 10–7, Sat. 10–5.*

NEED A BREAK? **Café Øieblikket** (⌧*Søren Kierkegaards Pl. 1, Centrum* ☎*33/47–47–47*) operates out of a prime corner on the ground floor of the Royal Library's Black Diamond. It's named after a literary journal to which philosopher Søren Kierkegaard once contributed. In summer the café sets up outdoor tables. The simple fare includes croissants, brownies, and sandwiches made on fluffy round buns.

⑤ Nationalmuseet (*National Museum*). An 18th-century royal residence, peaked by massive overhead windows, has contained—since the 1930s—what is regarded as one of the best national museums in Europe. Extensive permanent exhibits chronicle Danish cultural history from prehistoric to modern times. The museum has one of the largest collections of Stone Age tools in the world as well as Egyptian, Greek, and Roman antiquities. The exhibit on Danish prehistory features a great section on Viking times. The children's museum, with replicas of period clothing and a scalable copy of a real Viking ship, makes history fun for the under-12 set. Displays have English labels, and the do-it-yourself walking tour "History of Denmark in 60 Minutes" offers a good introduction to Denmark; the guide is free at the information desk. ⊠*Ny Vesterg. 10, Centrum* ☎*33/13–44–11* ⊕*www.natmus. dk* ⊠*Free* ☉*Tues.–Sun. 10–5.*

❹ ★ **Ny Carlsberg Glyptotek.** Among Copenhagen's most important museums—thanks to its exquisite antiquities and a world-class collection of impressionist masterpieces— the neoclassical New Carlsberg

WORD OF MOUTH

"If you can only see one museum, make it either the National Museum (very friendly) or the Glyptoteket Museum (there's a nice atrium café). . . . The city is a very walkable . . . you could walk from castle to castle in a day; follow the Royal Guard from Rosenborg Castle to Amalienborg, the residence of the royal family. [However] take a boat tour from Nyhavn and save walking to see the Mermaid." —MilenaM

Museum was donated in 1888 by Carl Jacobsen, son of the founder of the Carlsberg Brewery. Surrounding its lush indoor garden, a series of rooms house works by Pissarro, Degas, Monet, Sisley, Rodin, and Gauguin. The museum is also renowned for its extensive assemblage of Egyptian and Greek pieces, not to mention Europe's finest collection of Roman portraits and the best collection of Etruscan art outside Italy. A modern wing, designed by the acclaimed Danish architect Henning Larsen, provides a luminous entry to the French painting section. From June to September, guided English-language tours start at 2. The café overlooking the winter garden is well-known among Copenhageners for its Sunday Brunch. ⊠*Dantes Pl. 7, Centrum* ☎*33/41–81–41* ⊕*www. glyptoteket.dk* ⊠*DKr 50; free Sun.* ☉*Tues.–Sun. 10–4.*

❶❹ **Nyhavn** (*New Harbor*). This harbor-front neighborhood was built 300 years ago to attract traffic and commerce to the city center. Until 1970 the area was a favorite haunt of sailors. Though restaurants, boutiques, and antiques stores now outnumber tattoo parlors, many old buildings have been well preserved and retain the harbor's authentic 18th-century maritime character; you can even see a fleet of old-time sailing ships from the quay. Hans Christian Andersen lived at various times in the Nyhavn houses at numbers 18, 20, and 67.

NEED A BREAK?

Dozens of restaurants and cafés line Nyhavn. **Nyhavns Færgekro** (⊠*Nyhavn 5, Centrum* ☎ *33/15–15–88*) is among the best, with moderately priced Danish treats served in a cozy dining room. The windows still in place date back to the building's early incarnation as a home to the shipping company White Star Line, which ominously sold tickets to the *Titanic.* For lunch, try the all-you-can-eat buffet of pickled herring or a range of other Danish specialties. The restaurant is also known for its own flavored snaps collection, which is made in-house.

1 Tivoli. Copenhagen's best-known attraction, conveniently next to its main train station, attracts an astounding 1 million people from mid-April to mid-September. Tivoli is more sophisticated than a mere amusement park: among its attractions are a pantomime theater, an open-air stage, 38 restaurants (some of them very elegant), and frequent concerts, which cover the spectrum from classical to rock to jazz. Fantastic flower exhibits color the lush gardens and float on the swan-filled ponds.

Fodor'sChoice ★

WORD OF MOUTH

"Don't go to Tivoli during the day, go in the evening. We went twice—each time having dinner in a nice place. Although we went on a couple of rides we mostly enjoyed just strolling the beautifully lit areas, listening to the music, and watching the fireworks display that happens as the park closes."   —nytraveler

The park was established in the 1840s, when Danish architect George Carstensen persuaded a worried King Christian VIII to let him build an amusement park on the edge of the city's fortifications, rationalizing that "when people amuse themselves, they forget politics." The Tivoli Guard, a youth version of the Queen's Royal Guard, performs every day. Try to see Tivoli at least once by night, when 100,000 colored lanterns illuminate the Chinese pagoda and the main fountain. Some evenings there are also fireworks displays. Call to check the season's opening and closing dates as well as family discounts. Tivoli is also open select hours around Halloween and from late November until late December. The **Nimb** (⊠ *Bernstorffsgade 5, Centrum*), accessed from inside the gardens as well as from outside year-round, is a complex dating from 1909. It has Moorish-inspired architecture and was, indeed, once a bazaar. It was also one of the first buildings here to house a restaurant— a place for the jet-set crowd in the '20s and '30s. A DKr 100-million investment (roughly $20 million) has transformed the building into a multipurpose high-class playground with a luxury all-suite hotel, a bar, a gourmet restaurant, a bistro, a dairy, a chocolate factory, and a well-stocked wine cellar. ⊠ *Vesterbrog. 3, Centrum (on border of Vesterbro district)* ☎ *33/15–10–01* ⊕ *www.tivoli.dk* 🎫 *Grounds DKr 85, unlimited ride pass DKr 200* ⊙ *Mid-Apr.–mid-Sept., Sun.–Wed. 11–11, Fri. 11 AM–12:30 AM, Sat. 11 AM–midnight.*

 NEED A BREAK?

The **Løgismose Shop, Dairy & Grill-Bar** (⊠ *The Nimb, Tivoli Gardens, Bernstorffsgade 5, Centrum* ☎ *88/70–00–00*) is a combined gourmet deli, dairy, and chocolate factory sells its own brand of Summerbird chocolates. Watch organic butter being churned behind the glassed-in working dairy or grab some take-away for a picnic. You could also try gourmet hot dog—it's roasted in duck fat and rosemary and comes with soft onions. Wash it down with organic chocolate milk.

WORTH NOTING

11 Børsen (*Stock Exchange*). This masterpiece of fantasy and architecture is Europe's oldest stock exchange. Børsen was built between 1619 and 1640, with the majority of the construction in the 1620s. Christian IV commissioned the building in large part because he wanted to make Denmark the economic superpower and crossroads of Europe. Rumor has it that when it was being built he was the one who twisted the dragons' tails on the spire that tops the building. When it was first opened, it was used as a sort of medieval mall, filled with shopping stalls. Though parts of Børsen still operate as a stock exchange, the bulk of the building houses the chamber of commerce, and therefore the interior isn't open to the public. Across the canal, look for a square, modern building: the Nationalbanken (*the Danish National Bank*), designed by the famed Danish designer and architect Arne Jacobsen, is another key financial building. ⊠*Slotsholmsgade 3, Centrum.*

❸ Dansk Design Center (*Danish Design Center*). This sleek, glass-panel structure looms in sharp contrast to the old-world ambience of Tivoli just across the street. More a design showroom than a museum, the center's highlights are the innovative temporary exhibits (some great, others less so) on the main floor. One-third of these showcase Danish design; the rest focus on international design. The semipermanent collection on the ground floor (renewed every other year) often includes samples from the greats, including chairs by Arne Jacobsen, several artichoke PH lamps (designed by Poul Henningsen), and Bang & Olufsen radios and stereos. Wall labels are in English. The center's shop carries a wide range of Danish design items and selected pieces from the temporary exhibits. You can enjoy light organic meals in the café. ⊠*H. C. Andersens Blvd. 27, Centrum* ☎*33/69–33–69* ⊕*www.ddc.dk* ☜*DKr 50* ☉ *Weekdays 10–5, Wed. 10–9, weekends 11–4.*

❿ Dansk Jødisk Museum (*Danish Jewish Museum*). In a wing of the Royal Library, this national center of Jewish culture, art, and history opened in June 2004. Objects of both secular and religious interest are on display, including paintings, prints, jewelry, scrapbooks, films, and much more. The site was designed by Daniel Libeskind, the architect behind the winning design proposal for the World Trade Center memorial in New York City. The museum also gives extensive coverage to the Danish resistance movement, whose work during World War II helped bring nearly all of Denmark's 7,000 Jews to safety in Sweden. The museum has information in English. ⊠*Proviantpassegen. 6, Centrum* ☎*33/ 11–22–18* ⊕*www.jewmus.dk* ☜*DKr 40* ☉*June–Aug., Tues.–Sun. 10–5; Sept.–May., Tues.–Fri. 1–4, weekends 11–5.*

⓭ Kongens Nytorv. A mounted statue of Christian V dominates King's New Square. Crafted in 1688 by the French sculptor Lamoureux, the subject is conspicuously depicted as a Roman emperor. Every year, at the end of June, graduating high school students arrive in truckloads and dance beneath the furrowed brow of the sober statue.

Charlottenborg (⊠*Nyhavn 2, Centrum* ☎*33/13–40–22* ⊕*www.kun sthalcharlottenborg.dk*), a Dutch baroque–style castle on the square, was built by Frederik III's half brother in 1670. Since 1754 the garden-flanked property has housed the faculty and students of the Danish Academy of Fine Art. A section of the building is devoted to exhibitions of contemporary art and is open to the public. Tuesday through Sunday noon to 5. Admission is DKr 60. The old, pillared **Det Kongelige Teater** (*The Royal Danish Theater*) (✉*Kongens Nytorv 9* ☎*33/69–69–69 for tickets* ⊕*www.kgl-teater.dk*), now dubbed Gamle Scene since the recent openings of The Opera and the Royal Danish Playhouse, was established in 1748, although the facade dates from 1874. Since the division of the Royal Theatre into separate venues, the original building is primarily devoted to ballets performed by the world-renowned Royal Danish Ballet. Statues of Danish poet Adam Oehlenschläger and author Ludvig Holberg—whose works remain the core of Danish theater—flank the facade. The theater closes for part of the summer. There are guided tours, but they're only in Danish. ✉*Kongens NytorvCentrum.*

⑫ Nikolaj Kirke. Though the green spire of the imposing Nicholas Church—named for the patron saint of seafarers—appears as old as the surrounding medieval streets, it's actually relatively young. The current building was finished in 1914; the previous structure, which dated from the 13th century, was destroyed in the 1795 fire. Today the church is a contemporary art gallery that often shows good contemporary art exhibitions. ✉*Nikolaj Pl. 10, Centrum* ☎*33/18–17–80* ⊕*www.kunsthallennikolaj.dk* 🖮*DKr 20, free Wed.* ☉*Tues.–Sun. noon–5.*

❷ Rådhus Pladsen. City Hall Square is dominated by the 1905 mock-Renaissance Rådhus (City Hall). Architect Martin Nyrop's creation was popular from the start, perhaps because he envisioned that it should give "gaiety to everyday life and spontaneous pleasure to all . . ." A statue of Copenhagen's 12th-century founder, Bishop Absalon, sits atop the main entrance.

Besides being an important ceremonial meeting place for Danish VIPs, the intricately decorated Rådhus contains the first World Clock. The multidial, superaccurate astronomical timepiece has a 570,000-year calendar and took inventor Jens Olsen 27 years to complete before it was put into action in 1955.

Topped by two Vikings blowing an ancient trumpet called a *lur,* the Lurblæserne (Lur Blower Column) displays a good deal of artistic license—the lur dates from the Bronze Age, 1500 BC, whereas the Vikings lived a mere 1,000 years ago. City tours often start at this landmark, which was erected in 1914. Look up to see one of the city's most charming bronze sculptures, created by the Danish artist E. Utzon Frank in 1936. Across H. C. Andersens Boulevard, atop a corner office building, are an old neon thermometer and a gilded barometer. On sunny days there's a golden sculpture of a girl on a bicycle; come rain, a girl with an umbrella appears. ✉*Between H. C. Andersens Blvd., Vester Voldgade, and Bag Rådhuset Centrum* ☎*33/66–25–82* 🖮*Free; guided tours DKr 20–DKr 30* ☉*Mon.–Sat. 10–4; English-language tours weekdays at 3, Sat. at 10.*

NEED A BREAK? **Vandkunsten** (✉*Rådhusstr. 1 /, Centrum* ☎*33/13–90 40*) is a mom-and-pop joint near the Rådhus that makes great Italian-inspired sandwiches and salads. The shop is tiny, but the efficient service keeps customers moving.

There's only one table inside and it's usually surrounded by customers; so long as the weather is nice, get something to go and seek out a sunny spot for munching.

⑮ Skuespilhuset (*The Playhouse*). Completed in 2008, the newest addition to the Danish Royal Theatre focuses mainly on drama. While theater stagings are primarily in Danish, more accessible dance and music performances are also featured. A beautiful wooden ramp extends in front of the striking glass building. In summer, the café and restaurant move onto this deck and offer one of the best views of the Copenhagen harbor. The theater closes for part of the summer. ⊠ *Sankt Annæ Plads 36, Centrum* ☎ *33/69–69–69 for tickets* ⊕ *www.skuespilhus.dk.*

❼ Thorvaldsens Museum. The 19th-century artist Bertel Thorvaldsen (1770–1844) is buried at the center of this museum in a simple, ivy-covered tomb. Strongly influenced by the statues and reliefs of classical antiquity, he's recognized as one of the world's greatest neoclassical artists, having completed commissions all over Europe. The museum, once a coach house for Christiansborg, now houses Thorvaldsen's interpretations of classical and mythological figures, and an extensive collection of paintings and drawings by other artists that Thorvaldsen assembled while living—for most of his life—in Rome. The outside frieze by Jørgen Sonne depicts the sculptor's triumphant return to Copenhagen after years abroad. A free English audioguide is available. ⊠ *Bertel Thorvaldsen Pl. 2, Centrum* ☎ *33/32–15–32* ⊕ *www.thorvaldsensmuseum.dk* ⊠ *DKr 20, free Wed.* ☉ *Tues.–Sun. 10–5. Free audio tours available.*

❽ Tøjhusmuseet (*Royal Danish Arsenal Museum*). This Renaissance struc-
ⓒ ture—built by King Christian IV and one of central Copenhagen's oldest—contains impressive displays of uniforms, weapons, and armor in a 600-foot-long arched hall. Children are usually captivated by this museum, but it's very much a look-but-don't touch place. Each artifact has a label in English. ⊠ *Tøjhusg. 3, Centrum* ☎ *33/11–60–37* ⊕ *www. thm.dk* ⊠ *DKr 30* ☉ *Tues.–Sun. noon–4; July daily 10–4.*

CENTRUM: NORTH OF STRØGET

To the north of Strøget, you will find the smaller, more peaceful shopping streets of Købmagergade, Fiolstræde, and Nørregade. Kronprinsensgade, off Købmagergade, is another street known for trendy boutiques and café. Nørrebro (Northern Bridge), a neighborhood that grew enormously to accommodate working people during the industrial revolution, is now known for its large immigrant populations and its multitude of ethnic stores and restaurants. Intersecting the whole neighborhood is the long street, Nørrebrogade, which is packed with shops and kebab joints. Around Sankt Hans Torv, a square popular with the young and the hip, you will find a variety of trendy shops, cafés, restaurants, and clubs.

GETTING AROUND

For a 45-minute walk, go north on Købmagergade and pass Rundetårn. Climb its spiraling ramps and enjoy the view before heading to Kongens Have, a beautiful park where Danes congregate as the minute

The Artlessness of Danish Design

"There is one art—no more, no less—to do all things—with artlessness," Danish inventor and poet Piet Hein once wrote in the daily paper *Politiken*. The poem sums up the essence of the Danish design, where less really is more.

What's now commonly recognized as Danish Modern design flourished here during the years of economic depression around WW II. With a firm rooting in tradition—materials used in Denmark for centuries and age-old local craftsmanship—the basic principle of this new ethos was simplicity, followed by the probing question: "It might look pretty, but is it comfortable?"

Among the most famous products are Poul Henningsen's PH lamps; Arne Jacobsen's Egg, Swan, and Ant Chairs; and Hans J. Wegner's Round Chair. These objects become more interesting when learning stories about their makers, how they dreamed up their creations, and where these objects later turned up. For example, Poul Henningsen invented the world's tallest stilts at the age of 14—and an inflatable bicycle! Henningsen also designed a blackout lamp for Tivoli in 1941. The lamp, which couldn't be seen from overflying airplanes, allowed the park to stay open until midnight during the war. Arne Jacobsen designed the space-age cutlery used in Stanley Kubrick's movie *2001: A Space Odyssey*. And, for the famous 1961 Nixon–Kennedy debate, the rivals sat in Wegner's Round Chairs. So many Americans subsequently ordered the chair that Wegner and his workers could not keep up.

The central tenet of producing an object with the simplest, most efficient means is still being followed and developed by Danish designers today. On a smaller scale, Lego blocks, invented in Denmark, teach children worldwide that great things can be constructed with the most elementary of pieces. Danes are increasingly becoming occupied with designing products for a more sustainable future that reaches beyond the borders of the little country. Vestas, for example, the world's leading company for modern windmill technology, today has 33,500 wind turbines in 63 countries.

When in Denmark, it's fun to discover design in the context of everyday life. Upon arrival, take a rest after your long journey in one of Poul Kjærholm's chairs in **Copenhagen Airport**'s Terminal 3. Henningsen's spiral lamps are strung throughout **Tivoli**. Jacobsen has designed a gas station (Kystvejen 24, Charlottenlund), a housing complex (**Bellavista,** Strandvejen 419–451, Klampenborg), and a theater (**Bellevue Teatret,** Strandvejen 451, Klampenborg) north of Copenhagen (take Bus 14 from Klampenborg Station; *see* Copenhagen Side Trips, *below*). He's also the architect of the **Nationalbanken** (The National Bank), the **Radisson SAS Hotel** in Copenhagen, and, in Århus, **Århus Rådhus.**

For all of the above, you will find that the basic Danish design credo still holds: design is first and foremost intended to be used, not just looked at.

—by Sarah Lookofsky

the sun peers through the clouds. The garden is also home to Christian IV's castle, Rosenborg.

You can also walk north on Fiolstræde to see the main university buildings, Vor Frue Kirke, and the synangogue, before momentarily pleasing your sweet tooth at Sømods Bolcher. Farther north are the workers' museum and the botanical gardens. Just beyond, three lakes separate the city center from the Nørrebro and the neighborhood of Østerbro.

TOP ATTRACTIONS

㉑ **Arbejdermuseet** (*Workers' Museum*). The vastly underrated museum
★ chronicles the working class from 1870 to the present, with evocative life-size "day-in-the-life-of" exhibits, including reconstructions of a city street and re-creations of apartments, including the home of a brewery worker, his wife, and eight children. Changing exhibits focusing on Danish and international social issues are often excellent. The exhibitions have explanatory texts in English. The museum also has a 19th-century-style café and beer hall serving old-fashioned Danish specialties and a '50s-style coffee shop. ⊠*Rømersg. 22, Centrum* ☎*33/93–25–75* ⊕*www.arbejdermuseet.dk* ⊠*DKr 50* ☉*Daily 10–4.*

NEED A BREAK? At the popular ice cream shop, ParadIS (⊠*Sankt Hans Torv 24, Nørrebro* ☎*35/35–79–09* ⊕*www.paradis-is.dk*), Danes flock to eat the delicious, preservatives-free ice cream that is made on-site every day. If it isn't ice cream weather, opt for one of the many cafés on Sankt Hans Torv, such as Café Plenum, which offers inexpensive light fare. To get here, make a right off Noørrebrogade onto the pleasant Elmegade, which leads into Sankt Hans Torv.

㉒ **Rosenborg Slot.** The Dutch Renaissance Rosenborg Castle contains
Fodor's Choice ballrooms, halls, and reception chambers, but for all of its grandeur
★ there's an intimacy that makes you think the king might return any minute. Thousands of objects are displayed, including beer glasses, gilded clocks, golden swords, family portraits, a pearl-studded saddle, and gem-encrusted tables; an adjacent treasury contains the crown jewels. The castle's setting is equally welcoming: it's in the middle of the Kongens Have (King's Garden), amid lawns, park benches, and shady walking paths.

King Christian IV built Rosenborg Castle as a summer residence but loved it so much that he ended up living and dying here. In 1849, when the absolute monarchy was abolished, all the royal castles became state property, except for Rosenborg, which is still passed down from monarch to monarch. Once a year, during the fall holiday, the castle stays open until midnight, and visitors are invited to explore its darkened interior with bicycle lights. Textual information is also in English. ⊠*Øster Voldg. 4A, Centrum* ☎*33/15–32–86* ⊠*DKr 70* ☉*Castle: May.–Oct., daily 10–4; Nov.–Dec., Tues.–Sun. 11–2. Treasury: Tues.–Sun. 11–4.*

㉓ **Rundetårn** (*Round Tower*). Instead of climbing the stout Round Tower's
★ stairs, visitors scale a smooth, 600-foot spiral ramp on which—legend

has it—Peter the Great of Russia rode a horse alongside his wife, Catherine, who took a carriage. From its top, you enjoy a panoramic view of the twisted streets and crooked roofs of Copenhagen. The unusual building was constructed as an observatory in 1642 by Christian IV and is still maintained as Europe's oldest such structure.

The art gallery has changing exhibits, and occasional concerts are held within its massive stone walls. An observatory and telescope are open to the public evenings mid-October through March, and an astronomer is on hand to answer questions. ⊠*Købmagerg. 52A, Centrum* ☎*33/73–03–73* ⊕*www.rundetaarn.dk* ⊠*DKr 25* ⊙*Sept. 21–May 20, daily 10–5; May 21–Sept. 20, daily 10–8. Observatory mid-Oct.–mid-Mar., Tues. and Wed. 7 PM–10 PM.*

OFF THE BEATEN PATH

Assistens Kirkegård (*Assistens Cemetery*). This peaceful, leafy cemetery in the heart of Nørrebro is the final resting place of numerous great Danes, including Søren Kierkegaard (whose last name actually means "cemetery"), Hans Christian Andersen, and physicist Niels Bohr. In summer the cemetery takes on a cheerful, city-park air as picnicking families, young couples, and sunbathers relax on the sloping lawns amid the dear departed. ⊠*Kapelvej 4, Nørrebro* ☎*35/37–19–17* ⊕*www.assistens.dk* ⊠*Free* ⊙*Jan., Feb., Nov., and Dec., daily 8–4; Mar.–Apr., Sept. and Oct., daily 8–6; May–Aug., daily 8–8; Sept. and Oct., daily 8–6.*

WORTH NOTING

㉒ **Botanisk Have** (*Botanical Garden*). Trees, flowers, ponds, sculptures, and a spectacular 19th-century Palmehuset (Palm House) of tropical and subtropical plants blanket the garden's 25-plus acres. There's also an observatory and a geological museum. Take time to explore the gardens and watch the pensioners feed the birds. Some have been coming here so long that the birds actually alight on their fingers. ⊠*Øster Farimagsgade 2B, Centrum* ☎*35/32–22–22* ⊕*www.botanic-garden.ku.dk* ⊠*Free* ⊙*May–Sept., daily 8:30–6; Oct.–Apr., Tues.–Sun. 8:30–4.*

⑱ **Københavns Synagoge.** The contemporary architect Gustav Friedrich Hetsch borrowed from the Doric and Egyptian styles to create the ark-like Copenhagen Synagogue. Women sit in the upper galleries, while the men are seated below. Access to the synagogue is limited, so call ahead. ⊠*Krystalg. 12, Centrum* ☎*33/12–88–68* ⊙*Services Fri. at sundown and Sat. at 9 AM.*

⑰ **Københavns Universitet** (*Copenhagen University*). The main building of Denmark's leading institution for higher learning was constructed in the 19th century on the site of a medieval bishops' palace. The university was founded nearby in 1479. ⊠*Nørreg. 10, Centrum* ☎*35/32–26–26* ⊕*www.ku.dk.*

NEED A BREAK?

Near Copenhagen University is **Sømods Bolcher** (⊠*Nørreg. 24 or 36, Centrum* ☎ *33/12-60-46*), a Danish confectioner that has been on the scene since the late 19th century. Children and candy-lovers relish seeing the hard candy pulled and cut by hand.

🔟 **Vor Frue Kirke.** The site of Denmark's principle cathedral, the Church of Our Lady, has drawn worshippers since the 13th century, when Bishop Absalon built a chapel here. The previous church, consecrated in 1738, was burned to the ground in 1807 during the Napoleonic wars. Despite the country's poverty after the defeat, it was decided to build a new place of worship in the then modern neoclassical style. Inside you can see Thorvaldsen's marble sculptures depicting Christ and the 12 Apostles, and Moses and David cast in bronze. The funerals of both Kirkegaard and H. C. Andersen were held here. ✉ *Nørreg. 8, Frue Pl., Centrum* ☎ *33/37–65–40* ⊕ *www.domkirken.dk* ✂ *Free* ⊙ *Mon.–Wed. and Fri. 10–1, Thurs. 10–6.*

FREDERIKSSTADEN AND EAST

Northeast of Kongens Nytorv is the posh thoroughfare of Bredgade, which intersects Frederiksstaden, a royal quarter commissioned by Frederik V in the mid-1700s. The area is home to the royal castle of Amalienborg, which is symmetrically aligned with the majestic Marble Church. It's fun to time your visit here with the changing of the guard, which happens daily at noon. Farther northeast is the calm residential neighborhood of Østerbro, where young families stroll amid tall trees, grand old apartment buildings, and international embassies.

The old sailors' neighborhood of Nyboder is west of the fortification of Kastellet. From here, Øster Voldgade leads to Østre Anlæg park, which surrounds the art museums, Statens Museum for Kunst and Den Hirschsprungske Samling.

GETTING AROUND

For a pleasant 1½-hour stroll, depart from Kongens Nytorv, loop around the Nyhavn before continuing northeast along Bredgade. Turn off to see the Marble Church and admire the rococo palace of Amalienborg. Carry on to the water or head down Amaliegade to the Resistance Museum, Gefion Fountain, and Kastellet fortress, ending up at the *Little Mermaid* in Langelinie.

TOP ATTRACTIONS

㉛ ★ **Amalienborg.** The four identical rococo buildings occupying this square have housed royals since 1784. It's still the queen's winter residence. The Christian VIII palace across from the royal's wing houses the Amalienborg Museum, which displays the second part of the Royal Collection (the first is at Rosenborg Slot) and chronicles royal lifestyles between 1863 and 1947. Here you can view the study of King Christian IX (1818–1906) and the drawing room of his wife, Queen Louise. Rooms are packed with royal heirlooms and treasures.

In the square's center is a magnificent equestrian statue of King Frederik V by the French sculptor Jacques François Joseph Saly. It reputedly cost as much as all the buildings combined. Every day at noon, the Royal Guard and band march from Rosenborg Slot through the city for the changing of the guard. At noon on Queen Margrethe's birthday, April 16, crowds of Danes gather to cheer their monarch, who stands and waves from her balcony. On Amalienborg's harbor side is the garden of Amaliehaven, at the foot of which the queen's ship often docks. Since the royal family leaves Amalienborg during the summer months, guided tours of Christian VII's Palace are available July–September. English tours depart at 1 and 2:30 pm, DKr 75. ⊠ *Christian VIII's Palace–Amalienborg Pl., Frederiksstaden* 🏠 *33/12 21 86* 📧 *Museum: DKr 55* ⊙ *Museum: Tues.–Sun. 10–4.*

㉕ **Kastellet.** At the end of Amaliegade, the beautiful Churchill Park sur-
★ rounds the spired Anglican (or Episcopal) church St. Alban's. From here, walk north on the main path to reach the fortification of Kastellet. The peaceful walking paths, grazing sheep, and greenery welcome joggers and lovebirds to this still-operative military structure. Built in the aftermath of the Swedish siege of the city on February 10, 1659, the double moats were among the improvements made to the city's defense. The Citadel served as the city's main fortress into the 18th century; in a grim reversal during World War II, the Germans used it as headquarters during their occupation. ⊠ *Kastellet 68, Østerbro* 📧 *Free* ⊙ *Daily 6* AM–*10* PM.

㉓ **Statens Museum for Kunst.** Old-master paintings—including works by
🐾 Rubens, Rembrandt, Titian, El Greco, and Fragonard—as well as a
★ comprehensive array of antique and 20th-century Danish art make up the National Art Gallery collection. Also notable is the modern art, which includes pieces by a very small but select group of artists, including Henri Matisse, Edvard Munch, Henri Laurens, Emil Nolde, and Georges Braque. The space also contains a children's museum, which puts on shows for different age groups at kids' eye-level. Wall texts are in English. The bookstore and café are also worth a visit. ⊠ *Sølvg. 48–50, Østerbro* 🏠 *33/74–84–94* ⊕ *www.smk.dk* 📧 *Free for permanent collection, DKr 80 for special exhibitions* ⊙ *Tues. and Thurs.–Sun. 10–5, Wed. 10–8.*

WORTH NOTING

㉔ **Den Hirschsprungske Samling.** The Hirschsprung Collection showcases paintings from the country's Golden Age—Denmark's mid-19th-century school of naturalism—as well as a collection of paintings by the late-19th-century artists of the Skagen School. Their luminous works capture the play of light and water so characteristic of the Danish countryside. Texts are in English. ⊠ *Stockholmsg. 20, Østerbro* 🏠 *35/42–03–36* ⊕ *www.hirschsprung.dk* 📧 *DKr 50* ⊙ *Mon. and Wed.–Sun. 11–4.*

㉖ **Den Lille Havfrue** (*The Little Mermaid*). On the Langelinie promenade, this somewhat overhyped 1913 statue commemorates Hans Christian Andersen's lovelorn creation. Donated to the city by Carl Jacobsen, the son of the founder of Carlsberg Breweries, the innocent waif has also been the subject of some cruel practical jokes, including decapitation and the loss of an arm, but she's currently in one piece. Especially on a sunny Sunday, the Langelinie promenade is thronged with Danes and visitors making their pilgrimage to the statue. On this occasion, you may want to read the original Hans Christian Andersen tale; it's a heart-wrenching story that's a far cry from the Disney animated movie. Although the statue itself is modest, the views of the surrounding harbor are not. ⊠ *Langelinie promenade, Østerbro.*

The Danish Royals

The equitable Danes may believe that excessive pride is best kept hidden, but ask about their queen and this philosophy promptly flies out the window. The passion for Queen Margrethe II is infectious, and before long you may find yourself waving the Dannebrog flag along with the rest of them when the queen passes through. Graceful and gregarious, Queen Margrethe II is the embodiment of the new Danish crown, a monarchy that is steeped in history yet decidedly modern in its outlook.

Denmark's royal lineage has its roots in the 10th-century Kingdom of Gorm the Old. His son, Harald Bluetooth, established the royal headquarters in Zealand, where it remains to this day. Copenhagen's stately Amalienborg Slot has been the official royal residence since 1784. From here Queen Margrethe reigns in a true Danish style marked by sociability, not stuffiness. Renowned for her informal charm, the Queen has fostered an open, familial relationship between the royal house and the Danish public. Queen Margrethe's nurturing role has evolved naturally in a country of Denmark's petite size and population. Though she lives in Copenhagen, the Queen is far from Zealand-bound.

Margrethe wasn't always destined to be queen. When she was born in 1940, the law of succession was limited to sons, and it wasn't until 1953 that the law was ratified to include female accession of the throne. She was groomed to become queen, and on her 18th birthday stepped into her position as heir apparent to the crown. She studied archaeology and political science both at home and abroad, at the Universities of Copenhagen, Århus, Cambridge, and the Sorbonne. In 1967 Margrethe married the French-born Prince Henrik, born a count near Cahors, France.

Today's modern monarchy is perhaps best exemplified by what the queen does when she takes off her crown. An accomplished artist and illustrator, she designed the costumes for an acclaimed television production of Hans Christian Andersen's *The Shepherdess and the Chimney Sweep.* She also illustrated an edition of J. R. R. Tolkien's *The Lord of the Rings.* Her paintings have been exhibited in galleries, where they command top prices, all of which she donates to charity.

If there's anyone in the royal circle who has captured the public's hearts like Queen Margrethe, it's the elegant, stylish, Tasmanian-born Crown Princess Mary, who married Crown Prince Frederik in 2004 at Copenhagen Cathedral. Some 180 million people worldwide watched the event. The couple now has two children; the first-born, Christian, who will one day become king, was born in 2005.

Frederik's younger brother also went abroad for love. Prince Joachim married Hong Kong–born Alexandra in 1995, but the couple divorced in 2004. Both have since remarried—Joachim to the French Marie Cavallier, who is fast catching up to Mary in terms of style and popularity. When in Denmark, you will become familiar with the faces of all of these royals, since they always occupy the front pages of the Danish tabloids sold at the front of every convenience store.

2

28 Frihedsmuseet (*Resistance Museum*). Evocative, sometimes moving displays commemorate the heroic Danish resistance movement, which saved 7,000 Jews from the Nazis by hiding and then smuggling them to Sweden. The homemade tank outside was used to spread the news of the Nazi surrender after World War II. There's information on the displays in English-language. ☒*Churchillparken, Frederiksstaden* ☎*33/47–39–21* ⊕*www.frihedsmuseet.dk* ☒*Free* ☉*Oct.–Apr., Tues.– Sat. 10–3; May–Sept., Tues.–Sat. 10–5.*

27 Gefion Springvandet (*Gefion Fountain*). Not far from *The Little Mermaid* yet another dramatic myth is illustrated. The goddess Gefion was promised as much of Sweden as she could plough in a night. The story goes that she changed her sons to oxen and used them to portion off what is now the island of Zealand. ☒*East of Frihedsmuseet, Frederiksstaden.*

29 Kunstindustrimuseet. Originally built in the 18th century as a royal hospital, the fine rococo Museum of Decorative Art houses a large selection of European and Asian crafts. Also on display are ceramics, silverware, tapestries, and special exhibitions that often focus on contemporary design. There are labels in English. A small café serving organic treats also operates here. ☒*Bredg. 68, Frederiksstaden* ☎*33/18–56–56* ⊕*www.kunstindustrimuseet.dk* ☒*DKr 50* ☉*Permanent collection Tues.–Sun. 11–5.*

30 Marmorkirken (*Marble Church*). Officially the Frederikskirke, this ponderous baroque sanctuary of precious Norwegian marble was begun in 1749 and remained unworked on from 1770 to 1874 due to budget constraints. It was finally completed and consecrated in 1894. Around the exterior are 16 statues of various religious leaders from Moses to Luther, and below them stand sculptures of outstanding Danish ministers and bishops. The hardy can scale 273 steps to the outdoor balcony. Afterwards, you can continue along Bredgade to the exotic gilded onion domes of the Russiske Ortodoks Kirke (Russian Orthodox Church). ☒*Frederiksg. 4, off Bredg., Frederiksstaden* ☎*33/15–01–44* ⊕*www. marmorkirken.dk* ☒*Church free, dome DKr 25* ☉*Mon.–Thurs. 10–5, weekends noon–5. Dome access daily at 1 and 3* PM.

CHRISTIANSHAVN

Across the capital's main harbor, Inderhavn, is the smaller, 17th-century Christianshavn. In the early 1600s this area was mostly a series of shallows between land, which were eventually dammed. Today Christianshavn's colorful boats and postcard maritime character make it one of the toniest parts of town. To get there, walk from the Christiansborg area in Centrum across the Knippelsbro Bridge.

Cobbled avenues, antique street lamps, and bohemian charm are all part of one of the city's oldest neighborhoods. Even the system of earthworks—the best preserved of Copenhagen's original fortification walls—still exists. In the 17th century, Christian IV offered what were patches of partially flooded land for free, and with additional tax benefits; in return, takers would have to fill them in and construct sturdy

SOCCER

Danish soccer fans call themselves Roligans, which loosely translates as "calm fans," as opposed to the rowdy and often violent British hooligans. These Roligans idolize the national team's players as superstars. When the rivalry is most intense (especially against Sweden and Norway), fans belt out the national anthem, wear head-to-toe red and white, incessantly wave the Dannebrog (Danish flag), and have a good time whether or not they win. If national games aren't being played, the local team FCK and their loyal fans put on a good show, especially if they are playing against their archrivals from the western suburb of Brøndby. Prices are about DKr 160 at local matches; DKr 120 if purchased in advance; international matches are more expensive.

The biggest stadium, and the best place to watch local and international matches, is Copenhagen's main stadium, **Parken.** It's a 15-minute walk from Østerport Station, and Bus 15 takes you from Copenhagen Central Station to the door. (⊠ *Øster Allé 50, Østerbro* ☎ *35/43–31–31*). **Billetnet** (☎ *70/15–65–65*) sells tickets to national matches **Billet-lugen** (☎ *70/26–32–67*) sells tickets for local games.

buildings for trade, commerce, housing for the shipbuilding workers, and defense against sea attacks.

Gentrified today, the area harbors restaurants, cafés, and shops, and its ramparts are edged with green areas and walking paths, making it the perfect neighborhood for an afternoon or evening amble. The central square, Christianshavn Torv, is where all activity emanates from, and Torvegade, a bustling shopping street, is the main thoroughfare. For a pleasant break, relax at one of the cafés along Wilders Canal, which streams through the heart of town.

🟢 ★ **Christiania.** If you're nostalgic for 1960s counterculture, head to this anarchists' commune. You can walk here from Christianshavn: take Torvegade and make a left on Prinsessegade, which takes you to the main gate. You can also take Bus 2A from Rådhuspladsen, Tivoli, Christiansborg, and Christianshavn Station. Founded in 1971, when students occupied army barracks, it's now a peaceful community of nonconformists who run a number of businesses, including a bike shop, a rock-music club, and good organic eateries. Wall cartoons preach drugs and peace, but the inhabitants are less fond of cameras—picture-taking is forbidden. A group of residents recount their experiences as well as the history of Christiania on daily English-language tours conducted from June 26 through August 31. Tours depart at 3 from the main gate and are 1- to 1½-hours long. They cost DKr 30 per person and are a great way to discover the nooks and crannies of this quirky community. ⊠ *Prinsesseg. and Bådsmansstr., Christianshavn* ☎ *32/57–60–05 guided tours* ⊕ *www.christiania.org.*

🟢 **Dansk Arkitektur Center.** The Danish Architecture Center occupies an old wharf-side warehouse built in 1880. The center hosts rotating exhibitions that cover trends and trendsetters in architecture and architectural design. Things are labeled in English, and the museum's Web site has a guide for discovering noteworthy architecture in Denmark's major cities. ⌑*Strandg 27B, Christianshavn* ☎*32/57–19–30* ⊕*www.dac. dk* ⌑*DKr 40; exhibitions vary* ⊙*Daily 10 5.*

㉞ Holmen. Previously isolated from central Copenhagen, this former navy base north of Christianshavn, dating from the 17th century, has in recent years become an attractive area for arts, culture and chic living, all housed in converted military facilities. The Royal Academy's schools of Theatre, Film, Music, and Architecture are all housed in old barracks here. The most famous resident is the new opera house designed by the famous Danish architect Henning Larsen and placed symmetrically opposite the Marble Church and Amalienborg Castle. Operas are in their original language with Danish subtitles. The building opens three hours prior to performances, including a café and restaurant, the latter only for ticket-holders. The area is most easily accessed by harbor bus ferries that depart from Nyhavn, the Black Diamond, and Knippelsbro. ✉*Ekvipagemestervej 10, Holmen 1438* ☎*33/69–69–69* ⊕*www.operaen. dk* ⌑*Tickets DKr 70–DKr 833.*

VESTERBRO

To the west of Centrum is the vibrant neighborhood of Vesterbro. Formerly home to mostly working-class inhabitants and a red-light district, immigrants and trendy young folk have since moved in and seem to live quite harmoniously with the original populations. The buildings date from the late 1800s and were constructed during the industrial revolution. A number of popular cafés now surround the spruced-up Halmtorvet Square, which was previously notorious for its late-night prostitution.

Istedgade is a main artery in the neighborhood, leading from the Central Station to Enghave Plads. Istedgade has diversified over the past several years; no longer an area reserved for porn shops and massage parlors, the colorful neighborhood is now full of low-key cafés and trendy boutiques that serve the neighborhood's rapidly growing population of artists and students. It is a nice place to enjoy a snack, a coffee, or a beer in the sun. Though Istedgade is relatively safe, you may want to avoid the area near Central Station late at night.

The street of Vesterbrogade runs west from Rådhuspladsen to the neighborhoods of Valby and Frederiksberg. Originally a farming area that supplied the royal households with fresh produce, Frederiksberg is now known for its residences of the well-heeled and the city zoo. Valby is home to the world-renowned Carlsberg breweries.

㉟ Carlsberg Bryggeri (*Carlsberg Brewery*). A large, ornate chimney makes this mid-19th-century brewery visible from a distance. J. C. Jacobson, one of Denmark's most important historical figures, named the brewery after his son Carl; "Berg," or mountain, signifies the brewery's location on Valby Hill. The four giant granite elephants that guard the main entrance illustrate that Jacobsen was a well-traveled man who adored art. The elephants are in fact inspired by Bernini's famous obelisk in Rome. In the visitor center, new interactive displays, also in English,

SWIMMING

Swimming is very popular, particularly in the ocean and in select cordoned-off areas of the city's harbors. Some Danes who aptly call themselves "Vikings" or "polar bears" bathe year-round, even as water temperatures fall below freezing. If you're not soothed by cool or frigid waters, there are plenty of indoor pools around the city. Admission to most of these (DKr 20–DKr 50) includes a locker key, but you have to bring your own towel.

For free outdoor swimming, head to **Islands Brygge Havnebad** (⊠ *Islands Brygge*), where city dwellers cool off in harbor pools just minutes from the city center. The pool is a 10–15 minute walk from Rådhuspladsen. Follow H.C. Andersens Boulevard, which borders the square, over Langebro Bridge to Islands Brygge; the pool will be on your right. On the eastern coast of Amager is **Amager Strandpark** (⊠ *Along Amager Strandvej, Amager*), a landscaped beach with sand dunes, lookout points, grill pits,

and bike paths. The M2 Metro line takes you from Noøreport and Kongens Nytorv to this beach.

DGI Byen Swim Center (⊠ *Tietgensg. 65, Vesterbro* ☎ *33/29–80–00* ⊕ *www.dgi-byen.dk*), immediately behind Copenhagen Central Station, contains a massive oval pool with 100-meter lanes. The swim center also has a children's pool and a "mountain pool," with a climbing wall, wet trampoline, and several diving boards. Massages and other spa services are offered.

Frederiksberg Svømmehal (⊠ *Helgesvej 29, Frederiksberg2000*) is an old, beautiful indoor pool that also has modern spa facilities. **Øbrohallen** (⊠ *Gunnar Nu Hansens Plads 3, Østerbro*) is a grand neoclassical indoor pool built in 1930. A quiet spa experience is also available in the basement. Many locals enjoy swimming in the pools at **Vesterbro Svømmehal** (⊠ *Angelgade 4, Vesterbro*) that are naturally illuminated by the facility's floor-to-ceiling windows.

take you step by step through the brewing process. At the end of your visit, you're rewarded with a complimentary beer sampling. The Carlsberg Museum, also on the grounds, tells the story of the Jacobsen family, their beer empire, and Carlsberg's extensive philanthropy that still greatly benefits Danish culture. Large-scale beer production has now moved outside of the city and there are plans to convert the old brewery complex into a combined neighborhood for arts, culture, and living. ⊠ *Gamle Carlsberg Vej 11, Valby* ☎ *33/27–13–14* ⊕ *www.visitcarlsberg. com* ⊠ *DKr 50* ☉ *Tues.–Sun. 10–4.*

㊱ Københavns Bymuseum (*Copenhagen City Museum*). For an evocative collection detailing Copenhagen's history, head to this 18th-century building in the heart of Vesterbro. A meticulously maintained model of 16th-century Copenhagen is in front of the building. Inside there's also a memorial room for philosopher Søren Kierkegaard, the father of existentialism. ⊠ *Vesterbrog. 59, Vesterbro* ☎ *33/21–07–72* ⊕ *www. bymuseum.dk* ⊠ *DKr 20, free Fri.* ☉ *Daily 10–4, Wed. until 9.*

2

③ **Tycho Brahe Planetarium.** Situated at ✆ the western end of the lakes that divide Copenhagen, this modern, cylindrical planetarium, which appears to be sliced at an angle, features astronomy exhibits. It's Denmark's most advanced center for popularizing astronomy and space research and promoting knowledge of natural science. The on-site IMAX Theater is devoted to visual odysseys of the natural environment—below the sea, through the jungle, or into outer space. These films aren't recommended for children under age seven. ⊠ *Gammel Kongevej 10, Vesterbro* ☎ *33/12–12–24* ∰ *www.tycho.dk/ in_english* ⊠ *DKr 125 includes access to one IMAX movie and one 3-D movie* ⊙ *Daily 10:30–9.*

RUNNING

The 6 km (4-mi) loop around the three lakes just west of city center—Sankt Jørgens, Peblinge, and Sortedams, colloquially known as "Søerne," or the lakes—is a runner's nirvana. There are other good paths in Kongens Have; Fælledparken (near the stadium, between the neighborhoods of Nørrebro and Østerbro); Frederiksberg Garden (near the zoo, corner of Frederiksberg Allé and Pile Allé); and Dyrehaven, north of the city near Klampenborg.

OFF THE BEATEN PATH

Zoologisk Have. Children love the Zoological Gardens, which are home to 3,300 animals and 264 species. The small petting zoo and playground includes cows, horses, rabbits, goats, and hens. The indoor rain forest has butterflies, sloths, alligators, and other tropical creatures. The ✆ newly completed elephant house by the acclaimed architect Norman Foster is an elegant structure topped by two glass domes, providing its inhabitants with plenty of light and stomping ground. Sea lions, lions, and elephants are fed in the early afternoon. Be warned: on sunny weekends, the line to enter can be long, so come early. Check in advance for extended weekend and summer opening hours. ⊠ *Roskildevej 32, Frederiksberg* ☎ *70/20–02–00* ∰ *www.zoo.dk* ⊠ *DKr 130* ⊙ *Sept.– May 9–4, June–Aug. 9–6.*

WHERE TO EAT

Copenhagen, considered Scandinavia's culinary capital, has experienced a gastronomical revolution over the past decade. There's no shortage of talented chefs and innovative, fine-dining experiences. A rising interest in a concept known as new Nordic cooking has put an emphasis on the use of locally sourced raw materials and high-quality seasonal ingredients. Wild game, cured or smoked fish and meats, and specialties like Limfjord oysters, Læsø langoustine, as well as eel and plaice are a few examples.

There's also been a revival of traditional Danish fare and keeping age-old traditions alive. Don't miss the chance to try pickled or smoked herring, smørrebrød (open-face sandwiches), a street-side *pølser* (sausage), and the famous Danish pastries.

There are plenty of bistros serving moderately priced meals, and if you're looking for even more affordable fare, try one of the city's ethnic restaurants, which are concentrated in Vesterbro, Nørrebro, and the side streets off Strøget. For inexpensive savory noshes in stylish surroundings, consider lingering in a café.

A good number of restaurants offer fixed-priced menus with wine-pairing menus, and most restaurants require reservations. Many restaurants tack a surcharge of between 3.75% and 5.75% to the bill for the use of foreign credit cards, so you can save good money by paying cash.

CENTRUM

$ ✕**Café Victor.** Excellent people-watching and good bistro fare are the
FRENCH calling cards at this French-style corner café. It's best during weekend lunches, when young and old gather for rib roast, homemade pâté, and smoked salmon and cheese platters. This place also serves the best brunches in town. Be warned: the formal restaurant in the back of the space is expensive; order from the front café for a more affordable meal. ⊠*Ny Østerg. 8, Centrum* ☎*33/13–36–13* ⊕*www.cafevictor. dk* ⊟*AE, DC, MC, V.*

$–$$ ✕**Custom House.** British entrepreneur Terrance Conran expanded his
ECLECTIC empire with the renovation of the art-deco harborfront customs office. The complex now houses three restaurants and a trendy lounge-bar frequented by expats. The Italian restaurant, **Bacino,** offers simple dishes: think fresh pastas and risottos. Try the braised veal cheeks in Barolo with truffles or the *panna cotta* (caramel custard) with cherries and blood oranges. There's a five-course tasting menu, a theater menu, and an à la carte menu. **Ebisu,** the Japanese restaurant, is modeled after an Izakayan-type establishment where you're encouraged to share dishes. An open kitchen offers a glance into the preparation of such dishes as miso-marinated sea bass as well as tempura, sushi, and sashimi. You can choose from either an à la carte or one of several set menus. **Custom House Bar & Grill** is a European brasserie with a Scandinavian bent that's particularly good for lunch (try an open-face sandwich) or a late-night nosh as the kitchen is open until midnight every day. ⊠*Havnegade 44, Centrum* ☎*33/31–01–30* ⊕*www.customhouse.dk* ⚑*Reservations essential* ⊟*AE, DC, MC, V* ⊗*Bacino and Ebisu closed Sun.*

$ ✕**Ida Davidsen.** This five-generations-old, world-renowned lunch spot is
DANISH synonymous with smørrebrød. The often-packed dining area is dimly
★ lighted, with worn wooden tables and news clippings of famous visitors on the walls. Creative sandwiches include the H. C. Andersen, with liver pâté, bacon, and tomatoes. The terrific duck is smoked by Ida's husband, Adam, and served alongside a horseradish-spiked cabbage salad. ⊠*Store Kongensg. 70, Centrum* ☎*33/91–36–55* ⊕*www.idadavidsen. dk* ⚑*Reservations essential* ⊟*AE, DC, MC, V* ⊗*No dinner. Closed weekends and July.*

$$$$ ✕**Kong Hans Kælder.** Five centuries ago this was a vineyard. Now it's
ECLECTIC one of Scandinavia's finest restaurants. Chef Thomas Rode Andersen's
★ French-Danish–inspired dishes employ local ingredients and are served in a medieval subterranean space with whitewashed walls and vaulted ceilings. Try the foie gras with raspberry-vinegar sauce or the Belgian oysters from Marenne and Baerii caviar served with horseradish and rye croutons. ⊠*Vingårdstr. 6, Centrum* ☎*33/11–68–68* ⊕*www.konghans.dk* ⊟*AE, D, MC, V* ⊗*No lunch. Closed Sun.*

$$ ✕ **L'Alsace.** Set in the cobbled courtyard of Pistolstræde and hung with
FRENCH paintings by Danish surrealist Wilhelm Freddie, this restaurant is peaceful and quiet, and has attracted such diverse diners as Queen Margrethe,
Elton John, and the late Pope John Paul II. The hand-drawn menu lists
oysters from Brittany, terrine de foie gras, and *choucrôute à la Strasbourgeoise* (a hearty mélange of cold cabbage, homemade sausage, and
pork). Try the superb fresh-fruit tarts and cakes for dessert, and ask to
sit in the patio overlooking the courtyard. Although the restaurant is
generally closed on Sunday, it does serve lunch the first Sunday of each
month. ⊠ *Ny Østerg. 9, Centrum* ☎*33/14–57–43* ⊕*www.alsace.dk*
▤*AE, DC, MC, V* ⊘*Closed Sun.*

$$ ✕ **Le Sommelier.** The grande dame of Copenhagen's French restaurants
FRENCH is appropriately named. The cellar boasts more than 800 varieties of
Fodor'sChoice wine, and you can order many of them by the glass—with or without
★ the help of a sommelier. Exquisite French dishes are complemented by
an elegant interior of off-white walls, rough-hewn wooden floors, brass
chandeliers, and hanging copper pots. Dishes include guinea fowl in a
foie-gras sauce or lamb shank and crispy sweetbreads with parsley and
garlic. While waiting for your table, head to the burnished dark-wood
and brass bar and begin sampling the wine. ⊠ *Bredg. 63–65, Centrum*
☎*33/11–45–15* ⊕*www.lesommelier.dk* ▤*AE, DC, MC, V.*

$ ✕ **Nyhavns Færgekro.** Locals pack into this waterfront café every day at
SCANDINAVIAN lunchtime, when the staff unveils a buffet with 10 kinds of herring and
a variety of smørrebrød. Once an unsavory sailors' bar when Nyhavn
was the city's port, the red-and-blue building retains a rustic charm.
Waiters duck under rough wood beams when they deliver your dinner
specials, of, say, salmon with dill sauce or steak with shaved truffles.
In summer, sit outside and order an aquavit, the local spirit that tastes
like caraway seeds. ⊠ *Nyhavn 5, Centrum* ☎*33/15–15–88* ⊕*www.*
nyhavnsfaergekro.dk ▤*DC, MC, V.*

$$$$ ✕ **The Paul.** From the champagne aperitif to the dessert of blackberries
CONTINENTAL with licorice ice cream, dining at the Paul is never dull. Located in the
Fodor'sChoice middle of Tivoli and only open during the park's season, this exquisite
★ glass-enclosed pavilion is favored by those in the entertainment industry
and members of the Danish royal family. Chef Paul Cunningham combines local products with items from elsewhere to create such interesting
dishes as Danish turbot served with Jerusalem artichokes poached in
Noilly Prat dry vermouth and paired with a French Chardonnay. Dishes
on the seven-course tasting menu and the three-course menu known as
"ma cuisine" are lovingly prepared in an open kitchen. There is no à
la carte menu. Service is flawless. ⊠ *Tivoli, Verserbrogade 3, Centrum*
☎*33/75–07–75* ⊕*www.thepaul.dk* ⚠*Reservations essential* ▤*AE,*
DC, MC, V ⊘*Closed mid-Sept.–mid-May.*

$ ✕ **Peder Oxe.** On a 17th-century square, this lively, countrified bistro
ECLECTIC has rustic tables and 15th-century Portuguese tiles. All entrées—among
them grilled steaks, fish, and the best burgers in town—come with
salad from the excellent self-service bar. Tables are set with simple
white linens, heavy cutlery, and opened bottles of hearty French wine.
A clever call-light for the waitress is above each table. In spring, when
the high northern sun is shining but the warmth still hasn't kicked in,

you won't do badly sitting outside in the Gråbrødretorv (Gray Friars' Square) sipping drinks wrapped in one of the blankets left out on the wicker chairs. ✉ *Gråbrødretorv 11, Centrum* ☎ *33/11–00–77* ⊕ *www. pederoxe.dk* ⊟ *DC, MC, V.*

$$$$ ✗ **Restaurant Herman.** Thomas Herman is one of Denmark's most tal-
SCANDINAVIAN ented young chefs and the former head chef at the praised restaurant
Fodor'sChoice Kong Hans Kælder. Herman's philosophy is that taste is attached to
★ memories and emotions. At his restaurant in the Nimb hotel, he set out to honor the old Danish kitchen, and his meticulously crafted modern remakes of classic country-style dishes delight all the senses. The menu changes seasonally, but you might find smoked duck served with brined walnuts, marjoram, red cabbage and morrel mayonnaise. Four-, five-, and six-course tasting menus are available at dinner with matching wines; lunch sees two- and three-course menus starting at DKr 395. ✉ *Nimb Hotel, Tivoli Gardens, Bernstorffsgade 5, Centrum* ☎ *88/70–00–00* ⊕ *www.nimb.dk* ⚑ *Reservations essential* ⊟ *AE, DC, MC, V* ⊘ *No lunch Sat. Closed Sun.*

$ ✗ **The Royal Café.** Tucked between the Royal Copenhagen and Georg
CAFÉ Jensen shops, this eatery is part Danish design museum, part shop, and
Fodor'sChoice part café. High ceilings, Holmegaard glass chandeliers, and a whim-
★ sical mural evoke *Alice's Adventures in Wonderland.* Created in collaboration with design legends like Fritz Hansen, Arne Jacobsen, Royal Copenhagen, and Bang & Olufsen, the café is truly a showcase for what is quintessentially Danish. It's perhaps most known for its modern twist on traditional smørrebrød called "smushi." The staff delicately assembles these artful, sushi-ish–size, open-face sandwiches, and a pastry and cake bar tempts sweet tooths. ✉ *Amagertorv 6, Centrum* ☎ *38/14–95–27* ⊕ *www.theroyalcafe.dk* ⚑ *Reservations not accepted* ⊟ *AE, DC, MC, V* ⊘ *No dinner Sun.*

$ ✗ **Søren K.** Occupying a bright corner of the Royal Library's modern
CONTINENTAL Black Diamond extension, this cool-tone restaurant, with clean lines, blond-wood furnishings, and recessed lighting, serves French-Scandinavian concoctions. For waterfront views, choose a table up against the glass walls or outside. Signature dishes include dried Danish ham with thyme and beurre noir or scallops, corn puree, and watercress. The menu always has vegetarian dishes and a fish of the day. It's the perfect lunchtime spot, with a two-course menu for DKr 195. ✉ *Søren Kierkegaards Pl. 1, Centrum* ☎ *33/47–49–49* ⊕ *www.soerenk.dk* ⊟ *AE, DC, MC, V* ⊘ *Closed Sun.*

NØRREBRO

$ ✗ **Laundromat Café.** Here's a way to not only wash your clothes (in a
AMERICAN soundproofed room), but also enjoy breakfast, lunch, or dinner, or have a coffee or a beer. Best of all is the library, containing approximately 5,000 used books. The café serves salads, burgers, steaks, pastas, fish soups, and homemade desserts. ✉ *Elmegade 15, Nørrebro* ☎ *35/35–26–72* ⊟ *MC, V.*

$$ ✗ **Nørrebro Bryghus.** This award-winning microbrewery opened in a one-
ECLECTIC time metals factory in September 2003 and was an instant hit. The brewery has 160 seats in a two-story restaurant as well as a beer garden in summer. It has made over 50 beers and always has 12 on tap. Lunches

include salads, sandwiches, and burgers; in the evening you can order prix-fixe dinners of between three and four courses. Dishes feature beer as an ingredient, and knowledgeable staffers can suggest beer pairings. Brewery tours are offered. ☒*Ryesgade 3, Nørrebro* ☎*35/30–05–30* ⊕*www.noerrebrobryghus.dk* ☱*DC, MC, V* ☉*No dinner Sun.*

$$$$ ✕**Restaurant Kiin Kiin.** This ultratrendy yet authentic Thai restaurant,
THAI whose name means "eat, eat" (implying dinner's ready), transports
★ you instantly to Southeast Asia. Gilded Buddhas grace walls, hand-oven wicker chairs made from water hyacinth beckon, and cream-color bamboo lamps illuminate. The fragrance of cinnamon may well whet your appetite for such typical Thai street snacks as lotus-flower chips, satay, and fish cakes. Green curry, fresh coriander, and ginger flavor the dishes on the set menu presented on Asian-inspired Royal Copenhagen porcelain. (A four-course theater menu is available from 5:30 to 7:30 PM for DKr 450.) Kiin Kiin's famous Table 9, in a discreet corner, offers snug seclusion for romantics. ☒*Guldbergsgade 21, Nørrebro* ☎*35/35–75–55* ☖*Reservations essential* ☱*AE, DC, MC, V* ☉*No lunch. Closed Sun.*

FREDERIKSSTADEN

$ ✕**BioM.** The country's only government-certified organic restaurant
CONTINENTAL takes cooking and operating ecologically seriously. Everything here is organic, from the food, wine, and spirits to the paper on which the menu is printed to the earthtone paint on the walls. It's in a quiet residential area, just beside the old sailors' neighborhood of Nyboder, and it has a street-corner terrace. The French-inspired kitchen prepares seasonal hearty dishes made with local and fair trade ingredients. Try the weekend brunch, or come for lunch, when the menu has the most choices for under 100 DKr. ☒*Fredericiagade 78, Frederiksstaden* ☎*33/32–24–66* ⊕*www.biom.dk* ☖*Reservations essential* ☱*AE, MC, V* ☉*No dinner Sun. Closed Mon.*

$$ ✕**Bistro Boheme.** Within walking distance of such attractions as *The*
FRENCH *Little Mermaid* statue and the Kastellet, this bistro serves classic French cuisine in casual, stylish surroundings. A former showroom of an American car dealership, the open two-story space has a large dining area, a lounge with soft leather chairs, and a second-floor cocktail bar and glassed-in dining area for large groups. Owner and executive chef Per Thøstesen crafts such old-fashioned dishes as a terrine that mixes duck confit, veal shank, and foie gras with calvados and pistachios. Enjoy a glass of wine from the extensive list while French music plays in the background, or try street-side dining under the bright red awning. It can get very busy so you might have to work a little to get your waiter's attention. ☒*Esplanaden 8, Frederiksstaden* ☎*70/22–08–70* ⊕*www.bistroboheme.dk* ☖*Reservations essential* ☱*AE, DC, MC, V* ☉*Closed Sun.*

$$$$ ✕**Geranium.** Located in the beautiful Kongens Have, "the King's Gar-
SCANDINAVIAN den," is this modern northern European kitchen. You can dine in
Fodor's Choice the simple white interior, with its rustic detailing and abundant win-
★ dows, or on a sculpture-laden terrace with its open fire. Chefs Rasmus Kofoed and Søren Ledet put a modern touch on classic Scandinavian cooking by using advanced techniques including intriguing molecular

configurations. They source products from biodynamic farmers (that is, those who follow system of organic and holistic cultivation) to create vegetable-centric masterpieces. A seven-course menu features venison covered with a thin layer of smoked lard and served with beet root, mushrooms, and forest herbs. For dessert, there's elderberry jelly. An organic vegetarian menu and individual courses are also on offer. All are served with matching wines or juices. ⊠ *Kronprinsessegade 13, Frederiksstaden* ☎ *33/11–13–04* ⊕ *www.restaurantgeranium.com* ⚐ *Reservations essential* ⊟ *AE, DC, MC, V* ⊘ *No lunch Sat. Closed Sun. and Mon.*

$ ✕ **Madklubben.** The city's best-value kitchen offers meals of between one
SCANDINAVIAN   and four courses for as little as DKr 100. It's known for its satisfying traditional Danish dishes with a twist: *brændende kælighed* (literally, "burning love," but actually glazed pork cheeks, pickled pearl onions, and chives in a foamy potato puree) or *smilende økoæg* ("smiling organic egg"; cured ham from Skågen, peanut mayo, and watercress). Be aware of added charges and a timed seating schedule. Service can be slow due to crowds. A sister restaurant, Den Anden, meaning "The Second," serves traditional French cuisine in a historic building dating from 1750. It's where H. C. Andersen once dined. ⊠ *Store Kongensgade, 66Frederiksstaden* ☎ *33/32–32–34* ⚐ *Reservations essential* ⊟ *MC, V* ⊘ *No lunch. Closed Sun.*

$ ✕ **Pastis.** This lively eatery is the place to go for French brasserie-style
FRENCH   dishes. Accomplished chef and owner Mikkel Egelund satisfies with classics like entrecôte with béarnaise and crispy fries, *moules mariniere* (mussels steamed in white wine and herbs), or salad Niçoise. Also good is the *plateau de fruits de mer* (a platter of "fruit" of the sea), with lobster, oysters, and shrimp. Enjoy a predinner drink at the brass bar or have after-dinner coffee or a cognac on the patio. The restaurant has an à la carte menu for lunch and dinner, and a three-course dinner prix-fixe for DKr 255. ⊠ *Gothersgade 52, Frederiksstaden* ☎ *33/93–44–11* ⚐ *Reservations essential* ⊟ *AE, DC, MC, V* ⊘ *Closed Sun.*

$ ✕ **Told & Snaps.** This authentic Danish smørrebrød restaurant adheres
DANISH   to tradition by offering a long list of Danish delights, and the fare is
Fodor's Choice   somewhat cheaper than the city's benchmark smørrebrød restaurant,
★   Ida Davidsen. The butter-fried sole with rémoulade is a treat, as is the steak tartare. Wine is of course an option, but as this is true Danish cuisine, why not beer and *snaps* (Danish grain alcohol)? This place has one of largest selections in town and makes its own. ⊠ *Toldbodg. 2, Frederiksstaden* ☎ *33/93–83–85* ⊕ *www.toldogsnaps.dk* ⊟ *DC, MC, V* ⊘ *No dinner. Closed Sun.*

$$$ ✕ **Umami.** Enter through an acrylic curtain and find yourself seduced not
JAPANESE   only by the menu but also by the interior. Stone walls, ebony tables, and
★   subtly changing lighting provide a glamorous and refined mixture of texture and style. This Japanese-French hot spot draws an international crowd and the sexy and sophisticated. The lounge serves inventive cocktails and a wide array of sake (tastings are also an option). Try the ginger passion signature drink mixing *shochu* (a distilled spirit made from barley, potatoes, and rice), litchi liquor, ginger, and lime. Umami, meaning savory, serves small courses that you combine to create a full meal.

Start with fried langoustines with mango chutney or katafi-wrapped prawns with chili-mayonnaise. The Wagyu beef—also known as Kobe beef, with a truffle and wasabi sauce—the sushi, and the tempura do not disappoint. ⊠ *Store Kongensgade 59, Frederiksstaden* ☎ *33/38–75–00* ⊕ *www.restaurantumami.dk* ⌕ *Reservations essential* ⊟ *AE, DC, MC, V* ⊘ *No lunch. Closed Sun.*

CHRISTIANHAVN

$$$$ ✕ **Era Ora.** Since 1983 this premier Italian restaurant has been known for
ITALIAN its changing set menu and its climate-controlled wine cellar containing
★ 90,000 bottles of Italian vintages. Burnt-umber walls and black, chocolate brown, and white accents predominate in the dining room. You'll be served between nine and 17 (small) courses, depending on your appetite and time commitment. There's no à la carte menu. The tiny seafood antipasti, including octopus with homemade pasta and a touch of mascarpone cheese, fares well opposite a later main course of St. Peter fish; it's light and delicate in a fresh tomato sauce. This is a full, special night out; prepare to spend at least four hours dining leisurely. ⊠ *Overgaden neden Vandet 33-B, Christianshavn* ☎ *32/54–06–93* ⊕ *www.era-ora.dk* ⌕ *Reservations essential* ⊟ *AE, DC, MC, V* ⊘ *Closed Sun.*

¢ ✕ **Lagkagehuset.** Most everyone is familiar with Danish pastries, but did
BAKERY you know that they have their origin in Vienna, and the Danes call them *weinerbrød* meaning Vienna bread? This bakery is considered one of the city's best. Besides the scrumptious varieties of weinerbrød, fresh baked breads, and cakes, there are also delicious sandwiches, tea, and coffee available. This branch is on the picturesque Christianhavns' canal, but there's also a location in the Wonderful Copenhagen tourist office in Centrum. ⊠ *Torvegade 45, Christianshavn* ☎ *32/57–36–07.*

$$$ ✕ **L'Altro.** A few blocks southeast of Era Ora is this sister trattoria serving
ITALIAN rustic Italian dishes with many of the same ingredients but at slightly lower prices. Umbrian and Tuscan cuisine the way mama used to make is served family-style on colorful mismatched Sicilian ceramic dishes, which are also for sale. Choose between two menu options and enjoy them with wine from the 30-page menu. Take a trip downstairs through the giant birdcage and visit the wine cellar to make a selection by hand. ⊠ *Torvegade 62, Christianshavn* ☎ *32/54–54–06* ⊕ *www.laltro.dk* ⌕ *Reservations essential* ⊟ *AE, DC, MC, V* ⊘ *Closed Sun.*

$ ✕ **Spiseloppen.** Round out your visit to the Free State of Christiania with
ECLECTIC a meal at Spiseloppen, a 160-seat warehouse restaurant that was a military storage facility and an army canteen in its former life. Upon entering Christiania, wind your way past shaggy dogs, their shaggy owners, graffiti murals, and wafts of patchouli. (There are few street signs, so just ask; Spiseloppen is the neighborhood's best-known restaurant.) From the outside, this run-down warehouse may seem forbidding, but inside it's a different story. Climb up rickety stairs to the second floor and you're rewarded with a loft-size dining room with low, wood-beam ceilings and candles flickering on the tables. The menu highlights are fresh and inventive vegetarian and fish dishes, which might include artichokes stuffed with eggplant or portobello mushrooms served with squash, mango, and papaya. ⊠ *Bådsmandsstr. 43, Christianshavn* ☎ *32/57–95–58* ⊟ *MC, V* ⊘ *No lunch. Closed Mon.*

VESTERBRO

$$
CONTINENTAL
✕**Cofoco.** The name is an acronym for Copenhagen Food Consulting, and its reasonably priced three-course meals and fashionable surroundings have made it a hit. Lamb, beef, poultry, and fish are all on the menu, and appetizers may include foie gras, salmon tartare, or gazpacho. The restaurant has two seatings per night, and you can reserve a table online or by phone. Cofoco also runs sister restaurants, Les Trois Cochons, a brasserie style kitchen also in Vesterbro, and Auberge, a more refined restaurant in Østrerbro. All restaurants serve exceptionally well-made French-Danish cuisine at relavtively low prices. ⊠ *Abel Cathrines Gade. 7, Vesterbro* ☎ *33/13–60–60* ⊕ *www.cofoco.dk/kontakt.asp* ⚘ *Reservations essential* ⊟ *MC, V* ⊗ *No lunch. Closed Sun.*

$$$
ITALIAN
✕**Il Grappolo Blu.** "The Blue Cluster," is an upscale Italian restaurant offering intimate dining behind a facade of dark wood planks and heavily draped windows. Inside, handmade Vilca crystal glassware and baroque-style Italian textiles and furniture give a feeling of grandiose eloquence. The restaurant serves a variety of tasters such as virgin lobster with mascarpone, Jerusalem artichoke and shaved chocolate, and sole wrapped in prosciutto and zucchini on pomegranate sauce. Dishes are prepared with delicacies imported from Italy, including seasonal black truffles from Nocia in Umbria. Choose from a set menu of four to six courses and pair your meal with, among other things, one of 130 varieties of Brunello di Montalcino, a specialty here. The staff is knowledgeable and attentive. ⊠ *Vester Farimagsgade 35, Vesterbro* ☎ *33/11–57–20* ⚘ *Reservations essential* ⊟ *AE, DC, V* ⊗ *Closed Sun.*

$
CHINESE
✕**Yan's Wok.** Hong Kong-born chef Yan mans the wok here, serving regional cuisine, such as peppery dishes from the Szechuan province; aromatic shredded duck; or stir-fried lamb with ginger, spring onion, and chili. Yan's is unconventionally decorated with simple white linens and black leather chairs, and is a longtime favorite among locals. Regardless of the hour, you can be sure of getting tasty meals at bargain prices. The restaurant offers two five-course menus for DKr 198 and DKr 230, and an à la carte menu. ⊠ *Bagerstr. 9, Vesterbro* ☎ *33/23–73–33* ⊟ *AE, DC, MC, V* ⊗ *No lunch. Closed Mon.*

FREDERIKSBERG

$
CONTINENTAL
☾
✕**Belis Bar.** It's worth traveling a little outside of the city center to enjoy one of the best brunches in town. This restaurant-bar-café occupies a corner of the historic Frederiksberg city hall building and has a reasonably priced à la carte and one- to five-course dinner menus. Danish specialties like herring, pork meatballs with red beets, or fried plaice are typical lunch options. It's a child-friendly place with smaller portions available; you need only ask. Sit outside right on the square, indoors behind a glass atrium, at the bar, or in the restaurant deep inside. Regardless of where you sit, the friendly staff provides exceptional service. ⊠ *Frederiksberg Smallegade, 1Frederksberg* ☎ *33/11–03–13* ⊟ *AE, MC, V* ⊗ *No dinner Sun.*

$$$$
ECLECTIC
★
✕**Formel B.** The name stands for "basic formula," but this French-Danish fusion restaurant is anything but basic. White tablecloths, antique silver cutlery, custom-designed chairs (for sale), and Italian travertine

2

walls create a stylish setting. Dishes might include roasted turbot with wild local mushrooms, rye bread, and sauce *vin jaune* (a sauce made with white wine from late harvest Savagnin grapes grown in the Jura region of France)— served on an array of Royal Copenhagen dishes. Desserts are works of art. The wine list includes around 400 varieties, the majority are classic French, with an impressive selection from Burgundy. On offer are a six-course tasting or four-course signature menus plus wines; there is no à la carte menu. ⊠ *Vesterbrog. 182, Frederiksberg* ☎ *33/25–10–66* ⊕ *www.formel-b.dk* ⚖ *Reservations essential* ▤ *AE, DC, MC, V* ⊙ *No lunch. Closed Sun.*

$$$$ ✕ **Mielcke & Hurtigkarl.** This restaurant in the Fredriksberg gardens and on
ECLECTIC   grounds of the Royal Danish Garden Society serves contemporary inter-
Fodor'sChoice   national cuisine. Industry veteran Jan Hurtigkarl and head chef Jakob
★   Mielcke, collaborated with Danish artists to create an airy, welcoming space that stimulates all the senses. Green textiles bring the surrounding garden inside, as does an acoustic soundscape of forest creatures. Light reflecting off a prism dances on crystals hanging from the ceiling. Art installations make restroom visits an adventure. The innovative kitchen perfectly pairs ingredients from around the world—some of the rare. Foie gras placed atop "bark" made of bull kelp from Vancouver Island and dessert of deconstructed berries, lavender ice cream, "spherified" (that is, gelled) ruccula and apricot, and fresh clovers contrasts playfulness with serious cooking. The restaurant has a set lunch and dinner menu, both with matching wines. ⊠ *Frederiksberg Runddel 1, Frederiksberg2000* ☎ *38/34–84–36* ⊕ *www.mielcke-hurtigkarl.dk* ⚖ *Reservations essential* ▤ *AE, DC, MC, V* ⊙ *Closed Mon. and Tues., Apr.–Sept. No lunch Thurs.–Sat., Oct.–Dec. Closed Jan.–Mar.*

WHERE TO STAY

Copenhagen has plenty of hotel options ranging from five-star to budget accommodation. That said, rates are on the high end of the scale and rooms are on the small side. The city has, in recent years, increased its capacity with new design hotels, a luxury all-suite hotel in Tivoli gardens, and a youth hostel in the city center. Many existing properties have undergone renovation and expansion and emphasizing eco-friendly, sustainable business practices.

Copenhagen is a compact, eminently walkable and likable city, and most of the hotels are in or near Centrum, usually within walking distance of the major sights and thoroughfares.

Note that in Copenhagen, as in the rest of Denmark, rooms usually only have showers (while the rest have showers and bathtubs), so make sure to state your preference when booking.

AMAGER

$$ ▥ **Radisson SAS Scandinavia.** South across the Stadsgraven from Christianshavn is one of Denmark's largest hotels and Copenhagen's token skyscraper. An immense lobby, with recessed lighting and streamlined furniture gives access to the city's only casino. Guest rooms are large though somewhat institutional. The hotel's highly rated Dining Room

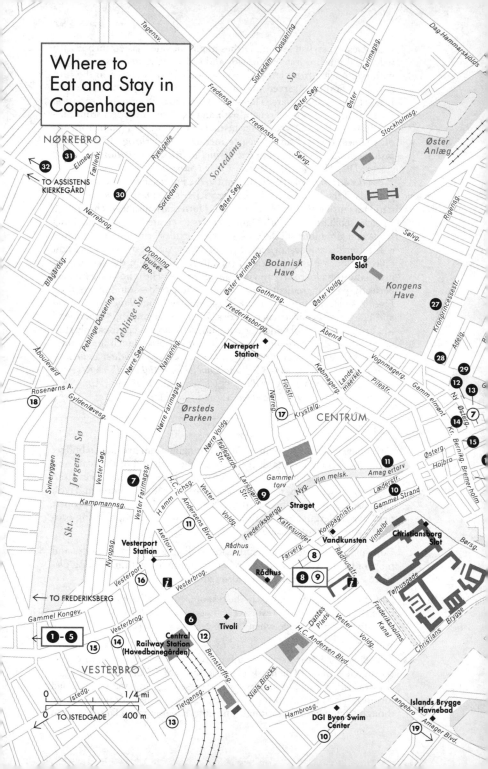

Where to Eat and Stay in Copenhagen

NØRREBRO

TO ASSISTENS KIERKEGÅRD

Tagensv.

Sortedam Dossering

Sø

Øster Søg.

Fredensbro.

Sølvg.

Dag Hammarskjölds

Øster Anlæg

Stockholmsg.

Rosenborg Slot

Botanisk Have

Kongens Have

Sølvg.

Rigensg.

Adelg.

Kronprincessegt.

CENTRUM

Rosenørns A.

Jørgens Sø

Skt.

Peblinge Sø

Ørsteds Parken

Nørreport Station

Strøget

Amagertorv

Gammel Strand

Vandkunsten

Christiansborg Slot

Børsg.

Christians Brygge

Tøjhusgade

Frederiksholms Kanal

Rådhus

Tivoli

Central Railway Station (Hovedbanegården)

VESTERBRO

Vesterport Station

TO FREDERIKSBERG

Gammel Kongev.

TO ISTEDGADE

1/4 mi

400 m

DGI Byen Swim Center

Islands Brygge Havnebad

H.C. Andersen Blvd.

Amager Blvd.

Langebro

Den Lille Havfrue ◆

KEY

ℹ Tourist Information

┼──── Rail Lines

① Restaurants

① Hotels

restaurant overlooking Copenhagen's copper towers and skyline, is a fine site for a leisurely lunch; dinner is also tempting with changing seasonal menus. **Pros:** good-size rooms with great city views; several on-site dining options. **Cons:** distance to Centrum (about a mile); feels like a business hotel. ✉*Amager Blvd. 70, Amager* ☎*33/96–50–00* ⊕*www. radissonsas.com* ⏎*542 rooms, 42 suites* ⚭*In-room: Wi-Fi. In-hotel: 4 restaurants, room service, pool, laundry service, Wi-Fi, parking (fee)* ▭*AE, DC, MC, V* ❙◎❙*EP.*

WORD OF MOUTH

"I've stayed in the Marriott twice. It's an easy walk to the train station and Tivoli, and it overlooks a wide canal. The executive floor rooms are particularly nice. I'd definitely stay at the Marriott again because I've had positive experiences in the past." —Dukey

CENTRUM

$$$ 🏨**Copenhagen Marriott Hotel.** This large Marriott on the waterfront is a well oiled-machine. However, the great view of the canal and Christianshavn through floor-to-ceiling windows is the only indication you're in Copenhagen, let alone Denmark. It has superior business and conference facilities and great fitness facilities with separate sauna and steam rooms for men and women. Rooms are comfortable and of a good size. **Pros:** all rooms have both tub and shower combo and either city or canal-side views. **Cons:** no restaurants nearby; small windows in the rooms, slightly institutionalized. ✉*Kalvebod Brygge 5, Centrum* ☎*88/33–99–00* ⊕*www.marriott.com/cphdk* ⏎*401 rooms, 10 suites* ⚭*In-room: safe, Internet. In-hotel: restaurant, room service, bar, gym, laundry services, parking (fee), some pets allowed, no-smoking rooms* ▭*AE, DC, MC, V* ❙◎❙*EP.*

$$ 🏨**Copenhagen Strand.** You can't stay closer to the harbor than here. Just a five-minute walk from Nyhavn, this pleasant hotel is housed in a waterfront warehouse dating from 1869. The cozy lobby has brown leather couches and old maritime pictures on the walls. Rooms are small but comfortable, with traditional-style wooden furnishings, blue color schemes, and sparkling baths. **Pros:** close to city attractions, most bathrooms have both a tub and shower. **Cons:** restaurant only serves breakfast; tight quarters; morning street noise. ✉*Havneg. 37, Centrum* ☎*33/48–99–00* ⊕*www.copenhagenstrand.dk* ⏎*174 rooms, 2 suites* ⚭*In-room: Internet. In-hotel: restaurant, bar, laundry service, Internet terminal, some pets allowed, no-smoking rooms* ▭*AE, DC, MC, V* ❙◎❙*BP.*

¢ 🏨**Danhostel Copenhagen Downtown.** This modern member of a hostel chain has a variety of room configurations, including double rooms. Its location next to Strøget and city hall means that you can be close to sights, restaurants, and bars even if you're on a tight budget. The hostel also hosts events and exhibitions, making it something of a cultural hub. The street-side café serves breakfast, lunch, and dinner and offers free fruit during the day. **Pros:** central location; inexpensive breakfast. **Cons:** small rooms; quiet time required 11 PM–4 AM; potential for lots of street noise. ✉*Vandkunsten 5, Centrum* ☎*70/23–21–10* ⊕*www.danhostel.*

dk ⇨*280 rooms* ⇨*In-hotel: restaurant, bicycles, no-smoking rooms* ▭*AE, DC, MC, V* ⓞ*EP.*

> **WORD OF MOUTH**
>
> "The best hotel in Copenhagen is Hotel Sankt Petri. You will be stunned! Justin Timberlake has stayed there. And my family."
>
> —traveller1959

$$$–$$$$ **First Hotel Skt. Petri.** For the better part of a century, a beloved budget department store nicknamed Dalle Valle occupied this site. It has been supplanted by this luxury hotel that's a hit with interior designers, fashionistas, and celebrities. It has everything you'd expect from a member of the Design Hotels, a collection of properties committed to design and cultural authenticity: a talking elevator telling you how fabulous the place is, contemporary Danish furnishings throughout, front desk staffers who could be models. Guest rooms, designed by Per Arnoldi, have a functional, modern aesthetic that's softened by bright, cheery colors. Many units have a terrace or balcony. The breakfast buffet and weekend brunch are among the city's best. **Pros:** great design everywhere; beautiful terrace; sleek cocktail bar. **Cons:** on the pretentious side; small rooms; street noise. ✉*Krystalg. 22, Centrum* ☎*33/45–91–00* ⊕*www.hotelsktpetri.com* ⇨*241 rooms, 27 suites* ⇨*In-room: safe, Internet. In-hotel: 2 restaurants, room service, bar, gym, laundry service, parking (paid), no-smoking rooms* ▭*AE, DC, MC, V* ⓞ*EP.*

$$ **Hotel Alexandra.** This singular boutique hotel honors the most influential furniture designers and artists from the Scandinavian modern era, including Klint, Wegner, Mogensen, Jacobsen, and Juhl. Rooms are outfitted with original design classics; details like door handles and faucets also reflect another era. The hotel has adopted many green practices and encourages guests to do the same: if you tell the front desk that you don't want your room cleaned, you'll receive a discount at the on-site restaurant (where many items are homemade and/or organic). **Pros:** authentic Danish design experience; friendly and helpful staff; buffet breakfast. **Cons:** lack of amenities; some furnishings are worn and torn; noisy location. ✉*H. C. Andersens Blvd. 8, Centrum* ☎*33/74–44–44* ⊕*www.hotel-alexandra.dk* ⇨*59 rooms, 2 suites* ⇨*In-room: Wi-Fi. In-hotel: bar, restaurant, laundry service, Wi-Fi* ▭*AE, D, MC, V* ⓞ*BP.*

$$$$ Fodor's Choice ★ **Hotel D'Angleterre.** The famed 250-year-old hotel welcomes royalty, politicians, and rock stars—from Margaret Thatcher to Madonna. An imposing New Georgian facade leads into an English-style sitting room. Standard guest rooms are individually decorated, many in pastels with overstuffed chairs and a mix of modern and antique furniture. The spit-and-polish staff accommodates every wish. The elegant Restaurant D'Angleterre serves excellent French cuisine. In winter the square in front of the hotel is converted into a skating rink. **Pros:** superb location; rich in history; full-service spa; large fitness center; decent quality restaurant. **Cons:** expensive; formal and straightlaced; some rooms could use a face-lift. ✉*Kongens Nytorv 34, Centrum* ☎*33/12–00–95* ⊕*www.dangleterre.com* ⇨*104 rooms, 19 suites* ⇨*In-room: safe, Internet. In-hotel: restaurant, room service, bar, pool, gym, spa, bicycles, laundry service, Internet terminal* ▭*AE, DC, MC, V* ⓞ*EP.*

$$$$ ⛄ **Hotel Nimb.** It's the first hotel in Tivoli Gardens and the most exclusive one in the city, with prices to match. Each of the 13 country-style, individually appointed suites has a view over the gardens; fine art, antiques, and textiles; and such amenities as Egyptian cotton towels and robes, a working fireplace, four-poster beds, and Bang & Olufsen electronics. Pros: very comfortable; superb location; great views. Cons: awkward spaces throughout due to building limitations; only a few guest rooms. ⊠*Bernstorffsgade 5, Centrum* ☎*88/70–00–00* ⊕*www.nimb.dk* ⚓*13 suites* ⚲*In-room: Wi-Fi, DVD (some). In-hotel: restaurant, bar, Wi-Fi, no-smoking rooms* ⊟*AE, DC, MC, V* ⦿*EP.*

$$ – $$$ ⛄ **Hotel Twentyseven.** This stylish Scandinavian lifestyle hotel is on a relatively quiet street, yet right across from the Rådhus Pladsen and a block from Strøget. Swedish interior designers shopped at Fritz Hansen to outfit this hotel with things like Series 7 bar stools, Arne Jacobsen Egg and Swan chairs, and Poul Henningsen PH-lamps. Vending machines offer everything from snacks to liquor to sex toys. Rooms have black, gray, and brown fabrics; wooden floors; plump bedding; slate bathrooms; and the occasional piece of red-lacquer furniture. The three on-site drinking establishments include the Wine Room, with 40 varieties by the glass; the Honey Ryder Cocktail Lounge, with a *Saturday Night Fever*–theme bathroom; and the Absolut Icebar. An organic breakfast and a light dinner buffet are included in the price. Pros: superb location; modern look and feel; meals included in rates. Cons: clock tower across the way rings on the hour 8 AM–midnight; not ideal for small children. ⊠*Løngangstræde 27, Centrum* ☎*70/27–56–27* ⊕*www.hotel27.dk* ⚓*200 rooms* ⚲*In-room: safe, Wi-Fi. In-hotel: restaurant, Wi-Fi, no-smoking rooms* ⊟*AE, DC, MC, V* ⦿*MAP.*

FREDERIKSSTADEN

$$ ⛄ **Best Western Hotel City.** This no-frills Best Western is tucked away on a side street a short walk from Kongens Nytorv, Nyhavn, the royal theater, the opera house, and the royal palace. The lobby has a calming fountain and a common area filled with sleek Danish furniture. Breakfast is included in the price, and a small corner bar offers drinks in the evenings. Rooms are done in black, gray, beige, and brown and have black leather Danish Gubi chairs and large black-and-white photos of jazz musicians. Pros: great location; good number of amenities; reasonable price. Cons: some room furnishings are outdated; not all rooms have tubs; restaurant only serves breakfast. ⊠*Peder Skrams Gade 24, Frederiksstaden* ☎*33/13–06–66* ⊕*www.hotelcity.dk* ⚓*81 rooms* ⚲*In-room: Wi-Fi. In-hotel: restaurant, laundry service, Wi-Fi, no-smoking rooms* ⊟*AE, DC, MC, V* ⦿*BP.*

$$ ⛄ **Copenhagen Admiral Hotel.** A five-minute stroll from Nyhavn, over-
★   looking old Copenhagen and Amalienborg Palace, the massive Admiral was once a grain warehouse (circa 1787). Today it's one of the least expensive top hotels, cutting frills and prices but retaining charm. Thick stone walls are broken by rows of windows; guest rooms mix maritime accents with modern furnishings and prints. Each room has a sitting area with leather sofas surrounded by 200-year-old exposed rafter beams. Rooms on the first through fourth floors also have French balconies. The SALT bar and restaurant lends Nordic touches to modern

HOTEL DEVELOPMENTS

At this writing a number of properties are under development in Copenhagen, many in the fast-growing Øresund region consisting of the southern part of Sweden or Skåne and Copenhagen metro area. Despite being about 8 km (5 mi) and 10 minutes from Centrum, these properties are easily accessible by train and may be more affordable than those in the city. Ørestad, the name for Copenhagen's part of the region, is home to Bella Center, a major conference and exhibition center, and Fields, Scandinavian's largest shopping center. The area is also home to tech companies and universities as well as innovative residential architectural projects and a nature preserve. There are also several properties in the works in Centrum.

Denmark's first floating hotel, **Copenhagen Living** (⊕ www.cphliving.com) is scheduled to open late in 2008 and on the inner harbor, a 10-minute walk from Centrum. Rooms are to incorporate Scandinavian classic design with floor-to-ceiling French windows that provide excellent harbor and city views. The extensive renovation of the historic **Palace Hotel** (⊕ www.palacehotel. dk), dating from 1910 and right on Centrum's Rådhus Pladsen, should

be completed in early 2009. The hotel is slated to be part of the Méridien chain. The family-owned Danish chain, Arp-Hansen Hotel Group is behind the upcoming 400-room **Tivoli Hotel** (⊕ www. arp-hansen.com) and Tivoli Congress Center complex (both set to open in the second half of 2010 near the central train station), which is being designed by Danish architect Kim Utzon. The **Bella Hotel** (⊕ www. bellacenter.dk), being built as part of the Øresund region's Bella convention center, is scheduled to open in 2011. It will be Scandinavia's largest hotel, with 814 luxury rooms in two 250-foot-tall towers. Plans also call for a large wellness center, a restaurant, a café, and a bar on the 23rd floor. **CABINN Metro** (⊕ www. cabinn.com/english/kbh/metro/ metro.html), operated by the Danish budget hotel chain CABINN and designed by the renowned American architect Daniel Libeskind, is slated to open its doors in Øresund in summer 2009. It will be a sizable hotel with 710 rooms. The **Crowne Plaza Copenhagen Towers** (⊕ www. copenhagentowers.com), a 365-room hotel with office, conference, and shopping facilities and near Bella Center and Field's shopping center in Øresund, is on track to open in 2010.

French brasserie food. A beautiful harborfront café offers great views. **Pros:** renovated rooms; great restaurant; quiet waterfront location. **Cons:** short walk to main attractions and other conveniences. ✉ Toldbodg. 24–28, Frederiksstaden ☎ 33/74–14–14 ⊕ www.admiralhotel. dk ➯ 314 rooms, 52 suites ⚿ In-room: Internet. In-hotel: restaurant, room service, bar, bicycles, laundry service, parking (paid), some pets allowed, no-smoking rooms ☰ AE, DC, MC, V ❑ EP.

$$–$$$ ⛴ **Front.** Huge purple flowerpots stand at the entrance to this funky harborside boutique property. Inside, a chalkboard on the wall welcomes you into the lounge with hot pink Danish-design chairs, tall black candleholders, and floral-pattern sofas. There's also an on-site American-

style diner that serves milk shakes, burgers, and fries. Simple, modern guest rooms—many with harbor views—have bold-color walls, black wooden accents, coordinating bedspreads, and pebble-stone bathroom floors. Free mineral water, soda, and beer from the minibar are a nice touch. The hotel is a showcase for Danish-design, with pieces from Normann Copenhagen, Ikea, and Gub, to name a few; some of the items are for sale in the on-site shop. **Pros:** great views; good-size rooms; laid back. **Cons:** street noise during rush hour. ⊠*Sankt Annæ Plads 21, Frederiksstaden* ☎*33/13–34–00* ⊕*www.front.dk* ➩*131 rooms* ⅏*In-room: Internet. In-hotel: restaurant, gym, laundry service, Internet terminal, parking (paid), some pets allowed* ⊟*AE, D, MC, V* ⧖⏐*EP.*

$$$ – $$$$
★
🔡**Nyhavn 71.** It's in a well-preserved 200-year-old building—a one-time spice warehouse—that overlooks the old ships of Nyhaven. Inside you'll find lots of exposed brick beams. The thick plaster walls are adorned with paintings by prominent Danish painters, including Jens Jørgen Thorsen; Asger Jorn; and the hotel's own founder, Alf Arp-Hansen. Rooms are tiny but cozy, with warm woolen spreads, dark woods, soft leather furniture, and crisscrossing timbers. Dishes on the menu at the Parkhuskælderen restaurant are made with seasonal Danish products. **Pros:** superb location; elegant furnishings; excellent service. **Cons:** small rooms and bathrooms; no off-street parking. ⊠*Nyhavn 71, Frederiksstaden* ☎*33/43–62–00* ⊕*www.71nyhavnhotel.com* ➩*150 rooms, 8 suites* ⅏*In-room: Wi-Fi. In-hotel: restaurant, room service, bar, laundry service, Internet terminal, Wi-Fi, some pets allowed, no-smoking rooms* ⊟*AE, DC, MC, V* ⧖⏐*EP.*

$$$
🔡**Phoenix.** The hotel was originally built in the 1680s but was torn down and rebuilt—rising from its rubble, just like the mythical Phoenix rose from its ashes—in 1847 as a plush, Victorian-style hotel. Suites are large and adorned with faux antiques and 18-karat-gold-plated bathroom fixtures; standard rooms are very small, measuring barely 9 by 15 feet. The hotel is close enough to city-center attractions that it gets a fair amount of street noise; light sleepers should ask for rooms above the second floor. Downstairs is Murdoch's Books & Ale, a snug pub done up in mahogany and brass that serves smørrebrød and light meals. **Pros:** central location; most baths have tubs. **Cons:** small rooms; slightly run down; less-than-efficient service. ⊠*Bredg. 37, Frederiksstaden* ☎*33/95–95–00* ⊕*www.phoenixcopenhagen.com* ➩*206 rooms, 7 suites* ⅏*In-room: safe, Wi-Fi. In-hotel: restaurant, room service, bar, laundry service, Internet terminal, Wi-Fi, some pets allowed, no-smoking rooms* ⊟*AE, DC, MC, V* ⧖⏐*EP.*

2

VESTERBRO

$$ ★ ✈ **AXEL Hotel Guldsmeden.** The newest member of the Hotel Gulds-meden chain is a boutique hotel with a green conscience. Among the eco friendly endeavors here are motion-sensor lighting that saves on electricity, an organic restaurant, and a bar that serves organic cocktails. Rooms have herringbone parquet floors, handmade oriental rugs, original art, and teak furniture imported from Bali (including four-poster beds). A spa with hot and cold-water tubs, sauna, and steam room lets you take a break from city life. **Pros:** eco-friendly amenities; pleasant courtyard garden; affordable breakfast and dinner. **Cons:** some bathrooms are very small; location in the "red light" district can make rooms susceptible to street noise. ⊠ *Helgolandsgade 11, Vesterbro* ☎ *33/31–32–66* ⊕ *www.hotelguldsmeden.dk* ↵ *107 rooms, 22 suites* ᏉＩ*n-room: Wi-Fi. In-hotel: restaurant, bar, spa, Wi-Fi, some pets allowed* ☰ *AE, D, MC, V* ＴOＩ*EP.*

$$ ✈ **DGI-byen.** This place seemingly has everything: rooms with an exquisite blend of Danish design; breakfast included in the rates; and a state-of-the-art recreation center with a bowling alley, climbing wall, shooting range, swimming pool, and spa. Though most rooms have double windows, you can sometimes hear the distant rumble of trains entering nearby Central Station. (The last train passes by at around 12:30 AM, so ask for a quiet room if you're a light sleeper.) As a hotel guest you receive a 10% discount at the on-site Vestauranten restaurant. **Pros:** lots of recreational activities; good amenities and discounts. **Cons:** far from main attractions; noise from trains at nearby station. ⊠ *Tietgensg. 65, Vesterbro* ☎ *33/29–80–00* ⊕ *www.dgi-byen.dk* ↵ *104 rooms* ᏉＩ*n-hotel: restaurant, pool, gym, spa, bicycles, Wi-Fi, parking (paid), no-smoking rooms* ☰ *AE, DC, MC, V* ＴOＩ*BP.*

$ ✈ **First Hotel Vesterbro.** Looming over Vesterbrogade—and a five-minute walk from Tivoli—this deluxe hotel is Denmark's third largest. The sun-drenched lobby, with floor-to-ceiling windows, has white pillars, blond-wood tables, and gray Dansk design armchairs. Rooms have pale yellow walls, cherrywood furnishings, and contemporary lithographs. Female travelers may want try out the First Lady rooms, which include adjustable mirrors and makeup remover in the bathrooms, fluffy bathrobes, an electric kettle, and women's magazines. Complimentary access is offered to a full-service fitness center nearby. A simple breakfast "to go" is included in the rate. It consists of coffee, tea, orange juice, and pastries and is served in the lobby until 9 AM. **Pros:** close to shops, restaurants, and main train station; breakfast included in rate. **Cons:** very small rooms; near the sometimes dodgy "red light" district. ⊠ *Vesterbrog. 23–29, Vesterbro* ☎ *33/78–80–00* ⊕ *www.firsthotels.com* ↵ *400 rooms* ᏉＩ*n-room: safe. In-hotel: restaurant, room service, bar, gym, laundry service, parking (paid), some pets allowed, no-smoking rooms* ☰ *AE, DC, MC, V* ＴOＩ*EP.*

$$$ Fodor'sChoice ★ ✈ **Radisson SAS Royal.** This high-rise was originally designed by Arne Jacobsen in 1960. The owners spent several years—and plenty of kroner—in re-embracing its Jacobsen look, and the result is a paean to the legendary designer. The graceful lobby has brown and green leather Jacobsen Swan and Egg chairs that are arranged in circles and

illuminated by the ceiling's recessed lights. Rooms are paneled in light maple and outfitted with Jacobsen chairs and lamps. Even the heavy door handles, functionally designed to fill the palm, were created by Jacobsen. The most famous room is 606, which looks just like it did in 1960, with all the original furnishings, including a nifty desktop that opens to reveal a lighted makeup mirror. Many of the rooms have views over Tivoli and the city center's copper-top buildings. The top-floor restaurant, Alberto K, serves top-notch Scandinavian-Italian cuisine. Sometimes the weekend rates include breakfast so be sure to ask. **Pros:** great views; beautiful Danish design throughout; large fitness area. **Cons:** some furnishings are worn; slightly institutionalized; service can be spotty. ⊠*Hammerichsg. 1, Vesterbro* 🕾*33/42–60–00* ⊕*www. radissonsas.com* ⇝*260 rooms, 24 suites* ⅃*In-hotel: restaurant, room service, bar, gym, Internet terminal, parking (paid), no-smoking rooms* ⊟*AE, DC, MC, V* ℩⊙℩*EP.*

> **WORD OF MOUTH**
>
> "The Royal is about a block from the central station, and Tivoli is at your doorstep along with Radhuspladen and Strøget. The inside of this hotel is lovely and so perfectly Scandinavian as it was fully designed by famed Danish designer Arne Jacobson." —MNP

FREDERIKSBERG

¢ 🖪 **Hotel CABINN Scandinavia.** This bright budget hotel is just west of the lakes and Vesterport Station. Its impeccably maintained rooms are very small but are designed with efficiency to include ample showers and foldaway and bunk beds. The hotel is popular with business travelers in winter and kroner-pinching backpackers and families in summer. There's no restaurant or bar, but you can buy refreshments at the front desk, and there's a continental breakfast for DKr 60. **Pros:** functional; affordable. **Cons:** tiny rooms; the need to reconfirm your reservation to prevent mix-ups. ⊠*Vodroffsvej 55, Frederiksberg* 🕾*35/36–11–11* ⊕*www.cabinn.com* ⇝*201 rooms* ⅃*In-hotel: Wi-Fi, parking (paid)* ⊟*AE, DC, MC, V* ℩⊙℩*EP.*

AFTER DARK

Nightspots are concentrated in several areas including in and around Strøget; in Vesterbro, with its main drag on Vesterbrogade just across from Tivioli Gardens; and on Istegade where you'll find some of the trendier bars and cafés. The area just off Kongens Nytorv on Gothersgade is also a nightlife hub. Nørrebro has lots of student cafés and bars, many around Sankt Hans Torv, and there are some upscale spots in Østerbro.

Copenhagen used to be famous for jazz, but that has changed, with many of the best clubs closing down. However, you can find nightspots catering to almost all musical tastes, from ballroom music to house, rap, and techno. There are also plenty of trendy clubs where DJs provide the sound tracks.

Restaurants, cafés, bars, and clubs stay open after midnight, a few until 5 AM. The club scene can be fickle—new venues crop up regularly, often replacing last year's red-hot favorites. Call ahead or check out *Copenhagen This Week* (⊕*www.ctw.dk*) and the English newspaper, *The Copenhagen Post* (⊕*www.cphpost.dk*) for current listings.

BARS AND LOUNGES

Copenhagen is peppered with wine bars and traditional bars where you can sample foreign and domestic beer. The city has seen a rise in places that specialize in cocktails—both traditional and experimental. A number of hotels have also become hot spots.

Hviids Vinstue (⊠*Kongens Nytorv 19, Centrum* ☎33/15–10–64 ⊕*www. hviidsvinstue.dk*) dates from the 1720s and attracts all kinds, young and old, singles and couples, for a glass of wine or cognac. **Karriere Bar** (⊠*Flæsketorvet 57, Vesterbro* ☎33/21–55–09 ⊕*www.karrierebar. com*) is a trendy restaurant-café-bar in the meatpacking district featuring interactive installations by international artists. DJs spin almost every weekend starting at 11 PM. The restaurant serves dinner and brunch on weekends.

Oak Room (⊠*Birkegade 10, Nørrebro* ☎38/60–38–60 ⊕*www.oak room.dk*) is a specialist cocktail bar in the popular nightlife corridor near Elmegade. Try a Venezuelan Butterfly (rum, passion fruit, lime, raw sugar syrup, and mint) or a La Cucaracha (tequila, apple, passion fruit, lime, and powdered sugar). **Peder Oxe's Vinkælder** (⊠*Gråbrødretorv 11, Centrum* ☎33/11–11–93) is the wine "basement" of the Peter Oxe restaurant. It's a casual and cozy bar, though nearly impossible to squeeze into on weekends.

Simply named and discretely located in an unmarked building **Ruby** (⊠*Nybrogade 10, Centrum* ☎33/93–12–03 ⊕*www.rby.dk*) feels more like a party in a luxury apartment than a cocktail lounge. It buzzes with a mixed clientele—from the "in" crowd to artists to businesspeople. The service-minded staff stir up exceptionally well-made drinks that are worth their high prices.

Vinbaren (⊠*Dronningens Tværgade 6, Centrum* ☎33/32–09–82 ⊕*www.vinbaren.dk*) is a wine bar with more than 70 bottles on offer. It's more than a wine bar, though. You can also find cocktails, champagne, and beer in addition to several wines by the glass. Although it's geared to a more adult crowd, Vinbaren is one of the livelier places in the city, with DJs playing after 10 on weekends. **Y's Café and Cocktailbar** (⊠*Nørre Voldgade 102, Centrum* ☎33/14–20–44) is a low-key cocktail bar with a 110 drinks on its menu, each one concocted by award-winning mixologist and owner Yvonne Kubach.

BEACH CLUBS

In the summer, beach clubs come alive along Copenhagen's harbor. **Docken** (⊠*Færgehavnsgade 35, Østerbro* ☎39/29–92–00 ⊕*www. docken.dk*) is a chill-out and cultural area with a sand bar, a concert hall, a club, a theater, and an art exhibition center. It's on the north end of the harbor (Nordhavn), facing the Øresund.

TOP HOTEL BARS

Many hotels have bars and lounges where even locals enjoy a cocktail and stylish surroundings.

Absolut Icebar Copenhagen (✉ *Løngangstræde 27, Centrum* ☎ *70/27–56–27* ⊕ *www.hotel27.dk/ icebar*) is literally one of the coolest bars in Copenhagen. Part of the trendy Hotel Twentyseven (which also houses the Honey Ryder lounge serving "molecular" cocktails), it's basically a –31°C (–23°F) ice box (don't worry, a coat is provided during your 40-minute visit), where you drink vodka concoctions in glasses made of ice.

Bar D'Angleterre (✉ *Kongens Nytorv 34, Centrum* ☎ *33/37–06–45* ⊕ *www.dangleterre.com*) is a distinguished bar in the Hotel D'Angleterre where you can look out on Copenhagen's most beautiful square, Kongens Nytorv. Stop here before heading to the nightspots two blocks over on Gothersgade. **Bar Rouge** (✉ *Krystalg. 22, Centrum* ☎ *33/45–91–00* ⊕ *www.hotelsktpetri.com*), a very

swanky cocktail lounge at the design hotel First Hotel Skt. Petri has DJs spinning records on weekends. It even produces and sells its own CDs. The **Library Bar** (✉ *Bernstorffsg. 4, Vesterbro* ☎ *33/14–92–62* ⊕ *www. profilhotels.se/en.aspx*) in the Plaza is an elegant spot for a quiet but pricey drink.

Nimb Bar & Vinotek (✉ *Bernstorffsgade 5, Centrum* ☎ *88/70–00–00*) on the second floor and in the former ballroom of the Nimb hotel, has an enormous fireplace and crystal chandeliers. You can come for a delightful afternoon tea and coffee service or for a drink. The impressive basement wine cellar has candlelit wooden picnic tables and glass-lined walls displaying bottles from every corner of the globe. The list has an unprecedented 1,300 varieties, many available by the glass. You can order Danish-inspired tapas (oysters, smoked salmon, quail eggs, Skågen ham and cheese) to accompany tastings.

Halvandet (✉ *Refshalevej 325, Holmen* ☎ *70/27–02–96*), sits on Refshaleøen, Copenhagan's old shipyard just across from the Little Mermaid. On summer days it's an urban beach club with activities like sunbathing, beach volleyball, kayak polo, and miniature golf. The party vibe continues the night, with DJs playing into the wee hours. The kitchen stays open until 10 PM, and a grill offers simple eats.

CAFÉS

Café life appeared in Copenhagen in the 1970s and quickly became a compulsory part of city living. The cheapest sit-down eateries (a cappuccino and sandwich often cost less than DKr 150), cafés transform into lively and relaxed nightspots. The crowd is usually an interesting mix. On weekends many cafés offer brunch, a Copenhagen classic. Once run-down and neglected, the up-and-coming Istedgade strip has several cheery cafés and restaurants.

Bang & Jensen (✉ *Istedg. 130, Vesterbro* ☎ *33/25–53–18* ⊕ *www.bang ogjensen.dk*) is a trendy café and cocktail bar with DJs on weekends. **Delicatessen** (✉ *Vesterbrog. 120, Vesterbro* ☎ *33/22–16–33* ⊕ *www. delicatessen.dk*) serves international cuisine by day and quality brunch on weekends. After 11 PM Thursday through Saturday, though, it's time for cocktails and dancing to DJ-spun house, hip-hop, and rock.

At the fashionable **Café Europa** (⊠ *Amagertorv 1, Centrum* ☎ *33/14–28–89*), just across from the Royal Copenhagen shop, people watching and coffee naturally go together. **Café Norden** (⊠ *Østerg. 61, Centrum* ☎ *33/11–77–91*) sits at the intersection of Købmagergade and Strøget, catercorner to Café Europa. Substantial portions make up for minimal table space at this art nouveau–style café.

At night **Café Zirup** (⊠ *Læderstræde 32, Centrum* ☎ *33/13–50–60*) is a modern lively hangout. The café has a good variety of sandwiches and a popular "hangover" brunch. **Café Zeze** (⊠ *Ny Østergade 20, Centrum* ☎ *33/14–23–90*) attracts the most attractive (and richest and most famous) at midday and in the early evening.

CASINO

The **Casino Copenhagen** (⊠ *Amager Blvd. 70, Amager* ☎ *33/96–59–65* ⊕ *www.casinocopenhagen.dk*), at the SAS Scandinavia Hotel, has American roulette, blackjack, poker, and slot machines. You must be 18 years old to enter, and there's a strictly enforced dress code—jackets are required and no athletic clothing is allowed. Outerwear must be left at the coat check, for a fee. Dealers and croupiers aren't shy about reminding winners that a tip of a certain percentage is customary. The casino is open daily 2 PM to 4 AM, and admission is DKr 90.

DANCE CLUBS

Most discos open at 11 PM, charging covers of about DKr 75 and selling drinks at steep prices. **Culture Box** (⊠ *Kronprinsessegade 54a, Centrum* ☎ *33/32–50–50*) holds club events on weekends with DJs playing anything from techno and hip-hop to reggae and electronic jazz. Check the calendar to see what's on as the venue is sometimes closed for private events. **K3** (⊠ *Knabrostræde 3, Centrum* ☎ *33/11–37–84*) is a four-room club with two separate dance floors in the formerly gay Pan Club. Now a mixed crowd—men and women, straight and gay (though all over age of 24)—enjoys electronica, DJs, and disco from the '70s, '80s, and '90s.

Nasa (⊠ *Gothersg. 8F, Boltens Gård, Frederiksstaden* ☎ *33/93–74–15* ⊕ *www.nasa.dk*) has an exclusive "members only" policy, which has earned it a legendary status. You can get on the guest list through your hotel or a concierge service like American Express. Once inside, you get to hobnob with the city's chic and moneyed set. The club opens at midnight on weekends. Underneath Nasa is Kulørbar, and, next door is Pink with a more casual vibe and a more lax door policy. **Nord** (⊠ *Vesterbrogade 2E, Vesterbro* ☎ *33/36–25–00* ⊕ *www.nordlounge. dk*) is a lounge and nightclub for people over 30 and plays music to match its clientele. It's one of the city's most popular and is open only on Saturday.

Park Café (⊠ *Østerbrog. 79, Østerbro* ☎ *35/42–62–48*) has an old-world café with live music downstairs, a disco upstairs, and a movie theater just next door. **Den Røde Pimpernel** (⊠ *Bernstorffsg. 3, Vesterbro*

WHERE TO TRY DANISH BEER

Beer remains a defining element of Danish culture. In fact, Denmark has the most breweries per capita of any country in the world. Although the traditional Carlsberg and Tuborg pilsner varieties are still the main options at most bars and restaurants, there are more brews on offer than ever before. The number of brewpubs with handcrafted brews has increased, and so has the number of places offering beer-pairing menus.

Charlie's Bar (⊠ *Pilestr. 33, Centrum* ☎ *33/32–22–89*) has 19 drafts, six of which are cask-conditioned ale—unfiltered, unpasteurized beer served from casks. There's a wide range of international and Danish beer, including house lagers Hancock and Thisted. **Den Tatoverede Enke** (⊠ *Gothersgade 8C, Centrum* ☎ *33/91–88–77*) is a bar–restaurant specializing in Belgian food and beer. There are 16 brews on tap and 100 varieties in bottles. Many of the dishes are prepared with beer (try the mussels here, which are some of the best in town), and there's a beer and food pairing menu.

Ølbaren (⊠ *Elmegade 2, Nørrebro* ☎ *35/35–45–34*) is a local favorite with a wide selection of international and Danish beers—about 120 of them bottled and 16 of them on tap. Ølbaren also offers beer tastings "on demand." At **Plan B** (⊠ *Frederiksborggade 48, Centrum* ☎ *33/36–36–56*) a retro-style café, expect beer bottles lining the walls; cozy couches; tapas and other café fare; and more than 400 varieties of beer, including several Danish microbrews.

The **Brew Pub** (⊠ *Vestergade 29, Centrum* ☎ *33/32–00–60* ⊕ *www.*

brewpub.dk) microbrewery and restaurant has a beer garden and 11 beers on tap as well as a beer-sampler menu and dishes made using beer. Near the main entrance to Tivoli is **Bryggeriet Apollo** (⊠ *Vesterbrogade 3, Vesterbro* ☎ *42/14–00–50* ⊕ *www.bryggeriet.dk/engelsk*), which opened in 1990 and is one of the first restaurants in Copenhagen to brew its own beer. It offers traditional draft and specialty brews. In Tivoli Gardens, **Færgekroen Bryghus** (⊠ *Centrum, on border of Vesterbro district* ☎ *33/75–06–80*) serves traditional Danish fare with home-brewed blonde and amber ales.

Nørrebro Bryghus (⊠ *Ryesgade 3, Nørrebro* ☎ *35/30–05–30* ⊕ *www.noerrebrobryghus.dk*), is one of Denmark's most popular brewpubs thanks, in part, to its beer-pairing menu and the tours of its brewing facility. **Vesterbro Bryghus** (⊠ *Vesterbrogade 2B, Vesterbro* ☎ *33/11–17–05*) is just across the street from Tivoli Gardens and has five brews on tap as well as beer tastings until 10:30 PM.

The **Carlsberg Visitors Center & The Jacobsen Brewhouse** (⊠ *Gammel Carlsberg Vej 11, Valby* ☎ *33/27–12–82* ⊕ *www.visitcarlsberg.com*) is in a building dating from 1860 in the original Carlsberg brewery. Take one of the self-guided tours to learn all there is about Carlsberg. The entry fee of DKr 50 includes two beers in the Jacobsen brewpub at the end of the tour, which takes approximately 1½ hours. To get here hop Bus 26 (the trip takes 10–15 minutes from Centrum) any day but Monday, when the facility is closed.

☎ 33/75–07–60) draws an adult crowd for dancing to live orchestras, trios, and old-time music—some of it classic Danish. The very popular English-style pub **Rosie McGee's** (✉ *Vesterbrog 2A, Vesterbro* ☎ 70/33–31–11 ⊕ *www.rosiemcgees.dk*) serves American and Mexican eats and encourages dancing, with DJs every night except Sunday and live bands on Thursday.

Rust (✉ *Guldbergsg. 8, Nørrebro* ☎ 35/24–52–00) is a constantly crowded dance club and live music venue on Nørrebro's main square, Skt. Hans Torv. Music ranges from indie to electronica to hop-hop. **Sofiekælderen** (✉ *Overgaden oven Vandet 32, Christianshavn* ☎ 32/57–27–87 ⊕ *www.sofiekaelderen.dk*) is a veteran of the Copenhagen night scene and serves as a hangout for local musicians. Live music plays on Thursday, a DJ spins on Friday, and live jazz on Saturday afternoon gives way to piano-bar tunes in the evening. The kitchen serves simple fare to accompany cocktails.

Vega (✉ *Enghavevej 40, Vesterbro* ☎ 33/25–70–11 ⊕ *www.vega.dk*) is a three-story complex consisting of Store Vega where larger concerts are held and Little Vega, which hosts smaller concerts and turns into a nightclub on Friday and Saturday. In the basement is Nano Vega for small acts. Next door is Ideal Bar, a good place to have a drink before entering or upon exiting Vega.

GAY AND LESBIAN SPOTS

Given Denmark's longtime liberal attitudes toward homosexuality, it's not surprising that Copenhagen has a thriving and varied gay nightlife scene. In August, the city holds Mermaid Pride, its boisterous annual gay-pride parade. Check out the free paper *Panbladet* (⊕ *www.panbladet.dk*) or the gay guides *Gayguide* (⊕ *www.gayguide.dk*) and *Copenhagen Gay Life* (⊕ *www.copenhagen-gay-life.dk*) for nightlife listings and other information. The **Landsforeningen for Bøsser og Lesbiske** (*The Danish National Association of Gays and Lesbians* ✉ *Nygade 7, Centrum* ☎ 33/13–19–48 ⊕ *www.lbl.dk*) is a good local contact.

Café Intime (✉ *Allegade 25, Frederiksberg* ☎ 38/34–19–58 ⊕ *www. cafeintime.dk*) is a great place to sit and sip cocktails. Every day a pianist plays on the grand piano, and every Sunday sees live jazz. This is a place for the "free minded," one that welcomes all walks of life. The small **Central Hjørnet** (✉ *Kattesundet 18, Centrum* ☎ 33/11–85–49 ⊕ *www.centralhjornet.dk*) is in a house that dates from 1802. It's been a bar for the past seven years, providing entertainment like drag shows for gays and lesbians alike.

Code (✉ *Rådhusstræde 1, Centrum* ☎ 33/26–36–26 ⊕ *www.code.dk*) a straight-friendly gay-and-lesbian dance club and lounge that holds events including drag shows and live DJs on weekends. The dark, casual **Cosy Bar** (✉ *Studiestr. 24, Downtown* ☎ 33/12–74–27) is one of the oldest men's bars in Copenhagen and is the place to go in the wee hours (it usually stays open until 8 AM).

Foxy (✉ *Meldahlsgade 4, Vesterbro* ☎ 32/62–20–90), is a disco for both gays and lesbians that has affordable drinks and themed parties. **Jailhouse**

Event Bar & Restaurant (⊠ *Studiestræde 12, Centrum* ☎ *33/15–22–55* ⊕ *www.jailhousecph.dk*) isn't as odd a place as the name sounds, even if it is decorated like a city jail. Waiters wear police uniforms, and overall, it's a fun, convivial atmosphere attracting men in a wide range of age groups.

Masken Bar & Café (⊠ *Studiestræde 33, Centrum* ☎ *33/91–09–37* ⊕ *www. maskenbar.dk*) is a relaxed bar welcoming both men and women, young and old. **Men's Bar** (⊠ *Teglgårdstr. 3, Centrum* ☎ *33/12–73–03* ⊕ *www. mensbar.dk*) is, as its name suggest, a men-only bar where wearing leather and rubber is encouraged. **Oscar Café & Bar** (⊠ *Rådhus Pl. 77, Centrum* ☎ *33/12–09–99*) is a relaxed spot for a drink or a cup of coffee and a chat with locals. There's also a menu of café food. It's a hot spot for both gays and lesbians.

JAZZ CLUBS

Although hard times have thinned Copenhagen's once-thriving jazz scene, you can still groove to local talent and international headliners, especially in July, when the Copenhagen Jazz Festival spills over into the clubs. Many clubs host Sunday-afternoon sessions that draw spirited crowds of Danes.

The large **Copenhagen Jazzhouse** (⊠ *Niels Hemmingsensg. 10, Centrum* ☎ *33/15–47–00* ⊕ *www.jazzhouse.dk*) attracts international names to its chic, modern, barlike interior. The downstairs concert hall turns into a dance club on Friday and Saturday after the jazz acts end. You can buy tickets at the door only one hour before start time.

Drop Inn (⊠ *Kompagnistr. 34, Centrum* ☎ *33/11–24–04*) draws a mixed crowd for its nightly live music sessions featuring rock, pop, blues, and jazz. The stage also welcomes songwriters and choirs, and the place puts on occasional Sunday-afternoon jazz sessions. As the name suggests, you're welcome to drop in and sit at the big wooden bar and enjoy the laid-back atmosphere. The eclectic decor includes iron statues of winged bacchanalian figures and an M. C. Escher–style ceiling fresco.

Huset Magstræde (⊠ *Magstraede 14, Centrum* ☎ *33/69–32–00*), is a cultural "house" with four floors of entertainment. The first floor is dedicated to jazz of all genres with big band nights and jam sessions. The other floors offer independent theater—everything from Shakespeare to experimental plays—an art house cinema, and the Musikcafeén with live rock and pop bands playing rock and pop. **La Fontaine** (⊠ *Kompagnistr. 11, Centrum* ☎ *33/11–60–98*) is Copenhagen's quintessential jazz dive, with sagging curtains, impenetrable smoke (although there are filters), and hep cats. This is a must for jazz lovers.

ROCK CLUBS

Copenhagen's rock clubs almost all are filled with young, fashionable crowds. Clubs tend to open and go out of business frequently, but you can get free entertainment newspapers and flyers advertising gigs at almost any café.

Isola Music Club (⊠ *Linnesgade 16A, Centrum* ☎ *27/28–14–28* ⊕ *www. isolabar.dk*) is a bar and club that pays tribute to classics like Iggy Pop,

David Bowie, and Nick Cave as well as modern rock. It's only open Thursday through Saturday. **Lades Kælder** (⊠*Kattesundet 6, Centrum* ☎*33/14–00–67* ⊕*www.lades.dk*), a local hangout just off Strøget, hosts good old-fashioned rock and-roll bands. It's one of the few places with live music every night.

Loppen (⊠*Bådsmandsstr. 43, Christianshavn* ☎*32/57–84–22* ⊕*www. loppen.dk*), in Christiania, is a medium-size venue featuring some of the bigger names in Danish music (pop, rock, and urban) and budding artists from abroad. Covers range from DKr 50 to DKr 150. The **Pumpehuset** (⊠*Studiestr. 52, Centrum* ☎*35/36–09–38* ⊕*www.pumpehuset.dk*) is the place for pop, soul, and rock, and gets some big names. Tickets can be steep. **Stengade 30** (⊠*Steng. 18, Nørrebro* ☎*35/39–09–20* ⊕*www.stengade30.dk*), named after its previous address, is a two-story club with two stages. Look for live rock, electronic/techno, and hip-hop performers as well as DJs. There's something happening most nights.

SHOPPING

A showcase for world-famous Danish design and craftsmanship, Copenhagen seems to have been set up with shoppers in mind. In fact, the city name Copenhagen (København in Danish), actually means the "merchant's harbor," because it was once a major center of trade. The spirit of those days remains with countless specialty shops in almost every corner of the city. The best buys are such luxury items as amber, crystal, porcelain, silver, and furs. Danish clothing design is now coming into fashion and is considered one of the nation's most important exports.

Look for offers and sales (*tilbud* or *udsalg* in Danish) and check antiques and secondhand shops for classics at cut-rate prices. Although prices are inflated by a hefty 25% value-added tax (Danes call it *moms*), non–European Union citizens can receive about an 18% refund. For more details and a list of all tax-free shops, ask at the tourist office for a copy of the *Tax-Free Shopping Guide*.

The **Information Center for Danish Crafts and Design** (⊠*Amagertorv 1, Downtown* ☎*33/12–61–62* ⊕*www.danishcrafts.dk*) provides helpful information on galleries, shops, and workshops specializing in Danish crafts and design—from jewelry to ceramics to wooden toys to furniture. Its Web site has listings and reviews of the city's best crafts shops.

AREAS

The pedestrian-only Strøget and adjacent Købmagergade are *the* shopping streets, but wander down the smaller streets for lower-priced, offbeat stores. The most exclusive shops are at the end of Strøget, around Kongens Nytorv, and on Ny Adelgade, Grønnegade, and Pistolstræde. Kronprinsensgade has become the in vogue fashion strip, where a number of young Danish clothing designers have opened boutiques. On the western end of Strøget, Nørre Voldgade, and Nørregade is the Latin Quarter with record stores and hip new and secondhand clothes shops specializing in street wear.

Running parallel to Strøget is Kompagnistræde and Læderstræde (together known as Strædet), featuring antiques shops selling silver, porcelain, toys, books, and other collectibles. Bredgade, just off Kongens Nytorv, is lined with elegant antiques and silver shops, furniture stores, and auction houses. In addition, the area around Ravnsborggade in Nørrebro is home to many collector and antiques stores.

DEPARTMENT STORES
Illum (✉ *Østerg. 52, Centrum* ☎ *33/14–40–02*), not to be confused with Illums Bolighus, is well stocked, with a lovely rooftop café and excellent basement grocery. **Magasin** (✉ *Kongens Nytorv 13, Downtown* ☎ *33/11–44–33* ⊕ *www.magasin.dk*), Scandinavia's largest department store, also has a top-quality basement marketplace.

> ## VAT REFUNDS
>
> Non-EU citizens can obtain a 13%–19% refund on the 25% value-added tax (VAT). The more than 1,500 shops that participate in program have a white TAX FREE sticker on their windows. Purchases must be at least DKr 300 per store and must be sealed and unused in Denmark. The shopkeeper will ask you to fill out a form and show your passport. You then turn in the forms at any airport or ferry customs desk and get a credit. Keep receipts and buys handy; occasionally customs authorities ask to see purchases.

MALLS
A popular mall is the gleaming **Fisketorvet Shopping Center** (☎ *33/36–64–00*), built in what was Copenhagen's old fish market. It's near the canal, south of Centrum and within walking distance of Dybbølsbro Station and the Marriott Hotel. It includes 100 shops, from chain clothing stores (Mang, H&M) and shoe shops (including the ubiquitous Ecco) to a smattering of jewelry, watch, and stereo retailers, such as Swatch and Bang & Olufsen. Fast-food outlets abound, and there are 10 cinemas.

Field's (✉ *Next to Ørestad Metro Station, or E20 Frakørsel, Exit 19* ⊕ *www.fields.dk*) is Scandinavia's largest mall with more than 140 retail shops. It's near the Copenhagen Airport and has a full floor devoted to food, entertainment, and leisure pursuits. It's open weekdays 10–8, Saturday 10–5, and the first Sunday of the month 10–5.

Galleri K, an elegant and modern complex at the intersection of Pilestræde, Antonigade, and Kristen Bernikows Gade, houses a number of popular Danish designers including By Marlene Birger (*www.bymalenebirger.com*), Designers Remix Collection (*www.designersremix.com*), and Dyrberg/Kern (*www.dyrbergkern.com*).

MARKETS
Throughout summer and into autumn, there are six major markets every weekend, many of which concentrate on selling antiques and secondhand porcelin, silver, and glassware. Bargaining is expected. Two of the sites are right downtown. Check with the tourist office or the magazine *Copenhagen This Week* (⊕ *www.ctw.dk*) for street markets.

At **Gammel Strand** on Friday and Saturday, the "market" is more of an outdoor antiques shop; you might find porcelain and crystal figurines, silver, or even, on occasion, furniture. **Israel Plads** (✉*Near Nørreport Station, Centrum*) has a Saturday flea market from May through October, open 9–3. Professional dealers sell classic Danish porcelain, silver, jewelry, and crystal, plus books, prints, postcards, and more.

Kongens Nytorv hosts a Saturday flea market in the shadow of the Royal Theater; the pickings aren't so regal, but if you arrive early enough, you might nab a piece of jewelry or some Danish porcelain. The side street **Ravnsborggade** (✉*Nørrebro* ⊕*www.ravnsborggade.dk*) is dotted with antiques shops that move their wares outdoors on Sunday.

SPECIALTY STORES
AUDIO EQUIPMENT
For high-tech design and acoustics, **Bang & Olufsen** (✉*Kongens Nytorv 26, Centrum* ☎*33/11–14–15* ⊕*www.bang-olufsen.dk*) is so renowned that its products are in the permanent design collection of New York's Museum of Modern Art. (Check prices at home first to make sure you are getting a deal.)

CLOTHING AND ACCESSORIES
If you're on the prowl for the newest Danish threads, you'll find a burgeoning number of cooperatives and designer-owned stores around town, particularly along Kronprinsensgade, near the Strøget.

Artium (✉*Vesterbrog. 1, Vesterbro* ☎*33/12–34–88*) offers an array of colorful, Scandinavian-designed sweaters and clothes alongside useful and artful household gifts. **Bruuns Bazaar** (✉*Kronprinsensg. 8, Centrum* ☎*33/32–19–99* ⊕*www.bruunsbazaar.com*) has its items hanging in the closet of almost every stylish Dane. Here you can buy the Bruuns label—inspired designs with a classic, clean-cut Danish look—and other high-end names, including Gucci.

House of Amber (✉*Kongens Nytorv 2, Centrum* ☎*33/11–67–00* ⊕*www.dyrbergkern.com*) is a shop and amber museum with a wide selection of amber jewelry and other objects situated at the beginning of Nyhavn. Another location can be found on Strøget. **Hennes & Mauritz** (✉*Amagertorv 23, Centrum* ☎*33/73–70–90*), H&M for short, the Swedish chain, has stores all over town. They offer reasonably priced clothing and accessories for men, women, and children. Best of all are the to-die-for baby clothes.

ICCompanys (✉*Frederiksberggade 24, Centrum* ☎*33/11–35–55*) carries a trendy, youthful style, typified by the Danish Matinique label. **Munthe plus Simonsen** (✉*Grønneg. 10, Centrum* ☎*33/32–03–12* ⊕*www.muntheplussimonsen.com*) sells innovative and playful—and pricey—Danish designs.**Petitgas Herrehatte** (✉*Købmagerg. 5, Centrum* ☎*33/13–62–70*) is a venerable shop for old-fashioned men's hats.

CRYSTAL AND PORCELAIN
Danish classics such as Holmegaard Glassworks and Royal Copenhagen porcelain are timeless treasures to take back home. Many department stores hold the latest collections and settings, however you can often

find secondhand pieces at antique stores and markets for reduced prices. Signed art glass is always more expensive, but be on the lookout for seconds as well as secondhand and unsigned pieces.

Bodum Hus (⊠ Østerg. 10, on Strøget, Centrum 📧33/36–40–80 ⊕www. bodum.com) shows off a wide variety of reasonably priced Danish-designed, functional—and especially kitchen-oriented—accoutrements. The French-press is a must for true coffee lovers.

The flagship store for **Royal Copenhagen** (⊠ Amagertorv 6, Centrum 📧33/13–71–81 ⊕www.royalcopenhagen.dk) beautifully displays its famous porcelain ware and settings fit for a king. The shop also has a museum on the second floor where you can see the painters in action. The **Royal Copenhagen Factory Outlet** (⊠ Søndre Fasanvej 9, Frederiks-berg 📧38/34–10–04 ⊕www.royalcopenhagen.com) has a good deal of stock, often at reduced prices, and is open on weekdays from 10 to 5 and Saturday 10 to 2. You can also buy Holmegaard Glass at the Royal Copenhagen store on in Centrum and this factory outlet.

Stilleben (⊠ Læderstræde 14, Centrum 📧33/91–11–31 ⊕www.stilleben. dk) is a quaint shop in the Latin Quarter run by two young potters and ceramic designers who sell their own work as well as items from other Scandinavian brands.

FURNITURE AND DESIGN
Dansk Møbelkunst (⊠ Bredg. 32, Frederiksstaden 📧33/32–38–37 ⊕www.dmk.dk) is spacious and elegant and home to one of the city's largest collections of vintage furniture. Some of the pieces are by such great Danish designers as Arne Jacobsen, Kaare Klint, and Finn Juhl. **Designer Zoo** (⊠ Vesterbrogade 137, Vesterbro 📧33/24–94–93 ⊕www. dzoo.dk) is run by eight talented designers who work on-site and sell unique furniture, jewelry, knitwear, and glass items.

Hay House (⊠ Østergade 61, 2nd fl., Centrum 📧99/42–44–40 ⊕www. hay.dk) is one of the most popular contemporary Danish furniture design houses. **Illums Bolighus** (⊠ Amagertorv 10, Downtown 📧33/14–19–41) is part gallery, part department store, showing off cutting-edge Danish and international design—art glass, porcelain, silverware, carpets, and loads of grown-up toys.

Paustian (⊠ Kalkbrænderiløbskaj 2, Østerbro 📧39/16–65–65, 39/18–55–01 for restaurant ⊕www.paustian.dk) sells furniture and accessories in a three-story building designed by Dane Jørn Utzon, the architect of the Sydney Opera House. You can also have a gour-met meal at the highly acclaimed Bo Bech at Restaurant Paustian (it's open for lunch and dinner). **Tage Andersen** (⊠ Ny Adelg. 12, Centrum 📧33/93–09–13) has a fantasy-infused floral gallery, shop, and museum filled with one-of-a-kind gifts and arrangements designed by the owner; browsers are charged a DKr 40 admission.

SILVER
Check the silver standard of a piece by its stamp. Three towers and "925S" (which means 925 parts out of 1,000) mark sterling. Two tow-ers are used for silver plate. The "826S" stamp (also denoting sterling,

but less pure) was used until the 1920s. Even with shipping charges, you can expect to save 50% versus American prices when buying Danish silver (especially used) at the source.

Danish Silver (⊠ *Bredg. 12, Frederiksstaden* ☎*33/11 52 52*), owned by longtime collector Gregory Pepin, houses a remarkable collection of classic Jensen designs from holloware and place settings to art-deco jewelry. Pepin, an American who has lived in Denmark for many years, is a font of information on Danish silver design, so if you're in the market, it's well worth a visit.

Georg Jensen (⊠ *Amagertorv 4, Centrum* ☎*33/11–40–80* ⊕ *www. georgjensen.com*) is one of the most recognized names in international silver, and his elegant, austere shop is aglitter with sterling. Jensen has its own museum next door. **Sølvkælderen** (⊠ *Kompagnistr. 1, Centrum* ☎*33/13–36–34*) is the city's largest (and brightest) silver store, carrying an endless selection of tea services, place settings, and jewelry.

SIDE TRIPS FROM COPENHAGEN

EXPERIMENTARIUM

8 km (5 mi) north of Copenhagen.

In the beachside town of Hellerup is the **Experimentarium,** where more than 300 exhibitions are clustered in various "Discovery Islands," each exploring a different facet of science, technology, and natural phenomena. A dozen body- and hands-on exhibits allow you to do things like blow giant soap bubbles, feel an earthquake, stir up magnetic goop, play ball on a jet stream, and gyrate to gyroscopes. Once a bottling plant for the Tuborg Brewery, this center also organizes interactive temporary exhibitions. Exhibit texts are in English. From downtown Copenhagen, take Bus 14 (from Rådhuspladsen) or 1A (from Kongens Nytorv or the Central Station). Alternatively, take the S-train to Svanemøllen Station, then walk north for 10 minutes. ⊠ *Tuborg Havnevej 7, Hellerup* ☎*39/27–33–95* ⊕ *www.experimentarium.dk* ☎*DKr 135* ⊗ *Mon. and Wed.–Fri. 9:30–5, Tues. 9:30–9, weekends and holidays 11–5.*

CHARLOTTENLUND

10 km (6 mi) north of Copenhagen.

Just north of Copenhagen is the leafy, affluent coastal suburb of Charlottenlund, with a small, appealing beach that gets predictably crowded on sunny weekends. A little farther north is Charlottenlund Slot (Charlottenlund Palace), a graceful mansion that has housed various Danish royals since the 17th century. The castle isn't open to the public, but the surrounding peaceful palace gardens are open to all, and Copenhageners enjoy coming up here for weekend ambles and picnics.

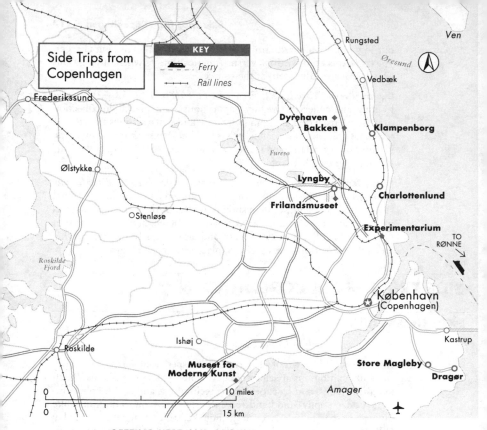

Side Trips from Copenhagen

KEY
🚢 Ferry
┼┼┼┼ Rail lines

Frederikssund

Rungsted

Ven

Øresund

Vedbæk

Dyrehaven ◆
Bakken ◆

Klampenborg

Ølstykke

Furesø

Lyngby

Charlottenlund

Stenløse

Frilandsmuseet

Experimentarium

TO RØNNE

Roskilde Fjord

København
(Copenhagen)

Kastrup

Roskilde

Ishøj

Store Magleby

Museet for
Moderne Kunst

Dragør

Amager

0 ___ 10 miles

0 ___ 15 km

GETTING HERE AND AROUND

Charlottenlund is a 15-minute S-train ride from the Central Station on the C line. Trains leave every 10 minutes. Alternatively, take Bus 14, which leaves from several points in Copenhagen. For the Ordrupgaard museum, take the S-train from major Copenhagen stations to Klampenborg or Lyngby Stations where you can catch Bus 388. Bus 169 leaves from Charlottenlund Station. Get off at Hovmarksvej, a 15-minute walk from the museum. Alternatively, take the train from Charlottenlund Station to Klampenborg Station and follow the above directions. Bus and train rides from Copenhagen to Charlottenlund traverse three zones, so a one-way ticket costs DKr 30.

EXPLORING

The **Danmarks Akvarium** (*Danmarks Aquarium*) is a sizable, well-designed aquarium near the palace. Expect all the usual aquatic suspects, from gliding sharks to brightly colored tropical fish to snapping crocodiles. ⊠*Kavalergården 1, Charlottenlund* ☎*39/62–04–16* ⊕*www.akvarium. dk* ⊠*DKr 90* ☉*Nov.–Jan., daily 10–4; Feb.–Apr., daily 10–5; May– Aug., daily 10–6; Sept. and Oct., daily 10–5.*

Fodor'sChoice
★

While in Charlottenlund, don't miss the remarkable **Ordrupgaard,** one of the largest museum collections of French impressionism in Europe outside France. Most of the great 19th-century French artists are represented, including Manet, Monet, Matisse, Cézanne, Renoir, Degas, Gauguin, Sisley, Delacroix, and Pissarro. Ordrupgaard also has a superb collection of Danish Golden Age painters and spectacular works by Vilhelm Hammershøi, whose deft use of light and space creates haunting settings for his mostly solitary figures. The paintings hang on the walls of what was once the home of museum founder and art collector Wilhelm Hansen. The interior of this manor dating from 1918 has been left just as it was when Hansen and his wife Henny lived here. In 2005 a black, curvaceous addition, designed by the acclaimed architect Zaha Hadid, joined the main building. In addition to extra exhibition space, the new structure made room for a spacious café that overlooks the park. Things are labeled in English. ⊠ *Vilvordevej 110, Charlottenlund* ☎*39/64–11–83* ⊕*www.ordrupgaard.dk* ⊠*DKr 65* ☉*Tues., Thurs., and Fri. 1–5, Wed. 10–8, weekends 11–5.*

NEED A BREAK? Situated on Strandvejen–the coastal road that showcases private mansions like beads on a string—**Café Jorden Rundt** (⊠ *Strandvejen 152, Charlottenlund* ☎*39/63–73–81* ⊕*www.cafejordenrundt.dk*), or "around the world," offers striking views of Øresund, the sound between Denmark and Sweden. The menu includes sizable sandwiches, soups, salads, and cakes. The café is open Sunday to Friday 10–9 and Saturday 10–7.

WHERE TO STAY

$$$ ⌂ **Skovshoved.** This delightful, art-filled inn is near a few old fishing cottages beside the yacht harbor. It's been licensed since 1660 and has retained its provincial charm. Larger rooms overlook the sea, smaller ones rim the courtyard; all have both modern and antique furnishings. The best way to get here is to take Bus 14 from Rådhus Pladsen or the S-train to Charlottenlund and walk 15 minutes from the station. **Pros:** quiet; close to the beach; highly regarded restaurant. **Cons:** far from shopping or other conveniences; slightly pretentious. ⊠*Strandvejen 267, Charlottenlund* ☎*39/64–00–28* ⊕*www.skovshovedhotel.com* ⟳*22 rooms, 2 suites* ⌂*In-room: safe, Wi-Fi. In-hotel: restaurant, bar* ⊟*AE, DC, MC, V* ⊚*EP.*

DRAGØR AND STORE MAGLEBY

★ *22 km (14 mi) southeast of Copenhagen.*

On the island of Amager, less than a half hour from Copenhagen, the quaint fishing towns of Dragør (pronounced *drah*-wer) and Store Magleby feel far away in distance and time. The two adjacent villages are part of Dragør municipality. Were it not for the planes whizzing to and from the nearby Copenhagen Airport, bobbing wooden boats, cobbled streets, small squares, and well-preserved thatched-roof houses would create the illusion of time travel.

GETTING HERE AND AROUND

Bus 30 leaves for Dragør every 20 minutes from Rådhuspladsen. Bus 350S leaves every 5 to 10 minutes from Nøreport; the trip takes about 45 minutes. From Kongens Nytorv, take the M1 Metro to Bella Center

Street and change to Bus 75E (approximately 30 minutes in transit), which leaves you at Dragør Rådhus. Bus 75E and 76E both run along the water from the airport, through Dragoør, to Store Magleby. The ride from Copenhagen traverses three zones (DKr 30 for a one-way ticket); that from the airport covers only two zones (DKr 20).

ESSENTIALS
Visitor Info Dragør Harbor Office (⊠ *Dragoør Havn 2, Dragør* ☎ *32/53–05–32* ⊕ *www.visitdragoer.dk*).

EXPLORING
The town is set apart from the rest of the area around Copenhagen because it was settled by Dutch farmers in the 16th century. King Christian II ordered the community to provide fresh produce and flowers for the royal court. Today neat rows of terra-cotta–roof houses trimmed with wandering ivy, roses, and the occasional waddling goose characterize the still meticulously maintained community. If there's one color that characterizes Dragør, it's the lovely pale yellow (called Dragør gul, or Dragør yellow) of its houses. According to local legend, the former town hall's chimney was built with a twist so that meetings couldn't be overheard.

As you're wandering around Dragør, and other old Danish villages, notice that many of the older houses have an angled mirror contraption attached to their street-level windows. This *gade spejl* (street mirror), unique to Scandinavia, was—and perhaps still is—used by the occupants of the house to "spy" on the street activity. Usually positioned at seat level, this is where the curious (often the older ladies of town) could pull up a chair and observe all the comings and goings of the neighborhood from the warmth and privacy of their homes.

WHERE TO EAT AND STAY
$$ ✕**Restaurant Beghuset.** This handsome restaurant in the center of the
DANISH town with rustic stone floors and green-and-gold painted doors is named Beghuset (Pitch House), because this is where Dragør's fishermen used to boil the pitch that waterproofed their wooden ships. The Danish dishes on the menu include baked goose breast served with rhubarb and horseradish-flavored compote. ⊠*Strandg. 14, Dragør* ☎*32/53–01–36* ⊕*www.beghuset.dk* ⊟*AE, DC, MC, V* ⊙*Closed Sun. and Mon.*

¢–$ ⊡**Dragør Badehotel.** Built in 1907 as a seaside hotel for vacationing Copenhageners, this plain, comfortable hotel is still geared to the summer crowds, yet manages to maintain low prices (you'd easily pay twice the price in Copenhagen). The basic rooms have dark-green carpets and simple furniture; half the rooms include little terraces that face toward the water, so make sure to ask for one when booking. The bathrooms are small and basic, most with a shower only. Breakfast is served on the outside terrace in summer. **Pros:** ocean views; price is right. **Cons:** few amenities; breakfast not included in rate; relatively far from Copenhagen. ⊠*Drogdensvej 43, Dragør* ☎*32/53–05–00* ⊕*www.badehotellet. dk* ⇖*34 rooms* ⚲*In-hotel: restaurant, bar, some pets allowed* ⊟*AE, DC, MC, V* ⦿*EP.*

KLAMPENBORG, BAKKEN AND DYREHAVEN

15 km (9 mi) north of Copenhagen.

As you follow the beautiful coast north of Copenhagen, you'll come upon the wealthy enclave of Klampenborg. Flocks of deer munch away on the well-kept soccer pitches in Dyrehaven—the "animal garden" that was planned as official royal hunting terrain in the 1670s—while sausages, lollypops, and beers are eagerly consumed by roller coaster–fatigued revelers in the amusement park of Bakken.

GETTING HERE AND AROUND

To reach Klampenborg take a regional train (in the direction of Nivå) or S-Train C to Klampenborg Station; both leave from the major train stations in Copenhagen. The trip takes about 15 minutes and traverses four zones (DKr 40 for a one-way ticket). Both Bakken and Dyrehaven are walking distance from Klampenborg Station. For Bellevue Beach, take Bus 14 from Klampenborg Station. Horse-drawn carriages are available for hire in Dyrehaven.

EXPLORING

The residents of Klampenborg are lucky enough to have the pleasant **Bellevue Beach** nearby. In summer this luck may seem double-edged, when scores of city-weary sun-seekers pile out at the Klampenborg S-train station and head for the sand. The Danes have a perfect word for this: they call Bellevue a *fluepapir* (flypaper) beach. Bellevue is still an appealing seaside spot to soak up some rays, especially considering that it's just a 15-minute train ride from Copenhagen.

Klampenborg is no stranger to crowds. Just a few kilometers inland, within the peaceful Dyrehaven, is **Bakken,** at 425 years of age, the world's oldest amusement park—and one of Denmark's most popular attractions. If Tivoli is champagne in a fluted glass, then Bakken is a pint of beer. Here a mostly working-class crowd lunches on hot dogs and cotton candy. Tivoli, with its trimmed hedges, dazzling firework displays, and evening concerts, is still Copenhagen's reigning queen, but unpretentious Bakken is unabashedly about having a good time. Bakken has more than 30 rides, from quaint, rickety roller coasters (refreshingly free of that Disney gloss) to newer, faster rides to little-kid favorites such as Kaffekoppen, the Danish version of twirling teacups, where you sit in traditional Royal Copenhagen–style blue-and-white coffee cups. ⊠ *Dyrehavevej 62 Klampenborg 2930 ⊹ take trains to Klampenborg Station* ☎ *39/63-35-44* ⊕ *www.bakken.dk* ☒ *Free; DKr 199 for a day pass to all rides in peak season* ⊙ *Season is mid-Mar.–Sept. Opening hours vary from noon to 10 PM or midnight and from 2 PM to 10, 11, or midnight; call for details.*

★ The Bakken amusement park sits within the verdant, 2,500-acre **Dyrehaven** (*Deer Garden*), where herds of wild deer roam freely. Once the favored hunting grounds of Danish royals, today the park has become a cherished weekend oasis for Copenhageners. Hiking and biking trails traverse the park, and lush fields beckon nature-seekers and families with picnic baskets. The deer are everywhere; in the less-trafficked regions of the park you may find yourself surrounded by an entire herd of deer delicately stepping through the fields. The park's centerpiece is the copper-top, 17th-century Eremitagen, formerly a royal hunting lodge. It is closed to the public. Dyrehaven is a haven for hikers and bikers, but you can also go in for the royal treatment and enjoy it from the high seat of a horse-drawn carriage. The carriages gather at the park entrance near the station. The cost is DKr 400–DKr500 for 50 minutes, but shorter, cheaper trips are also available. ⊠*Park entrance is near Klampenborg S-train station, Klampenborg* ☎*39/97–39–00.*

WHERE TO EAT

$ – $$ ✕ **Strandmøllekroen.** The 200-year-old beachfront inn is filled with
SEAFOOD   antiques and hunting trophies. The best views are of the Øresund from
★   the back dining room. Elegantly served seafood and steaks are the mainstays, but game is also often available. For a bit of everything try the seafood platter for a selection of ocean-derived treats. ⊠*Strandvejen 808, Klampenborg* ☎*39/63–01–04* ⊕*www.strandmoellekroen.dk* ▭*AE, DC, MC, V.*

FRILANDSMUSEET

16 km (10 mi) northwest of Copenhagen.

☺ North of Copenhagen is Lyngby, its main draw **Frilandsmuseet,** an openair museum. About 50 Danish farmhouses and cottages from the period 1650–1950 have been painstakingly dismantled, moved here, reconstructed, and filled with period furniture and tools. Trees, farm animals, and gardens surround the museum; bring lunch and plan to spend the day. For DKr 25, you can take a horse-drawn carriage tour around the museum. For children, the farm animals and history-theme pantomime performances are the biggest draw. To get here, take the B Line S-train from all major Copenhagen stations to Sorgenfri station, then walk right and follow the signs. The trip from Copenhagen traverses five zones, the equivalent of a DKr 50 one-way ticket. ⊠*Kongevejen 100, Lyngby* ☎*33/13–44–41* ⊕*www.frilandsmuseet.dk* ▣*Free* ☉*Mid-Mar.–late Oct., Tues.–Sun. 10–5. Also open during weekends in Dec.*

MUSEET FOR MODERNE KUNST

20 km (12 mi) southwest of Copenhagen.

Architect Søren Robert Lund was just 25 and a student when awarded the commission for the **Museet for Moderne Kunst,** which is set against the flat coast southwest of Copenhagen. Arken, or "the ark," which opened in 1996, is a building with a ship's features; sail-like protrusions and narrow red corridors that provoke submarine associations. The museum's massive sculpture room exhibits both modern Danish and international art. Notice how this hall is narrow in one end and wider in the other to provoke illusions of space and proximity, depending on where you stand. The café, which looks like a ship's bridge, offers nice views of Køge Bugt. S-trains C and E leave from all major Copenhagen train stations. From Copenhagen, you traverse five zones, the equivalent of a DKr 50 one-way ticket. From there, take Bus 128, which lets you off in front of the museum. ⊠ *Skovvej 100, Ishøj* ☏ *43/54–02–22* ⊕ *www.arken.dk* ⊠ *DKr 85* ⊙ *Tues.–Sun. 10–5, Wed. 10–9.*

ZEALAND

2

The goddess Gefion is said to have carved Zealand (Sjælland) from Sweden. If she did, she must have sliced the north deep with a fjord, while she chopped the south to pieces and left the sides bowing west. Though the coasts are deeply serrated, Gefion's myth is more dramatic than the flat, fertile land of rich meadows and beech stands.

Slightly larger than the state of Delaware, Zealand is the largest of the Danish islands. From Copenhagen, almost any point on it can be reached in an hour and a half, making it the most traveled portion of the country—and it's especially easy to explore thanks to the extensive road network.

Along the pretty beach highway between Copenhagen and Helsingør are the suburbs that play home to Denmark's wealthiest citizens. This area is still referred to as the "whiskey belt"—so named because whiskey was a preferred drink of the wealthy residents in this area. At the northeast tip of the island sits Helsingør's Kronborg Castle, which Shakespeare immortalized in *Hamlet*. Frederiksborg, considered one of the most magnificent Renaissance castles in Europe, also lies to the north. Beaches with summer cottages, white dunes, and calm waters surround Hornbæk. To the west of Copenhagen is Roskilde, medieval Denmark's most important town, home to a UNESCO-listed cathedral that served as northern Europe's spiritual center 1,000 years ago, and a famous rock music festival. To the south are rural towns and fine white beaches, often surrounded by forests. Even more unspoiled are the tiny islands around southern Zealand, virtually unchanged over the past century.

HUMLEBÆK

31 km (19 mi) north of Copenhagen.

Historically a fishing village, this elegant seaside town with a population of about 6,000 is now a suburb of Copenhagen. It's also home to a fantastic modern art museum—Louisiana. In summer the town's many cottages fill with vacationers, and the gardens come alive with vibrant colors. The town takes its name from the plant *humle* (hops), which is abundant in the area.

GETTING HERE AND AROUND

Trains run to Humlebæk from Copenhagen every 20 minutes. These trains originate in the Swedish city of Malmö and run in the other direction from Helsingør. The 30-minute trip costs DKr 90, and you can buy tickets from machines in any station.

ESSENTIALS

Train Info DSB (☎ 70/13–14–15 ⊕ www. dsb.dk).

EXPLORING

☾ The must-see **Louisiana** is a modern-
Fodor's Choice art museum with fresh, witty tempo-
★ rary exhibitions and an impressive
permanent collection that includes
Picasso, Giacometti, and Warhol.
Even if you're not an art lover,
it's well worth the 30-minute trip
from Copenhagen to see this beau-

tiful combination of a 19th-century
villa and modern Danish architecture, with its large sculpture garden
and dramatic view of the Øresund waters. There's a children's section as well, where kids can draw and paint under the supervision of
museum staff. To get here from the station, walk north about 10 minutes. ⊠ *Gammel Strandvej 13* ☎49/19–07–19 ⊕*www.louisiana.dk*
🎫*DKr 90* ⊙*Tues.–Fri 11–10, weekends 11–6.*

The **Karen Blixen Museum** in Rungstedlund, is in the elegant, airy manor
of Baroness Karen Blixen, who wrote *Out of Africa* under the pen name
Isak Dinesen. The manor house, to which she returned in 1931 to write
her most famous works, now displays Blixen's manuscripts, sketches,
photographs, and memorabilia documenting her years in Africa. Leave
time to wander around the gorgeous gardens, which also function as
a bird sanctuary. You can take Bus 388 from Louisiana to the Blixen
museum. ⊠*Rungsted Strandvej 111, Rungsted Kyst* ☎45/57–10–57
⊕*www.karen-blixen.dk* 🎫*DKr 45* ⊙*May–Sept., Tues.–Sun. 10–5;
Oct.–Apr., Wed.–Fri. 1–4, weekends 11–4.*

HELSINGØR

*14 km (8½ mi) north of Humlebæk, 45 km (28 mi) north of
Copenhagen.*

Helsingør's name is derived from "hals," or neck, after the narrow neck
of water separating it from Sweden's Helsingborg. That slim waterway
made the town wealthy in the in the 1420s, when Erik of Pomerania
established a tariff for all ships passing through it. Shakespeare angli-
cized the town's name to "Elsinore" and made its massive castle the
home of his fictional character Hamlet. Today about 34,000 people live
in Helsingør, which still has a maritime flavor.

GETTING HERE AND AROUND

Trains run every 20 minutes from Copenhagen, and the 45-minute journey to Helsingør costs DKr 110. These trains originate in the Swedish
city Malmö. Ferries, including some that take cars, also run every half
hour between Helsingør and its Swedish twin city, Helsingborg, with
a round-trip costing DKr 46. Helsingør is also the starting point for
a regional railway that provides excellent connections to Fredensborg

and Hornbæk. Antique trains—"Veterantog"—periodically run on this line in the summer.

ESSENTIALS

Ferry Info ACE Link (✉ *Jernbanevej 10A, Helsingør* ☎ *49/71–02–00* ⊕ *www.acelink. dk).* **H-H Ferries** (✉ *Færgevej 12, Helsingør* ☎ *49/26–01–55* ⊕ *www.hhferries.dk).*

Hospital Helsingør Hospital (✉ *Esrumvej 145, Helsingør* ☎ *48/29–49–49* ⊕ *www. helsingorhospital.dk).*

Pharmacies Axeltorv Apotek (✉ *Groskenstræde 2, Helsingør* ☎ *49/21–12–23).* **Stengades Apotek** (✉ *Stengade 46, Helsingør* ☎ *49/21–86–00).*

Train Info DSB (☎ *70/13–14–15* ⊕ *www.dsb.dk).*

Visitor Info Helsingør Tourist Information Office (✉ *Havneplads 3, Helsingør* ☎ *49/21–13–33* ⊕ *www.visithelsingor.dk).*

EXPLORING

Fodor's Choice ★ **Kronborg Slot** (*Kronborg Castle*) dominates the city of Helsingør. Built in the late 1500s, it's the inspiration for Elsinore castle in Shakespeare's *Hamlet* (1601). Shakespeare probably never saw the castle in person, but he managed to capture its spirit—it's a gloomy, chilly place, where it's clear that an ordinary person today lives much better than kings once did. The castle was built as a Renaissance tollbooth: from its cannon-studded bastions, forces collected a tariff from all ships crossing the sliver of water between Denmark and Sweden. Well worth seeing are the 200-foot-long dining hall and the dungeons, where there is a brooding statue of Holger Danske (Ogier the Dane). According to legend, the sleeping Viking chief will awaken to defend Denmark when it's in danger. (The largest Danish resistance group during World War II called itself Holger Danske.) ✉ *At point, on harbor front* ☎ *49/21–30–78* ⊕ *www.ses.dk/kronborgcastle* 🎫 *DKr 60* ☉ *May–Sept., daily 10:30–5; Oct. and Apr., Tues.–Sun. 11–4; Nov.–Mar., Tues.–Sun. 11–3.*

Whole streets of medieval-era Helsingør can still be seen on its downtown shopping streets, where merchants' and ferrymen houses have been converted into modern shops. On the corner of Stengade and Sankt Annægade near the harbor is **Sankt Olai Kirke** (*St. Olaf's Church*), worth a peek for its elaborately carved wooden altar. ✉ *Sct. Anna Gade 12* ☎ *49/21–04–43* ⊕ *www.helsingordomkirke.dk* 🎫 *Free* ☉ *May–Aug., daily 10–16; Sept.–Apr., daily 10–2.*

Close to Sankt Olai Kirke is Sankt Marie Kirke with the 15th-century **Carmelite Kloster** (*Carmelite Convent*), one of the best-preserved examples of medieval architecture in Scandinavia. ✉ *Skt. Annæ G. 38* ☎ *49/21–17–74* 🎫 *Free; tour costs DKr 20* ☉ *Mid-May–mid-Sept., daily 10–3; tour at 2 mid-June–mid-Sept. Mid-Sept.–mid-June, daily 10–2; no fixed tour time.*

WHERE TO EAT

Most simple cafés and inexpensive eateries are in the city center, along the main shopping street on Stengade and around Axeltorv, the city's main square. If you are in Helsingør mainly to visit Kronborg, consider having a picnic on the castle grounds at the picnic area just left of the main entrance.

$ **⨉Madam Sprunck.** Tucked back
ECLECTIC   behind the walking street is a popular restaurant-café in a half-timber building with a lovely garden courtyard that has picnic tables and an outdoor beer tap. The restaurant has a café menu with open-face sandwiches and the best burgers and brunch in town. Dinner options consist of set and à la carte menus of French-inspired dishes. The place is romantic and is usually packed with locals. It also has a good beer and wine selection and serves cocktails in the evenings. ⊠ *Stengade 48* ☎ *49/26–48–49* ⊕ *www.madamsprunck.dk* ♺ *Reservations essential* ⊟ *AE, MC, V.*

$ **⨉Phonoteket.** A combined shop selling music (including vinyl), pottery,
CAFÉ   and books, and retro café with stark white exterior welcomes a crowd for breakfast and lunch only. The café offers cakes, pastries, and sandwiches. ⊠ *Stengade 36* ☎ *49/21–23–11* ♺ *No reservations* ⊟ *AE, DC, MC, V* ⊘ *No dinner. Closed Sun.*

¢   **⨉Radmand Davids Hus.** This classic Danish lunch restaurant is in a
SCANDINAVIAN   creaky, half-timber building dating from 1694 with off-kilter floors, low ceilings, and lots of charm. It's a good place to stop for the "shopping lunch," a hearty lunch platter with homemade Danish specialties. The outdoor terrace is surrounded by a cozy garden. ⊠ *Strandgade 70* ☎ *49/26–10–43* ⊟ *MC, V* ⊘ *No dinner. Closed Sun.*

> **TO BE OR NOT TO BE?**
>
> In summer Kronborg Castle is the site of the Hamlet Festival (⊠ *Havnepl. 1* ☎ *49/21–69–79* ⊕ *www.hamletscenen.dk*), during which internationally renowned theater troupes offer outdoor performances of *Hamlet.* The schedule varies from year to year.

WHERE TO STAY

$$ **☷Hotel & Casino Marienlyst.** The historic hotel dates from 1860, when
★   it was the country's first waterfront property. Now modernized, the rooms, suites, and apartments feature simple Scandinavian style with pastels and blues. Rooms on the sound side, many with balconies, present a magnificent view of Kronborg Castle and the Swedish coast. The hotel has direct beach access, a large outdoor terrace, and an on-site pool with a water slide. Enjoy the evenings at the on-site casino or at the stylish bar and lounge. **Pros:** beach location; super views; family-friendly; close to Copenhagen. **Cons:** a major conference and party hotel that can be noisy, particularly on weekends; some room furnishings show signs of wear. ⊠ *Nordre Strandvej 2* ☎ *49/21–40–00* ⊕ *www. marienlyst.dk* ⇱ *223 rooms, 16 suites* ♿ *In-room: Internet. In-hotel: restaurant, room service, bar, pool, gym, Wi-Fi, some pets allowed, no-smoking rooms* ⊟ *AE, DC, MC, V* ☉⎮ *BP.*

$ **☷Hotel Hamlet.** A few minutes from the harbor and train station, this overly renovated hotel with yet another renovation taking place in 2008 has lost some of its charm but makes an attempt at character with raw timbers and deep-green walls. The rooms are furnished in dark wood and are comfortable, if nondescript. **Pros:** close to main train station and shopping street. **Cons:** no-frills hotel; lacks a lounge or common area; basic service. ⊠*Bramstr. 5* ☎*49/21–05–91* ⊕*www.hotelhamlet. dk* ⇆*36 rooms* ⟁*In-hotel: restaurant, bar, some pets allowed, no-smoking rooms* ☰*AE, DC, MC, V* ♜⌐*CP.*

¢ ♜**Hotel Sleep2night.** If you're traveling by car, this motel-like place is
ⓒ ideal. It's clean and simple and offers rooms with basic amenities and minimalistic design. The hotel also has apartments, some with Jacuzzi and sauna. Breakfast is included in the rate, and a dinner buffet is on offer Monday through Saturday. There's miniature golf out back. **Pros:** five minutes from central Copenhagen; good for families; good base for touring the area. **Cons:** in an industrial area with a shipping company just across the street; no restaurants, shops, or other entertainment nearby. ⊠*Industrivej 21* ☎*49/27–01–00* ⊕*www.sleep2night. com* ⇆*95 rooms, 24 apartments* ⟁*In-hotel: restaurant, bar, public Internet* ☰*AE, DC, MC, V* ♜⌐*CP.*

¢ ♜**Villa Moltke Vandrerhjem.** This youth hostel is in an old villa on a
ⓒ private beach facing the Kattegat Sea. It's 2 km (1 mi) from city center and is well served by both bus and train. It has outdoor table tennis, a sheltered grill area on the beach, and nearby soccer field and tennis courts. **Pros:** great location on the water; lots of family activities; well run. **Cons:** restaurant only serves breakfast; not close to major sights. ⊠*Nordre Strandvej 24* ☎*49/21–16–40* ⊕*www.helsingorhostel.dk* ⇆*190 beds* ⟁*In-hotel: restaurant, bicycles, laundry facilities* ☰*MC, V* ♜⌐*EP.*

AFTER DARK

Most of the nightlife is around the shopping streets and consist of discos and cocktail bars. Axeltorv Square comes alive in summer, especially on Friday nights. Many cafés host live music acts for people of all ages.

Annexet (⊠*Stengade 26E* ☎*49/21–60–90*) is known for its live-music performances. **Club Retro** (⊠*Bjergegade 1* ☎*25/30–73–07*) is a disco chain that attracts young party goers with DJs, live bands, and comedians. **Envy** (⊠*Stengade 81* ☎*49/26–18–49*) is one of the most popular dance clubs with great cocktails. There's a mixed-age crowd.

SHOPPING

Beneath its well-restored medieval charm, Helsingør is a working-class town with a substantial population of immigrants. Although you won't find the fancy boutiques that dot the rest of northern Zealand on Helsingør's pedestrian shopping streets—Stengade, Sternegade, and Bjergegade—there's a great selection of traditional food providers that will offer memorable snacks. From April to November an outdoor market with fresh fruit, cheese, and fish takes place on Wednesday, Friday, and Saturday at Axletorv, in the center of town.

Follow the delectable smell of home-baked waffle cones—or just follow the crowds—to **Brostræde Fløde-Is** (⊠*Brostræde 2* ☎*49/21–35–91*). It has been making summer days more tasty since 1922. Antique toys and antique-style paper dolls, along with newly made dollhouse furniture, are some of the items for sale at the eccentric handicrafts store, **CoCo & Co** (⊠*Stengade 31H* ☎*49/26–30–80*).

Møllers Konditori (✉*Stengade 39* ☎*49/21–02–16*) is Denmark's oldest pastry shop. Try its "beer bread," a traditional treat that's often the first solid food given to Danish babies.

FREDENSBORG

15 km (9 mi) southwest of Helsingør, 33 km (20 mi) northwest of Copenhagen.

Fredensborg means "town of peace," earning the name after a peace treaty ending the Great Northern War was signed here in 1720. Fredensborg Castle, also known as Fredensborg Slot, is the unofficial favorite residence of the Danish royal family and a frequent site of elaborate state dinners. On its grounds is a historical baroque garden and nearby is Lake Esrum.

GETTING HERE AND AROUND
If you're not traveling by car, Fredensborg is easiest to reach from Helsingør, the base for a regional train that runs every half-hour. A ticket for the 20-minute journey costs DKr 50. From Copenhagen, take Bus 173E to the stop Fredensborg Slot. The trip takes an hour and costs DKr 90.

ESSENTIALS
Train and Bus Info DSB (☎70/13–14–15 ⊕www.dsb.dk).

EXPLORING
Fredensborg Palace (*Castle of Peace*), was built by Frederik IV to commemorate the 1720 peace treaty in which Denmark relinquished much of southern Sweden. Originally inspired by French and Italian castles, its style was diluted by later reconstructions, but it has long been a place where the royals actually enjoy living. Today, it's one of the most-used residences of the Danish royal family, particularly in the spring and fall. Crown Prince Frederik and his Australian-born wife Princess Mary make their full-time home in the castle's Chancellery House, and little prince Christian goes to a local public school. When the Queen is present, the Royal Life Guards sound taps at 10 PM. At noon every day there's the changing of the guard. The palace is open to the public in July only.

Open year-round is the stately **Slotshave** (castle garden), inspired by the French gardens of Versailles. Denmark's largest historical garden is well worth a stroll. A small section called *den reserverede have* (the reserved garden) is used privately by the royal family but open to the public in July. The reserved garden includes a flower garden, a vegetable garden that supplies the castle, and the orangerie where Denmark's oldest myrtles, which date from the 1750s, are preserved. ✉*Fredensborg* ☎*33/40–31–87* ⊕*www.ses.dk/398d55f0* ✉*With guided tour only: DKr 50. Reserved gardens: DKr 40. Combined ticket: DKr 75* ۞*July: castle daily 1–4:30 (guided tours every 15 mins); reserved garden daily 9–5.*

WHERE TO EAT AND STAY

$ ECLECTIC Fodor's Choice ★ **Skipperhuset.** On the grounds of the Fredensborg Slot, this 18th-century former royal boathouse is on the shore of Lake Esrum. When weather permits, sunset alfresco meals are pure enchantment. Warm, smoked wild Baltic salmon served with spinach flash-fried in soy sauce and balsamic vinegar is a delightful favorite and a fabulous buy for the money. *Skipperallé 6 48/48–17–17 www.skipperhuset.dk MC, V Closed mid-Oct.–Easter.*

¢ **Danhostel Fredensborg Vandrerhjem.** This youth and family hostel offers a wide selection of sleeping arrangements. It has private rooms (accommodating up to five people) many with shower facilities in the room available. It's next to the Fredensborg Palace and has a large surrounding park that leads directly to the castle. You can order breakfast for DKr 55. The restaurant serves dinner for groups only, but the kitchen is available to all guests. **Pros:** great location next to the castle; large park near the lake. **Cons:** no full-service restaurant; no group rooms. *Østrupvej 3 48/48–03–15 www.fredensborghostel.dk 42 rooms (21 without bath) In-hotel: restaurant, Wi-Fi MC, V EP.*

$$$ ★ **Hotel Fredensborg Store Kro.** Built by King Frederik IV, this magnificent Renaissance annex to Fredensborg Palace is the archetypal stately inn. Inside are European antiques and paintings; outside, glass gazebos and classical statues overlook a garden. The individually decorated rooms are sumptuous, with delicate-pattern wallpapers and antiques. The romantic Restaurant Anna Sophie serves Danish-French fare and has a fireplace and grand piano. **Pros:** historic hotel with pleasant surroundings; down the street from Fredensborg Palace. **Cons:** potentially pretentious, aging property that undergoes renovation often; not the best value for the money. *Slotsg. 6 48/40–01–11 www.storekro.dk 48 rooms, 6 suites In-hotel: restaurant, bar, public Internet, Wi-Fi, parking (free) AE, DC, MC, V BP.*

SPORTS AND THE OUTDOORS

Magnificent displays of hawks and eagles in flight can be seen at **Falkonergården.** Located 1 km (½ mi) northeast of Fredensborg, this former farm keeps alive the Viking tradition of hunting with hawks. Falcons swooping at speeds approaching 300 kph (186 mph) over the audience's head in the hour-long shows. *Davidsvænge 11 48/48–25–83 www.falkonergaarden.dk DKr 80 Show times, regardless of weather: Apr.–May, Sun. at 2; June, Sept., andOct., weekends at 2; July, Wed. at 10 and 5, Thurs. at 10, weekends at 5; Aug., Wed. and weekends at 5.*

HILLERØD

10 km (6 mi) southwest of Fredensborg, 40 km (25 mi) northwest of Copenhagen.

Surrounded by forests, Hillerød is an ordinary small city with some extraordinary features: it's home to the lovely Frederiksborg Castle and within a short drive of the ruins of two medieval monestaries, at

Æbelholt and Esrum. Nowadays the town, founded in the 15th century, is an important industrial area.

GETTING HERE AND AROUND

S trains run every 10–20 minutes between Copenhagen and Hillerød. The 40-minute trip costs DKr 90.

ESSENTIALS

Train Info DSB (☎ *70/13-14-15* ⊕ *www.dsb.dk*).

EXPLORING

★ The Danish royal family's castles are a motley lot, and Hillerød's **Frederiksborg Slot** (*Frederiksborg Castle*) is one of the few that can be called a true beauty. Danish builder king Christian IV tore down a previous castle on the site and built this Dutch Renaissance version in the early 1600s. The building is enclosed by a moat, covers three islets, and is topped by with dozens of gables, spires, and turrets. Devastated by a fire in 1859, the castle was reconstructed with the support of the Carlsberg Foundation and now includes Denmark's Nationalhistoriske Museum (National History Museum), which contains the country's best collection of portraits and historical paintings. It also has an activity area where kids can dress up as historical figures.

Don't miss the gorgeous castle chapel Slotskirke, with its lacy ornamentation: Danish monarchs were crowned here for more than 200 years, and the house organ dates from 1610. The lovely Baroque Gardens, rebuilt according to J.C. Krieger's layout from 1725, include a series of wide waterfalls that make the neatly trimmed park a lovely place for a stroll. Don't miss the floral sculptures of the current royals' official monograms. ✉ *Hillerød* ☎ *48/26-04-39* ⊕ *www.frederiksborg museet.dk; www.ses.dk/1d90029* 🎟 *DKr 60; gardens free* ⏱ *Castle and museum: Mar. 15–Oct., daily 10–5; Nov.–Mar. 14, daily 11–3. Gardens: Apr.–Sept. 8* AM*–9* PM*; Oct.–Mar. 8–6.*

WHERE TO EAT AND STAY

$$ ✕ **La Perla.** Simple but good Italian food is served in this beautiful old
ITALIAN house in the very center of town. The decor is an interesting mix of Italian and Danish styles, a thoroughly modern twist on the Mediterranean. ✉ *Torvet 1* ☎ *48/24-35-33* ⊕ *www.laperla.dk* 🍴 *Reservations essential* 🗖 *AE, DC, MC, V* ⏱ *Closed Sun. and Mon.*

$ ✕ **Spisesteder Leonora.** In the shadow of Frederiksborg Castle, this family
DANISH restaurant bustles in what used to be the castle stables. Inside, walls feature
⏱ hanging prints and paintings of royalty and the castle and outside you'll find a large patio with great views of the castle. It's a popular stopover for castle visitors. The Danish menu ranges from quick openface sandwiches to savory stews, soups, and steaks. There's brunch on Sunday. ✉ *Frederiksborgslot 5* ☎ *48/26-75-16* ⊕ *www.leonora. dk* 🗖 *DC, MC, V* ⏱ *No dinner.*

$ 🏨 **Hotel Hillerød.** The decor consists of sensible Danish design and luxurious lighting. Most rooms have kitchenettes and private terraces. Packages that include greens fees at a local golf course can be arranged. The entire hotel is accessible to wheelchair users. The restaurant serves

Danish fare featuring fresh herbs, and offers breakfast, lunch, and dinner. **Pros:** central location, near shopping and sights; friendly, helpful staff. **Cons:** often used as a conference hotel, lack cultural charm. ✉ *Milnersvej 41* ☎ *48/24–08–00* ⊕ *www.hotelhillerod.dk* 🖵 *111 rooms, 2 suites* ⚹ *In-room: kitchen (some), Wi-Fi. In-hotel: restaurant, bicycles, Wi-Fi, some pets allowed, no-smoking rooms* ▤ *AE, DC, MC, V* ⦿ *BP.*

HORNBÆK

27 km (17 mi) northeast of Hillerød, 14 km (8 mi) southwest from Helsingør, 47 km (29 mi) north of Copenhagen.

Hornbæk, considered Denmark's answer to France's Riviera because the society's upper echelon maintain summer homes here, has lovely beaches and typical small fishing village feeling like nearby neighbors Gilleleje and Tilsvildeleje. Thatch-roofed holiday homes here sell for a pretty penny, and the central street, Nordre Strandvej, is lined with boutiques selling high-end clothing and housewares.

GETTING HERE AND AROUND
If you're not traveling by car, the easiest way to reach Hornbæk is from Helsingør, where a regional train leaves every 30 minutes. The 25-minute trip costs DKr30. From Copenhagen, take a train to Hillerød or Helsingøor and take the regional railway on to Hornbæk; the journey will take you around 90 minutes.

ESSENTIALS
Train Info DSB (☎ *70/13–14–15* ⊕ *www.dsb.dk*).

WHERE TO EAT
$$
SEAFOOD
★

✕ **Hansen's Café.** This intimate restaurant, in a National Trust building constructed in 1783, is just steps from the harbor. The Danish art hanging from the timber walls provides a cozy ambience for a casual crowd that often lingers for drinks well after dinner. The daily menu is short but provides a taste of what's fresh—especially seafood. Try the lumpfish roe for a tasty local treat. Business hours vary so it's wise to call in advance. ✉ *Havnevej 19* ☎ *49/70–04–79* ⊕ *www.hansenscafe. dk* ▤ *DC, MC, V* ⊘ *No lunch.*

$$$$
ECLECTIC

✕ **Søstrene Olsen.** This thatched-roof harbor establishment feels more like a home than a restaurant. It's owned and run by a husband-wife and has served classic French-Danish specialties since 1982. In the evening there are three-course and à la carte menus; the lunch menu has such local dishes as Danish herring (try the fried version) and smoked eel. The enclosed garden area out back is the perfect place relax. ✉ *Øresundsvej 10, Hornbæk* ☎ *49/70–05–50* ⊕ *www.sostreneolsen.dk* ▤ *AE, DC, MC, V* ⊘ *Closed Tues. and Wed.*

WHERE TO STAY
$$$$
Fodor's Choice
★

▦ **Havreholm Slot.** A few miles southwest of Hornbæk beach, this small former castle is surrounded by wooded grounds and overlooks the Havrehrolm Lake. Rooms and suites are in separate cabinlike quarters with designer furniture, Bang & Olufsen TVs, and balconies or terraces.

A sitting room and library, private golf course, four tennis courts, horseback riding arrangements and indoor and outdoor pool offer plenty of opportunity for outdoor activity. The restaurant serves elaborate French cuisine at dinner and smørrebrød and Danish comfort food at lunch. **Pros:** elegant; beautiful location; lots of activities. **Cons:** main building is often booked for wedding parties, so restaurant not always open to all guests. ⊠*Klosterrisvej 4, Havreholm* ☎*49/75–86–00* ⊕*www.havreholm.dk* ⊅*22 rooms, 6 suites* ⚒*In-hotel: restaurant, golf course, pool, Internet terminal, Wi-Fi* ⊟*AE, DC, MC, V* ⊗*BP.*

¢ ☷**Hotelpension Ewaldsgaarden.** This basic, casual but well-run pension is just blocks from the marina and the beach. It's also in a residential neighborhood off one of the town's main (though quiet) streets. There are sinks in the rooms but toilets and showers are shared. **Pros:** quiet; good service; well maintained. **Cons:** open only in summer; no frills; shared bathrooms only. ⊠*Johannes Ewaldsvej 5* ☎*49/70–00–82* ⊕*www.ewaldsgaarden.dk* ⊅*12 rooms* ⚒*In-hotel: restaurant, Internet terminal, Wi-Fi* ⊟*No credit cards* ⊗*BP.*

SHOPPING

Boomerangkaninen (⊠*Nordre Strandvej 336* ☎*49/76–17–17*) is a children's clothing boutique that sells toys as well as adorable-but-pricey Danish labels like Katvig, Mojo, and Joha. Making a virtue out of necessity, **Ilse Jacobsen** (⊠*A.R. Friis Vej 1 and 2,* ☎*49/70–16–98*) designs and sells sophisticated women's rain boots and jackets. Her line is sold in five countries, but Hornbæk is her base, with one shop that sells footwear across from another that sells clothing. **Sylvest Stentøj** (⊠*Klosterrisvej 2* ☎*49/70–11–20*) sells unique, witty pottery of all sizes and shapes. Its specialty is a fun blue spiky vase. Opening hours are odd, so call in advance; the owner speaks English.

ODSHERRED

58 km (36 mi) southwest of Hornbæk, 80 km (50 mi) northwest of Copenhagen (via Roskilde).

Humans have lived on the Odsherred peninsula since the Stone Age—and who can blame them, since its steep cliffs, white-sand dunes, and acres of forests provide both natural beauty and a defense from intruders? Dragsholm Castle, which once belonged to the bishop at Roskilde Cathedral and later to a local nobleman, has since been converted to a hotel. There's also plenty of beach life on the silky sand surrounding Sejerø Bugt (Sejerø Bay).

GETTING HERE AND AROUND

The drive to Odsherred is lovely, but getting here by public transportation is tricky, requiring at least two changes from just about anywhere. Go to rejseplanen.dk to get the latest bus and train information. Ferries are another option: there are lines that run to Århus and Ebeltoft.

ESSENTIALS

Ferry Info Mols-Linien (☎*70/10–14–18* ⊕*www.mols-linien.dk*).

Train Info DSB (☎*70/13–14–15* ⊕*www.dsb.dk*).

Visitor Info **Visit Odsherred** (⊠ *Algade 43 4500 Nykøbing SJ* ☎ *59/91–08–88* ⊕ *www.visitodsherred.dk)*.

EXPLORING

Sjællands Odde, the tiny strip of land north of the Sejerø Bay, offers slightly marshy but secluded beaches. Inside the bay, the beaches are once again smooth and blond.

Ⓒ **Sommerland Sjælland,** caters to visitors of all ages. The dozens of activities include a roller coaster, an aqua park, and a small zoo with pony rides. Children under 10 especially enjoy Miniland. ⊠ *Gammel Nykøbingvej 169, Nykøbing Sjælland* ☎ *59/31–21–00* ⊕ *www.sommerlandsj.dk* ⚏ *DKr 185* ⊙ *May 30–Aug. 30; check for opening hours.*

WHERE TO STAY

$$$$ ⌖ **Dragsholm Slot.** Dragsholm Castle, originally built in the 12th century, has been a home since the 18th century. Today it's a hotel with an acclaimed restaurant, where food from the local fields, forests and markets is prepared by Claus Henriksen, former sous-chef from one Denmark's highest acclaimed restaurants. Book well in advance for their popular "gourmet weekends." **Pros:** romantic; four challenging golf courses nearby. **Cons:** not on the beach; far from the nearest train station, making a car essential. ⊠ *Dragsholm Allé 1, Hørve* ☎ *59/65–33–00* ⊕ *www.dragsholm-slot.dk* ⟿ *33 rooms, 3 suites* ⏚ *In-hotel: restaurant* ▤ *AE, DC, MC, V* ⦿ *BP*.

ROSKILDE

36 km (22 mi) west of Copenhagen (on Rte. 156).

Roskilde is Zealand's second-largest town and one of its oldest, having been founded in 998. The town is named for a Viking king called Ro, who, according to legend, built the city around a lovely spring—"kilde" in Danish. In the Middle Ages Roskilde was one of northern Europe's largest and most important cities with a population of 5,000 to 10,000. Its eccentric, enormous cathedral, built in 1170, is a UNESCO World Heritage Site. These days Roskilde is a university town known for hosting an enormous rock festival every summer. It makes a great base for exploring nearby historic areas like Lejre and Skibby.

GETTING HERE AND AROUND

Trains run from Copenhagen to Roskilde every half hour. The 20-minute journey costs DKr 80. Within Roskilde, there's an excellent bus network. If you'd like to take a scenic boat ride, the M/S *Sagafjord* makes regular trips on Roskilde Fjord and has a restaurant onboard. Tickets cost DKr 98.

ESSENTIALS

Hospital Roskilde Amts Sygehus (⊠ *Køgevej 7-13, Roskilde* ☎ *46/32–32–00).*

Ferry Info Saga Fjord (☎ *46/75–64–60* ⊕ *www.sagafjord.dk).*

24-Hour Pharmacy Roskilde (⊠ *Dom Apotek, Algade 52* ☎ *46/32–32–77).*

EXPLORING

Construction began on **Roskilde Domkirke** (*Roskilde Cathedral*) around 1170 on the site of a church erected 200 years earlier by the Viking hero Harald Bluetooth. The building of it was made possible by the introduction of brick making to Denmark—it is made up of more than 3 million bricks—and a commission by the powerful Bishop Absalon, who's also considered one of the founders of Copenhagen. The cathedral made the city one of the spiritual capitals of Northern Europe. These days, its best known as the mausoleum of the royals: 38 Danish monarchs are entombed here, including the first Queen Margrethe (1353–1412), and there's reason to believe that Queen Margrethe II will ultimately find her resting place in or near the cathedral, like her father, Frederik IX. Don't miss the 16th-century clock depicting St. George charging a dragon, whose hisses and howls throughout church cause Peter Døver, "the Deafener," to sound the hour. A squeamish Kirsten Kiemer, "the Chimer," shakes her head in fright but manages to strike the quarter-hours. ⊠ *Domkirkestr. 10* ☎ *46/35–16–24* ⊕ *www.roskildedomkirke. dk/uk* ⊠ *DKr 25* ⊙ *Apr.–Sept., Mon.–Sat. 9–4:45, Sun. 12:30–4:45; Oct.–Mar., Tues.–Sat. 10–3:45, Sun. 12:30–3:45.*

Less than 1 km (½mi) north of the cathedral, on the fjord, is the modern **Vikingeskibsmuseet** (*Viking Ship Museum*), containing five Viking ships sunk in the fjord 1,000 years ago. Submerged to block the passage of enemy ships, they were discovered in 1957. The painstaking recovery involved building a watertight dam and then draining the water from that section of the fjord. The splinters of wreckage were then preserved and reassembled. A deep-sea trader, warship, ferry, merchant ship, and fierce 92½-foot man-of-war attest to the Vikings' sophisticated and aesthetic boat-making skills. ⊠ *Vindeboder 12* ☎ *46/30–02–00* ⊕ *www.vikingeskibsmuseet.dk* ⊠ *May–Sept. DKr 95, Oct.–Apr. DKr 55* ⊙ *Daily 10–5.*

Skibby is the main town of the little peninsula situated between Roskilde Fjord and Isefjord, 31 km (19 mi) northwest of Roskilde. Four kilometers (2½ mi) east of the town is **Selsø Slot** (*Selsø Castle*), constructed in 1576 and reworked in high-baroque style in 1734. The museum here displays original 17th-century interiors, including Denmark's oldest working kitchen, with a 250-year-old mechanical spit still going around. ⊠ *Selsøvej 30A, Skibby* ☎ *47/52–01–71* ⊕ *www.selsoe.dk* ⊠ *DKr 40* ⊙ *May–mid-June and mid-Aug.–Oct., weekends 1–4; mid-June–mid-Aug., daily 11–4.*

OFF THE BEATEN PATH

Jægerspris Slot. When King Frederik VII and his accomplished wife, Countess Danner, inherited this medieval castle in 1854, they gave it an "extreme makeover" in the style of the day. It remains an excellent example of mid-19th-century decorating, heavy on portraits in gilded frames and silk-covered chairs. To the north extends Nordskoven, a forest of 100-year-old oaks. ⊠ *Slotsgården 20, Jægerspris* ☎ *47/53–10–04* ⊕ *www.kongfrederik.dk* ⊠ *DKr 50* ⊙ *Open Mar. 15–Oct., Tues.–Sun. 11–4.*

Back in the Iron Age, Lejre was the **Fodor'sChoice** capital of the Lejre Kingdom; some ★ scholars believe it's mentioned in *Beowulf*. These days it's best known as the home of the 50-acre **Lejre Forsøgscenter** (*Lejre Archaeological Research Center*), a pioneer in the field of "experimental archeology." In summer a handful of hardy Danish families live here under the observation of researchers; they go about their daily routine grinding grain, herding goats, and wearing furs and skins, providing a clearer picture of ancient ways of life. You can experience a Stone Age camp, a Viking market, and 19th-century farmhouses, and there's a large children's area. ⊠*Slangealleen 2* ☎*46/48–08–78* ⊕*www. lejre-center.dk* ☜*DKr 110* ☉*Mid-June–mid-Aug., daily 10–5; other times irregular hrs.*

> **ROCK ON**
>
> At the end of June, Roskilde hosts one of Europe's biggest rock and pop music gatherings, the **Roskilde Festival** (⊕*www. roskilde-festival.dk*). Some 75,000 people show up every year to see the world's biggest names play outdoor concerts.

WHERE TO EAT

$$$ ✕**Raadhuskælderen.** The basement of city hall, near the cathedral, houses
ECLECTIC this charming and popular café–restaurant. Try open-face sandwiches or cake and coffee after sightseeing. The dinner menu features French-Danish inspired dishes and various cuts of beef and lamb grilled on a lava-rock barbecue. Exposed brick walls, curved white ceilings, and low lights give some local flavor as does a courtyard with town views. ⊠*Fondens Bro 1, Roskilde* ☎*46/36–01–00* ⊕*www.raadhuskaelderen. dk* ☐*AE, DC, MC, V* ☉*Closed Sun.*

$$$ ✕**Restaurant Store Børs.** Located on the Roskilde harbor with views of the
SEAFOOD Roskilde Cathedral is this seafood restaurant with a changing monthly menu. Its seven-course Torve Taste menu, with matching wines, represents the best of each season. There's also a beer menu that pairs handmade local brew from Gourmetbryggeriet with the cuisine. The kitchen smokes its own salmon, produces its own cheese, and uses herbs from its own garden. ⊠*Havnevej 43, Roskilde* ☎*46/32–50–45* ⊕*www. store-bors.dk* ☐*AE, DC, MC, V* ⬧*Reservations essential* ☉*Closed Sun. and Mon.*

$$ ✕**Svogerslev Kro.** Three kilometers (2 mi) west of Roskilde is the village
DANISH of Svogerslev, a peaceful location for this traditional thatch-roof Danish inn. Exposed wooden beams make the interior a cozy place to tuck into the hearty Danish fare. The menu includes a vegetarian option as well as some international dishes such as Wiener schnitzel and steak. ⊠*Hovedg. 45, Svogerslev* ☎*46/38–30–05* ⊕*www.svogerslevkro.dk* ☐*AE, DC, MC, V.*

WHERE TO STAY

$$ ☷**Hotel Prindsen.** Licensed since 1695 this hotel is one of Denmark's oldest. It's in the middle of the pedestrian shopping street t the heart of the city. The elegant dark-wood lobby leads to the simple but homey rooms. The restaurant has a pleasant street-side terrace and serves quality Danish-French meals; weekend brunches are popular. The hotel's

H. C. Andersen suite is named after the legendary writer because he frequented the hotel. **Pros:** superb location; good service; historic building. **Cons:** rooms and bathrooms are small; some street noise. ⊠*Alg. 13* ☎*46/30–91–00* @*www.prindsen.dk* ➯*74 rooms, 2 suites* ⟨*Inroom: Internet. In-hotel: restaurant, bar, Wi-Fi, parking (free), some pets allowed, no-smoking rooms* ☐*AE, DC, MC, V* ⦿|*BP*.

¢ ⌂**Roskilde Vandrerhjem.** This youth hostel is on Roskilde Fjord, close to the town's green areas and attractions. A stay here gets you use of the kitchen. The hostel offers breakfast for DKr 45 and discounts for the restaurant Snekken just across the street. **Pros:** good location; good budget option. **Cons:** plain interior; basic amenities. ⊠*Vindeboder 7* ☎*46/35–21–84* @*www.rova.dk* ➯*152 beds* ⟨*In-hotel: restaurant, laundry facilities* ☐*MC, V* ⦿|*EP*.

AFTER DARK

At **Bryggergården** (⊠*Alg. 15* ☎*46/35–01–03* @*www.restaurantbryg gergaarden.dk*), or the Draft Horse as it used to be called, you can have a late supper and beer—try one of many local varieties from Roskilde and Herslev on offer—in cozy surroundings.

In summer, **Café Mulle Rudi** (⊠*Djalma Lunds Gård 7* ☎*46/37–03–25*) is an arty spot with indoor and outdoor seating and live jazz.

When the town's youth are in the mood for live rock, they head to **Gimle** (⊠*Ringstedg. 30* ☎*46/37–19–82* @*www.gimle.dk*) on weekends.

SHOPPING

Between Roskilde and Holbæk is **Galleri Kirke Sonnerup** (⊠*Englerupvej 62, Såby* ☎*46/49–26–70*), with a good selection of pottery, glass, clothing, and woodwork produced by more than 50 Danish artists. Roskilde has many active artists, and **Jeppe.art** (⊠*Skomagergade 33,* ☎*46/36–94–35*) is a cooperative of craftspeople who sell their own jewelry, glassware, ceramics, clothing, knitwear, textiles, and paintings. On a busy shopping street **The Lützhøft Købmandsgård** (*Lützhøft's Old Grocer's Shop*), (⊠*Ringstedgade 6-8* ☎*46/35–00–61*) is actually part of Roskilde Museum. It's a re-created version of a 1920s general store. You can buy crockery, hardware, and groceries typical of the time period. A "lifestyle house where everything is for sale," **Outsidein** (⊠*Køgevej 3* ☎*46/32–00–50*) is a unique establishment. It carries Danish fashion from international names like DAY Birger et Mikkelsen, tin lamps and porcelain, furniture, and art—in fact, it has a resident artist on the first floor.

MØN

122 km (75 mi) south of Copenhagen.

The island of Møn makes for a wonderful side trip from Copenhagen, especially in summer. Its main attraction is the white chalk cliffs along the coast. The local beaches are unspoiled and uncrowded. Hikers will enjoy its network of trails, bird-watchers can observe local and migrating specimens, and lovers of wild orchids will find the greatest selection in all of Denmark. Although it has fewer than 12,000 year-round inhabitants, Møn comes alive in summer, with vacationers from around Europe attracted to its holiday cottages.

GETTING HERE AND AROUND

You can reach Møn by car across bridges linking it to Zealand and the nearby island of Falster. It's about a 90-minute drive from Copenhagen. There's no direct train link to Møn: you must take a train to Falster and then switch to a bus.

ESSENTIALS

Visitor Info Møn Turistbureau (⊠ *Storegade 2, Stege* ☎ *55/86–04–00* ⊕ *www. visitvordingborg.dk*).

EXPLORING

The island of Møn is most famous for its dramatic chalk cliffs, known in Danish as **Møns Klint.** Circled by a beech forest, the milky-white 75-million-year-old bluffs plunge 400 feet to a small, craggy beach—accessible by more than 500 steps. Down on the beach, join the Danish families hunting for fossils. You can have your fossils identified at the **GeoCenter Møns Klint,** a spectacular natural history museum with aquariums and a Mossasaurus skeleton. ⊠ *Stengårdvej 8, Borre* ☎ *55/86–36–00* ⊕ *www.moensklint.dk* ⌛ *DKr 100* ⊙ *Easter–Oct., daily 10–5; July and Aug. 10–6.*

Near Møns Klint is **Liselund Slot,** built by an 18th-century nobleman so his wife could "play at being a peasant," an idea inspired by Marie-Antoinette's peasant village at Versailles. The tiny structure is the world's only thatch-roof palace, and the place where Hans Christian Andersen wrote his fairy tale *The Tinder Box.* Behind it you'll find lakes with islands, an ideal spot for a romantic picnic. ⊠ *Langebjergvej 4, Borre* ☎ *55/81–21–78* ⌛ *DKr 25* ⊙ *Castle open May–Oct., Wed.–Fri. 10:30–2:30.*

Møn's largest city, **Stege** (population 2,000), began as a fishing village and expanded slowly around a castle erected in the 12th century. By the 15th century the town was encircled with moats and ramparts with three entranceways, each controlled by a gate tower: one of these gates, Mølleporten, still stands. Storegade, Stege's main street, has small shops selling food, wine, and local goods, and on Tuesday in the summer is transformed into a giant marketplace.

Stege's **Empiregården Museum** is a tiny museum in an old merchant home, with a local historical collection that includes toys, coins, and weaponry. ⊠ *Storegade 75, Stege* ☎ *55/81–40–67* ⊕ *www.museerne.dk/content/ us5* ⌛ *DKr 30* ⊙ *Tues.–Sun. 10–4.*

Ten kilometers (6 mi) west of Stege is **Kong Asgers Høj** (*King Asger's Hill*). Bring your own flashlight if you'd like to explore this Stone Age burial mound. During daylight hours you can go right into the long, thin burial chamber of this "passage grave."

WHERE TO EAT

$$ **✕Bryghuset Møn.** This café–restaurant serves its own beer produced on
CAFÉ the premises, with up to six varieties on tap and many more bottled. The
café serves sandwiches and a popular fresh-vegetable-laden "brewery
burger." A quality carvery buffet, with freshly sliced roasted meats and
salads, and an à la carte menu are available in the restaurant. Try the
classic pork shank marinated in brown ale at either the restaurant or
the café. ⊠ *Søndersti 3, Stege* ☎ *55/81–20–00* ⊕ *www.bryghusetmoen.
dk* ⚒ *Reservations not accepted* ⊟ *MC, V.*

¢ **✕David's.** Situated in the "glass house" on the main street is a charming
ECLECTIC café with a garden patio. The kitchen satisfies its many patrons with
☺ delicious Danish-French inspired dishes. Brunch is served every day
as are a good variety of sandwiches, tapas, vegetarian options, warm
dishes like quiche Lorraine and soups, and children's plates. There's a
three-course dinner menu on Friday and Saturday for DKr 225. ⊠ *Stor-
egade 11, Stege* ☎ *33/13–80–57* ⊕ *www.davids.nu* ⚒ *Reservations
essential* ⊟ *MC, V* ⊙ *No dinner. Closed Mon.*

WHERE TO STAY

¢ **▦Pension Bakkegården.** Between the view of the Baltic Sea and the
☺ Klinteskov forest, this small hotel farm dating from 1910 offers the
best of the island. From here it's a relaxing 20-minute stroll through
the beech forest to the cliffs of Møn. Six of the 12 rooms overlook
the sea. Every room is decorated by an artist from Møn and works
are available for sale. Children will enjoy the gardens with beautiful
views of the surrounding hills. **Pros:** lots of comfortable common areas;
nice views; accessible by bus. **Cons:** rooms have sinks but toilets and
baths are shared; 17 km (10 mi) from the city. ⊠ *Busenevej 64, Busene
Borre* ☎ *55/81–93–01* ⊕ *www.bakkegaarden64.dk* ⟷ *12 rooms with-
out bath* ⚘ *In-hotel: restaurant, bicycles, laundry service, Internet ter-
minal* ⊟ *No credit cards* ⊺⊙*BP.*

¢ **▦Præstekilde Hotel.** On a small island, this hotel has a splendid view of
Stege Bay from the middle of the golf course. Small, simply equipped
rooms are decorated in light colors. Staffers are efficient yet warm.
The restaurant serves good French-inspired Danish food. **Pros:** a bus
comes to the hotel's door every day; golf, hiking, and biking oppor-
tunities. **Cons:** rooms are small and simple; location about 5 km (3
mi) from shopping. ⊠ *Klintevej 116, Keldby* ☎ *55/86–87–88* ⊕ *www.
praestekilde.dk* ⟷ *42 rooms, 4 suites* ⚘ *In-hotel: restaurant, golf
course, pool, bicycles, Internet terminal, Wi-Fi, some pets allowed, no-
smoking rooms* ⊟ *AE, DC, MC, V* ⊺⊙*BP.*

FUNEN AND THE CENTRAL ISLANDS

Christened the Garden of Denmark by its most famous son, Hans Chris-
tian Andersen, Funen (Fyn) is the smaller of the country's two major
islands. A patchwork of vegetable fields and flower gardens, the flat-
as-a-board countryside is relieved by beech glades and swan ponds.
Manor houses and castles pop up from the countryside like magnificent
mirages. Some of northern Europe's best-preserved castles are here: the

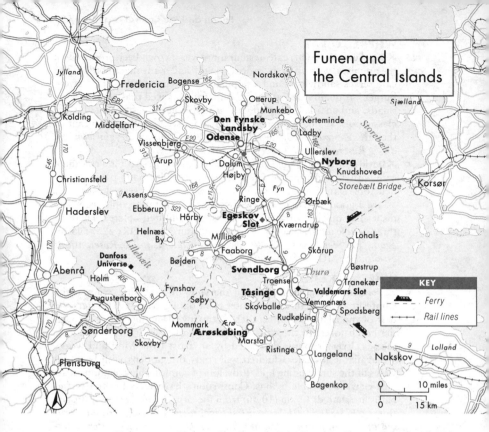

12th-century Nyborg Slot, travel pinup Egeskov Slot, and the lavish Valdemars Slot. The fairy-tale cliché often attributed to Denmark springs from this provincial isle, where the only place with modern vigor or stress seems to be Odense, its capital. Trimmed with thatch-roof houses and green parks, the city makes the most of the Andersen legacy but surprises with a rich arts community at the Brandts Klædefabrik, a former textile factory turned museum compound.

Towns in Funen are best explored by car. It's even quick and easy to reach the smaller islands of Langeland and Tåsinge—both are connected to Funen by bridges. Slightly more isolated is Ærø, where the town of Ærøskøbing, with its colorfully painted half-timber houses and winding streets, seems caught in a delightful time warp.

NYBORG

136 km (85 mi) southwest of Copenhagen (including the bridge across the Great Belt); 30 km (19 mi) southeast of Odense.

Like most visitors, you should begin your tour of Funen in Nyborg, a 13th-century town that was Denmark's capital during the Middle Ages.

WHERE TO EAT

$$$$ ✕**Den Gamle Kro.** Built within the courtyards of several 17th-century
FRENCH homes, this popular restaurant has walls of ancient stone topped by a
sliding glass roof. Though the menu is mostly French, you can still order
an inexpensive smørrebrød. ✉*Overg. 23* ☎*66/12–14–33* ⊕*www.
dengamlekro.ou* ☐*DC, MC, V.*

$$ ✕**Den Grimme Ælling.** The name of this chain restaurant means "the
DANISH ugly duckling," but inside it's simply homey, with pine furnishings and
Ⓒ a boisterous family ambience. It's extremely popular with tourists and
★ locals alike, thanks to an all-you-can-eat buffet heaped with cold and
warm dishes. Reservations are recommended. ✉*Hans Jensens Str. 1*
☎*65/91–70–30* ⊕*www.grimme-aelling.dk* ☐ *MC, V.*

$ ✕**Franck A.** Overlooking the pedestrian street, this spacious, styl-
ECLECTIC ish café-restaurant-bar with exposed brick walls is Odense's answer
to Copenhagen's trendy venues—minus the pretension. Hipsters and
media types mingle over cocktails but, this being Odense, informality
prevails. Brunch is served until 4. The lunch and dinner menu of global
cuisine runs the gamut from Thai chicken curry to hefty grilled burg-
ers. On Friday Franck A often hosts a popular '80s music night, with
lively cover bands. ✉*Jernbaneg. 4* ☎*66/12–27–57* ⊕*www.francka.
dk* ☐*MC, V.*

$$$$ ✕**Klitgaard.** This chic, cool-tone restaurant serves a changing menu of
ECLECTIC innovative Nordic-French fusion fare. Stuffed quail is seasoned with
rosemary and accompanied by an endive salad; a fricassee of scallops
and asparagus is enveloped in a tangy lemon sauce. The fresh cuisine
is complemented by a soothing decor of tan walls, hardwood floors,
and cane furniture that glow softly under recessed lights. ✉*Gravene 4*
☎*66/13–14–55* ⊕*www.restaurantklitgaard.dk* ⚭*Reservations essential*
☐*AE, DC, MC, V* ⊘*Closed Sun. and Mon. and mid-Dec.–early Jan.*

¢ ✕**Målet.** A lively crowd calls this sports club its neighborhood bar. The
GERMAN schnitzel is served in a dozen creative ways from traditional schnitzel
with sautéed potatoes and peas to Indian curry schnitzel with rice,
chutney, and pineapple. After the steaming plates of food, watching and
discussing soccer are the chief delights of the house. Reservations are a
good idea. ✉*Jernbaneg. 17* ☎*66/17–82–41* ⊕*www.restaurantmaalet.
dk* ☐*No credit cards.*

$$$$ ✕**Restaurant Under Lindetræet.** The snug corner restaurant, situated in the
ECLECTIC same cozy, cobblestone neighborhood as the Hans Christian Andersen
House, serves seasonal Italian and French-inspired dishes using Danish
ingredients, such as grilled redfish with boiled potatoes. Reservations
are recommended. ✉*Ramsherred 2* ☎*66/12–92–86* ☐*AE, DC, MC,
V* ⊘*Closed Sun. and mid-Dec.–early Jan.*

WHERE TO STAY

$ ▥**Clarion Collection Hotel Plaza Odense.** A five-minute walk from the train
station, this stately hotel dates from 1915 and overlooks Odense's leafy
central park, Kongens Have. An old-fashioned wooden elevator takes you
up to the ample, comfortable rooms outfitted in traditional dark-wood
furniture. Adjoining the cream-color lobby is the glass-walled Restau-
rant Rosenhaven, which serves contemporary Danish fare. **Pros:** five-
minute walk from train station; charming park view. **Cons:** some rooms

noisy. ⊠*Østre Stationsvej 24* ☎*66/11–77–45* ⊕*www.hotel-plaza.dk*
↪*68 rooms, 7 suites* ᕫ*In-hotel: restaurant, room service, bar, gym,
laundry service, parking (free), some pets allowed, no-smoking rooms*
☰*AE, DC, MC, V* ⏀*BP.*

¢–$$ ⊡ **First Hotel Grand Odense.** More than a century old, with renovated fin-
de-siècle charm, this imposing four-story, brick-front hotel greets guests
with old-fashioned luxury. The original stone floors and chandeliers
lead to a wide staircase and upstairs guest rooms that are modern with
plush furnishings and sleek marble bathrooms. Pros: close to Odense
attractions; close to train. Cons: not recommended for people with
disabilities. ⊠*Jernabaneg. 18* ☎*66/11–71–71* ⊕*www.firsthotels.com*
↪*138 rooms, 3 suites* ᕫ*In-room: safe, refrigerator, Wi-Fi. In-hotel:
restaurant, room service, bar, laundry service, Wi-Fi, parking (paid),
some pets allowed, no-smoking rooms* ☰*AE, DC, MC, V* ⏀*BP.*

¢   ⊡ **Hotel Ydes.** This well-kept, bright, and colorful hotel is a good bet for
Fodor's Choice students and budget-conscious travelers tired of barracks-type accom-
★   modations. The well-maintained rooms are spotless and comfortable.
Pros: affordable. Cons: small rooms; restaurant only serves breakfast.
⊠*Hans Tausens G. 11* ☎*66/12–11–31* ⊕*www.ydes.dk* ↪*25 rooms*
ᕫ*In-room: safe, DVD (some), Wi-Fi. In-hotel: restaurant, Wi-Fi, some
pets allowed, no-smoking rooms* ☰*AE, DC, MC, V* ⏀*BP.*

$$$ ⊡ **Radisson SAS–Hans Christian Andersen Hotel.** Around the corner from
the Hans Christian Andersen House, this blocky brick conference hotel
has a plant-filled lobby and rooms done in shades of red and yellow.
Pros: close to top attractions; casino. Cons: lacks charm; no single
rooms. ⊠*Claus Bergs G. 7* ☎*66/14–78–00* ⊕*www.radissonsas.com*
↪*145 rooms* ᕫ*In-room: safe, refrigerator, Wi-Fi. In-hotel: restaurant,
room service, bar, gym, laundry service, Wi-Fi, parking (free), some pets
allowed, no-smoking rooms* ☰*AE, DC, MC, V* ⏀*BP.*

AFTER DARK

CAFÉS AND BARS

Odense's central arcade is an entertainment mall, with bars, restaurants, and live music ranging from corny sing-alongs to hard rock.
The **Air Pub** (⊠*Kongsg. 415000* ☎*66/14–66–08* ⊕*www.airpub.dk*) is
a Danish pub that caters to a thirty- and fortysomething crowd, with
meals and a small dance floor. At the **Boogie Dance Café** (⊠*Nørreg. 21,*
☎*66/14–00–39*) a laid-back crowd grooves to pop and disco.

For a quiet evening, stop by **Café Biografen** (⊠*Brandts Passage*
☎*66/13–16–16* ⊕*www.cafebio.dk*) for an espresso, beer, or light snack,
or settle in to see one of the films screened here. In the heart of town is
Franck A (⊠*Jernbaneg. 4* ☎*66/12–27–57* ⊕*www.francka.dk*), a spirited café-restaurant with arched windows overlooking the pedestrian
street. Live music on Thursday—from pop to '80s to jazz—draws a
stylish crowd.

CASINO

You'll find this casino in the slick glass atrium of the **SAS Hans Christian Andersen Hotel** (⊠*Claus Bergs G. 7, Odense* ☎*66/14–78–10*
⊕*www.casinoodense.dk*), where you can play blackjack, roulette, and
baccarat.

JAZZ CLUBS

Dexter (⊠ *Vinderg. 65* ☎ *63/11–27–28* ⊕ *www.dexter.dk*) has all kinds of jazz—from Dixieland to fusion—Friday and Saturday nights. **Grøntorvet Café and Bar** (⊠ *Sortebrødre Torv 9* ☎ *63/12–33–00*) presents live jazz every other Sunday at 2 PM.

SHOPPING

Odense's compact city center has clothing, furniture, and shoe stores, and a Magasin department store. The main shopping strips are Vestergade and Kongensgade. Rosengårdcentret, one of northern Europe's largest malls, is 5 km (3 mi) west of Odense. It has more than 125 shops and food outlets, including trendy clothing stores; jewelry, woodwork, and antiques shops; a multiplex cinema; and a post office.

Denmark is well known for its paper cutouts, inspired, in part, by Hans Christian Andersen. Using a small pair of scissors and white paper, he would create cutouts to illustrate his fairy tales. Today replicas of Andersen's cutouts are sold at several Odense gift stores. Also popular are mobiles, often depicting Andersen-inspired themes like swans and mermaids. Uniquely Danish—and light on the suitcase—they make great gifts to take home.

Jam-packed with mobiles, cutouts, and Danish flags and dolls, **Klods Hans** (⊠ *Hans Jensens Str. 34* ☎ *66/11–09–40*) opened just after World War II to cater to all the American soldiers on leave who wanted to bring back Danish gifts. For fine replicas of Scandinavian Viking jewelry, head to **Museums Kopi Smykker** (⊠ *Klareg. 3* ☎ *66/12–06–96* ⊕ *www. museum-jewelry.dk*). Each piece, in either sterling silver or gold, comes with a printed leaflet explaining its Viking origins.

SVENDBORG

44 km (28 mi) south of Odense.

Svendborg is Funen's second-largest town and one of the country's most important cruise harbors. It celebrates its eight-centuries-old maritime traditions every July, when old Danish wooden ships congregate in the harbor for the circular Funen *rundt*, or regatta. Play your cards right, and you might hitch aboard and shuttle between towns. Contact the tourist board or any agreeable captain. With many charter-boat options and good marinas, Svendborg is an excellent base from which to explore the hundreds of islands of the South Funen archipelago.

GETTING HERE AND AROUND

From Odense, drive Route 9 south to Svendborg. The drive should take approximately 25 minutes. DSB also operates a train service from Odense to Svendboørg every half-hour. A ticket for the 55-minute trip costs DKr 63 (one-way).

The Svendborg Maritime Centre organizes charters and cruises on well-kept schooners, including summer excursions aboard the century-old schooner *Meta*. If you prefer traveling by land, Svendborg Nærtrafik runs buses around Svendborg and into its surrounds.

ESSENTIALS

Bus Info Svendborg Nærtrafik (☎63/11–22–00 ⊕ www.fynbus.dk).

Car Rental See Automobiler (✉Grønnemosevej 12, Svendborg ☎62/21–07–86 ⊕ www.seeauto.dk).

Ferry Info M/S Helge (⊕www.mshelge.dk). **Ærøærgerne** (✉Havnepladsen 1, Svendborg ☎62/52–40–00 ⊕ www.aeroe-ferry.dk). **Svendborg-Skarø-Drejø** (✉Havnepladsen 2, Svendborg ☎62/23–30–85).

Tour info Maritimt Center Danmark (For cruises and charters ✉Havnepladsen 2, Svendborg ☎62/23–30–25 ⊕www.maritimt-center.dk).

Train Info Svendborg Banegaard (Train Station) (✉Klosterpl. 10, Svendborg).

Visitor Info Sydfyns Touristbureau (✉Centrumpl. 4, Svendborg ☎62/21–09–80 ⊕ www.visitsydfyn.dk).

EXPLORING

Bagergade (Baker's Street) is lined with some of Svendborg's oldest half-timber houses. At the corner of Grubbemøllevej and Svinget is the **Viebæltegård,** the headquarters of the Svendborg County Museum and a former poorhouse. You can wander through dining halls, washrooms, and the "tipsy clink," where, until 1974, inebriated citizens were left to sober up. ✉Grubbemøllevej 13 ☎62/21–02–61 ⊕www. svendborgmuseum.dk 🎫DKr 40 ⏱June–Sept., Tues.–Sun. 10–5; Oct.– May, Tues.–Sun. 10–4.

In the heart of Svendborg, tucked behind the main street of Brogade, is a small, cobblestone courtyard surrounded by red half-timber houses. Dating from 1650, this charming square used to house Svendborg's general store. **Vintapperiet,** a snug, low-ceiling wine bar and shop, now occupies the square, and here you can taste your way—by the glass or by the bottle—through a range of top-notch French and Italian wines. Wine barrels line the entranceway; the small dining room, with less than a half dozen tables, overlooks the courtyard. They serve a light menu to complement the wines, including pâté and pungent cheese with hunks of bread and olives. It is open for lunch only, and closed on Sunday; in winter it's also closed on Monday. ✉Brog. 37 ☎62/22–34–48.

Fodor's Choice The moated Renaissance **Egeskov Slot,** one of the best-preserved island-
★ castles in Europe, presides over the town of Kværndrup, 15 km (9 mi) north of Svendborg. Peaked with copper spires and surrounded by Renaissance, baroque, English, and peasant gardens, the castle is still a private home, though visitors can see a few of the rooms, including the great hall, the hunting room, and the Riborg Room, where the daughter of the house was locked up from 1599 to 1604 after giving birth to a son out of wedlock. The castle also has an antique vehicle museum. ✉5700Kværndrup ✈15 km (9 mi) north of Svendborg ☎62/27–10–16 ⊕www.egeskov.com 🎫Castle and museum: DKr 175 ⏱Castle: May, June, Aug., and Sept.–Oct. 4, daily 10–5; July, daily 10–7. Museum: June and Aug., daily 10–6; July, daily 10–8 (Wed. open until 11 PM). May and Sept., daily 10–5.

WHERE TO EAT AND STAY

$$ DANISH **Hotel Ærø.** A hodgepodge of ship parts and nautical doodads, this dimly lighted restaurant and inn looks like it's always been here. Brusque waitresses take orders from serious local trenchermen. The menu is staunchly old-fashioned, featuring *frikadeller* (fried meatballs), fried *rødspætte* (plaice) with hollandaise sauce, and dozens of smørrebrød options. ✉*Brog. 1, Ærøfærgen, at Ærø ferry* ☎*62/21–07–60* 🌐*www.hotel-aeroe.dk* ▭*DC, MC, V.*

$$$ DANISH **Svendborgsund.** In a harborside building dating from 1682, this warm, maritime-theme restaurant serves traditional Danish cuisine, including pork tenderloin heaped with grilled onions and mushrooms and served with potatoes and pickled cucumbers. The extensive smørrebrød lunch menu includes marinated herring topped with egg yolk and fried fillet of plaice with shrimp, caviar, and asparagus. The summertime terrace is an inviting spot to soak up sun, beer, and the waterfront views. ✉*Havnepl. 5* ☎*62/21–07–19* 🌐*www.restaurantsvendborgsund.dk* ▭*AE, DC, MC, V.*

$ ★ **Missionhotellet Stella Marris.** Southwest of Svendborg, this lovely seaside villa dates from 1904. An old-fashioned English-style drawing room, complete with piano, stuffed chairs, and an elegant chandelier, overlooks the villa's spacious gardens; follow a path through the greenery. Each of the rooms has its own color scheme; one room has flowery wallpaper and white lace curtains, while another has a simple tan-and-rose decor. Bathrooms are basic and include a shower only. The hotel is part of Missionhotel, a Christian hotel chain in operation since the early 1900s. The Stella Marris is one of the few Missionhotels that still maintains an alcohol- and smoke-free environment. **Pros:** seaside views; surrounding gardens. **Cons:** No in-room phones; alcohol-free; no leisure facilities. ✉*Kogtvedvænget 3* ☎*62/21–38–91* 🌐*www.stellamaris.dk* *24 rooms, 20 with bath* *In-room: Wi-Fi. In-hotel: restaurant, laundry service, parking (free), some pets allowed, no-smoking rooms* ▭*AE, DC, MC, V* *EP.*

AFTER DARK

BARS AND LOUNGES

The beer flows freely at the cavernous pub **Børsen** (✉*Gerritsg. 31* ☎*62/22–41–41* 🌐*www.borsenbar.dk*), in a building dating from 1620. A young rowdy crowd of tourists and locals packs the place nightly. **Crazy Daisy** (✉*Frederiksg. 6* ☎*62/21–67–60* 🌐*www.svendborg.crazydaisy.dk*) attracts a casual, over-21 crowd that dances to oldies and rock on Saturday night; a younger crowd pours in on Friday. The restaurant **Oranje** (✉*Jessens Mole (Jessens Pier)* ☎*62/22–82–92* 🌐*www.oranjen.dk*), in an old sailing ship moored in the harbor, sometimes has live jazz in summer.

CAFÉ

In the heart of town is the spacious **Under Uret Café** (✉*Gerritsg. 50* ☎*62/21–83–08* 🌐*www.under-uret.com*), playfully decorated with watches on the wall—"Under Uret" means "under watch." For prime people-watching, settle in at one of the outdoor tables. The café menu includes brunch, club sandwiches, burritos, and a range of salads, from Greek to Caesar.

SHOPPING

Svendborg's city center is bustling with shops, particularly on Gerritsgade and Møllergade, which are peppered with clothing stores, gift shops, and jewelers. For colorful, handblown glassworks head to **Glas Blæseriet** (⊠*Brog. 37A* ☎*62/22–83–73*), which shares a half-timber courtyard in the center of town with the wine restaurant Vintapperiet. Glassblower Bente Sonne's lovely nature-inspired creations—in pale greens, oranges, and blues—are decorated with seashells, starfish, lizards, fish, and lobsters. You can watch Sonne blowing glass weekdays 10–3:30. On Saturday the shop is open 10–3:30, with no glassblowing demonstration.

TÅSINGE

3 km (2 mi) south of Svendborg (via the Svendborg Sound Bridge), 43 km (27 mi) south of Odense.

Tåsinge Island is known for its local 19th-century drama involving Elvira Madigan and her married Swedish lover, Sixten Sparre. The drama is featured in the 1967 Swedish film *Elvira Madigan*. Preferring heavenly union to earthly separation, they shot themselves and are now buried in the island's central Landet churchyard. Brides throw their bouquets on the lovers' grave.

GETTING HERE AND AROUND

From Svendborg, follow Johannes Joergensens Vej and turn left on Sundbrovej, which takes you across the Svendborgsound bridge (toll DKr 205). Once across, turn left at the first traffic light, and continue along Eskaervej. Follow this until it becomes Troense Strandvej. The trip should take approximately 25 minutes.

Bus 200, run by Fynbus, takes passengers from Svendborg to Troense every hour. The trip takes 30 minutes and costs DKr 17. From mid-May through mid-September, the century-old schooner *M/S Helge* sails to Vindebyoere, Troense, and Valdemars Castle on Tåsinge.

ESSENTIALS

Bus Info Fynbus (☎*63/11—22–00* ⊕ *www.fynbus.dk*).

Ferry Info M/S Helge (⊕ *www.mshelge.dk*).

EXPLORING

Fodor's Choice ★ Troense is Tåsinge's main town, and one of the country's best-preserved maritime villages, with half-timber buildings and their hand-carved doors. South of town is **Valdemars Slot** (*Valdemars Castle*), dating from 1610, one of Denmark's oldest privately owned castles, now owned and run by Caroline Fleming. You can wander through almost all of the sumptuously furnished rooms, libraries, and the candlelit church. There's also an X-rated 19th-century cigar box not to be missed. A yachting museum explores Denmark's extensive yachting history. There are also toy and trophy museums within the castle. ⊠*Slotsalleen 100,*

Troense ☎*62/22–61–06* ⊕*www.valdemarsslot.dk* 🎫*DKr 110* ⊘*May, June, and Aug., daily 10–5; July, daily 10–6; Sept., Tues.–Sun. 10–5; Oct., weekends 10–5.*

WHERE TO EAT AND STAY

¢–$ ✗**Bregninge Mølle.** If you've ever wondered what the inside of a wind-
DANISH mill looks like, this is your chance to find out. Within the Bregninge
Fodor'sChoice windmill, built in 1805, circular stairs lead to this restaurant's three
★ levels, each with 360-degree views of the surrounding sea and Tåsinge
countryside. The traditional Danish menu features *frikadeller* (fried
meatballs) served with rice and peas. ⊠*Kirkebakken 19, Bregninge*
☎*62/22–52–55* ⊕*www.bregningemoelle.dk* ▤*MC, V* ⊘*Closed mid-
Oct.–Mar.*

¢ ⊞**Hotel Troense.** Dating from 1908, this harborside hotel has bright,
simply furnished rooms with fringed white bedcovers. The restaurant,
with a fireplace, serves a Danish menu with such dishes as oven-baked
salmon served with fresh asparagus. It also offers a couple of vegetarian dishes, including a pie stuffed with seasonal vegetables. The hotel
often has discounted weekend deals that include breakfast and dinner.
Pros: harborside with lovely views; close to Troense attractions. **Cons:**
no leisure facilities. ⊠*Strandg. 5, Troense* ☎*62/22–54–12* ⊕*www.
hoteltroense.dk* ⏦*36 rooms* ⚬*In-room: Wi-Fi. In-hotel: restaurant,
room service, Wi-Fi, parking (free), some pets allowed, no-smoking
rooms* ▤*AE, DC, MC, V* ⏉*BP* ⊘*Mid-Dec.–1st wk Jan.*

SHOPPING

For delicate handblown glass, visit **Glasmagerne** (⊠*Vemmenæsvej 10,
Tåsinge* ☎*62/54–14–94* ⊕*www.glasmagerne.dk*).

ÆRØSKØBING

★ *30 km (19 mi) south of Svendborg, 74 km (46 mi) south of Odense,
plus a 1-hr ferry ride from Svendborg.*

The island of Ærø, where country roads wind through fertile fields,
is aptly called the Jewel of the Archipelago. About 27 km (16 mi)
southeast of Søby on the island's north coast, the storybook town of
Ærøskøbing is the port for ferries from Svendborg. Established as a
market town in the 13th century, it didn't flourish until it became a
sailing center during the 1700s. Today Ærøskøbing is a bewitching
tangle of cobbled streets lined with immaculately preserved half-timber
houses. Stop by the red 17th-century home at the corner of Vestergade
and Smedegade, considered to be one of the town's finest examples of
its provincial architecture.

As you wander through town, you'll notice that many of the homes
display a pair of ceramic dogs on their windowsills. Traditionally, these
were used by sailors' wives to signal to outsiders—and, as rumor has it,
potential suitors—the whereabouts of their husbands. When the dogs
were facing in, it meant that the man of the house was home, and when
the dogs were facing out, that he was gone.

GETTING HERE AND AROUND

Ferries run by ÆrøfÆrgerne provide the only access to Ærø. The ferry from Svendborg to Ærøskøbing takes 1 hour 15 minutes and departs approximately every three hours. In addition, there's a one-hour ferry from Faaborg to Søby, a town on the northwest end of the island; and another from Rudkøbing—on the island of Langeland—to Marstal, on the eastern end of Ærø. Fynbus operates a service from Æroøskøbing to Søby for DKr 35 and Ær øskøbing to Marstal, which costs DKr 25.

ESSENTIALS

Car Rental Ærøskøbing Bilservice (*Ærøskøbing Car Service*) (⊠ *Vesterg. 2, Ærøskøbing* ☎ *62/52-10-96*).

Bus Info Fynbus (☎ *63/11-22-00* ⊕ *www.fynbus.dk*).

Ferry Info Ærøærgerne (☎ *62/52-40-00* ⊕ *www.aeroe-ferry.dk*).

Medical Assistance Ærøskøbing Sygehus (*Ærøskøbing Hospital* ⊠ *Sygehusvej. 18, Ærøskøbing* ☎ *63/52-14-00*).

Visitor Info Ærø Touristbureau (⊠ *Ærøskøbing Havn 4, Ærøskøbing* ☎ *62/ 52-13-00*).

EXPLORING

History is recorded in miniature at the **Flaske-Peters Samling** (*Bottle-Ship Collection*), thanks to a former ship's cook known as Peter Bottle, who built nearly 2,000 bottle ships in his day. ⊠ *Smedeg. 22, Ærøskøbing* ☎ *62/52-29-51* ⊕ *www.arremus.dk* 🖃 *DKr 25* ☉ *End Oct.–Mar., Thurs. and Fri. 1–3, weekends 10–noon; Apr.–last wk June., mid-Aug.– last wk Oct., daily 10–4; last wk June–mid-Aug., daily 10–5.*

Ærø Museum houses numerous relics—including some from the Stone Age—culled from archaeological digs on the island. Also displayed are antique domestic furnishings from the homes of skippers on the island. Call ahead or check at the tourist office, because nonsummer hours can vary. ⊠ *Brog. 3–5, Ærøskøbing* ☎ *62/52-29-50* ⊕ *www.arremus.dk* 🖃 *DKr 25* ☉ *Mar.–mid-Oct., weekdays 10–4, weekends 11–3; mid-Oct.–mid.-Mar., weekdays 10–1.*

The two-story half-timber **Hammerichs Hus** (*Hammerich's House*) was once the home of sculptor Gunnar Hammerich. Today it has reconstructed period interiors of ancient Ærø homes, including maritime paintings, furniture, and porcelain pieces. ⊠ *Gyden 22, Ærøskøbing* ☎ *65/52-29-50* 🖃 *DKr 25* ☉ *Mid-June–Aug., daily noon–4.*

★ Southeast of Ærøskøbing, 12 km (7.5 mi) along a lush landscape of green and yellow hills rolling toward the sea, is the sprightly shipping town of **Marstal**. From its early fishing days in the 1500s to its impressive rise into a formidable shipping port in the 1700s, Marstal's lifeblood has always been the surrounding sea. At its seafaring height, in the late 1800s, Marstal had a fleet of 300 ships. Today Marstal is home port to 20 vessels, from tall-masted schooners to massive trawlers. Much of the town's activity—and its cobbled streets—radiates from the bustling port. In a nod to its seafaring heritage, the Marstal harbor is one of the few places in the world still constructing wooden ships.

WHERE TO EAT AND STAY

$$ ✕**Restaurant Addi's.** In the heart of town is this amiable restaurant. The
DANISH dining room, with low white ceilings and a black-and-white checkered
★ floor, is nicknamed the *kongelogen* (the royal box) because of the royal
portraits, past and present, that line the walls. Steaks, thick-cut and
juicy, come with large salads. In summer the outside terrace and beer
garden overflow with day-trippers from the mainland. ✉ *Vesterg. 39*
☎ *62/52–21–43* ▤ *MC, V* ✆ *Closed Nov. and Feb.*

¢ ▦**Det Lille Hotel.** Six large, simply furnished rooms make up the second
floor of this friendly *lille* (little) hotel. Flowery curtains frame small win-
dows that overlook the garden below. On the bottom floor are a popu-
lar restaurant and bar, both of which draw a daily crowd of regulars
(reservations are essential for the restaurant). The Danish menu includes
fried plaice topped with butter sauce and pork fillet with tomatoes,
mushrooms, and a white-wine cream sauce. The snug bar is decorated
with a ship's wheel and lanterns. **Pros:** popular bar-restaurant; intimate
feel. **Cons:** no in-room phones. ✉ *Smedeg. 33* ☎ *62/52–23–00* ⊕ *www.
det-lille-hotel.dk* ➹ *6 rooms without bath* ♿ *In-room: DVD, Wi-Fi.
In-hotel: restaurant, bar, Wi-Fi, parking (free), some pets allowed, no-
smoking rooms* ▤ *DC, MC, V* ¶ *BP.*

$$$ ▦**Hotel Ærøhus.** A half-timber building with a steep red roof, the
Ærøhus looks like a rustic cottage on the outside and an old, but overly
renovated, aunt's house on the inside. Pine furniture and cheerful duvets
keep the guest rooms simple and bright. The garden's five cottages
have small terraces. **Pros:** in middle of town; near ferry landing; some
cottages have a sauna. **Cons:** fussy interior, not all rooms have bath.
✉ *Vesterg. 38* ☎ *62/52–10–03* ⊕ *www.aeroehus.dk* ➹ *67 rooms, 56
with bath* ♿ *In-room: kitchen (some), refrigerator, Wi-Fi. In-hotel: restaurant, room service, bar, tennis courts, bicycles, laundry facilities,
laundry service, Wi-Fi, parking (free), some pets allowed, no-smoking
rooms* ▤ *MC, V* ¶ *BP.*

¢ ▦**Pension Vestergade 44.** Rising over Ærøskøbing's main street are two
superbly maintained patrician homes. Standing side by side, they are
mirror images of each other, built by two ship captains, brothers, who
wanted to raise their families in identical surroundings. One of the
homes has been converted into this small hotel that has been lovingly
restored by its owners, a friendly British-German couple, to recapture
all of the building's former charms. A claw-foot iron stove heats up the
breakfast room that overlooks a sprawling back garden with clucking
chickens who lay the eggs for the morning meal. White lace curtains
frame the windows and an antique wooden plate rack displays blue-
and-white English porcelain dishes. The beautifully appointed rooms,
each with its own color scheme, have naturally sloping floors and vintage wooden towel racks laden with fluffy, bright-white towels. **Pros:**
beautiful building; organic breakfast. **Cons:** no private bath in July; no
leisure facilities; no in-room phones. ✉ *Vesterg. 44* ☎ *62/52–22–98*
⊕ *www.vestergade44.com* ➹ *6 rooms, no private bath in July* ♿ *In-
room: Wi-Fi. In-hotel: restaurant, bar, Internet terminal, parking (free),
some pets allowed, no-smoking rooms* ▤ *No credit cards* ¶ *BP.*

AFTER DARK

Of Ærøskøbing's few bars, one of the most popular is **Arrebo** (✉ *Vesterg. 4* ☎ *62/52-28-50* ⊕ *www.arrebo.com*), with yellow walls, wooden tables, and local art on the walls. On weekends it hosts live music, from blues to rock to jazz. A bell dangles at one end of the bar, and in the sailor tradition, whoever rings it must buy the whole bar a round of drinks.

SHOPPING

Ærøskøbing is sprinkled with a handful of craft and gift shops. Unfortunately, there are virtually no more bottle-ship makers on the island. Instead, the labor-intensive curiosities are made in Asia and modeled on original Ærø bottle-ship designs. For souvenir bottle ships, head to **Kolorit** (✉ *Moseager 3* ☎ *62/52-25-21*), a small gift shop crammed with Danish mementos.

JUTLAND

Jutland (Jylland), Denmark's western peninsula, is the only part of the country naturally connected to mainland Europe; its southern boundry is the frontier with Germany. In contrast to the smooth land of Funen and Zealand, the Ice Age–chiseled peninsula is bisected at the north by the craggy Limfjord and spiked below by the Danish "mountains." Himmelbjerget, the zenith of this modest range, peaks at 438 feet. Farther south, the Yding Skovhøj plateau rises 568 feet—modest hills just about anywhere else. The windswept landscapes trace the west coast north to Skagen, a luminous, dune-covered point.

To the east, facing Funen, Jutland is cut by deep fjords rimmed with forests. The center is dotted with castles, parklands, and the famed Legoland. Denmark's oldest and youngest towns, Ribe and Esbjerg, lie in southwest Jutland. In Ribe's medieval town center is the country's earliest church; modern Esjberg, perched on the coast, is the departure point for ferries to nearby Fanø, and island of windswept beaches and traditional villages. Århus and Aalborg, respectively Denmark's second- and fourth-largest cities, face east and have nightlife and sights to rival Copenhagen's.

Nearly three times the size of the rest of Denmark, with long distances between towns, the peninsula of Jutland can easily take several days, even weeks, to explore. If you are pressed for time, concentrate on a single tour or a couple of cities. Delightful as they are, the islands are suitable only for those with plenty of time, as many require an overnight stay.

KOLDING

71 km (44 mi) northwest of Odense (via the Little Belt Bridge), 190 km (119 mi) west of Copenhagen.

Kolding is an interesting city that screams "design." It's the home of the Danish School of Art & Design, as important to this country as the

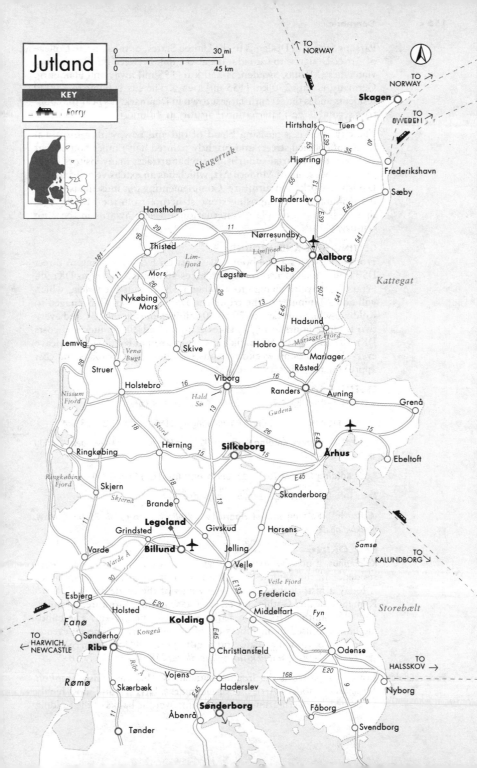

Parsons School of Design is to the United States, or the Ontario College of Art & Design is to Canada. It's also a link between other Scandinavian cities (Malmö, Sweden, is 250 km [155 mi] away and Hamburg, Germany, is only 250 km [155 mi] away). The city is home to 63,000 residents and is the seventh-largest town in Denmark. It's near the country's second-largest international airport at Billund.

The city itself is a pleasing blend of old and new, with a historical center of cobbled streets and brightly painted half-timber houses that give way to industrial suburbs. But what attracts many visitors is the Trapholt Museum of Modern Art, which has an extensive collection of Danish artworks and furniture. Complementing this museum is, oddly, the Koldinghus, an imposing stone structure from the Middle Ages that itself won a couple of international design awards in the 20th century.

GETTING HERE AND AROUND

From Odense, it's a one-hour drive west on E20 to Kolding. A direct DSB train from Odense to Kolding takes 40 minutes and costs DKr 99. (You may have to change to another DSB train at Fredericia, which will add 20 minutes to the trip.) The DSB train from Copenhagen to Kolding, which runs every 20 to 30 minutes during the day and every two to three hours at night, takes 2 hours and 20 minutes and costs DKr 287 (one-way). Sydtrafik runs buses around Kolding. They leave every 20 minutes on weekdays and every hour on weekdays and cost approximately DKR 19 (one-way).

ESSENTIALS

Bus Info Sydtrafik (☎ 76/60–86–00 ⊕ www.sydtrafik.dk).

Car Rental Avis Biludlejning (⊠ Ndr. Ringvej 1186000 ☎ 75/52–93–99).

Medical Assistance Kolding Sygehus (*Kolding Hospital*) (⊠ Skovvangen 2-86000 ☎ 76/33–20–00).

Taxis Kolding Taxi (☎ 75/52–15–00). **Krone Taxi** (☎ 75/50–27–00).

Train Info DSB (☎ 70/13–14–15 ⊕ www.dsb.dk).

Visitor Info Kolding Tourist Board (⊠ Akseltorv 8 ☎ 76/33–21–00 ⊕ www.visitkolding.dk).

EXPLORING

Koldinghus, a massive structure that was once a fortress, then a royal residence in the Middle Ages (and the last royal castle in Jutland), is today a historical museum. The wings of the castle are devoted to Romanesque and Gothic church art and sculpture, furniture, ceramics, and silversmithing from the 13th century to the present. The building has been used by members of the royal family for special events. There's also a popular café and a gift shop. ⊠ Markdanersgade 11 ☎ 76/33–81–00 ⊕ www.koldinghus.dk ⊠ DKr 55 ⊙ Daily 10–5.

Fodor'sChoice Just east of town is the **Trapholt Museum for Moderne Kunst** (*Trapholt* ★ *Museum of Modern Art*), one of Denmark's largest—and most highly acclaimed—modern-art museums. Rising over the banks of the Kolding

Fjord, this sprawling white complex has been artfully incorporated into its surroundings, affording lovely water and parkland views from its floor-to-ceiling windows. A collection of 20th-century Danish paintings is displayed in the light-filled galleries; it includes works by Anna Ancher, Ejler Bille, Egill Jakobsen, J. A. Jerichau, Jais Nielsen, Richard Mortensen, Aksel Jørgensen, and Franciska Clausen. A true highlight is the Danish Furniture Museum, housed in a specially designed annex that is accessed via a circular ramp topped by a skylight. The superbly displayed collection includes the world's largest assemblage of Danish-designed chairs, offering a unique historical overview of the birth and popularization of the nation's furniture design. The museum keeps its furniture storage room open to the public, so you can peruse the entire collection even when it's not officially on display.

The Danish ceramics collection, one of the largest in Denmark, is also well worth a look, featuring works by Thorvald Bindesbøll and one-of-a-kind ceramics by Axel Salto, whose pieces often resemble living organisms. Famous designer Arne Jacobsen's summer cottage was moved to Trapholt and opened on its grounds. Café Trapholt serves coffee, beverages, and light meals. The gift shop sells local and international art and design-related gifts. ⊠ *Æblehaven 23* ☎ *76/30–05–30* ⊕ *www. trapholt.dk* 🖃 *DKr 65* ⊙ *Tues.–Sun. 10–5, Wed. 10–8.*

WHERE TO EAT AND STAY

$$$
SEAFOOD
★

✕ **Admiralen.** Across from the harbor is this elegant seafood restaurant, with pale yellow tablecloths, white walls, and blue-suede chairs. It serves excellent fish dishes, including grilled salmon with spinach and steamed lemon sole with scallops. Reservations are a good idea. ⊠ *Toldbodeg. 14* ☎ *75/52–04–21* ⊕ *www.admiralen.dk* ⊟ *AE, DC, MC, V* ⊙ *Closed Sun., last wk Dec., and last 3 wks Jan.*

$$$

☷ **Hotel Koldingfjord.** This impressive neoclassical hotel has mahogany floors and pyramid skylights. The rooms vary in size (with 39 in a separate annex), but all have pale-wood furnishings and bright prints. The motto of the excellent French-Danish restaurant is "good food is art"; expect well-presented seafood dishes, as well as other intriguing seasonal options. **Pros:** good restaurant; sauna; pool. **Cons:** few on-site amenities. ⊠ *Fjordvej 154, Strandhuse* ☎ *75/51–00–00* ⊕ *www. koldingfjord.dk* 🛏 *134 rooms, 7 junior suites* ♿ *In-room: safe (some), refrigerator, Wi-Fi. In-hotel: 2 restaurants, room service, bar, pool, bicycles, Wi-Fi, parking (free), some pets allowed, no-smoking rooms* ⊟ *AE, DC, MC, V* ⫶◯⫶ *BP.*

$
★

☷ **Saxildhus Hotel.** This oh-so-Danish property, with gables, black-painted beams, and clunky antiques in its hallways and guest rooms is steps from the train station and has long been Kolding's premier hotel. Its rooms come in a range of styles, some with mahogany four-poster beds and others with more contemporary furnishings. The hotel's restaurant, Latin, serves breakfast and dinner. **Pros:** free minibar; free access to gym across the street. **Cons:** street rooms get noisy. ⊠ *Jern-baneg. 39, Banegårdspl.* ☎ *75/52–12 00* ⊕ *www.saxildhus.dk* 🛏 *80 rooms, 7 suites* ♿ *In-room: refrigerator, Wi-Fi. In-hotel: restaurant,* *room service, bar, laundry service, Internet terminal, parking (free), no-smoking rooms* ☰*AE, DC, MC, V* ⎀⊙⏐*BP.*

AFTER DARK
In the heart of town, on Lilletorv (Little Square), is the stylish and amiable **Den Blå Café** (✉*Slotsg. 4* ☎*75/50–65–12* ⊕*www.denblaacafe.dk*), with live Danish, British and American rock and blues bands playing to a backdrop of colorful art and posters every Thursday. In the afternoon, locals sidle up to the picture windows overlooking the square and enjoy coffee and warm baguette sandwiches or chips and guacamole. In the evening, beer and cocktails flow freely, and on summer weekends there's live jazz on the terrace. The café is open until midnight Monday through Wednesday and until 2 AM Thursday through Saturday.

SHOPPING
Kolding's town center is a jumble of walking streets dotted with clothing and jewelry stores and ice-cream shops. **Furiosa** (✉*Blæsbjergg. 2A* ☎*75/50–88–87*) is the best store in Kolding for interior design. The two-story **Sinnerup** (✉*Sønderg. 9* ☎*75/50–56–22* ⊕*www.sinnerup. dk*) sells all the big names in Danish design, from Stelton and Georg Jensen tableware to functional wooden furniture made by the design firm Trip Trap.

SØNDERBORG

90 km south of Kolding.

This town of 30,000 is the center of what is marketed as a "holiday region" of the country—indeed, there are four castles in this area alone. It's deep in southeast Jutland, and has its own airport and train and bus stations. It's the obvious base for a visit to the island of Als, Denmark's seventh largest, which is connected by two bridges from Sønderborg (and a car ferry just north of the town).

Southern Jutland was part of Germany between 1864 and 1920, and because of this the art nouveau movement flourished in Sønderborg, whereas in other parts of Denmark the preference was for a traditional arts and crafts style. Sønderborg is a wonderful spot for a walking tour, admiring the buildings constructed between 1905 and 1915. A brochure explaining the route is available from the local tourist office.

GETTING HERE AND AROUND
From Kolding, head south on Route E45 through Åbenrå and take Exit 71 to Route 41 to Sønderborg. The drive should take 1 hour and 30 minutes. X-bus runs from Kolding to Sønderborg regularly throughout the day; it costs DKr 126 for the 1-hour-and-45-minute trip. In Sønderborg, Sydrafik buses will take you around town for DKr 30 (adult, one-way).

The DSB train from Copenhagen to Sønderborg, which stops at Kolding along the way, runs every two hours and costs approximately DKr 200 (or DKr 129 for the 1½-hour trip from Kolding to Sønderborg).

Cimber Air is the only direct carrier from Copenhagen to Sønderborg. Flights cost approximately DKr 1,200 and take 45 minutes. Car rental is available at the airport and at Europcar in Sonderborg.

ESSENTIALS

Airport Info **Sonderborg Airport** (⊠ *Lufthavnsvej 1* ☎ *74/42—21—30* ⊕ *www. eksb.dk*). **Cimber Air** (☎ *33/47–35–16* ⊕ *www.cimber.dk*).

Bike Rental **Cykel Hjørnet** (⊠ *Nørrekobbel 26400* ☎ *74/43–63–00*). **Jønne's Cykler** (⊠ *Alsgade 54* ☎ *74/42–63–26*).

Bus Info **Rutebilstation** (*Sonderborg Bus Station*) (⊠ *Jernbaneg. 1* ☎ *74/42–26–25*). **Xbus** (☎ *98/90–09–00* ⊕ *www.xbus.dk*).

Medical Assistance **Sønderborg Sygehus og Skadeklinik** (*Hospital and Emergency Clinic*) (⊠ *Sydvang 1* ☎ *74/18–25–00*).

Train Info **DSB** (☎ *70/13–14–15* ⊕ *www.dsb.dk*). **Sønderborg Banegaard** (*Sønderborg Train Station*) (⊠ *Alsion 2*).

Visitor Info **Sønderborg Turistbureau** (⊠ *Rådhustorvet 7* ☎ *74/42–35–55*).

EXPLORING

The **Museum at Sønderborg Castle** exhibits a wonderful array of artifacts outlining southern Jutland's history and the building itself. The castle has the most intact royal chapel preserved from the time of Reformation. For a unique visit, take part in the guided Ghostwalking Tours, which take place on Monday and Wednesday night at 10 PM from June 1 to mid-August. The cost is DKr 95 and you can buy tickets at the Sønderborg Turistbureau. ⊠ *Sønderbro 1* ☎ *74/42–25–39* ⊕ *www. museum-sonderjylland.dk* ⛶ *DKr 45* ⊗ *May–Sept., daily 10–5; Oct.– Mar., weekdays 1–4; Apr., weekdays 10–4.*

WHERE TO EAT AND STAY

$$
DANISH
★

✕ **Skipperkroen Als.** This restaurant may be the second-most-obvious reason to make a stop in Augustenborg—on the island of Als, 7 km (4 mi) northeast of Sønderburg—after seeing Sønderburg Castle. It's on the marina, and you can always stop by for coffee and cake or an icy Danish beer on the terrace if you don't want to commit to a whole meal. The dining room is at once elegant and cozy, with crisp white linens blending in with the modern Danish decor. Pricey prix-fixe meals are featured at dinner—venison in a red currant sauce is a good choice if it's in season—but you can get a traditional Danish luncheon platter of herring, smoked salmon, prawns, pâté, and cheese, for a very reasonable DKr 155. ⊠ *Langdel 6D, Augustenborg* ☎ *74/47–10–84* ⊟ *AE, MC, V* ⊗ *Closed Sun. and Mon. and Dec. and Jan.*

$

⛶ **Ballebro Færgekro.** This inn, overlooking the calm waters of the Als fjord, seems like a location for an Ingmar Bergman film. Mists hover over the water; a gingerbread-style house is surrounded by broad lawns. The country-inspired guest rooms are very comfortable, with large bathrooms and good-quality amenities. A traditional Danish breakfast of cold cuts, cheeses, fresh breads, and jellies is served buffet-style or brought to your table on a three-tiered tray. This inn is a perfect spot for a romantic getaway—and it's steps from the car ferry that takes you on a five-minute ride to Als. **Pros:** beautiful setting, water views. **Cons:** not accessible to people with disabilities. ⊠*Færgevej 5, Blans, Sønderborg* ☎*74/46–13–03* ⊕*www.ballebro.dk* ⛱*11 rooms* ⛵*In-room: Wi-Fi. In-hotel: restaurant, room service, bar, beachfront, bicycles, Wi-Fi, parking (free), some pets allowed, no-smoking rooms* ⊟*AE, DC, MC, V* ⎮⚬⎮*BP.*

$$ 🔳**Baltic Hotel.** This beautifully restored hotel from the 1800s is in the village of Høruphav, which is a 15-minute drive east of Sønderborg. Rooms are plush, and five have an easterly ocean view. Meals are well worth having at the hotel's restaurant, with two-, three-, and eight-course options. For something more informal, there's the ground-floor Grill & Wine Bar. A stay here gets you a get 20% discount at a nearby golf course and on boat rentals. **Pros:** historical building; near scenic marina and walking/biking path to the seaside at Danish–German border. **Cons:** outside Sønderborg; few rooms with ocean view; not accessible for people with disabilities. ⊠*Havbo 29, Sydals, Høruphav* ☎*74/41–52–00* ⊕*www.hotel-baltic.dk* ⛱*8 rooms, 2 suites* ⛵*In-room: safe, kitchen (some), Wi-Fi. In-hotel: 2 restaurants, room service, bar, beachfront, bicycles, laundry service, Wi-Fi, parking (free), some pets allowed, no-smoking rooms* ⊟*DC, MC, V* ⎮⚬⎮*BP.*

RIBE

★ *60 km (36 mi) southwest of Kolding, 150 km (103 mi) southwest of Århus.*

In the southwestern corner of Jutland, the country's oldest town is well worth the detour for its medieval center preserved by the Danish National Trust. As you stroll around, note the detailed doors and facades of the buildings and the antique streetlights. From May to mid-September a night watchman circles the town, recalling its history and singing traditional songs. If you want to accompany him, gather at the main square at 10 PM.

GETTING HERE AND AROUND

From Sønderborg, take Route 41 to Åbenrå, then take E45, followed by Route 429 or Route 24 to Ribe. The drive takes approximately 1 hour and 30 minutes. Sydtrafik runs buses from Sonderborg to Ribe; the trip takes two hours and costs DKr 84.

From other parts of Denmark, the easiest way to get to Ribe is by train. Take DSB service to Tønder; if you're coming from Copenhagen or other cities in east Denmark, you'll transfer at Bramming to the Arriva service to Ribe (the trip costs DKr 311 from Copenhagen and takes four hours).

Once in Ribe, take Sydtrafik Bus 717 to the Viking Center and the 712 to Vadehavscentret in Vester Vedsted. In Vester Vedsted, you can buy the DKr 60 ticket for the so-called "tractor buses"—run by Manboebussem and Vadehadffafari—to Mandø, a small, verdant island accessible only at low tide.

ESSENTIALS

Bike Rental **Danhostel Ribe Vandrehjem** (⊠ *Sct. Pedersg. 16* ☏ *75/42-42-88* ⊕ *www.danhostel-ribe.dk*).

Bus and Train Info DSB (☏ *70/13-14-15* ⊕ *www.dsb.dk*). **Ribe Station** (⊠ *Dagmarsg. 16* ☏ *70/13-14-15*). **Sydtrafik** (☏ *76/60-86-00* ⊕ *www.sydtrafik.dk*). **Manboebussem** (☏ *73/44-51-07* ⊕ *www.mandoebussen.dk*). **Vadehadffafari** (☏ *75/44-59-12* ⊕ *www.vadehavssafari.dk*).

Visitor Info Ribe Tourist Office (⊠ *Torvet 3* ☏ *75/42-15-00* ⊕ *www.visitribe.dk*).

EXPLORING

The **Ribe Domkirke** (*Ribe Cathedral*) stands on the site of one of Denmark's earliest churches, built around AD 860. The present structure, which dates from the 12th century, is built of a volcanic tufa stone, transported by boats from quarries in Cologne, France. Note the Cat Head Door, said to be for the exclusive use of the devil. The 14th-century brick bell tower once clanged out flood and fire warnings to Ribe's citizens and today affords sweeping views of the town's red-slate rooftops and surrounding marshes. ⊠ *Torvet 15* ☏ *75/42–06–19* ⊕ *www.ribe-domkirke. dk* ▣ *DKr 10* ⊗ *Nov.–Mar., Mon.–Sat. 11–3; May–Sept., Mon.–Sat. 10–5; Oct. Mon.–Sat. 11–4. Hrs vary Sun. year-round.*

The **Ribes Vikinger** (*Ribe Viking Museum*) chronicles Viking history with conventional exhibits of household goods, tools, and clothing. There's a multimedia room with an interactive computer screen where you can search for more Viking information in the form of text, pictures, and videos. ⊠ *Odinspl.* ☏ *76/88–11–22* ⊕ *www.ribesvikinger.dk* ▣ *DKr 60* ⊗ *Apr.–June, daily 10–4; Sept.–Mar., Tues.–Sun. 10–4; July and Aug., Tues. and Thurs.–Sun. 10–6, Wed. 10–9.*

Bus 717 travels 2 km (1 mi) south from the Ribe railway station to the **Viking Center,** an outdoor exhibit detailing how the Vikings lived day-to-day, with demonstrations about homes, food, and crafts. ⊠ *Lustrupvej 4, Lustrupholm* ☏ *75/41–16–11* ⊕ *www.ribevikingecenter.dk* ▣ *DKr 75* ⊗ *May, June, and Sept., weekdays 10–3:30; July and Aug., daily 11–5.*

The lush island of **Rømø,** 35 km (22 mi) southwest of Ribe, has one of Denmark's widest beaches, which unfurls along a sunny western coast and has protected areas for windsurfers, horseback riders, nudists, and dune-buggy riders alike—space for everyone, it seems. Rømø has just 850 permanent residents, but masses of vacationing German and Danish families increase this number tenfold in summer. Indeed, it's a haven for campers, cyclists, and budget vacationers. A causeway crosses green fields and marshy wetlands to connect Rømø to the mainland. Many birds live here, feeding off the seaweed and shellfish washed up by the tides. Summerhouses dot the island; most of Rømø's services and accommodations are in and around the village of Havneby, 8 km (5 mi) south of the causeway, and in the camping and shopping complex of Lakkolk, in the west.

In the 19th century the tiny island of **Fanø** (30 km[19 m]) northwest of Ribe—plus a 12-minute ferry from Esbjerg—had an enormous ship-building industry and a fleet second only to Copenhagen's. The shipping industry deteriorated, but the maritime heritage remains. Today Fanø is a summer oasis for legions of Danes and other northern Europeans. Silky sand beaches unfold along the west coast, buffered by windswept dunes and green reeds. Cars are allowed on the beach, and it's well worth taking a ride along the flat sandy coast between the ferry port in Nordby, Fanø's capital, and the traditional town of Sønderho, 13 km (8 mi) to the south. Spinning along the white sandy expanse is like crossing a desert; only the dark blue sea off in the distance reminds you of your island whereabouts. The beach is so level and wide that the military used to train here. In the off-season, when summer visitors have returned home, the Fanø shore becomes a tranquil retreat, hauntingly silent save for the rustle of reeds and the far-off squawk of a bird.

WHERE TO EAT AND STAY

$$
DANISH
✕**Sælhunden.** The 400-year-old canal-side "Seal Tavern" can seat up to 60 people, but it feels smaller, and its coziness draws both wayfarers and locals. The only seal mementos left are a few skins and pictures, but you can still order a "seal's special" of cold shrimp, sautéed potatoes, and scrambled eggs. In summer, you can sit outside by the river or in the courtyard. ⊠*Skibbroen 13* ☎*75/42–09–46* ⊕*www.saelhunden. dk* ⚭*Reservations essential* ⊟*MC, V.*

¢ ▦**Danhostel Ribe.** In the town center, this plain, redbrick hostelry has four- and five-bed family rooms that can be arranged as double rooms. Many rooms have their own bath and toilet. All rooms are functional and childproof, with metal bunks and industrial carpeting. A kitchen is available. **Pros:** flexible room arrangements; center of town. **Cons:** almost no in-room amenties. ⊠*Ribehallen, Skt. Pedersg. 16* ☎*75/42–06–20* ⊕*www.danhostel-ribe.dk* ⤴*170 beds, 40 with bath* ⚲*In-room: no phone, no TV, Wi-Fi. In-hotel: restaurant, tennis court, gym, bicycles, laundry facilities, Wi-Fi, parking (free), no-smoking rooms* ⊟*AE, DC, MC, V* ⓞⅠEP ⊙*Closed mid-Dec.–mid-Jan.*

$ ▦**Den Gamle Arrest.** Spend the night in the clink at "The Old Jail," a simple yet cozy hotel housed in what was Ribe's main jail from 1893 to 1989. The artist-owner has done a brilliant job of modernizing the cells into comfortably habitable rooms, while preserving all the prison details. **Pros:** historical building; modern, with fun prison twist. **Cons:** few in-room amenities; no leisure facilities. ⊠*Torvet 11* ☎*75/42–37–00* ⊕*www.dengamlearrest.dk* ⤴*11 rooms, 4 with bath* ⚲*In-room: no phone, refrigerator (some), no TV (some). In-hotel: restaurant, parking (free), no-smoking rooms* ⊟*MC, V* ⓞⅠBP.

$$
Fodor'sChoice
★
▦**Hotel Dagmar.** The Dagmar, originally built in 1581 by a city alder-man, became an inn by 1800. Although ordinances prohibit such modern conveniences as an elevator, some contemporary touches are apparent. For a hotel of this vintage, standard rooms are quite comfort-able (though not lavish); some have canopy beds. The cheap amenities in the bathrooms are a bit of a surprise but shouldn't detract from the hotel's merits overall. The restaurant is fantastic, with seasonal set (two or six courses) and à la carte menus. The scallops topped with a sweet-

potato crisp and surrounded by vichyssoise is an excellent appetizer; the North Sea fish of the day in a lobster sauce is a smart idea for the main course. The hotel is next to the local tourist bureau and across the street from the 900-year old cathedral. **Pros:** well-regarded restaurant; historical hotel. **Cons:** no leisure facilities; parking fee DKr 90/day. ✉*Torvet 1* 📠*/5/42–00–33* ⊕*www.hoteldagmar.dk* ↘*48 rooms* ⌂*In-room: refrigerator, Wi-Fi. In-hotel: 2 restaurants, room service, but, laundry service, Wi-Fi, parking (paid), some pets allowed, no-smoking rooms* ▤*AE, DC, MC, V* ⛏*EP.*

SHOPPING

Antikgaarden (✉*Overdammen 5* 📠*75/44–19–47*) has a varied collection of Danish antiques, including old Royal Copenhagen plates. **Idé Butik Aps** (✉*Overdammen 4* 📠*75/42–14–14* ⊕*idebutikken-ribe.dk*) sells Danish crafts ranging from paper cutouts and glassware to figurines of Danish *nisser* (elves). For amber jewelry, head to **Rav I Ribe** (✉*Nedderdammen 32* 📠*75/42–03–99*), one of the largest amber purveyors in town.

BILLUND

40 km (25 mi) northwest of Kolding, 59 km (37 mi) northeast of Ribe, 101 km (63 mi) southwest of Århus.

Billund is the site of Denmark's second-biggest tourist attraction outside Copenhagen: Legoland. The son of the founder of the Lego Company, Godtfred Christiansen, invented the Lego toy brick in Billund in 1949; today the Lego Company employs approximately 6,500 people (2,500 of whom work in Billund). Over the years the company has manufactured more than 375 billion Lego bricks, all of which trace back to the modest facilities of the family home, which still stands on Main Street here.

Billund has grown exponentially with the Lego success, and today has its own international airport (constructed by Lego and then given to the community) and a large community center (also donated by Lego). However, outside of Legoland there's not much to keep you here—the bank in town is larger than the town hall, and you're in and out of the little metropolis before you know it.

GETTING HERE AND AROUND

Billund Airport is 3 km (2 mi) northeast of downtown. Car rentals are available here, but Buses 117, 406, and 907X can take you into the city center in approximately 15 minutes. (Bus 406 also runs directly to Kolding.) A free shuttle bus goes to Hotel Legoland. Other buses will take you to Århus, Esbjerg, Kolding, Vejle, or Odense.

If you're coming by car from Ribe, follow Route 32 approximately 10 km (6 mi) out of town, then take Route 425 toward Billund Airport. The drive takes approximately 45 minutes.

ESSENTIALS

Airport Info Billund Airport (📠*76/50–50–50* ⊕*www.billund-airport.dk*).

Pharmacy Billund Apoteksudsalg (✉ *Butikstorvet 3* ☎ *75/33–81–94*).

Taxis Billund-Give Taxa (☎ *75/35–35–06* ⊕ *www.billundgivetaxa.dk*).

Visitor Info Billund Erhvervs Fremme (✉ *Jorden Rundt 1, Grindsted* ☎ *79/72–72–02* ⊕ *www.visitbillund.dk*).

EXPLORING

☺ At the amazing **Legoland** everything is constructed from Lego bricks—
Fodor's Choice more than 50 million of them. Among its incredible structures are scaled-
★ down versions of cities and villages from around the world (Miniland),
with working harbors and airports; the Statue of Liberty; a statue of
Sitting Bull; Mt. Rushmore; a safari park; and Pirate Land.

Some of the park's other attractions are more interactive than the
impressive constructions. The Falck Fire Brigade, for example, allows
a family or group to race eight mini fire engines. The Power Builder
Robots allow children and adults to sit inside robots as they program
their own ride. ✉ *Normarksvej 9* ☎ *75/33–13–33* ⊕ *www.legoland.dk*
▨ *DKr 259* ☉ *Mid-Mar.–Oct. 25 open daily at 10; closing hrs vary
between 5 and 8 throughout the season; check the Web site.*

WHERE TO STAY

$$$$ ⛨ **Hotel Legoland.** It may be a bit pricier than other area hotels, but it is
☺ inside Legoland Village, and your room rate includes two days' admission to the park, breakfast, and access to Legoland through the hotel,
so you avoid the long lines at the park entrance. Many of the colorful
guest rooms overlook all the action. This hotel is beyond kid-friendly:
pictograms help children identify which room they are in and rooms
include the requisite Legos for kids of all ages to play with. The restaurant serves good meals, and, at lunch and dinner, a children's buffet
is also available. There's golf, tennis, and a pool nearby. **Pros:** family
friendly; activities for kids in summer; access to Legoland included in
rates. **Cons:** no in-room safes; rooms near the bar get noisy. ✉ *Aast-
vej 10* ☎ *75/33–12–44* ⊕ *www.hotellegoland.dk* ⇌ *199 rooms* ৬ *In-
room: refrigerator, Wi-Fi. In-hotel: restaurant, room service, bar, gym,
laundry service, Wi-Fi, parking (free), no-smoking rooms* ⊟ *AE, DC,
MC, V* ⎍ *BP.*

$ ⛨ **Hotel Propellen.** Very close to the airport (and to Legoland), this stylish
hotel is owned by the Danish Air Pilots Union; hence the name. Rooms
are tastefully furnished, if not as fun as those in Hotel Legoland. There's
a special summer menu in the restaurant, including an all-you-can-eat
ice-cream bar. Note that there's a DKr 30 discount if you pay in cash.
Pros: sauna. **Cons:** few overall amenities for the price. ✉ *Nordmarksvej
3* ☎ *75/33–81–33* ⊕ *www.propellen.dk* ⇌ *91 rooms, 3 suites* ৬ *In-
room: safe, refrigerator, Wi-Fi. In-hotel: restaurant, room service, bar,
pool, gym, laundry service, Wi-Fi, parking (free), some pets allowed,
no-smoking rooms* ⊟ *AE, DC, MC, V* ⎍ *BP.*

ÅRHUS

101 km (63 mi) northeast of Billund.

Århus is Denmark's second-largest city, and, with its funky arts and college community, one of the country's most pleasant. Cutting through the center of town is a canal called the Århus Å (Århus Creek). It used to run underground, but was uncovered a few years ago. Since then, an amalgam of bars, cafés, and restaurants has sprouted along its banks, creating lively thoroughfares. At all hours of the day and night this waterfront strip is abuzz with crowds that hang out on the outdoor terraces and steps that lead down to the creek.

The VisitÅrhus tourist office has information about the Århus Passport, which includes passage on buses, free or discounted admission to the 12 most popular museums and sites in the city, and tours.

GETTING HERE AND AROUND

From Copenhagen, follow E20 toward Esbjerg via the Storebælt Bridge (toll 205 DKr). At the highway, bear right after Exit 60 Fredericia V and continue on E45 north toward Århus/Vejle. Stay on E45 until you reach Århus. Alternativey, the DSB train takes approximately four hours and costs DKr 311. Abildskous Route 888 offers the cheapest bus service from Copenhagen to Århus at DKr 290.

From Billund, take Route 18 towards Horsens and pick up E45 toward Århus after taking Exit 57 Horsens south. At the Billund Airport, buses run directly to Århus. The trip takes about 1 hour and 30 minutes and costs DKr 180.

Århus airport, 45 km northeast of the city, has regular flights to Copenhagen, Gothenburg, Stockholm, Oslo, and London, as well as charters to southern Europe. Hourly buses run between Århus Airport and the train station in town. The trip takes around 50 minutes and costs DKr 90. There's also bus service (Bus 212) between Århus Airport and Randers and Ebeltoft. A taxi ride from the airport to central Århus takes 45 minutes and costs well over DKr 500.

For direct Zealand to Jutland passage, you can take a car-ferry hydrofoil from Zealand's Odden to Århus (one hour). You can also take the slower, but less expensive, car ferry from Kalundborg (on Zealand) to Århus (2 hours, 40 minutes). Both ferries travel five times daily on weekdays, and slightly less often on weekends. For ferry schedules and information, call Mols-Linien.

ESSENTIALS

Airport Info Århus Airport (☎ 87/75-70-00 ⊕ *www.aar.dk*).

Bus Info Abilskous Route 888 (☎ 70/21-08-88 ⊕ *www.abildskou.dk*).

Boat and Ferry Info Mols-Linien (☎ 70/10-14-18 ⊕ *www.molslinien.dk*).

Train Info DSB (☎ 70/13-14-15 ⊕ *www.dsb.dk*).

Visitor Info VisitÅrhus (✉ *Banegårdspl. 20*, ☎ 87/31-50-10 ⊕ *www.visitaarhus. com*).

EXPLORING

The **Rådhus** is probably the most unusual city hall in Denmark. Built in 1941 by noted architects Arne Jacobsen and Erik Møller, the pale Norwegian-marble block building is controversial, but cuts a startling figure when illuminated in the evening. The VisitÅrhus tourist board can arrange for a guide to take you through the building. Tours take about an hour and cost DKr 557. ⊠*Park Allé* ⊕*www.aarhus.dk* ⊙*Daily by guided tour only.*

WORD OF MOUTH

"I have dear friends who live near Århus, and so I've spent a great deal of time in that area. I love driving through the countryside, but for just a few hours; you'll find plenty to do in the city itself. One of the most interesting things is [Den Gamle By], a restoration of buildings typical for a city in that area from long, long ago."

—prizren

Rising gracefully over the center of town, the **Århus Domkirke** (*Århus Cathedral*) was originally built in 1201 in a Romanesque style but was expanded and redesigned into a Gothic cathedral in the 15th century. Its soaring, whitewashed nave is one of the country's longest. The cathedral's highlights include its chalk frescoes, in shades of lavender, yellow, red, and black, that grace the high arches and towering walls. Dating from the Middle Ages, they depict biblical scenes and the valiant St. George slaying a dragon and saving a maiden princess in distress. Also illustrated is the poignant death of St. Clement, who drowned with an anchor tied around his neck. Nonetheless, he became the patron saint of sailors. Climb the tower for bird's-eye views of the rooftops and thronged streets of Århus. ⊠*Bispetorv* ☎*86/20–54–00* ⊕*www.aarhus-domkirke.dk* ☜*Tower: DKr 10* ⊙*Oct.–Apr., Mon.–Sat. 10–3; May–Sept., Mon.–Sat. 9:30–4.*

★ Don't miss the town's open-air museum, known as **Den Gamle By** (*Old Town*). Its 75 historic buildings—including 70 half-timber houses, a mill, and millstream—were carefully moved from locations throughout Denmark and meticulously re-created, inside and out. ⊠*Viborgvej 2* ☎*86/12–31–88* ⊕*www.dengamleby.dk* ☜*DKr 50–DKr 100 depending on season and activities* ⊙*Jan. and Feb., daily 11–3; Feb.–mid-Mar., daily 10–4; mid-Mar.–June, and 2nd wk Sept.–3rd wk Nov., daily 10–5; July–1st wk Sept., daily 9–6; last wk Nov.–last wk Dec., Mon. and Tues., 9–5, Wed.–Fri. 9–7, weekends 10–7. Grounds always open.*

ARoS Århus Kunstmuseum, the city's newest art museum, was an immediate hit when it opened in April 2004, and 340,000 people passed through its doors in its first nine months of opening. On the top floor there's a restaurant as well as a rooftop patio—a photographer's dream. The art, of course, is paramount, and comprises the museum's own collection of more than 9,000 works dating from 1770 to the present, as well as internationally known visiting exhibits. ⊠*Aros Allé 2* ☎*87/30–66–00* ⊕*www.aros.dk* ☜*DKr 90* ⊙*Tues. and Thurs.–Sun. 10–5, Wed. 10–10.*

Just south of the city is **Marselisborg Slot** (*Marselisborg Castle*), the palatial summer residence of the royal family. The changing of the guard takes place daily at noon when the queen is here. When the royal family is away (generally in winter and spring), the grounds, including a sumptuous rose garden, are open to the public. You can get here on Bus 1, 18, or 19. ⊠*Kongevejen 100* ☎*No phone* ⊕*www.kongehuset. dk* ⊠*Free.*

In a 250-acre forest south of Århus is the **Moesgård Forhistorisk Museum** (*Prehistoric Museum*), with exhibits on ethnography and archaeology, including the famed Grauballe Man: a 2,000-year-old corpse so well preserved in a bog that scientists could determine his last meal. In fact, when the discoverers of the Grauballe Man stumbled upon him in 1952, they thought he had recently been murdered and called

ÅRHUS FESTIVALS

Århus comes most alive on the last Friday in August through the following week, when the Århus Festival (☎89/40-91-91 ⊕www.aarhusfestuge.dk) begins, combining concerts, theater, and art exhibitions with beer tents and sports. The **Århus International Jazz Festival** bills international and local greats in early or mid-July. In July the **Viking Moot** draws aficionados to the beach below the Museum of Prehistory at Moesgård. Activities and exhibits include market booths, ancient defense techniques, and rides on Viking ships.

the police. The Forhistorisk vej (Prehistoric Trail) through the forest leads past Stone- and Bronze Age displays to reconstructed houses from Viking times. ⊠*Moesgård Allé (Bus 6 from center of town), Høbjerg* ☎*89/42-11-00* ⊕*www.moesmus.dk* ⊠*DKr 45* ☉*Apr.–Sept., daily 10–5; Oct.–Mar., Tues.–Sun. 10–4.*

WHERE TO EAT

$$$
ECLECTIC
★
✕**Bryggeriet Sct. Clemens.** At this popular pub you can sit among copper kettles and quaff the local brew, which is unfiltered and without additives, just like in the old days. Between the spareribs and Australian steaks, you won't go hungry, either. ⊠*Kannikeg. 10–12* ☎*86/13–80–00* ⊕*www.bryggeriet.dk* ⊟*AE, DC, MC, V.*

$$$$
ECLECTIC
✕**Prins Ferdinand.** On the edge of old town, right next to the entrance of Den Gamle By, this premier Danish-French restaurant is named after the colorful Århus-based Prince Frederik (1792–1863), who was much loved despite (or perhaps because of) his fondness for gambling and carousing. Here elegant crystal chandeliers hang over large round tables with crisp linens and ceramic plates created by a local artist. Vases of sunflowers brighten the front room. Depending on the season, the three- or seven-course set menus might include grilled turbot topped with a cold salsa of radishes, cucumber, and dill or venison served with cabbage, foie gras, and new potatoes. A daily vegetarian option is offered, and might include grilled asparagus with potatoes, olives, and herbs. ⊠*Viborgvej 2* ☎*86/12–52–05* ⊕*www.prinsferdinand.dk* ⊟*AE, DC, MC, V* ☉*Closed Sun. and Mon.*

$$
DANISH
✕**Restaurant Margueritten.** Tucked into a cobbled courtyard, this cheery restaurant is housed in former stables, which accounts for the low wood beam ceiling. Well-worn wooden tables and tan walls round out the warm atmosphere. Contemporary Danish fare includes fish, veal,

and lobster dishes. In summer and early fall the back garden is open all day. ⊠ *Guldsmedg. 20* ☎ *86/19–60–33* ⊟ *AE, DC, MC, V* ⊘ *No lunch Sun. Closed mid-Dec.–mid-Jan.*

$$ ✕ **Seafood.** Just south of town is Marselis Harbor, a bustling little sail-
SEAFOOD boat cove surrounded by waterfront restaurants and cafés that draw
Fodor's Choice big crowds on sunny summer weekends. Here you'll find one of the best
★ seafood restaurants in Århus. Its signature dish, which draws moans of delight from diners, is a seafood bouillabaisse heaped with tiger prawns, squid, Norwegian lobster, and mussels, and served with aioli on the side. Other dishes include oven-baked catfish with asparagus and warm ginger butter. The restful interior has light-blue walls. ⊠ *Havnevej 44, Marselisborg* ☎ *86/18–56–55* ⊕ *www.seafoodaarhus.dk* ⊟ *AE, DC, MC, V* ⊘ *Closed Sun. Sept.–Apr.*

WHERE TO STAY

¢ ⊡ **Danhostel Århus.** As in all Danish youth and family hostels, the rooms here are clean, bright, and functional. The secluded setting in the woods near the fjord is downright beautiful. Unfortunately, the hostel can get noisy. Guests may use the kitchen. **Pros:** beautiful setting; games room. **Cons:** sometimes noisy; few in-room amenities; few leisure facilities. ⊠ *Marienlundsvej 10* ☎ *86/16–72–98* ⊕ *www.aarhus-danhostel.dk* ↩ *157 beds in 35 shared rooms, 11 with private shower* ♨ *In-room: no phone, no TV (some), Wi-Fi. In-hotel: restaurant, laundry facilities, Wi-Fi, parking (free), no-smoking rooms* ⊟ *AE, MC, V* ⊙ *EP* ⊘ *Closed mid-Dec.–mid-Jan.*

$$$ ⊡ **Hotel Ferdinand.** Occupying a prime spot along the canal, this hotel offers an original—but pricey—concept in lodging. Suites are in eight former studio apartments and four apartments in a later addition. Each suite has its own sumptuous style as well as original white wood-beam ceilings, huge gleaming bathrooms, and canal views. The plush restaurant, with wooden floors, black and white furnishings, and colored lights, serves French brasserie-style fare. **Pros:** large rooms; beautiful views. **Cons:** gets noisy outside; no no-smoking rooms, only two parking spaces. ⊠ *Åboulevarden 28* ☎ *87/32–14–44* ↩ *12 suites* ♨ *In-room: safe, kitchen (some), refrigerator, Internet, Wi-Fi. In-hotel: 2 restaurants, room service, bar, laundry facilities, Wi-Fi, parking (free), some pets allowed* ⊟ *AE, DC, MC, V* ⊙ *BP.*

$$$ ⊡ **Hotel Guldsmeden.** This intimate hotel is in a renovated 19th-century town house. Personal touches abound here. Rooms are done in natural tones and have teak shelves and Indonesian rugs; one has a claw-foot tub. The sunny garden blooms with flowers in summer, and the outdoor terrace is just the spot to enjoy breakfast of fruit, muesli, toast, and marmalade. **Pros:** organic breakfast; courtyard and terrace; French colonial rooms. **Cons:** only five parking spaces, only available at certain times of day; few leisure facilities. ⊠ *Guldsmedg. 40* ☎ *86/13–45–50* ⊕ *www.hotelguldsmeden.dk* ↩ *27 rooms, 20 with bath; 3 suites* ♨ *In-room: safe, refrigerator (some), DVD (some), Wi-Fi. In-hotel: restaurant, bicycles, Wi-Fi, parking (no fee), some pets allowed, no-smoking rooms* ⊟ *AE, DC, MC, V* ⊙ *BP.*

$$$ ⊡ **Hotel Royal.** In operation since 1838, Århus's grand hotel has wel-
★ comed such greats as musicians Artur Rubinstein and Marian Anderson.

Well-heeled guests enter through a stately lobby appointed with sofas, modern paintings, and a winding staircase. The layout of the rooms varies, but all have velour and brocade furniture and marble bathrooms. **Pros:** discounts at nearby golf course; luxurious decor; DVD players upon request. **Cons:** parking with fee DKr 100. ✉*Store Torv 4* ☎*86/12 00 11* 🌐*www.hotelroyal.dk* *69 rooms, 32 suites* *In-room: kitchen (some), refrigerator, Wi-Fi. In-hotel: restaurant, room service, bar, laundry service, Wi-Fi, parking (paid), no-smoking rooms* *AE, DC, MC, V* *BP.*

AFTER DARK

BARS AND LOUNGES

Café Svej (✉*Åboulevarden 22* ☎*86/12–30–31* 🌐*www.svej.dk*), on the canal, is a popular meeting spot for drinks and quiet chats in its Viennese-inspired decor. The friendly **Café Jorden** (✉*Badstueg. 3* ☎*86/19–72–22*) has a brass-and-wood bar and a heated outdoor terrace with a red awning. Students and young professionals mix with the chatty bar staff, who like to sing along to the pop and rock classics.

★ The **Café Under Masken** (*Under the Mask Café* ✉*Bispeg. 38000* ☎*86/18–22–66*), next door to the Royal Hotel, is the personal creation of Århus artist Hans Krull, who also designed the unique iron sculptures that grace the entrance to the hotel. The surreal bar is crammed with every type of mask imaginable, from grinning Balinese wooden masks to black-and-yellow African visages. Pygmy statues and stuffed tropical birds and fish line the shelves. Everything was collected by Krull and bar patrons. The back wall is lined with aquariums filled with exotic fish. As the manager puts it, "Everyone's welcome. This bar is a no-man's-land, a place for all the 'funny fish' of the world." If that's not enough of a draw, consider that the drink prices are some of the lowest in town, and more than 30 kinds of beer are on offer. It's open Monday through Saturday until 2 AM, and Sunday until midnight.

Carlton (✉*Rosensg. 23* ☎*86/20–21–22*) is a classy bar and restaurant, presided over by a carousel horse. Sip cocktails in the front bar-café, or dine on French fare in the dining room. The **Cockney Pub** (✉*Maren Smeds Gyde 8* ☎*86/19–45–77* 🌐*www.cockneypub.dk*) is just that, and a bit more. It offers an exclusive line of beers and a wide selection of whiskeys. It was awarded the Cask Marque medal in 2004, "for pubs which serve the perfect pint."

Delighting committed smokers everywhere (it advertises to them specifically), **Ris Ras Filliongongong** (✉*Mejlg. 24* ☎*86/18–50–06*), a self-described "sitting-room" with a major selection of beers, is never empty. **Sidewalk** (✉*Åboulevarden 56–58* ☎*86/18–18–66*) has a large waterfront terrace that draws crowds on warm nights; in the equally lively interior you can sip cocktails at the long bar or graze on tapas and light meals, including hummus with olives and salad topped with soy-roasted chicken.

CASINO

The **Royal Hotel** (✉*Store Torv 4* ☎*86/12–00–11*) houses the city's casino with blackjack, roulette, baccarat, and slot machines.

SHOPPING

With more than 800 shops and many pedestrian streets (Strøget, Frederiksgade, Sct. Clemensgade, Store Torv, and Lille Torv), this is a great place to play havoc with your credit cards. As befits a student town, Århus also has its "Latin Quarter," a jumble of cobbled streets around the cathedral, with boutiques, antiques shops, and glass and ceramic galleries that may be a little less expensive. In Vestergade street, you can turn on Grønnengade and stroll along Møllestien to see its charming old homes.

At the **Bülow Duus Glassworks** (⊠*Studsg. 14* ☎*86/12–72–86*) you can browse among delicate and colorful items from fishbowls to candleholders. While here, visit Mette Bülow Duus's workshop and witness the creation of beautiful glassware. **Folmer Hansen** (⊠*Sønderg. 43* ☎*86/12–49–00*) is packed with Danish tableware and porcelain, from sleek Arne Jacobsen–designed cheese cutters, ice buckets, and coffeepots to Royal Copenhagen porcelain plates.

For the best selection of Georg Jensen designs, head to the official **Georg Jensen** (⊠*Sønderg. 1* ☎*86/12–01–00* ⊕*www.georgjensen.com or www.damask.dk*) store. It stocks Jensen-designed and -inspired watches, jewelry, table settings, and art-nouveau vases. The textile designs of Georg Jensen Damask, in a separate department, are truly beautiful.

SILKEBORG

43 km (27 mi) west of Århus.

At the banks of the River Gudenå begins Jutland's Lake District. Here, you'll find Silkeborg, a small city surrounded by lakes and forests. The area between Silkeborg and Skanderborg contains some of Denmark's loveliest scenery and most of its meager mountains, including the 438-foot Himmelbjerget, at Julsø (Lake Jul), 15 km (10 mi) southeast of Silkeborg. You can climb the narrow paths through the heather and trees to the top, where an 80-foot tower stands sentinel. It was placed there on Constitution Day in 1875 in memory of King Frederik VII.

GETTING HERE AND AROUND

Trains by the Danish carrier Arriva leave Århus every half-hour for Silkeborg. The ride takes approximately 50 minutes, and costs DKr 78. By car, drive west on Route 15 toward Silkeborg. Local bus transportation is run by Midttrafik (⊕*www.midttrafik.dk*) and will take you all over Silkeborg, as well as into the surrounding areas for DKr 32. Buses run several times an hour, but service slows at night.

ESSENTIALS

Bus Info Midttrafik (☎*87/40–82–00* ⊕*www.midttrafik.dk*).

Medical Assistance Regionshospitalet Silkeborg (*Silkeborg Hospital*) (⊠*Falkevej 3* ☎*87/22–21–00*).

Train Info Arriva Skandinavien (☎*72/30–25–00* ⊕*www.arriva.dk*).

Visitor Info Silkeborg Tourist Office (⊠*Åhavevej 2A* ☎*86/82–19–11* ⊕*www.silkeborg.com*).

EXPLORING

The best way to explore the Lake District is by water, as the Gudenå winds its way some 160 km (100 mi) through lakes and wooded hillsides down to the sea. Take one of the excursion boats or the world's last coal-fired paddle steamer, *Hjejlen,* which departs in summer (mid-June through August) from Silkeborg Harbor. Since 1861 it has paddled its way through narrow stretches of fjord, where the treetops meet overhead, to the foot of the Himmelbjerget. ⊠*Havnen* ☎*86/82–07–66* ⊕*www.hjejlen.com* ☒*DKr 100.*

> ### SILKEBURG JAZZ FESTIVAL
>
> In late June, jazz-lovers from all over Europe come to celebrate Silkeborg's Riverboat Jazz Festival (☎ *86/80–16–17* ⊕ *www. riverboat.dk*), with live jazz performed on indoor and outdoor stages over four days. Attendance is consistent at 40,000–45,000 people, so be sure to reserve lodgings in advance.

The **Silkeborg Museum** isn't only the oldest building in the town, dating from 1767, it also houses the city's main attractions: the 2,400-year-old Tollund Man and Elling Girl, two bog people preserved by the chemicals in the soil and water. In addition, there are exhibits that showcase trades made famous in the area, such as clog and wheel making, and pottery and papermaking. The museum also has a fine collection of old Danish glass, a café, and a gift shop. ⊠*Hovedgårdsvej 7* ☎*86/82–14–99* ⊕*www.silkeborgmuseum.dk* ☒*DKr 45* ⊙*May–mid-Oct., daily 10–5; mid-Oct.–Apr., weekends noon–4.*

The eclectic **Silkeborg Museum of Art** contains Danish artist Asger Jorn's collection of more than 5,000 works by 150 international artists, including Max Ernst; Picabia; Le Corbusier; and such Danish contemporaries as Bjerke Petersen, Carl-Henning Pedersen, and Egill Jacobsen. Jorn's own works number around 100, in various mediums (paintings, ceramics, drawings, and graphics). ⊠*Gudenåvej 7-9* ☎*86/82–53–88* ⊕*www.silkeborgkunstmuseum.dk* ☒*DKr 60* ⊙*Apr.–Oct., Tues.–Sun. 10–5; Nov.–Mar., Tues.–Fri. noon–4, weekends 10–5.*

At the **Aqua Ferskvands Akvarium** (*Aqua Aquarium*), which is the largest freshwater aquarium in northern Europe, you can see beavers, otters, freshwater fish, and other animals in re-creations of their natural habitat. ⊠*Vejlsøvej 55* ☎*89/21–21–89* ⊕*www.aqua-ferskvandsakvarium. dk* ☒*DKr 95* ⊙*Jan.–June and mid-Aug.–mid-Dec., weekdays 10–4, weekends 10–5; July–mid-Aug., daily 10–6.*

WHERE TO EAT AND STAY

$$$

DANISH

×**Aalekroen.** Also known as Onkel Peters Hus (Uncle Peter's Place), this spot is noted for its house specialties: fried eel and seafood. The grilled meat dishes are also excellent. This old inn stands at the shore of a scenic lake. ⊠*Julsøvænget 5* ☎*86/84–60–33* ⊕*www.aalekroen.dk* ⚑*Reservations essential* ☐*AE, DC, MC, V* ⊙*Closed Mon. Oct.–Apr.*

$$

★

Radisson SAS Hotel Silkeborg. This business-class hotel was built within the main building of an old paper mill and is connected to a convention center (Jysk Musik & Teaterhus). Rooms are soothing, with slate-gray and warm yellow tones and relaxing river views. The Riverside Restaurant is considered Silkeborg's trendiest dining spot, and the food doesn't disappoint. **Pros:** close to city center; nice views; good restaurant. **Cons:** room-share fees for parents traveling with children; no on-site leisure facilities (you pay DKr 100 to access a nearby gym with pool and sauna). ⊠*Papirfabrikken 12* ☎*88/82–22–22* ⊕*www.radissonsas.com* ☞*100 rooms, 4 suites* ♿*In-room: safe, refrigerator, Internet. In-hotel: restaurant, room service, bar, laundry service, Wi-Fi, parking (free), some pets allowed, no-smoking rooms* ☰*AE, DC, MC, V* ⦿*BP.*

AALBORG

112 km (70 mi) north of Århus.

The gentle waters of the Limfjord cut off the top segment of Jutland completely. Perched on its narrowest point is Aalborg, Denmark's fourth-largest city, which includes the youthful Aalborg University, founded in 1974. Aalborg began in 692 as the gateway between north and mid-Jutland. It was granted a municipal charter in 1342, and the Limfjord has been crucial to the city's economy since the heyday of the herring industry.

GETTING HERE AND AROUND

From Silkeborg, drive east on Route 15 toward Århus, then north on E45 to Aalborg. The drive takes 1 hour and 40 minutes. City Bus 960X runs from Silkeborg to Aalborg. The ride takes just over two hours and costs DKr 162.

There's also a DSB train that runs between Silkeborg and Aalborg every hour. With an easy transfer in Skanderborg, the trip takes 2 hours and 20 minutes and costs DKr 216. Trains to Aalborg leave twice an hour from Copenhagen and take approximately five hours. A one-way ticket costs DKr 348.

Cimber and SAS have flights from Copenhagen to Aalborg several times a day, with tickets ranging DKr 300–DKr 2,000. Flights take approximately 45 minutes. Taxis and buses connect Aalborg Airport 7 km (4 mi) southeast of the city. A taxi costs around DKr 175 and takes roughly 10 minutes.

Nordjyllands Trafikselskab has buses connecting the airport to towns near Aalborg as well as those that take you around the city and its environs. Long-distance bus routes from Aalborg to Copenhagen (five hours) are available through Abildskou and cost approximately DKr 310.

ESSENTIALS

Airport Info Aalborg Airport (☎*98/17–11–44* ⊕*www.aal.dk*). **Cimber** (⊕*www.cimber.dk*). **SAS** (⊕*www.flysas.com*).

Bus Contacts Abildskou (⊠*Graham Bellsvej 40 Århus* ☎*70/21–08–88* ⊕*www.abildskou.dk*). **Nordjyllands Trafikselskab** (☎*98/11–11–11* ⊕*www.nordjyllandstrafikselskab.dk*).

Car Rental Avis (⊠*John F. Kennedys Plads 3A* ☎*70/24–77–40*). **Europcar**

(✉ *Jyllandsg. 6* ☎ *98/13–23–55* ⊕ *www.europcar.dk*). **PS Biludlejning** (✉ *Jyllandsg. 22* ☎ *96/30–01–04*).

Medical Assistance Aalborg Hospital (✉ *Hobrovej 18* ☎ *99/32–11–11*). **Budolfi Apotek** (*Pharmacy*) (✉ *Alg. 60* ☎ *98/12–06–77*).

Visitor Info VisitAalborg (✉ *Østeråg. 8* ☎ *99/31–75–00* ⊕ *www.visitaalborg.com*).

EXPLORING
TOP ATTRACTIONS

★ **Jens Bang Stenhus.** The local favorite landmark is the magnificent 17th-century *Jens Bang's Stone House*, built by the wealthy merchant Jens Bang in 1642. It was rumored that because he was never made a town council member, the cantankerous Bang avenged himself by caricaturing his political enemies in gargoyles all over the building and then adding his own face, its tongue sticking out at the town hall. The five-story building has been the home of Aalborg's oldest pharmacy for more than 300 years. Note that the Aalborg tourist office is directly across the street. ✉ *Østeråg. 99000.*

Jomfru Ane Gade. In the center of the old town is a street named, as the story goes, for an aristocratic maiden accused of being a witch, then beheaded. Now the it's fame is second only to that of Copenhagen's Strøget. Despite the flashing neon and booming music of about 30 discos, bars, clubs, and eateries, the street attracts a thick stream of pedestrian traffic and appeals to all ages.

Lindholm Høje. Just north of Aalborg at Nørresundby (still considered a part of greater Aalborg) is Lindholm Høje, a Viking and Iron Age burial ground where stones placed either in the shape of a ship or in triangles denote where men were buried; oval and circular groups of stones show where women were buried. In total, there are about 682 graves dating from AD 400 to shortly before AD 1000. At the bottom of the hill there is a museum that chronicles Viking civilization.

The **Viking Drama** (☎ *98/17–33–73* ⊕ *www.lindholmvikingespil.dk* 💳 *DKr 80*) is a musical and dramatic performance about the daily lives of the Vikings, held on the grounds of Lindholm Høje. It's performed in Danish, but the music, singing, dancing, and costumes don't need any translation. The show is performed mid-June through the month's end only at 7 PM on weekdays, 4:30 and 11 PM on Saturday, and 4:30 on Sunday. ✉ *Vendilavej 11* ☎ *99/31–74–40* 💳 *Burial ground free, museum DKr 30* ◷ *Apr.–Oct., daily 10–5; Nov.–Mar., Tues.–Sun. 10–4.*

V & S Distillers. In many parts of the world, Aalborg is identified more as a brand—a brand of schnapps, that is: the clear, potent liquor many Danes enjoy with herring. Since V & S Distillers bought Harald Jensen's still in 1883, the city's name has been linked with aquavit, and the world-famous schnapps still carries the name of Aalborg. You can take part in a two-hour guided tour of the plant, with a tasting and a stop at the company store. ✉ *C. A. Olesens Gade 1* ☎ *98/12–42–00* ⊕ *www. distillers.dk* 💳 *DKr 40–50* ◷ *July and Aug., 10–3, Sept.–June, 10–9.*

WORTH NOTING

Budolfi Kirke. The baroque *Cathedral Church of St. Botolph* is dedicated to the English saint. Eight cocks crow the hour from four identical clock faces on the tower. The stone church, replacing one made of wood, has been rebuilt several times in its 800-year history. It includes a copy of the original spire of the Rådhus in Copenhagen, which was taken down about a century ago. The money for the construction was donated to the church by a generous local merchant and his sister, both of whom, locals say, had no other family on which to lavish their wealth. ⊠ *Gammel Torv.*

Helligåndsklosteret. Next to Budolfi Kirke is the 15th-century *Monastery of the Holy Ghost.* One of Denmark's best-preserved monasteries—and perhaps the only one that admitted both nuns and monks. It's now a home for the elderly. The building was erected in several stages during the 15th century and the beginning of the 16th century, and coincidentally, the duties of the first nuns and monks were to look after the sick and aged. During World War II the monastery was the meeting place for the Churchill Club, a group of Aalborg schoolboys who became world famous for their sabotage of the Nazis—their schemes were carried out even after the enemy thought they were locked up. ⊠ *C. W. Obels Pl., Gammel Torv* ☎ *98/12–02–05* ☉ *Guided tours mid-June–mid-Aug., daily at 1:30.*

Nordjyllands Kunstmuseum. The blocky marble-and-glass structure of the *North Jutland Museum of Modern Art* was designed by architects Alvar and Elissa Aalto and Jacques Baruël. The gridded interior partition system allows the curators to tailor their space to each exhibition, many of which are drawn from the museum's permanent collection of 20th-century Danish and international art. On the grounds there are also a manicured sculpture park and an amphitheater that hosts occasional concerts. ⊠ *Kong Christians Allé 50* ☎ *98/13–80–88* ⊕ *www.nord jyllandskunstmuseum.dk* ☜ *DKr 40* ☉ *Tues.–Sun. 10–5; Feb.–Apr., Sept.–Nov., Tues. 10–9.*

WHERE TO EAT

¢
★
DANISH ✕**Duus Vinkjælder.** Most people come to this cellar—part alchemist's dungeon, part neighborhood bar—for a drink, but you can also get a light bite. In summer enjoy smørrebrød; in winter sup on grilled meats and the restaurant's special liver pâté. ⊠ *Østeråg. 9* ☎ *98/12–50–56* ▭ *DC, V* ☉ *Closed Sun.*

$$
DANISH ✕**Mortens Kro.** The chef-owner of Mortens Kro, Morten Nielsen, is a celebrity in these parts, and the food here is a delight, both visually and gastronomically. The menu changes monthly, but a starter might be steamed white asparagus with leeks in a mousseline sauce, with herbs and freshly shelled shrimp. A main course could be free-range veal tenderloin from North Jutland, marinated in basil and served with slow-baked small tomatoes and the ubiquitous new potatoes. Every inch of the restaurant is thoughtfully designed, even the washrooms—they're equipped with waterfalls and nature sound effects emanating from invisible speakers. Jackets aren't required, but a "business casual" look is a good way to go. ⊠ *Mølleå Arkaden* ☎ *98/12–48–60* ⊕ *www.*

mortenskro.com ⚲*Reservations essential* ▤*AE, DC, MC, V* ⊘*Closed Sun. Closed last 3 wks in July and last wk in Jan.*

$$$ ✕ **Søgaards Bryghus.** Microbreweries normally aren't upscale, but this
STEAK brew house is a cut above the rest. The spotless interior; piping hot food from the kitchen; attractive glassware, brass, and exposed brick; and lots of smiles make this pub special. It serves great food, like barbecued ribs, steaks, and fries; it even has its own in-house butcher. Tastings and tours can also be arranged, and if you're in Aalborg for a couple of days you can buy a liter of your favorite homemade brew in a Danish-designed bottle and return for refills. ✉*C. W. Obels Pl. 1A* ☎*98/16–11–14* ⊕*www.soegaardsbryghus.dk* ▤*AE, DC, MC, V.*

WHERE TO STAY

$ ▦ **Helnan Phønix.** In a central and sumptuous old mansion, this hotel is popular with vacationers as well as business travelers. Rooms are luxuriously furnished with plump chairs and polished, dark-wood furniture; in some, the original wooden ceiling beams are still intact. The Brigadier restaurant serves excellent French and Danish food. **Pros:** centrally located, well furnished. **Cons:** parking isn't free, no elevator to fifth floor (walk up from fourth). ✉*Vesterbro 77* ☎*98/12–00–11* ⊕*www.helnan.dk* ⌔*210 rooms, 2 suites* ⌖*In-room: safe, kitchen (some), refrigerator, Wi-Fi. In-hotel: restaurant, room service, bar, gym, laundry service, Wi-Fi, parking (paid), some pets allowed, no-smoking rooms* ▤*AE, DC, MC, V* ⏐◯⏐*BP.*

¢ ▦ **Hotel Hvide Hus.** This Best Western property is one of the city's few "high-rises," at 16 stories. The bright rooms have balconies overlooking Kildepark. It's a five-minute walk to the train station diagonally across the park or a 10-minute walk to the city center. Breakfasts in the topfloor Restaurant Kilden are more than adequate, and it's worth checking out the daily dinner specials in the same room. Meals are well presented in a relaxed atmosphere with a wonderful view of the city. Weekend rates are very reasonable. **Pros:** close to attractions; city and park views. **Cons:** street traffic makes rooms on lower floors noisy. ✉*Vesterbro 2* ☎*98/13–84–00* ⊕*www.hotelhvidehus.dk* ⌔*196 rooms, 2 suites* ⌖*Inroom: refrigerator, Wi-Fi. In-hotel: restaurant, room service, bar, gym, laundry service, Wi-Fi, parking (free), some pets allowed, no-smoking rooms* ▤*AE, DC, MC, V* ⏐◯⏐*BP.*

AFTER DARK

Consider a pub crawl along the famed Jomfru Ane Gade, popular for its party atmosphere and rock-bottom drink prices. Opt for the house drink of the night (usually a Danish beer), and you'll often pay one-third of the normal cost. There's variety in music and ambience, so if one place doesn't fit your mood, maybe the one next door will.

BARS

Dimly lighted and atmospheric, **Duus Vinkjælder** (✉*Østeråg. 9* ☎*98/ 12–50–56*) is one of the most classic beer and wine cellars in all of Denmark. It's an obligatory stop for anyone who wants a taste of Aalborg's nightlife. **L. A. Bar** (✉*Jomfru Ane Gade 7* ☎*98/11–37–37*) is a chatty, American-style bar. **Spirit of America** (✉*Jomfru Ane Gade 16* ☎*98/16–99–44* ⊕*www.spiritofamerica.dk*) is a good spot to catch an international soccer match on the bar's big-screen TV.

CASINO

The city's sole casino is at the **Radisson SAS Limfjord Hotel** (✉ *Ved Stranden 14–16* ☎*98/10–15–50* ⊕*www.casinoaalborg.dk*).

MUSIC AND DANCE CLUBS

Gaslight (✉*Jomfru Ane Gade 23* ☎*98/10–17–50*) plays rock and grinding dance music for a young crowd. **Le Bar Bat** (✉*Jomfru Ane Gade 25* ☎*98/13–32–41*) offers live music Thursday and Friday. The cozy, ground-floor bar of **Pusterummet** (✉*Jomfru Ane Gade 12* ☎*98/16–06–39*) is open during the day, but the second floor turns into a dance club on Friday and Saturday nights.

Rock Caféen (✉*Jomfru Ane Gade 7* ☎*98/13–66–90*) is for serious rock-and-roll lovers, with occasional metal concerts. **Rock Nielsen** (✉*Jomfru Ane Gade 9-11* ☎*98/13–99–29*) is a rock-and-roll dance club where disco music would most likely never be heard.

SKAGEN

88 km (55 mi) northeast of Aalborg.

For more than a century, Skagen (pronounced *skane*), a picturesque area where the North Sea meets the Baltic Sea, has been a favorite destination of well-off travelers, artists, and architects. This 600-year-old market town on Jutland's windswept northern tip has long pebbly beaches and huge open skies. Sunsets are tremendous events, so much so that idlers on the beach stop and applaud. Its main industry has traditionally been fishing, but tourism now seems to be eclipsing that.

GETTING HERE AND AROUND

From Aalborg, drive north on E45 to Frederikshavn, then continue north on Route 40 to Skagen. The drive should take approximately 90 minutes. Those traveling by train must transfer at Frederikshavn to Nordjyske Jernbaner, a local service that operates hourly on most days. The ride from Aalborg to Skagen costs DKr 120 and takes just over two hours.

ESSENTIALS

Car Rental Autohjoernet (✉*Kattegatvej 16* ☎*98/44–23–66*).

Train Info Nordjyske Jernbaner (☎*98/45–45–10* ⊕*www.njba.dk*).

Visitor Info Skagen Turistforening (✉*Vestre Strandvej 10* ☎*98/44–13–77* ⊕*www.skagen-tourist.dk*).

EXPLORING

★ The 19th-century Danish artist and nationally revered poet Holger Drachmann (1846–1908) and his friends, including the well-known P. S. Krøyer and Michael and Anna Ancher, founded the Skagen School of painting, which sought to capture the special quality of light and idyllic seascapes here. They and their contemporaries mostly enjoyed depicting everyday life in Skagen from the turn of the 20th century until the 1920s, and you can see their efforts on display in the **Skagen Museum**. It's a wonderful homage to this talented group of Danes, and you'll become mesmerized by some of the portraits, which seem more like a photographic collection of days gone by. Some of the more famous canvases may be on loan at museums throughout the world, but do try to visit, even if you're only in Skagen for a half day. The museum store sells posters, postcards, and other souvenirs depicting the Skagen paintings. ⊠*Brøndumsvej 4* ☎*98/44–64–44* ⊕*www.skagensmuseum. dk* ⊠*DKr 80* ☉*Feb.–Apr. and Sept.–Dec., Tues–Sun. 10–5; May–Aug., Thurs.–Tues. 10–5, Wed. 10–9.*

Michael and Anna Ancher are Skagen's—if not Denmark's—most famous artist couple, and their meticulously restored 1820 home and studio, **Michael og Anna Ancher's Hus,** is now a museum. Old oil lamps and lace curtains decorate the parlor; the doors throughout the house were painted by Michael. Anna's studio, complete with easel, is awash in the famed Skagen light. More than 240 paintings by Michael, Anna, and their daughter, Helga, grace the walls. ⊠*Markvej 2–4* ☎*98/44–30–09* ⊕*www.anchershus.dk* ⊠*DKr 40* ☉*Nov., Feb., and Mar., Sat. 11–3; Apr. and Oct., Sat.–Thurs. 11–3; May–Sept., daily 11–5.*

Fodor's Choice Danes say that in Skagen you can stand with one foot on the Kattegat, ★ the strait between Sweden and eastern Jutland, the other in the Skagerrak, the strait between western Denmark and Norway. It's possible to do this, but by no means go swimming here—it's very dangerous. The point is so thrashed by storms and roiling waters that the 18th-century **Tilsandede Kirke** (*Sand-Buried Church*), 2 km (1 mi) south of town, is covered by dunes, except for its tower. ⊠*Tower: DKr 10* ☉*Tower: June–Aug. 11–5.*

Even more famed than the Sand-Buried Church is the west coast's dramatic **Råbjerg Mile,** a protected migrating dune that moves about 50 feet a year and is accessible on foot from the Kandestederne.

WHERE TO EAT AND STAY

$$ ✕**Skagen Fiske Restaurant.** At first this place seems very unassuming, DANISH but it actually faces one of the two marinas that dock private yachts— in summer the restaurant's terrace is the place to see and be seen by the denizens of these vessels. On the ground floor a sand floor (over wood) greets you in the restaurant's pub; upstairs, the blue-and-white restaurant might reminder you of a warehouse attic, but this is Danish chic, and that's Russian abstract art on the walls. Upstairs or down, the Pandestegte *fiskefrikadelier* (fish cakes) are a must-try. Made from three Nordic fish and gently creamed with herbs and potatoes, they may be the restaurant's most popular item. Wash them down with a frosty Danish beer or lemon soda. Note that there's no dress code, but you'll want wear your best casual chic threads. Reservations are recommended. ⊠*Fiskehuskaj 13* ☎*98/44–35–44* ⊕*www.skagen-fiskerestaurant.dk* ⊟*DC, MC, V* ☉*Closed weekends in Nov. and for all Jan.*

$$ 🏨**Plesner Hotel & Restaurant.** This appealing hotel is a three-minute walk from the train station. Ulrik Plesner, a famous local architect responsible for many buildings in Skagen, designed this one as well. Rooms are bright, airy, and spotless. All have a private bath; rooms 21 and 22 have French windows. Guest quarters in the hotel's annex, although smaller, are charming and have little terraces. The dining room has

popular lunch specials, though note that it's only open from June 16 to August 14. **Pros:** fresh and clean; close to train station. **Cons:** no leisure facilties. ⊠*Holstvej 8* ☎*98/44–68–44* ⊕*www.hotelplesner.dk* ⤴*24 rooms, 2 suites* ⟋*In-room: Wi-Fi (some). In-hotel: restaurant, room service, Wi-Fi, no-smoking rooms* ☰*AE, DC, MC, V* ⦶*BP.*

\$\$\$\$ ⚏ **Ruths Hotel.** This is definitely the grande dame of Old Skagen, originally built by Emma and Hans Christian Ruth. It has been completely rebuilt with modern facilities, and its main restaurant, Ruth's Gourmet, is operated by Chef Michel Michaud, known for heading up the kitchens at such renowned venues as Kong Hans in Copenhagen. (The only drawback is that you have to call ahead at least a month in advance for a reservation during high season!) There's also a brasserie that serves French food prepared with local ingredients by any of Chef Michaud's 17 cooks. Rooms are typically lavish, in an understated way, and all have balconies or terraces and Swedish-made DUX beds; some have hot tubs. The Wellness Centre provides regular spa and beauty treatments, as well as some forms of laser cosmetic surgery. **Pros:** luxury amenities; all rooms have balconies or terraces. **Cons:** north wing gets noisy with street traffic; difficult to reserve table in Ruth's Gourmet during high season. ⊠*Hans Ruths Vej 1* ☎*98/44–11–24* ⊕*www.ruths-hotel.dk* ⤴*15 rooms, 18 suites* ⟋*In-room: safe, kitchen (some), DVD (some), Internet (some), Wi-Fi. In-hotel: 2 restaurants, pool, gym, spa, bicycles, laundry facilities, Wi-Fi, parking (free)* ☰*AE, DC, MC, V* ⦶*CP.*

\$\$\$\$ ⚏ **Strandhotellet.** Also in Old Skagen, this bright and romantic hotel is the perfect foil to the wild, windy sea- and sandscapes nearby. Built in 1912, it's filled with gently curved wicker furnishings, painted woods, and original art. Rooms are done in pastels, and are reminiscent of those from a country estate—a country estate that just happens to have Bang & Olufsen flat-screen televisions. The staff is accommodating, though in the off-season they may leave at 10 PM (returning the next morning to prepare a continental breakfast, of course). **Pros:** guests can use pool, spa, and gym at Ruths Hotel without charge; romantic setting. **Cons:** few on-site facilities; staff not on duty 24/7. ⊠*Jeckelsvej 2* ☎*98/44–34–99* ⊕*www.strandhotellet.glskagen.dk* ⤴*8 rooms, 12 suites, 2 houses* ⟋*In-room: safe, kitchen (some), DVD (some), Internet (some), Wi-Fi. In-hotel: restaurant, room service, bar, bicycles, laundry facilities, Wi-Fi, parking (free)* ☰*AE, DC, MC, V* ⦶*CP.*

SHOPPING

Skagen's artistic heritage and light-drenched landscapes continue to draw painters and craftspeople, meaning you'll find better-than-average souvenirs in town. The pedestrian street has a fascinating and intimate shopping atmosphere with stores as fine as those you'd see in Copenhagen.

For colorful, innovative handblown glass, for example, head for **Glaspusterblæser** (⊠*Sct. Laurentii Vej 33* ☎*98/44–58–75*), a large glassblowing workshop housed in what was once Skagen's post office. The amber store and workshop **Ravsliberen I Skagen** (⊠*Algade 12A* ☎*98/44–55–27* ⊕*www.ravsliberen.dk*) sells top-quality amber jewelry, including pieces with insects trapped inside.

Finland

WORD OF MOUTH

"We went to a neat town called Porvoo, also Turku, and did a lot of walking in Helsinki and visited the outdoor market on the waterfront. We also went to the ballet one night—beautiful building. The architecture in Helsinki is really interesting, and it's just a beautiful city where you can sit and enjoy coffee and cakes on the waterfront—weather permitting!"
— Nancy

"I appreciated the fact that local stores (including the famous Stockmann department store) had absolutely no "kitsch" on display. In general I thought Helsinki was one gorgeous and very stylish town."

— hsv

Updated by
Robert Brenner

IF YOU LIKE MAJESTIC OPEN spaces, fine architecture, and courteous locals, Finland is for you. Mother Nature dictates life in this Nordic land, where winter brings perpetual darkness, and summer, perpetual light. Crystal clear streams run through vast forests lighted by the midnight sun, and reindeer roam free. Even the arts mimic nature: witness the music of Jean Sibelius, Finland's most famous son, which can swing from a somber nocturne of midwinter darkness to the tremolo of sunlight slanting through pine and birch, or from the crescendo of a blazing sunset to the pianissimo of the next day's dawn. The architecture of Alvar Aalto and the Saarinens—Eliel and son Eero, visible in many U.S. cities, also bespeaks the Finnish affinity with nature, with soaring spaces evocative of Finland's moss-floored forests.

Until 1917, Finland was under the domination of its nearest neighbors, Sweden and Russia, who fought over it for centuries. After more than 600 years under the Swedish crown and 100 under the Russian czars, the country inevitably bears many traces of the two cultures, including a small (just under 6%) but influential Swedish-speaking population and a scattering of Orthodox churches.

There is a tough, resilient quality to the Finns, descended from wandering tribes who probably migrated from the south and southwest before the Christian era. Finland is one of the few countries that shared a border with the Soviet Union in 1939 and retained its independence. Indeed, no country fought the Soviets to a standstill as the Finns did in the grueling 105-day Winter War of 1939–40. This resilience stems from the turbulence of the country's past and from the people's determination to work the land and survive the long, dark winters.

The country's role as a crossroads between East and West is vibrantly reflected in Helsinki, from which it has become increasingly convenient to arrange brief tours to Tallinn (the capital of Estonia), and St. Petersburg, Russia. The architectural echoes of St. Petersburg in Helsinki are particularly striking in the "white night" light of June. Tallinn, with its medieval Old Town and bargain shopping, is a popular trip that can be done in a day. Traveling there takes an hour and a half by hydrofoil, three and a half by ferry.

"The strength of a small nation lies in its culture," noted Finland's leading 19th-century statesman and philosopher, Johan Vilhelm Snellman. As though inspired by this thought, Finns—who are among the world's top readers—continue to nurture a rich cultural climate, as is illustrated by its 900 museums and the festivals throughout Finland that continue to attract the top performers, in jazz (Pori), big bands (Imatra), opera (Savonlinna), folk music (Kaustinen), and rock (Ruisrock in Turku).

The average Finn volunteers little information, but that's a result of reserve, not indifference. Make the first approach and you may have a friend for life. Finns like their silent spaces, though, and won't appreciate backslapping familiarity—least of all in the sauna, still regarded by many as a spiritual as well as a cleansing experience.

ORIENTATION AND PLANNING

GETTING ORIENTED

Finland's capital, Helsinki, commands the southern coast and shelters more than one-tenth of the country's population. Towns were first settled in the southwest, where the culture of the South Coast and the Åland Islands has a decidedly Swedish influence. Northern Finland—Finnish Lapland—straddles the Arctic Circle and is sparsely populated. Finland's central region is dominated by the Lakelands, the country's vacation belt.

Helsinki. The mark of a storied Swedish and Russian heritage is overlaid with cool and calm Finnish character in the seaside capital city. Helsinki is a place to work as it hosts innumerable conferences and power-meetings and, increasingly, a place to play, owing to its repertoire of fine restaurants and its chic bar-lounge scene.

Southwestern Coast and the Ålands. Along the southwest coast resides the former capital, home to the country's most impressive medieval fortress, as well as Finland's best beaches set among former Russian villas. In summer, the living is breezy as many Finns and Swedes head to cottages on one of the thousands of gorgeous Åland Islands or party shamelessly on the ferries crossing to and from Stockholm.

The Lakelands. The recipe for a traditional Finnish summer requires a cabin, a sauna, a lake, and little else, and many Finns maintain all three ingredients here. Other regional attractions include the city of Tampere, a curious combination of high-tech industry and high culture, and a number of towns with medieval castles and big summer music and theater festivals.

Lapland. Europe's largest wilderness is the scene of hiking trails among brilliant foliage, endlessly skiable snowfields before the breathtakingly beautiful Northern Lights, the Sami (Northern Europe's indigenous people), and Santa Claus. It falls almost entirely within the Arctic Circle and its forests, rivers, and mountains are both at the root of *sisu* (unwaivering determination) and a great source of tranquillity, two qualities Finns value almost above all else.

PLANNING

WHEN TO GO

Finland's tourist season begins in June, when the growing daylight hours herald the opening of summer restaurants and outdoor museums, and the start of boat tours and cruises. Summer is by far the best time to visit Helsinki, the Lakelands, and the Southwestern Coast and Ålands, which come out of hibernation for the long, bright, but not overly hot, summer days. A special draw in the Lakelands is the Savonlinna Opera Festival, held in late July or early August.

Finland can also be exhilarating on clear, brisk winter days. For a real treat, visit Lapland—home of Santa Claus in December. Operating on a different schedule altogether, the tourist season in the north focuses on

TOP REASONS TO GO

■ **East Meets West.** Helsinki displays a provocative blend of Swedish and Russian influences. Admire the double headed golden eagle symbolizing imperial Russia in the market square as well as the clean lines of the Scandinavian-designed wares in stores around it, and taste Russian-style Baltic Herring and the delicacies of a Swedish smörgåsbord in the same meal.

■ **Feel the Heat.** Finns love their saunas. There are more than 2 million hot spots here, the majority in small cabins separate from their owners' summer cottages. The best of 'em are located at water's edge, ensuring a short commute from stifling heat to an invigorating dip in a lake or the Baltic.

■ **Arctic Wonder.** Finns' characteristic modesty concerning their country is cast aside when they speak of cross-country skiing under the Northern Lights or hiking during the short autumn in Lapland's deciduous forests.

■ **A Mind for Design.** In big-name stores like Marimekko and Iittala, as well as the boutique shops of the Design District in Helsinki and smaller towns and cities, you'll find homewares, furniture, clothing, and accessories of exceptional craftsmanship and style.

winter events, when the snow is deep and the northern lights bright. Ski trips in Lapland in early spring are popular and many resorts offer tourist packages. Summer weather in Lapland offers a different repertoire to the traveler, when the snow and ice of the north give way to flowing rivers and greenery. The Midnight Sun Film Festival in Sodankylä offers round-the-clock screenings in tents.

CLIMATE

Yours truly, can expect warm (not hot) days in Helsinki from mid-May, and in Lapland from mid-June until September. The midnight sun can be seen from May to July, depending on the region. For a period in midwinter, the northern lights almost make up for the fact that the sun does not rise at all. Even in Helsinki, summer nights are brief and never really dark, whereas in midwinter, daylight lasts only a few hours.

The following are average daily maximum and minimum temperatures for Helsinki.

Jan.	16°F	8°C	May	41°F	5°C	Sept.	43°F	6°C
	26°F	3°C		59°F	15°C		56°F	13°C
Feb.	15°F	-9°C	June	49°F	9°C	Oct.	36°F	2°C
	27°F	2°C		66°F	18°C		46°F	7°C
Mar.	23°F	-5°C	July	53°F	11°C	Nov.	28°F	-2°C
	34°F	1°C		70°F	21°C		36°F	2°C
Apr.	31°F	-1°C	Aug.	51°F	10°C	Dec.	20°F	-6°C
	45°F	7°C		66°F	18°C		30°F	1°C

BUSINESS HOURS

Banks are open weekdays 9 to 4 or 5. Many offices and embassies close at 3 from June to August. Stores are generally open weekdays 9 to 6 and Saturday 9 to 1 or 2 and are closed Sunday.

Major holidays include: New Year's Day, Easter Sunday and Monday, May Day ("Vappu," May 1), Whitsunday (between mid- and the end of May), Midsummer Eve and Day (late June), Independence Day (December 6), Christmas Eve and Day, and Boxing Day (day after Christmas).

GETTING HERE AND AROUND
AIR TRAVEL

Finnair offers domestic and international flights, with daily direct service from New York (JFK) and twice-weekly from Boston in summer, and flights six times a week from New York during the rest of the year. Scandinavian Airlines operates two flights a day from both Newark and Chicago, one to Stockholm and one to Copenhagen, with connections on to Helsinki. It also offers service from Seattle and Washington D.C. to Copenhagen. Flying time from New York to Helsinki is eight hours, nine hours for the return trip.

All international flights arrive at Helsinki–Vantaa International Airport (HEL), 20 km (12 mi) north of city center.

Air Contacts Helsinki–Vantaa International Airport (⊕ *www.ilmailulaitos.fi*). **Finnair** (⊕ *www.finnair.com*). **SAS Scandinavian Airlines** (⊕ *www.scandinavian. net*).

BOAT TRAVEL

From Stockholm, Silja and Viking Line ships cross to the Finnish Åland Islands (7 hours), Turku (11 hours), and Helsinki (15 hours), generally with one departure daily in each direction.

Finland is still a major shipbuilding nation, and the ferries that cruise the Baltic to the Finnish Åland Islands and Sweden seem more like luxury liners. Facilities might include saunas, children's playrooms, casinos, a host of bars and cafés, and superb restaurants. There are storage boxes for luggage in the Helsinki and Stockholm terminals if you are planning a day of sightseeing in either city.

In Helsinki the Silja Line terminal for ships arriving from Stockholm is at Olympialaituri (Olympic Harbor), on the west side of the South Harbor. The Viking Line terminal for ships arriving from Stockholm is at Katajanokkanlaituri (Katajanokka Harbor), on the east side of the South Harbor. Both Silja and Viking have downtown agencies where information and tickets are available. Ask about half-price fares for bus and train travel in conjunction with ferry trips.

Boat and Ferry Info Silja Line (☎ *09/18041 in Helsinki* ⊕ *www.silja.com*). **Viking Line** (☎ *09/12351 in Helsinki* ⊕ *www.vikingline.fi*).

BUS TRAVEL

The Finnish bus network, Matkahuolto, is extensive, and the fares reasonable. You can travel the network between Finland and Norway, Sweden, or Russia.

Bus Info **Matkahuolto** (☎ *0200/4000 in Helsinki €1.50 per minute plus local charge for national timetable, 09/0136 8133 ⊕ www.matkahuolto.com*).

CAR TRAVEL

Driving is pleasant on Finland's relatively uncongested roads. That said, car rental here isn't cheap: regular daily rates range from about €80 to €160, and unlimited mileage rates are the norm.

Late autumn and spring are the most hazardous times to drive. Roads are often icy in autumn (*kelivaroitus* is the slippery road warning), and the spring thaw can make for *kelirikko* (heaves). Driving is on the right-hand side of the road. You must use headlights at all times, and seat belts are compulsory for everyone. Yield to cars coming from the right at most intersections. The use of cell phones while driving is not permitted. There are strict drinking-and-driving laws in Finland, and remember to watch out for elk and reindeer signs, placed where they are known to cross the road.

Outside urban areas, speed limits vary between 60 kph and 100 kph (37 mph and 62 mph), with a general speed limit of about 80 kph (50 mph). In towns the limit is 40 kph to 60 kph (25 mph to 37 mph) and on motorways it's 100 kph to 120 kph (62 mph to 75 mph).

Car Travel Info **Automobile and Touring Club of Finland** (☎ *09/7258–4400 in Helsinki, 0200/8080 24-hr road service ⊕ www.autoliitto.fi*).

GASOLINE Gasoline costs about €1.50 per liter. Nearly all gas stations are self-service. Those in Helsinki and on major roadways are open 24 hours.

PARKING You can usually park on the right-hand side of the road. In town, you'll find meters everywhere you're required to pay for parking; there are also a few pay-by-the-hour garages. In winter, signs in Finnish posted a week in advance will announce snow plowing. Metered parking can cost up to €2 per hour.

TAXI TRAVEL

Taxis go everywhere in Finland. The meter starts at about €5 daytime and about €7.70 evenings and weekends. The price per-kilometer increases with the number of passengers. In cities people generally go to one of the numerous taxi stands and take the first one available. You can hail a cab, but most are on radio call. Most taxi drivers take credit cards. Tipping is unnecessary; if you want to leave something, round up to the nearest euro. A receipt is a *kuitti*.

Taxi Info **Taxi Center** (☎ *0100/0700 €1.15 plus 8 cents per 10 seconds plus local charge, 0100/06000 €1.15 plus 8 cents per 10 seconds plus local charge for advance bookings ⊕ www.taksihelsinki.fi*).

TRAIN TRAVEL

Passenger trains leave Helsinki twice daily for St. Petersburg (5½ hours) and once daily on an overnighter to Moscow (13 hours). Remember that you need a visa to travel to Russia. To get to northern Sweden or Norway, you must combine train–bus or train–boat travel.

The Finnish State Railways, or VR, serve southern Finland well, but connections in the central and northern sections are scarcer and are supplemented by buses. Helsinki is the main junction, with Riihimäki to the north a major hub. You can get as far north as Rovaniemi and Kemijärvi by rail, but to penetrate farther into Lapland, you'll need to rely on buses, domestic flights, or local taxis.

Note that all train travelers in Finland must have a reserved seat, but it is possible to buy a seat ticket on the train. Special fast trains (Intercity and the Helsinki-Turku Pendolino) are more expensive but also more comfortable. First- and second-class seats are available on all express trains.

Train Info Finnish Railways (*VR* ☏ *0600/41–902 €1 plus local network charge* ⊕ *www.vr.fi*). **Rail Europe** (☏ *888/382-7245* ⊕ *www.raileurope.com*).

RESTAURANTS

Most restaurants open at 11 for lunch, switch to a dinner menu at 4, and close their kitchens around 11; virtually all non-hotel restaurants are closed on Sunday. Finns generally prefer to eat at 7 or 7:30 when dining out, thus rarely is it necessary to make a reservation for a seating before 7 or after 9. No dress codes are stated and jackets are rarely required, however at top restaurants it is expected that patrons look sharp. Take note that restaurants in the bigger cities are often closed in July.

Finnish food emphasizes freshness rather than variety, although in keeping with European trends, restaurants are becoming more innovative and expanding on classic Finnish ingredients—from forest, lake, and sea.

The better Finnish restaurants offer some of the country's most stunning game—pheasant, reindeer, hare, and grouse—accompanied by wild-berry compotes and exotic mushroom sauces. The chanterelle grows wild in Finland, as do dozens of other edible mushrooms, the tasty morel among them. Fish wears many hats in Finland, and is especially savored smoked. Come July 21, crayfish season kicks in.

Other specialties are *poronkäristys* (sautéed reindeer), *lihapullat* (meatballs in sauce), *uunijuusto* (light, crispy baked cheese), and *hiilillä paistetut silakat* (charcoal-grilled Baltic herring). *Seisova pöytä*, the Finnish version of the smorgasbord, is a cold and hot buffet available at breakfast, lunch, or dinner, and is particularly popular on cruise ships.

Local yogurt and dairy products are extremely good and ice cream is popular; an increasing number of places sell low-fat flavors or frozen yogurts, although the fat-free craze hasn't completely taken over. Finnish desserts and baked goods are renowned. *Mämmi*, a dessert made of wheat flour, malt, and orange zest and served with cream and sugar, is a treat during Easter. More filling are *karjalan piirakka*, thin, oval rye-bread pierogi filled with rice or mashed potatoes and served warm with *munavoi*, a mixture of egg and butter. *Munkki* (doughnuts), *pulla*

CUTTING COSTS

Travelers posting in the Travel Talk Forums at Fodors.com recommend the following budget saving tips.

BUS AND CAR TRAVEL

For trips on Matkahuolto (the Finnish bus network) that are longer than 80 km (50 mi) one-way, children ages 4–11 get a discount of 50%; senior citizens and teens between 12 and 16 get 30%. Adults in groups of three or more are entitled to a 25% discount. Children under 4 travel free with an adult.

For car rentals, look into package rates for three- and seven-day trips, and watch for weekend and summer discounts. It's cheaper to rent directly from the United States before coming to Finland; most agencies allow booking through their Web sites. Some Finnish service stations also offer car rentals at reduced rates.

TRAIN TRAVEL

Children ages 6–16 travel half-fare. There is a 15% reduction when 3–10 people travel together and a 20% discount for groups of 11 or more. Senior citizens (over 65) can get 50% discounts on train fares. With a Familyticket, children under 17 travel free when accompanied by an adult with a full-priced ticket.

The Finnrail Pass gives unlimited first- or second-class travel within a month's time for passengers living permanently outside Finland; the 3-day pass costs €131, the 5-day pass €175, and the 10-day pass €237 (€195, €260, and €353, respectively, for first-class). Children under 17 receive a 50-percent discount. Passes can be purchased from the Finnish Railways, or VR. TourExpert at

the Helsinki City Tourist Office also sells Finnrail passes.

Eurail's Scandinavia rail pass allows unlimited second-class travel throughout Denmark, Finland, Norway, and Sweden, and comes in various denominations. It is valid for 4 days of unlimited travel in any two-month period ($367); 5 days of unlimited travel in two months ($407); 6 days in two months ($463); 8 days ($515); 10 days ($571). It must be used within six months of purchase. A rail pass with similar conditions is available for travel solely within Finland.

Contacts DER Travel Services (☎ 800/782-2424 ⊕ www.der. com). **Finnish Railways** (VR ☎ 0600/41–902 €1 plus local network charge ⊕ www.vr.fi). **Rail Europe** (☎ 888/382-7245 ⊕ www. raileurope.com).

SHOPPING

Residents of countries outside the EU can recover 10% to 16% of the value-added tax (VAT) by going through the "tax-free for tourists" procedure: when you ask for your tax rebate—and be sure to ask for it at the point of purchase—you'll get a tax-free voucher and your goods in a sealed bag. The minimum purchase required is €40. Present the voucher and unopened bag at tax-free cashiers when leaving Finland or when departing the EU. These are located at most major airports, at the departure terminals for most long-distance ferries, and at major overland crossings into Norway and Russia. The tax refund can also be credited to a credit card account.

(sweet bread), and other confections are consumed with vigor by both young and old.

Alcohol is expensive here, but beer lovers should not miss the well-made Finnish brews. That more coffee is consumed per capita in Finland than in any other country is evidenced by the staggering number of cafés and coffee bars throughout the country. Particularly in Helsinki, patrons of cafés downtown and around the waterfront spill outside onto the streets.

HOTELS
Every lodging class exists in Finland, from luxurious urban hotels to rustic cabins on lake shores and in the forest. Expect private baths in rooms unless otherwise noted. Prices almost always include a generous breakfast and sauna privileges.

Look for room-rate discounts on weekends and in summer months, especially between *Juhannus* (Midsummer, the summer solstice holiday in late June) and July 31, when prices are usually 30% to 50% lower.

COTTAGE RENTALS
Those looking for the genuine Finnish experience should rent a cottage. Sun Cottages offers 30 one- and two-bedroom retreats in the Korpilampi area of northern Espoo. Lomarengas is one of the largest Web resources, listing and booking cottages for rent throughout the country.

Contacts Sun Cottages (☎ *0400/602–108* ⊕ *www.aurinkohuvilat.fi*). **Lomarengas** (☎ *306/502–502* ⊕ *www.lomarengas.fi*).

WHAT IT COSTS IN EUROS				
¢	$	$$	$$$	$$$$
MAIN CITIES				
Restaurants under €10	€10–€17	€17–€23	€23–€29	over €29
Hotels under €80	€80–€140	€140–€190	€190–€240	over €240
ELSEWHERE				
Restaurants under €10	€10–€16	€16–€20	€20–€25	over €25
Hotels under €70	€70–€105	€105–€140	€140–€175	over €175

Restaurant prices are based on the median main course price at dinner. Hotel prices are for two people in a standard double room in high season.

HOSTELS
During the summer season (June–August) many university residence halls open their doors to visitors. Accommodation in dormitories is usually in double rooms with shared toilet, shower, and cooking facilities among two to three rooms. In addition, regular youth hostels are available to all travelers year-round regardless of age and have various types of accommodations, including single and double rooms. Prices can range from €10 to €30 per person. Meals are generally available in a coffee shop or cafeteria.

Contacts **Finnish Tourist Board** (☎ *09/417–6911 in Helsinki* ⊕ *www.visitfinland. com*). **Finnish Youth Hostel Association** (☎ *09/565–7150 in Helsinki* ⊕ *www. srmnet.org*).

ESSENTIALS

ELECTRICITY The electrical current in Finland is 220 volts, 50 Hz. Outlets take the Continental plugs, with two round prongs. To use your North American blow-dryer, for example, you'll need both a converter and an adapter.

EMERGENCIES The nationwide emergency number is 112. Late-night pharmacies are only in large towns. Look under *Apteekki* in the phone book; listings include pharmacy hours. The U.S. embassy is in Helsinki.

Contact U.S. Embassy (✉ *Itäinen Puistotie 14B, Helsinki* ☎ *09/616–250, 09/6162–5730 consular section inquiries Mon.–Thurs. 3–4* ⊕ *www.usembassy.fi*).

ENTRY REQUIREMENTS U.S. citizens need a valid passport for stays of up to three months.

LANGUAGE Finnish, the principal language, is a Finno-Ugric tongue related to Estonian with distant links to Hungarian. The country's second official language is Swedish, although only about 6% of the population speaks it as their primary language. In the south, most towns have Finnish and Swedish names; if the Swedish name is listed first, it indicates more Swedish than Finnish speakers live in that area. A third language, Sami, is actually a group of languages spoken by the Sami, the original dwellers of Lapland in the north, and has semiofficial status in certain northern areas. English is spoken in most cities and resorts.

MONEY MATTERS **Currency and Exchange.** Finland uses the euro, abbreviated as EUR or the symbol €. Euro bills are divided into 5, 10, 20, 50, 100, 200, and 500. The euro is divided into 100 cents in denominations of 1-, 2-, 5-, 10-, 20-, and 50-cent coins as well as €1 and €2 coins. At this writing the exchange rate was €0.79 to the U.S. dollar, €1.18 to the pound sterling, and €0.64 to the Canadian dollar.

There are exchange bureaus in all bank branches and major hotels; Forex booths in major cities; and at Helsinki–Vantaa Airport. Some large harbor terminals also have exchange bureaus, and international ferries have exchange desks. Local banks and Forex offices usually give the best rates and charge a minimal commission. You can also change back any unused currency (no coins) at no fee with the original receipt. An exchange cart moves through the trains to Russia.

Pricing. The strength of the euro may make Finland seem somewhat expensive to travelers from non-euro countries.

Sample Prices. A cup of coffee, €2.50; glass of beer, starting from €4; soft drink, €3; ham sandwich, €4.50; 2-km (1-mi) taxi ride, €6–€9 (depending on time of day).

Taxes. There's a 22% sales tax on most consumer goods, 17% on food, and 8% on transportation; all taxes are included in the listed price of an item. Residents of countries outside the EU can recover 12% to 16% on unopened purchases over €40 by going through the "tax-free for tourists" procedure (⇨ *"Cutting Costs" box*).

Tipping. Tipping is not the norm in Finland but is becoming more of a habit, so use your own discretion. Finns normally do not tip cab drivers, but if they do they round up to the nearest euro. Give one euro to train or hotel porters. Coat-check fees are usually posted, and tips above this amount are not expected.

PHONES   The country code for Finland is 358. You must begin all direct overseas calls with 990, 996, 999, or 00, plus country code (e.g., 1 for the United States and Canada). If you're dialing out of your immediate area within Finland, dial 0 first; drop the 0 when calling Finland from abroad.

Dial ☎020–208 for overseas information or to place collect calls. Dial 118 or 020202 for information in Helsinki and elsewhere in Finland; 020208 for international information (€3.49 per minute plus local charge).

Major urban areas in Finland have moved to a phone-card system, and most phones only accept cards (no coins), which fortunately are usually available nearby at post offices, R-kiosks, and some grocery stores. Public phones charge a minimum of about €0.50. Most pay phones have picture instructions illustrating how they operate. Note that regional phone companies have their own cards that don't work in telephones in other regions. The main companies include Sonera, Elisa (Helsinki), and Soon Communications (Tampere).

Finland, like most European countries, has a different cellular-phone switching system from the one used in North America. Newer phones can handle both technologies; check with the dealer where you purchased your phone to see if it can work on the European system, in which case you can rent prepaid SIM cards from R-Kiosks throughout the country. Telephone companies including Sonera and DNA rent and sell old phones.

VISITOR INFO   **Contact Finnish Tourist Board** (✉ *Suomen Matkailun edistämiskeskus, Töölönk. 11, Helsinki* ☎ *09/417–6911 in Helsinki, 212/885–9700 or 800/346–4636 in New York* ⊕ *www.visitfinland.com*).

HELSINKI

A city of the sea, Helsinki was built along a series of odd-shape peninsulas and islands jutting into the Baltic coast along the Gulf of Finland. Streets and avenues curve around bays, bridges reach to nearby islands, and ferries ply among offshore islands.

Having grown dramatically since World War II, Helsinki now absorbs more than one-tenth of the Finnish population and the metropolitan area covers a total of 764 square km (474 square mi) and 315 islands. Most sights, hotels, and restaurants cluster on one peninsula, forming a compact central hub. The greater Helsinki metropolitan area, which includes Espoo and Vantaa, has a total population of more than a million people.

Helsinki is a relatively young city compared with other European capitals. In the 16th century, King Gustav Vasa of Sweden decided to woo trade from the Estonian city of Tallinn and thus challenge the Hanseatic League's monopoly on Baltic trade. Accordingly, he commanded the people of four Finnish towns to pack up their belongings and relocate at the rapids on the River Vantaa. The new town, founded on June 12, 1550, was named Helsinki.

For three centuries, Helsinki (Helsingfors in Swedish) had its ups and downs as a trading town. Turku, to the west, remained Finland's capital and intellectual center. Ironically, Helsinki's fortunes improved when Finland fell under Russian rule as an autonomous grand duchy. Czar Alexander I wanted Finland's political center closer to Russia and, in 1812, selected Helsinki as the new capital. Shortly afterward, Turku suffered a disastrous fire, forcing the university to move to Helsinki. The town's future was secure.

Just before the czar's proclamation, a fire destroyed many of Helsinki's traditional wooden structures, precipitating the construction of new buildings suitable for a nation's capital. The German-born architect Carl Ludvig Engel was commissioned to rebuild the city, and as a result, Helsinki has some of the purest neoclassical architecture in the world. Add to this foundation the influence of Stockholm and St. Petersburg with the local inspiration of 20th-century Finnish design, and the result is a European capital city that is as architecturally eye-catching as it is distinct from other Scandinavian capitals. You are bound to discover endless delightful details—a grimacing gargoyle; a foursome of males supporting a balcony's weight on their shoulders; a building painted in striking colors with contrasting flowers in the windows. The city's 400 or so parks make it particularly inviting in summer.

Today, Helsinki is still a meeting point of eastern and western Europe, which is reflected in its cosmopolitan image, the influx of Russians and Estonians, and generally multilingual population. Outdoor summer bars ("terrassit" as the locals call them) and cafés in the city center are perfect for people-watching on a summer afternoon.

GETTING HERE AND AROUND

AIR TRAVEL All domestic and international flights to Helsinki use Helsinki-Vantaa International Airport, 20 km (12 mi) north of the city center.

Local bus 615 runs between the airport and the main railway station downtown from 1:50 AM to 1:20 AM. The fare is €3.60 and the trip takes about 40 minutes. Finnair buses carry travelers to and from the railway station (Finnair's City Terminal) every 20 minutes, with a stop at the Scandic Hotel Continental Helsinki. Stops requested along the route from the airport to the city are also made. Travel time from the Scandic Hotel Continental to the airport is about 35 minutes from the main railway station; the fare is €5.90. Buses to most airport hotels are free.

A limousine ride into central Helsinki will cost €95–€236, depending on size and make of vehicle. Contact Limousine Service if ordering from abroad. There's a taxi stop at the arrivals building. A cab ride into central Helsinki costs about €30. Driving time is 20 to 35 minutes, depending on the time of day. Airport Taxi costs €30–€35 for one to four passengers, and operates shuttles between the city and the airport. If you are going to the airport, you must reserve by 7 PM the day before departure. Leaving from the airport, you do not need a reservation—just look for the Airport Taxi stands in the arrivals halls. The yellow line taxi stand at the airport also offers fixed-rate trips into the city.

BOAT TRAVEL   A ferry to the Suomenlinna fortress island runs about twice an hour, depending on the time of day, and costs €2 one-way and €3.80 round-trip. Ten-trip tickets issued for city public transport can be used on the ferry, too. From June to August, private water buses run from Kauppatori to Suomenlinna, charging €3.50 one-way and €5.50 round-trip.

CAR TRAVEL   Ring Roads One and Three are the two major highways that circle the city. Mannerheimintie and Hämeentie are the major trunk roads out of Helsinki. Mannerheimintie feeds into Highway E12, which travels north and takes you to the ring roads. Hämeentie leads you to Highway E75 as well as Roads 4 and 7. From either route, you will find directions for Highway 45 to the airport or, from the eastern edge of the city, you can take Mäkelänkatu, which merges into 45. For specific route information, contact the Automobile and Touring Club of Finland or the tourist office.

PUBLIC   Bus and tram networks are compact but extensive, and service is fre-
TRANSIT   quent, with more infrequent service nights and on Sunday. Pick up a route map at the tourist office—many stops do not have them. Tickets bought from the driver cost €2.20 for buses and €2 for trams. You can also buy a tourist ticket for unlimited travel on public transportation within the city (€6 one day, €12 three days, €18 five days), or purchase the Travel Card, loaded with an amount or for a time period. Purchase your tickets from the automated machine at stops and stations, rather than on-board, in order to avoid a service charge. Extensive information on routes, fares, and timetables is available from the Helsinki City Transport Web site. The Helsinki Kortti (Helsinki Card) allows unlimited travel on city public transportation, free entry to many museums, a free sightseeing tour, and other discounts. It's available for one, two, or three days (€30, €40, or €50, respectively). You can buy it at more than 70 places, including the airport (information desks), ferry terminals, some hotels and travel agencies, Stockmann's department store, the Hotel Booking Centre, the Helsinki City Tourist office, or online through Helsinki Expert; contact them for more information.

TAXI TRAVEL   There are numerous taxi stands; central stands are at Rautatientori at the station, the main bus station, Linja-autoasema, and in the Esplanade. Taxis can also be flagged, but this can be difficult, as many are on radio call and are often on their way to stands, where late-night lines may be very long. An average taxi ride in Helsinki can cost around €10; a taxi from the airport can cost €30 or more. All taxis in Helsinki go through the Taxi Center, or you can call Kovanen, a private company for taxis, vans, luxury minibuses, and limousine services.

TRAIN TRAVEL   Helsinki's suburbs and most of the rest of southern, western, and central Finland are well served by trains. Travel on trains within the city limits costs the same as all public transport, €2 or less if you use a Travel Card (which carries an initial fee of €9 but reduces the cost of each trip; you can buy the card for specific amounts or time periods). A single regional ticket costs €4 and is good for 80 minutes, including transfers. Regional tourist tickets are available for one day (€12), three days (€24), and five days (€36).

ESSENTIALS

3

Airport Info Airport Taxi (☎ *0600/555–555*). **Helsinki-Vantaa Airport** (☎ *09/82771* ⊕ *www.ilmailulaitos.fi*). **Limousine Service** (☎ *09/2797–800 in Helsinki* ⊕ *www.limousineservice.fi*).

Boat and Ferry Info Suomenlinna Ferry (☎ *0100–111*).

Car Info Automobile and Touring Club of Finland (☎ *09/7258–4400, 0200/8080 24-hr road service* ⊕ *www.autoliitto.fi*).

Hospitals Meilahden Sairaala (✉ *Haartmaninkatu 4, Meilahti* ☎ *09/4711*). **Töölön Sairaala** (✉ *Töölönk. 40, Töölö* ☎ *09/4711*).

Public Transport Info Helsinki City Transport (☎ *09/310-1071* ⊕ *www.hel.fi/hkl*).

Taxis Kovanen (☎ *0200/6060 €1.25 per minute plus local charge, open 24 hrs* ⊕ *www.kovanen.com*). **Taxi Center** (☎ *0100/0700 €1.15 plus 8 cents per 10 seconds plus local charge, 0100/06000 € 1.15 plus 8 cents per 10 seconds plus local charge for advance bookings* ⊕ *www.taksihelsinki.fi*).

24-Hour Pharmacy Yliopiston Apteekki (✉ *Mannerheim. 96, Töölö* ☎ *0300/20200 (€0.40 per minute plus local charge)*.

Visitor Info Helsinki City Tourist and Convention Bureau (✉ *Pohjoisespl. 19, Esplanadi Helsinki* ☎ *09/3101–3300* ⊕ *www.hel.fi/tourism*).

EXPLORING HELSINKI

The city center, characterized by its large multistory malls, is densely packed and easily explored on foot, the main tourist sites grouped in several clusters; nearby islands are easily accessible by ferry. Just west of Katajanokka, Senaatintori and its Tuomiokirkko (Luthern Cathedral) mark the beginning of the city center, which extends westward along Aleksanterinkatu. The wide street Mannerheimintie is comparable to New York's Broadway, moving diagonally past the major attractions of the city center before terminating beside the Esplanade. Southern Helsinki is a tangle of smaller streets, some of them curving and some of which run for just a few blocks before changing their names; carry a good map while exploring this area.

IN AND AROUND KAUPPATORI

The orange tents of the Kauppatori market brighten even the coldest snowy winter months with fresh flowers, fish, crafts, and produce. In warm weather, the bazaar fills with shoppers who stop for the ubiquitous coffee and munkki, the seaborne traffic in Eteläsatama or South

Harbor a backdrop. From here you can take the local ferry service to Suomenlinna (Finland's Castle), Korkeasaari (Korkea Island), home of the zoo, or take a walk through the neighborhoods of Helsinki, encompassing the harbor; city center shopping district; tree-lined Bulevardi; and the indoor Hietalahden Tori, another marketplace.

TOP ATTRACTIONS

❻ **Havis Amanda.** This fountain's brass centerpiece, a young woman perched on rocks surrounded by dolphins, was commissioned by the city fathers to embody Helsinki. Sculptor Ville Vallgren completed her in 1908 using a Parisian girl as his model. Partying university students annually crown the Havis Amanda with their white caps on the eve of Vappu, the May 1 holiday. ⊠*Eteläespl. and Eteläranta, Keskusta/ Kauppatori.*

❷ **Kauppatori** *(Market Square).* At this Helsinki institution, open year-
★ round, wooden stands with orange and gold awnings bustle in the mornings when everyone—tourists and locals alike—comes to shop, browse, or sit and enjoy coffee and conversation. You can buy a freshly-caught perch for the evening's dinner, a bouquet of bright flowers for a friend, or a fur pelt. In summer the fruit and vegetable stalls are supplemented by an evening arts-and-crafts market. The crepes made-to-order by one of the tented vendors are excellent. ⊠*Eteläranta and Pohjoisespl., Keskusta/Kauppatori* ۞*Sept.–May, weekdays 6:30–2, Sat. 6:30–3; June–Aug., weekdays 6:30–2 and 3:30–8, Sat. 6:30–3, Sun. 10–4; hrs can vary.*

❽ **Obeliski Keisarinnan Kivi** *(Czarina's Stone).* This obelisk with a double-headed golden eagle, the symbol of Imperial Russia, was erected in 1835, toppled during the Russian Revolution in 1917, and fully restored in 1972. ⊠*Kauppatori along Pohjoisespl., Keskusta/Kauppatori.*

㉙

★ A former island fortress, **Suomenlinna** *(Finland's Castle)* is a perennially popular collection of museums, parks, and gardens, and has been designated a UNESCO World Heritage Site. In 1748 the Finnish army helped build the impregnable fortress, long referred to as the Gibraltar of the North; since then it has expanded into a series of interlinked islands. Although Suomenlinna has never been taken by assault, its occupants surrendered once to the Russians in 1808 and came under fire from British ships in 1855 during the Crimean War. Today Suomenlinna makes a lovely excursion from Helsinki, particularly in early summer when the island is engulfed in a mauve-and-purple mist of lilacs, introduced from Versailles by the Finnish architect Ehrensvärd.

Suomenlinna is easily reached by public ferry (€2.20 one-way, €3.50 round-trip) or private boat (€3.50 one-way, €5.50 round-trip), both of which leave from Helsinki's Kauppatori. The ferry ride from South Harbor to Suomenlinna takes about 15 minutes. Plan to spend an afternoon on the islands; you'll need about four hours to explore the fortress and museums. Note that days open and hours of sites are limited off-season.

Although its fortification occupied six islands, its main attractions are now concentrated on three: Iso Mustasaari, Susisaari, and Kustaanmiekka. There are no street names on the island, so get a map for about €2 from the Helsinki City Tourist Office before you go, or buy one at the visitor center on the island. From June 1 to August 31, guided English-language tours leave daily at 11 AM and 2 PM from the Suomenlinna Visitor Centre (⊠*Suomenlinna* ☎*09/684–1880, 09/684–1850 tours* ⊕*www. suomenlinna.fi*); call to arrange tours at other times. The center, which is in the same building as the Suomenlinna Museum, is on the shore of Tykistölahti Bay, about 400 yards south of the main ferry terminal

Fodor's Choice ★ The **Suomenlinna Museo** *(Suomenlinna Museum)* is housed in the same building as the visitor center, and exhibits cover the building of the fortress and the fleet and early life on islands; the ticket price includes the *Suomenlinna Experience* multimedia show. ⊠*Iso Mustasaari, Suomenlinna* ☎*09/4050–9691* ⊠*€5* ⊙*May–Aug., daily 10–6; Oct.– Apr., daily 10–4.*

❶ ★ **Vanha Kauppahalli** *(Old Market Hall).* From piles of colorful fish roe to marinated Greek olives, the old brick market hall on the waterfront is a treasury of delicacies. The vendors set up permanent stalls with decorative carved woodwork. ⊠*Eteläranta, along South Harbor, Kauppatori* ⊙*Weekdays 8–6, Sat. 8–4.*

WORTH NOTING

Ehrensvärd Museo. *This museum* is named for Augustin Ehrensvärd, the military architect who directed the fortification of the islands of Suomenlinna from 1748 until 1772, the year of his death. Exhibits include a model-ship collection and officers' quarters dating from the 18th century. Ehrensvärd's tomb is in the adjacent castle courtyard. ⊠*Suomenlinna B 40, Suomenlinna* ☎*09/684–1850* ⊠*€3* ⊙*Apr., weekends 11–4; early May–Aug., daily 10–5; Sept., daily 11–4; guided tour in English 11 AM and 2 PM, €6.50.*

❼ **Jugendsali.** Originally designed as a bank in 1906, this now serves as a cultural information office and the main booking point for Helsinki Expert tours. In addition to brochures, the office has free publications detailing the city's nightlife, dining, and arts scenes. ⊠*Pohjoisespl. 19, Kauppatori* ☎*09/310–11111* ⊙*May–Sept., weekdays 9–8, weekends 9–6; Oct.–Apr., weekdays 9–6, weekends 10–4.*

⓫ **Hietalahden Tori** *(Hietalahti Market).* The brick market hall is crammed with vendors selling fish, flowers, produce, and meat. You can also find antiques, collectibles, and art. A simultaneous outdoor flea market has tables piled with the detritus of countless Helsinki attics and cellars. Shoppers can stop amid the action for coffee, doughnuts, and meat pies. This market is especially popular with Helsinki's Russian community. ⊠*Bulevardi and Hietalahdenk., Hietalahti* ⊙*Regular market weekdays 6:30–2, Sat. 6:30–3; flea market weekdays 8–2, Sat. 8–3; market hall weekdays 10–5, weekends 10–3; summer evening flea market weekdays 3:30–8, Sun. 10–4.*

196 <

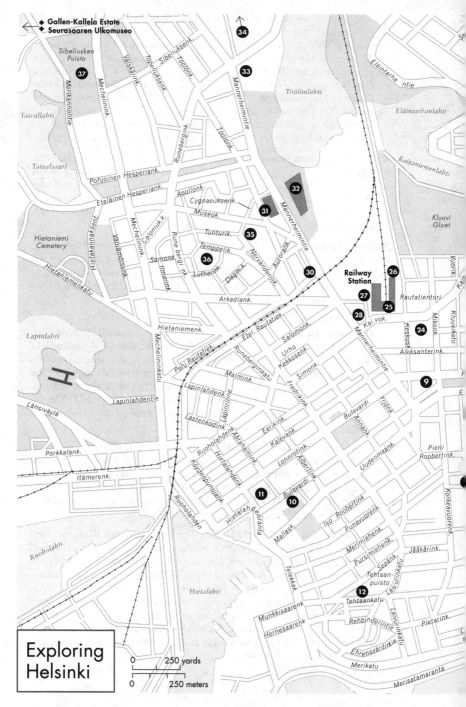

◆ Gallen-Kallela Estate
◆ Seurasaaren Ulkomuseo

Sibeliuksen Puisto
37

Taivallahti

Taivalsaari

Hietaniemi Cemetery

Lapinlahti

Pohjoinen Hesperiank.
Eteläinen Hesperiank.

Apollonk.
Cygnaeuksenk.
Museok.
31
32
Tunturik.
35
Temppelik.
36
Lutherink.
Dagm. k.
Samonk.
30

Arkadiank.

Hietaniemenk.

Etel. Rautatiek.

Pohj. Rautatiek.

Hietaniemenkatu

Mechelininkatu

Länsiväylä

Lapinlahdentie

Porkkalank.

Itämerenk.

Ruoholahti

Hietalahti

Merikannontie
Mechelinink.
Välskärink.
Topeliuksenk.
Sibeliuksenk.
Töölönk.
Runebergink.
Töölönk.

Mannerheimintie

Töölönlahti

Eläintarha ntie

Eläintarhanlahti

Kaisaniemenlahti

Kluuvi Gloet

Mannerheimintie

Runebergintie
Salomonk.
Urho Kekkosenk.
Simonk.
Fredrikink.

Malmink.

Lapinlahdenk.

Lastenkodink.

Ruoholahdenk.
Abrahamink.
Eerikink.
Kalevank.
Lonnrotink.
Albertink.

Bulevardi
11
10

Hietalahdenranta

Hietalahdenk.
Köydenpunojank.

Ruoholahden

Mallask.

Telekak.

Munkkisaarenk.
Hernesaarenk.

Railway Station
27
28
Kai vok.
26
25
Rautatientori

Keskusk.
Mikonk.
Aleksanterink.
24

9

Yrjönk.
Annank.

Bulevardi

Uudenmaank.

Pieni Roobertink.

Iso Roobertink.
Punavuoren.
Merimiehenk.
Pursimiehenk.
Sepänk.
Jääkärink.
Korkeavuoren.

Tehtaan-puisto
12
Tehtaankatu

Rehbinderintie

Laivurinkatu

Pietarink.

Ehrensvärdintie

Merikatu

Merisatamaranta

Vuorik.
Kluuvikatu

Exploring
Helsinki

0   250 yards

0   250 meters

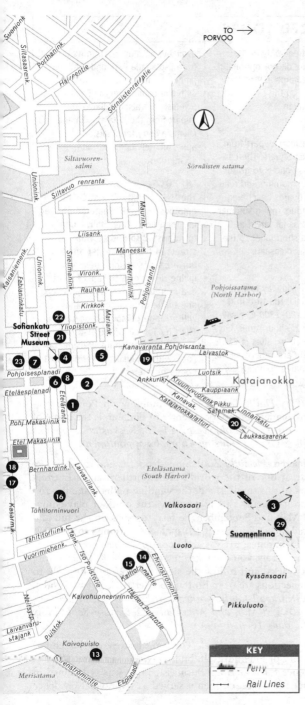

3

ORGANIZED TOURS

Tours run most frequently in the summer yet some do not operate in early June or September. Visit the city tourist office on the Esplanade for more information.

BY BOAT

Most major boat tours depart from Kauppatori Market Square. The easiest way to choose one is to go to the square in the morning and read the information boards describing the tours. Most tours run in summer only. You can go as far afield as Porvoo or take a short jaunt to the Helsinki Zoo on Korkeasaari.

BY BUS

Bus tours are a good way to get oriented in Helsinki. The **Helsinki Expert** (☎ *09/2288–1600* ⊕ *www. helsinkiexpert.fi*) 1½-hour Audio City Tour of central Helsinki sites is €11 with the Helsinki Card; otherwise the cost is €25. Recorded commentary is available on a headset. Tours leave from Esplanade Park and the Katajanoka Terminal. Guided city tours, with live commentary in English and Swedish, are also available; they depart from the Katajanokka and Olympia Ferry terminals and last approximately one hour and 45 minutes.

ON FOOT

The Helsinki City Tourist Office employs "Helsinki Helpers," dressed in green and white. Daily, June to August, 8 to 8, they walk the streets in the city center and harbor area, answering questions and giving directions. Helsinki Expert is a multipurpose travel agent and guide-booking center that will arrange personal tour guides. The City Tourist Office also has an excellent brochure, *Helsinki on Foot*, with six walks covering most points of interest.

4 **Kaupungintalo** *(City Hall).* The light blue building on Pohjoisesplanadi (North Esplanade), the political center of Finland, is the home of city government offices. ⊠ *Pohjoisespl. 11–13, Keskusta/Kauppatori* ☎ *09/169–2598* ☉ *Guided tours on Thurs. by appointment.*

3 **Korkeasaari Eläintarha** *(Helsinki Zoo).* Snow leopards and reindeer like
⟳ the cold climate at one of the world's most northern zoos. Entirely within the limits of this small island, the winding paths make the zoo seem larger than it actually is. Children love the outdoor play equipment. Between May and September the ferry departs on the full and half-hour from Market Square; (€10) includes entrance to the zoo. The trip takes 15 minutes; arrival and departure times are posted at the harbor. Alternatively, you can take the metro to the Kulosaari stop, cross under the tracks, and follow the signs for a 20-minute walk to the zoo. Bus connections are from Erottaja or Herttoniemi (weekends). ⊠ *Korkeasaari (Korkea Island), Korkeasaari* ☎ *0600/95911* ⊕ *www. korkeasaari.fi* ☜ *€5* ☉ *Mar. and Apr., daily 10–6; May–Sept., daily 10–8; Oct.–Feb., daily 10–4.*

5 **Presidentinlinna** *(President's Palace).* The long history of this edifice mirrors the history of Finland itself: built between 1813 and 1820 as a private residence for a German businessman, it was redesigned in 1843 as a palace for the czars; then it served as the official residence of Finland's presidents from 1919 to 1993. Today it houses the offices of Finland's first female president, Tarja Halonen, and is the venue for official receptions. The best part of the house is said to be its hall of mirrors. It is closed to the public except for prearranged group tours organized by Helsinki Expert, the Helsinki Tourist Association, on Wednesday and Saturday 11–3. ✉*Pohjoisespl. 1, Keskusta/Kauppatori* ☎*09/2288–1222.*

⑩ **Sinebrychoffin Taidemuseo** *(Sinebrychoff Museum of Foreign Art).* The wealthy Russian Sinebrychoffs owned a brewing company and lived in this splendid yellow-and-white 1840 neo-Renaissance mansion filled with wildly opulent furniture. The family's home and foreign art collection are now a public museum; you'll find a staid collection of Dutch and Swedish 17th- and 18th-century portraits, a lively collection of landscapes, miniatures, and porcelain, and the mansion's original decorative furniture. Concerts are occasionally held in the museum's main salon. ✉*Bulevardi 40, Hietalahti* ☎*09/1733–6460* ⊕*www.fng.fi* ✉*€7* ⊙*Tues. and Fri. 10–6, Wed. and Thurs. 10–8, weekends 11–5.*

⑨ **Svenska Teatern** *(Swedish Theater).* Dating from 1827, the first wooden theater on this site was considered too vulnerable to fire and was replaced by a stone building in 1866. Ironically, the stone building was itself nearly destroyed by a fire. In 1936, a team of architects—Eero Saarinen and Jarl Eklundhe among them—renovated it. The white-washed round theater today displays an attractive shape and dignified simplicity of design. The Swedish Theater's own company performs plays in Swedish year-round. ✉*Pohjoisespl. 2, Esplanadi/Erottaja* ☎*09/6162–1411* ⊕*www.svenskateatern.fi* ⊙*Box office daily noon–6* PM; *closed May–Aug.*

NEED A BREAK?

The **Café Aalto** (✉*Pohjoisespl. 39, Esplanadi* ☎*09/121–4446*), on the Academic Bookstore's mezzanine, is pleasant for lunch or a snack. Choose one of the sandwiches, which usually include cold-smoked salmon, herring, tuna, mozzarella, and vegetarian options, or a fresh soup or salad, which change daily. It's a good place for a traditional afternoon *pulla* (Finnish sweet bread) and coffee.

RESIDENTIAL AND SEASIDE HELSINKI

Bordered by the sea, the south side of Helsinki is resplendent with elegant 20th-century residences and parks with winding paths. The waterfront Kaivopuisto, the city's oldest and best-known park, leads into the upscale embassy neighborhood. Bordering this is another posh waterfront neighborhood, Eira, which has some of the city's most expensive and highly coveted old apartments, built in Jugend style.

TOP ATTRACTIONS

⓯ **Cygnaeuksen Galleria** *(Cygnaeus Gallery)*. This diminutive gallery, in a cottage with a tower overlooking the harbor, is the perfect setting for works by various Finnish painters, sculptors, and folk artists. This was once the summer home of Fredrik Cygnaeus (1807–81), a poet and historian who generously left his cottage and all the art inside to the Finnish public. ⊠*Kalliolinnantie 8, Kaivopuisto* ☎*09/4050–9628* ⌨*€4* ⊗ *Wed. 11–7, Thurs.–Sun. 11–4.*

⓲ **Designmuseo** *(Design Museum)*. **Fodor'sChoice** The best of Finnish design can be ★ seen here in displays of furnishings, jewelry, ceramics, and more. ⊠*Korkeavuorenk. 23, Keskusta* ☎*09/622–0540* ⊕*www.design museum.fi* ⌨*€7* ⊗*Sept.–May, Tues. 11–8, Wed.–Sun. 11–6; June– Aug., daily 11–6.*

Gulf of Finland Archipelago. In winter Finns walk across the frozen sea with dogs and even baby buggies to the nearby islands. On the land side, the facades of the Eira and Kaivopuisto districts' grandest buildings form a parade of architectural splendor. One tradition that remains, even in this upscale neighborhood, is rug-washing in the sea—an incredibly arduous task. You may be astounded to see people leave their rugs to dry in the sea air without fear of theft. ⊠*South of Merisatamaranta, Merisatama.*

WORTH NOTING

⓭ **Kaivopuisto** *(Well Park)*. This large, shady, path-filled park was once the site of a popular spa that drew people from St. Petersburg, Tallinn, and all of Scandinavia until its popularity faded during the Crimean War. All the spa structures were eventually destroyed (the main spa building was destroyed during WWII) except one, the **Kaivohuone,** now a popular bar-restaurant. Across from the entrance of Kaivohuone, take Kaivohuoneenrinne through the park past a grand Empire-style villa built by Albert Edelfelt, father of the famous Finnish painter who bore the same name. Built in 1839, it is the oldest preserved villa in the park. ⊠*South of Puistok. on water, Kaivopuisto.*

⓮ **Mannerheim Museo** *(Mannerheim Museum)*. Marshal Karl Gustaf Mannerheim (1867–1951) was a complex character sporting a varied résumé: he served as a high-level official in the Russian czar's guard, was a trained anthropologist who explored Asia, and is revered as a great general who fought for Finland's freedom and later became the country's president. The Mannerheim Museo is inside the great Finnish military leader's well-preserved family home and exhibits his letters

> **BIKING**
>
> Helsinki and environs make for excellent biking through a decent network of trails, many traversing the downtown area and running through parks, forests, and fields. The free area sporting map ("Ulkoilukartta") gives details of all trails; pick up a copy at the tourist office. Daily rentals, including mountain bikes, are available from **Green Bike** (☎*50/550–1020* ⊕*www.greenbike.fi*). The city also has bikes with fluorescent wheels for free—drop a coin in the slot as a deposit, take a ride, and drop it off at any of 26 sites around the city.

and personal effects. European furniture, Asian art, and military medals and weaponry are on display. ⊠*Kalliolinnantie 14, Kaivopuisto* ☎*09/635–443* ⊕*www.mannerheim-museo.fi* ⊠*€8, includes guided tour* ⊙*Fri.–Sun. 11–4, Mon.–Thurs. by appointment.*

⑫ **Mikael Agricolan Kirkko** *(Mikael Agricola Church)*. Built in 1935 by Lars Sonck, this church is named for the Finnish religious reformer considered to be the father of written Finnish. Mikael Agricola (circa 1510–57) wrote the first Finnish children's speller, the *Abckirja* (published around 1543), and translated the New Testament into Finnish (published in 1548). The church's sharp spire and tall brick steeple are visible amid **Tehtaanpuisto,** a small neighboring park. The inside of the church is quite bare, and no visitors are allowed except during Sunday services. ⊠*Tehtaank. 23A, Eira* ☎*09/709–2255* ⊙*Open only during Sun. services.*

⑰ **Suomen Rakennustaiteen Museo** *(Museum of Finnish Architecture)*. Stop in to buy an architectural map of Helsinki that includes locations of several buildings by Alvar Aalto, the most famous being Finlandiatalo in Töölö. The permanent exhibits of this museum are far from comprehensive, and specialists will want to visit the extensive library and bookstore. ⊠*Kasarmik. 24, Keskusta* ☎*09/8567–5100* ⊕*www.mfa.fi* ⊠*€3.50* ⊙*Tues., Thurs., Fri. 10–4, Wed. 10–8, weekends 11–4.*

⑯ **Tähtitorninvuori** *(Observatory Tower Hill)*. Named for the astronomical observatory within its borders, this park has sculptures, winding walkways, and a great view of the South Harbor. The observatory belongs to the astronomy department of Helsinki University and is closed to the public. ⊠*West of Laivasillank. and South Harbor, Kaivopuisto.*

NEED A BREAK?

Café Ursula (⊠*Ehrenströmintie. 3, Kaivopuisto* ☎*09/652–817)* **by the sea,** with views across to Suomenlinna, is a favorite among locals for coffee, ice cream, pastries, and light lunches that include soups and salads made with traditional Finnish ingredients. The lunch menu, which changes daily, includes fresh fish specialties, fish or root-vegetable soups, and a steak dish.

KATAJANOKKA AND SENAATINTORI

Katajanokka is separated from the mainland by a canal and begins just east of Kauppatori. A charming residential quarter as well as a cargo- and passenger-ship port, this area also has one of the city's main landmarks, the dazzling Orthodox Uspenskin Katedraali, one of the biggest cathedrals in Europe. Not far from Katajanokka is the elegant Lutheran Cathedral that dominates Senaatintori. The Ateneumin Taidemuseo is also nearby.

TOP ATTRACTIONS

㉔ ★ **Ateneumin Taidemuseo** *(Atheneum Art Museum of the Finnish National Gallery)*. The best traditional Finnish art is housed in this splendid neoclassical complex, one of three museums organized under the Finnish National Gallery umbrella. The gallery holds major European works, but the outstanding attraction is the Finnish art, particularly the works of Akseli Gallen-Kallela, inspired by the national epic *Kalevala.* The rustic portraits by Albert Edelfelt are enchanting, and many contemporary Finnish artists are well represented. The two other museums that make up the National Gallery are **Kiasma** and **Synebrychoff.** ⊠ *Kaivok. 2, Keskusta* ☎ *09/1733–6401* ⊕ *www.fng.fi* ⌨ *€6, additional charge for special exhibits* ⊙ *Tues. and Fri. 9–6, Wed. and Thurs. 9–8, weekends 11–5.*

㉗ **Nykytaiteenmuseo (Kiasma)** *(Museum of Contemporary Art).* Praised for
★ the boldness of its curved steel shell but condemned for its encroachment on the territory of the Mannerheim statue, this striking museum displays a wealth of Finnish and foreign art from the 1960s to the present. Look for the "butterfly" windows, and don't miss the view of Töölönlahti from the north side of the fifth floor gallery. ⊠ *Mannerheiminaukio 2, Keskusta/Pääposti* ☎ *09/1733–6501* ⊕ *www.kiasma. fi* ⌨ *€7, free first Wed. of every month 5–8* ⊙ *Tues. 10–5, Wed.–Sun. 10–8:30.*

㉕ **Rautatieasema** *(train station).* This outdoor square and the adjoining train station are the city's bustling commuter hub. The station's huge granite figures are by Emil Wikström; the solid building they adorn was designed by Eliel Saarinen, one of the founders of the early-20th-century National Romantic style. ⊠ *Kaivok. 1, Rautatientori, Keskusta* ☎ *0600/41–902 for information in English (a €1 charge applies), 0307/23703 international fares* ⊕ *www.vr.fi.*

㉑ **Senaatintori** *(Senate Square).* You've hit the heart of neoclassical Hel-
★ sinki. The harmony of the three buildings flanking Senaatintori exemplifies one of the purest styles of European architecture, as envisioned and designed by German architect Carl Ludwig Engel. On the square's west side is one of the main buildings of **Helsingin Yliopisto** (Helsinki University), and up the hill is the university library. On the east side is the pale yellow **Valtionneuvosto** (Council of State), completed in 1822 and once the seat of the Autonomous Grand Duchy of Finland's Imperial Senate. At the lower end of the square, stores and restaurants now occupy former merchants' homes. ⊠ *Bounded by Aleksanterink. to south and Yliopistonk. to north, Senaatintori.*

㉒ **Tuomiokirkko** *(Lutheran Cathedral of Finland).* The steep steps and green
Fodor's Choice domes of the church dominate Senaatintori. Completed in 1852, it is the
★ work of famous architect Carl Ludwig Engel, who also designed parts of Tallinn and St. Petersburg. Wander through the tasteful blue-gray interior, with its white moldings and the statues of German reformers Martin Luther and Philipp Melancthon, as well as the famous Finnish bishop Mikael Agricola. Concerts are frequently held inside the church. The crypt at the rear is the site of frequent historic and architectural exhibitions and bazaars. ⊠ *Yliopistonk. 7, Senaatintori* ☎ *09/709–2455* ⊙ *June–Aug., Mon.–Sat. 9–midnight, Sun. noon (or when worship service ends)–midnight, other times Mon.–Sat. 9–6, Sun. noon (or when worship service ends)–6.*

NEED A BREAK? **Café Engel** (⊠ *Aleksanterink. 26, Senaatintori* ☎ *09/652–776*), named for the architect Carl Ludwig Engel, serves traditional lunch fare right on

Senaatintori. Portions are hearty—you can fill up on a huge bowl of the tomato-basil soup or the cold smoked salmon sandwich; for a lighter snack, try a savory *karjalanpiiraka* (egg or potato pie) or one of the smaller open-faced cold-cut sandwiches. Locals stop in for coffee, wine and desserts, which include seasonal treats such as lingonberry cheesecake, fruit tarts, and an excellent Sacher torte.

19 ★ Uspenski Katedraali *(Uspenski Cathedral).* Perched atop a small rocky cliff over the North Harbor in Katajanokka is the main cathedral of the Orthodox church in Finland. Its brilliant gold onion domes are its hallmark, but its imposing redbrick edifice, decorated by 19th-century Russian artists, is no less distinctive. The cathedral was built and dedicated in 1868 in the Byzantine-Slavonic style and remains the biggest Orthodox church in Scandinavia. ⊠ *Kanavak. 1, Katajanokka* ☎ *09/634–267* ⊙ *May–Sept., Mon. and Wed.–Fri. 9:30–4, Tues. 9:30–6, Sat. 9:30–3, 6–8, Sun. 10–noon; Oct.–Apr., Tues.–Fri. 9:30–4, Sat. 9:30–3, Sun. 10–noon; closed for weddings and other special events.*

WORTH NOTING

28 Mannerheimin Patsas *(Statue of Marshal Karl Gustaf Mannerheim).* The equestrian gazes down Mannerheimintie, the major thoroughfare named in his honor. ⊠ *Mannerheimintie, in front of main post office and Museum of Contemporary Art, west of station, Keskusta/Pääposti.*

OFF THE BEATEN PATH

Linnanmäki. Helsinki's amusement park to the north of the city can be reached by Trams 3B and 3T from in front of the railway station. ⊠ *Tivolikuja 1, Linnanmäki* ☎ *09/773–991* ⊕ *www.linnanmaki.fi* ☞ *Free entrance to park, €4 for individual rides for children under 120 cm, €6 for over 120 cm, day pass under 120 cm €21, over 120 cm €33* ⊙ *May–late Aug., daily, hrs vary, call ahead or visit Web site.*

23 Pörssitalo *(Stock Exchange).* Although the trading is fully automated, the beautiful interior of the Stock Exchange, with its bullet-shape chandeliers, is worth seeing. The Pörssitalo was designed by Lars Sonck and built in 1911. ⊠ *Fabianink. 14, Keskusta* ⊙ *Weekdays 8–5.*

26 Suomen Kansallisteatteri *(National Theater).* Productions in the three theaters are in Finnish. The elegant granite facade overlooking the railway station square is decorated with quirky relief typical of the Finnish National Romantic style. In front is a statue of writer Aleksis Kivi. ⊠ *Läntinen Teatterikuja 1, north side of Rautatientori, Keskusta/Rautatieasema* ☎ *09/1733–1331* ⊕ *www.nationaltheatre.fi.*

NEED A BREAK?

On the north flank of Katajanokka, near the end of Katajanokan Pohjoisranta, you'll see the **Katajanokan Casino** (⊠ *Laivastok. 1, Katajanokka* ☎ *09/622-2722*). It was built in 1911 as a warehouse, later became a naval officers' casino, and today is a seaside restaurant. Set on its own headland, the casino has a summer terrace from which you can gaze across the North Harbor to the Kruunuhaka district while sipping a cold beer.

㉚ Wanha Satama *(Old Harbor)*. Despite its old-brick-warehouse appearance, this is actually a small shopping center with several food stores, restaurants, and cafés. There's even an exhibition hall in the left-hand (north) wing. The "W" in Wanha is pronounced "V." ⊠ *Kanavak and Pikku Satamak, Katajanokka.*

TÖÖLÖ

Most of Helsinki's major cultural buildings—the opera house, concert hall, and national museum—are within a short distance of each other around the perimeter of the inlet from the sea called Töölönlahti. The inlet itself is lovely in all seasons, and the walking and biking paths are well trodden by locals. The winding streets just east of Mannerheimintie enfold the Temppeliaukio Kirkko (Temple Square Church), whose unexceptional facade gives way to an amazing cavernous interior. Also nearby, the Sibelius park cuts a large swath out of the neighborhood and borders the sea.

TOP ATTRACTIONS

㉜ Finlandiatalo *(Finlandia Hall)*. This white, winged concert hall was one of Alvar Aalto's last creations. It's especially impressive on foggy days or at night. If you can't make it to a concert here, try to take a guided tour. ⊠ *Karamzininkatu 4, Keskusta* ☎ *09/402–41* ⊕ *www.finlandiatalo.fi* ⊙ *Symphony concerts usually held Wed. and Thurs. nights.*

㉟ Helsingin Taidehalli *(Helsinki Art Gallery)*. Here you'll see the best of contemporary Finnish art, including painting, sculpture, architecture, and industrial art and design. ⊠ *Nervanderink. 3, Keskusta* ☎ *09/454–2060* 🔅 *€7, can vary for special exhibitions* ⊙ *Tues., Thurs., and Fri. 11–6, Wed. 11–8, weekends noon–5.*

㉛ Suomen Kansallismuseo *(National Museum of Finland)*. Architect Eliel Saarinen and his partners combined the language of Finnish medieval church architecture with elements of art nouveau to create this vintage example of the National Romantic style. The museum's collection of archaeological, cultural, and ethnological artifacts gives you insight into Finland's past. ⊠ *Mannerheimintie 34, Keskusta* ☎ *09/40501* ⊕ *www.nba.fi/en/nmf* 🔅 *€7* ⊙ *Tues. and Wed. 11–8, Thurs.–Sun. 11–6.*

㉝ Suomen Kansallisooppera *(Finnish National Opera)*. Grand gilded operas, classical ballets, and booming concerts all take place in Helsinki's splendid opera house, a striking example of modern Scandinavian architecture. All events at the opera house draw crowds, so buy your tickets early. ⊠ *Helsinginkatu 58, Keskusta* ☎ *09/4030–2210 house tours, 09/4030–2211 box office* ⊕ *www.operafin.fi* ⊙ *Tues.–Fri. 10–5; house tours, in English, in summer Tues. and Thurs. at 3, or by appointment.*

Fodor'sChoice
★

㊱ Temppeliaukio Kirkko *(Temple Square Church)*. Topped with a copper dome, the church looks like a half-buried spaceship from the outside. In truth, it's really a modern Lutheran church carved into the rock outcrops below. The sun shines in from above, illuminating the stunning interior with its birch pews, modern pipe organ, and cavernous walls. Ecumenical and Lutheran services in various languages are held throughout the week. ⊠*Lutherinkatu 3, Töölö* ☎*09/494–698* ⊙ *Weekdays 10–7:45, Sat. 10–6, Sun. noon–1:45 and 3:15–5:45; closed Tues. 1–2 and during weddings, concerts, and services.*

WORTH NOTING

③⓪ Eduskuntatalo *(Parliament House).* The imposing, colonnaded, Eduskuntatalo stands near Mannerheim's statue on Mannerheimintie. The legislature has one of the world's highest proportions of women. ⊠*Mannerheimintie 30, Keskusta* ☎*09/432–2027* ⊕*www.eduskunta.fi.*

③④ Olympiastadion *(Olympic Stadium).* At this stadium built for the 1952 Games, take a lift to the top of the tower for sprawling city views. ⊠*East of Mannerheim, Olympiastadion* ☎*09/436–6010* ⊕*www.stadion.fi* ⊠*€2* ⊙ *Weekdays 9–8, weekends 9–6.*

OFF THE BEATEN PATH

Seurasaaren Ulkomeseo. On an island about 3 km (2 mi) northwest of city center, the Seurasaari Outdoor Museum was founded in 1909 to preserve rural Finnish architecture. The old farmhouses and barns that were brought to Seurasaari come from all over Finland. Many are rough-hewn log buildings dating from the 17th century, of primary inspiration to the late 19th-century architects of the national revivalist movement in Finland. All exhibits are marked by signposts along the trails; don't miss the church boat and the gabled church. Seurasaari Island is connected to land by a pedestrian bridge and is a restful place for walking throughout the year, with its forest trails and ocean views. You can walk there in about 40 minutes from the opera house; follow Mannerheimintie northeast, then turn left onto Linnankoskenkatu and follow signs along the coast. Alternatively, take Bus 24 from city center, in front of the Swedish Theater at the west end of Pohjoisesplanadi; its last stop is by the bridge to the island. Plan on spending at least three hours exploring and getting to the museum. ⊠*Seurasaari* ☎*09/4050–9660 in summer, 09/4050–9568 in winter* ⊕*www.nba. fi* ⊠*€6. Guided tours in English available mid-June–mid-Aug., at 3, starting at ticket kiosk.* ⊙*Mid-May–late May and early Sept.–mid-Sept., weekdays 9–3, weekends 11–5; June–Aug., daily 11–5; closed mid-Sept.–mid-May.*

③⑦ Sibeliuksen Puisto. The **Sibelius-Monumentti** (Sibelius Monument) itself is worth the walk to this lakeside park. What could be a better tribute to Finland's great composer than this soaring silver sculpture of organ pipes? ⊠ *West of Mechelinin, Töölö.*

OFF THE BEATEN PATH

Urho Kekkonen Museum Tamminiemi. The grand house overlooking Seurasaari from the mainland is Tamminiemi, where the late Finnish president Urho Kekkonen lived from 1956 to 1986. Originally known as Villa Nissen, Tamminiemi was built in 1904. Inside are the scores of gifts presented to Finland's longest-serving president by leaders from around the world. His study is the most fascinating room, with its gift from the United States: a cupboard full of *National Geographic* maps of the world. To ensure an English-speaking guide, call ahead. ⊠*Seurasaarentie 15, Seurasaari* ☎*09/4050–9650* ⊕*www.nba.fi/en/ukk_museum* ⊠*€5, includes guided tour in English, daily at 1:30* ⊙*Mid-May–mid-Aug., daily 11–5; mid-Aug.–mid-May, Wed.–Sun. 11–5.*

WHERE TO EAT

Helsinki's recent restaurant scene expansion appears only to be gaining momentum as modern Finnish cuisine comes into its own. The city is dotted with cozy yet decidedly modern-looking venues offering reindeer, herring, and pike accompanied by delicious Finnish mushrooms or wild-berry sauces. Don't be turned off by menu descriptions such as "reindeer with lingonberry sauce and chanterelles,"—it's a classic example of the Finnish tendency toward understatement, and the skill will be evident in the taste. You'll find everything from Mexican to Nepalese (quite popular with locals) in the city, though not at every price point. Expect European-size entrées, excellent location, and service at a steep price. A strong café culture makes it easy to find a tasty, reasonably priced lunch.

AROUND ESPLANADE AND KATAJANOKKA

$$$
EASTERN
EUROPEAN

✕**Bellevue.** The spare lines of Bellevue belie its real age—it's been around since 1917, serving dishes inspired by Russian and Finnish cuisine. Try the *shashlik* (cubed lamb kebab served with mushroom rice) or the ox fillet à la Novgorod. The plush interior of this elegant town house has many shining samovars, but only some of them are functional; each table has lighted candles. ⊠*Rahapajank. 3, Keskusta* ☎*09/179–560* ⊟*AE, DC, MC, V* ⊘*Closed Sun. No lunch July.*

$$$$
FRENCH

✕**Chez Dominique.** Helsinki's most vaunted restaurant is everything you'd expect of a place that has maintained two Michelin stars since 2002. Celebrity chef Hans Välimäki uses locally produced ingredients wherever possible, creating his own Finnish take on high-end French cuisine. While the menu changes on a near-monthly basis, pigeon from Anju filled with duck foie gras and served with consumme or root vegetable salsify has held its own since 1998; a recurring dessert is chocolate canalone with liquid chocolate and raspberry mousse. The dining room, design by Finn Vertti Kivi, is a sexy combination of black carpet, white walls, leather chairs, and black tinted glass, with a few small veiled-glass windows into the kitchen. There's a 13-course degustation menu for around €135. ⊠*Rikhardink. 4* ☎*09/612–7393* ⚑*Reservations essential* ⊟*AE, DC, MC, V* ⊘*Mid-Aug.–late-June: Closed Sun. No lunch Mon. or Sat. Late-June to mid-Aug.: closed Sun. and Mon. No lunch Tues.–Sat.*

$$$
SEAFOOD
Fodor'sChoice
★

✕**Havis.** Across the street from the Market Square and the South Harbor, this restaurant specializes in traditional Scandinavian fish dishes with contemporary twists. Begin with the savory blue-mussel soup, and move on to specialties like the slow-fried *lavaret* (whitefish). Vegetarians will appreciate the mushroom crepes with glazed vegetables and the daily vegetarian special. The dessert menu includes old-time Finnish standards like strawberry milk and doughnuts with coffee pudding. ⊠*Etelärantatie 16, Kauppatori* ☎*09/6869–5660* ⊕*www.royalravin tolat.com* ⊟*AE, DC, MC, V* ⊘*Closed Sun. mid-Sept.–Apr. No lunch weekends.*

$$$
ECLECTIC

✕**Mecca.** Step into the dark-hued, cozy lounge and it's clear even before you see a menu that this is one of Helsinki's hottest restaurants. Beyond the bar and the flame-enclosing decorative glass tanks is the airy dining room bordered on one side by an outdoor terrace, on another the open kitchen. The term "international fare" doesn't suffice for chef Petteri Luoto's funky, unique take on familiar dishes. Small dishes (four for €38 or two for €23) include "Kenzo Peace and Love Unicorn", a vegetable spring roll with a scoop of lemon sorbet, and "Peking Duck Fake"—the cucumber strips covered in a mango chutney and hoisin sauce replacing plum; try combining hot (from the left side of the menu page) and cold ones (right). The seven-course "Mystery Trip" (€65 per person) must be ordered by the whole table. ⊠ *Korkeavuorenk. 34* ☎ *09/1345–6200* ⚙ *Reservations essential* ⊟ *AE, DC, MC, V* ☾ *Sun. No lunch.*

$$$$
SCANDINAVIAN
★

✕ **Palace Gourmet.** This hotel restaurant has a magnificent view of the South Harbor. Its specialties are French and Finnish fare, including such creations as warm artichoke salad with smoked whitefish and basil sauce, and fillet of lamb with tarragon, tomatoes, and garlic sauce. Call ahead for the "Menu Surprise," a seven-course meal that changes daily and costs €106. There are also three- and four-course set menus. ⊠ *Palace Hotel, Eteläranta 10, Kauppatori* ☎ *09/1345–6715* ⊟ *AE, DC, MC, V* ☾ *Closed weekends and July.*

$$
ITALIAN

✕ **Raffaello.** In the heart of Helsinki's financial district, this cozy Italian restaurant with redbrick walls, parquet floors, and decorative frescoes has a reputation for friendly service, reasonable prices, and tasty pasta, salad, and meat dishes. Try the steak gratinated with Gorgonzola, rosemary potatoes, and a boletus sauce, or the grilled salmon fillet with a red onion mushroom gratin, saffron risotto, and crab sauce. ⊠ *Aleksanterink. 46, Keskusta* ☎ *09/8568–5730* ⊟ *AE, DC, MC, V.*

$$$$
SCANDINAVIAN
Fodor'sChoice
★

✕ **Savoy.** With its airy, Alvar Aalto–designed, functionalist dining room overlooking the Esplanade Gardens, the Savoy is a frequent choice for business lunches and was also Finnish statesman Marshal Karl Gustaf Mannerheim's favorite; he is rumored to have introduced the *vorschmack* (minced lamb and anchovies) recipe. Savoy's menu usually includes reindeer fillet and a changing menu of inventive fresh fish dishes like fried whitefish with new potatoes, smoked salmon roe, and vermouth sauce. ⊠ *Eteläespl. 14, Esplanadi* ☎ *09/684–4020* ⊟ *AE, DC, MC, V* ☾ *Closed weekends.*

$$$$
FRENCH

✕ **Sipuli.** Sipuli stands at the foot of the Russian Orthodox Uspenski Cathedral and gets its name—meaning onion—from the church's golden onionlike cupolas. The restaurant is in a 19th-century warehouse building, with redbrick walls and dark-wood panels, and a skylight with a spectacular view of the cathedral. Classic French-Finnish combinations may include fennel soup with forest mushroom ravioli, smoked fillet of pike perch with salmon mousse, and roasted fillet of veal with port sauce. ⊠ *Kanavaranta 7, Katajanokka* ☎ *09/622–9280* ⊟ *AE, DC, MC, V* ☾ *Closed weekends, except for group dinners, and July.*

$$$
ECLECTIC
★

✕ **Teatterin Grilli.** Located not *on* the Esplanade but in the gardens at the western end, this "it" complex includes a restaurant-lounge with outdoor seating, two bars, and a well-heeled nightclub with a coveted upstairs terrace. One of the spaces is usually being reconceptualized to keep things fresh; currently the dining room is splashed in orange, black, and green, accented with candelabras webbed in white sheets. Cozy banquette seating dominates the main space, separated from tables in nooks on either side by Louis Vuitton leather-padded thresholds, each of which has a mini-chandelier. The cuisine is well-made, from seasonal starters such as creamy crayfish soup with fennel foam to entrées like grilled tuna with mango, hemp seeds, and wasabi dip. ⊠*Pohjoisesplanadi 2* ☎*09/6128–5005* ♨*Reservations essential* ⊟*AE, DC, MC, V* ⊗*Closed Sun.*

$$$$
JAPANESE

✕**Yume.** Finland's finest Japanese restaurant offers a French-influenced version made with an emphasis on Finnish ingredients. The excellent tempura dishes include tiger prawns and vegetables rolled in filo pastry, lending them extra crispiness. The Finnish butterfish appears in sushi platters; small dishes include the fantastically fresh tuna tartar a la Yume served with a dollop of wasabi mayonnaise, and scallops in wasabi butter puddles with sake foam clouds. Water cascades down the sides of the glass entryway and a high-wire act of pillow-shaped bulbs is suspended over diners, many of whom are high-powered businesspeople from the adjoining Hotel Kämp, which owns—and lends its extremely high caliber service to—the restaurant. ⊠*Kluuvik. 2* ☎*050/561–4938* ♨*Reservations essential* ⊟*AE, DC, MC, V* ⊗*Closed Sun. and 3–5* PM *daily.*

$$
ECLECTIC

✕**Zetor.** Known as the tractor restaurant, Zetor is a haven for the weary traveler in need of some homey high-cholesterol cooking—choose from meatballs, Karelian stew, sausage, or schnitzel, washed down with the house brew. Wooden tables, farm equipment, and a witty menu make for an entertaining evening. Late nights the restaurant transforms into a hipster bar and disco. ⊠*Kaivopiha, Mannerheimintie 3–5, Keskusta/Kaivopiha* ☎*09/666–966* ⊟*AE, DC, MC, V* ⊗*No lunch weekends.*

WEST OF MANNERHEIMINTIE

$$
SCANDINAVIAN
Fodor's Choice
★

✕**Kosmos.** Just a short walk from Stockmann's department store, this cozy restaurant has become a lunchtime favorite among businesspeople working nearby. Come evening, it's given over to artists and journalists. Its high ceilings and understated interior give it a Scandinavian air of simplicity and efficiency. Menu highlights include reindeer fillet in a sauce of spruce shoots and rosemary served with roasted potatoes and vorschmack with duchesse potatoes (a rich version of mashed), pickles, and beets. ⊠*Kalevank. 3, Keskusta* ☎*09/647–255* ⊟*AE, DC, MC, V* ⊗*Closed Sun. and in July. No lunch Sat.*

$$
ECLECTIC
★

✕**Kynsilaukka.** This cozy yet sophisticated restaurant appeals to the senses with fresh, beautifully prepared food. It's also a garlic lover's dream. Stellar dishes include the garlic cream soup and bouillabaisse; for dessert try the classic crepes with cloudberry sauce. A reasonably priced lunch menu and the fact it's open on holidays help make it a local favorite. All portions are served in two sizes. ⊠*Fredrikink. 22, Keskusta* ☎*09/651–939* ⊟*AE, DC, MC, V.*

$
SCANDINAVIAN

✕**Ravintola Perho.** Helsinki's catering school operates this brasserie-style restaurant decorated in pine. The emphasis is on Finnish food, particularly salmon and reindeer. Its reasonable prices, central location (just west of Mannherheimintie), and own microbrew make it a favorite. ⊠*Mechelinkatu 7, Töölö* ☎*09/5807–8649* ⊟*AE, DC, MC, V* ⊗*Closed weekends June–mid-Aug.*

$$ ✕**Seahorse.** This institution opened in 1934 and is as comfortable serv-
FINNISH ing its calorie-rich traditional Finnish fare to resident rock stars as to the
mere mortal locals who use it to stifle a hangover—or turn to the worn-
looking bar (unchanged since 1950) to start on their way toward one. If
you make it past appetizer #8, a shot of the local liquor Koskenkorva,
try the pickle-and-sour-cream-laden Beefsteak a la Sea Horse or the
classic crispy fried Baltic Herring with mashed potatoes and beetroot.
No-frills decor (aside from the sea horse painting on the back wall) and
friendly service make this an unintimidating place to get local flavor.
✉*Kapteenink. 11* ☎*09/628–169* ▤*AE, DC, MC, V.*

¢ ✕**Zucchini.** For a vegetarian lunch or just coffee and dessert, Zucchini
VEGETARIAN is a cozy hideaway with quiet music, magazines, and a few sidewalk
tables. Pizzas, soups, and salads are all tasty. ✉*Fabianinkatu 4, Kes-
kusta* ☎*09/622–2907* ▤*AE, DC, MC, V* ⊘*Closed weekends. No
dinner.*

KESKUSTA AND TÖÖLÖ

$$ ✕**Elite.** A short distance from the town center, but a welcome oasis after
SCANDINAVIAN excursions to the Temppeliaukio Kirkko and the Sibelius monument,
★ Elite's simple art-deco interior and spacious layout are popular with
artists and writers. Traditional Finnish dishes to sample are fried Baltic
herring, salmon soup with rye bread, and select game. If you want more
contemporary dishes, try the salmon with lemon-anchovy butter, or the
rose-fried liver with capers and bacon-onion fry. The outdoor seating
in summer is popular. ✉*Etelä Hesperiank. 22, Töölö* ☎*09/434–2200*
▤*AE, DC, MC, V.*

$$ ✕**Kuu.** If you like finding the true character of a city and enjoy local
SCANDINAVIAN color, try looking in simple, friendly restaurants such as Kuu, literally
Moon. The menu combines Finnish specialties such as Baltic herring,
salmon, and reindeer with imaginative international fare. It's especially
convenient for nights at the opera, and the delightful terrace is open
year-round. ✉*Töölönk. 27, Töölö* ☎*09/2709–0973* ▤*AE, DC, MC,
V.*

$$ ✕**Töölönranta.** The upscale Töölönranta packs in plenty of operagoers,
CONTEMPORARY since it's right behind the National Opera House overlooking the bay.
★ An innovative water-cooled wok on display in the wide-open kitchen
turns out stir-fried specials. Other favorites include arctic char, wild
duck, and game dishes. In summer, when the patio catches the evening
sun, this is a superb place to savor a beer. ✉*Helsinginkatu 56, Töölö*
☎*09/454–2100* ▤*AE, DC, MC, V.*

$$$ ✕**Troikka.** The Troikka takes you back to czarist times with its samo-
EASTERN vars, icons, and portraits of Russian writers—as well as the excep-
EUROPEAN tionally good Russian food and friendly service. Try the *zakusky,* an
assortment of Russian appetizers including such delicacies as Baltic
herring, homemade poultry pâte, wild mushrooms, and marinated gar-
lic. ✉*Caloniuksenk. 3, Keskusta* ☎*09/445–229* ▤*AE, DC, MC, V*
⊘*Closed Sun. and Mon. and July. No lunch.*

WHERE TO STAY

In recent years, Helsinki has been noted for its high-end design hotels, which emphasize room decor, layout, and in-house restaurants and bars. Top hotels are notoriously expensive, generally have small rooms, and mostly cater to business travelers. Standards are high, and the level of service usually corresponds to the price. Rates can plummet by as much as 50% on weekends, and most include a generous breakfast buffet and sauna privileges.

CITY CENTER

$$$ ⛄ **Hotel Seurahuone.** Built in 1914, this Viennese-style town-house hotel across from the train station has a loyal clientele won over by its age-less charm and cosmopolitan interiors. A patina of well-worn elegance pervades all areas, from the grand main stairway and the chandeliered restaurant serving Finnish cuisine to the ornate, skylighted pub. Rooms come in many styles, from traditionally furnished with brass beds and high ceilings in the old section, to the newer rooms with a sleek, modern design. Standard rooms have slightly larger bathrooms than most "Club" rooms, though their bedrooms are smaller. **Pros:** regal decor; dead-center locale. **Cons:** small bathrooms; one old-fashioned elevator. ✉*Kaivokatu 12, Rautatieasema* ☎*09/69141* ⊕*www.hotelliseurahuone. fi* ⬅*114 rooms, 4 suites* ⌂*In-room: safe, Internet, Wi-Fi. In-hotel: restaurant, room service, bar, laundry service, Wi-Fi, parking (paid), some pets allowed, no-smoking rooms* ⊟*AE, DC, MC, V* ⚲*BP.*

$ ⛄ **Omenahotelli Eerikinkatu.** This relatively new hotel chain (its first location opened in 2001) emphasizes price and location over services and amenities. You'll find no receptionist and certainly no doorman—guests must use a numerical code they receive by e-mail when booking in order to access the building, then their floor, then their room. A 24-hour help desk can be reached by phone near the entrance if there's a problem. Rooms are small but livable, with space for a sofa bed, table, microwave, and a small bathroom. A €16-per-day "Business Pack" includes a modest breakfast, Internet and two movies. There's a comparable second location in Helsinki. Prices increase strictly based on the number of rooms taken, so book early. **Pros:** great value; privacy. **Cons:** drab-looking accommodations; modest breakfast costs extra and is served at local café; rooms only cleaned weekly. ✉*Eerikink. 24* ☎*0600/18018 €9 per reservation plus €1.97 per minute* ⊕*www.omena.com* ⬅*95* ⌂*In-room: no phone, Internet. In-hotel: parking (paid)* ⊟*AE, DC, MC, V.*

AROUND ESPLANADE AND KATAJANOKKA

$$$ ⛄ **Best Western Premier Katajanokka.** Featuring comfortable rooms with heated bathroom floors, this building originally opened as a county jail in 1888. You can step into one of the original cells in a far corner of the basement restaurant, and decor doesn't get more tongue-in-cheek than original cell bars lining small sections of the hallways. Rooms are decent-size with stylish white-and-gray-tile bathrooms and oversize rain-effect showerheads (some rooms have bathtubs as well). All in all, it's not a bad place to do time. **Pros:** friendly staff; good breakfast; prices cut almost in half on weekends. **Cons:** slightly removed from city center. ✉*Vyök. 1* ☎*09/670–290* ⊕*www.bwkatajanokka.fi* ⬅*106 rooms*

&In-room: safe, Internet, Wi-Fi. In-hotel: restaurant, room service, bar, gym, laundry service, Internet terminal, Wi-Fi, some pets allowed ☐AE, DC, MC, V ⦿BP.

$$$$ ⊡**Hotel Haven.** Opened in early 2009, Haven's prime harborside location and luxury amenities place it among Helsinki's finest hotels. Even "Comfort" rooms (the least expensive of the three categories) have a second TV in the bathroom, in addition to the larger Bang & Olufsen set with nearly 100 channels in the bedroom, and stylish-yet-cozy furnishings. "Style" rooms, a step up, have the same-size chic brown-and-white bathrooms with oversize showerheads but have slightly wider bedrooms, most of them facing the harbor. "Lux" rooms are largest and feature espresso machines and fantastic harborviews. The included breakfast is served downstairs in the superb restaurant Havis, one of many also owned by the company behind this hotel. **Pros:** lavish room amenities; harbor views; Elemis bath and spa products. **Cons:** some rooms face plain side streets. ⊠Unionink. 17 ☎09/6128–5850 ⊕www.hotelhaven.fi ⟳76 rooms, 1 suite &In-room: safe, Internet, Wi-Fi. In-hotel: 3 restaurants, room service, bars, spa, laundry service, Internet terminal, Wi-Fi, parking (paid), some pets allowed ☐AE, DC, MC, V ⦿BP.

$$$–$$$$ ⊡**Palace.** Built for the 1952 Olympic games, this clublike hotel is on the
★ 9th and 10th floors of a waterfront commercial building with splendid views of the South Harbor. Its faithful clientele—largely British, Swedish, and American—appreciates the personal service, such as daily afternoon tea, that comes with its small size. The hotel's restaurants, especially the Palace Gourmet, are among Helsinki's best. **Pros:** great views; excellent on-site restaurants. **Cons:** corporate feel. ⊠Eteläranta 10, Kauppatori ☎09/1345–6656 ⊕www.palacehotel.fi ⟳37 rooms, 2 suites &In-room: safe (some), Internet, Wi-Fi. In-hotel: 2 restaurants, room service, bar, laundry service, parking (paid) ☐AE, DC, MC, V ⦿BP.

$$–$$$ ⊡**Scandic Grand Marina Helsinki.** Housed inside an early-19th-century customs warehouse in the posh Katajanokka island neighborhood, the Grand Marina has one of the best convention centers in Finland. Its location, friendly service, modern facilities, and reasonable prices have made this hotel a favorite. Ask for a room with a view of South Harbor. **Pros:** free Wi-Fi; children under 13 stay free; 101 items on offer at breakfast. **Cons:** some rooms have poor views. ⊠Katajanokanlaituri 7, Katajanokka ☎09/16661 ⊕www.scandic-hotels.com ⟳442 rooms, 20 suites &In-room: safe, Wi-Fi. In-hotel: restaurant, bars, gym, laundry service, laundry facilities, Internet terminal, Wi-Fi, parking (paid), no-smoking rooms ☐AE, DC, MC, V ⦿BP.

NEAR MANNERHEIMINTIE

¢ ⊡**Hostel Academica.** This summer hostel is made up of what are, during the rest of the year, university students' apartments. You can choose between rooms in the old or new sections; the latter have higher rates. Each floor has a small lounge; the rooms are functional, modern, and have their own small kitchens. Family rooms and extra beds are also available, and there are special family rates. The central location is good for shopping and transport. **Pros:** social atmosphere; good value. **Cons:** spartan rooms; breakfast not included. ⊠Hietaniemenk. 14, Hietaniemi

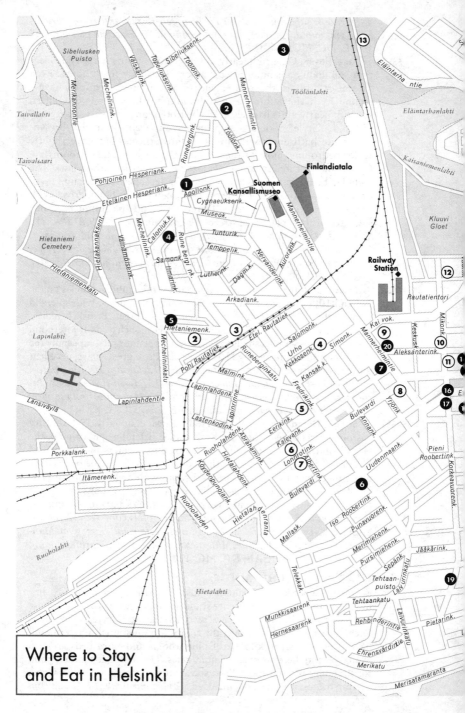

Where to Stay
and Eat in Helsinki

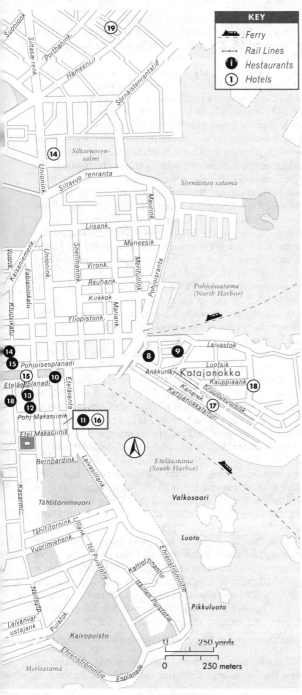

3

KEY

- 🚢 *Ferry*
- ⊢⊣ *Rail Lines*
- ❶ *Restaurants*
- ① *Hotels*

Restaurants ▼

Bellevue	9
Chez Dominique	18
Elite	1
Havis	10
Kosmos	7
Kuu	2
Kynsilaukka	6
Mecca	17
Palace Gourmet	11
Raffaello	14
Ravintola Perho	5
Savoy	13
Seahorse	19
Sipuli	8
Teatterin Grilli	16
Töölönranta	3
Troikka	4
Yume	15
Zetor	20
Zucchini	12

Hotels ▼

Best Western Premier Katajanokka	18
Cumulus Airport	13
Fenno	19
Hilton Helsinki Strand	14
Hostel Academica	2
Hotel Glo	10
Hotel Haven	15
Hotel Helka	3
Hotel Kämp	11
Hotel Seurahuone	9
Klaus K	8
Omenahotelli Eerikinkatu	5
Palace	16
Palace Hotel Linna	6
Radisson SAS Plaza Hotel Helsinki	12
Scandic Continental Helsinki	1
Scandic Grand Marina Helsinki	17
Scandic Simonkenttä Helsinki	4
Sokos Hotel Aleksanteri	7

☎09/1311–4334 ⊕*www.hostelacademica.fi* ⟿*260 rooms* ⏶*In-room: no phone, kitchen, no TV, Internet (some). In-hotel: pool, Internet terminal, no-smoking rooms* ☰*AE, DC, MC, V* ⊘*Closed Sept.–May.*

$$$$ 🖬 **Hotel GLO.** Well-dressed locals meet in the lobby lounge while a largely
★   international business clientele heads upstairs to unwind in what are
Helsinki's slickest hotel rooms. There are 70 different room configurations: GLO room XLs are the best value, being considerably larger than most entry-level GLO rooms and just a tad pricier. Deluxe rooms, one step above, are only slightly larger and include the otherwise €10-per-day access to the outstanding gym and sauna shared with the adjoining Hotel Kämp. There's a pillow menu with four choices and guests can order free-of-charge exercise equipment, such as yoga mats, Swiss balls, and stationary bikes, and relaxation accessories, such as a heated mattress and neck-and-back massager. Room rates can plunge by as much as 65% on weekends. **Pros:** gorgeous rooms; complimentary leisure accessories on-demand; fantastic spa. **Cons:** gym and sauna cost extra if in standard room. ⊠*Kluuvik. 4* ☏*010/3444–400* ⊕*www.palace kamp.fi* ⟿*132 rooms, 12 suites* ⏶*In-room: safe, Internet, Wi-Fi. In-hotel: restaurant, room service, bar, gym, spa, laundry service, parking (paid), some pets allowed* ☰*AE, DC, MC, V* ⌶◯❙*BP.*

$$ 🖬 **Hotel Helka.** Privately owned by the Finnish YWCA, this is a pleasant,
affordable alternative to the higher-price chain hotels. Although in the heart of the city, the Helka is surprisingly quiet, thanks to its double-paned windows. Furnishings are in light wood and mixed pastels. The restaurant, Helka Keittiö ("Helka's Kitchen"), specializes in classic Finnish dishes. Prices can drop to nearly €100 for a standard double on weekends. **Pros:** peaceful accommodations; central location; free Internet in lobby. **Cons:** some singles are tiny. ⊠*Pohjoinen Rautatiekatu 23, Keskusta* ☏*09/613–580* ⊕*www.helka.fi* ⟿*147 rooms, 3 suites* ⏶*In-room: Internet. In-hotel: restaurant, room service, bar, laundry service, Internet terminal, Wi-Fi, parking (free)* ☰*AE, DC, MC, V* ⌶◯❙*BP.*

$$$$ 🖬 **Hotel Kämp.** Opposite the Esplanade Park stands this splendid, luxuri-
Fodor'sChoice   ous, late-19th-century cultural landmark. In the past the hotel was the
★   site of a theater and was the meeting point for Finland's most prominent
politicians, artists, and celebrities, including Mannerheim, Saarinen, Gallen-Kallela, and former president Paasikivi, who became one of the hotel owners. Sibelius himself often visited the hotel and dedicated a song to it. Take the beautiful, sweeping staircase up to the grand ballroom, known as the mirror room. When not unwinding in one of the spa's three different saunas or its 10 treatment rooms, guests can borrow iPods, stereos, and video game systems from the lobby. **Pros:** lavish rooms; five-star service; fantastic spa. **Cons:** breakfast costs extra; gym and sauna costs €10 extra if in standard room. ⊠*Pohjoisesplanadi 29, Keskusta* ☏*09/576–1111* ⊕*www.hotelkamp.fi* ⟿*164 rooms, 15 suites* ⏶*In-room: DVD (some), Internet, Wi-Fi. In-hotel: 2 restaurants, room service, bar, gym, spa, laundry service, parking (paid), no-smoking rooms* ☰*AE, DC, MC, V.*

$$$$ 🖬 **Klaus K.** Short-stay business travelers love the aesthetics and atten-
tion to detail at Klaus K, one of Helsinki's chicest hotels. Reception, up a few steps past the bar-lounge-club and the Italian restaurant, is

set in white amid funky chairs. Beyond are a second, more upscale restaurant and a full-service day spa. Of the 137 rooms, there are 118 different configurations: "Desire" rooms, at around 82-square-feet, are generally a big step up in size from the standard-level "Passion" and "Mystical" rooms, which range from 40-square-feet for single travelers up to 62-square-feet. Vibrant color schemes, cool-yet-comfortable furniture, speakers in the bathrooms, and custom-made 900-spring beds are in all rooms. You'll certainly look cool here; just ensure you get a room large enough to make you feel it. **Pros:** Helsinki's best breakfast; fantastic location just off the Esplanade; gorgeous rooms. **Cons:** some standard rooms are tiny; no drawer space in most rooms. ⊠ *Bulevardi 2/4* ☎ *040/900–3711* ⊕ *www.klauskhotel.com* ⊷ *135 rooms, 2 suites* ♨ *In-room: safe, DVD, Internet, Wi-Fi. In-hotel: 2 restaurants, room service, bar, gym, spa, laundry service, Internet terminal, Wi-Fi, parking (paid), no kids under 18* ⊟ *AE, DC, MC, V* ❦ *BP.*

$$$
Fodor'sChoice
★

Palace Hotel Linna. On a quiet side street, this small luxury hotel distinguishes itself with a rare combination of character, consistency, and service. The front section is a handsome 1903 stone castle with wood-beam, medieval-style restaurants, lounges, conference rooms, and a cavernous banquet hall. A walkway across an inner court brings you to the modern building housing the guest rooms, which have comfortable, contemporary furnishings. **Pros:** central location; pleasant rooms; most drawer space in Helsinki. **Cons:** Internet costs extra; bath products not included. ⊠ *Lönnrotink. 29, Hietalahti* ☎ *10/344–4100* ⊕ *www. palace.fi* ⊷ *48 rooms* ♨ *In-room: Internet, Wi-Fi. In-hotel: restaurant, room service, bar, laundry service, Wi-Fi, parking (paid), some pets allowed, no-smoking rooms* ⊟ *AE, DC, MC, V* ❦ *BP.*

$$$

Radisson SAS Plaza Hotel Helsinki. This Renaissance-style former office building in the heart of the city has been adapted into a first-class hotel by renowned Finnish architects Ilmo Valjakka and Pervin Imaditdin. Rooms and suites come in three styles: Nordic, with light wood furnishings; classic, with darker wood furnishings; and Italian, with sunny bright colors and bold designs. The courtyardlike main restaurant, the Pääkonttori (headquarters), is brightened by a large skylight. The sophisticated Lasibaari bar has beautiful stained-glass windows. Rates drop considerably on weekends. **Pros:** choice of room style; central location. **Cons:** big hotel feel. ⊠ *Mikonkatu 23, Keskusta* ☎ *09/77590* ⊕ *www.radissonsas.com* ⊷ *195 rooms, 6 suites* ♨ *In-room: Internet (some), Wi-Fi. In-hotel: 2 restaurants, bars* ⊟ *AE, DC, MC, V* ❦ *BP.*

$$$–$$$$

Scandic Simonkenttä Helsinki. Located next to the bus station and the Forum shopping center, this hotel was specially designed to be environmentally friendly and to fulfill hypoallergenic standards. The rooms have blue, green, or red color schemes, wood floors, and cherrywood and leather furnishings. Rooms on the upper floors have good views of the city. **Pros:** extremely clean rooms; warm decor. **Cons:** mediocre views. ⊠ *Simonkatu 9, Keskusta* ☎ *09/683–80* ⊕ *www.scandic-hotels. com* ⊷ *360 rooms, 3 suites* ♨ *In-room: Wi-Fi. In-hotel: restaurant, room service, bar, gym, laundry service, Internet terminal, Wi-Fi, some pets allowed, no-smoking rooms* ⊟ *AE, DC, MC, V* ❦ *BP.*

NORTH OF CITY CENTER

$–$$
★
⊡ **Cumulus Airport.** This fully equipped, modern accommodation satisfies Helsinki's need for an airport hotel that meets the highest international standards. Convenient for layovers, the hotel borders the airport commercial zone and has the best conference facilities in the area. A standard room includes a comfy armchair and queen-size bed and has such soft touches as paisley bedspreads. All rooms are soundproofed. **Pros:** convenient to airport; comfortable rooms; pool. **Cons:** kitschy decor. ⊠*Robert Huberintie 4, Airport Vantaa* ☎*09/4157–7100* ⊕*www.cumulus.fi* ⇗*260 rooms, 4 suites* ⬦*In-room: Internet. In-hotel: restaurant, room service, bars, pool, gym, laundry facilities, laundry service, Internet terminal, some pets allowed, no-smoking rooms* ⊟*AE, DC, MC, V* ⦿|*BP.*

¢–$
⊡ **Fenno.** Ten minutes from the city center by tram (3B), in the Kallio neighborhood, this apartment hotel has simple, reasonably priced rooms. You can opt to stay in a private studio apartment with kitchenette and bathroom; an even less-expensive choice is an unpretentious, light-color economy room, which includes shared bath and kitchen facilities with other guests on the same floor. **Pros:** self-catering option; easy city access. **Cons:** not all rooms have stoves. ⊠*Kaarlenkatu 7, Kallio* ☎*09/774–980* ⊕*www.hotelfenno.fi* ⇗*68 apartments for 1–2 persons, 32 economy single rooms with shared facilities* ⬦*In-room: no a/c, kitchen. In-hotel: restaurant, Internet terminal, Wi-Fi, laundry facilities, parking (paid)* ⊟*AE, DC, MC, V* ⦿|*BP.*

$$$
Fodor's Choice
★
⊡ **Hilton Helsinki Strand.** From the tastefully furnished rooftop saunas and the large, crisply decorated rooms, to the bathrooms with heated floors and the car-wash service in the basement garage, this hotel pampers you for a price. The distinctive use of granite and Finnish marble in the central lobby is accentuated by a soaring atrium, where the Bridges restaurant is also located. The waterfront vistas are a pleasure. An entire floor is reserved for nonsmokers, and some of the suites have panoramic views of the sea. **Pros:** lavish rooms; regal lobby; great views. **Cons:** slightly removed from city center. ⊠*John Stenbergin Ranta 4, Hakaniemi* ☎*09/39351* ⊕*www.interconti.com* ⇗*192 rooms, 8 suites* ⬦*In-room: safe, Wi-Fi. In-hotel: restaurant, room service, bar, pool, laundry service, Wi-Fi, parking (paid), no-smoking rooms* ⊟*AE, DC, MC, V* ⦿|*BP.*

TÖÖLÖ AND MUNKKINIEMI

$$$$
★
⊡ **Scandic Continental Helsinki.** One of the most popular hotels in Helsinki, this local institution is modern and central and particularly popular with business travelers from the United States. It has hosted superpower summits and various diplomatic guests, and has a comprehensive range of business services. The hotel is close to Finlandia Hall and the Finnish National Opera. Lastu, the hotel's excellent restaurant, serves Scandinavian dishes and there's a separate bar. **Pros:** excellent location; lobby can be a scene. **Cons:** corporate feel. ⊠*Mannerheim. 46, Töölö* ☎*09/47371* ⊕*www.scandic-hotels.com* ⇗*500 rooms, 12 suites* ⬦*In-room: safe (some), Wi-Fi. In-hotel: restaurant, room service, bar, pool, gym, laundry service, Internet terminal, Wi-Fi, parking (paid), some pets allowed, no-smoking rooms* ⊟*AE, DC, MC, V* ⦿|*BP.*

CLOSE UP

Saunas

An authentic Finnish sauna is an obligatory experience, and not hard to find: there are 1.6 million saunas in this country of just more than 5 million people—even the parliament has its own sauna. The traditional Finnish sauna—which involves relaxing on wooden benches, pouring water onto hot coals, and swatting your neighbor's back with birch branches—is an integral part of cabin life and now city life, as apartments are outfitted with small saunas in their bathrooms. Almost every hotel has at least one sauna available free of charge, usually at standard times in the morning or evening for men and women to use separately. Larger hotels offer a private sauna in the higher-class rooms and suites. Public saunas (with swimsuits required) are becoming increasingly popular, even in winter, when sauna-goers momentarily leave the sauna to jump into the sea through a large hole in the ice (called *avantouinti*). Public swimming pools are also equipped with saunas that can be used at no extra charge. For information on saunas and the sauna tradition, contact the **Finnish Sauna Society** (☎ *09/686-0560* ⊕ *www. sauna.fi*).

3

AFTER DARK

Originally known for its rock and heavy metal clubs, Helsinki has recently developed a suave bar-lounge scene. What began as a love of mojitos is flourishing into a number of carpeted, couch-lined venues combining loungy tunes with magnificent cocktails, some as a separate part of chic restaurants. While the city is generally quiet Sunday–Tuesday nights, a well-dressed, mostly suit-clad clientele begins boozing and schmoozing in earnest on "little Saturday" (aka Wednesday), and you can expect lines at the most popular places starting at 11 on weekends. The compact size of the city center makes it easy to barhop. Almost any place with a terrace or courtyard is sure to be busy in summer, and cover charges, when required, average €5–€10. The free bimonthly magazine *We Are Helsinki,* available at the Helsinki City Tourist Office, has the lowdown on the city's nightlife.

BARS AND LOUNGES

Finland's finest cocktails are mixed at **A21** (⊠ *Annank. 21, Keskusta* ☎ *45/6387–500*), a cozy cocktail lounge owned by a Finnish duo who learned the trade in London; Remember to ring the doorbell. **Angleterre** (⊠ *Fredrikinkatu 47, Keskusta* ☎ *09/647–371*) is a cozy English ale house run by a well-known Helsinki cellar master; it's frequented by an upwardly mobile, professional crowd. **Ateljee Bar** (⊠ *Hotel Torni, Yrjönk. 26, Keskusta* ☎ *020/1234–604*) is a modest space boasting magnificent views from its porches nearly 200 feet (60 meters) above the city center, and serves innovative cocktails.

Grotesk (⊠ *Ludvigink. 10, Keskusta* ☎ *10/470–2100*) belies its name with black carpet, an ornate polished-wood ceiling, and well-dressed people sipping champagne and expertly made cocktails; its courtyard is packed in summer. **Kappeli** (⊠ *Eteläespl. 1, Esplanadi* ☎ *09/681–2440*) has a huge outdoor terrace, perfect for summer nights, and an à la carte menu. Its leaded windows offer an excellent view of the Havis Amanda statue.

Mecca (⊠ *Korkeavuorenk. 34, Esplanadi* ☎ *09/1345–6200*) has a DJ spinning chill international music in the lounge downstairs from 6 PM Wednesday and Thursday, and the vibe extends to its larger second-floor lounge overlooking the dining room on the weekends. It serves 10 varieties of mojito. **Molly Malone's** (⊠ *Kaisaniemenkatu 1C, Keskusta* ☎ *09/171–272*) is a popular Irish pub, with nightly live music. **O'Malley's** (⊠ *Sokos Hotel Torni, Yrjönkatu 26, Keskusta* ☎ *09/1311–3459*) is the first Irish pub in Helsinki.

Raffaello (⊠ *Aleksanterink. 46, Keskusta* ☎ *09/8568–5730*) attracts a young crowd of professionals from the Helsinki financial district. **Teatteri** (⊠ *Pohjoisesplanadi 2, Esplanadi* ☎ *09/6128–5005*) takes full advantage of its sexy in-the-esplanade-gardens locale with a perennially cool, if expensive, nightclub and two bar-lounges. **Vanha Ylioppilastalo** (⊠ *Mannerheim. 3, Keskusta* ☎ *09/1311–4368* ⊕ *www.vanha.fi*) has a large selection of beers and attracts students with live music and DJs in three spaces—everything from blues, folk, and jazz to reggae, hip-hop, and Latin.

The **William K** (⊠ *Annankatu 3, Keskusta* ☎ *010/766–4400* ⊠ *Mannerheim. 72, Töölönk* ☎ *09/409–484*) bars offer an excellent selection of European ales.

CASINO
Grand Casino Helsinki (⊠ *Mikonkatu 19, Keskusta* ☎ *09/680–800* ⊕ *www.grandcasinohelsinki.fi*) has roulette, blackjack, slot machines, and poker tournaments, as well as dinner shows and restaurants.

GAY AND LESBIAN BARS
For up-to-date details of the gay scene, contact the gay rights organization **SETA** (☎ *09/681–2580* ⊕ *www.seta.fi*). **dtm** (⊠ *Iso Roobertink. 28, Keskusta* ☎ *09/676–314*) short for "Don't Tell Mama," is one of the largest gay clubs in Finland.

Lost and Found (⊠ *Annank. 6, Keskusta* ☎ *09/680–1010*) is a bar as well as full-scale restaurant and is known for being straight-friendly. **Mann's Street** (⊠ *Mannerheim. 12A, 2nd fl., Keskusta* ☎ *09/612–1103*) is popular among older gay men and has karaoke daily and dancing on the first Saturday of the month.

JAZZ CLUBS
Helsinki's most popular jazz club, **Storyville** (⊠ *Museok. 8, Keskusta* ☎ *09/408–007* ⊕ *www.storyville.fi*), has live jazz, blues, rock-and-roll, and dancing Monday–Saturday.

NIGHTCLUBS
For an upscale evening of cocktails, dinner, and a live show (June–August), head over to Grand Casino Helsinki's **Fennia Salon** (⊠ *Mikonkatu 19, Keskusta* ☎ *09/680–800*). **Kaivohuone** (⊠ *Kaivohuone Kaivopuisto, Kaivopuisto* ☎ *09/621–2160*) is an old spa structure in beautiful

Kaivopuisto; its dance floor is often packed weekends. One of Finland's original megaclubs, **Lux** (⊠*Kamppi shopping mall, Kekkosenk. 1A, Keskusta* ☏*020/775–9350*) still packs 'em in and has large terraces.

On weekends, late night at **Manala** (⊠*Dagmarinkatu 2, Töölö* ☏*09/ 5807–7707*) is an extraordinary cocktail of elegant tango, bebop, and swing in the main hall and frenetic disco on the top floor. The first-floor restaurant in open until 4 AM. The university-owned **Tavastia Club** (⊠*Urho Kekkosenk. 4–6, Keskusta* ☏*09/7746–7423*) is one of the best rock clubs for top Finnish talent and some solid imports.

SHOPPING

From large, well-organized malls to closet-size boutiques, Helsinki has shopping for every taste. Most sales staff in the main shopping areas speak English and are helpful. Smaller stores are generally open weekdays 9–6 and Saturday 9–1. Small grocery stores are often open on Sunday year-round; other stores are often open on Sunday from June through August and December. The Forum and Kamppi complexes and Stockmann's department store are open weekdays 9–9, Saturday 9–6, and (in summer and Christmastime) Sunday noon–6. An ever-expanding network of pedestrian tunnels connects the Forum, Stockmann's, and the train-station tunnel.

The area south and west of Mannerheimintie has been branded Design District Helsinki. It includes roughly 170 venues, most of them smaller boutiques and designer-run shops selling handmade everything from jewelry to clothing to homewares. The majority are located on Fredrikinkatu and Annankatu; look for a black Design District Helsinki sticker in the window. You can pick up a map detailing the shops in the district at most participating stores. Kiosks remain open late and on weekends; they sell such basics as milk, juice, camera film, and tissues. Stores in Asematunneli, the train-station tunnel, are open weekdays 10–10 and weekends noon–10.

DEPARTMENT STORES
Stockmann's (⊠*Aleksanterink. 52B, Keskusta* ☏*09/1211* ⊕*www.stock mann.fi*) is Helsinki's premier department store. The 1950s showpiece landmark near the train station, **Sokos** (⊠*Asema-aukio 2C, Rautatieasema* ☏*010/765–000*) is a high-quality alternative to Stockmann's.

DISTRICTS
Pohjoisesplanadi (⊠*Esplanadi*), on the north side of the Esplanade, packs in most of Helsinki's trademark design stores. The southern part of **Senaatintori** has a host of souvenir and crafts stores, with several antiques shops and secondhand bookstores on the adjoining streets. Next to Senaatintori is the **Kiseleff Bazaar Hall** (⊠*Aleksanterinkatu 22–28*), an attractive shopping gallery.

A great place to begin your exploration of the Design District is at **Design Forum Finland** (⊠*Erottajank. 7, Punavouri*), which sells items from many of the nearby stores as well as items by designers without places of their own. It also puts on exhibitions featuring particular artists and it has a café. There is one pedestrian shopping street a few blocks south of the Esplanade, on **Iso Roobertinkatu**; stores here are conventional, and are more relaxed than around Mannerheimintie and the Esplanade. ✉ *Keskusta.*

MALLS

All of Helsinki's shopping malls have a good mix of stores plus several cafés and restaurants. **Forum** (✉ *Mannerheim. 20, Keskusta*) is the largest shopping complex in Helsinki, with 120 stores. The large **Itäkeskus** shopping complex in east Helsinki, perhaps the biggest indoor mall in Scandinavia, with 190 stores, restaurants, and other services, can be reached by metro. **Kaivopiha** (✉ *Kaivok. 10, Keskusta*) is across from the train station. The high-end **Kämp Galleria** (✉ *Pohjoisesplanadi 33, Keskusta*), bounded by Kluuvikatu, Pohjoisesplanadi, Mikonkatu, and Aleksanterinkatu, has 50 stores, including Finnish and international design shops.

The **Kamppi Center** (✉ *Urho Kekkosenkat. 1, Keskusta*), has 129 shops and each floor has a different theme.

Kluuvi (✉ *Aleksanterink. 9–Kluuvik. 5, Keskusta*) is a major shopping mall.

SPECIALTY STORES

CERAMICS AND ACCESSORIES

Aarikka (✉ *Pohjoisesplanadi 27, Esplanadi* ☎ 09/652–277) sells wooden jewelry, silver, and gifts. **Arabian Tehtaanmyymälä** (✉ *Hämeentie 135, Arabia* ☎ 020/4393–507) has Arabia, Hackman, and Iittala and Rörstrand tableware, glassware, cutlery, and cookware for outlet prices. **Nou Nou** (✉ *Uudenmaank. 2, Punavuori* ☎ 050/600–81) sells beautiful colored glassware by designer Anu Penttinen. A great place for cool, inexpensive gifts is **Secco** (✉ *Frederikink. 33, Punavuori* ☎ 09/678–782), which turns found materials into "treasures of wasteland" such as purses made from tire-rubber, messenger bags from old seat belts, and bowls from vinyl records.

The **Iittala Concept Store** (✉ *Pohjoisesplanadi 25, Esplanadi* ☎ 0204/ 393–501) sells the crisp, functional glass and tableware designs of Iittala and Arabia. **Pentik** (✉ *Mannerheimintie 5, Keskusta* ☎ 09/6124–0795) is known for its classy but homey style of ceramic dishes and other housewares. Inventive gift items and cards are also on sale. Combining "Nordic" and "Suomi" (meaning "Finnish"), **NORSU** (✉ *Kaisaniemenk. 9* ☎ 09/2316–3250) is both an exhibition space and a high-end shop with contemporary crafts from jewelry to glassware.

CLOTHING

A local favorite, **Helsinki 10** (✉ *Eerikink. 3, Keskusta* ☎ 10/548–9801) sells high-end clothing, shoes, and accessories for the young-and-stylish by a bevy of designers worldwide—a good place for parents hoping to buy teenagers and twentysomethings clothes they might actually wear. **IVANAhelsinki** (✉ *Uudenmaank. 15, Punavuori* ☎ 09/622–4422) has earned international recognition for its solid-color and brightly

Marimekko

When the world's fashion-conscious think Finland, they think Marimekko. Founded by a Finnish couple in 1949, the company got its big international break when Jacqueline Kennedy appeared in front of JFK on the cover of *Sports Illustrated* magazine wearing a Marimekko dress during the 1960 presidential campaign. More recently, Manolo Blahnik took the company's prints as one of the inspirations for his spring/summer 2008 collection. One of its best-known designs is artist Marija Isola's

"Unikko," comprising large poppies in bright, bold colors, created in 1964 and still in production on items from dresses to bedding. Another of the company's timeless designs is "Piccolo," a vivid striped pattern which first took the form of the "Jokapoika" shirt (1956) and is today printed on a range of clothing and accessories found in Marimekko stores. The company introduces dozens of new fabric designs every year with an emphasis on bold, uncluttered patterns.

patterned women's sweaters and dresses. At its four locations in central Helsinki, **Marimekko** (⊠ *Pohjoisespl. 2, Esplanadi* ☎ *09/686–0240* ⊠ *Pohjoisespl. 31, Kämp Galleria, Esplanadi* ☎ *09/6860–2411* ⊠ *Urho Kekkosen Katu 1, Kamppi shopping center, Keskusta* ☎ *010/344–3300*) sells bright, unusual clothes for men, women, and children in quality fabrics. Though the products are costly, they're worth a look even if you don't plan to buy.

JEWELRY
Anna Heino (⊠ *Uudenmaank. 34, Punavuori* ☎ *09/6220–0333*) uses stones in her cleverly designed women's necklaces, earrings, rings and bracelets, an example being a silver bracelet with removable links. She also does custom designs. **Kalevala Koru** (⊠ *Unionink. 25, Keskusta* ☎ *09/686–0400*) bases its designs on traditional motifs dating back as far as the Iron Age. Its designs are also available at most jewelry shops around Finland, and at Stockmann's and Sokos, at reasonable prices. **Union Design** (⊠ *Eteläranta 14, inner courtyard Kauppatori* ☎ *09/6220–0333*) is an atelier workshop of goldsmiths, silversmiths, and jewelers emphasizing limited series and unique pieces, displaying top-notch talent in Finnish design.

SAUNA SUPPLIES
For genuine Finnish sauna supplies such as wooden buckets, bath brushes, and birch-scented soap, visit the **Sauna Shop** (⊠ *Aleksanterink. 28, Keskusta*) in the Kiseleff Bazaar. The fourth floor of **Stockmann's** (⊠ *Aleksanterink. 52, Keskusta* ☎ *09/1211*) stocks accessories and supplies for the sauna.

STREET MARKETS
Helsinki's main street markets and market halls specialize in food, but all have some clothing (new and used) and household products. **Hakaniemi Street Market and Market Hall** (⊠ *North of town center, off Unionink., Hakaniemi* ⊙ *Indoor Market Hall: weekdays 8–6, Sat. 8–4; street market: weekdays 6:30–3*) has everything from Eastern spices to used

clothing and ceramics. Visit **Kauppatori** (⇨ *Exploring Helsinki*), Helsinki's Market Square, to browse among the colorful stalls or just relax with a coffee. At the **Old Market Hall** (◔ *Weekdays 8–7, Sat. 8–4*), almost adjacent to Kauppatori, you can browse and shop for anything from flowers to vegetables, meat, and fish. **Hietalahden Tori**, at Bulevardi and Hietalahdenkatu, is open weekdays 6:30–2 and Saturday 6:30–3 (with extended summer hours). At the outdoor flea market (open weekdays 8–2, Saturday 8–3) you can get an ever-changing assortment of used items; the indoor market is brimming with food, flowers, fish, and more.

SIDE TRIPS FROM HELSINKI

Helsinki's outskirts are full of attractions, most of them no more than a half-hour bus or train ride from the city center. From the idyllic former home of Finland's national artist to the utopian garden city of Tapiola in Espoo, options abound.

GALLEN-KALLELA ESTATE

10 km (6 mi) northwest of Helsinki.

Set at the edge of the sea and surrounded by towering, wind-bent pines, the turreted brick-and-stucco Gallen-Kallela Estate was the self-designed studio and home of the Finnish Romantic painter Akseli Gallen-Kallela. Gallen-Kallela (1865–1931) lived in the mansion on and off from its completion in 1913 until his death. Inside, the open rooms of the painter's former work spaces make the perfect exhibition hall for his paintings. Also displayed are some of his posters and sketches of the ceiling murals he made for the Paris Art Exhibition at the turn of the 20th century. To get to the estate, take Tram 4 from in front of the Sokos department store on Mannerheimintie. From the Munkkiniemi stop walk 2 km (1 mi) through Munkinpuisto Park. ⊠ *Gallen-Kallelantie 27, Tarvaspää* 🕾 *09/849–2340* ⊕ *www.gallen-kallela.fi* 🎫 *€8* ◔ *Mid-May–Aug., daily 10–6; Sept.–mid-May, Tues.–Sat. 10–4, Sun. 10–5.*

HVITTRÄSK

40 km (25 mi) west of Helsinki.

In an idyllic position at the top of a wooded slope is Hvitträsk, the studio home of architects Herman Gesellius, Armas Lindgren, and Eliel Saarinen. The property dates back to the turn of the 20th century, and is now a charming museum. The whimsical main house reveals the national art nouveau style, with its rustic detail and paintings by Akseli Gallen-Kallela; Saarinen lived here, and his grave is nearby. A café and restaurant are set up in one of the architects' houses. Hvitträsk can be reached from Helsinki by taking the L or U train to Luoma and walking 2.7 km (1.7 mi) or taking the E, L, S or U train to Kauklahti and then a taxi. ⊠ *Hvitträskintie 166, Kirkkonummi, Hvitträsk, Luoma* 🕾 *09/4050–9630* ⊕ *www.hvittrask.fi* 🎫 *€5* ◔ *Museum May–Sept., daily 11–6; Oct.–Apr., Tues.–Sun. 11–5.*

AINOLA

50 km (31 mi) north of Helsinki.

The former home of Finland's most famous son, composer Jean Sibelius was designed by Lars Sonck in 1904 and takes its name from his wife, Aino. From late spring through summer, the intimate wooden house set in secluded woodland is open to the public as a museum. Take a bus from the Helsinki Linja-autoasema (bus station) or a local train first to the town of Järvenpää; Ainola is 2 km (1 mi) farther by bus or taxi. ✉ *Ainolantie, Järvenpää* ☎ *09/287–322* ⊕ *www.ainola.fi* 🖃 *€5* ☉ *Early May–Sept., Tues.–Sun. 10–5.*

3

PORVOO

50 km (31 mi) east of Helsinki.

Porvoo is a living record of the past, with its old stone streets and painted wooden houses lining the riverbank. Artisan boutiques around the old Town Hall Square invite exploration. Take a stroll into the Old Quarter to see the multicolor wooden houses.

GETTING HERE AND AROUND

Part of the fun of visiting Porvoo is the journey you take to get there. On summer Saturdays (July through the end of August, except Midsummer) there's a train connection along the historical museum rail between Helsinki and Porvoo, on board the old trains from the 1950s and 1960s. Prices are €15 one-way, €25 round-trip. Once in Porvoo, you can take a historic ride on a steam train to Hinthaara and back. Contact the Porvoo Museum Railway Society for details.

Far more regular than the historic train journey is the **boat service.** May through September, cruises depart from Helsinki's South Harbor regularly (check the Web site for exact dates and times): the *J. L. Runeberg* takes 3½ hours, and the round-trip costs €33. The *King* takes three hours each way and costs €39 for a round-trip. You will be taken westward through dozens of islands before landing at Porvoo. For more information, contact the boat companies or the Porvoo City Tourist Office. By bus, take the Porvoo bus from Kanppi Station in Helsinki one-hour to Porvoo Station near the marketplace, which is a five-minute walk from the harbor. By car, take the E18 freeway to the old road 170 into Porvoo.

ESSENTIALS

Train Info Porvoo Museum Railway Society (☎ *0400/700–717* ⊕ *helsinkiww. net/pmr*).

Visitor Info Porvoo City Tourist Office (☎ *019/520–2316 tourist office, 019/524–3331 J. L. Runeberg, 019/524–3331 M/S King, Royal Line* ⊕ *www. msjlruneberg.fi*).

EXPLORING

The **Home of J. L. Runeberg** (⊠ *Aleksanterink 306100* ☎ *019/581–330*), Finland's national poet, is a fantastically authentic museum displaying the poet and his wife's original furnishings and paintings exactly as they were upon his death in 1877. The Runeberg story is told by museum staff and there's an exhibit related to Finnish history.

Visit the 15th-century stone-and-wood cathedral, **Porvoon Tuomiokirkko,** where the diet of the first duchy of Finland was held in the 1800s.

The **Walter Runebergin Veistoskokoelma** (*Walter Runeberg Sculpture Collection* ⊠ *Aleksanterink 506100* ☎ *019/582–186*) has some wonderful pieces and is well worth a visit.

The **Porvoo Museo** (⊠ *Välik. 1106100* ☎ *019/574–7500 or 019/574–7589* ⊕ *www.porvoonmuseo.fi*), inside the historic town hall built in 1764, captures the region's social and cultural history through exhibits on daily life and household objects. Next door to the Porvoo Museo, **Holm House** (⊠ *Välik. 1106100* ☎ *0400/407-475*) is the restored 18th-century home of the wealthy merchant Holm family.

Near Porvoo in Haikko, you can visit the **Albert Edelfeltin Atelje** (⊠ *Edelfeltsstigen 306400* ☎ *019/577–414*), the painter's studio.

SHOPPING

Atelier AN (⊠ *Jokik. 12A 4* ☎ *040/565–5625*) sells smart-looking handmade sweaters, hats, coats, and jackets produced from wool as well as local reindeer, lamb, and elk skins. At **Brunberg OY** (⊠ *Välik. 4* ☎ *019/548–4235*), 2 km (1.2 mi) from its factory, you can sample and buy chocolate-mint chips, chocolae-orange chips, and other combinations, as well as the individually wrapped fudgelike toffees adored throughout Finland, at the nation's best prices.

VANTAA

20 km (13 mi) north of Helsinki.

Though not remarkable, Vantaa—the municipality north of Helsinki proper and the home of the international airport—has a few notable attractions. A welcome surplus of open green space and trails for biking, hiking, and running create an oasis for outdoor enthusiasts. Don't miss the 15th-century Helsingin Pitajan Kirkko (Parish Church).

Consider using Vantaa as home base if your trip to Helsinki coincides with a convention and you can't find accommodations there: the airport is within the city's municipal boundaries and easily reached by public transport. The Helsinki Card also works in Vantaa.

GETTING HERE AND AROUND

From Helsinki's main railway station, it's a 20- to 25-minute ride on the K, N, or R trains, the R being the fastest. The main stop in Vantaa is Tekkurila in eastern Vantaa, which has a bus connection to the airport.

ESSENTIALS
Visitor Info Vantaa Travel Center (⊠ *Ratatie 7, Tikkurila* ☎ *09/8392–2133* ⊕ *www. vantaa.fi).*

EXPLORING
☾ The **Heureka Suomalainen Tiedekeskus** *(Heureka Finnish Science Center)* has interactive exhibits on topics as diverse as energy, language, and papermaking. There is also a cafeteria, a park, and a planetarium with taped commentary in English as well as the Verne IMAX-type theater. ⊠ *Tiedepuisto 1, Tikkurila* ☎ *09/85799* ⊕ *www.heureka.fi* ⊡ *€14.50 exhibitions only, €9 for Verne theater only, €19 for both* ☉ *Mon., Wed., and Fri. 10–5, Thurs. 10–8, weekends 10–6.*

3

The **Suomen Ilmailumuseo** *(Finnish Aviation Museum)* has more than 60 military and civilian aircraft on display. ⊠ *Tietotie 3* ☎ *09/870–0870* ⊕ *www.suomenilmailumuseo.fi* ⊡ *€6* ☉ *Daily 11–6.*

The peaceful **Viherpaja Japanese and Cactus gardens** in Vantaa include an exhibition of carnivorous plants. ⊠ *Meiramitie 101510* ☎ *09/822–628* ⊕ *www.viherpaja.fi* ⊡ *Japanese Garden and carnivorous plants €1, other gardens free* ☉ *June–Aug., weekdays 8–6, weekends 9–4; Sept.– May, weekdays 8–7, weekends 9–5.*

FISKARS VILLAGE

90 km (56 mi) west of Helsinki.

This ironworks village is best-known as the place where the Fiskars company began producing its eponymous orange scissors in 1967. The company has since relocated production but still owns much of the picturesque lake-dotted, tree-lined village, where it has encouraged artists, designers, and their families to settle. At any given time, the village features two exhibitions—one usually related to the Fiskars company, one to international art, a modest museum, a couple of surprisingly good restaurants, and a 15-room hotel.

GETTING HERE AND AROUND
From Helsinki, it's best to rent a car for the easy 75-minute drive. Alternatively, you can take a 50- to 55-minute train ride to Kaarja, from which point it's a 15-minute taxi ride; buses from Karjaa are infrequent and connections from the train are poor.

ESSENTIALS
Visitor Info Fiskars Village (⊠ *Peltorivi 1* ☎ *019/277-7504* ⊕ *www.fiskarsvil lage.fi).*

EXPLORING
☾ At **Bianco Blu** visitors can try their hand at blowing their own glass item during an hour-and-a-half-long guided session, or shop among the many professionally blown wares. ⊠ *Kuparivasarantie 14* ☎ *45/139–0020* ⊕ *www.biancoblu.fi* ⊡ *About €30 a session* ☉ *Tues.–Fri. 11–5, Sat. 11–4; May–July and Dec. also open Sun. 11–4.*

☾ The **Fiskars Museum** gives a modest overview of the things produced in the village, its culture, and the living conditions of the 19th-century

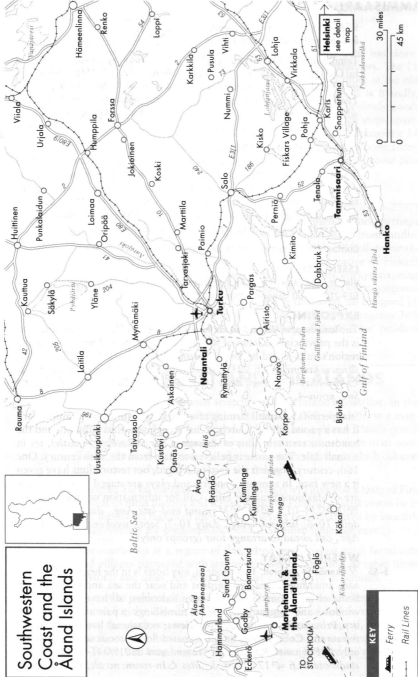

Southwestern Coast and the Åland Islands

Helsinki see detail map

30 miles
45 km

KEY

Ferry

Rail Lines

Hämeenlinna
Renko
Loppi
Viiala
Viiala
Urjala
Forssa
Humppila
Karkkila
Pusula
Vihti
Lohja
Virkkala
Karis
Snappertuna
Porkkalanselkä
Nummi
Kisko
Fiskars Village
Pohja
Jokioinen
Koski
Salo
Pernio
Tenala
Tammisaari
Punkalaidun
Oripää
Loimaa
Marttila
Paimio
Kimito
Dalsbruk
Hanko
Huittinen
Tarvasjoki
Hango västra fjärd
Kauttua
Säkylä
Yläne
Mynämäki
Turku
Pargas
Airisto
Gullkrona Fjärd
Laitila
Askainen
Naantali
Rymättylä
Nauvo
Bergham Fjärden
Gulf of Finland
Rauma
Uusikaupunki
Taivassalo
Kustavi
Iniö
Osnäs
Korpo
Björkö
Baltic Sea
Åva
Brändö
Kumlinge
Kumlinge
Bergham Fjärden
Sottunga
Kökar
Åland (Ahvenanmaa)
Sund County
Bomarsund
Lumparen
Föglö
Kökarsfjärden
Hammarland
Godby
Mariehamn & the Åland Islands
Eckerö
TO STOCKHOLM

In-hotel: restaurant, room service, bar, Wi-Fi, parking (fee) ⊟AE, DC, MC, V ❍❙*BP.*

HANKO

37 km (23 mi) southwest of Tammisaari, 141 km (88 mi) southeast of Turku.

In the coastal town of Hanko (Hangö), you'll find long stretches of beach—about 30 km (19 mi) of it—some sandy and some with sea-smoothed boulders. Sailing abounds here, thanks to Finland's largest guest harbor. A sampling of the grandest and most fanciful private homes in Finland dot the seacoast, their porches edged with gingerbread iron detail and woodwork, and crazy towers sprouting from their roofs. Favorite pastimes here are beachside strolls; bike rides along well-kept paths; and, best of all, long walks along the main avenue past the great wooden houses with their wraparound porches.

This customs port has a rich history. Fortified in the 18th century, Hanko defenses were destroyed by the Russians in 1854, during the Crimean War. Later it became a popular spa town for Russians, then the port from which more than 300,000 Finns emigrated to North America between 1880 and 1930.

GETTING HERE AND AROUND

Hanko can be reached by car along Route 25, by train from Helsinki or Turku with a connection at Karjaa, and by bus from either city.

Transportation Info Finnish Railways *(VR ☎0600/41–902 €1 plus local network charge ⊕www.vr.fi).* **Matkahuolto Bus** *(☎0200/4000€1.50 per minute plus local network charge ⊕www.matkahuolto.fi).*

ESSENTIALS

Visitor Info Hanko *(✉Raatihuoneentori 5, Box 14 ☎019/220–3411 ⊕www. hanko.fi).*

EXPLORING

⟳ Through the telescope of **Vesitorni** *(Hanko's Water Tower)*, you can follow the comings and goings of the town's marine traffic and get a grand view of some of the very small islands sprinkled around the peninsula's edges. *✉Vartiovuori ☎019/220–3411 tourist office ☎€1 ❍Early June–July, daily noon–5; Aug., daily 1–3.*

WHERE TO STAY

¢ ⛺**Camping Silversand.** There are various facilities at this large campground near the water, including eight-person cabins and full hookups for trailers, as well as trailers and tents for rent. **Pros:** close to nature; good facilities. **Cons:** rustic. *✉Hopeahietikko, Hanko ☎019/ 248–5500, 09/6138–3210 off-season ⊕www.lomaliitto.fi ❍Closed mid-Oct.–mid-Apr.*

$-$$ ⬚ **Hotel Villa Maija.** Comprised of three houses surrounding a courtyard, this seaside hotel offers 13 unique rooms, including some with balconies and some with full kitchens best suited to families. Its bed-and-breakfast feel is well suited to its quiet setting. **Pros:** Close to the water;

storied atmosphere. **Cons:** no nightlife. ⊠*Appelgrenintie 7, Hanko* ☏*050/505–2013* ⊕*www.villamaija.fi* ⟲*13 rooms* ◔*In-room: no a/c, kitchen (some), refrigerator (some). In-hotel: restaurant, room service, bar, beachfront, Wi-Fi, parking (free)* ⊟*AE, DC, MC, V* �|○|*BP.*

SPORTS AND THE OUTDOORS
BOATING
Boats can be rented at the guest harbor Info-Point in Hanko, or through the local tourist office. Young people and families race in and attend the annual **Hanko Regatta,** setting sail during a weekend at the end of June or beginning of July.

TURKU

140 km (87 mi) northwest of Hanko, 166 km (103 mi) west of Helsinki.

Founded at the beginning of the 13th century, Turku is the nation's oldest and fourth-largest city and was the original capital of newborn Finland. Its early importance in the history of Finland has earned Turku the title of "the cradle of Finnish culture." Turku has a long history as a commercial and intellectual center (the city's name means trading post); once the site of the first Finnish university, it has two major universities, the Finnish University of Turku and the Swedish-speaking Åbo Akademi. Turku has a population of about 200,000, and a busy, year-round harbor. In summer the banks of the river come alive with boat and ship cafés.

A lively artistic community thrives in Turku, and like most Finnish towns, it comes into its own in the summer. It is most active in July during the **Ruisrock Festival** (⊕*www.ruisrock.fi*), drawing international acts to the seaside park 5 km (3 mi) west of the city. August's **Turku Music Festival** (⊕*www.turkumusicfestival.fi*) features baroque and contemporary performances. The highlight of the festival is the well-attended, outdoor Down by the Laituri, with stages set up along the city's waterfront.

GETTING HERE AND AROUND
Turku's airport is a 20- to 25-minute taxi ride from the town's center, which will cost €20–€25. Alternatively, you can take the #1 bus, which leaves from in front of the Hamburger Bors Hotel every 20 minutes and goes straight to the airport for €2.50. Finnair provides service to and from Helsinki and Stockholm. The Helsinki–Turku drive is 166 km (103 mi) on E18.

In summer, Turku TouRing, the tourist office, has a three-hour tour of Turku's main sights, including the cathedral and castle. They also have tours geared to children. A TurkuCard includes unlimited travel on city public transportation, a guided city tour in summer, free entry to all the city's museums, and restaurant discounts. It's available for one or two days (€21 or €28, respectively) or as a family card for up to two adults and three children under 15 for one day (€40). You can buy it at museums, most hotels, or at the tourism information office; contact Turku Touring for more information.

ESSENTIALS
Airline Contact **Finnair** (⊕ *www.finnair.fi*).

Hospital TYKS Hospital (Turku University Hospital) (✉ *Luolavuorenk. 1, Turku* ☏ *02/269–7711, 112 in emergency*)

Steamship Info Steamship Company SS Ukkopekka (✉ *Linnank. 38, Turku* ☏ *02/515–3300* ⊕ *www.ukkopekka.fi*).

Taxi Turku Taxi (☏ *02/10–041*).

Visitor Info Turku TouRing (✉ *Aurakatu 4, Turku* ☏ *02/262–7444* ⊕ *www. turkutouring.fi*).

EXPLORING
TOP ATTRACTIONS
★ **Aboa Vetus/Ars Nova.** This museum displays a unique combination of history and art. Begun as a straightforward extension of the Villa von Rettig collection, the museum's concept changed when workers discovered archaeological remains, which were excavated and incorporated into the museum. Modern art in the old villa includes works by Auguste Herbin (1882–1960) and Max Ernst (1891–1976), as well as Picasso's *The Swordsman*, although not all works are always on display. The preserved excavations in the Aboa Vetus section date to as early as the 13th century. ✉ *Itäinen Rantakatu 4–6, Keskusta* ☏ *02/250–0552* ⊕ *www.aboavetusarsnova.fi* ☒ *€8* ☉ *Apr.–late Sept., daily 11–7; mid-Sept.–Mar., Tues.–Sun., 11–7.*

Fodor'sChoice **Turun Linna.** Where the Aura flows into the sea stands *Turku Castle*,
★ one of the city's most important historical monuments. The oldest part of the fortress was built at the end of the 13th century, and the newer part dates from the 16th century. The castle was damaged by bombing in 1941, and its restoration was completed in 1961. Many of its seemingly infinite rooms hold rather incongruous exhibits: next to a display on medieval life (featuring a dead rat to illustrate the Black Death) is a roomful of 1920s flapper costumes. The vaulted chambers themselves give you a sense of the domestic lives of the Swedish royals. A good gift shop and a pleasant café are on the castle grounds. ✉ *Linnank. 80, Keskusta* ☏ *02/262–0300* ⊕ *www.turku.fi/museo* ☒ *€7 without a guide, €9 with a guide* ☉ *Mid-Apr.–mid-Sept., daily 10–6; mid-Sept.–mid-Apr., Tues.–Fri. and Sun. 10–3, Sat. 10–5.*

Turun Taidemuseo. *The Turku Art Museum* holds some of Finland's most famous paintings, including works by Akseli Gallen-Kallela, and a broad selection of turn-of-the-20th-century Finnish art and contemporary works. The impressive granite building, situated along Puolala Park, was completed in 1904 and in itself is worth the visit. In summer, the museum features works from Estonia. Call ahead for information on guided tours. ✉ *Aurakatu 26, Keskusta* ☏ *02/262–7100* ⊕ *www. turuntaidemuseo.fi* ☒ *€7.50 summer, €6 other times* ☉ *Tues.–Fri. 11–7, weekends 11–5.*

Turun Tuomiokirkko. The 700-year-old *Turku Cathedral* remains the seat of the archbishop of Finland. It was partially gutted by fire in 1827 but has subsequently been completely restored. In the choir are R. W.

Ekman's frescoes portraying Bishop Henry (an Englishman) baptizing the then-heathen Finns, and Mikael Agricola offering the Finnish translation of the New Testament to Gustav Vasa of Sweden. The cathedral also houses a museum, which displays medieval church vestments, silver chalices, and wooden sculptures. ☒ *Turun Tuomiokirkko, Tuomiokirkkotori 20, Keskusta* ☎*02/261–7100* ☜*€2 for Cathedral Museum* ⊕*www.turunsrk.fi* ☉*Mid-Apr.–mid-Sept., daily 9–8; mid-Sept.–mid-Apr., daily 9–7.*

WORTH NOTING

Luostarinmäki Handicrafts Museum. This authentic collection of wooden structures escaped fire in the 19th century and now contain shops and workshops where traditional crafts are demonstrated and sold. Ask staff about the history of a particular workshop or call ahead for schedule of guided tours, offered several times daily in summer. ☒ *Vartiovuorenk. 4, Keskusta* ☎*02/262–0350* ⊕*www.turunmuseot.fi* ☜*€5 without guide, €7 with guide* ☉*Mid-Apr.–mid-Sept., daily 10–6; other times of year by appointment.*

WHERE TO EAT

$$
ECLECTIC

✕**Blanko.** Especially popular with locals for lunch, Blanko serves an eclectic mix of salads, pastas, Asian stir-fry, chicken, lamb, and beef. Pastas, such as minced lamb mixed with linguine over salad with red pesto are particularly popular. While no newcomer, the restaurant's quick service, funky artwork and its comfy lounge seating near the bar between dining areas maintain its trendy appeal. The sidewalk tables are generally a packed place to see and be seen during the summer. ☒*Aurak. 1* ☎*02/233–3966* ⚖*Reservations essential* ▤*AE, DC, MC, V.*

$$$
SCANDINAVIAN

✕**Herman.** Upstairs, a fine-dining restaurant complete with river views and a fish tank maître'd desk; downstairs, pub-style seating with a smaller menu where locals come to sip mugs of the restaurant's own light and dark brews. Both feature French-influenced Finnish cuisine, whether it be the five-course Menu Herman for €60–€70 (sound familiar? this restaurant actually predates Rocca, listed below) or à la carte entrees including fried white fish with sweet potato cake and fennel sauce and desserts such as a mocca crème brûlée with muscovado ice cream. Book early and request a table by the front windows. Downstairs is closed for dinner in winter but you can try the beer at a small lounge upstairs or come at lunch for the €8.60 all-you-can-eat buffet. ☒*Läntinen Rantak. 37* ☎*02/230–3333* ⚖*Reservations essential* ▤*AE, DC, MC, V* ☉*No lunch weekends.*

$$
ECLECTIC
Fodor's Choice
★

✕**Mami.** The name means "Mom" in Finnish and the regulars at this small-yet-airy riverside bistro feel right at home. The bright green-and-white dining room is outfitted with chairs from the '60s and floor-to-ceiling windows overlooking the river. The menu changes monthly and always includes seasonal ingredients in its fresh fish dishes, including charcoaled slightly-smoked salmon over potato salad or grilled whitefish with beetroot and cream spiced with anchovies. Prompt yet friendly service and individual hand-towels in the bathrooms complete the comfortable atmosphere. If only Mom cooked this well. ☒*Linnank. 3* ☎*02/231–1111* ▤*AE, DC, MC, V* ☉*Closed Sun. No lunch Sat.*

$$$$ ✕**Rocca.** Synonymous with "fine-dining in Turku," the city's most
SCANDINAVIAN   upscale restaurant is a waterfront white-linen-and-exposed-brick affair
a short riverside walk from the city center. The menu is decidedly Scandinavian with French and Italian influences, and features seasonal fish
and game in appetizers such as crayfish soup with lobster mousse and
entrees such as deer silverside with turnip puree and dark Banyuls sauce.
The five-course Menu Rocca ranges from €50 depending on the ingredients used (one of the five is a cheese course prior to dessert). The wine
list usually includes 160 bottles; wine tastings and special menus can
be arranged. ✉*Läntinen Rantak. 55* ☏*02/284–8800* ⚮*Reservations
essential* ▤*AE, DC, MC, V* ⊘*Closed Sun. and from Christmas until
New Year's Eve. No lunch Sat.*

$$$ ✕**Suomalainen Pohja.** This classic Finnish restaurant is decorated in dark
SCANDINAVIAN   wood with large windows offering a splendid view of an adjacent park.
Seafood, poultry, and game dishes have earned a good reputation here.
The menu changes every few weeks to accommodate regulars; highlights
include fillet of reindeer with sautéed potatoes or cold smoked rainbow
trout with asparagus. ✉*Aurak. 24, Keskusta* ☏*02/251–2000* ▤*AE,
DC, MC, V* ⊘*Closed weekends and July.*

WHERE TO STAY

¢ ⌂**Hostel Turku.** Turku's only year-round hostel features clean, unclut-
tered eight-bed, six-bed, four-bed, and twin-bed rooms. The staff mem-
bers take their jobs seriously and it shows in the cleanliness of the large
shared bathrooms, although there are private shower rooms as well.
A small lounge with the hostel's only television and two dining areas
encourage socializing, while families appreciate the baby-changing facil-
ities. Members of Youth Hostelling get a €2.50 discount per night. **Pros:**
good bus connections from doorstep; clean facilities. **Cons:** modest cold
breakfast costs extra (€5.20); 15-minute walk to the city center. ✉*Lin-
nank. 39* ☏*02/262–7680* ⊕*www.turku.fi/hostelturku* ☞*23 rooms*
⚮*In-room: no phone, refrigerator, no TV. In-hotel: laundry facilities,
Internet terminal, parking (free)* ▤*AE, DC, MC, V* ⦿*BP.*

$$$ ⌂**Park Hotel.** Built in 1904 in the art nouveau style for a British execu-
tive who ran the local shipyard, the castlelike Park Hotel is one of Fin-
land's most unusual lodgings. Rooms have high ceilings and antique
furniture but offer all the comforts of a modern hotel. It's in the heart
of Turku, two blocks from the main market square. **Pros:** central location; unique atmosphere. **Cons:** room sizes vary considerably (ask to
see a few options, if possible). ✉*Rauhank. 1, Turku* ☏*02/273–2555*
⊕*www.parkhotelturku.fi* ☞*20 rooms, 1 suite* ⚮*In-room: Wi-Fi.
In-hotel: room service, bar, laundry service, parking (free), some pets
allowed, no-smoking rooms* ▤*AE, DC, MC, V* ⦿*BP.*

$$$ ⌂**Radisson SAS Marina Palace.** Popular with business travelers and,
in summer, families for its excellent riverfront location just outside
of the city center, the Marina Palace does not disappoint. Riverside
rooms, which are always given first (so book early) are considerably
larger than their street-facing counterparts and include couches; all
are done in warm reds and browns with backlit, framed mirrors over
the beds. Bathrooms have marble-topped counters and clean-looking
white tile. The included breakfast is delicious. **Pros:** riverfront location;

outstanding men's and women's sauna facilities; friendly service. **Cons:** mediocre restaurant; corporate feel. ⊠*Linnank. 32* ☎*020/1234–700* ⊕*www.radissonsas.com* ⌨*180 rooms, 4 suites* ⚭*In-room: safe, Internet, Wi-Fi. In-hotel: restaurant, room service, bar, gym, laundry service, Internet terminal, Wi-Fi, parking (paid)* ⊟*AE, DC, MC, V* ⦿|*BP.*

$$–$$$ ▣ **Sokos Hotel Hamburger Börs.** This is one of Turku's best-known and finest hotels. Guest rooms have modern amenities. The German-style tavern is great for drinks; the main restaurant serves Continental cuisine and Finnish specialties such as fillet of reindeer with bacon. There's often live music in the nightclub. **Pros:** heart-of-it-all location; good restaurant. **Cons:** in-house nightclub can be loud. ⊠*Kauppiask. 6, Turku* ☎*02/337–381* ⊕*www.sokoshotels.fi* ⌨*396 rooms, 10 suites* ⚭*In-room: safe (some), Wi-Fi. In-hotel: 9 restaurants, room service, bar, pool, parking (paid), some pets allowed, no-smoking rooms* ⊟*AE, DC, MC, V* ⦿|*BP.*

AFTER DARK

Turku has several distinctive bars in historic buildings. **Koulu (School)** (⊠*Eerikinkatu 18, Keskusta* ☎*02/274–5757*) is a brewery restaurant in what used to be a school for girls built in the 1880s. **Old Bank** (⊠*Aurakatu 3, Keskusta* ☎*02/274–5700*), near the market square, is one of the most popular bars in Turku, housed in a former bank and offering 150 brands of beer from all over the world. A block closer to the river, **Blanko** (⊠*Aurakatu 1, Keskusta* ☎*02/233–3966*)is popular with twentysomethings for its wine and basic cocktails, such as its mojitos.

Puutorin Vessa (Toilet) (⊠*Puutori, Puu Square, Keskusta* ☎*02/233–8123*) is decidedly Turku's most unusual pub, in a functionalist building once serving as a public restroom but now housing what the owners call a "nice-smelling bar." The **Uusi Apteekki (New Pharmacy)** (⊠*Kaskenkatu 1, Keskusta* ☎*02/250–2595*) has a wide selection of beers on tap, served in an old apothecary.

SHOPPING

Hansa (⊠*Kristiinank. 9, Keskusta* ☎*02/251–8590* ⊕*www.hansainfo. fi*) is Turku's largest shopping mall with more than 150 shops, including Marimekko. The **Forum** (⊠*Linnank. 9-11, Keskusta*) is another large mall just off the market square.

STREET MARKETS

Market Square (⊠*Keskusta* ⊙*Weekdays 7–6, Sat. 8–3*) is a village of red tents selling flowers, fruits, and vegetables as well as baked goods, clothing, and trinkets. At **Market Hall** (⊠*Keskusta* ⊙*Weekdays 7–5:30, Sat. 7–3*), a redbrick building completed in 1896, you can buy everything from smoked ham to souvenirs.

NAANTALI

20 km (12 mi) west of Turku, 170 km (105 mi) west of Helsinki.

Built around a convent of the Order of Saint Birgitta in the 15th century, the coastal village of Naantali is an aging medieval town, former pilgrimage destination, artists' colony, and modern resort all rolled into one. Many of its buildings date from the 17th century, following a massive rebuilding after the Great Fire of 1628. You'll also see a number of 18th- and 19th-century buildings, which form the basis of the Old Town—a settlement by the water's edge. These shingled wooden buildings were originally built as private residences, and many remain so, although a few now house small galleries.

Naantali's extremely narrow cobblestone lanes gave rise to a very odd law. During periods when economic conditions were poor, Naantalians earned their keep by knitting socks and exporting them by the tens of thousands. Men, women, and children all knitted so feverishly that the town council forbade groups of more than six from meeting in narrow lanes with their knitting—and causing road obstructions.

The **Naantali Music Festival** (☎*02/434–5363* ⊕*www.naantalinmusiik kijuhlat.fi*) features chamber music, orchestra, and jazz performances and takes place in June.

GETTING HERE AND AROUND
From Turku, you can take the 11 and 110 bus from Turku Market Place, which runs frequently. By car, take route 185, 8, or E8 through the city of Raisio to either Route 40 or the Raisiontie to the Aurinkotie into Naantali. You can take a 3½- to 4-hour steamship cruise between Turku and Naantali, which includes a smorgasbord lunch or dinner while drifting around the archipelago (€13–€20 not including meals); cruises run from mid-June to mid-August and there's a lunch cruise in September. Contact the Naantali tourist office or the Steamship Company SS *Ukkopekka.*

ESSENTIALS
Taxi Info Lounais-Suonen Taxi (☎*02/10041* ⊕*www.taxivie.net in Finnish*).

Steamship Info Steamship Company SS Ukkopekka (✉*Linnank. 38, Turku* ☎*02/ 515–3300* ⊕*www.ukkopekka.fi*).

Visitor Info Naantali Tourist Board (✉*Kaivotori 2* ☎*02/435–9800* ⊕*www. naantalinmatkailu.fi*).

EXPLORING
Near Naantali's marina, a footbridge leads to **Kailo Island,** in summer abuzz with theater, beach, sports, picnic facilities, and a snack bar.

A major attraction in the village is **Kultaranta,** the summer residence for Finland's presidents, with its more than 3,500 rosebushes. During the winter, the area is only open on Friday evening; call ahead to arrange tours. ✉*Luonnonmaasaari, Kultaranta* ☎*02/435–9800* ⊕*www.naan talinmatkailu.fi* ⊙*Guided tours late June–mid-Aug., Tues.–Sun.; call Naantali tourist office or check Web site for times; mid-Aug.–mid-June, Fri. 6–8.*

☾ The **Moomin World** theme park brings to life all the famous characters of the beloved children's stories written by Finnish author Tove Jansson. The stories emphasize family, respect for the environment, and new adventures. ✉*Kailo Island, PL 48, Kailo* ☎*02/511–1111* ⊕*www.*

muumimaailma.fi ☎€20, €29 *for a 2-day ticket, which includes Adventure Väski Island* ⊙ *Mid-June–mid-Aug., daily 10–6.*

The convent **Naantalin Luostarikirkko** *(Naantali's Vallis Gratiae)* was founded in 1443 and completed in 1462. It housed both monks and nuns, and operated under the aegis of the Catholic church until it was dissolved by the Reformation in the 16th century. Buildings fell into disrepair, then were restored from 1963 to 1965. The church is all that remains of the convent. ✉*Nunnak, Keskusta* ☎*02/437–5420, 02/437–5413 to check current schedules* ☎*Free* ⊙*May, daily 10–6; June–Aug., daily 10–8; Sept.–Apr., Wed. noon–2, Sun. 11 (or after worship service ends)–3 or by arrangement.*

WHERE TO STAY

$$$$ 📺**Naantali Kylpylä Spa.** The emphasis here is on pampering, with foot massages, shiatsu physical therapy, mud packs, spa-water, and algae baths and a recreation program that includes yoga, tai chi, gymnastics, and water aerobics. All kinds of health packages can be arranged, including health-rehabilitation programs. It is set on a peninsula in several buildings; you can also choose to stay aboard the yacht hotel, which is attached to the spa by an indoor corridor. **Pros:** 100 listed spa treatments; 21 conference rooms. **Cons:** lacks the intimacy of smaller retreats. ✉*Matkailijantie 2* ☎*02/44550* ⊕*www.naantalispa.fi* ⇗*81 rooms, 40 apartments, 129 suites, 140 suites in yacht* ⅃*In-room: safe (some), kitchen (some), refrigerator (some), Internet (some). In-hotel: 6 restaurants, room service, bars, pools, spa, laundry facilities, laundry service, Wi-Fi, parking (free), some pets allowed* ⊟*AE, DC, MC, V* ⎮⊚⎮*BP.*

MARIEHAMN AND THE ÅLAND ISLANDS

155 km (93 mi) west of Turku.

The Ålands are composed of more than 6,500 small rocky islands and skerries, inhabited in large part by families that fish or run small farms. Virtually all of the more than 25,000 locals are Swedish speaking and very proud of their largely autonomous status, which includes having their own flag and stamps. Their connection with the sea is indelible, their seafaring traditions revered. Åland is demilitarized and has special privileges within the EU that allow duty-free sales on ferries between Finland and Sweden.

Mariehamn (Maariahamina), on the main island, is the capital (population more than 10,000) and hub of Åland life. At its important port, some of the greatest grain ships sailing the seas were built by the Gustav Eriksson family.

GETTING HERE AND AROUND

Mariehamn's airport is 5 km from the town center and a €10–€15 10-minute taxi ride. Finnair provides service to and from Helsinki and Stockholm.

Åland is most cheaply reached by boat from Turku and Helsinki. Call the TallinkSiljan or Viking Line in Turku, Mariehamn, Tampere, or Helsinki. You can also reach the islands by Alandstrafiken ferry, which also transports cars. Purchase tickets at the harbor.

ESSENTIALS
Airline Contact Finnair (⊕ *www.finnair.fi*).

Boat Contacts Alandstrafiken (☎ *018/525–100 Mariehamn* ⊕ *www.aland strafiken.ax*). **Silja Line** (☎ *02/335–6244 Turku, 018/16711 Mariehamn, 03/216–2000 Tampere, 09/18041 Helsinki* ⊕ *www.silja.fi*). **Viking Line** (☎ *02/333–1331 Turku, 018/26011 Mariehamn, 03/249–0111 Tampere, 09/12351 Helsinki* ⊕ *www. vikingline.fi*).

Taxi Info Mariehamn Taxi (☎ *18/26000* ⊕ *www.taxi.ax*).

Visitor Info Åland Tourist Board (✉ *Storagatan 8, Mariehamn* ☎ *018/24000* ⊕ *www.visitaland.com*).

EXPLORING
The **Museifartyget Pommern** *(Pommern Museum Ship)*, in Mariehamn West Harbor at town center, is one of the last existing grain ships in the world. Once owned by the sailing fleet of the Mariehamn shipping magnate Gustaf Erikson, the ship carried wheat between Australia and England from 1923 to 1939. ✉ *On western harbor, Mariehamn* ☎ *018/531–421* ⊕ *www.pommern.aland.fi* ☜ *€5* ⊙ *May, June, and Aug., daily 9–5; July, daily 9–7; Sept., daily 10–4.*

In prehistoric times the islands were, relatively speaking, heavily populated, as is shown by traces of no fewer than 10,000 ancient settlements, graves, and strongholds. A visit to **Sund County** will take you back to the earliest days of life on the islands, with its remains from prehistoric times and the Middle Ages. **Kastelholm** is a medieval castle built by the Swedes to strengthen their presence on Åland. ✉ *Kastelholm* ☎ *018/432–150* ☜ *€5* ⊙ *Guided tours May, June, and early–mid-Aug., daily 10–5; July, daily 10–6; mid-Aug.–Oct. daily 10–5.*

Jan Karlsgården Friluftsmuseum *(Jan Karlsgården Open-air Museum)* is a popular open-air museum, with buildings and sheds from the 18th century that portray farming life on the island 200 years ago. ✉ *Kastelholm* ☎ *018/432–150* ☜ *Free* ⊙ *May–Sept., daily 10–5.*

About 8 km (5 mi) from the village of Kastelholm in Sund are the scattered ruins of **Bomarsund Fortress,** a huge naval fortress built by the Russians in the early 19th century. It was only half finished when it was destroyed by Anglo-French forces during the Crimean War. The fortress is open for touring at all times and features signs but for more information, you'll want to pick up a pamphlet from the small visitor center during its opening hours. ☎ *018/432–120* ⊙ *June and Aug., weekdays 10–4; July, daily 10–4; call ahead, as times can vary.*

WHERE TO STAY
$$$ ⊞ **Arkipelag.** In the heart of Mariehamn, the bayside Arkipelag Hotel is known for its fine marina and lively disco-bar. Rooms are modern and comfortable, with huge picture windows and balconies. Ask

for a seaside room. The restaurants, set in long, wood-panel rooms with wide windows overlooking an ocean inlet, serve fresh Åland seafood. **Pros:** indoor and outdoor pool; party goes late; great views from seaside rooms. **Cons:** party goes late. ⊠*Strandgatan 31, Mariehamn* ☎*018/24020* ⊕*www.hotellarkipelag.com* ⬩*78 rooms, 8 suites* ⬩*In-room: Internet, Wi-Fi. In-hotel: restaurant, room service, bar, pool, laundry service, Internet terminal, Wi-Fi, parking (free), some pets allowed* ⊟*AE, DC, MC, V* ⎮◯⎮*BP.*

$$ 	⊞**Björklidens Stugby.** The cabins are small, but the draw here is the out-
☾ 	doors. You can take out one of the free rowboats, or relax on the lawns and the tree swings. It is 25 km (16 mi) north of Mariehamn. Each cabin, as well as each of the five apartments, which sleep 4–7 people, has a full kitchen. There are outdoor grills and washing machines for guests to use, but they're more likely to be taken with the beachside sauna. **Pros:** beautiful setting; activities for kids. **Cons:** very basic amenities. ⊠*Björklydn 1, Hammarland* ☎*018/37800* ⊕*www.bjorkliden.aland. fi* ⬩*14 cabins, 5 apartments* ⬩*In-room: kitchen, refrigerator, no TV (some). In-hotel: restaurant, bar, beachfront, laundry facilities, Internet terminal, parking (free)* ⊟*AE, DC, MC, V* ⊙*Closed late Oct.–Apr.*

SPORTS AND THE OUTDOORS

BIKING

Most towns have bikes for rent from about €10 per day (€50 per week). The fine scenery and the terrain, alternately dead flat and gently rolling, make for ideal cycling. The roads are not busy once you leave the highway. **Suomen Retkeilymajajärjestö** (*Finnish Youth Hostel Association* ⊠*Yrjönk. 38B 15, Helsinki* ☎*09/565-7150* ⊕*www.hostellit.fi*) has reasonably priced bicycle rental–hostel packages for one to two weeks starting in Helsinki.

For Åland bicycle routes and tour packages, contact **Ålandsresor Ab** (⊠*PB 158, Mariehamn* ☎*018/28040* ⊕*www.alandsresor.fi*). **Viking Line** (⊠*Storagatan 2, Mariehamn* ☎*018/26211*) is a bike-friendly outfit that also offers cottage rentals in Åland.

BOATING AND FISHING

These are great sailing waters for experienced mariners. Boats can be rented through the Åland tourist office. Try **Ålandsresor** (⊠*Torggatan 2, Mariehamn* ☎*018/28040*) for fishing packages in the Ålands, which typically include equipment, a cottage, and a license for three or four days. **Viking Line** (⊠*Storagatan 2, Mariehamn* ☎*018/26211*) also offers packages for anglers.

THE LAKELANDS

Finland is perhaps best known for its lakes, numbering about 188,000, and you don't need to travel far in this region to appreciate their beauty, whether in winter or summer. Almost every lake, big or small, is fringed with tiny cabins. The lake cabin is a Finnish institution, and until the advent of cheap package tours abroad, nearly every Finnish family vacationed in the same way—in its cabin on a lake.

Savonlinna is the best-placed town in the Lakelands and can make a convenient base from which to begin exploring the region. Savonlinna also stands out among the towns, for both its stunning, water-bound views—it is hugged by gigantic Lake Saimaa—and its cultural life. The monthlong Savonlinna Opera Festival in July is one of Finland's—and Europe's—greatest. Most events, including opera, ballet, drama, and instrumental performance, are staged at the 14th-century Olavinlinna Castle, splendidly positioned just offshore.

To the west, the smaller Hämeenlinna has its own lakeside castle. North of Hämeenlinna, high-tech Tampere has the cultural variety of a city and is nestled between two large lakes. There are small medieval churches scattered through the Lakelands, the most famous of which is the stone church in Hattula, its interior a gallery of medieval painted scenes.

For centuries the lakeland region was a much-contested buffer zone between the warring empires of Sweden and Russia. After visiting the people of the Lakelands, you should have a basic understanding of the Finnish word *sisu* (guts), a quality that has kept Finns independent. Savonlinna, Tampere, and Hämeenlinna are only short train rides from Helsinki; all three make good daylong excursions from the capital city.

SAVONLINNA

335 km (208 mi) northeast of Helsinki.

One of the larger Lakelands towns, Savonlinna is best known for having the finest castle in all of Finland. The town takes advantage of this stunning attraction by holding major events, such as the annual opera festival, in the castle courtyard.

GETTING HERE AND AROUND

Buses are the best form of public transport into the region, with frequent connections to lake destinations from most major towns. An express bus from Helsinki can take five to six hours. It's a six-hour ride/drive from Helsinki to Savonlinna traveling Route 5 to Route 14 in Juva, then another 60 km (37 mi) from Juva. The train trip from Helsinki to Savonlinna takes 4½ hours. Savonlinna is one of the Lakelands towns with an airport. It's 15 km (9 mi) from the city center. A taxi is your only option: the 20-minute ride costs €12 per person when booked in advance. The flight time from Helsinki on Finnair is roughly one hour, and some flights stop in Varkaus.

The islands that make up Savonlinna center are linked by bridges. First, stop in at the tourist office for information; then cross the bridge east to the open-air market that flourishes alongside the main passenger quay. From here you can catch the boat to Kuopio and Lappeenranta. VIP Cruise offers scenic and lunch cruises aboard two 100-year-old steamboats June through August.

ESSENTIALS

Airline Contacts Finnair (⊕ www.finnair.fi).

Cruises VIP Cruise (☎ 15/516–130 ⊕ www.vipcruise.info).

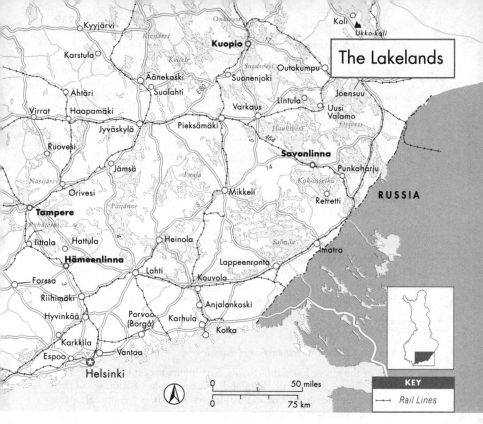

Taxi Info Taxi (☎ *15/106–0100*).

Tourist Board (✉ *Puistokatu 1* ☎ *015/517–510* ⊕ *www.savonlinnatravel.com*).

EXPLORING

A 10-minute stroll from the quay to the southeast brings you to Savonlinna's most famous site, the castle **Olavinlinna.** First built in 1475 to protect Finland's eastern border, the castle retains its medieval character and is one of Scandinavia's best-preserved historic monuments. Still surrounded by water that once bolstered its defensive strength, the fortress rises majestically out of the lake. Every July the **Savonlinna Opera Festival** (✉ *Olavinkatu 27* ☎ *015/476–750* ⊕ *www.operafestival.fi*) is held in the castle's courtyard, which creates a spellbinding combination of music and surroundings. The festival is a showcase for Finnish opera but it also hosts foreign companies such as the Los Angeles Opera and the Royal Opera. You will need to make reservations well in advance for both tickets and hotel rooms (note higher hotel rates during the festival), as Savonlinna draws many music lovers. The festival also includes arts and crafts exhibits around town. ✉ *Olavinlinna* ☎ *015/531–164* ⊕ *www.nba.fi/en/olavinlinna_castle* 🖙 *€5 entrance to Olavinlinna* ⊙ *June–mid-Aug., daily 10–5; mid-Aug.–May, daily 10–3. Guided tours daily on the hr.*

For a glimpse into the history of lake traffic, including the fascinating floating timber trains still a common sight on Saimaa today, visit the **Savonlinnan maakunta museo** (*Savonlinna Provincial Museum*), to which belong the 19th-century steam schooners, the SS *Salama*, the SS *Mikko*, and the SS *Savonlinna*. ⊠*Riihisaari island, near Olavinlinna, Riihisaari* ☎*015/571–4712* ⊕*www.savonlinna.fi/museo* ☜€4 ☉*Sept.–June, Tues.–Sun. 11–5; July–mid-Aug., daily 11–5. Boats: mid-May–end of Aug. during museum hrs.*

3

OFF THE BEATEN PATH

Old Mine of Outukumpu. This child-friendly complex 187 km (116 mi) north of Savonlinna consists of a mining museum and activities that include a trip on a mining train and a mineral exhibition. ⊠*Kaivosmiehenpolku 2* ☎*013/554–795* ⊕*www.vanhakaivos.fi* ☜€9 ☉*June–Aug., daily 10–6.*

© **Visulahden Matkailukeskus.** Five kilometers (3 mi) outside of Mikkeli, the Visulahti Travel Center includes a waxworks, an old car museum, and an amusement park with waterslides and a motor park. Restaurants, cabins, camping, lakeside sauna, boating, and swimming are also available at this all-purpose travel and vacation spot that caters to families and is especially popular with kids. Most activities are open only during the summer, but cabins can be rented throughout the year. From Savonlinna, you can take the Mikkeli bus or, if driving yourself, Route 14 to Route 5. It's 100 km (62 mi) from Savonlinna. ⊠*Visulahdentie 1, Mikkeli* ☎*015/182–81* ⊕*www.visulahdenmatkailu.fi* ⊟*DC, MC, V.*

★ One of the most popular excursions from Savonlinna is to the eastward **Taidekeskus Retretti** (*Retretti Art Center*). It's accessible via a two-hour boat ride or a 30-minute, 29-km (18-mi) bus trip. It consists of a modern art complex of unique design and has a cavern section built into the 8-km (5-mi) Punkaharju Ridge, which rises from the water and separates the Puruvesi and Pihlajavesi lakes. (At times the pine-covered rocks narrow to only 25 feet, yet the ridge still manages to accommodate a road and train tracks.) ⊠*Tuunaansarintea 3, Punkaharju* ☎*015/775–2200* ⊕*www.retretti.fi* ☜€15 ☉*June and Aug., daily 10–6 (ticket office open until 5); July, daily 10–7.*

WHERE TO EAT

$$

SCANDINAVIAN

✕**Huvila Brewery Restaurant.** Boasting nine homemade brews (mostly British-style ales), a waterfront locale with an outdoor patio, and a gastronomic cuisine, Huvila is a fantastic surprise so far from a big city. Tasty appetizers include malt-fried goat cheese with herb salad and apple vinaigrette; among the "splendid sequels" might be pike perch fried with malt crumbs and served with a tomatoes-and-crab risotto and a spinach puree. Vegetarians will be satisfied and everyone will be happy with the raspberry sherbet accompanied by chocolate mousse. ⊠*Puistok. 4* 🕾*015/5550–555* ⚑*Reservations essential* ⊟*AE, DC, MC, V* ⊗*No lunch. June–Aug., closed Sun.; Sept.–May, closed Sun. and Mon.*

$$–$$$ ✗ **Majakka.** The centrally located Majakka feels intimate due to its
FINNISH   booths and abundant greenery. Some tables offer nice views of the adjacent park and the Haukivesi Lake harbor. The menu changes twice a year, although there are some standards—try the steak topped with a pepper-and-cream sauce. Reservations are essential during festival season. ⊠*Satamak. 11, Keskusta* 🕾*015/206–2825* ⊟*AE, DC, MC, V.*

$ ✗ **Paviljonki.** Just 1 km (½ mi) from the city center is Paviljonki, the
SCANDINAVIAN   restaurant of the Savonlinna restaurant school. The menu is short but sweet; try the fried *vendace* (the tiny, tasty fish abundant in the lakes) with herb-spiced potato salad, or the classic pepper steak. The restaurant closes early (7 PM) and has a lunch buffet. ⊠*Rajalahdenk. 4, Nojanmaa* 🕾*015/550–6303* ⊟*DC, MC, V.*

¢   ✗ **Pizzeria Capero.** This Savonlinna institution has been satisfying locals
ECLECTIC   with its excellent pizzas in its split-level, tavernlike space for more than 25 years. An equally big draw, however, are its "pots"—combinations of rice and ingredients including chicken, shrimp, mussels, and mushrooms, baked together with a crispy cheese overlay. The pots take a while to prepare; start with a small pizza to try the best of both worlds. ⊠*Olavink. 51* 🕾*015/533–955* ⊟*AE, DC, MC, V.*

WHERE TO STAY

$–$$ 🏨 **Family Hotel Hospitz.** In the heart of Savonlinna overlooking Saimaa Lake, this charming YMCA hotel is in a 1930s brick building on historic Linnankatu. It has small, unpretentious rooms, all individually decorated in period styles. **Pros:** friendly staff; lake views from some rooms. **Cons:** simple bathrooms. ⊠*Linnank. 20* 🕾*015/515–661* ⊕*www.hospitz. com* ⊅*21 rooms* ⅋*In-room: Wi-Fi. In-hotel: bar, Wi-Fi, parking (free), some pets allowed* ⊟*AE, DC, MC, V* ⅋◯*BP.*

$$ 🏨 **Punkaharju Valtion Hotelli.** Near Retretti Art Center, the Punkaharju National Hotel was constructed as a gamekeeper's lodge for Czar Nicholas I in 1845. Enlarged and restored, it is now a restful spot for a meal or an overnight visit. The manor house with small rooms is decorated in the old Finnish country style. The restaurant serves simple local dishes such as fried vendace. It's a half-hour drive from Savonlinna. **Pros:** ocean-view rooms; authentic Finnish feel. **Cons:** basic rooms. ⊠*Harutia 596, Punkaharju* 🕾*020/752–9800* ⊕*www.lomaliitto.fi* ⊅*18 rooms, 3 suites, 3 with shared baths* ⅋*In-hotel: restaurant, room service, bar, beachfront, parking (free)* ⊟*DC, MC, V.*

$$–$$$ 🏨 **Seurahuone.** This hotel in a 1950s town house is near the market and passenger harbor. Rooms are small but comfortable and have modern fittings; be sure to ask for one that overlooks the picturesque harbor. If you don't plan to be in the nightclub until closing, request a room on the other side of the hotel. **Pros:** one of city's best nightclubs; some rooms have lake views. **Cons:** nightclub noise filters up to some rooms. ⊠*Kauppatori 4–6* 🕾*015/5731* ⊕*www.savonlinnanseurahuone.fi* ⊅*84 rooms* ⅋*In-room: Internet. In-hotel: 2 restaurants, room service, bar, Internet terminal, parking (paid)* ⊟*AE, DC, MC, V* ⅋◯*BP.*

$$–$$$ ⚇**Spa Hotel Casino.** A 1960s relic, the Spa Hotel Casino has a restful lakeside location on an island linked to town by a pedestrian bridge. Rooms are basic with brown cork floors, white walls, and simple furnishings; all except one have a balcony. **Pros:** Savonlinna's most luxurious facilities; lake views. **Cons:** dated decor. ⊠ *Kylpylaitoksentie, Kasinonsaari* ☎*015/73950* ⌨*80 rooms* ♿ *In-room: Internet. In-hotel: 2 restaurants, room service, bar, pool, spa, Wi-Fi, parking (free), some pets allowed, no-smoking rooms* ⊟*AE, DC, MC, V* ⵔ|*BP.*

$$ ⚇**Summer Hotel Vuorilinna.** The simple white rooms of this modern student dorm become hotel rooms in summer. Guests may use the facilities, including the restaurant, of the nearby Spa Hotel Casino. **Pros:** central location. **Cons:** no-frills dorm housing. ⊠ *Kylpylaitoksentie, Kasinonsaari* ☎*015/739–5495* ⌨*220 rooms* ♿ *In-room: no TV. In-hotel: parking (free)* ⊟*AE, DC, MC, V* ⵔ|*BP* ⊘*Closed mid-Aug.–May.*

KUOPIO

185 km (115 mi) northwest of Savonlinna.

See firsthand Finland's proximity to Russia in Kuopio, with its Russian Orthodox monastery and museum. The area is characterized by forest-covered hills, countless lakes and is a great place for boating, hiking and fishing.

GETTING HERE AND AROUND

Kuopio's airport, 20 km (12 mi) from the town center, is a one-hour flight from Helsinki on either Finnair or Blue 1. It's a 10–15-minute drive into town; both airlines provide regular shuttle service for €5, while a taxi booked in advance will cost €10 and may pick up other passengers along the way; a direct, non-prebooked ride will cost €20. A drive to Kuopio from Helsinki takes four hours along route E63, passing through Mikkeli; ExpressBus service from Helsinki runs up to seven times a day and takes six or seven hours depending on how many stops it makes. VR trains run from Helsinki seven times a day, with the fastest Pendolino train making the journey in five hours. Saimaan Laivamatkat Oy offers tours to the Lintulan Luostari (Lintula Convent).

ESSENTIALS

Airline Contacts Finnair (⊕ *www.finnair.fi*). **Blue 1** (⊕ *www.blue1.fi*).

Taxi Info Taxi (☎ *017/106–400 €0.65/call plus local rate*).

Train Info Finnish Railways (*VR* ☎ *0600/41–902 €1 plus local network charge* ⊕ *www.vr.fi*).

Visitor and Tour Info Saimaan Laivamatkat Oy (⊠ *Kauppatori 2, Savonlinna* ☎ *15/250–250*). **Kuopio Tourist Board** (⊠ *Haapaniemenk. 17* ☎ *017/182–584* ⊕ *www.kuopioinfo.fi*).

EXPLORING

TOP ATTRACTIONS

★ **Ortodoksinen Kirkkomuseo.** *The Orthodox Church Museum* possesses one of the most interesting and unusual collections of its kind. When Karelia (the eastern province of Finland) was ceded to the Soviet Union after World War II, religious art was taken out of the monasteries and brought to Kuopio. The collection is eclectic, and includes one of the most beautiful icon collections in the world, as well as embroidered church textiles. ⊠*Karjalank. 1, Kuopio* ☎*20/610–0266* ⊠*€5* ⊗*May–Aug., Tues., Thurs.–Sun. 10–4, Wed. 10–6; Sept.–Apr., Tues.–Fri. noon–3, weekends noon–4.*

Tori. Kuopio's tourist office is close to this *marketplace.* Coined *maailman napa*—the belly button of the world—Kuopio's market square should be one of your first stops, for it is one of the most colorful outdoor markets in Finland. Try the famous *kalakukko pie* (fish and bacon in a rye crust). ⊗*May–Sept., weekdays 9–5, Sat. 9–3; Oct.–Apr., Mon.–Sat. 9–3.*

WORTH NOTING

Lintulan Luostari. You can reach the Lintula Convent by boat from Valamo, or you can visit both the convent and the monastery by boat on scenic day excursions from Kuopio. Boat tours from Kuopio are available mid-June to mid-August from Saimaan Laivamatkat. Tours depart from Kuopio's main pier; upon arrival at Palokin pier, taxi transport is arranged to Lintulan Luostari and Valamo, and the return trip to Kuopio is made by bus. The trip can be made in reverse, going by bus and returning by boat to the harbor, to Valamo only. You can also take a two-hour local cruise operated by Kuopio Roll Cruises for €11. ☎*017/266–2466 Kuopio Roll Cruises* ⊠*Tours approximately €70 including boat and ground transportation* ⊗*Convent June–Aug.*

Puijon Näkötorni. The slender *Puijo Tower*, 3 km (2 mi) northwest of Kuopio, is best visited at sunset, when the lakes shimmer with reflected light. It has two observation decks and is crowned by a revolving restaurant with marvelous views. ☎*017/255–5250* ⊕*www.puijo.com* ⊠*€4* ⊗*May–Aug., daily 9–9; Sept., daily 11–6; check Web site for winter hrs.*

Valamon Luostari. If you were fascinated by the treasures in the Orthodox Church Museum, you'll want to visit the Orthodox convent of Lintula and the *Valamo Monastery* in Heinävesi, between Varkaus and Joensuu. As a major center for Russian Orthodox religious and cultural life in Finland, the monastery hosts daily services. Precious 18th-century icons and sacred objects are housed in the main church and in the icon conservation center. The Orthodox library is the most extensive in Finland and is open to visitors. A café-restaurant is on the grounds, and very modest hotel and hostel accommodations are available at the monastery. ⊠*Uusi Valamo, Valamontie 42* ☎*017/570–111, 017/570–1810 hotel reservations* ⊕*www.valamo.fi* ⊠*€4 for guided tour* ⊗*June.–Aug., daily 7:30 AM–9 PM; Sept.–Apr., daily 8–8; guided tours daily June–Aug., other times by appointment.*

WHERE TO EAT

$$
ECLECTIC
✕ Isä Camillo. This popular restaurant is in a former Bank of Finland building and serves Finnish and international cuisine—steaks and pastas are particularly popular—at reasonable prices. Ask to eat in the bank vault. ⊠*Kauppak. 25–27, Keskusta/Tori* ☎*017/581–0450* ▤*AE, DC, MC, V.*

$$$
SCANDINAVIAN

✕**Musta Lammas.** Near the passenger harbor, Musta Lammas is in the basement of a brewery founded in 1862. It has been attractively adapted from its beer-cellar days, retaining the original redbrick walls and beer barrels. The specialty here is Finnish fish and game specialties such as *muikku* (vendace), whitefish, and lamb, prepared with innovative sauces and side dishes. ⊠*Satamak. 4, Keskusta* ☎*017/581–0458* ▤*AE, DC, MC, V* ⊗*Closed Sun. No lunch.*

¢–$
SEAFOOD

✕**Restaurant Sampo.** In the town center, Sampo was founded in 1931, and its Scandinavian furniture dates from the 1950s. High ceilings and large chandeliers impart an elegant look. Try the muikku, which comes smoked, fried, grilled, or in a stew with pork, potatoes, and onions. ⊠*Kauppak. 13, Keskusta/Tori* ☎*017/261–4677* ▤*AE, DC, MC, V.*

WHERE TO STAY

$$

▦**Quality Hotel Iso-Valkeinen.** On the lakeshore 5 km (3 mi) from town center, this hotel has large, quiet rooms in four one-story buildings. Several rooms have balconies with views of the nearby lake. **Pros:** lake views from some rooms; great nightlife in club. **Cons:** rooms in separate building from restaurant. ⊠*Mataniementie 2, Päiväranta* ☎*017/539–6100* ⊕*www.isovalkeinen.com* ⤶*100 rooms* ⌂*In-room: Wi-Fi. In-hotel: 3 restaurants, room service, bars, gym, beachfront, Wi-Fi, parking (free), some pets allowed, no-smoking rooms* ▤*AE, DC, MC, V* ⊟*BP.*

$$–$$$
☾

▦**Scandic Kuopio.** One of the most modern local hotels, rooms here are spacious by European standards, with large beds and generous towels. It's on the lakefront and also close to town. The restaurant Mesimarja specializes in traditional Finnish fare. **Pros:** spacious rooms; lake views; kids stay free. **Cons:** large chain-hotel feel. ⊠*Satamakatu 1* ☎*017/195–111* ⊕*www.scandichotels.com* ⤶*138 rooms* ⌂*In-room: Wi-Fi. In-hotel: 2 restaurants, room service, bar, pool, gym, laundry service, Wi-Fi, parking (free), some pets allowed* ▤*AE, DC, MC, V* ⊟*BP.*

$$
☾

▦**Spa Hotel Rauhalahti.** About 5 km (3 mi) from town center, Rauhalahti is near Kallavesi Lake and has no-frills rooms and apartments. A number of amenities cater to families and a full-service spa will please guests looking to be pampered. The hotel has six restaurants and has live dance music three times a week. **Pros:** range of room types; waterslide for kids; nightclub for grown-ups. **Cons:** removed from city center. ⊠*Katiskaniementie 8* ☎*030/608–30* ⊕*www.rauhalahti.com* ⤶*104 rooms, 2 suites, 40 apartments, 6 luxury apartments* ⌂*In-room: safe (some), Internet. In-hotel: 6 restaurants, room service, bars, pool, gym, spa, parking (free), no smoking rooms* ▤*AE, DC, MC, V* ⊟*BP.*

TAMPERE

293 km (182 mi) southwest of Kuopio, 174 km (108 mi) northwest of Helsinki.

From about the year 1000, this was the base traders and hunters set out from on their expeditions to northern Finland; it was not until 1779 that a Swedish king, Gustav III, founded the city itself. In 1828 a Scotsman named James Finlayson came to the infant city and established a factory for spinning cotton. This was the beginning of "big business" in Finland.

The Finlayson firm is today one of the country's major industrial enterprises, but its local factory complex has been converted to house software firms, restaurants, a museum, and a multiplex cinema.

Although cotton and textile manufacturers put Tampere on the map as a traditional center of industry, the city is now known for its high-tech companies and large universities. Tampere's more than 200,000 inhabitants also nurture an unusually sophisticated cultural environment, with the international festivals of short film (March) and theater (August) among the most popular offerings. An isthmus little more than a half-mile wide at its narrowest point separates the lakes Näsijärvi and Pyhäjärvi, and at one spot the Tammerkoski Rapids provide an outlet for the waters of one to cascade through to the other. Called the Mother of Tampere, these rapids once provided the electrical power on which the town's livelihood depended. Their natural beauty has been preserved in spite of the factories on either bank. Don't be surprised to see people fishing for salmon off a bridge in the shadow of a pulp mill, a reminder of conscious efforts since the 1970s to keep the city's environment clean.

GETTING HERE AND AROUND

Finnair, Ryanair, and Blue1 all fly to Tampere. Tampere's airport is 17 km (11 mi) from the city center. You can take a Ryanair bus from Tampere train station straight to the airport for €6. Public bus #61 will take you from the city center for €4.10. The 30-minute taxi ride from the airport to the city center will cost around €30. You can also go by airport taxi, which must be booked at least 30 minutes prior to pickup time, for €14. Because it may pick up other passengers, it's recommended that you schedule your pick-up for at least three hours prior to your flight's departure. Finnish Railways offers excellent train connections from Helsinki, ranging 1½–2 hours, depending on the train.

Driving from Helsinki, take Highway 3. The drive will take around an hour and 45 minutes in the summer and longer between late October and early April, when the speed limits drop by 20 km per hour. The Tampere tourist office offers helpful services such as walking and bus tours and free bicycle rentals. You can also buy a Tourist Card for one or more days (€6 first day plus €4 each additional day), which allows unlimited travel on city buses.

ESSENTIALS

Transportation Info Blue1 (☎ *060/002–5831 €1.75 per minute plus local network charge* ⊕ *www.blue1.com).* **Finnair** (⊕ *www.finnair.com).* **Finnish Railways** (*VR* ☎ *0600/41–902 €1 plus local network charge* ⊕ *www.vr.fi).* **Ryanair** (☎ *020/039–000 €1.5 per minute plus local network charge* ⊕ *www.ryanair.com).* **Taxi and Airport Taxi** (☎ *100/4131).*

Hospital Tampereen Yliopistollinen Sairaala (TAYS) (✉ *Teiskontie 35, Tampere* ☎ *03/311–611).*

Visitor Info Ähtäri Tourist Board (✉ *Ostolank. 4* ☎ *06/533–1754* ⊕ *www.ah tari.fi).* **Tampere Tourist Board** (✉ *Rautatienk. 25 A* ☎ *03/5656–6800* ⊕ *www. gotampere.fi).*

EXPLORING

TOP ATTRACTIONS

Fodor's Choice **Amurin Työläiskorttelimuseo.** While in western Tampere, be sure to visit
★ the *Amuri Museum of Workers' Housing,* one of the city's best muse-
ums. It consists of more than 30 apartments in a collection of wooden
houses, plus a sauna, a bakery, a haberdashery, and more from the
1880s to the 1970s. Its cozy café has garden seating in summer and
serves fresh bread baked on the premises. ⊠ *Satakunnankatu 49, Amuri*
☎ *03/716–6690* ⊕ *www.tampere.fi/amuri* ☜ *€5* ⊙ *Mid-May–mid-
Sept., Tues.–Sun. 10–6.*

Fodor's Choice **Runoilijan Tie.** One of the most popular excursions from Tampere is the
★ Poet's Way steamboat tour along Lake Näsijärvi. The Tarjanne, built
in 1908, passes through the agricultural parish of Ruovesi, where J. L.
Runeberg, Finland's national poet, once lived. Shortly before the boat
docks at Virrat, you'll pass through the straits of Visuvesi, where many
artists and writers spend their summers. ⊠ *Laukontori 10A 3, Tampere*
☎ *010/422–5600* ⊕ *www.runoilijantie.fi* ☜ *Same-day round-trip fare
for boat–bus package €57 round-trip Tampere—Ruovesi* ⊙ *June–Aug.
17, Tues., Thurs., and Sat.*

★ **Tuomiokirkko.** Most buildings in Tampere, including this cathedral, are
comparatively modern. It was built in 1906 and houses some of the
best-known masterpieces of Finnish art, including Magnus Enckell's
fresco *The Resurrection* and Hugo Simberg's *Wounded Angel* and
Garden of Death. ⊠ *Tuomiokirkonkatu 3, Keskusta* ☎ *03/219–0265*
⊙ *May–Aug., daily 9–6; Sept.–Apr., daily 11–3.*

WORTH NOTING

⟳ **Ähtäri.** Not far north of Virrat is Ähtäri, where you will find the Ähtäri
Animal Park, Finland's first wildlife park. In a beautiful countryside
setting, it has a "holiday village," several good hotels, including the
Scandic Mesikämmen, and recreation facilities. The park, home to
many indigenous species, including bears, lynx, snow owls, wolves,
elk, reindeer, and snow leopards, is set on 148 forested acres. Hiking,
golf, swimming, skiing, and horseback riding is plentiful in this area
surrounded by lakes and coniferous forests. Contact the tourist office
for more information. ⊠ *Karhunkierros 130, Ähtäri* ☎ *06/5393–555*
⊕ *www.ahtarinelainpuisto.fi* ☜ *€13 in summer, €8 in winter* ⊙ *Jan.–
May and mid Aug.–Oct., daily 10–4; June–mid-Aug., daily 10–7; Nov.–
Dec., daily 10–2.*

Lenin Museo (*The Lenin Museum*), the only one of its kind left in the
world, occupies the hall where Lenin and Stalin first met in the historic
Tampere Workers' Hall. Photos, memorabilia, and temporary exhibits
document the life of Lenin and the Russian Revolution, as well as modern Russia. ⊠ *Hämeenpuisto 28, 3rd fl., Hämeenpuisto* ☎ *03/276–8100*
⊕ *www.lenin.fi* ☜ *€5* ⊙ *Weekdays 9–6, weekends 11–4.*

⟳ **Museokeskus Vapriikki.** Not far from Amuri Museum, in the old Tampella
factory area, is the *Vapriikki Museum Center,* which consolidates the
collections of five museums (700,000 pieces) to illustrate the city's role
in Finnish industrial history. Housed in a former textile and turbine

factory complex that dates from the 1880s, the permanent exhibit focuses on local history, while other displays cover archaeological finds and modern art. The eclectic changing exhibitions, of which there are around 10 annually, run the gamut from Sitting Bull to photography. The center also includes an excellent café and gift shop. ✉ *Veturiaukio 4, Tampella* ☎*03/5656–6966* ⊕*www.tampere.fi/vapriikki* 🎟*€6* ⊙*Tues. and Thurs.–Sun. 10–6, Wed. 11–8.*

Ⓒ **Särkänniemen Huvikeskus.** A 1½-km (1-mi) walk west, then north from the heart of Tampere brings you to the Särkänniemi Recreation Center, a major recreation complex for both children and adults. Its many attractions include an amusement park, a children's zoo, a planetarium, and a well-planned aquarium with a separate dolphinarium. Within Särkänniemi, the Sara Hildénin Taidemuseo (Sara Hildén Art Museum) is a striking example of Finnish architecture, with the works of modern Finnish and international artists, including Giacometti, Klee, Miró, and Picasso. Särkänniemi's profile is punctuated by the 550-foot Näsinneulan Näkötorni (Näsinneula Observatory Tower), Finland's tallest observation tower and the dominant feature of the Tampere skyline. The top of the tower holds an observatory and a revolving restaurant. The views are magnificent, commanding the lake, forest, and town—the contrast between the industrial maze of Tampere at your feet and the serenity of the lakes stretching out to meet the horizon is unforgettable. ✉*Särkänniemi* ☎*03/248–8111, 020/714–3500 museum* ⊕*www.sarkanniemi. fi* 🎟*€8 for observation tower and museum; €6 for admission to either one ride, the aquarium, planetarium or dolphinarium; 1-day Särkänniemi Adventure Key (pass to all sights and rides in park) €30, 2-day €40* ⊙*Summer hrs: Museum daily noon–7; children's zoo, adventure park, rides, and aquarium noon–9; planetarium every 30 mins 12:15–8:15; tower noon–11:30; check Web site or call for other hrs.*

WHERE TO EAT

$$
SCANDINAVIAN
✕**Astor.** Here you'll find a moderately priced brasserie menu and a more expensive selection on the main menu. In the restaurant, try the salmon, whitefish, duck, or reindeer dishes, many prepared in red-wine or game sauces. Brasserie favorites include salads and open-faced sandwiches (called toasts) with smoked-reindeer, smoked salmon, and chicken. ✉*Aleksis Kivenk. 26, Keskusta* ☎*03/260–5700* ▤*AE, DC, MC, V.*

$$$
SPANISH
✕**Bodega Salud.** Salud mixes Spanish specialties with classics such as lamb chops and steaks. A salad bar with cheese and fruit is a favorite. Try the tapas prix-fixe lunch served 11–4 PM. ✉*Tuomiokirkonkatu 19, Keskusta* ☎*03/233–4400* ⊕*www.salud.fi* ⚘*Reservations essential* ▤*AE, DC, MC, V.*

$$–$$$
SCANDINAVIAN
✕**Harald.** The Viking details and the hearty fare make this quirky restaurant in the heart of the city a nice change of pace. Choose from steaks and fillets of fish and game at sturdy wooden tables, along with beer served in earthenware mugs. ✉*Hämeenkatu 23, Keskusta* ☎*04/4766–8203* ▤*AE, DC, MC, V.*

$$
EASTERN
EUROPEAN
✕**Laterna.** In a czarist-era hotel with antique bay windows and light fixtures, oil paintings, and elegant dark-wood furniture, Laterna specializes in Russian fare with a Finnish twist. Once the haunt of artists and

writers, the scene here is still lively—occasional performances on the weekends can include the famous Finnish tango. Classic dishes include vorschmack (a hash of beef, lamb, and herring), blini, and borscht with sour cream. ✉ *Puutarhakatu 11, Keskusta* ☎ *03/272–0241* ☰ *AE, DC, MC, V.*

$$–$$$
SCANDINAVIAN
✕ **Teatteriravintola Tillikka.** Long known as a hangout for leftist intellectuals, Tillikka now prepares hearty meals overlooking the rapids for patrons of every political persuasion. House specialties include meatballs, herring fillets, fried pike perch, and pepper steak; try any of them with one of the local brews. The restaurant is housed in the same building as the city theater. ✉ *Teatteritalo, Hämeenkatu 14, Keskusta* ☎ *10/767–2300* ☰ *AE, DC, MC, V.*

$$$
SCANDINAVIAN
✕ **Tiiliholvi.** A romantic cellar in an art-nouveau building with a colorful past, Tiiliholvi serves Finnish haute cuisine and the best wine selection in town. Fresh, seasonal ingredients like mushrooms, reindeer, partridge, and salmon are often paired with unexpected wine or liquor sauces or fresh herb vinaigrettes. ✉ *Kauppak. 10, Keskusta* ☎ *03/272–0231* ☰ *AE, DC, MC, V* ☯ *Closed Sun. No lunch in July.*

WHERE TO STAY

$$$
🏨 **Scandic Tampere City.** This Scandic property in the heart of the city center, opposite the train station, caters to business travelers and tourists. The hotel was completely renovated in 2005. **Pros:** great location; excellent service. **Cons:** chain-hotel feel. ✉ *Hämeenkatu 1* ☎ *03/244–6111* ⊕ *www.scandichotels.com* ↘ *262 rooms, 1 suite* ⚐ *In-room: safe, Wi-Fi. In-hotel: restaurant, room service, bar, gym, laundry service, Internet terminal, Wi-Fi, parking (paid), some pets allowed, no-smoking rooms* ☰ *AE, DC, MC, V* ⏛ *BP.*

$$–$$$
🏨 **Sokos Hotel Ilves.** Soaring above a gentrified area of old warehouses near city center, this 18-story hotel is Tampere's tallest building. All rooms above the sixth floor have spectacular views of the city and Pyhäjärvi and Näsijärvi lakes. **Pros:** nightclub; Scandinavian breakfast; lavish feel. **Cons:** removed from the city center. ✉ *Hatanpään valtatie 1* ☎ *020/1234–631* ⊕ *www.sokoshotels.fi* ↘ *327 rooms, 9 suites* ⚐ *In-room: safe, Wi-Fi. In-hotel: 3 restaurants, room service, bars, pool, gym, laundry service, Wi-Fi, parking (paid), some pets allowed, no-smoking rooms* ☰ *AE, DC, MC, V* ⏛ *BP.*

$$$
🏨 **Sokos Hotel Tammer.** A beautiful historic hotel overlooking a park, the Hotel Tammer has a grand dining room. Guest rooms are individually decorated and have modern fittings. **Pros:** lovely decor; excellent service. **Cons:** slightly corporate feel. ✉ *Satakunnankatu 13* ☎ *020/1234–632* ↘ *87 rooms* ⚐ *In-room: safe, Internet, Wi-Fi (some). In-hotel: restaurant, room service, bar, laundry service, Wi-Fi, parking (free), some pets allowed, no-smoking rooms* ☰ *AE, DC, MC, V* ⏛ *BP.*

AFTER DARK

Tampere has a lively pub and beer-bar scene. Don't be surprised if you see a quiz competition going on in one of the local pubs, a popular Tampere pastime, particularly in the winter. The Irish theme is at its best at **O'Connell's** (✉ *Ratatienkatu 24, Keskusta* ☎ *03/222–7032*) with occasional live music.

For live jazz music, visit **Paapan Kapakka** (⊠*Koskikatu 9, Keskusta* ☎*03/211–0037*). Stroll down from Koskikekus to Kehräsaari island, with its old brick buildings converted to shops and restaurants, to **Fall's Cafe** (⊠*Kehräsaari, Keskusta* ☎*03/223–0061*), in a cozy cellar, with an international beer selection and central European beers on tap.

Try the in-house brew at **Plevna** (⊠*Itäinenk. 8, Keskusta* ☎*03/260–1200*). A lively German-style brass band plays during Oktoberfest and at Christmas. The English-style **Salhojankadun Pub** (⊠*Salhojank. 29, Keskusta* ☎*03/255–3376*) is an old favorite. The converted post office is now **Wanha Posti** (⊠*Hämeenk. 13, Keskusta* ☎*03/223–3007*), lauded for its wide selection of Finnish and international brews.

Tampere's most unique bar, **Telakka** (⊠*Tullikamarin aukio 3, Keskusta* ☎*03/225–0700*), is in an old granary. Founded by a cooperative of actors, who also serve tables, it has live music and a theater upstairs. There's a menu of pub food and a grill on the terrace in summer. The **Ilves Night Club** (⊠*Hotel Ilves, Hatanpään valtatie 1, Keskusta* ☎*03/262–6262*) is one of the most popular nightspots in Tampere, drawing a mixed crowd of professionals and students, for dancing and drinks.

HÄMEENLINNA

78 km (49 mi) southeast of Tampere, 98 km (61 mi) north of Helsinki (via Hwy. 12).

Founded in 1639, Hämeenlinna is the birthplace of Finnish composer Jean Sibelius and today further encourages its resident artists with an impressive urban park. Its big castle and small museums make the town a good place for a day trip from Helsinki.

GETTING HERE AND AROUND
From both Tampere and Helsinki, Hämeenlinna is a one-hour drive along Highway 3. Every train from Helsinki to Tampere or Vaasa passes through Hämeenlinna; the journey takes about 45 minutes.

ESSENTIALS
Taxi Info Alue Taxi (☎*03/106–2500*).

Visitor Info Hämeenlinna Tourist Board (⊠*Raatihuoneenk. 11* ☎*03/621–3373* ⊕*www.hameenlinna.fi/english*).

EXPLORING
Swedish crusaders began construction on **Hämeen Linna** *(Häme Castle)* in the 13th century to strengthen and defend the Swedish position in the region. What began as a fortified camp evolved over the centuries into a large castle of stone and brick. In modern times, the castle, one of Finland's oldest, has served as a granary and a prison, and it is now restored and open to the public for tours and exhibitions. The castle sits on the lakeshore, 1 km (½ mi) north of Hämeenlinna's town center. Tours in English take place every hour in the summer and are available every hour in winter by appointment only. ⊠*Kustaa III:n k. 6, Hämeenlinna* ☎*03/675–6820* ⊕*www.nba.fi/en/hame_castle* 🎫*€5*

includes guided tour ☉*May–mid-Aug., daily 10–6; mid-Aug.–mid-May., weekdays 10–4, weekends 11–4.*

The **Hämeenlinnan Taidemuseo** *(Hämeenlinna Art Museum)*, housed partly in a 19th-century granary designed by Carl Ludvig Engel, exhibits Finnish art from the 19th and 20th centuries and foreign art from the 17th century; works evacuated from Vyborg in 1939 form the core of the collection. ✉*Viipurintie 2, Keskusta* ☎*03/621–2669* 🖭*€6* ☉*Tues.– Thurs. noon–6, Fri.–Sun. noon–5.*

★ At the **Iittala Lasikeskus** *(Iittala Glass Center)*, top designers produce magnificent glass; the ones in the factory shop are bargains you won't find elsewhere. Museum tours are available. ✉ *Könnöläencie 2C* ☎*0204/396–230* 🖭*€3* ☉*Museum May–Aug., daily 10–6; Sept.–Apr., weekends, daily 10–5 or by appointment; shop May–Aug., daily 9–8; Sept.–Apr., daily 10–6.*

Hämeenlinna's secondary school has educated many famous Finns, among them composer Jean Sibelius (1865–1957). The only surviving timber house in the town center is the **Sibeliuksen syntymäkoti** *(Sibelius birthplace)*, a modest dwelling built in 1834. The museum staff will play your favorite Sibelius CD as you tour the rooms, one of which contains the harmonium Sibelius played as a child. ✉*Hallitusk. 11, Keskusta* ☎*03/621–2755* 🖭*€4* ☉*May–Aug., daily 10–4; Sept.–Apr., daily noon–4.*

OFF THE BEATEN PATH

Pyhän Ristin Kirkko. Six kilometers (3½ mi) north of Hämeenlinna is Hattula, whose Church of the Holy Cross is the most famous of Finland's medieval churches. Its interior is a fresco gallery of biblical scenes whose vicious little devils and soulful saints are as vivid and devious as when they were first painted around 1510. ✉*Hattula1* ☎*03/672–3383 during open hrs, 03/631–1540 all other times* 🖭*€3* ☉*Mid-May–mid-Aug., daily 11–5; open at other times by appointment.*

If you're driving between Helsinki and Hämeenlinna along Highway 12, consider stopping at Riihimäki, home of the **Suomen Lasimuseo** *(Finnish Glass Museum)*; it's 35 km (22 mi) south of Hämeenlinna. Here you can examine an outstanding display on the history of glass from early Egyptian times to the present, artfully arranged in an old glass factory. ✉*Tehtaankatu 23, Riihimäki* ☎*019/758–4108* ⊕*www.riihimaki.fi* 🖭*€5* ☉*Tues.–Sun. 10–6.*

WHERE TO EAT AND STAY

$$
SCANDINAVIAN

✗**Huviretki.** In the heart of the city, Huviretki has specialties such as garlic steak with cherry tomatoes and roasted whitefish or smoked salmon. There are many salads, pasta dishes, and pizzas on the menu. ✉*Cumulus Hotel, Raatihuoneenk. 16–18, Keskusta* ☎*03/648–8210* ⊟*AE, DC, MC, V.*

$$$
SCANDINAVIAN

✗**Piiparkakkutalo.** In a renovated old-timber building designed by famed architect Selim Lindquist, and finished in 1907, Piiparkakkutalo (Gingerbread House) specializes in meat dishes; try the pepper steak, fillet of reindeer, or wild duck. ✉*Kirkkorinne 2, Keskusta* ☎*03/648–040* ⊟*AE, DC, MC, V.*

$$$$ 🏨 **Rantasipi Aulanko.** One of Finland's top hotels sits on the lakeshore
Fodor's Choice   in a beautifully landscaped park 4½ km (3 mi) from town. All rooms
★   have wall-to-wall carpeting, and some overlook the golf course, park,
or lake. **Pros:** serene location; 9-hole and 18-hole golf courses. **Cons:**
removed from town. ✉*Aulangontie 93, Hämeenlinna* 🕾*03/658–801*
⊕*www.rantasipi.fi* ⟁*241 rooms, 5 suites* ⌂*In-room: Internet, Wi-Fi.
In-hotel: restaurant, room service, bar, golf course, tennis court, pool,
spa, laundry facilities, Internet terminal, Wi-Fi, parking (free), some
pets allowed, no-smoking rooms* ▤*AE, DC, MC, V* ¶◎*BP.*

SPORTS AND THE OUTDOORS
SKIING
The **Finlandia Ski Race Office** (✉*Urheilukeskus, Lahti* 🕾*03/816–813*
⊕*www.finlandiahiihto.fi*) has details on events. In February, you can
attend the **Finlandia-hiihto,** a 60-km (37-mi) ski race. The **Lahti Ski Games**
(🕾*03/816–810* ⊕*www.lahtiskigames.com*) take place in March.

LAPLAND

Lapland is often called Europe's last wilderness, a region of endless
forests, fells, and great silences. Settlers in Finnish Lapland walked
gently and left the landscape almost unspoiled. Now easily accessible
by plane, train, or bus, this arctic outpost offers comfortable hotels and
modern amenities, yet you won't have to go very far to find yourself in
an almost primordial setting.

Only about 4,000 native Sami (also sometimes known as Lapps) still
live in Lapland; the remainder of the province's population of 203,000
is Finnish. Though modern influences have changed many aspects of
their traditional way of life, there is still a thriving Sami culture. Sami
crafts make use of natural resources, reflected in skilled woodwork,
bonework, and items made of reindeer pelts. In March, on Maria's Day,
a traditional church festival takes place in Hetta, a village near Enontekiö. It is particularly colorful, attended by many Sami in their most
brilliant dress, and usually has reindeer racing or lassoing competitions.
Contact the Enontekiö tourist office for details.

Although the cities have fine facilities and cultural events, it is the lonely
moors with the occasional profile of a reindeer herd crossing, the clear
forest streams, and the bright trail of the midnight sun reflected on a
lake's blackest waters that leave the most indelible impressions. Summer
in Lapland has the blessing of round-the-clock daylight, and beautiful
weather typically accompanies the nightless days. In early fall the colors
are so fabulous that the Finns have a special word for it: *ruskaa.* If you
can take the intense but dry cold, winter in Lapland is full of fascinating
experiences, from the northern lights to reindeer roundups. Depending
on how far north of the Arctic Circle you travel, the sun might not rise
for several weeks around midwinter. But it is never pitch-black; light
reflects from the invisible sun below the horizon even in the middle of
the night, and there is luminosity from the ever-present snow.

While you're here sample such local foods as cloudberries; lingonberries; fresh salmon; and reindeer, served smoked and sautéed, roasted, and as steaks. Restaurants serve hearty soups, crusty rye bread, delicious baked Lappish cheese, and dark brewed coffee in wooden cups with meals—you won't leave hungry.

ROVANIEMI

832 km (516 mi) north of Helsinki.

The best place to start your tour of Lapland is Rovaniemi, where the Ounas and Kemi rivers meet almost on the Arctic Circle. Often called the Gateway to Lapland, Rovaniemi is also the administrative hub and communications center of the province.

If you're expecting an Arctic shantytown, you're in for a surprise. After Rovaniemi was all but razed by the retreating German army in 1944, Alvar Aalto directed the rebuilding and devised an unusual street layout: from the air, the layout mimics the shape of reindeer antlers! During rebuilding, the population rose from 8,000 to its present-day size of around 36,000—so be prepared for a contemporary city, university town, and cultural center on the edge of the wilderness.

GETTING HERE AND AROUND

Rovaniemi is connected with Helsinki and the south by road, rail, and air links; there is even a car-train from Helsinki. There is Finnair service every day but Sunday between Rovaniemi and Ivalo. You can also fly to Sodankylä. The airpot is 10 km (6 mi) from the town center. An Airport Express shuttle goes to the major hotels then heads to the airport one hour before scheduled flights and costs €5. A taxi to or from the airport will cost around €20 and take 10–15 minutes. Trains leave twice daily from Helsinki, with one in the morning and one overnight. Sodankyla, 130 km (81 mi) north of the Rovaniemi airport, can be reached by a one-and-a-half-hour bus ride. There is no train service north of Rovaniemi.

If you are driving north, follow Arctic Highway 4 (national highway) to Kuopio–Oulu–Rovaniemi, or go via the west coast to Oulu, then to Rovaniemi. From Rovaniemi, the national highway continues straight up to Lake Inari via Ivalo. Roads are generally good, but some in the extreme north may be rough. Bus service into the region revolves around Rovaniemi; from there you can switch to local buses.

If you'd rather not rent a car, all but the most remote towns are accessible by bus, train, or plane. Buses leave three to four times daily from Rovaniemi to Inari (five to six hours) and five to six times a day to Ivalo (four hours). You can take countryside taxis to your final destination; taxi stands are at most bus stations. Taxi drivers invariably use their meters, and specially negotiated fares—even for long distances—are unusual, but you can ask for an estimate before starting the trip.

THE GREAT OUTDOORS

Winter sports reign in Lapland, from the quirky ice golfing to the traditional cross-country skiing. Ylläs, Levi, and Saariselkä are Lapland's leading centers for both downhill and cross-country skiing; Kiilopää is known for cross-country skiing. Other popular resorts include Pyhä, Luosto, Salla, Suomu, Pallas, and Olos. In western Lapland, the **Levi resort** (⊠ *Levi Tourist Info, Myllyjoentie 2, Levi* ☎ *016/639–3300* ⊕ *www.levi.fi*) has 44 slopes and 27 lifts.

Pyhä and Luosto (⊠ *Pyhä-Luosto Travel Ltd., Laukotie 1, Luosto* ☎ *0207/303–020* ⊕ *www. pyha-luostomatkailu.fi*), in the Pyhätunturi National Park in southern Lapland, offers cabins near to cross-country and downhill skiing, and snowboarding possibilities.

In the middle of the fells near Urho Kekkonen National Park, **Saariselkä** (⊠ *Pohjois-Lapin Matkailu, Kelotie, Seula, Saariselkä* ☎ *016/668–402* ⊕ *www.saariselka.fi*) is an international tourist center with a network of well-marked hiking, skiing, and biking trails. Downhill and cross-country skiing are popular at **Ruka** (⊠ *Rukakeskus, Rukatunturi* ☎ *08/860–0200* ⊕ *www.ruka.fi*), which is also one of the most unrestricted areas in the world for snowmobiling.

In summer, canoeing is a popular pursuit; you can take canoe trips on Lake Inari, or, for the intrepid, forays over the rapids of the Ivalojoki River. Summer golf takes on such unusual guises as midnight-sun golf and Green Zone Tornio-Haparanda Golf—you'll play 9 holes in Finland and the other 9 in Sweden **Meri-Lapin Golfklubi** (⊠ *Näräntie, Tornio* ☎ *016/431–711* ⊕ *www.golf.fi/ mlgk*). In the summer it is so light that you can play during the night. The course is famous for its one-hour putt.

Karttakeskus (⊠ *Vuorik. 14, Helsinki* ☎ *020/577-7580* ⊕ *www.karttakeskus.fi*), by the railway station in Helsinki, provides maps of marked cross-country skiing trails in Lapland.

Lapland Travel Ltd. (Lapin Matkailu OY) and Lapland Safaris offer fly-fishing and combined canoe-and-fishing trips, in addition to reindeer and snowmobile safaris and ski treks.

ESSENTIALS

Transportation Info Airport Express (☎*16/362–222*). **Finnair** (⊕ *www.finnair. com*). **Finnish Railways** (*VR* ☎*0600/41–902 €1 plus local network charge* ⊕ *www.vr.fi*). **Rovaniemi Taxi** (☎*16/106–410* ⊕ *www.finnair.com*). **Sodankyla Taxi** (☎*020/099-600*).

Hospital Lapin Keskussairaala (⊠ *Ounasrinteentie 22, Rovaniemi* ☎*016/3281, 016/328-2100 evenings and weekends*).

Tour Info Lapland Safaris (⊠ *Koskikatu 1, Rovaniemi* ☎*016/331–1200* ⊕ *www. lapinsafarit.fi*). **Lapland Travel Ltd. (Lapin Matkailu Oy)** (⊠ *Valtak. 18 L9, Rovaniemi* ☎*10/8300–400* ⊕ *www.laplandtravel.fi*).

Visitor Info Rovaniemi (⊠ *Lorvi Square, Maakuntak. 31* ☎*016/346–270* ⊕ *www.rovaniemi.fi*). **Sodankylä** (⊠ *Jäämerentie 3* ☎*40/746-9776* ⊕ *www.sodankyla.fi*).

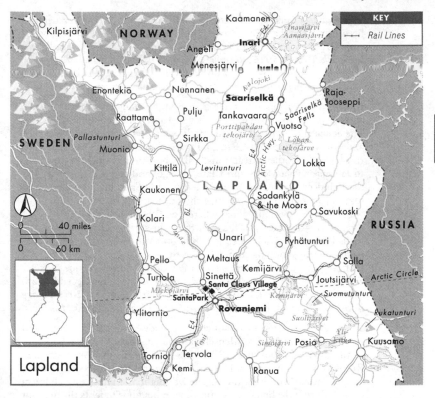

3

Lapland

EXPLORING

Fodor's Choice ★ One of the best ways to tune in to the Finish far north culture is to visit the **Arktikum** *(Arctic Research Center)*, 1 km (½ mi) north of Lappia-Talo. The Arktikum houses the Lapland Provincial Museum, whose riveting exhibit on Sami life tells the full story of their survival. ✉ *Pohjoisranta 4, Keskusta* ☎ *016/322–3260* ⊕ *www.arktikum.fi* 💵 *€12* ⊙ *Early June–mid-June, daily 10–6; mid-June–mid-Aug., daily 9–7; mid-late Aug., daily 10–6; Sept.–May, Tues.–Sun. 10–6; some extended hrs in winter.*

One of the town's architectural wonders is **Lappia-Talo** *(Lappia House)*, the Aalto-designed concert and congress center that houses the world's northernmost professional theater. ✉ *Hallitusk. 11, Keskusta* ☎ *016/322–2495 ticket office* ⊙ *Closed June–Aug.*

OFF THE BEATEN PATH Lapland is dominated by great moorlike expanses. The modern tourist center of **Luosto,** 105 km (65 mi) north of Rovaniemi, is in the heart of the moor district of southern Lapland—an area of superb hiking, mountain cycling, orienteering, and skiing. If you don't have a car, a daily bus makes the 60-km (37-mi) trip from Kemijärvi to Luosto. Kemijarvi is 87 km (54 mi) north of Rovaniemi and can be reached via local train. ⊕ *www.laplandluosto.fi.*

⟳ **Salla Reindeer Park.** In winter, visitors can obtain a reindeer driver's license and feed the animals at this farm 150 km (93 mi) east of Rovaniemi. ⊠*Hautajärventie 111, Salla* ☎*016/837–771* ⊕*www.sallarein deerpark.fi* ☎*€7.50 in summer; in winter, license to drive reindeer for 10-mins €10, 3-hr excursion €69* ⊗ *Weekdays 10–4, weekends 10–3; hrs can vary according to weather, call ahead in winter.*

⟳ Rovaniemi's real claim to fame is that Santa Claus lives in its suburbs, as reflected in the growing number of tourist attractions in the area. The **SantaPark** Christmas theme park is set deep inside a rocky cavern and offers a Magic Sleigh Ride, a Puppet Circus, and a Christmas Carrousel, among other attractions. Take the Santa Train from the Park to **Joulupukin Pajakylä** (Santa Claus Village) and stop along the way at the Reindeer Park to see Santa's sleigh team. Sami in native dress and reindeer hauling sleighs enhance the authenticity of the village. (This is likely to be the only place where your children will be able to pet a reindeer—the ones you'll see in the wild are shy.) Postcards can be mailed from the special Arctic Circle post office. There's also a complete souvenir shopping complex, plus the impressive mountains of mail that pour in from children all over the world. And yes, he does answer every letter. The village is closed when he is abroad, on December 25. ⊠*96930 Arctic Circle* ☎*016/333–0000 park, 016/356–2096 village info* ⊕*www.santapark.com* ☎*Park €25, village free* ⊗ *Call for hrs.*

The Sodankylä region has some of the oldest Sami settlements, and today it is one of the most densely populated areas of Finnish Lapland. In the town of **Sodankylä**, 130 km (81 mi) north of Rovaniemi (via Rte. 4 or 5), is a Northern Lights Observatory (for professionals only) and an ancient wooden church. The Midnight Sun Film Festival draws crowds during the height of summer, running films in tents throughout the night. ☎*400/856–080 in Helsinki* ⊕*www.msfilmfestival.fi.*

WHERE TO EAT

$$$ ✗**Fransmanni.** This restaurant, with friendly service and Kemijoki River
ECLECTIC views from the bar, specializes in French cuisine but also features Finnish and Lapp casserole dishes. Try the grilled beef fillet in honey-and-bacon sauce. ⊠*Vaakuna Hotel, Koskik. 4, Keskusta* ☎*016/332–2515* ☐*AE, DC, MC, V.*

$$$$ ✗**Ounasvaaran Pirtit.** This holiday village and ski center includes two
SCANDINAVIAN of Rovaniemi's classic restaurants, Kota and Aurora, which focus on traditional Finnish and Lapp food. At either restaurant you'll find dishes with fresh salmon and reindeer, and a dessert of soft cheese with arctic cloudberries. There's a buffet and a set menu at the Kota Restaurant and an à la carte menu at Aurora. Hours vary for both restaurants throughout the year, so call ahead. ⊠*Antinmukka 4, Ounasvaara* ☎*016/333–0100* ⊗*Reservations essential* ☐*AE, DC, MC, V.*

WHERE TO STAY

$$$ ⊞**Lapland Hotels Sky Ounasvaara.** On a hilltop 3 km (2 mi) from the town, Sky Ounasvaara is the top choice in Rovaniemi for views, hiking, and skiing—both slalom and cross-country—especially for those with a car. Some rooms have bathtubs, a rarity, and 47 rooms have saunas.

Larger rooms with kitchenettes are available for families. At the restaurant dine on roasted whitefish or arctic char with crayfish or fruit sauce, and try one of the desserts based on local fruits such as cloudberries. Pros: restaurant ranked among Finland's finest. Cons: outside of town. ⊠ Ounasvaara, Rovaniemi ☎016/323–400 ⊕www.laplandhotels.com ➡60 rooms, 1 suite, 11 apartments, 5 cabins ♿In-hotel: restaurant, room service, bar, laundry service, Wi-Fi, parking (free), some pets allowed ⊟AE, DC, MC, V ⫴◯⫵BP.

$$$ **Rantasipi Pohjanhovi.** Stretched along the shore of the Kemijoki River, this hotel combines modern amenities with quick access to the moors. Rooms are large, with low ceilings and big windows. Some are white-walled with autumn-tone upholstery and wood trim, while others have black walls with light upholstery—for those who have trouble sleeping during the days of the midnight sun. Pros: stylish room; nightclub for partiers; complimentary evening saunas. Cons: only 10 TV channels. ⊠Pohjanpuistikko 2 ☎016/33711 ⊕www.rantasipi.fi ➡212 rooms, 17 suites ♿In-room: Wi-Fi. In-hotel: restaurant, room service, bars, pool, laundry service, Internet terminal, parking (free), some pets allowed, no-smoking rooms ⊟AE, DC, MC, V ⫴◯⫵BP.

$$–$$$ **Scandic Luosto.** Amid the plains southeast of Sodankylä, this small-scale hotel is modern and comfortable. It is built in a unique kelo (dead-wood) timber style. Each cabin has a fireplace, sauna, and kitchenette. If you get tired of cross-country skiing, visit the amethyst mine nearby. Pros: three restaurants to choose from; skiing on your doorstep. Cons: can feel isolated. ⊠Luppokeino 3, Luosto ☎016/624–400 ⊕www.scandichotels.com ➡54 cabins, 5 rooms ♿In-room: kitchen (some), Wi-Fi (some). In-hotel: 3 restaurants, room service, bars, Wi-Fi, some pets allowed, no-smoking rooms ⊟AE, DC, MC, V ⫴◯⫵BP.

$$ **Scandic Rovaniemi.** This modern hotel is in the heart of Rovaniemi, five minutes from the railway station. Guest rooms are simply furnished and comfortable. Nine rooms have individual saunas and eight have Jacuzzis. Pros: children under 13 stay free; saunas and Jacuzzis in superior rooms. Cons: large chain-hotel feel. ⊠Koskik. 23 ☎016/4606–000 ⊕www.scandic-hotels.com ➡167 rooms ♿In-room: Wi-Fi. In-hotel: restaurant, room service, bar, laundry service, Wi-Fi, some pets allowed, no-smoking rooms ⊟AE, DC, MC, V ⫴◯⫵BP.

$$$ **Sokos Hotel Vaakuna.** The Vaakuna has small but comfortable guest rooms decked in neutral shades. The lobby is dotted with armchairs and has marble floors. There are two restaurants, Fransmanni and Rosso, the latter of which turns out pastas and pizzas. Pros: Wi-Fi in restaurants; nightclub. Cons: corporate feel; gym is nearby and costs €2. ⊠Koskikatu 4, Rovaniemi ☎020/1234–695 ⊕www.sokoshotels.fi ➡157 rooms, 2 suites ♿In-room: Wi-Fi. In-hotel: 2 restaurants, room service, bars, laundry facilities, laundry service, Wi-Fi, parking (paid), some pets allowed, no-smoking rooms ⊟AE, DC, MC, V ⫴◯⫵BP.

SAARISELKA

265 km (165 mi) north of Rovaniemi.

You could hike and ski for days in the area around Saariselka without seeing another soul. The town has many hotels and is a good central base from which to set off on a trip into the true wilderness. Marked trails traverse forests and moors, where little has changed since the last Ice Age. The town of Tankavaara, 40 km (25 mi) south of Saariselka, is the most accessible and the best developed of several gold-panning areas.

GETTING HERE AND AROUND

A one-hour Airport Express shuttle connects Saariselka and the Ivalo Airport. From Saariselka, you can take one of four daily local bus connections to Tankavaara for €6. However, if you arrive in Saariselka at night and destined for Tankavaara, you will miss the bus and will have to either take a taxi or spend the night.

ESSENTIALS

Taxi Info Taxi Koskinen (☎ *400/394–862*). **Taxi Katajamaa** (☎ *400/731–973*).

Visitor Info Saariselkä (✉ *Kelotie, Seula* ☎ *016/668–402* ⊕ *www.saariselka.fi*).

EXPLORING

ⓒ The **Kultamuseo** *(Gold Museum)* tells the century-old story of Lapland's hardy fortune seekers. Guides will show you how to pan for gold dust and tiny nuggets from the silt of an icy stream. ✉ *Kultakylä, Tankavaara* ☎ *016/626–171* ⊕ *www.tankavaara.fi* ✑ *€7 museum, €4 an hr for gold panning* ⊙ *June–mid-Aug., daily 9–6; mid-Aug.–Sept., daily 9–5; Oct.–May, weekdays 10–4.*

More than 2,500 magnificent square km (962 square mi) make up the **Urhokekkosen Kansallispüisto** *(Urho Kekkonen National Park).* The park guide center is at Tankavaara. The western side of the park has marked trails accessible to hikers of all experience levels while wilderness zones present more demanding terrain. It is also popular for fishing and hunting, and reindeer herding remains the largest source of income in the region.

WHERE TO EAT

$ ✕ **Wanha Waskoolimies.** In the tradition of the old gold prospectors, this
SCANDINAVIAN   rustic restaurant consists of three rooms hewn from logs. Daily specials such as traditional sautéed reindeer with mashed potatoes and lingonberry sauce will give you a taste of simple but high-quality Lapland fare. ✉ *Tankavaaran Kultakylän* ☎ *016/626–158* ▭ *AE, DC, MC, V.*

WHERE TO STAY

$$$–$$$$ 🛏 **Holiday Club Saariselkä.** This hotel is known for its luxurious spa cen-
ⓒ   ter. The glass-dome swimming area is crammed with foliage, fountains, waterslides, wave machines, and a hot tub. The solarium, saunas, and Turkish baths are adjacent. Guest rooms have blond and dark-wood fittings and slate-blue carpets. Moderately priced cabin accommodations are also available. Note that the breakfast and spa facilities are included in prices. Children 4 to 14 can stay in their parents' room for the price of an extra bed, around €25; children under four stay free. The bus stops

at the hotel. **Pros:** nightclub party without nightclub noise in rooms; many amenities and activities. **Cons:** spa can be overrun with families. ⊠*Saareseläntie 7, Saariselkä* 🕾*016/6828* ⊕*www.holidayclubhotels. fi* ☞*134 rooms, 5 suites* ♿*In-room: Internet. In-hotel: 2 restaurants, room service, bars, tennis court, gym, spa, parking (free), some pets allowed, no-smoking rooms* ⊟*AE, DC, MC, V* 🍴*BP.*

¢ 🏨**Hotel Korundi.** Just off the Arctic Highway, this hotel has quiet surroundings and cozy, contemporary rooms for two to five people; most have a fireplace. You can try your luck at panning for gold here. The restaurant is in a separate building. **Pros:** close-to-nature feel with limited electronics. **Cons:** breakfast costs extra. ⊠ *Tankavaara* 🕾*016/626–158* ☞*8 rooms, 10 cabins with shared bathhouse* ♿*In-room: no phone, kitchen (some), no TV. In-hotel: restaurant, bar, laundry service, Internet terminal, parking (free), some pets allowed* ⊟*AE, DC, MC, V.*

$$ 🏨**Hotelli Kieppi.** The piney comfort of the rooms and the quiet countryside make this a good Lapland retreat. Five wood buildings with 12 to 16 rooms each make it especially popular with families. The restaurant has a cozy fireplace and pine furniture. Its regional and Continental menu is strong on reindeer and fish. **Pros:** evening sauna included; away-from-it-all feel; good restaurant. **Cons:** separate buildings. ⊠*Raitopolku 1, Saariselkä* 🕾*016/554–4600* ⊕*www.hotellikieppi.fi* ☞*64 rooms* ♿*In-room: refrigerator. In-hotel: restaurant, room service, bar, laundry facilities, Internet terminal, Wi-Fi, parking (free), some pets allowed, no-smoking rooms* ⊟*AE, DC, MC, V* 🍴*BP.*

$$$–$$$$ 🏨**Riekonlinna.** On the fringes of the wilderness treeline, the pinewood
☾ fittings and neutral-tone textiles of this contemporary Lappish hotel go well with its natural surroundings. All rooms have a balcony, and many have a sauna. The restaurant serves fresh local specialties, including reindeer, salmon, and snow grouse. The hotel is only 30 minutes from Ivalo airport, and its location provides excellent cross-country and downhill skiing; snowmobiling and reindeer safaris are also offered. There is a children's playroom. **Pros:** activites on your doorstep; great restaurant. **Cons:** can feel isolated. ⊠*Saariseläntie 13, Saariselkä* 🕾*016/679–4455* ⊕*www.laplandhotels.com* ☞*192 rooms, 4 suites, 36 apartments* ♿*In-room: Internet (some). In-hotel: restaurant, room service, bar, gym, laundry facilities, Wi-Fi, parking (free), some pets allowed* ⊟*AE, DC, MC, V* 🍴*BP.*

IVALO

40 km (25 mi) north of Saariselkä, 193 km (116 mi) north of Rovaniemi.

The village of Ivalo is the main center for northern Lapland and the largest village in the Inari region, with 4,300 inhabitants. It connects major snowmobile routes in winter and attracts anglers to its lakes, which have a reputation for bountiful fishing, in summer.

GETTING HERE AND AROUND
Finnair runs five 1½-hour flights a day to Ivalo in high season, one a day in low season. In winter, groups sometimes charter flights from London

and Paris to Ivalo en route to visiting the Santa Clause Village. Despite Ivalo's being 10 km (6 mi) from the airport, FInnair's airport shuttles do not go here. From the airport, your only option is a 10-minute, €15 taxi ride into town; there are usually taxis waiting. Buses leave six times daily from Rovaniemi to Ivalo (four hours). For tourist information, contact Saariselka.

ESSENTIALS

Taxi Info **Ivalo Taxi** (☎ *10/087–888*)..

EXPLORING

With its first-class hotel, airport, and many modern amenities, Ivalo offers little to the tourist in search of a wilderness experience, but on the huge island-studded expanses of **Inarijärvi** (Lake Inari), north of Ivalo, you can go boating, fishing, and hiking.

SPORTS AND THE OUTDOORS

☾ **Tunturikeskus Kiilopää** (✉ *Saariselkä* ☎ *016/6700–700* ⊕ *www.suomen latu.fi/kiilopaa*) is a multiactivity center at the edge of Urho Kekkonen National Forest that has guided ski and snowshoe tours, accommodations, and a smoke sauna. There are summer activities, too.

BOATING

A three-hour trip up the Lemmenjoki River can be arranged by **Lemmenjoen Lomamajat Oy Ahkuntupa** (✉ *Lemmenjoki* ☎ *016/673–475* ☾ *Mar.–Sept.*)

WHERE TO STAY

$$ ⊡ **Hotel Ivalo.** Modern and well equipped for business travelers and families, this hotel is 1 km (½ mi) from Ivalo, right on the Ivalojoki River. The lobby has marble floors, the lounge a brick fireplace. The rooms are spacious and modern, with oatmeal carpets and lots of blond birch-wood trimming; ask for one by the river. The restaurant serves Continental fare, as well as delicious Lappish dishes. **Pros:** regal lobby; luxurious decor; river views. **Cons:** slightly corporate feel. ✉ *Ivalontie 34, Ivalo* ☎ *016/688–111* ⊕ *www.hotelivalo.fi* ↩ *91 rooms, 3 suites* ☾ *In-hotel: restaurant, room service, bars, pool, Internet terminal, Wi-Fi, some pets allowed, no-smoking rooms* ☰ *AE, DC, MC, V* ⦿ *BP.*

$ ⊡ **Kultahippu.** In the heart of Ivalo, along the Ivalojoki River, Kultahippu
☾ claims to have the northernmost nightclub in Finland. Guest rooms are cozy, with simple birch-wood furnishing; larger rooms with a sauna are available for families. The restaurant serves traditional Lapp meals à la carte. **Pros:** good nightlife; authentic restaurant. **Cons:** simple amenities. ✉ *Petsamontie 1, Ivalo* ☎ *016/661–825* ⊕ *www.kultahippuhotel. fi* ↩ *30 rooms* ☾ *In-hotel: restaurant, bar, beachfront, laundry service, Internet terminal, Wi-Fi, parking (free)* ☰ *AE, DC, MC, V* ⦿ *BP.*

$ ⊡ **Tunturikeskus Kiilopää.** This "fell center" is in the midst of hiking and cross-country skiing territory in the Urho Kekkonen National Park district, 45 km (28 mi) south of Ivalo Airport. Accommodations are in beautifully crafted log cabins, apartments, or individual hotel rooms, all made of wood and stone. Apartments have picture windows and fireplaces. Eighteen new log cabins were completed in 2007. The restaurant serves reindeer and other game entrées. **Pros:** activities at your door-step; range of high-quality accommodation options. **Cons:** can feel iso-lated. ⊠ *Kiilopää, Saariselkä* ☎ *016/670–0700* ⊕ *www.suomenlatu.fi/ kiilopaa* ↪ *26 cabins, 8 apartments, 34 rooms, 9 youth-hostel rooms* ⚐ *In hotel restaurant, no-smoking rooms* ☐ *AE, DC, MC, V* ⏸*CP.*

INARI

40 km (24 mi) northwest of Ivalo, 333 km (207 mi) north of Rovaniemi.

It is a stunning drive northwest from Ivalo along the lakeshore to Inari, home of the *Sami Parlamenta* (Sami Parliament) and the center of Sami culture. Lake Inari is Finland's second largest and includes more than 3,000 islands, around which locals and visitors fish in summer and snowmobile in winter. Other popular activities include visiting a rein-deer farm, canoeing the nearby rivers, hiking, and cross-country skiing in the Arctic wilderness.

GETTING HERE AND AROUND

Buses leave from the Ivalo town center to Inari and cost €7. A taxi from Ivalo will take about 40 minutes. Buses leave four times daily from Rovaniemi to Inari (five to six hours). Lake Lines Inari offer Sami tours that include a visit to SIIDA, the Sami Museum in Inari, and a cruise on Lake Inari (operated by Lake Lines Inari).

ESSENTIALS

Taxi Info **Taxi Rikhard Ranta** (☎ *400/959–375*). **Taxi Ilmar Slant** (☎ *400/ 180–771*).

Tour Info **Lake Lines Inari** (⊠ *Meska-Set Oy, Ruskatie 3, Inari* ☎ *0400/391–017*).

Visitor Info **Inari Tourist Board** (⊠ *Northern Lapland Tourism Ltd., Kelotie, Seula, Saariselkä* ☎ *016/668–402* ⊕ *www.inarilapland.org*).

EXPLORING

The **SIIDA Center,** on the village outskirts, hosts exhibits on the Sami people and the northern seasons. The center houses the **Saamelaismu-seo** (Sami Museum) (☎ *410/898–212*) and the **Ylä-Lapin luontokeskus** (Northern Lapland Nature Center). The museum's permanent exhi-bitions include one on the evolution of nature and culture from the Ice Age to the present, while the main exhibit focuses on the unique natural features of northern Finland's arctic environment. Temporary exhibitions might focus on Sami history or art, nature photographs, or conservation. The Nature Center includes the **Metsähallitus** (*Forest and Park Service* ☎ *0205/647–740*), which can provide camping and fish-ing permits along with advice on exploring the wilderness. A 17-acre open-air museum complements the indoor exhibits at the center during the summer with displays of old Sami dwellings, trapping, and fishing gear. ⊠ *Rte. 4 by Lake Inari, Inari* ☎ *410/898–212 or 0205/647–740* ⊕ *www.siida.fi* 🎫 *€8* 🕐 *Saamelaismuseo: June–Sept., daily 9–8; Oct.– May, Tues.–Sun. 10–5.*

**OFF THE
BEATEN
PATH**

Inarin Porofarmi. At this working reindeer farm 14 km (9 mi) southeast of Inari, you can drive a reindeer sled or be pulled on skis by the magical animals. ⊠ *Kaksamajärvi, Ivalo* ☎ *016/663–005* ☉ *June–Aug., weekdays at noon; other times and seasons by appointment and only for groups of 10 or more.*

WHERE TO STAY

$-$$

Inarin Kultahovi. This cozy inn is on the wooded banks of the swiftly flowing Juutuajoki Rapids. The no-frills double rooms are small, with handwoven rugs and birch-wood furniture. In summer you might need a reservation to get a table at Kultahovi's restaurant; the specialties are red trout and reindeer, but try the tasty whitefish caught from nearby Lake Inari. A television channel shows the view from an underwater camera in the river, which in summer captures the red trout spawning. The hotel completed a second building with 16 rooms in December 2007. **Pros:** rooms in new building have own saunas; river views. **Cons:** river rapids too strong for swimming. ⊠ *Saarikoskentie 2, Inari* ☎ *016/671–221* ⊕ *www.hotelkultahovi.fi* ⇨ *45 rooms* ⌂ *In-room: Internet (some), Wi-Fi (some). In-hotel: restaurant, room service, bar, laundry service, parking (free), some pets allowed* ▤ *DC, MC, V* ⊙| *BP.*

SPORTS AND THE OUTDOORS

Many local travel agencies throughout Lapland offer different types of tours of the region. **Arctic Safaris** (⊠ *Koskikatu 6, Rovaniemi* ☎ *016/ 340–0400* ⊕ *www.arcticsafaris.fi*) offers summer and winter tours including canoeing, hiking, and snowmobiling.

Norway

WORD OF MOUTH

"Norway is an incredible country. The people are so friendly, the landscapes are absolutely beautiful, and their government is people-focused (as opposed to corporate-focused). Transportation was very accessible, there were no language barriers, and the food was delicious. It was expensive (they are on the kroner), but not as bad as the euro. We plan to go back and visit the northern part of the country and either see the northern lights or midnight sun."

—danielsonkin

Updated by
Marie Peyre

ONE OF THE WORLD'S MOST beautiful countries, Norway has long been a popular cruising destination, famed for its stunning fjords. Formed during the last ice age's meltdown when the inland valleys carved by huge glaciers filled with seawater, fjords are undoubtedly Norway's top attractions—they shape the country's unique landscape and never fail to take your breath away.

But while the fjords are Norway's most striking and dramatic scenic features, there is much else to see, from the vast expanses of rugged tundra in the north to the huge evergreen forests along the Swedish border, from the fertile coastal plains of the Jæren region in the southwest to the snow-covered peaks and glaciers of the center.

One of the least densely populated countries in Europe, Norway is also one of the richest (thanks to the discovery of oil and gas in the North Sea in the late 1960s), and this newfound wealth has changed the country significantly in the past decades, transforming cities like Stavanger into global players and boosting both the economy and the self-confidence of the Norwegian people.

Norway also regularly tops surveys as the country with the highest quality of life in the world, owing a great deal to the well-developed welfare system. The country's social democratic political system is to a large extent based on compromise, cooperation, and tolerance. These qualities are also at the heart of the country's reputation as a diplomatic mediator in world affairs.

It wasn't always like this. In the Middle Ages, the Vikings, accomplished seamen, crossed over to continental Europe and the British Isles on their famed longships (a few well-preserved examples of which you can see at the Viking Ship Museum in Oslo) and waged, in their attempt to establish new trade links and settlements, a campaign of violence that lasted for 200 years. The Vikings' tough nature, coupled with their excellent skills as navigators, lived on in their descendants, and it's no coincidence that some of the foremost explorers of modern times (Fridtjof Nansen, Thor Heyerdahl, and of course Roald Amundsen among them) hail from Norway.

So do many professional skiers and ice skaters; winter sports is another thing Norwegians have always excelled at, as they proved during the Lillehammer Winter Olympics in 1994, and keep reminding the rest of the world at every major international competition.

From 1537 to 1814, Norway was under the rule of Denmark, and after that it was forced into a union with Sweden until 1905, during which time the rise of the Norwegian romantic nationalism cultural movement took root. Composer Edvard Grieg, playwright Henrik Ibsen, and artist Edvard Munch were among those who helped put Norway on the international cultural map. Today Oslo, Bergen, and Stavanger are all vibrant cities with rich culture, including many festivals and world-class artists (homegrown and imported) performing regularly to discerning audiences.

But it's nature tourists come to see, and the Norwegians themselves have a strong attachment to the natural beauty of their homeland. In almost any kind of weather, blasting or balmy, large numbers of Norwegians are outdoors, fishing, biking, skiing, hiking, or sailing. Everybody— from cherubic children to hardy, knapsack-toting seniors—bundles up for just one more ski trip or hike in the mountains.

When discussing the size of their country, Norwegians like to say that if Oslo remained fixed and the northern part of the country were swung south, it would reach all the way to Rome. Perched at the very top of the globe, this northern land is long and rangy, stretching 2,750 km (1,705 mi) from north to south, and offers vast expanses of unspoiled terrain—a fantastic playground for nature lovers, wildlife enthusiasts, and sporty types.

4

ORIENTATION AND PLANNING

GETTING ORIENTED

Norway is long and narrow, with a jagged coastline carved by deep, dramatic fjords. Oslo, Norway's capital, is in the east, only a few hours from the Swedish border. The coast, from Oslo around the southern tip of the country up to Stavanger, is filled with wide beaches and seaside communities. North of here, in Norway's central interior, the country is blanketed with mountains, creating dramatic valleys and plateaus. Bergen, on the west coast, is considered the gateway to fjord country. Moving north, the land becomes wild and untouched. Outside the north's two main cities, Trondheim and Tromsø, the land stretches for miles into the Arctic Circle and up to the Russian border. We describe each of these regions in its own section below.

Oslo. The Norwegian capital is home to just over 500,000 inhabitants, but it boasts great museums, top restaurants, and a stunning new Opera House. Check out the Royal Palace, at the end of Karl Johans Gate (Oslo's main thoroughfare) before ambling down to Aker Brygge, the trendy area by the harbor. Then visit Vigeland's statue park or Holmenkollen ski jump, before ending your day in one of Grünerløkka's many buzzing restaurants.

The Oslo Fjord. The islands dotting the Oslo Fjord make for a popular boat trip and a great day out in summer. Go on a mini cruise to explore the area, while away an afternoon fishing on the rocks, or laze in the sun in Drøbak or Åsgårdstrand, two of the many seaside resorts along the fjord. Fredrikstad's Old Town, northern Europe's best preserved fortress town, is well worth a visit, and so is Hadeland Glassverk, inland to the north.

Southern Norway. The southern coast, or Sørlandet, is a popular summer destination with Norwegians, not least because of its mild climate. Cute white wooden towns and thousands of little islands are dotted along the shore, making this a boating paradise. Inland you can take a cruise on the Telemark Canal, or see wild reindeers on the Hardangervidda, Europe's largest mountain plateau.

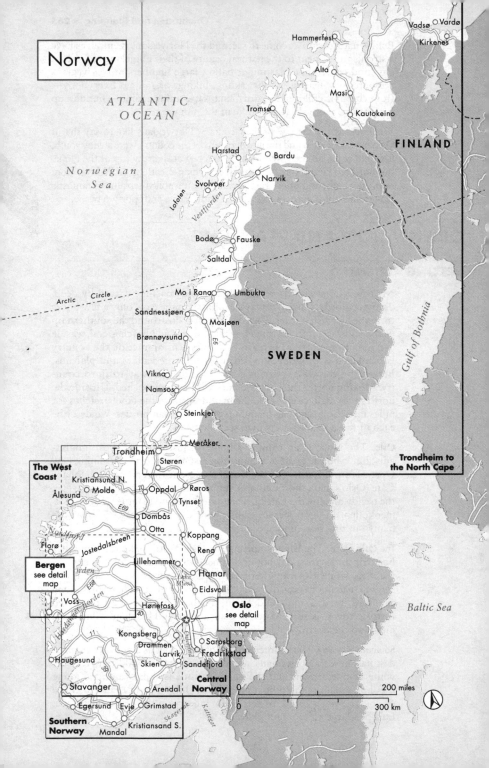

Bergen. The "Gateway to the Fjords," as it's known, is Norway's second-largest city. Built around a pretty harbor and surrounded by seven hills, Bergen has much to offer visitors, not least those in search of history and culture. Highlights include the UNESCO-listed Hanseatic wharf of Bryggen, the famous fish market, the aquarium, and the Fløibanen funicular. Nearby you can also visit the homes of composer Edvard Grieg and violin virtuoso Ole Bull.

The West Coast. Norway's spectacular fjords are what draw most visitors to the country, and it's easy to see why. Whether driving along the water's edge or taking the views in from a boat, you can expect fantastic scenery, whatever the weather. Stavanger, Norway's oil capital and one of its most cosmopolitan cities, is also worth a visit, as are Bergen and Ålesund.

4

Central Norway. Mountains and huge forests cover a great part of Central Norway, where you'll also find some of the best ski resorts in the country, including Trysil and Lillehammer (home of the 1994 Winter Olympics). The Jotunheimen, or "Home of the Giants," is popular with hikers in summer, as is Rondane National Park. If a gentler kind of landscape is what you're after, Mjøsa, Norway's biggest lake, or Gudbrandsdalen, one of its longest valleys, will both appeal.

Trondheim to the North Cape. Trondheim is home to the biggest cathedral in Norway, Nidarosdomen, an impressive early gothic-style structure, while Røros, 100 km (62 mi) to the south, is a picturesque old mining town famed for its wooden buildings and church. The region is also one of the best for angling, and salmon is plentiful in the Namsen River. Further north the Lofoten Islands, with their rugged peaks, quaint little fishermen's villages, and many bird cliffs, draw artists and wildlife enthusiasts, while the North Cape remains a goal for many travelers.

PLANNING

WHEN TO GO

The tourist season peaks in June, July, and August, when daytime temperatures are often in the 70s (21°C to 26°C) and sometimes rise into the 80s (27°C to 32°C). In general, the weather is not overly warm, and a brisk breeze and brief rainstorms are possible anytime. Nights can be chilly, even in summer.

Visit in summer if you want to experience the endless days of the midnight sun; the best time to visit is mid-May to late July. Hotels, museums, and sights have longer opening hours and the modes of transportation run on more frequent schedules. If you decide to travel in May, try to be in the country on the 17th, or *Syttende Mai,* Norway's Constitution Day, when flag-waving Norwegians bedecked in national costumes, or *bunader,* fill the streets. Fall, spring, and even winter are pleasant, despite the Nordic reputation for gloom. The days become shorter quickly, but the sun casts a golden light not seen farther south. On dark days, fires and candlelight will warm you indoors.

Winter Norway is a wonderland of snow-covered mountains glowing under the northern lights, and few tourists are around to get in

TOP REASONS TO GO

■ **Explore Norway's Fjords.** The Norwegian fjords are known for their majestic beauty, and should top your agenda. From the spring cherry tree blossoms in Hardangerfjord to the rugged scenery and barren cliffs of windswept Lysefjord, no two fjords are the same. Geirangerfjord, the most photographed, and Sognefjord, the longest and deepest, are possibly the most popular, but some of the smaller fjords are just as stunning, so make sure you include a few different ones on your itinerary.

■ **Enjoy the Great Outdoors.** Get close to nature. Whether you fancy hiking in the Hardangervidda or Jotunheimen, skiing in one of

Northern Europe's best resorts, sailing along the southern coast or fishing in some of the world's best salmon rivers, the choice is yours. Wildlife is plentiful, too, so if you can't see the elusive moose, you're guaranteed to spot other mammals and birds.

■ **Catch the Midnight Sun.** Seeking 24-hour sunlight? Travel north of the Arctic Circle in summer, where the sun never drops below the horizon, to experience this unique phenomenon, and make the most of the longest days of the year. Or go between November and February to witness the awe-inspiring spectacle of the Northern Lights brightening up the dark winter sky.

your way (although many tourist attractions are also closed). The days may seem perpetually dark, and November through February can be especially dreary. If it's skiing you're interested in, plan your trip for March or April, as there's usually still plenty of snow left. Take note that during Easter Week, many Norwegians head for the mountains, so it's hard to get accommodations—cities are virtually shut down, and even grocery stores close.

CLIMATE

The climate on the west coast of Norway is surprisingly moderate, due to the influence of the Gulf Stream. Inland and to the north, temperatures are more extreme, with warm summers and bitingly cold winters (November to March). You can expect snow pretty much anywhere north of Oslo in winter. The mildest climate is to be found along the southern coast, while Bergen is the town that receives the most rain. The following are average daily maximum and minimum temperatures for Oslo.

Jan.	19°F	-7°C	May	43°F	6°C	Sept.	46°F	8°C
	28°F	-2°C		61°F	16°C		60°F	16°C
Feb.	19°F	-7°C	June	50°F	10°C	Oct.	38°F	3°C
	30°F	-1°C		68°F	20°C		48°F	9°C
Mar.	25°F	-4°C	July	55°F	13°C	Nov.	31°F	-1°C
	39°F	4°C		72°F	22°C		38°F	3°C
Apr.	34°F	1°C	Aug.	54°F	12°C	Dec.	25°F	-4°C
	50°F	10°C		70°F	21°C		32°F	0°C

BUSINESS HOURS

Banks are open weekdays 9 to 4. Many offices and embassies close at 3 from June to August. Stores are generally open weekdays 9 to 5 or 6 and Saturday 9 to 1 or 2 and are closed Sunday.

Major holidays include: New Year's Day, Holy (Maundy) Thursday, Good Friday, Easter Sunday and Monday, May Day, Ascension (40 days after Easter), Whitsun/Pentecost (Sunday and Monday 10 days after Ascension), Constitution Day (17 May), Christmas Day, and Boxing Day (day after Christmas).

GETTING HERE AND AROUND

AIR TRAVEL

Gardermoen Airport (OSL), about 45 km (28 mi) north of Oslo, is the major entry point for most visitors. Most flights from North America have at least one connection, though Continental is the exception with direct flights from New York. American Airlines flies via London and Brussels; Finnair connects through Helsinki; Iceland Air flies via Reykjavík. Scandinavian Airlines System (SAS), partnering with United, has flights via Copenhagen and Stockholm. A flight from New York to Oslo takes about eight hours.

Within Norway, Norwegian, SAS and Widerøe connect many of the cities by regular flights. SAS and low-cost airline Norwegian also serve many destinations in Europe, while Widerøe also has flights to a handful of destinations in Sweden, Denmark and the United Kingdom.

Contacts American Airlines (⊕ *www.aa.com*). **Continental** (⊕ *www.continental. com*). **Finnair** (⊕ *www.finnair.com*). **Iceland Air** (⊕ *www.icelandair.com*). **Norwegian** (⊕ *www.norwegian.no*). **SAS** (⊕ *www.flysas.com*). **Widerøe** (⊕ *www. wideroe.no*).

BOAT AND FERRY TRAVEL

Taking a ferry isn't only fun, it's often necessary in Norway, as they remain an important means of transportation along the west coast. More specialized boat service includes hydrofoil (catamaran) trips between Stavanger, Haugesund, and Bergen. There are also fjord cruises out of these cities and others in the north. Fjord1 and Tide are the main ferry companies, and Route Information Norway is a company that has comprehensive links to all forms of transport within Norway.

Norway's most renowned boat is *Hurtigruten*, which literally means "Rapid Route." Also known as the Coastal Steamer, the boat departs from Bergen and stops at 36 ports along the coast in six days, ending with Kirkenes, near the Russian border, before turning back. Tickets can be purchased for the entire journey or for individual legs.

Ferry Contacts Tide (☎ *05505 in Bergen* ⊕ *www.tide.no*). **Fjord1** (☎ *71–21–95–00 in Molde* ⊕ *www.fjord1.no*). **Route Information Norway** (⊕ *www.ruteinfo.no*).

Cruise Contacts Hurtigruten (☎ *810–30–000 in Narvik* ⊕ *www.hurtigruten.com*). **Hurtigruten US (formerly Norwegian Coastal Voyage Inc)** (☎ *866/257–6071 in New York* ⊕ *www.nhurtigruten.us*).

CUTTING COSTS

Norway is a notoriously expensive country, but there are several ways to keep down costs.

AIR TRAVEL

The SAS Visit Scandinavia/Europe Air Pass offers up to eight flight coupons for one-way travel between Scandinavian cities (and participating European countries). One-way tickets within Scandinavia start at $72, (unless you're headed to the far north; these flights range from $108 to $370). These passes can be bought only in conjunction with a round-trip ticket between North America and Europe on SAS and must be used within three months of arrival.

Widerøe Airline's Explore Norway by Plane plan, available between late June and mid-August, divides Norway into three parts with boundaries at Trondheim and Tromsø, and you can fly as much as you like within a 14-day period. This costs €490 for the whole country, €331 for one zone, and €417 for two zones. An extra week costs €221. (Widerøe lists its prices in Euros for the ease of the majority of its customers.)

FOOD

Most restaurants have good value lunch menus, while dinner is often costly. Or do as many Norwegians do and pack your own, a great way to sample different local breads and cheeses. Alcohol is prohibitively expensive in Norway, so stick to tap water and soft drinks wherever possible.

GROUND TRANSPORTATION

ScanRail Passes get you discounts on train, ferry, and car transportation in Norway, Sweden, Denmark, and Finland. Also look into the EurailPass, which you can buy only in the United States through ScanAm. A Eurail

Norway Rail Pass, for example, is available for three, four, five, six, and eight days of unlimited rail travel for nonresidents on Norwegian State Railways (NSB). Low-season prices are offered from October through April. Discounted fares also include family, student, senior-citizen (including their not-yet-senior spouses), and off-peak "mini" fares, which must be purchased a day in advance.

Rail Passes ScanAm World Tours (⊕ *www.scandinaviantravel.com*). **Rail Europe** (⊕ *www.raileurope.com*).

HOTELS

Special summer and weekend rates may save you money in cities, while prices tend to be higher in holiday areas during the same period. Fjordpass, at NKr 120, is the biggest hotel pass in Norway, with preferential rates in 170 hotels all over the country. Buy it online or at participating hotels. Breakfast is usually included, but check before you book.

Contact Fjordpass (⊕ *www. fjord-pass.com*).

SHOPPING

Value-added tax, VAT for short but called *moms* all over Scandinavia, is a hefty 25% on all purchases except books; it is included in the prices of goods. All purchases of consumer goods totaling more than NKr 315 for export by nonresidents are eligible for VAT refunds. (Carry your passport when shopping to prove you are a nonresident.) Look for shops carrying the sticker "Tax-Free Shopping." VAT refunds save you 11 to 19% of the price paid by residents; head to the Cash Refund offices at airports, ferries, cruise ships and border crossings. Find more info on ⊕ *www. globalrefund.com*.

BUS TRAVEL

Bus tours can be effective for smaller regions within Norway, but the train system is excellent and offers much greater coverage in less time. Buses do, however, tend to be less expensive.

Every ond station of the railroad is supported by a number of bus routes, some of which are operated by the Norwegian State Railway (NSB), others by local companies. Long-distance buses usually take longer than the railroad, and fares are only slightly lower. Virtually every settlement on the mainland is served by bus, and for anyone with a desire to get off the beaten track, a pay-as-you-go, open-ended bus trip is the best way to see Norway.

Most long-distance buses leave from Bussterminalen close to Oslo Central Station. Nor-Way Bussekspress, a chain of 50 Norwegian bus companies serving 500 destinations, can arrange any journey.

Contacts Ruteinformasjonen (☎177); for timetables and fares for the area you are situated in [except Svalbard]. **Bussterminalen** (⊠ Galleriet Oslo, Schweigaardsgt. 10 ☎ 23-00-24-00 bus information). **Nor-Way Bussekspress** (☎815-44-444 ⊕ www.norway.no). **Norwegian State Railway (NSB)** (☎815-00-888 ⊕ www.nsb.no).

CAR TRAVEL

You can drive in Norway with your valid U.S. driver's license. Excellent, well-marked roads make driving a great way to explore Norway, but it can be an expensive choice. Ferry costs can be steep, and you should turn up early in peak season for the most popular crossings, as ferry companies no longer take bookings. Tolls on some major roads and to enter Oslo, Bergen, Trondheim, Stavanger, and Kristiansand add to the expense, as do the high fees for city parking. Tickets for illegal parking are painfully costly.

If you're planning to drive around Norway, call or check the Web site of the Statens Vegvesen (Public Roads Administration), which monitors and provides information about roads, conditions, tolls, distances, and ferry timetables. Phones are open 24 hours a day.

Four-lane highways are found only around major cities. Elsewhere, roads tend to be narrow and twisting, with only token guardrails. The southern part of Norway is fairly compact—all major cities are about a day's drive from each other. Along the west coast, waits for ferries and passage through tunnels can be significant. Don't expect to cover more than 240 km (150 mi) in a day, especially in fjord country.

In a few remote areas, especially in northern Norway, road conditions can be unpredictable in autumn, winter, or spring. Some high mountain roads are closed as early as October due to snow, and do not open again until June. When driving in remote areas, especially in winter, let someone know your travel plans, use a four-wheel-drive vehicle, and travel with at least one other car.

Contacts Norsk Automobil-Forbund (NAF) (Norwegian Automobile Association ☎ 92-60-85-05 in Oslo, 08-505 for 24-hr service ⊕ www.naf.no). **Statens Vegvesen** (☎175 in Norway, 815-48-991 from abroad ⊕ www.vegvesen.no).

GASOLINE
Gas is expensive and costs approximately NKr 13 per liter (that's around US$9.10 per gallon). Stations are mostly self serve, and hours vary greatly. Those marked *kort* are 24-hour pumps, which take oil-company credit cards or bank cards, either of which is inserted directly into the pump.

RULES OF
THE ROAD
Driving is on the right. The maximum speed limit is 90 kph (55 mph) on major highways. On other highways the limit is 80 kph (50 mph) or 70 kph (43 mph). The speed limit in cities and towns is 50 kph (30 mph), and 30 kph (18 mph) in residential areas. Speeding is punished severely.

By law, you must keep your headlights on at all times, and everyone, including infants, must wear seat belts. Children under four years of age must ride in a car seat, and children over four years must ride in the back. Norway has strict drinking-and-driving laws, and there are routine roadside checks. The legal limit is a blood-alcohol level of 0.02%, which effectively means that you should not drink any alcohol before driving. If you are stopped, you may be required to take a breath test. If it is positive, you must submit to a blood test. No exceptions are made for foreigners, who can lose their licenses on the spot. Other penalties include fines and imprisonment. An accident involving a driver with an illegal blood-alcohol level usually voids all insurance agreements, so the driver becomes responsible for his own medical bills and damage to the cars.

PARKING
You can usually park on the side of the road, though not on main roads and highways. Signs reading PARKERING/STANS FORBUDT mean no parking or stopping. For most downtown parking you must either buy a ticket from an automatic vending machine and display it on the dash, or use a public car park. The latter is more expensive (about NKr 250 a day in Oslo, and NKr 100– NKr 150 in other major cities).

TAXI TRAVEL
Even the smallest villages have some form of taxi service. Towns on the railroad normally have taxi stands just outside the station. All city taxis are connected with a central dispatching office, so there is only one main telephone number for calling a cab. Look in the telephone book under "Taxi" or "Drosje." Never use an unmarked, or pirate, taxi, since their drivers are unlicensed and in some cases may be dangerous.

TRAIN TRAVEL
NSB, the Norwegian State Railway System, has five main lines originating from the Oslo S Station. Its 4,000 km (2,500 mi) of track connect all main cities. Train tickets can be purchased in railway stations or from travel agencies. NSB has its own travel agency in Oslo. Note that many travelers assume that rail passes guarantee them seats on the trains they wish to ride. Not so. You need to book seats ahead even if you are using a rail pass.

NSB trains are clean, comfortable, and punctual. Most have special compartments for travelers with disabilities and for families with children younger than age two. First- and second-class tickets are available.

Norway's longest rail route runs north to Trondheim, then extends onward as far as Fauske and Bodø. The southern line hugs the coast to

Stavanger, while the stunning western line crosses Hardangervidda, the scenic plateau that lies between Oslo and Bergen. An eastern line to Stockholm links Norway with Sweden, while another southern line through Göteborg, Sweden, is the main connection with Continental Europe. Narvik, north of Bodø, is the last stop on Sweden's Ofot line, the world's northernmost rail system, which runs from Stockholm via Kiruna.

Contact **NSB** (☎ *81-50-08-88 in Oslo* ⊕ *www.nsb.no).*

RESTAURANTS

Major cities like Oslo, Bergen, and Stavanger offer a full range of restaurants, from traditional to international. Expect fewer options in more rural areas. Pizza restaurants are very popular, particularly in the south, and often offer the best value for money. Chains like Peppes and Dolly Dimples have outlets throughout the country. Norwegians usually eat their dinner, or *middag,* early (5 PM is not unusual if eating at home, a bit later if dining out). Reservations are required for the most sought-after restaurants in major cities, but are not always necessary otherwise. It is generally much cheaper to eat out at lunchtime than in the evening, as many establishments have good value lunch menus.

Although not widely known abroad, Norwegian food is surprisingly tasty and varied. Fish, as one would expect from a country with such a long coastline, is a strong component of the Norwegian diet, with cod a particular favorite. The latter appears in many dishes, including *lutefisk,* a traditional Christmas dish (usually eaten with a dash of aquavit, or schnapps). Shellfish is also excellent—from prawns to lobster, the choice is ample, and the *kongekrabbe,* or giant crab, is a local specialty much prized by tourists and locals alike. Game is another specialty in season; make sure you try moose or reindeer if you get the chance. And do seek out the Lofoten lamb (organic, free-range lamb reared on the Lofoten archipelago in the north). Last but not least, leave room for desserts—the pastries, from *boller* to *skolebrød,* are delicious, as are the many different breads.

HOTELS

Norwegian hotels have high standards in cleanliness and comfort and prices to match. Even the simplest youth hostels provide good mattresses with fluffy down comforters and clean showers or baths. Breakfast, usually served buffet style, is often included in the room price at hotels. Rustic cabins and campsites are also available all over the countryside, as are independent hotels.

HYTTER

Quintessentially Scandinavian, *hytter,* or rentals that range from small wooden cabins to bigger chalet type houses, are as ubiquitous on the coast as they are in mountainous areas. Ideally suited to families and small groups, they offer good value for money, and allow you to be close to nature while still enjoying some degree of comfort. Local and regional tourist offices can help you book accommodation in a *hytte,* as well as the company Norges Booking.

Contact **Norges Booking** (☎ *32-08-57-10* ⊕ *www.norgesbooking.com).*

WHAT IT COSTS IN NORWEGIAN KRONER				
¢	$	$$	$$$	$$$$
OSLO and BERGEN				
Restaurants	under 130	130–200	200–270	270–350	over 350
Hotels	under 900	900–1,300	1,300–1,700	1,700–2,100	over 2,100
ELSEWHERE				
Restaurants	under 100	100–150	150–200	200–250	over 250
Hotels	under 600	600–1,000	1,000–1,400	1,400–1,800	over 1,800

Restaurant prices are based on the median main course price at dinner, excluding tip. Hotel prices are for two people in a standard double room in high season.

ESSENTIALS

ELECTRICITY The electrical current in Norway is 220 volts, 50 cycles alternating current (AC). Outlets take the Continental plugs, with two round plugs. To use your North American appliances, you'll need both a converter and an adapter.

EMERGENCIES Ambulance, fire, and police assistance is available 24 hours. Norsk Automobil-Forbund (NAF) offers roadside assistance. They patrol major roads and mountain passes from mid-June to mid-August. Another roadside assistance agency is Falken.

Contacts Ambulance (☎113). **Norsk Automobil-Forbund (NAF)** (*Norwegian Automobile Association* ☎92–60—85–05 in Oslo, 08505 for 24-hr service ⊕ *www.naf.no*). **Falken** (☎02222 for 24-hr service ⊕ *www.falken.no*). **Fire** (☎110). **Police** (☎112). **U.S. Embassy** (✉*Henrik Ibsens gt. 48, SentrumOslo* ☎22-44-85-50 ⊕ *norway.usembassy.gov*).

ENTRY U.S. citizens need only a valid passport for stays of up to three months. Your passport must be valid for at least three months beyond the length of your stay.

LANGUAGE Despite the fact that Norwegian is in the Germanic family of languages, it is a myth that someone who speaks German can understand it. Fortunately, English is widely spoken.

Norwegian has three additional vowels: æ, ø, and å. Æ is pronounced as a short "a." The ø, sometimes printed as *oe*, is the same as ö in German and Swedish, pronounced very much like a short "u." The å is a contraction of the archaic "aa" and sounds like long "o." These three letters appear at the end of alphabetical listings, such as those in the phone book.

There are two officially sanctioned Norwegian languages, Bokmål and Nynorsk. Bokmål is used by 84% of the population and is the main written form of Norwegian and the language of books, as the first half of its name indicates. Nynorsk, which translates as "new Norwegian," is actually a compilation of older dialect forms from rural Norway. Every Norwegian also receives at least seven years of English instruction, starting in the second grade. The Sami (or Lapps), who inhabit the northernmost parts of Norway, have their own language, which is distantly related to Finnish.

MONEY
MATTERS

Currency and Exchange. The Norwegian *krone* (plural: *kroner*) translates as "crown," written officially as NOK. Price tags are seldom marked this way, but instead read "Kr" followed by the amount, such as Kr 10. (In this book, the Norwegian krone is abbreviated NKr.) One krone is divided into 100 *øre*, and coins of 50 øre and 1, 5, 10, and 20 kroner are in circulation. Bills are issued in denominations of 50, 100, 200, 500, and 1,000 kroner. At this writing, the rate of exchange was NKr 5.82 to the U.S. dollar and NKr 8.33 to the euro.

Pricing and Taxes. Costs are high in Norway, and so is the value-added tax VAT (aka *moms*) of 25% (generally included in the prices of goods). Residents of countries outside the EU can recover some of this tax with the Global Refund scheme (⇨ *Cutting Costs box, above*).

You can buy liquor and strong beer (over 3% alcohol) only in state-owned shops, at very high prices, during weekday business hours, usually 9:30 to 6 and in some areas on Saturday until mid-afternoon. (When you visit people in Norway, a bottle of liquor or fine wine bought duty-free on the trip over is much appreciated.) Weaker beers and ciders are usually available in grocery stores, except in certain rural areas.

Sample Prices. Cup of coffee, NKr 20–NKr 30; a half liter of beer, NKr 50–NKr 60; the smallest hot dog (with bun plus *lompe*—a flat Norwegian potato bread—mustard, ketchup, and fried onions) at a convenience store, NKr 20–NKr 30; bottle of wine, from NKr 80; urban transit fare in Oslo, NKr 34; soft drink, NKr 25–NKr 35; sandwich, NKr 40–NKr 50; 1½-km (1-mi) taxi ride, NKr 50–NKr 70.

Tipping. Tipping is kept to a minimum in Norway because service charges are added to most bills. It is, however, handy to have a supply of NKr 5 or NKr 10 coins for less formal service. Tip only in local currency. Room service usually includes a service charge in the bill, so tipping is discretionary. Round up a taxi fare to the next round digit, or tip anywhere from NKr 5 to NKr 10, a little more if the driver has been helpful. All restaurants include a service charge, ranging from 12% to 15%, in the bill. It's customary, but not obligatory, to add up to 10% for exceptional service.

PHONES

The country code for Norway is 47. There are no area codes—you must dial all eight digits of any phone number wherever you are. Telephone numbers that start with a 9 or 4 are usually mobile phones, and are considerably more expensive to call. Telephone numbers starting with the prefix 82 cost extra. Toll-free numbers begin with 800 or 810. Numbers beginning with 815 cost NKr 1 per call.

Dial 1881 for information in Norway, 1882 for international information. To place a collect or an operator-assisted call to a number in Norway, dial 115. Dial 117 for collect or operator-assisted calls outside of Norway. All international operators speak English.

Local calls cost NKr 3 or NKr 5 from a pay phone. If you hear a short tone, it means that your purchased time is almost up. Push-button public phones—which accept NKr 1, 5, and 10 coins (some also accept NKr 20 coins)—are easy to use: lift the receiver, listen for the dial tone, insert the coins, dial the number, and wait for a connection. The digital screen at the top of the box indicates the amount of money in your "account." Green-card public phones only accept credit cards or Tellerskritt (phone cards), which you can buy in various denominations at Narvesen and Norsk Tipping shops and kiosks.

Scandinavia has been one of the world leaders in mobile phone development; almost 90% of the population owns a mobile phone. Although standard North American cellular phones will not work in Norway, some companies rent cellular phones to visitors. Contact the Norwegian Tourist Board for details.

VISITOR INFO **Contacts Norwegian Tourist Board** (☎ *22-00-25-00* ⊕ *www.visitnorway.com*). **Royal Norwegian Embassy in the United States** (☎ *202/333-6000* ⊕ *www. norway.org*). **Scandinavian Tourist Board** (☎ *212/885-9700 in New York* ⊕ *www. goscandinavia.com*).

OSLO

What sets Oslo apart from other European cities is not so much its cultural traditions or its internationally renowned museums as its simply stunning natural beauty. How many world capitals have subway service to the forest, or lakes and hiking trails within city limits? But Norwegians will be quick to remind you that Oslo is a cosmopolitan metropolis with prosperous businesses and a thriving nightlife.

Once overlooked by travelers to Scandinavia, Oslo is now a major tourist destination and the gateway to what many believe is Scandinavia's most scenic country. That's just one more change for this town of 500,000—a place that has become good at survival and rebirth throughout its nearly 1,000-year history. In 1348 a plague wiped out half the city's population. In 1624 a fire burned almost the whole of Oslo to the ground. It was redesigned and renamed Christiania by Denmark's royal builder, King Christian IV. After that it slowly gained prominence as the largest and most economically significant city in Norway.

During the mid-19th century, Norway and Sweden were ruled as one kingdom, under Karl Johan. It was then that the grand main street that's his namesake was built, and Karl Johans Gate has been at the center of city life ever since. In 1905 the country separated from Sweden, and in 1925 an act of Parliament finally changed the city's name back to Oslo. Today, Oslo is Norway's political, economic, industrial, and cultural capital.

GETTING HERE AND AROUND

AIR TRAVEL The spacious and bright Oslo Airport in Gardermoen, 45 km (28 mi) north of the city, is a 50-minute car or taxi ride (expensive at around NKr 700 a trip) via the E6 from Oslo's city center. From Oslo S Station, it's a 19-minute ride by Flytoget (express train, NKr 170 one-way, or NKr 160 if booked online), with trains scheduled every 10 minutes (from 5:36 AM to 12:56 AM every day).

Flybussen buses, operated by SAS, depart from Oslo Bussterminalen Galleriet daily every 20 minutes and reach Oslo Airport approximately 40 minutes later (NKr 140 one-way, NKr 240 round-trip).

Two additional airports serve Oslo: Torp Airport in Sandefjord, on the west side of the Oslofjord, and the new Rygge Airport in Moss, which opened in 2008, on the east side. They are served by low-cost airlines only, with flights to several Norwegian destinations and a few European cities, but no direct routes from the US.

BOAT AND FERRY TRAVEL   A ferry to Hovedøya and other islands in the harbor basin leaves from Aker Brygge. These are great spots for picnics and short hikes. From April through September, ferries run between Rådhusbrygge 3, in front of City Hall, and Bygdøy, the western peninsula, where many of Oslo's major museums are located. There is also ferry service from Aker Brygge to the town of Nesodden, as well as to popular summer beach towns along the fjord's coast, including Drøbak. Several ferry lines also connect Oslo with the United Kingdom, Denmark, Sweden, and Germany.

BUS AND TRAIN TRAVEL   The main bus station, Oslo Bussterminalen, is across from the Oslo S Station. You can buy local bus tickets at the terminal or on the bus. Tickets for long-distance routes on Nor-Way Bussekspress can be purchased here or at travel agencies.

Norway's state railway, NSB (Norges Statsbaner), has two train stations downtown—Oslo Sentralstasjon (Oslo S), and a station at Nationaltheatret. Long-distance domestic and international trains arrive at and leave from Oslo S Station. Suburban commuter trains use one or the other station. Commuter cars reserved for monthly pass holders are marked with a large black "M" on a yellow circle. Trains marked "C," or InterCity, offer such upgraded services as breakfast and office cars—with phones and power outlets—for an added fee.

CAR TRAVEL   The E18 connects Oslo with Göteborg, Sweden (by ferry between Sandefjord and Strömstad, Sweden); Copenhagen, Denmark (by ferry between Kristiansand and Hirtshals, Denmark); and Stockholm directly overland. The land route from Oslo to Göteborg is the E6. All routes leading into Oslo have tollbooths a certain distance from the city center, forming an "electronic ring." The toll is NKr 25. If you have the correct change, drive a lane marked "Mynt." If you don't, use a "Manuell" lane. "AutoPASS" is for residents who have taken up an annual subscription.

If you plan to do any amount of driving in Oslo, buy a copy of the *Stor Oslo* map, available at bookstores and gasoline stations. It may be a small city, but one-way streets and few exit ramps on the expressway make it very easy to get lost.

BIKING

Oslo is a great biking city. One scenic ride starts at Aker Brygge and takes you along the harbor to the Bygdøy peninsula, where you can visit the museums or cut across the fields next to the royal family's summerhouse. Many regions of Norway have many cycling paths, some of them old roads that are in the mountains and along the western fjords. The Rallarvegen, from Haugastøl in the Hardangervidda National Park to Flåm, is very popular among cyclists. The southern counties of Vestfold and Rogaland have a well-developed network of cycling paths.

Many counties have produced brochures that have touring suggestions and maps. Most routes outside large cities are hilly and can be physically demanding. If you want to travel with your bike on an NSB long-distance train, you must make a reservation and pay an additional fee (10% of the full-price ticket, minimum NKr 57; NKr 150 on the Bergen Railway; NKr 80 on the Flåm Railway). On local or InterCity trains, bikes are transported if space is available. You can use the City Cycle Scheme to borrow a bike in Oslo. Pay an annual subscription to get access to many cycle stands around the city and more than 1,000 bikes that can be borrowed for up to three hours at a time. An electronic tourist card can be rented for the day (for a deposit) at tourist information offices. ☎815-00-250 ⊕ www. oslobysykkel.no. If you feel like roughing the terrain of the Holmenkollen marka, you can rent mountain bikes from **Tomm Murstad** (⊠ Tryvannsvn. 2, Holmenkollen, Oslo ☎ 22-13-95-00) in summer. Just take T-bane line 1 to Frognerseteren and get off at Voksenkollen Station. Cycling maps are available online at www.oslosykkelkart.no.

Syklistenes Landsforening (⊠ Storgt. 23C, Operapassajen, Oslo ☎ 22-47-30-30 ⊕ www.slf. no) has maps and general information, as well as the latest weather conditions. Several companies, including Lillehammer's **Trollsykling** (⊠ Box 373, Lillehammer ☎ 61-28-99-70 ⊕ www.troll sykling.com), organize cycling tours in most parts of Norway.

Parking is very difficult—many spaces have one-hour limits and can cost more than NKr 25 per hour. Instead of individual parking meters in P-lots, a machine dispenses validated tickets to display in your car windshield. If you buy an Oslo Pass (from a tourist board or hotel), which offers discounts on many things, you can park for free in city-run street spots or at reduced rates in lots run by the city (P-lots). Just be mindful of time limits and where the card truly is valid.

PUBLIC TRANSIT Within Oslo subways and most buses and tramways (*trikk*) start running at 5:30 AM, with the last run after midnight. On weekends, there's night service on certain routes. Trips on all public transportation within Oslo cost NKr 34 (NKr 24 if purchased from the machine before boarding), with a one-hour free transfer; tickets that cross municipal boundaries have different rates. It often pays to buy a pass or multiple-travel card, which includes transfers. A day card (*dagskort*) costs NKr 60 and a seven-day pass costs NKr 200. Tickets can be used on subway, bus, or tramway. Trafikanten provides transit information.

The NKr 160 *flexikort*—available at Narvesen newsstands, 7-Eleven stores, tourist information offices, T-bane stations, and on some routes—is valid for eight trips by subway, bus, or tramway. The Oslo Pass (from NKr 220 for one day, NKr 320 for two days and NKr 410 for three days) offers unlimited travel on all public transport in greater Oslo as well as free admission to several museums and sights, discounts at specified restaurants, and other perks. You can buy the cards tourist offices and hotels.

TAXI TRAVEL Taxis are radio dispatched from a central office, and it can take up to 30 minutes to get one during peak hours. There are also taxi stands all over town, usually near Narvesen newsstands and kiosks. It's possible to hail a cab on the street, but cabs aren't allowed to pick up passengers within 100 yards of a stand. It's not unheard of to wait for more than an hour at a taxi stand in the wee hours of the morning, after everyone has left the bars. Never take pirate taxis; all registered taxis should have their roof lights on when they're available. Rates start at around NKr 40 for hailed or rank cabs, and NKr 60 for ordered taxis, depending on the time of day and the company.

ESSENTIALS

Airport Info Oslo Airport Gardermoen (☎ *915-06-400* or *64-81-20-00* ⊕ *www.osl.no*). **Torp Airport** (☎ *33-42-70-00* ⊕ *www.torp.no*). **Rygge Airport** (☎ *69-23-00-00* ⊕ *www.ryg.no*).

Airport Transfers Flybussen (☎ *22-80-49-71* ⊕ *www.flybussen.no/oslo*). **Flytoget** (☎ *815-00-777* ⊕ *www.flytoget.no*). **Oslo Airport Taxi** (☎ *02-323* ⊕ *www.oslotaxi.no*).

Boat and Ferry Contacts Bygdøyfergene (operated by Norway Yacht Charter) (☎ *23-35-68-90* ⊕ *www.nyc.no*). **Nesodden Bundefjord Dampskibsselskap** (☎ *23-11-52-20* ⊕ *www.nbds.no*).

Bus and Train Info Nor-Way Bussekspress (☎ *81-54-44-44* ⊕ *www.nor-way.no*). **NSB Customer Service** (☎ *815/00-888* ⊕ *www.nsb.no*). **Oslo Bussterminalen** (⊠ *Oslo Bussterminalen Galleriet, Sentrum* ☎ *23-00-24-00*).

Car Rentals Avis (☎ *64-81-06-60 airport, 815/33-044 downtown* ⊕ *www.avis. no*). **Budget/SIXT** (☎ *64-81-06-80 at airport only* ⊕ *www.budget.no*). **Europcar** (☎ *64-81-05-60 airport, 22-83-12-42 downtown* ⊕ *www.europcar.no*). **Hertz** (☎ *64-81-05-50 at airport, 22-21-00-00 downtown* ⊕ *www.hertz.no*).

Public Transit Info Trafikanten (*public transportation information* ☎ *815-00-176, 177 within Oslo* ⊕ *www.trafikanten.no*).

Taxis Norgestaxi (☎ *08-000* ⊕ *www.norgestaxi.no*). **Oslo Taxi** (☎ *02323* ⊕ *www. oslotaxi.no*). **Taxi 2** (☎ *800-TAXI2* ⊕ *www.taxi2.no*).

Visitor Info Oslo Sentralstasjonen (Oslo S Station) (⊠ *Jernbanetorget, Sentrum* ☎ *No phone* ⊗ *Daily 8 AM–11 PM*). **Tourist Information Center in Oslo** (⊠ *Fridtjof Nansens pl. 5, by town hall, entrance from Roald Amundsens gt., or Jernbanetorget 1, at main train station, both in Sentrum* ☎ *81-53-03-55* ⊕ *www.visitoslo.com*).

EXPLORING OSLO

Karl Johans Gate, starting at Oslo Sentralstasjon (Oslo Central Station, also called Oslo S Station and simply *Jernbanetorget,* or "railway station" in Norwegian) and ending at the Royal Palace, forms the backbone of downtown Oslo. Many major museums and historic buildings lie between the parallel streets of Grensen and Rådhusgata.

West of downtown are Frogner and Majorstuen, residential areas known for their fine restaurants, shopping, cafés, galleries, and the Vigeland sculpture park. Southwest is the Bygdøy Peninsula, with a castle and five interesting museums that honor aspects of Norway's taste for exploration.

Northwest of town is Holmenkollen, with its stunning bird's-eye view of the city and the surrounding fjords, a world-famous ski jump and museum, and three historic restaurants. On the more multicultural east side, where a diverse immigrant population lives alongside native Norwegians, are the Munch Museum and the Botanisk Hage og Museum (Botanical Gardens and Museum). The trendy neighborhood of Grünerløkka, with lots of cafés and shops, is northeast of the center.

DOWNTOWN: THE ROYAL PALACE TO THE PARLIAMENT

Although the city region is huge (454 square km [175 square mi]), downtown Oslo is compact, with shops, museums, historic buildings, restaurants, and clubs concentrated in a small, walkable center that's brightly illuminated at night.

TOP ATTRACTIONS

⑬ Det Kongelige Slottet *(The Royal Palace).* At one end of Karl Johans Gate, the vanilla-and-cream-color neoclassical palace was completed in 1848. Although generally closed to the public, the palace is open for guided tours (in English) in summer Monday to Thursday and Saturday at 12:00, 2 and 2:20 PM, and Friday and Sunday at 2, 2:30 and 4 PM. The rest of the time, you can simply admire it from the outside. An equestrian statue of Karl Johan, King of Sweden and Norway from 1818 to 1844, stands in the square in front of the palace. ⊠*Drammensvn. 1, Sentrum* ☎*22–04–89–25* ⊕*www.kongehuset.no* ☎*Tour NKr 95* ☉*Mid-June–mid-Aug., guided tours only.*

⑭ Historisk Museum *(Historical Museum).* In partnership with the Vikingskiphuset (in Bygdøy), this forms the University Museum of Cultural Heritage, which concentrates on national antiquities as well as ethnographic and numismatic collections. See the intricately carved *stavkirke* (wood church) portals and exhibitions on subjects ranging from the Arctic to Asia. You can also gain a deeper understanding of Norway's Viking heritage through artifacts on display here. ⊠*Frederiksgt. 2, Sentrum* ☎*22–85–19–00* ⊕*www.ukm.uio.no* ☎*Free* ☉*Mid-May–mid-Sept., Tues.–Sun. 10–5; mid-Sept.–mid-May, Tues.–Sun. 11–4.*

⑮ Nasjonalgalleriet *(National Gallery.)* The gallery, part of the National
★ Museum of Art, Architecture and Design, houses Norway's largest collection of art created before 1945. The deep-red Edvard Munch room holds such major paintings as *The Dance of Life,* one of two existing

oil versions of *The Scream,* and several self-portraits. Classic landscapes by Hans Gude and Adolph Tidemand—including *Bridal Voyage on the Hardangerfjord*—share space in galleries with other works by major Norwegian artists. The museum also has works by Monet, Renoir, Van Gogh, and Gauguin ⊠ *Universitetsgt. 13, Sentrum* ☎ *21-98-20-00* ⊕ *www.nasjonalmuseet.no* ⊠ *Free* ◷ *Tues., Wed., and Fri. 10–6, Thurs. 10–7, weekends 11–5.*

㉑ **Rådhuset** *(City Hall).* This redbrick building is best known today for
Fodor'sChoice the awarding of the Nobel peace prize, which takes place here every
★ December. In 1915, the mayor of Oslo made plans for a new City Hall, and ordered the clearing of slums that stood on the site. The building was finally completed in 1950. Inside, many museum-quality master- pieces are on the walls. After viewing the frescoes in the Main Hall, walk upstairs to the Banquet Hall to see the royal portraits. In the East Gallery, Per Krogh's mosaic of a pastoral scene covers all four walls, making you feel like you're part of the painting. On festive occasions, the Central Hall is illuminated from outside by 60 large spotlights that simulate daylight. ⊠ *Rådhuspl., Sentrum* ☎ *23–46–16–00* ⊕ *www. radhusets-forvaltningstjeneste.oslo.kommune.no* ⊠ *NKr 40* ◷ *May– Aug., daily 9–6; Sept.–Apr., daily 9–4.*

WORTH NOTING

⓫ **Ibsenmuseet.** Famed Norwegian dramatist Henrik Ibsen, known for *A Doll's House, Ghosts,* and *Peer Gynt,* among other classic plays, spent his final years here, in the apartment on the second floor, until his death in 1906. Every morning Ibsen's wife, Suzannah, would encour- age the literary legend to write before allowing him to head off to the Grand Café for his brandy and foreign newspapers. His study gives striking glimpses into his psyche. Huge, intense portraits of Ibsen and his Swedish archrival, August Strindberg, face each other. On his desk still sits his "devil's orchestra," a playful collection of frog and troll- like figurines that inspired him. Take a guided tour by well-versed and entertaining Ibsen scholars. Afterward, visit the museum's exhibition of Ibsen's drawings and paintings and first magazine writings. ⊠ *Henrik Ibsens gate 26, Sentrum* ☎ *22–12–35–50* ⊕ *www.norskfolkemuseum. no/ibsenmuseet* ⊠ *NKr 85* ◷ *Tues.–Sun., guided tours at 11, noon, 1, 2, and 3; June–Aug., additional guided tours at 4 and 5.*

⓱ **Nationaltheatret** *(National Theater).* In front of this neoclassical theater, built in 1899, are statues of Norway's great playwrights, Bjørnstjerne Bjørnson, who also composed the national anthem, and Henrik Ibsen. Most performances are in Norwegian, so you may just want to take a guided tour of the interior, which can be arranged by appointment. Some summer performances are in English. ⊠ *Stortingsgt. 15, Sentrum* ☎ *22–00–14–00* ⊕ *www.nationaltheatret.no.*

⓳ **Stenersen-museet.** Named for art collector Rolf E. Stenersen, this city- owned museum opened in 1994 displays highly regarded and some- times provocative temporary exhibitions. It also houses three private art collections donated to the city at various times by Rolf E. Stenersen, Amaldus Nielsen, and Ludvig Ravensberg. ⊠ *Munkedamsvn. 15, Vika*

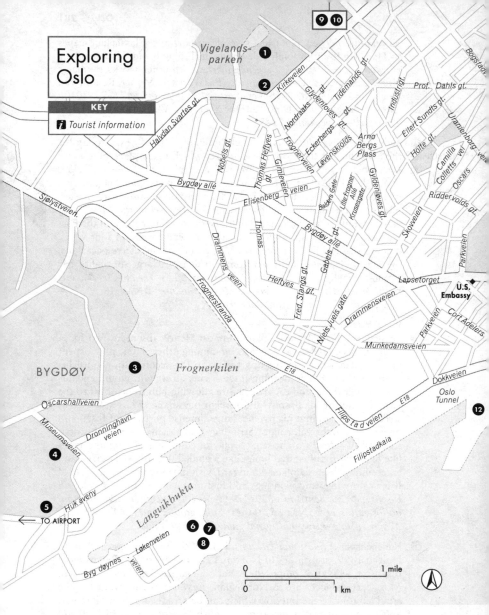

Exploring Oslo

KEY

🛈 Tourist information

BYGDØY

Frognerkilen

Langvikbukta

← TO AIRPORT

U.S. Embassy

Oslo Tunnel

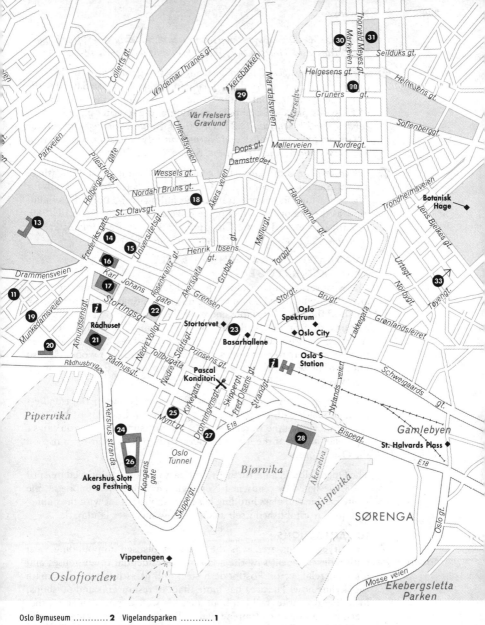

☎23–49–36–00 ⊕*www.stenersen.museum.no* ⊠*NKr 45, free in winter* ⊙*Tues. and Thurs. 11–7, Wed., Fri., and weekends 11–5.*

㉒ Stortinget *(Norwegian Parliament).* Informative guided tours of this classic 1866 building are conducted daily in summer, and on Saturday the rest of the year. In front of the Parliament building, the park benches of Eidsvolls plass are a popular meeting and gathering place. ⊠*Karl Johans gate 22, Sentrum* ☎23–31–31–80 ⊕*www.stortinget.no* ⊠*Free* ⊙*Guided tours in English and Norwegian July–mid-Aug., weekdays at 10, 11:30, and 1; mid-Aug.–June, Sat. at 10, 11:30, and 1.*

⑯ Universitet *(The University).* The great hall in the middle building (there are three in all) is decorated with murals by Edvard Munch. Look for *The Sun*, which shows penetrating rays falling over a fjord. This building was the site of the Nobel peace prize award ceremony until 1989, when it was moved to the City Hall. ⊠*Aulaen, Karl Johans gt. 47, Sentrum* ☎22–85–97–11 ⊠*Free* ⊙*July, weekdays 10–2.*

KVADRATUREN, AKERSHUS CASTLE, AND AKER BRYGGE

The Kvadraturen is the oldest part of Oslo still standing. In 1624, after the town burned down for the fourteenth time, King Christian IV renamed the city Christiania and moved it from the area that is southeast of Oslo S Station, called Gamlebyen, rebuilding it adjacent to the Akershus Fortress. In order to prevent future fires, the king decreed that houses were to be built of stone or brick instead of wood. He also built a stone wall around the rebuilt city to protect it from his enemies, the Swedes.

Aker Brygge, on the other side of Pipervika, is one of the trendiest areas in Oslo, with several shopping centers and dozens of bars and restaurants lining the waterfront. On a sunny summer day, you can sit and relax at one of the many terraces, or hop on a boat for a trip on the Oslo Fjord.

The Opera House, a bit further to the east in Bjørvika, opened in April 2008. Designed by renowned Norwegian architect firm Snøhetta, the white marble and glass building has been an instant hit with the public, and quickly established itself as Oslo's new must-see landmark.

TOP ATTRACTIONS

⑫ Aker Brygge. This area was the site of a disused shipbuilding yard until redevelopment saw the addition of residential town houses and a commercial sector. Postmodern steel and glass buildings dominate the skyline now. The area has more than 40 restaurants and 60 shops, including upmarket fashion boutiques, as well as pubs, cinemas, theaters, and an indoor shopping mall. There is outdoor dining capacity of 2,500 as well as an open boulevard for strolling. Service facilities include banks, drugstores, and a parking lot for 1,600. ⊠*Aker Brygge* ☎22–83–26–80 ⊕*www.akerbrygge.no* ⊠*Free* ⊙*Shopping hrs weekdays 10–8, Sat. 10–6.*

⑯ Akershus Slott og Festning *(Akershus Castle and Fortress).* Dating to 1299, this stone medieval castle and royal residence was developed into a

Fodor'sChoice
★

fortress armed with cannons by 1592. After that time, it withstood a number of sieges and then fell into decay. It was finally restored in 1899. Summer tours take you through its magnificent halls, the castle church, the royal mausoleum, reception rooms, and banqueting halls. ✉️*Akershus Slott, Festningspl., Sentrum* ☎️*23–09–35–53* 🌐*www.nas jonalefestningsverk.no/akershus* 🎫*Grounds and concerts free, castle NKr 65* 🕐*Grounds: daily 6 AM–9 PM. Castle: May–end Aug., Mon.–Sat. 10–6, Sun. 12:30–4; mid-Sept.–Apr., Thurs. tours at 1. Guided tours: May–mid-Sept., daily at 11, 1, and 3; mid-Sept.–Apr., Thurs. at 1.*

㉘ The Opera House. Oslo's brand new opera house opened with great fanfare on April 12, 2008, in the presence of the Norwegian King and a host of celebrities. The white marble and glass building, designed by renowned Norwegian architect firm Snøhetta, is a stunning addition to the Oslo waterfront, and the pride of Norwegians. It doesn't just look good; accoustics inside the dark oak auditorium are excellent, too. The program includes ballet, orchestra concerts, rock, and opera. ✉️*Kirsten Flagstads pl. 1* ☎️*21–42–21–00 or 815-444–88* 🌐*www.operaen.no* 🎫*Free* 🕐*Guided tours available every day.*

Fodor'sChoice ★

WORTH NOTING

㉗ Astrup Fearnley Museet for Moderne Kunst *(Astrup Fearnley Museum for Modern Art).* This privately funded museum opened in 1993 and earned an international reputation for its collections of postwar Norwegian and international art. In its smaller gallery, British artist Damien Hirst's controversial installation *Mother and Child Divided* is on display. The museum's permanent collection includes works by international artists, such as Andy Warhol, Jeff Koons, Damien Hirst, Cindy Sherman, Bruce Neumann, Matthew Barney, Charles Ray, Sherrie Levine, and Bjarne Melgaard. ✉️*Dronningensgt. 4, Sentrum* ☎️*22–93–60–60* 🌐*www. afmuseet.no* 🎫*Free* 🕐*Tues., Wed., and Fri. 11–5, Thurs. 11–7, weekends noon–5. Guided tours weekends at 1.*

㉕ Museet for Samtidskunst *(National Museum of Contemporary Art).* A stunning granite-and-marble example of art nouveau architecture, this 1906 former bank building is the largest museum of postwar Norwegian and international art. Its ornate gilded interior contrasts with the modern and contemporary art shown in its permanent and temporary exhibitions. The permanent collection of 4,700 works spans the genres of graphic art, drawing, photography, sculpture, decorative arts, installations, and video. Take time to ponder the two fascinating permanent installations: Ilya Kabakov's *The Garbage Man* and Per Inge Bjoørlo's *Inner Room V.* ✉️*Bankpl. 4, Sentrum* ☎️*22–86–22–10* 🌐*www.nas jonalmuseet.no* 🎫*Free* 🕐*Tues., Wed., and Fri. 11–5, Thurs. 11–7, weekends noon–5. Guided tours by appointment only.*

⑳ Nobels Fredssenter *(Nobel Peace Center).* Every year the Nobel Peace Prize is awarded in Oslo. Learn about past and present laureates and their work in an original installation featuring 1,000 fiber optic lights; read about Alfred Nobel's inventions and travels in a huge interactive book; and see a documentary on the current laureate in the Passage of Honor room at this new high-tech attraction by the harbor. There are special activities for young would-be peace activists, and changing exhibitions throughout the year. ⊠*Brynjulf Bulls pl. 1, Sentrum* ☎*48–30–10–00* ⊕*www.nobelpeacecenter.org* ⊠*NKr 80* ☉*June–Aug., daily 10–6; Sept.–May, Tues.–Sun. 10–6.*

㉔ **Norges Hjemmefront Museum** *(Norwegian Resistance Museum).* Striped prison uniforms, underground news sheets, and homemade weapons tell the history of the resistance movement that arose before and during Norway's occupation by Nazi Germany. A gray, winding path leads to two underground stone vaults in which models, pictures, writings, and recordings trace the times between Germany's first attack in 1940 to Norway's liberation on May 8, 1945. Every year, on the anniversaries of these dates, Norwegian resistance veterans gather here to commemorate Norway's dark days and honor those who lost their lives. The former ammunitions depot and the memorial lie at the exact spot where Norwegian patriots were executed by the Germans. ⊠*Akershus Slott, Sentrum* ☎*23–09–31–38* ⊕*www.nhm.mil.no* ⊠*NKr 30* ☉*June–Aug., Mon.–Sat. 10–5, Sun. 11–5; Sept.–May, weekdays 10–4, weekends 11–4.*

㉓ **Oslo Domkirke** *(Oslo Cathedral).* Consecrated in 1697 as Oslo's third cathedral, this dark-brown brick structure has been Oslo's main church ever since. The original pulpit, altarpiece, and organ front with acanthus carvings still stand. Take a look at the ceiling murals painted between 1936 and 1950 by artist Hugo Louis Mohr, and stained-glass windows by Emanuel Vigeland. In the 19th century the fire department operated a lookout from the bell tower, which you can visit. At press time, the cathedral was closed for major renovations that were due to be completed in late 2009. ⊠*Stortorvet 1, Sentrum* ☎*23–31–46–00* ⊕*www.oslodomkirke.no* ⊠*Free* ☉*Daily 10–4.*

NEED A BREAK?

Pascal Konditori (⊠ *Tollbugt. 11, Sentrum* ☎ *22–42–11–19* ⊕ *www.pascal.no*), a trendy, Parisian-style patisserie inside an old-fashioned Norwegian *konditori* (café), is known for its French coffee, homemade pastries, and ice cream. It's a place to see and be seen.

MUNCH MUSEUM AND DAMSTREDET

The Munch Museum is east of the city center in Tøyen, an area in which Edvard Munch spent many of his years in Oslo. The Tøyen district has a much different feel than Oslo's cushy west side—it's ethnic and more industrial.

West of Tøyen, north of the city center near Vår Frelsers Gravlund, is the quiet, old-fashioned district of Damstredet, one of the few areas with original, 18th-century wooden houses.

TOP ATTRACTION

㉝ **Munchmuseet** *(Munch Museum).* Edvard Munch, Norway's most famous

Fodor'sChoice ★ artist, bequeathed his enormous collection of works (about 1,100 paintings, 3,000 drawings, and 18,000 graphic works) to the city when he died in 1944. The museum is a monument to his artistic genius, housing the largest collection of his works and changing exhibitions. Munch actually painted several different versions of *The Scream,* the image for which he's best known. An important one of his Scream paintings, as well as another painting, *The Madonna*, were stolen from the Munch Museum in an armed robbery in 2004 but were fortunately recovered in 2006, and put back on display in 2008 after extensive restoration work. While most of the Munch legend focuses on the artist as a troubled, angst-ridden man, he moved away from that pessimistic and dark approach to more optimistic themes later in his career. ✉*Tøyengt. 53, Tøyen* 🕿*23–49–35–00* ⊕*www.munch.museum.no* 🕭*NKr 75* ⊘*June– Aug., daily 10–6; Sept.–May, Tues.–Fri. 10–6, weekends 11–5.*

WORTH NOTING

㉙ **Gamle Aker Kirke** *(Old Aker Church).* Dating to circa 1150, this medieval
★ stone basilica is Oslo's oldest church—it's still in use as a parish church. Inside, the acoustics are outstanding, so inquire about upcoming concerts. ✉*Akersbakken 26, St. Hanshaugen* 🕿*23–62–91–20* ⊕*www. gamle-aker.no* 🕭*Free* ⊘*June–mid-Sept., Mon.–Sat. noon–4, Sun. 10 –2; rest of year Tues. and Fri. noon–2.*

⑱ **Kunstindustrimuseet** *(Museum of Decorative Arts and Design).* Rich Baldishol tapestries from 1100, Norwegian dragon-style furniture, and royal apparel (including Queen Sonja's wedding gown from 1968) make this a must-see museum. Founded in 1876, it also has exquisite collections of Norwegian 18th-century silver, glass, and faience. A contemporary Scandinavian section follows the history of design and crafts in the region. ✉*St. Olavs gt. 1, Sentrum* 🕿*21–98–20–00* ⊕*www.nasjonal museet.no* 🕭*Free* ⊘*Tues., Wed., and Fri. 11–5, Thurs. 11–7, weekends noon–5.*

GRÜNERLØKKA

Once a simple working-class neighborhood north of the center, Grünerløkka has undergone a revival since the '90s and now hosts a number of trendy bars, cafés, eateries, eclectic galleries, and gift stores. Popular with young people, the area is now known as Oslo's little Greenwich Village. Take a shopping tour here during the day or come for dinner and a drink at night.

TOP ATTRACTIONS

㉛ **Birkelundenparken.** This green lung and center of Grünerløkka features concerts, fairs, weekend markets, and political rallies in summer, as well as the usual host of stripped-down sun worshippers. The square and fountain were built in the late 19th century by merchant Thorvald Meyer and city planner G. A. Bull. ✉*Off Thorvald Meyers gt., Grünerløkka.*

㉚ **Markveien and Thorvald Meyers Gate.** The two main streets in Grünerløkka run parallel from north to south over about 1 km, ending at the Aker River in the south. Markveien is the swankier of the two, and boasts many small galleries and boutiques, while Thorvald Meyers Gate has more of a buzz, with many cafés, restaurants, and convenience shops. Olaf Ryes Plass, about halfway down, is a small park lined with cafés and restaurants that are packed in summer. The Ankerbrua, where Markveien crosses the Aker River, is a massive granite bridge with four impressive bronze sculptures featuring creatures from Norwegian folk tales. ⊠ *Off Schleppegrells gt., Grünerløkka.*

㉜ Parkteatret. This atmospheric art deco–style movie house (built in 1907) has been converted into a funky bar, café, restaurant, and venue. Live music gigs, literary evenings, films, and theater are held in the converted cinema room inside, which has seating for 250. To get a sense of the laid-back Grünerløkka lifestyle, chill out here with a cocktail. Free jazz is held on weekends in the front bar. ⊠ *Olaf Reyes pl. 11, Grünerløkka* ☎ *22–35–63–00* ⊕ *www.parkteatret.no* ⊠ *Free* ⊙ *Daily, noon until performances end (around 1* AM*).*

FROGNER, MAJORSTUEN, AND HOLMENKOLLEN

Among the city's most stylish neighborhoods, Frogner and Majorstuen combine classic Scandinavian elegance with contemporary European chic. Hip boutiques and galleries coexist with embassies and ambassadors' residences on the streets near and around Bygdøy Allé. Holmenkollen, the hill past Frogner Park, has the famous ski jump and miles of ski trails.

TOP ATTRACTIONS

❿ Holmenkollen Ski Museum and Ski Jump. A distinctive part of the city's skyline, Oslo's ski jump holds a special place in the hearts of Norwegians. Originally built in 1892, it has been rebuilt 18 times since, the last time for the World Championships in 1982, and is still a popular site for international competitions. It attracts a million visitors, both skiers and non, every year. The ski museum and jump tower are currently closed because the hill is being rebuilt for the Nordic World Ski Championships 2011, and Holmenkollen will reopen in January 2010. In the meantime, you can stop at the nearby **visitor center** (⊠ *Kollenstua* ☎ *22–92–32–00*) in Kollenstua, where you'll be able to learn more about the history of Holmenkollen, watch archive movies taken during earlier competitions, and see models of the hill over the years, as well as the impressive model of the new Holmenkollen Ski Jump currently under construction. ⊠ *Kongevn. 5, Holmenkollen* ☎ *22–92–32–00* ⊕ *www.skiforeningen.no* ⊠ *Free* ⊙ *Oct.–Apr., weekdays 10–3, weekends 10–4; May–Sept., daily 10–4.*

Fodor's Choice ★

❶ Vigelandsparken *(Vigeland's Park).* Also known as Frogner Park, Vigelandsparken has 212 bronze, granite, and wrought-iron sculptures by Gustav Vigeland (1869–1943). Most of the stunning park sculptures are placed on a nearly 1-km-long (½ mi-long) axis and depict the stages of life: birth to death, one generation to the next. See the park's 56-foot-high granite *Monolith Plateau,* a column of 121 upward-striving nude figures surrounded by 36 groups on circular stairs. The most beloved sculpture is a bronze of an enraged baby boy stamping his foot and scrunching his face in fury. Known as *Sinnataggen* (The Angry Boy), this famous statue has been filmed, parodied, painted red, and even stolen from the park. It is based on a 1901 sketch Vigeland made of a little boy in London. There is also a museum on-site for those wishing to delve deeper into the artist's work. ⊠ *Kirkevn., Frogner* ☎ *23–49–37–00* ⊕ *www.vigeland.museum.no* ⊠ *Free; NKr 50 for museum* ⊙ *Daily.*

Fodor's Choice ★

WORTH NOTING

❾ ☪ **Internasjonale Barnekunstmuseet** *(International Museum of Children's Art).* The brainchild of Rafael Goldin, a Russian immigrant, the museum showcases her collection of children's drawings from more than 150 countries. You can see the world though the eyes of a child in its exhibitions of textiles; drawings; paintings; sculptures; and children's music, dancing, and other activities. ✉ *Lille Frøens vei 4, Blindern* ☎ *22–46–85–73* ✇ *www.barnekunst.no* ✆ *NKr 50* ◷ *Late June–early Aug., Tues.–Thurs. and Sun. 11–4; mid-Sept.–mid-Dec. and late Jan.– late June, Tues.–Thurs. 9:30–2, Sun. 11–4.*

❷ **Oslo Bymuseum** *(Oslo City Museum).* One of the world's largest cities, Oslo has changed and evolved greatly over its thousand years. A two-floor, meandering exhibition covers Oslo's prominence in 1050, the Black Death that came in 1348, the great fire of 1624 and subsequent rebuilding, and the urban development of the 20th century. Among the more interesting relics are the red coats that the first Oslo police, the watchmen, wore in 1700, and the first fire wagon in town, which appeared in 1765. Plan to visit the museum near the beginning of your stay for a more informed understanding of the Norwegian capital. Since 2006 the museum has become part of the Oslo Museum, which also incorporates the Teatermuseet and the Interkulturelt Museum. ✉ *Frognervn. 67, Frogner* ☎ *23–28–41–70* ✇ *www.oslobymuseum.no* ✆ *NKr 50* ◷ *Tues.–Sun. 11–4.*

4

◤ **NEED A BREAK?** Generations of families have warmed themselves by the open fires of **Frognerseteren** (✉ *Holmenkollen 200* ☎ *22–92–40–40* ✇ *www.frognerseteren. no*) with a cup of hot chocolate after a long day skiing on the slopes. This restaurant and lookout occupies a special place in the hearts of Norwegians. The two-story log cabin has earthy wooden tables decked with iron candelabras, and traditional rose paintings and taxidermied animals adorning the walls. Try to get a seat on the upper floor to enjoy the view over the Oslo fjord, or use the telescopes on the terrace.

BYGDØY

Several of Oslo's best-known historic sights are concentrated on the Bygdøy Peninsula (west of the city center), as are several beaches, jogging paths, and the royal family's summer residence. The most pleasant way to get to Bygdøy—available from May to September—is to catch Ferry 91 from the rear of the Rådhuset on Pier 3. Times vary, so check with Trafikanten (☎ *177*) for schedules.

An alternative is to take Bus 30, marked "Bygdøy," from Stortingsgata at Nationaltheatret along Drammensveien to Bygdøy Allé, a wide avenue lined with chestnut trees. The bus passes Frogner Church and several embassies on its way to Olav Kyrres plass, where it turns left, and soon left again, onto the peninsula. The royal family's summer residence, actually just a big white frame house, is on the right. Block out a day for this trip.

OUTDOORS AROUND OSLO

Oslo's natural surroundings and climate make it ideally suited to outdoor pursuits. Frogner Park has many paths, and you can jog or hike along the Aker River, but take extra care late at night or early in the morning. Or you can take the Sognsvann trikk to the end of the line and walk or jog along Sognsvann Lake. The Oslo Archipelago is a favorite destination for sunbathing urbanites, who hop ferries to their favorite isles. You can also spend a sunny summer afternoon at Oslo's harbor, Aker Brygge, admiring the docked boats; or venture out into the fjords on a charter or tour.

The Oslo fjord and its islands, the forested woodlands called the *marka*, (or Oslomarka) make the Norwegian capital an irresistible place for outdoor activities like swimming in lakes or hiking. Nine alpine ski areas have activities until late at night. More than 2,600 km (1,600 mi) of prepared cross-country ski trails run deep into the forest, of which 90 km (50 mi) are lighted for special evening tours. The Oslomarka is also just 15 minutes north of the city center by tram.

The **Villmarkshuset** (⊠ *Christian Krohgs gt. 16, Sentrum* ☎ *22–05–05–22*) is an equipment, activities, and excursion center specializing in hiking, climbing, fishing, cycling, and canoeing. You can rent a canoe from here, drop it into the Akers River at the rear of the store, and paddle out into the Oslo fjord. There's also an indoor climbing wall, a pistol range, and a diving center and swimming pool.

The **Skiforeningen** (⊠ *Kongevn. 5* ☎ *22–92–32–00* ⊕ *www.skiforeningen.no*) provides national snow-condition reports and can give tips on cross-country trails. They also offer cross-country classes for young children (three- to seven-year-olds), downhill classes for older children (7- to 12-year-olds), and both kinds of classes, as well as instruction in telemark-style racing and snowboarding techniques, for adults.

Oslo's most accessible ski center is the **Tryvann Winter Park** (⊠ *Tryvannsveien 64, Holmenkollen* ☎ *40–46–27–00* ⊕ *www.tryvann.no*). It has 11 downhill slopes, six lifts, and a terrain park with a half-pipe for snowboarders. It's open weekdays until 10 PM, and you can rent equipment here, too.

Sky-high masts and billowing white sails give the *Christian Radich* (☎ *22–47–82–70* ⊕ *www.radich.no*) a majestic, old-fashioned style. This tall ship makes nine different sailing trips, varying from a three-day voyage to an autumn sail across the Atlantic. Although you aren't required to have prior sailing experience, do expect rough seas, high waves, lots of rain, and being asked to participate in crew-members' tasks.

TOP ATTRACTIONS

❼ **Fram-Museet.** Once known as the strongest vessel in the world, the enormous, legendary Norwegian polar ship *Fram* has advanced farther north and south than any other surface vessel. Built in 1892, it made three arctic voyages conducted by Fridtjof Nansen (1893–96), Otto Sverdrup (1898–1902), and Roald Amundsen (1910–12). Climb on board and peer inside the captain's quarters, which has explorers' sealskin jackets and other relics on display. Surrounding the ship are many expedition artifacts. ⊠*Bygdøynesvn 36, Bygdøy* ☎*23–28–29–50* ⊕*www.fram. museum.no/en* ✉*NKr 50* ☉*Nov.–Feb., weekdays 10–3; Mar., Apr., and Oct., daily 10–4; May and Sept., daily 10–5; June–Aug., daily 9–6.*

❻ **Kon-Tiki Museum.** The museum celebrates Norway's most famous 20th-
☾ century explorer. Thor Heyerdahl made a voyage in 1947 from Peru to
★ Polynesia on the *Kon-Tiki,* a balsa raft, to lend weight to his theory that the first Polynesians came from the Americas. His second craft, the *Ra II,* was used to test his theory that this sort of boat could have reached the West Indies before Columbus. The museum also has a film room and artifacts from Peru, Polynesia, and the Easter Islands. ⊠*Bygdøynesvn. 36, Bygdøy* ☎*23–08–67–67* ⊕*www.kon-tiki.no* ✉*NKr 60* ☉*Apr., May, and Sept., daily 10–5; June–Aug., daily 9:30–5:30; Oct. and Mar., daily 10:30–4; Nov.–Jan., daily 10:30–3:30.*

❹ **Norsk Folkemuseum** *(Norwegian Folk Museum).* One of the largest open-
☾ air museums in Europe, this is a perfect way to see Norway in a day.
Fodor'sChoice From the stoic stave church to farmers' houses made of sod, the old
★ buildings here span Norway's regions and history as far back as the 14th century. Indoors, there's a fascinating display of folk costumes. The displays of richly embroidered, colorful *bunader* (national costumes) from every region includes one set at a Telemark country wedding. The museum also has stunning dragon-style wood carvings from 1550 and some beautiful *rosemaling,* or decorative painted floral patterns. The traditional costumes of the Sami (Lapp) people of northern Norway are exhibited around one of their tents. If you're visiting in summer, inquire about Norwegian Evening, a summer program of folk dancing, guided tours, and food tastings. On Sundays in December, the museum holds Oslo's largest Christmas market. ⊠*Museumsvn. 10, Bygdøy* ☎*22–12–37–00* ⊕*www.norskfolke.museum.no* ✉*NKr 95* ☉*Mid-Sept.–mid-May, weekdays 11–3, weekends 11–4; mid-May– mid-Sept., daily 10–6.*

❺ **Vikingskiphuset** *(Viking Ship Museum).* The Viking legacy in all its glory
Fodor'sChoice lives on at this classic Oslo museum. Chances are you'll come away fas-
★ cinated by the three blackened wooden Viking ships *Gokstad, Oseberg,* and *Tune,* which date to AD 800. Discovered in Viking tombs around the Oslo fjords between 1860 and 1904, the boats are the best-preserved Viking ships ever found and have been exhibited since the museum's 1957 opening. In Viking times, it was customary to bury the dead with food, drink, useful and decorative objects, and even their horses and dogs. Many of the well-preserved tapestries, household utensils, dragon-style wood carvings, and sledges were found aboard ships. The museum's rounded white walls give the feeling of a burial mound. Avoid summertime crowds by visiting at lunchtime. ⊠*Huk Aveny 35, Bygdøy* ☎*22–13–52–80* ⊕*www.ukm.uio.no/vikingskipshuset* ✉*NKr 50* ☉*May–Sept., daily 9–6; Oct.–Apr., daily 10–4.*

WORTH NOTING

⑧ Norsk Sjøfartsmuseum *(Norwegian Maritime Museum).* Traditional
wooden Norwegian fishing boats, maritime paintings by by well-known
Norwegian artists, and intricate ship models are all on display here. The
arctic vessel *Gjøa* is docked outside. The breathtaking panoramic movie
The Ocean: A Way of Life delves into Norway's unique coastal and
maritime past. ⊠ *Bygdøynesvn. 37, Bygdøy* ☎ *24–11–41–50* ⊕ *www.
norsk-sjofartsmuseum.no* ☜ *NKr 40* ⊙ *Mid-May–Aug., daily 10–6;
Sept.–mid-May, daily 10–4, Thurs. 10–6.*

③ Oscarshall Slott. This small country palace was built (1847–52) in eccentric English Gothic style for King Oscar I. There's a park, pavilion, fountain, and stage on the grounds. The original interior has works by the
Norwegian artists Adolph Tidemand and Hans Gude. At this writing,
revised admission fees and opening hours were still under wraps, but a
quick call or look at the website when you're ready to visit will be well
worth the effort. ⊠ *Oscarshallvn., Bygdøy* ☎ *22–56–15–39* ⊕ *www.
kongehuset.no* ☜ *NKr 20* ⊙ *Late May–mid-Sept., Tues., Thurs., and
Sun. noon–4.*

WHERE TO EAT

Many Oslo chefs have developed menus based on classic Norwegian recipes but with exciting variations, like Asian or Mediterranean cooking
styles and ingredients. You may read about "New Scandinavian" cuisine on some menus—a culinary style that combines seafood and game
from Scandinavia with spices and sauces from any other country.

Spend at least one sunny summer afternoon harborside at Aker Brygge
eating in one of the many seafood restaurants and watching the world
go by. Or buy steamed shrimp off the nearby docked fishing boats and
plan a picnic in the Oslo fjords or Vigeland or another of the city's
parks. Note that some restaurants close for a week around Easter, in
July, and during the Christmas holiday season. Some restaurants are
also closed on Sunday. Like more and more cities worldwide, smoking
in indoor public spaces isn't allowed, but terraces and other outdoor
spaces are alright; aim for upwind if you're sensitive to smoke (or down-
wind to be polite if you're a smoker yourself).

DOWNTOWN: ROYAL PALACE TO THE PARLIAMENT

Restaurants downtown along Karl Johans Gate cater to tourists and
offer a range of cuisines, including Indian, Chinese, and traditional
Norwegian. Many are high-quality restaurants, and prices are generally steep.

$$$$
ITALIAN
Fodor'sChoice
★

✕ **Baltazar Ristorante & Enoteca.** Celebrating its 10th anniversary in 2008,
this gem of a restaurant, tucked away in the arcades behind the cathedral, is well worth seeking out. There is a gourmet venue upstairs, serving top modern Italian food, and a more informal enoteca downstairs
(with more informal prices; think $ to $$), offering simpler, more tra-
ditional dishes. In summer, tables spill out on the big outside terrace
and you can enjoy your meal alfresco. Whichever floor you decide to
visit, the antipasti are always superb, and so is the homemade pasta;

veal with tuna sauce and parmesan is a delicious starter. The stunning wine list features some 450 Italian wines, with all regions well represented, and a choice of vintages for several labels. Our favorite Italian in Oslo. ⊠Dronningensgt. 27. Domkirkeparken ☎23–35–70–60 ⊕www.baltazar.no ⊟AE, DC, MC, V ⊘Closed Sun., July, and for Easter and Christmas.

$$ ✕**Brasserie France.** As its name suggests, this wine bar near the Parlia-
FRENCH ment building is straight out of Paris. The waiters' long, white aprons; the art nouveau interior; old French posters; and closely packed tables all add to the illusion. The tempting menu includes a delicious, steaming-hot bouillabaisse and duck confit, as well as more modest dishes such as onion soup, steak tartare and entrecote grillée. There is also, in true Gallic style, a strong wine list. ⊠Øvre Slottsgt. 16, Sentrum ☎23–10–01–65 ⊕www.brasseriefrance.no ⊟AE, DC, MC, V ⊘Closed Sun. Lunch Sat. only.

$ ✕**Dinner.** The simple name belies the fact that this is one of the best
CHINESE places in Oslo for Chinese food, particularly spicy Szechuan, Canton-
Fodor'sChoice ese dishes, and seafood in general. Peking duck is a specialty here, or,
★ for a lighter meal, try the delectable dim sum basket. ⊠Stortingsgt. 22, Sentrum ☎23–10–04–66 ⊕www.dinner.no ⊟AE, DC, MC, V ⊘No lunch Sun.

¢ ✕**Kaffistova.** Norwegian home cooking is served cafeteria-style at this
NORWEGIAN downtown restaurant on the ground floor of the Hotell Bondeheimen. Daily specials come in generous portions and include soup and a selection of entrées. There is always at least one vegetarian dish, as well as fish (including salmon and cod) and homemade meatballs. Whale and reindeer often feature on the menu, too. A good option for lunch. ⊠Hotell Bondeheimen, Rosenkrantz gt. 8, Sentrum ☎23–21–42–10 ⊟AE, DC, MC, V.

$$$$ ✕**Restaurant Eik.** This is Norway's first smoke-free restaurant, although
CONTEMPORARY if it were allowed, cigar smoke would not be out of place among the plush chairs, deep-red sofa, dark-toned artwork, and soft music. The food, in contrast, is thoroughly up to date. The well-priced three- and five-course prix-fixe menus change weekly but might include porcini soup with chorizo, arugula, and parmigiano to start, followed by veal with asparagus and a celeriac and truffle puree. ⊠Hotel Savoy, Universitetsgt. 11, Sentrum ☎22–36–07–10 ⊕www.restauranteik.no ⊟AE, DC, MC, V ⊘Closed Sun., Mon., and July.

$$$$ ✕**Smak av Oro.** A great place for adventurous and playful gourmets,
MEDITERRANEAN with a concept that might seem a bit gimmicky (you order "tastes," not
★ conventional dishes) but works well thanks to chef Esben Holmboe's dexterity in the kitchen. Ingredient pairings are daring, and combinations unexpected; try salmon and imperial oysters with apple, for example, or crayfish and lobster mousse with lard and pomelo. The wine-pairing options are spot on, too. Cheap it ain't, but it's money well spent. ⊠Tordenskjoldsgt. 6, Sentrum ☎23–01–02–40 ⊕www. smakavoro.no ⊟AE, DC, MC, V ⊘Closed Sun. No lunch.

¢ ✕**Vegan.** This innovative buffet-style vegetarian restaurant was estab-
VEGETARIAN lished in 1938, and is one of Europe's oldest. Its success has been such that it recently had to move to bigger premises, and it now

4

accommodates 100 customers. Vegan is a godsend for vegetarians in a town with meat- and fish-centric menus. A wide variety of meals are on offer here, including vegetarian pasta dishes, pizza, curries, salads, soups and quiches. ⊠*Akersgt. 74, Sentrum* ☎*91–18–88–32* ⊕*www. vegano.no* ⊟*AE, DC, MC, V* ⊘*Closed Sat.*

KVADRATUREN AND AKER BRYGGE

If you're after typical Norwegian dining, try the restaurants around Kvadraturen in Sentrum (the center), which offer very traditional meals in typical Norwegian settings. The patrons are mostly locals and the food is usually quite simple, based on seasonal fish and game. Aker Brygge caters to tourists and young professionals with pricier restaurants that have a more international flavor. This is also where you'll find many of the best fish restaurants.

$ ✕**Beach Club.** This American-style diner in Aker Brygge has been draw-
AMERICAN ing the crowds with great burgers since it opened in 1989. The classics
Ⓒ are all there, but for something a bit different try the Favorite (hamburger with cheese, bacon and chili con carne) or the Zorba (chicken burger with tzatziki). If you're feeling homesick, tucking into the full American breakfast will no doubt cheer you up. There is a kids' menu for the little ones, original Keith Haring on the walls, and a big terrace for sunny days. ⊠*Bryggetorget 14* ☎*22–83–83–82* ⊕*www.beachclub. no* ⊟*AE, DC, MC, V.*

$$ ✕**Det Gamle Rådhus.** Housed in Oslo's first town hall, in a building
NORWEGIAN dating back to 1641, this is the city's oldest restaurant. Its reputation is based mostly on traditional fish and game dishes such as the moose entrecote or the Røros reindeer. An absolute must, if you're lucky enough to be visiting at the right time, is the house specialty, the pre-Christmas lutefisk platter. The backyard has a charming outdoor area for dining in summer. ⊠*Nedre Slottsgt. 1, Sentrum* ☎*22–42–01–07* ⊕*www.gamleraadhus.no* ⊟*AE, DC, MC, V* ⊘*Closed Sun.*

$$$ ✕**Engebret Café.** This somber old-fashioned restaurant at Bankplas-
NORWEGIAN sen was a haunt for bohemian literati at the turn of the 20th century and the building itself dates from the 17th century. The formal, French-tinged Norwegian dinner menu includes traditional seasonal fare around *Juletide* (Christmastime), including lutefisk and *pinnekjøtt* (sticks of meat), which is lamb steamed over branches of birch. For a real taste of Norway, try the *smalahove* (a whole sheep's head). Many Norwegian families consider it a treat to visit the restaurant around Christmas, so book early if that's your plan, too. During the rest of the year, try the reindeer in cream sauce or the poached catfish. ⊠*Bankpl. 1, Sentrum* ☎*22–82–25–25* ⊕*www.engebret-cafe.no* ⊟*AE, DC, MC, V* ⊘*Closed Sun.*

$$$ ✕**Lofoten Fiskerestaurant.** Named for the Lofoten Islands off the north-
SEAFOOD west coast, this Aker Brygge restaurant is considered one of Oslo's best
★ for fish, from salmon to cod to monkfish. It has a bright, fresh, minimalistic interior with harbor views and a summertime patio. From January through March, try the cod served with its own liver and roe; April through September, the shellfish; and, from October through December, the lutefisk. Call ahead, since sometimes only large groups are served.

⊠*Stranden 75, Aker Brygge* ☎*22–83–08–08* ⊕*www.lofoten-fiske restaurant.no* ▤*AE, DC, MC, V.*

$$–$$$
SEAFOOD
Fodor'sChoice
★

✕**Solsiden.** With its high ceiling and huge windows, this restaurant, housed in a former warehouse right by the harbor, is the perfect place for dinner on a sunny summer evening. Heed the locals and splash out on a plateau de fruits de mer (the house specialty) or opt for the well-priced menu of the day. Dishes like turbot with mustard purée and lobster sauce, or halibut with mushroom risotto and blue mussel sauce, come highly recommended. The desserts, from passionfruit Pavlova to strawberry clafoutis, don't disappoint either. There is also a good wine list with decent by-the-glass options. The restaurant attracts the odd celebrity—the Rolling Stones and Bruce Springsteen all ate here recently. Fifteen years since opening it still draws sizeable crowds, so book ahead. ⊠*Søndre Akershus Kai 34* ☎*22–33–36–30* ⊕*www.sol siden.no* ▤*AE, DC, MC, V* ☉*Open in summer only, from mid-May to end of Aug., dinner only.*

$$$$
FRENCH

✕**Statholdergaarden.** Onetime Bocuse d'Or champion Bent Stiansen's Asian-inspired French dishes have long been popular with locals. The six-course gastronomic menu changes daily; you can also order from the à la carte menu. Try the pigeon with sweet-corn compote, celery cream, and cherry sauce or the fried sea bass with bok choy, risotto, parmesan croquettes, and tomato and saffron sauce. More than 400 years old, the rococo dining room is one of Norway's largest. ⊠*Rådhusgt. 11, Sentrum* ☎*22–41–88–00* ⊕*www.statholdergaarden.no* ⚐*Reservations essential; jacket and tie* ▤*AE, DC, MC, V* ☉*Closed Sun. and 3 wks in July.*

TØYEN AND GRØNLAND

The most internationally diverse group of restaurants can be found east of downtown, particularly in multicultural Tøyen and Grønland. This area also has the most reasonable dining prices in Oslo.

¢
NORWEGIAN
☺

✕**Asylet.** This popular pub right by Grønland Torg serves homemade traditional Norwegian food in an atmospheric setting. The building, which dates from the 1730s, was once an orphanage. The big lunch menu features a good selection of smørbrød, and Christmas specialties are served in December. There is a fireplace inside, and a beer garden in which to enjoy the sun in summer. ⊠*Grønland 28* ☎*22–17–09–39* ⊕*www.asylet.no* ▤*AE, DC, MC, V.*

$
THAI

✕**Bangkok Thai.** Some of the best Thai food in Oslo can be had here, including *tom yum*, a hot-and-sour seafood-based soup; Thai beef salads; and perennial favorites such as green curry and pad thai. Spacious and carefully decorated with Thai paintings and artifacts, this restaurant is a bit more upmarket than other eateries in this neighborhood. Sharp service here makes for pleasant dining. ⊠*Grønlandsleiret 27, Grønland* ☎*22–17–70–03* ▤*MC, V* ☉*Closed Mon.*

¢
INDIAN

✕**Punjab Tandoori.** Plastic tables, a kitschy decor, and a refrigerator that hums will not suit picky diners. However, the homemade tandoori is a treat here, and prices go as low as NKr 70 for a main course. The chicken with rice, raita, and naan is one of the most popular dishes on the menu, but there are many other options, including several vegetarian

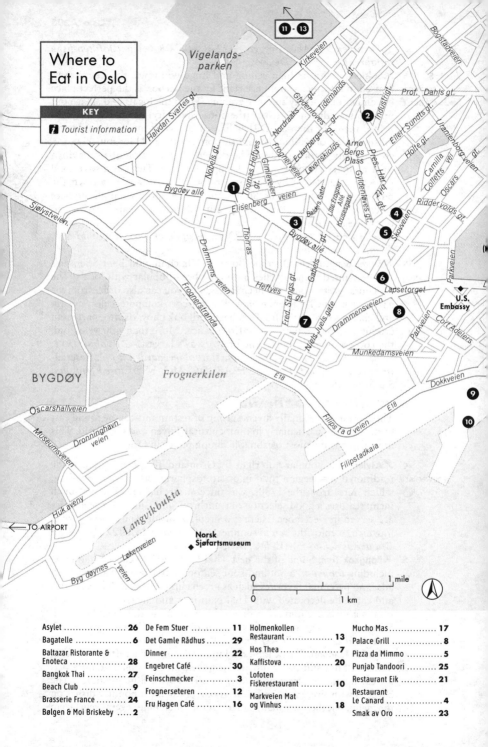

Where to Eat in Oslo

KEY

ℹ Tourist information

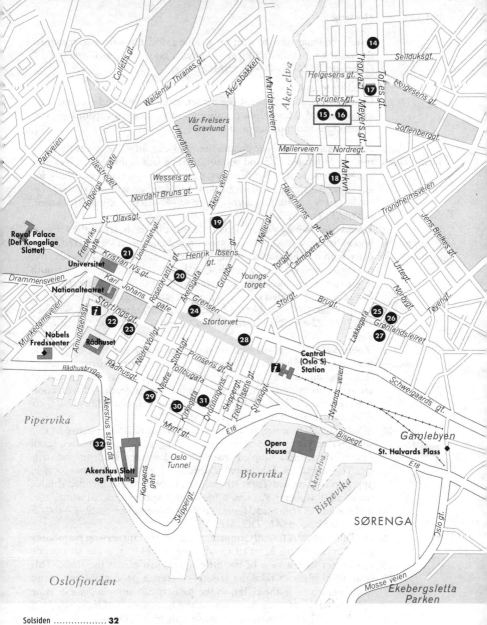

dishes. You may have to wait for a table as local Indians also recognize the value of Punjab Tandoori—always a good sign. ⊠*Grønland 24, Grønland* ☎22–17–20–86 ⊟*MC, V.*

GRÜNERLØKKA

Grünerløkka, just north of the center, is Oslo's up-and-coming artsy neighborhood. Most of its restaurants serve modern versions of Norwegian fare and international dishes.

$ ✕**Fru Hagen Café.** Classic chandeliers and elegant velvet sofas decorate
MEDITERRANEAN this old-fashioned café and restaurant. The fare is simple and inexpensive—American-style hamburgers, pastas, and spicy chicken salads, for example. At night, Fru Hagen doubles as a bar with a DJ. ⊠*Thorvald Meyers gt. 40, Grünerløkka* ☎45–49–19–04 ⊕*www.fruhagen. no* ⊟*AE, DC, MC, V.*

$$ ✕**Markveien Mat og Vinhus.** This restaurant in the heart of the Grünerløkka
NORWEGIAN løkka district serves fresh French-inspired cuisine. It's a relaxed, artsy
★ place with a bohemian clientele. Paintings cover the yellow walls, and the tables are laid with white linen. Veal and baked halibut are both house specialties, but it's the stunning wine list that draws the crowds— it was recently singled out by Wine Spectator magazine as among the best in Oslo. ⊠*Torvbakkgt. 12, entrance on Markvn. 57, Grünerløkka* ☎22–37–22–97 ⊕*www.markveien.no* ⊟*AE, DC, MC, V* ☉*Closed Sun.*

$ ✕**Mucho Mas.** Large servings are the order of the day here but a table
MEXICAN may be hard to find, such is Mucho Mas's popularity. Burritos, nachos, tacos, and quesadillas (not to mention the ever-popular chili con carne) are served as spicy as you like in a simple setting decorated with cool-hued pastels. ⊠*Thorvald Meyers gt. 36, Grünerløkka* ☎22–37–16–09 ⊕*www.muchomas.no* ⊟*AE, DC, MC, V.*

$$ ✕**Sult.** Trendy Norwegian bohemian informality is the essence of this
NORWEGIAN small restaurant, whose name means "hunger." Large windows, small square tables, and a simple homemade look attracts students and writers. Try one of the fish or pasta specials. Next door, the bar-lounge, appropriately named *Tørst* (thirst), has it own unique blended drinks, including Raspberry Parade, a blend of raspberry juice, champagne, and vodka. ⊠*Thorvald Meyers gt. 26, Grünerløkka* ☎22–87–04–67 ⊕*www.sult.no* ⊟*AE, DC, MC, V.*

$ ✕**Villa Paradiso.** A friendly, unpretentious restaurant serving reasonably
ITALIAN priced pizzas in the heart of trendy Grünerløkka. You can sit outside
☾ in summer with a view of the little square just across the street. This is an ideal place to take the family—thereis a good children's menu and a playroom in the cellar, so the parents can enjoy a glass of wine upstairs while the kids have fun in the basement. ⊠*Olaf Ryes pl. 8* ☎22–35–40–60 ⊕*www.villaparadiso.no* ⊟*AE, DC, MC, V.*

FROGNER AND MAJORSTUEN

Some of Oslo's best restaurants are here in the wealthier western side of the city. The upmarket international dining scene includes many French-inspired kitchens.

$$$$
NORWEGIAN
Fodor's Choice
★

✕ **Bagatelle.** Chef and owner Eyvind Hellstrøm has established an international reputation for his modern Norwegian cuisine and superb service. Bagatelle attracts the who's who of Oslo society, and is widely recognized as the city's best restaurant. Artworks by contemporary artists accent the understated, elegant dining room. Three-, five-, and seven-course menus change daily. The lobster is always a standout. ⊠*Bygdøy Allé 3, Frogner* ☎*22–12–14–40* ⊕*www.bagatelle.no* ⊟*AE, DC, MC, V* ⊘*Closed Sun. mid-July–mid-Aug. No lunch.*

$$
ECLECTIC
★

✕ **Bølgen & Moi Briskeby.** Restaurateurs Toralf Bølgen and Trond Moi have a winner in this minimalistic restaurant. If you're tired of eating breakfast in your hotel, rise and shine here instead. Housed in a former power station, the restaurant incorporates the past with a long, eye-catching cement dining table and open fires. Well-known Norwegian artists such as photographer Knut Bry showcase their work in the restaurant's bar, brasserie, and formal dining room. Try the oversize Thorenfeldt burger, or the three-course set menu, which changes daily. Most dishes are cooked in the wood-burning oven in the corner. ⊠*Løvenskioldsgt. 26, Frogner* ☎*24–11–53–53* ⊕*www.bolgenogmoi. no* ⊟*AE, DC, MC, V* ⊘*Lunch only on Sun.*

$$$$
SCANDINAVIAN

✕ **Feinschmecker.** The name is German, but the food is international and Scandinavian. Modern and stylish, the dining room's warm, earthy tones give it a cozy look. Finnish chef Filip Langhoff previously worked at Ferran Adria's much acclaimed restaurant El Bulli in Spain, and qualified for the Bocus d'Or 2009. He excels at everything, but has a particular fondness for Norwegian scallops and reindeer. Feinschmecker is a haven for vegetarians with a three-course menu of local produce that changes according to the season. ⊠*Balchensgt. 5, Frogner* ☎*22–12–93–80* ⊕*www.feinschmecker.no* ⊛*Reservations essential* ⊟*AE, DC, MC, V* ⊘*Closed Sun. and last 3 wks July. No lunch.*

$$
CONTEMPORARY
★

✕ **Hos Thea.** An intimate yet lively dining experience awaits in this white-and-blue restaurant that recently celebrated 20 years in business. From the open kitchen, owner Sergio Barcilon and the other chefs often serve the French and Spanish food themselves. The small menu lists four or five choices for each course, but every dish is superbly prepared. Noise levels can be high late at night, as can smoke levels on the terrace. ⊠*Gabelsgt. 11, entrance on Drammensvn., Skillebekk* ☎*22–44–68–74* ⊕*www.hosthea.no* ⊛*Reservations essential* ⊟*AE, DC, MC, V* ⊘*No lunch.*

$$–$$$
CONTEMPORARY

✕ **Palace Grill.** Don't let the "grill" part fool you: it may be relaxed, but Palace Grill's French-inspired cuisine is anything but fast food. This tiny, eight-table restaurant near the Royal Palace is one of the most fashionable spots on the Oslo dining scene. It doesn't take reservations, however, and is usually full, so try to get here before 5 PM for a table. ⊠*Solligt. 2, off Drammensvn., Frogner* ☎*23–13–11–40* ⊕*www.palace grill.no* ⊟*AE, DC, MC, V* ⊘*Closed Sun. and Mon.*

$
PIZZA
Fodor's Choice
★

✕ **Pizza da Mimmo.** Named for owner Domenico Giardina, aka Mimmo, this is Oslo's best pizzeria. In 1993 Mimmo, who's originally from Calabria, was the first to bring thin-crust Italian pizza to the city. Taste his perennially popular panna and prosciutto pizza, and the Pizza Calabrizella. The casual restaurant is on the basement level in a white-

4

brick building; earthy colors, hanging rugs, and small cellar windows give it a cavelike appearance. ✉ *Behrensgt. 2, entrance on Skovvn., Frogner* ☎ *22–44–40–20* ⊕ *www.pizzadamimmo.no* ⌕ *Reservations essential* ⊟ *AF, DC, MC, V.*

$$$
CONTEMPORARY

✕ **Restaurant Le Canard.** Behind the Royal Castle, this elegant restaurant is in what looks like a brick manor house. Inside are such antique furnishings as a stained-glass window by Maria Vigeland, the wife of Emanuel. Chef Trond Andresen shows off his simple, French-inspired compositions in a menu that changes weekly. The wine cellar of 30,000 bottles includes rare champagne from 1928. In summer you can dine in special style on Le Canard's stunning garden terrace. ✉ *Pres. Harbitz gt. 4, Frogner* ☎ *22–54–34–00* ⌕ *Reservations essential* ⊟ *AE, DC, MC, V* ☾ *Closed Sun. No lunch.*

$
INDIAN

✕ **Village Tandoori.** Walking through this restaurant feels like what a nighttime wander through an Indian or Pakistani village about a hundred years ago might have been like. Antique rugs, including vibrant silk ones with embroidery and beadwork, adorn the walls of the many small dining rooms. The chicken and lamb curries and tandooris are delicious, and there are several vegetarian dishes to choose from. ✉ *Bygdøy Allé 65, Frogner* ☎ *22–56–10–25* ⊕ *www.village-tandoori.no* ⊟ *AE, DC, MC, V* ☾ *No lunch.*

HOLMENKOLLEN

This small, wealthy neighborhood is a 15-minute drive northwest of the center, halfway into the forest. It's a popular place for downhill and Nordic skiing, and the few restaurants here are popular in winter and serve hearty, traditional Norwegian meals.

$$$–$$$$
NORWEGIAN
Fodor's Choice
★

✕ **De Fem Stuer.** Near the famous Holmenkollen ski jump, in the historic Holmenkollen Park Hotel Rica, this restaurant serves first-rate food in a grand setting, with stunning views over Oslo. Chef Are Nortvedt's modern Norwegian dishes blend classic ingredients with more exotic ones; just try not to be intrigued by the pigeon with Japanese noodles or the pan-fried Arctic char with pickled shiitake mushrooms and caviar sauce. For something a bit more traditional, opt for the four-course menu called A Taste of Norway—you'll get exactly that. ✉ *Holmenkollen Park Hotel Rica, Kongevn. 26, Holmenkollen* ☎ *22–92–27–34 Jacket and tie* ⊟ *AE, DC, MC, V.*

$$–$$$
NORWEGIAN

✕ **Frognerseteren.** Located just above the Holmenkollen ski jump and therefore a great spot to take in sweeping mountain views, this is possibly Oslo's most famous restaurant. Popular with locals and travelers, it specializes in fish and game. The scrumptious apple cake is legendary, and perfect for dessert or for an afternoon treat with coffee. Eating reindeer in brown sauce with local *tittebær* (red berries) at Frognerseteren would have to be the ultimate Norwegian experience. You can eat in the less formal café downstairs, or in the more exclusive restaurant upstairs. Take the Holmenkollbanen to the end station and then follow the signs downhill to the restaurant. ✉ *Holmenkollvn. 200, Holmenkollen* ☎ *22–92–40–40* ⊕ *www.frognerseteren.no* ⊟ *AE, DC, MC, V.*

$$ **✕ Holmenkollen Restaurant.** An old-fashioned, luxury mountain cabin
NORWEGIAN café, restaurant, and banquet hall, this Oslo institution dates to 1892.
The spacious café is perfect for an afternoon coffee and cake after
walking or skiing. In the smaller, formal restaurant, the small menu
focuses on Norwegian fish and game dishes served with innovative
sauces. ⊠ *Holmenkollvn. 119, Holmenkollen* ☎ *22–13–92–00* ⊕ *www.*
holmenkollen-restaurant.oslo.no ⊟ *AE, DC, MC, V.*

WHERE TO STAY

Most lodgings are central, just a short walk from Karl Johans Gate.
Many are between the Royal Palace and Oslo S Station, with the newer
ones closer to the station. For a quiet stay, choose a hotel in either
Frogner or Majorstuen, elegant residential neighborhoods behind the
Royal Palace and within walking distance of downtown. Television and
phones can be expected in most Oslo hotel rooms, and Internet con-
nection is found in all but budget hotels. Most hotels in Oslo include
either a full or Continental breakfast in their rates, and all of them have
no-smoking rooms.

DOWNTOWN: ROYAL PALACE TO THE PARLIAMENT

Downtown has many traditional Norwegian hotels dating from the
19th and early 20th centuries. These establishments are pricey, but they
cater to travelers with the best service and amenities.

$$ 🖼 **Best Western Hotell Bondeheimen.** Founded in 1913 for country folk
☾ visiting the city, Bondeheimen, which means "farmers' home," still gives
discounts to members of Norwegian agricultural associations. Rooms
have a minimalistic look, in dark greens and earthy reds. This is a
good choice for families. If you are looking for quiet, ask for a room
in back. The Kaffistova restaurant is in the same building. **Pros:** family
rooms cost the same as double rooms; breakfast is substantial. **Cons:**
the rooms overlooking the street can be noisy in the evening. ⊠ *Rosen-*
krantz gt. 8, entrance on Kristian IVs gt., Sentrum ☎ *23–21–41–00*
⊕ *www.bondeheimen.com* ⮐ *127 rooms, 5 suites* ♿ *In-room: Internet.*
In-hotel: restaurant ⊟ *AE, DC, MC, V* ⦿ *BP.*

$$$ 🖼 **Grand Hotel.** In the center of town on Karl Johans Gate, the Grand
opened in 1874. The hotel is the choice of visiting heads of state, and
there is even a Nobel suite. Ibsen used to drink brandy at the Grand
Café in the company of journalists. Munch was also a regular guest;
you can see him with his contemporaries in Per Krohg's painting on the
café's far wall. Norwegians book several years in advance for National
Day, May 17, in order to have a room overlooking the parades below.
Pros: period features have been preserved throughout the hotel; there's
a Ladies Floor, with 13 unique rooms designed for women travelers;
the beautiful pool in the new Artesia Spa. **Cons:** the hotel is so big you
could get lost easily; the gym is tiny. ⊠ *Karl Johans gt. 31, Sentrum*
☎ *23–21–20–00* ⊕ *www.grand.no* ⮐ *290 rooms, 52 suites* ♿ *In-room:*
Internet. In-hotel: 3 restaurants, bars, pool, gym, spa ⊟ *AE, DC, MC,*
V ⦿ *BP.*

4

$$$ ⛶ **Hotel Bristol.** With its interior design inspired by Edwardian England, the Bristol has a dignity and class all its own. Rooms are elegant and understated. The lounge and bar were decorated in the 1920s with an intricate Moorish theme and recall Fez more than Scandinavia. Josephine Baker performed in the piano bar in the 1920s. The Library Bar and Wintergarden, with its red, burnished leather sofas, is a great place to while away an evening. **Pros:** good location; professional staff; elegant lobby and bar. **Cons:** the lifts are tiny; some rooms are a bit dated. ⊠*Kristian IVs gt. 7, Sentrum* ☎*22–82–60–00* ⊕*www.bristol. no* ⥱*251 rooms, 10 suites* ⚘*In-hotel: 2 restaurants, bars, gym* ▤*AE, DC, MC, V* ⏁*BP.*

$$$–$$$$ ⛶ **Hotel Continental.** With its elegant early-20th-century facade, the
Fodor'sChoice   Continental is an Oslo landmark that continues to attract with stylish
★   rooms, gracious service and two wonderful restaurants—Theatercafeen, an Oslo landmark, and since 2006, Annen Etage, another great choice for dinner. Opposite Nationaltheatret and close to many cafés, clubs, and movie theaters, the hotel is ideal for leisure as well as business travelers. Dagligstuen (The Sitting Room) has original Munch's lithographs on the walls, and is a popular meeting place for drinks and quiet conversation. **Pros:** exemplary service; beautiful, well-appointed rooms; brand-new gym **Cons:** steep prices; corridors are a bit dated (though they're due to begin refurbishment by this writing). ⊠*Stortingsgt. 24–26, Sentrum* ☎*22–82–40–00* ⊕*www.hotel-continental.no* ⥱*155 rooms, 23 suites* ⚘*In-room: Internet. In-hotel: 2 restaurants, bars, gym* ▤*AE, DC, MC, V* ⏁*EP.*

$–$$$ ⛶ **Norlandia Karl Johan Hotel.** The late-19th-century Karl Johan Hotel, once known as the Nobel, is elegant, with stained-glass windows that line the circular staircase, bringing to mind 19th-century Paris. Half of the rooms were renovated in 2008, so ask for one of those when booking. **Pros:** good location; friendly staff; period features. **Cons:** some rooms are noisy. ⊠*Karl Johans gt. 33, Sentrum* ☎*23–16–17–00* ⊕*www.karljohan.norlandia.no* ⥱*114 rooms, 8 suites* ⚘*In-room: Internet. In-hotel: restaurant, bar* ▤*AE, DC, MC, V* ⏁*BP.*

$$$$ ⛶ **Radisson SAS Scandinavia Hotel.** Popular with business travelers, this 1974 hotel has a winning combination of service and classic style. Simple, elegant rooms come in different designs: art deco, Italian, Asian, Continental, Scandinavian, and—predictably, for a hotel run by an airline—69 high-tech business-class rooms. The Summit Bar has a stunning, panoramic view of Oslo—it's a great place for an evening cocktail. **Pros:** generous size rooms; fares are much lower on weekends and summer holidays; good views from the upper floors. **Cons:** breakfast room can get packed; front desk is often understaffed at peak times. ⊠*Holbergsgt. 30, Sentrum* ☎*23–29–30–00* ⊕*www.radissonsas.com* ⥱*488 rooms, 9 suites* ⚘*In-room: Internet. In-hotel: 2 restaurant, bar, pool, gym* ▤*AE, DC, MC, V* ⏁*BP.*

$$ ⛶ **Rica Victoria.** This modern business hotel occupies one of the city center's taller buildings, giving some top-floor rooms views of Oslo's rooftops. The rooms, built around a center atrium, are elegant and stylish: they're furnished with Biedermeier reproductions, brass lamps, and paisley fabrics in bold reds and dark blues. **Pros:** modern decor; great

breakfast; friendly staff. **Cons:** ugly facade; it might be tricky to find a table at breakfast when the hotel is fully booked. ⊠ *Rosenkrantz gt. 13, Sentrum* ☎ *24–14–70–00* ⊕ *www.rica.no* ⊃ *199 rooms, 5 suites* ⚒ *In-room: Internet. In-hotel: restaurant, bar* ⊟ *AF, DC, MC, V* ⦿ *BP.*

$ **Thon Hotel Cecil.** A short walk from Parliament, this modern hotel is a
★   relatively inexpensive option in the center of town. Although the rooms are basic, they are perfectly suited to the active, on-the-go traveler. The second floor opens onto a plant-filled atrium, the hotel's "activity center." In the morning it's a breakfast room, but in the afternoon it becomes a lounge, serving coffee, juice, and fresh fruit. **Pros:** friendly staff; good value for money; the heated shower floors are a nice touch. **Cons:** Internet connection is not included in the rate; facilities are limited. ⊠ *Stortingsgt. 8, Sentrum* ☎ *23–31–48–00* ⊕ *www.thonhotels.no/ cecil* ⊃ *111 rooms, 2 suites* ⚒ *In-room: Internet. In-hotel: bar* ⊟ *AE, DC, MC, V* ⦿ *BP.*

$$ **Thon Hotel Stefan.** A home away from home, this hotel tries hard to make guests feel well looked after. Hot drinks are served to late arrivals, and breakfast tables come with juice boxes and plastic bags for packing a lunch (request this service in advance). The top-floor lounge has magazines in English, and the restaurant serves one of the best buffet lunches in town. **Pros:** newly refurbished business and family rooms; in-room tea- and coffee-making facilities. **Cons:** Internet not included in the rate; some rooms are a bit small and in need of refurbishing; some rooms can be noisy. ⊠ *Rosenkrantz gt. 1, Sentrum* ☎ *23–31–55–00* ⊕ *www.thonhotels.no/stefan* ⊃ *150 rooms, 11 suites* ⚒ *In-room: Internet. In-hotel: restaurant, bar* ⊟ *AE, DC, MC, V* ⦿ *BP.*

FROGNER, MAJORSTUEN, AND HOLMENKOLLEN

These leafy suburbs west of the center are known for large, beautiful homes inhabited by prosperous Norwegians. The hotels are mainly from the 19th century and range from upmarket boutique properties to affordable bed-and-breakfasts.

$$ **Clarion Collection Hotel Gabelshus.** In a blending of old and new styles, the Gabelshus became part of the Choice Hotels Scandinavia Group in 2005 when it literally joined together with a neighboring hotel, formerly the Oslo Ritz. The original building of the Gabelshus retains its old-world English charm, while its newer counterpart offers rooms with a modern, minimalistic Scandinavian style. **Pros:** charming period building; quiet residential area; free evening meal. **Cons:** some rooms are better than others; the staff is not always very helpful. ⊠ *Gabelsgt. 16, Frogner* ☎ *23–27–65–00* ⊕ *www.gabelshus.no* ⊃ *114 rooms* ⚒ *In-room: Internet. In-hotel: restaurant, bar, spa* ⊟ *AE, DC, MC, V* ⦿ *MAP.*

¢   **Cochs Pensjonat.** A stone's throw from the Royal Palace, this no-frills guesthouse has reasonably priced, comfortable, but rather spartan rooms. Most of the 88 rooms have private bathrooms, but check when you make your reservation; some also have kitchenettes. **Pros:** central location; good value for money. **Cons:** basic facilities; value rooms are tiny; no on-site restaurant. ⊠ *Parkvn. 25, Majorstuen* ☎ *23–33–24–00*

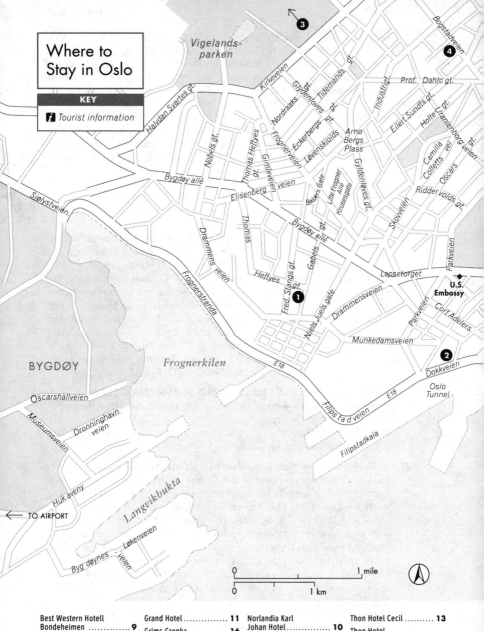

Where to Stay in Oslo

KEY

i Tourist information

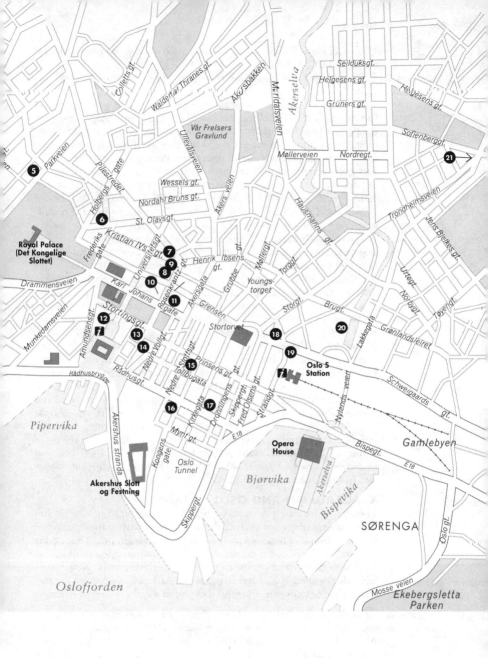

⊕*www.cochspensjonat.no* ⇌*88 rooms* ⚭*In-room: no phone, no TV (some)* ⊟*MC, V* ⫷⦾⫸*EP.*

$$–$$$ ⊞**Holmenkollen Park Hotel Rica.** Dating to 1894, this stunning and distinguished hotel has a peaceful mountaintop setting with unparalleled views of the city below. Guest rooms have earth tones and dark-wood furniture. Next to the Holmenkollen Ski Arena, the property provides the perfect base for outdoor pursuits such as cycling, skiing, and running. It's worth a visit even if you don't stay here; we suggest heading to De Fem Stuer, the wonderful restaurant. **Pros:** great views over Oslo; very good restaurant; environmentally friendly (the hotel composts its organic waste for its extensive garden). **Cons:** far from the city center. ⊠*Kongevn. 26, Holmenkollen* ☎*22–92–20–00* ⊕*www.holmenkollenparkhotel.no* ⇌*220 rooms* ⚭*In-room: Internet. In-hotel: 3 restaurants, bar, pool, gym, spa* ⊟*AE, DC, MC, V* ⫷⦾⫸*BP.*

$–$$ ⊞**Thon Hotel Gyldenløve.** Nestled among the many shops and cafés on Bogstadveien, this hotel is a very good value for its location. Rooms are light and airy and have stylish Scandinavian furniture. It is within walking distance of Vigelandparken, and the tramway stops just outside the door. **Pros:** modern, functional design; bright, airy rooms **Cons:** it's a bit of a walk to the center; limited facilities. ⊠*Bogstadvn. 20, Majorstuen* ☎*23–33–23–00* ⊕*www.thonhotels.no/gyldenlove* ⇌*164 rooms* ⚭*In-room: Internet. In-hotel: restaurant* ⊟*AE, DC, MC, V* ⫷⦾⫸*BP.*

$$–$$$ ⊞**Thon Vika Atriumøve.** It won't win any awards for its design, but this hotel is conveniently located for Aker Brygge, and the rooms, although plain, are well appointed (all have a safe, hair dryer, iron, flat-screen TV, and tea- and coffee-making facilities). There is a big gym downstairs, and extensive meeting and facilities, and the staff are helpful and friendly. **Pros:** good location a stone's throw from Aker Brygge; bright breakfast room; friendly, knowledgeable staff. **Cons:** rooms are a bit boring and bathrooms tiny; there is a busy road just outside the main entrance. ⊠*Munkedamsvn. 45, Frogner* ☎*22–83–33–00* ⊕*www.thonhotels.com/vikaatrium* ⇌*79 rooms, 18 suites* ⚭*In-room: Internet. In-hotel: restaurant* ⊟*AE, DC, MC, V* ⫷⦾⫸*BP.*

KVADRATUREN AND OSLO S STATION

The area immediately around Oslo S, which was until now a bit run down, is experiencing a revival, due in no small part to the opening of the opera house in Bjørvika in April 2008. As a result, prices have gone up, but you'll still find a decent choice of accommodation in this area, from well established chains to exciting boutique hotels. New hotels have also opened in Kvadraturen, the old part of town behind the fortress, offering convenient central location in a quieter part of town.

$$–$$$ ⊞**Clarion Royal Christiania Hotel.** What was once bare-bones hous-
★ ing for 1952 Olympians is now a luxury, 100% no-smoking hotel. Although the original plain exterior remains, the interior is more modern, designed using feng shui principles. Rooms have white walls and mahogany furniture. **Pros:** welcoming lobby; organic breakfast; on-site parking. **Cons:** the size can seem daunting to some; the location—right by a busy intersection—is convenient but not particularly charming. ⊠*Biskop Gunnerus gt. 3* ☎*23–10–80–00* ⊕*www.royalchristiania.*

no ⚓*412 rooms, 91 suites* Ꮸ*In-hotel: restaurant, bar, pool, gym, spa* ☰*AE, DC, MC, V* ⍣○⍣*BP.*

$$–$$$ 🖭 **First Hotel Millennium.** This hotel is comfortable, with an understated, downtown chic. Guest rooms are simple, with a dark blue, green, and yellow color theme; all have bathtubs. Several rooms are geared toward women and come with a bathrobe, skin products, and women's magazines. The main-floor lounge has games, a music room, Internet access, and a library. The restaurant-bar, Primo, serves an impressive international menu, which includes quail and swordfish. **Pros:** good location; friendly staff. **Cons:** noise from traffic; rooms get hot in summer and there's no a/c. ✉*Tollbugt. 25* 🕾*21–02–28–00* ⊕*www.firsthotels.com* ⚓*112 rooms, 8 suites* Ꮸ*In-room: no a/c, Internet. In-hotel: restaurant, bar* ☰*AE, DC, MC, V* ⍣○⍣*BP.*

$$$–$$$$ 🖭 **Grims Grenka.** Opened in March 2008, this stylish hotel was the only one in Scandinavia to make the top 50 list in *Wallpaper** magazine this year. Expect stylish design throughout, with smart lighting, striking colors, clever use of mirrors, and glassed-in bathrooms. The on-site Madu restaurant specializes in dim sum and Asian dishes, there is a rooftop terrace with a bar and sun-loungers for guests to enjoy in summer, and a relaxation area that should be completed in 2009. **Pros:** modern, Asian-inspired rooms; huge bathtubs and rain showerheads; superb location. **Cons:** the emphasis on design sometimes overlooks functionality; minimalistic breakfast. ✉*Kongensgt. 5* 🕾*23–10–72–00* ⊕*www.grimsgrenka.no* ⚓*66 rooms, 42 suites* Ꮸ*In room: Internet. In hotel: restaurant, bars* ☰*AE, DC, MC, V* ⍣○⍣*BP.*

$$$–$$$$ 🖭 **Radisson SAS Plaza Hotel.** Standing out from other buildings on the
★ city's skyline, northern Europe's largest hotel is the jewel of the Radisson SAS chain. The understated, elegant rooms have gilded fixtures and marble, and many have spectacular views. Since it's next to Oslo S Station, buses and other local transit are convenient. **Pros:** great top floor bar; fit-for-a-king breakfast buffet; luxuriously grand bathtubs **Cons:** crowds outside the Oslo Spektrum, right opposite the hotel, a nuisance when there is a concert on; lifts seem to have a mind of their own when it comes to heading up or down; the huge reception area looks more like a station concourse than a hotel lobby. ✉*Sonja Henies pl. 3* 🕾*22–05–80–00* ⊕*www.radissonsas.com* ⚓*673 rooms, 20 suites* Ꮸ*In-room: Internet. In-hotel: 2 restaurants, bars, pool, gym* ☰*AE, DC, MC, V* ⍣○⍣*BP.*

$$–$$$ 🖭 **Scandic Byporten.** Right above Oslo main train station, the Scandic Byporten offers well-priced accommodation in the center of town. Especially suited for this place are families (kids stay free) and those with a big appetite (a huge organic breakfast is included in the rate). **Pros:** convenient, central location; good shopping nearby; friendly, helpful staff. **Cons:** drug dealing and prostitution are not uncommon around the station late at night, although the area is safe; you might struggle to find the entrance when coming from the station (it's hidden at the far end of the shopping center). ✉*Jernbanetorget 6* 🕾*23–15–55–00* ⊕*www. scandichotels.no* ⚓*240 rooms, 4 suites* Ꮸ*In-room: Internet. In-hotel: restaurant, bar, no-smoking rooms* ☰*AE, DC, MC, V* ⍣○⍣*BP.*

$$–$$$ 🏨 **Thon Hotel Oslo Panoramaøve.** Located in Kvadraturen, close to Akershus Festning, this is the latest hotel in the popular Thon chain, opened in September 2008. The rooms, although they have a slightly unusual layout, are functional, spacious and light, with modern furniture and wooden floors; some even have a kitchenette. The two huge suites on the top floor are stunning, with great views over Oslo and the Oslo Fjord. **Pros:** brand new hotel; convenient location; friendly staff. **Cons:** limited facilities; tiny lifts; small bathrooms. ⊠*Rådhusgt. 7b, Kvadraturen* ☎*23–31–08–00* ⊕*www.thonhotels.com/oslopanorama* ↘*116 rooms, 2 suites* ⚴*In-room: Internet.* ⊟*AE, DC, MC, V* ⑩|*BP.*

FARTHER AWAY

¢ 🏨 **Haraldsheim Youth Hostel.** Located 4 km (2.5 mi) northeast of Oslo, but with easy access to the city center, Haraldsheim Youth Hostel is a smart budget choice for young (and young at heart) travelers. Facilities are basic but clean, with a huge outside area, where big barbecues can be used by guests in summer. Two- and four-bed rooms are available (ideal for families), as well as accommodation in small dorms. **Pros:** great bargain; informal atmosphere; nice bright common areas with billiards and TV. **Cons:** limited facilities; can be noisy when groups turn up. ⊠*Haraldsheimvn. 4* ☎*22–22–29–65* ⊕*www.haraldsheim.no* ↘*70 rooms* ⚴*In-room: no TV (some).* ⊟*DC, MC, V* ⑩|*BP.*

AFTER DARK

More than ever, the Oslo nightlife scene is vibrant and varied. Cafés, restaurant-bars, and jazz clubs are laid-back and mellow. But if you're ready to party, there are many pulsating, live-rock and dance clubs to choose from. Day or night, people are usually out on Karl Johans Gate, and many clubs and restaurants in the central area stay open until the early hours. Aker Brygge, the wharf area, has many bars and some nightclubs, attracting mostly tourists, couples on first dates, and other people willing to spend extra for the waterfront location. Grünerløkka and Grønland have even more bars, pubs, and cafés catering to a younger crowd. A more mature upmarket crowd ventures out to the less-busy west side of Oslo, to Frogner and Bygdøy.

Drinking out is very expensive, starting at around NKr 70 for a beer or a mixed drink. Many Norwegians save money by having drinks at friends' houses—called a *forschpiel*—before heading out on the town. Some bars in town remain quiet until 11 PM or midnight when the first groups of forschpiel partyers arrive.

For nightlife listings, pick up a copy of the free monthly paper *Natt og Dag* or Friday's edition of *Avis 1.*

BARS AND LOUNGES

With its 1970s theme, **Café Con Bar** (⊠*Brugt. 11, Grønland* ☎*22–05–02–00* ⊕*www.cafeconbar.no*), is one of Oslo's trendy crowd-pleasers. The kitchen closes at 10 and guest DJs spin on weekends. For cheap beer and an informal crowd, visit the popular student hangout **Stargate Pub** (⊠*Grønlandsleiret 33, Grønland* ☎*22–04–13–77*) at Brugata, just alongside the bridge. **Parkteatret** (⊠ *Olaf Ryes pl. 11, Grünerløkka* ☎*22–35–63–00* ⊕*www.parkteatret.no*), set in a converted art deco theater, has either theater, film, live music, or DJs every night of the week. If you're more partial to lounging than drinking, the **Biblioteki baren og Vinterhaven** at the Hotel Bristol (⊠ *Kristian IVs gt. 7, Sentrum* ☎*22–82–60–00*) is a stylish hangout with old-fashioned leather armchairs, huge marble columns, and live piano music.

Onkel Donald (⊠ *Universitetsgt. 26, Sentrum* ☎*23–35–63–10* ⊕*kafe. onkeldonald.no*) is the trendiest meeting place in the center and has a capacity for hundreds. For a change of pace, try **Lorry** (⊠ *Parkvn. 12, Sentrum* ☎*22–69–69–04* ⊕*www.lorry.no*), behind the Royal Palace grounds. It has stuffed wildlife and early-20th-century sketches of famous Norwegians adorning the walls. It also advertises 180 different types of beer, but don't be surprised if not all of them are in stock.

Serious beer drinkers may find **Oslo Mikrobryggeriet** (⊠ *Bogstadvn. 6, Majorstuen* ☎*22–56–97–76* ⊕*www.omb.no*) worth a stop. Eight different beers are brewed on the premises, including the increasingly popular Oslo Pils. The **Underwater Bar** (⊠ *Dalsbergstien 4, St. Hanshaugen* ☎*22–46–05–26* ⊕*www.underwater.no*) is a pub with an undersea theme, complete with fish tanks and scuba gear, and live opera on Tuesday and Thursday at 9 PM.

CAFÉS
As a mark of Oslo's growing cosmopolitanism, the city now has a Continental café culture, with bohemian coffeehouses and chic cafés dotting the sidewalks. Grünerløkka especially has lots of cafés to suit every taste; they're great for people-watching and whiling away warm summer afternoons.

Following in the tradition of the grand Continental cafés, the **Theatercafe** in the Continental Hotel (⊠ *Stortingsgt. 24–26, Sentrum* ☎*22–82–40–50* ⊕*www.theatercafeen.no*) is an Oslo institution. A meeting place for artists and intellectuals for several decades, today it still attracts Oslo's beau monde, and is a good bet for celebrity spotting. Also in the center, **Café Bacchus** (⊠ *Dronningensgt. 27, Sentrum* ☎*22–33–34–30*), in the old Basarhall at the rear of Oslo Domkirke, is tiny but serves a mean brownie. Background music is classical during the day, jazz at the night. **Kaffebrennerlet** (⊠ *Storgt. 2, Sentrum* ☎*22–42–01–31* ⊕*www.kaffebrenneriet.no*), meanwhile, is Oslo's answer to Starbucks, with good coffee and shops throughout town.

The **Tea Lounge** (⊠ *Thorvald Meyers gt. 33B, Grünerløkka* ☎*22–37–07–07* ⊕*www.tealounge.no*) serves alcoholic and nonalcoholic tea drinks. It's very stylish, with mellow music, a mosaic tile bar, picture windows, high-backed plush red sofas, and a trendy crowd to match. For a slightly more bohemian experience, head to **Fru Hagen** (⊠ *Thorvald Meyers gt. 40, Grünerløkka* ☎*45–49–19–04* ⊕*www.fruhagen. no*), with its classical-looking chandeliers and elegant velvet-furnished sofas. Aim for a window seat to check out the passing traffic.

In the west of the city, **Clodion Art Café** (⊠ *Bygdøy Allé 63, Frogner* ☎ *22–44–97–26* ⊕ *www.clodion.no*) with its multicolor furniture, oversize coffee mugs, and children's play area, is popular with families.

DANCE CLUBS

Most dance clubs open late, so the beat doesn't really start until midnight. Many establishments have a minimum age for entry, which can be as high as 25. There's also usually a cover of around NKr 50–NKr 100. Oslo's beautiful people congregate at **Cosmo,** (⊠ *Ruseløkkvn. 14, Sentrum* ☎ *40–00–33–97*), Norway's biggest club, bar, and lounge, spread over three floors. Another one of Oslo's best clubs is **Sikamikanico** (⊠ *Møllergata 2, Sentrum* ☎ *22–41–44–09* ⊕ *www.sikamikanico.no*) with DJs playing anything from hip-hop to progressive house and jazz. Expect big crowds and a big party atmosphere. Serious clubbers should try **Skansen** (⊠ *Rådhusgt. 25, Sentrum* ☎ *22–42–28–88*) for house and techno music. It has a good dance floor and DJs on weekends. Most of the big hotels have discos that appeal to the over-thirty crowd. **Smuget** (⊠ *Rosenkrantz gt. 22, Sentrum* ☎ *22–42–52–62*) is an institution: it hosts live rock and blues bands every night except Sunday, when crowds flock to the in-house discotheque.

Over in the east of the city, **Kafe Kaos,** (⊠ *Thorvald Meyers gate 56, Grünerløkka* ☎ *22–04–69–90*) is a new addition to Grünerløkka's groovy music scene with a large outdoor area, terrific cocktails, and a funky vibe.

GAY BARS

For information about gay and lesbian clubs and bars in Oslo, you can read *Pink Planet,* the gay newsletter; check out www.gaysir.no; or call **LLH** (*Landsforening for Lesbisk og Homofil Frigjøring* ☎ *22–41–11–33* ⊕ *www.llh.no/oslo*), the national gay and lesbian liberation association.

A fixture on Oslo's gay scene since the 1970s, **London Pub** (⊠ *C.J. Hambros pl. 5, Sentrum* ☎ *22–70–87–00* ⊕ *www.londonpub.no*) has a piano bar on the top floor and Sunday theme parties. A younger breed of clientele frequents the bar **Chairs** on the ground floor.

JAZZ CLUBS

Norwegians take their jazz seriously. **Blå** (⊠ *Brennerivn. 9C, Grünerløkka* ☎ *40–00–42–77* ⊕ *www.blaaoslo.no*), on the Akers River, is considered the leading club for jazz and related sounds in the Nordic countries. The riverside patio is popular in summer.

At **Herr Nilsen** (⊠ *C.J. Hambros pl. 5, Sentrum* ☎ *22–33–54–05* ⊕ *www. herrnilsen.no*), some of Norway's most celebrated jazz artists perform in a stylish space. There's live music three nights a week and jazz on weekend afternoons. **Belleville** (⊠ *Mariboes gt. 2b, St. Hanshaugen/ Sentrum* ☎ *22–11–33–08*) is a small, intimate venue with gigs every nights of the week. For more information on jazz in Oslo, visit www. jazzinoslo.no/english.

OSLO MUSIC FESTIVALS

The popular outdoor music festival **Norwegian Wood** (☎815-50-333 or 67-10-34-50 ⊕ www.norwegian wood.no) is held at the Frognerbadet (Frogner Swimming Pool) in June. Begun in the early '90s, the festival hosts big names such as Iggy Pop, Bob Dylan, Alanis Morisette, the Foo Fighters, and Rufus Wainwright, as well as fledgling Norwegian bands. The large **Øya Music Festival** (☎815-33-133 for tickets ⊕ www. oyafestivalen.com) is held at Mid-delalderparken in Gamlebyen in August and features a mix of talents, from Sigur Ros to Sonic Youth.

Every August, the **Oslo Jazz Festival** (☎22-42-91-20 ⊕ www.oslojazz.

no) brings in major international artists and big crowds to various venues throughout town.

You should also check out Oslo Opera Festival, ⊕ www.kulturentu siastene.no; All Ears (improvisation in Grünerløkka), ⊕ www.all-ears. no; Ultimafestivalen (contemporary music), ⊕ www.ultima.no; Oslo World Music Festival, ⊕ www.rik skonsertene.no/osloworldmusicfes tival; Kongene på Haugen (rock and pop, with big names and emerging talent), www.kongenepahaugen.no; and Inferno (heavy metal, a genre very popular in Norway), ⊕ www. infernofestival.net.

MUSIC CLUBS

At Oslo's numerous rock clubs, the cover charges are low, the crowds young and boisterous, and the music loud. **Oslo Spektrum** (✉ *Sonia Henies pl. 2, Sentrum* ☎ *22–05–29–00 or 815–11–211 for tickets* ⊕ *www.oslospektrum.no*), one of Norway's largest live-music venues, is just behind the Oslo City shopping center. Past acts have included big names such as Radiohead, Britney Spears, Bob Dylan, Bruce Springsteen, and Neil Young.

Cosmopolite (✉ *Soria Moria, Vogtsgt. 64, Sentrum* ☎ *22–11–33–08* ⊕ *www.cosmopolite.no*) features live music acts from all over the world, especially Latin America. Look for jazz here, too.

The lineup at **Rockefeller/John Dee** (✉ *Torggt. 16, Sentrum* ☎ *22–20–32–32* ⊕ *www.rockefeller.no*) features everything from hard-rock to alternative and hip-hop acts, including Nick Cave, Blondie, and Ashe, while **Oslo Garage** (✉ *Grensen 9Sentrum* ☎ *22–42–37–44* ⊕ *www.gara geoslo.no*)promotes Norwegian and international rock.

SHOPPING

Oslo is the best place in the country for buying anything Norwegian. Popular souvenirs include knitwear, wood and ceramic trolls, cheese slicers, boxes with rosemaling, gold and silver jewelry, items made from pewter, smoked salmon, caviar, *akvavit* (a white spirit), chocolate, and goat cheese.

Established Norwegian brands include Porsgrund porcelain, Hadeland and Magnor glass, David Andersen jewelry, and Husfliden handicrafts. You may also want to look for popular, classical, or folk music CDs;

English translations of Norwegian books; or clothing by a Norwegian designer.

Prices in Norway, as in all of Scandinavia, are generally much higher than in other European countries. Prices of handmade articles, such as knitwear, are controlled, making comparison shopping useless. Otherwise, shops have both sales and specials—look for the words *salg* and *tilbud*. In addition, if you are a resident of a country other than Norway, Sweden, Finland, or Denmark, you can have the Norwegian value-added tax (*moms*) refunded at the airport when you leave the country. When you make a purchase, you must clearly state your country of residence in order to have the necessary export document filled in by store staff.

SHOPPING NEIGHBORHOODS

Basarhallene, the arcade behind the cathedral, is worth a browse for glass and crystal and handicrafts made in Norway. Walk 15 minutes west of the city center and you can wander up the tree-lined Bygdøy Allé and browse the fashionable **Frogner** and **Bygdøy** areas, which are brimming with modern and antique-furniture stores, interior design shops, food shops, art galleries, haute couture, and Oslo's beautiful people. The streets downtown around **Karl Johans Gate** draw many of Oslo's shoppers. The concentration of department stores is especially high in this part of town. **Majorstuen** starts at the T-bane station with the same name and proceeds down Bogstadveien to the Royal Palace. Oslo is not famed for its markets, but there's a small flower market on Stortorget in front of the Oslo Cathedral, and a few stalls selling souvenirs and second-hand records on Youngstorget. Every Saturday, a flea market is open at **Vestkanttorget,** at Amaldus Nilsens plass near Frognerparken. **Grünerløkka,** a 15-minute walk north of the center, is blooming with trendy new and bohemian fashion boutiques, and many quirky little shops.

DEPARTMENT STORES

GlasMagasinet (⊠*Stortorvet 9, Sentrum* ☎*22–90–87–00* ⊕*www.glasmagasinet.no*), opposite Oslo Domkirke, is more accurately an amalgam of shops under one roof rather than a true department store. Many of its stores sell handcrafted items made with glass, silver, and pewter. Traditionally, families visit GlasMagasinet at Christmastime, so the store is usually open on Sunday in December.

Steen & Strøm (⊠*Kongensgt. 23, Sentrum* ☎*22–00–40–00* ⊕*www.steenogstrom.no*), one of Oslo's first department stores, sells the usual: cosmetics, clothing, books, and accessories. It also has a well-stocked floor of accoutrements for outdoor activities.

SHOPPING CENTERS

Aker Brygge, Norway's first major shopping center, is right on the water across from the Tourist Information Center at Vestbanen. Shops are open until 8 most days, and some open on Sunday (☎*22–83–26–80* ⊕*www.akerbrygge.no*). **ByPorten** (⊠*Jernbanetorget 6, Sentrum* ☎*23–36–21–60* ⊕*www.byporten.no*) is a shopping center with more than 70 fashion, food, and gift stores next to Oslo S Station. **Oslo City**

(⊠*Stenersgt. 1, Sentrum* ☎*815/44–033* ⊕*www.oslocity.no*), at the other end of downtown, with access to the street from Oslo S Station, is the city's largest indoor mall, and the country's most visited, with almost 100 shops and cateries over five floors. The elegant **Paleet** (⊠*Karl Johans gt. 37–43, between Universitetsgt. and Rosenkrantz gt., Sentrum* ☎*22–03–38–88* ⊕*www.paleet.no*) opens up into a grand, marbled atrium and has many clothing, accessories, and food stores, including a basement food court.

SPECIALTY STORES
ANTIQUES
Norwegian rustic antiques (those objects considered of high artistic and historic value) cannot be taken out of the country, but just about anything else can with no problem. The Frogner district has many antiques shops, especially on Skovveien and Thomas Heftyes Gate between Bygdøy Allé and Frogner plass. Deeper in the heart of Majorstuen, Industrigate is famous for its good selection of shops. The rare volumes at **Damms Antikvariat** (⊠*Tollbugt. 25, Sentrum* ☎*22–41–04–02* ⊕*www.damms.no*) will catch the eye of any antiquarian book buff, with volumes in English as well as Norwegian.

Esaias Solberg (⊠*Kirkeristen, Sentrum* ☎*22–86–24–80* ⊕*www.esaias. no*), behind Oslo Cathedral, has exceptional small antiques. **Marsjandisen** (⊠*Fridtjof Nansens pl. 2, Sentrum* ☎*22–42–71–68*), specializes in Hadeland glass, silver, cups, and mugs. **West Sølv og Mynt** (⊠*Niels Juels gt. 27, Frogner* ☎*22–55–75–83*) has the largest selection of antique silver in town.

ART GALLERIES
Kaare Berntsen (⊠*Universitetsgt. 12, Sentrum* ☎*22–99–10–10* ⊕*www. kaare-berntsen.no*) is Northern Europe's biggest art dealer and gallery and sells paintings as well as furniture and small antique items. **Galleri Elenor** (⊠*Kirkevn. 50, Frogner* ☎*22–46–16–90* ⊕*www.gallerielenor. com*), near Frognerparken west of the center, displays modern Norwegian and international art.

Galleri Markveien (⊠*Markveien 30, Grünerløkka* ☎*22-38—00–26* ⊕*www.gallerimarkveien.com*) displays the abstract work of the commercially successful artists Tone Granberg and Geir Sletten. **Kunstnernes Hus** (*The Artists' House* ⊠*Wergelandsvn. 17, Sentrum* ☎*22–85–34–10* ⊕*www.kunstnerneshus.no*) exhibits contemporary art, and hosts an art show every fall. The gallery also has a bar/restaurant that is a weekend hot spot for artists and local celebrities.

BOOKS
In Oslo bookshops, you can always find some English-language books. You may want to pick up some classic works by Henrik Ibsen and Knut Hamsun in translation, as well as some by contemporary writers such as Jostein Gaarder, Linn Ullmann, and Nikolaj Frobenius.

ARK Qvist (⊠*Drammensvn. 16, Sentrum* ☎*22–54–26–00*), considered Oslo's "English bookshop," specializes in fiction, crime, and Norwegian-Scandinavian translations. **Norli** (⊠*Universitetsgt. 24, Sentrum*

☏22–00–43–00 ⊕*www.norli.no*) is a bookstore chain that has the largest number of titles in Norway. This store keeps a substantial number of Scandinavian-language fiction and travel books on hand. **Tanum** (✉*Karl Johans gt. 43, Sentrum* ☏22–41–11–00 ⊕*www.tanum.no*) is strong in the arts, health and healing, and travel.

CLOTHING

H & M (*Hennes & Mauritz* ✉*Stortorvet 13, Sentrum* ☏22 00 81 00 ✉*Bogstadvn. 4, Frogner* ☏22 59 09 00 ⊕*www.hm.com/no*) carries fresh, up-to-date looks at reasonable prices. **Cubus** (✉*Grensen 12* ☏22 47 43 30 ⊕*www.cubus.no*) is a good bet for well-priced staples. **Bik Bok** (✉*Karl Johans gt. 3, Sentrum* ☏22 42 40 68 ✉*Bogstadvn. 22, Frogner* ☏22 59 46 11 ⊕*www.bikbok.com*), a popular Norwegian chain, has several outlets in the capital. **Indiska** (✉*Karl Johans gt. 6, Sentrum* ☏22 42 65 00 ✉*Storgt. 1, Sentrum* ☏22 41 38 00 ⊕*indiska.com*) is a Swedish chain selling colorful, ethnic-inspired clothes and accessories for women.

Grünerløkka, north of the city center, is an alternative shopping district filled with hip little boutiques. **Probat** (✉*Thorvald Meyers gt. 52, Grünerløkka* ☏22–37–94–22 ⊕*www.probat.no*) sells hip T-shirts from all around the world, as well as T-shirts with inscriptions in Norwegian. **Rebella** (✉*Thorvald Meyers gt. 52, Grünerløkka* ☏22–37–94–22 ⊕*rebella.no*), next door to Probat, showcases edgier clothes by young Norwegian fashion designers.

In the city center, **Oleana** (✉*Stortingsgt. 8, Sentrum* ☏22–33–31–63 ⊕*www.oleana.no*) is a popular Norwegian brand known for its original and elegant women's sweaters. Designer Solveig Hisdal, behind Oleana's success story since 1992, has won many awards for her collections, which she now exports as far as Australia.

For more Norwegian designs, you could also try the **Design Forum** (various locations in town, check their Web site www.designforum.no), which specializes in colorful clothes and accessories made with natural materials.

Norwegian sportswear chain stores are easy to spot in the city's malls and on Karl Johans Gate, but also consider checking out some specialty shops. **Peak Performance** (✉*Bogstadvn. 13, Majorstuen* ☏22–96–00–91 ⊕*www.peakperformance.com*) is a top choice for fashionable sportswear. **Skandinavisk Høyfjellutstyr** (✉*Bogstadvn. 1, Majorstuen* ☏23–33–43–80 ⊕*skandinaviskhoyfjellsutstyr.no*) has a great selection of traditional mountain sportswear.

FOOD

Throughout Oslo there are bakeries, delis, fishmongers, and gourmet food shops to tempt all tastes. In west Oslo **Åpent Bakeri** (✉*Inkognito Terrasse 1, Frogner* ☏22–44–94–70 ⊕*www.apentbakeri.no*) bakes the city's best-tasting bread for devoted locals and top restaurants. **Fjelberg Fisk og Vilt** (✉*Bygdøy Allé 56, Frogner* ☏22–44–60–41 ⊕*www.fjelberg.no*) has a reputation for its high-quality fish and seafood, including salmon (smoked, tartare, fresh, and cured), lobster, shrimp, and fish soup. A good restaurant is also on the premises. **Skafferiet** (⊠*Elisenbergvn. 7, Frogner* ☎*22–44–52–96*), open daily from 10 to 10, is popular with sophisticated Oslo residents for its gourmet foods and fresh flowers.

In the east of the capital **Hotel Havana** (⊠*Thorvald Meyers gt. 36, Grünerløkka* ☎*23–23–03–23* ⊕*www.hotelhavana.no*) is a hip delicatessen with cheeses, Cuban coffee and cigars, tapas plates, and fresh fish. The ethnic shops of Grønland and Grünerløkka are also your best bet for a nice selection of fruit and vegetables, including more exotic specimens.

GLASS, CERAMICS, AND PEWTER
The shops at **Basarhallene**, behind the cathedral, sell glass and ceramics. **Gastronaut** (⊠*Bygdøy Allé 56, Frogner* ☎*22–44–60–90*) sells top-quality china, cutlery, linen, and glass, as well as spices and condiments from Spain and Italy. If there's no time to visit a glass factory outside of town, department stores are the best option: **GlasMagasinet** (⊠*Stortorvet 8, Sentrum* ☎*22–90–87–00* ⊕*www.glasmagasinet.no*) stocks both European and Norwegian designs in glass, pewter, and silver. **Norway Designs** (⊠*Stortingsgt. 28, Sentrum* ☎*23–11–45–10* ⊕*www.norwaydesigns. no*) showcases Scandinavian art glass, kitchenware, ceramics, silver, and other household items. Swedish company **Design Torget** (⊠*House of Oslo, Ruseløkkvn. 26, Aker Brygge* ☎*21–55–28–25* ⊕*www.design torget.se*) (there is another branch in the Byporten Shopping Center) specializes in funky, fun and colorful articles ranging from stationery to kitchen utensils.

HANDICRAFTS
Basarhallene, the arcade behind the cathedral, is worth a browse for handicrafts made in Norway. **Heimen Husflid A/S** (⊠*Rosenkrantz gt. 8, enter at Kristian IVs gt., Sentrum* ☎*23–21–42–00* ⊕*www.heimen. net*) has small souvenir items and a department dedicated to traditional Norwegian costumes, or *bunad*.

Husfliden (⊠*Rosenkrantz' gate 19, Sentrum* ☎*22–42–10–75* ⊕*www. dennorskehusfliden.no*), one of the finest stores for handmade goods in the country, has an even larger selection than that at Heimen Husflid. You can find pewter, ceramics, knits, and Norwegian handmade textiles, furniture, felt boots and slippers, loafers, sweaters, traditional costumes, wrought-iron accessories, Christmas ornaments, and wooden kitchen accessories. **Norsk Kunsthandverkeri** *(Norwegian Association of Arts and Crafts)* (⊠*Rådhusgt. 24, Sentrum* ☎*22–01–55–70* ⊕*www. kunsthandverk.no*) has beautiful, colorful pieces.

JEWELRY
Gold and precious stones are no bargain, but silver and enamel jewelry and Viking period productions can be. Some silver pieces are made with Norwegian stones, particularly pink thulite. **David-Andersen** (⊠*Karl Johans gt. 20, Sentrum* ☎*24–14–88–00* ⊕*www.david-andersen.no* ⊠*Bogstadvn. 23, Majorstuen* ☎*22–59–50–00* ⊠*Stranden 3, Aker Brygge* ☎*22–83–42–00*) is Norway's best-known goldsmith. He makes stunning silver and gold designs.

The **ExpoArte** (⊠*Henrik Ibsens gt. 100, Frogner* ☎*22–55–93–90* ⊕*www.expoarte.no*) gallery specializes in custom pieces and displays the work of avant-garde Scandinavian jewelers. **Smykketeatret** (⊠*Kristian Augusts gt. 3, Sentrum* ☎*21–53–12–22* ⊕*www.smykketeatret. no*) also showcases alternative jewelry from both Norwegian and other Scandinavian/European designers at reasonable prices. **Heyerdahl** (⊠*Roald Amundsensgt. 6, Sentrum* ☎*22–41–59–18* ⊕*www.heyer dahl.no*), near City Hall, is a good dependable jeweler.

KNITWEAR

Norway is famous for its colorful hand-knit wool sweaters, and even mass-produced (machine-knit) models are of top quality. Prices are regulated, and they are always lower than buying a Norwegian sweater abroad.

Maurtua Husflid (⊠*Akershusstranda, Sentrum* ☎*22–41–31–64* ⊕*www. maurtua.no*), on the waterfront beneath Akershus Castle, has a large selection of sweaters and blanket coats. So have **Oslo Sweater Shop** (⊠*SAS Scandinavia Hotel, Tullinsgt. 5, Sentrum* ☎*22–11–29–22* ⊕*www. sweater.no*), **Rein og Rose** (⊠*Ruseløkkvn. 3, Sentrum* ☎*22–83–21–39*), in the Vika shopping district, and **Norway Shop,** (⊠*Fridtjof Nansens pl. 2, Sentrum* ☎*22–33–41–90* ⊕*www.norwayshop.com*).

SIDE TRIPS FROM OSLO

There is much to see and do around Oslo, particularly in the Oslo Fjord area. The coast, on both the east and west side, offers ample opportunities for swimming, walking, and fishing. Farther away from the sea, expect gentle rolling fields, big *gård* (farms), and forested areas. This region is one of the most populated in Norway, so public transport links and roads are good, making for quick travel.

DRØBAK

35 km (21 mi) south of Oslo.

Drøbak's pretty collection of white wooden houses and small winding streets gives the impression of a typical Sørlander (southern) town, yet it is only one hour's drive from the capital. Oslovians often take day trips to Drøbak to sit by the beach and eat fresh shrimp. During World War II Norwegian forces sank the German cruiser *Blucher* here.

GETTING HERE AND AROUND

From May to September you can take the scenic one-hour ferry ride from Oslo's Aker Brygge to Drøbak on the M/S *Prinsessen*. By car, follow Route E18 southeast from Oslo to Route E6. Follow signs to Drøbak.

The trip on Bus 541 or 542 from Strandgata at the corner of Prinsensgata in Oslo to Drøbak affords great glimpses of the fjord (and bathers in summer). The trip takes an hour, and buses depart hourly at 15 minutes to and 15 minutes past the hour during the week, with reduced service on weekends.

There is no rail station in Drøbak itself. The nearest station is in Ski. But the boat trip from Oslo is really the best option and much more pleasant.

ESSENTIALS

Boat Contact M/S *Prinsessen* (⊠ *Stranden 1* ☎ *23–11–52–20* ⊕ *www.nbds.no*).

Bus Info Norgesbuss AS (☎ *40––00––11–66 or 177* ⊕ *www.trafikanten.no*).

Visitor Info Drøbak (*Drøbak Turistinformasjon* ☎ *64–93–50–87* ⊕ *www.visitoslo.com*).

EXPLORING

More than 1,000 species of fish and marine life from the Oslo Fjord are exhibited in the **Drøbak Akvarium** *(aquarium)*. There's a children's area where kids can handle a variety of shellfish, and a special exhibit explains how you can make lutefisk, the Norwegian fish delicacy popular at Christmastime. ⊠ *Havnegata 4* ☎ *95–90–39–27* ⊕ *www.akvarium.net* ⌦ *NKr 40* ⊙ *June–Aug., daily 10–7; Sept.–May, daily 10–4.*

Jegstad Gård farm, a traditional Norwegian dairy, has animals to visit and horse carriages to ride. Wander along the nature trail or visit the stable, farm museum, and Viking burial mounds. You can play sports or relax on the large lawn. The farm is between Drøbak and Vestby, to the south. ⊠ *Rte. E6, junction 17 Vestby* ☎ *41–60–62–58* ⊕ *www.jegstad.no* ⌦ *NKr 50* ⊙ *July–mid-Aug., noon–4; by special arrangement rest of yr.*

The inviting **Tregaardens Julehus** *(Christmas House)* dominates the town's central square. Just around the corner from the post office, this 1876 building was once a mission for seafarers unable to reach Oslo because the fjord was frozen over. Now it's a retail store that sells Christmas wares and gifts such as wooden dolls and mice made of cloth—all handmade by Eva Johansen, the store's creator and owner. Many Norwegian children believe Father Christmas resides in Drøbak because there's a Santa's post office in this store. ⊠ *Main Sq.* ☎ *64–93–41–78* ⊕ *www.julehus.no.*

WHERE TO EAT

$ ╳ On the main square, stop in **Det Gamle Bageri Ost & Vinstue** *(The Old*
CAFÉ *Bakery Wine and Cheese Room)* for salads, pies, and hearty sandwiches. The wood interior dates from 1740, and classical music soirees are held on weekends. ⊠ *Havnebakken 1* ☎ *64–93–21–05* ▭ *AE, DC, MC, V.*

FREDRIKSTAD

34 km (20 mi) south of Moss.

Fredrikstad's Gamlebyen (Old Town), Norway's oldest fortified city, lies peacefully at the mouth of the Glomma, the country's longest river. Its bastions and moat date from the 1600s. After spending time in the Old Town browsing the shops and museum, take a boat or drive on to the Hvaler archipelago (20 minutes away), a popular vacation spot.

GETTING HERE AND AROUND

If driving from Oslo, follow the E6 south and turn right onto Route 110 toward Fredrikstad just past Rygge Airport in Moss. The journey takes an hour and 30 minutes. Buses also link Fredrikstad with Oslo; they're operated by Nor-Way Bussekspressen.

Trains run regularly from Oslo S to Fredrikstad, several times a day (journey time is just over an hour). The train station is located in Cicignon, and you need to take the little ferry to cross over to Gamlebyen.

ESSENTIALS

Bus Contact Nor-Way Bussekspress (☎ 815-44-444 ⊕ www.nor-way.no).

Train Contact NSB (Norwegian State Railways ☎ 815-00-888 ⊕ www.nsb.no).

Visitor Info Fredrikstad Turistkontoret (⊠ Tøihusgt. 41, Gamle Fredrikstad ☎ 69-30-46-00 ⊕ www.opplevfredrikstad.com).

EXPLORING

★ In the center of town is **Fredrikstad Domkirke** *(Fredrikstad Cathedral).* Built in 1860 in a flamboyant neo-Gothic style, it contains stained-glass decorations by Emanuel Vigeland, whose work also adorns Oslo Cathedral. ⊠ *Nygaardsgt. 29/31* ☎ *69-30-79-00* ⊡ *Free* ☉ *Tues.– Fri. 11–3.*

The **Fredrikstad Museum** documents the town's history from 1860 to 1960 through objects related to its industrial, commercial, hospital, and day-to-day life. There is also a collection of photographs and paintings by local artists. ⊠ *Tøihusgt. 41* ☎ *69-95-85-00* ⊡ *NKr 40* ☉ *Tues.– Fri. noon–3:30, weekends 11–4.*

Fodor'sChoice
★
Named after a king who never bothered to visit the city (Fredrerik II), and designed by one of the most prominent military engineers of the time (J. C. de Cicignon), **Gamlebyen,** Fredrikstad's Old Town, is the best-preserved fortress town in the whole of Scandinavia. Its cobbled streets, old wooden houses, and quaint boutiques evoke a time gone by. The local marching band is often seen (and heard) rehearsing in full regalia, and many of the original 200 cannons that used to guard this garrison town can still be seen on the thick rampart walls. Check out Bastion 5, a cluster of galleries featuring ceramics, paintings and jewelry by local artists, housed in the old slavery building, and stop at the old-fashioned bakery for coffee and *skolebrød* (custard pastry with coconut flakes) on the way back. There is a lively market every Saturday on the main square in summer.

WHERE TO EAT AND STAY

$$$ ✕⊡ **Radisson SAS.** Fredrikstad's newest hotel is ideally located on the main pedestrian street, within easy walking distance of all the shops and restaurants. The stylish rooms are modern and comfortable, and come in two themes: Urban or Ocean. The Filini restaurant, which serves Mediterranean fare, is one of the best in town. **Pros:** stylish contemporary design throughout, including black granite floors, fiber-optic lighting and a huge fireplace; the Sky Bar, on the top floor, with great views over the city and river; helpful, professional staff. **Cons:** the hotel is not on the riverside itself; the restaurant is on the expensive side. ⊠ *Nygaten*

2-6 ☎*69–39–30–00* ⊕*www.radisson.com* ⇄*172 rooms* ⌂*In-room: Internet. In-hotel: restaurant, bars* ⊟*AE, DC, MC, V* ⦶*BP.*

SHOPPING

Glashytte (⊠*Torsnesvn. 1* ☎*69–32–28–12* ⊕*www.glashytta.net*) is a well-known glassblowing studio and shop; its glassware is exhibited and sold in galleries throughout Norway. You can watch glassblowers perform their magic, creating everything from schnapps glasses to vases in primary colors. If you're in the area, you can place a special order and go see your glass object blown. You can pick it up a few days later after it's been cooled slowly in a kiln, which makes it less fragile.

JEVNAKER

70 km (42 mi) northwest of Oslo.

A day trip to Jevnaker combines a drive along picturesque Tyrifjord (a lake, not a fjord, despite the name) with a visit to Norway's oldest glassworks, in operation since 1762. It's lovely, but other than this there isn't much else to do.

GETTING HERE AND AROUND

To get to Jevnaker by road, follow the E16 from Sandvika (west of Oslo) to Hønefoss, and turn east just before Hønefoss on Route 241 toward Jevnaker. If leaving from the east, follow Route 4 to Gjøvik and take Route 35 west to Jevnaker at Roa. It's about two hours. The bus company Timekspressen line 4 links Hønefoss with Oslo with departures every hour.

There is no train station in Jevnaker. The nearest station is in Hønefoss, with departures for Oslo several times daily (journey time 1 hour 45 minutes).

ESSENTIALS

Bus Contact Timekspressen (linje 4) (⊕ *www.timekspressen.no*).

Train Contact NSB (*Norwegian State Railways* ☎ *815–00–888* ⊕ *www.nsb.no*).

EXPLORING JEVNAKER

☾ At **Hadeland Glassverk,** one of the country's most popular attractions, you can watch artisans blowing glass, or you can blow your own for NKr 95 (weekends and school holidays only). Both practical table crystal and one-of-a-kind art glass are produced here, and you can buy first-quality pieces as well as seconds in the gift shop. Learn the history of glass at the Glass Museum. For children, there's a Honey House of bees and a Children's House that celebrates Christmas every weekend from April through December. There is also a bakery and a restaurant, Kokkestua, which serves traditional Norwegian meals. ⊡*Rte. 241, Postboks 85 Glassverksvn. 9, 3520* ☎*61–31–66–00* ⊕*www.hadeland-glassverk.no* ▧*Glass museum and factory NKr 40* ⊙ *Weekdays 10–6, Sat. 10–5, Sun. 11–6.*

ÅSGÅRDSTRAND

11 km (7 mi) south of Horten.

Since 1920 the coastal town of Åsgårdstrand has been a popular vacation and bathing spot. A couple of decades before that, it was known as an artists' colony for outdoor painting, attracting Edvard Munch, Fritz Thaulow, and others. In summer the local tourist office can arrange guided history tours of the area, led by well-versed guides.

GETTING HERE AND AROUND

From Oslo take the E18 and head south toward Tønsberg. Åsgårdstrand is 11 km (7 mi) south of Horten, you'll see signs shortly after you've past Horten. Timekspressen line 8 links Tønsberg with Oslo with departures every hour.

There is no train station in Åsgårdstrand. The nearest station is located in Tønsberg. There are regular departures from Oslo, and the journey takes about 1 hour 30 minutes.

ESSENTIALS

Bus Contact Timekspressen (line 8) (⊕ *www.timekspressen.no*).

Train Contact NSB (*Norwegian State Railways* ☎ *815–00–888* ⊕ *www.nsb.no*).

Visitor Info Horten Tourist Office (☎ *33–03–17–08* ⊕ *www.visithorten.com*).

EXPLORING

Fodor's Choice
★

Munchs Lille Hus (*Munch's Little House*) was the summer house and studio in which the artist spent seven summers. Now a museum, it was here that he painted *Girls on the Bridge* and earned a reputation as a ladies' man. ⊠*Munchsgt. 25* ☎*33–08–21–31* ⊠*NKr 30* ☉*May, weekends 11–6; June–Aug., Tues.–Sun. 11–6; Sept., weekends 11–3.*

WHERE TO EAT

$

CAFÉ

✕ **Munch's Café og Frantzens Konditori.** Steps away from the harbor, this a good option for lunch, be it a sandwich and coffee or a full-on meal. The on-site bakery has some wonderful cakes and breads, and it's possible to sit outside in summer. ⊠*Stangsgt. 5* ☎*33–08–10–26* ⊟*AE, DC, MC, V.*

SOUTHERN NORWAY

In summer, many of Oslo's residents migrate to the forests of Telemark and the sunny southern coast. Southern Norway is an ideal area for those who want to get close to nature, with a mild summer climate and terrain varying from inland mountains and forests to coastal flatland.

South of Telemark, you reach the famed beaches and fjords of the coast. Many splendid points mark the route of the North Sea Road. Beginning in the relaxed resort town of Kristiansand, the road winds west along the major section of Norway's southern coast, Sørlander. Wide, sun-kissed, inviting beaches have their blue waters warmed by the Gulf Stream. Sandy terrain turns to coastal flatlands, inland mountain peaks and green forests ideal for cycling, hiking, and mountaineering.

Freshwater lakes and rivers, and this section of the ocean, are some of the best places to go salmon fishing—they're also superb for canoeing, kayaking, and rafting. The region is the perfect habitat for such wildlife as beavers, deer, foxes, and many birds. When the North Sea Road reaches its final destination, it's in a landscape of fjords, islands, mountains, and valleys. Stavanger, Norway's oil capital, is here; a cosmopolitan city yet with small-town charm, it has some of the country's best restaurants, hotels, and cultural life.

NOTODDEN

112 km (69 mi) west of Oslo.

The town of Notodden isn't much more than a small industrial town (albeit with a really great annual blues festival usually held some time in the beginning of August). It's believed that the area was prosperous in the Middle Ages because of the size of the town's *stavkirke* (stave church).

GETTING HERE AND AROUND
By car follow the E18 from Oslo to Drammen, and then the E134. Several trains serve Notodden from Oslo S every day, although you'll have to change trains on the way. The journey can take anything between two to six hours, depending on connections. Buses also depart regularly from Oslo Bus Terminal to Notodden, and take about two hours.

ESSENTIALS
Bus Contact Timekspressen (line 1, Oslo-Notodden) (☎ *35–02–60–00 or 177* ⊕ *www.timekspressen.no*).

Train Contact Norwegian State Railway (NSB) (☎ *815–00–888* ⊕ *www.nsb.no*).

Visitor Info Notodden (✉ *Teatergt. 3* ☎ *35–01–50–00*).

EXPLORING
★ At 85 feet high and 65 feet long, the **Heddal Stave Church** is Norway's largest still in use, and it dates back to the 12th century. The structure is resplendent with rosemaling (decorative flower painting from the 17th century), a bishop's chair, and incense vessels from the Middle Ages. Look out for the stylized animal ornamentation and the grotesque human heads on the portals. ✉ *Heddalsvn. 412* ☎ *35–01–39–90* ⊕ *www.heddalstavkirke.no* 🎫 *NKr 50* ☉ *Mid-May–mid-June and mid-Aug.–mid-Sept., daily 10–5; mid-June–mid-Aug., daily 9–7.*

MORGEDAL

200 km (124 mi) west of Oslo.

In the heart of Telemark is Morgedal, the birthplace of modern skiing, thanks to the persistent Sondre Norheim, who in the 19th century perfected his skis and bindings and practiced jumping from his roof. His innovations included bindings that close behind the heel and skis that narrow in the middle to facilitate turning. In 1868, he took off for a 185-km (115-mi) trek to Oslo just to prove it could be done. A hundred years ago skiers used one long pole, held diagonally, much

Southern Norway

Bergen

Voss

Hardangerfjord

Kinsarvik

Odda

134

134

Gol

Geilo

7

40

Hønefoss

7

Oslo

Hokksund

Drammen

Oslofjorden

Drammensfjorden

Rjukan

TELEMARK

Kongsberg

Lågen

Morgedal

Dalen

Seljord

134

Notodden

Heddal
Stave
Church

Åsgårdstrand

Tønsberg

Skien

Larvik

Valle

Porsgrunn

E18

Stavern

Ryfylke

ROGALAND

Kragerø

Jomfruland

Preikestolen

9

AUST-AGDER

Risør

Stavanger

Lyngør

E18

Sandnes

VEST-AGDER

Tvedestrand

Orre

Jæren

Obrestad

Evje

42

405

41

Arendal

Ogna

Egersund

E39

Vennesla

Grimstad

44

Flekkefjord

Mosby

Lillesand

E39

Kristiansand

Mandal

Skagerrak

0   40 miles

0   60 km

like high-wire artists. Eventually the use of two short poles became widespread, although purists still feel that the one-pole method is the "authentic" way to ski.

GETTING HERE AND AROUND

By car, follow the E18 from Oslo to Drammen, and then take the E134. There is no train station in Morgedal. The nearest station is in Bø, with several direct trains a day from Oslo (journey time: 2 hours). Buses also depart regularly from Oslo Bus Terminal to Morgedal; these take about 3½ hours.

ESSENTIALS

Bus Contact Nor-Way Bussekspress (☎ *815–44–444* ⊕ *www.nor-way.no*).

Visitor Info Morgedal (⊠ *No street address* ☎ *35–05–42–50 or 41–25–38–07* ⊕ *www.morgedal.com*).

EXPLORING

The **Norsk Skieventyr** *(Norwegian Skiing Adventure Center)* in Morgedal guides you through the 4,000-year history of the winter sport with life-size exhibits of typical ski cottages and authentic skis and costumes. Displays include the inside of Norway's original and last ski-wax factory, where specialists melted a variety of secret ingredients, including cheese, to make uphill and downhill slides smoother. Visit Norheim's cottage, Øvrebø, above the edge of the forest, where the Olympic flame was lighted. Several action-packed skiing films can be seen here. ⊠ *Rte. 11 between Brunkeberg and Høydalsmo* ☎ *35–05–42–50* ᠍ *NKr 60* ☉ *Late May–mid-June, daily 11–5; mid-June–mid-Aug., daily 9–7; mid-Aug.–late Aug., daily 11–5; Sept.–mid-Dec. and mid-Jan–late May, Mon.–Thurs. 10–3:30, Fri. 10–5, Sat. 11–5, Sun. 11–6.*

GRIMSTAD

53 km (33 mi) east of Kristiansand.

Grimstad is a pretty coastal town with a charming wharf. In the mid- to late 19th century, the town was famous as a shipbuilding center, and from 1844 to 1850 the teenage Henrik Ibsen worked as an apprentice at the local apothecary shop. Later, in the early 20th century, author Knut Hamsun, winner of the Nobel Prize for Literature yet infamous for his support of Nazi Germany, lived here. Today Grimstad is called the "Town of Poets," and is still home to many artists. A popular Norwegian short-film festival is held here in early summer.

GETTING HERE AND AROUND

Grimstad is on the E18, the main highway between Oslo and Kristiansand. There is no train station in Grimstad itself; the nearest one's in Arendal. There are regular coaches from Oslo to Grimstad that take under 4½ hours.

ESSENTIALS

Transport Bus Station (⊠ *Storgt. 1* ☎ *37–00–47–00 or 177 for bus information*).

Visitor Info Grimstad (⊠ *Sorenskrivergården, Storgt. 1A* ☎ *37–25–01–68* ⊕ *www. grimstad.net*).

EXPLORING

★ Grimstad Apotek is now a part of **Ibsenhuset–Grimstad Bymuseum** *(the Ibsen House)* and has been preserved with its 1837 interior intact. Ibsen wrote his first play, *Catlina*, here. Every summer Grimstad holds an Ibsen festival celebrating the famous playwright. The museum also has a maritime department and a section honoring Terje Vigen, a folk hero who was the subject of a poem by Ibsen. He is credited with riding to Denmark to bring back food for the starving Norwegians. ⊠*Henrik Ibsens gt. 14* ☎*37–04–04–90* ⊕*www.ibsen.net* ☎*NKr 50* ⊙*Mid-May–mid-Sept., Mon.–Sat. 11–5, Sun. noon–5.*

KRISTIANSAND

4

326 km (202 mi) southwest of Oslo and 232 km (144 mi) southeast of Stavanger.

Nicknamed "Sommerbyen" ("Summer City"), Norway's fifth-largest city has 78,000 inhabitants. Norwegians come here for its sun-soaked beaches and beautiful harbor.

Kristiansand has also become known internationally for the outdoor **Quart Festival** (☎*38–14–69–69* ⊕*www.quart.no*), which hosts local and international rock bands every July.

According to legend, in 1641 King Christian IV marked the four corners of Kristiansand with his walking stick, and within that framework the grid of wide streets was laid down. The center of town, called the Kvadraturen, still retains the grid, even after numerous fires. In the northeast corner is Posebyen, one of northern Europe's largest collections of low, connected wooden house settlements, and there's a market here every Saturday in summer. Kristiansand's Fisketorvet (fish market) is near the south corner of the town's grid, right on the sea.

GETTING HERE AND AROUND

From Oslo take the E18, from Stavanger the E39. There are regular train departures for Kristiansand from both Oslo (between 4½ and 5 hours) and Stavanger (3 hours 15 minutes). Buses also serve these cities; they take roughly the same time as trains to get to Oslo, and a solid 4 hours for Stavanger.

Kristiansand is served by SAS, with nonstop flights from Oslo, Bergen, and Trondheim. Widerøe and Norwegian also link Kristiansand with other cities within Norway. Kjevik Airport is about 16 km (10 mi) northeast of the town center. The *Flybussen* airport bus departs from the coach station, *rutebilstasjon*, throughout the day and proceeds to Kjevik, stopping at downtown hotels along the way. A similar bus makes the return trip from the airport. The journey takes 25 minutes and costs NKr 80.

Several bus companies have daily departures for the 5½- to 6-hour journey between Oslo and Kristiansand, and for the 4-hour trip to Stavanger. All leave from Kristiansand bus terminal. Sørlandsruta has various buses covering the local area.

Trains leave Oslo S Station five times daily for the 4½- to 5-hour journey to Kristiansand. There are departures throughout the day for the 3½-hour Kristiansand–Stavanger route. Kristiansand's train station is at Vestre Strandgata.

From Oslo it is 320 km (199 mi) to Kristiansand. Route E18 parallels the coastline but stays slightly inland on the eastern side of the country and farther inland in the western part. Although seldom wider than two lanes, the route's very flat and makes for some very easy driving. Kristiansand taxis are connected with a central dispatching office; fare to the airport runs about NKr 250.

Walking tours of Kristiansand are offered only in summer; ask at the tourist office. The City Train is a 15-minute tour of the center part of town, and runs from June to August and around the winter holidays. If you're not in the mood for an organized tour, Kristiansand is best gotten around by foot or bus, depending on your mood or the weather.

ESSENTIALS

Air Contacts Norwegian (☎ 815-21-815 in Norway, 21-49-00-15 from outside Norway ⊕ www.norwegian.no). **SAS** (☎ 800/221-2350 in U.S., 91-50-54-00 in Norway ⊕ www.flysas.com). **Widerøe** (☎ 810-01-200 in Norway ⊕ www. wideroe.no).

Bus Contacts Kristiansand Bus Information (☎ 38-00-28-00, 177 for all routes and timetables ⊕ www.177-agder.no). **Agder Kollektivtrafikk AS** (☎ 815-00-194 ⊕ www.agderkollektivtrafikk.no). **Sørlandsruta** (☎ 38-27-82-00 ⊕ www.sorland sruta.no). **Flybussen** (☎ 37-93-44-00 ⊕ www.flybussen.no/kristiansand).

Taxis Taxi Sør (☎ 38-02-80-00 ⊕ www.taxisor.as). **Agder Taxi** (☎ 38-00-20-00 ⊕ www.agdertaxi.no).

Train Contacts Kristiansand Train Station (☎ 38-07-75-32 ⊕). **NSB** (Norwegian State Railways ☎ 815-00-888 ⊕ www.nsb.no).

Visitor and Tour Info City Train (☎ 41-78-88-88 ⊕ www.citytrain.no). **Kristiansand Tourist Office (Inspirasjon Sørlandet AS)** (✉ Rådhusgt. 6 ☎ 38-12-13-14 ⊕ www.sorlandet.com).

EXPLORING
TOP ATTRACTIONS

The **Agder naturmuseum og botaniske hage** (Agder Nature Museum and Botanical Gardens) takes on Sørlandet's natural history from the Ice Age to the present, examining the coast and moving on to the high mountains. There's a rainbow of minerals on display, as well as a rose garden with varieties from 1850. There's even the country's largest collection of cacti. ✉ Gimlevn. 23 ☎ 38-09-23-88 ⊕ www.naturmuseum. no ⊠ NKr 40 ☉ Mid-June–mid-Aug., daily 11–5; mid-Aug.–mid-June, Tues.–Fri. 10–3, Sun. noon–4; closed Mon. and Sat.

☾ One of Norway's most popular attractions, **Kristiansand Dyreparken** is
★ actually five separate parks, including a water park (bring bathing suits and towels); a forested park; an entertainment park; a theme park; and a zoo, which contains an enclosure for Scandinavian animals such as wolves, snow foxes, lynxes, and elks. The theme park, **Kardemomme By**

(Cardamom Town), is named for a book by Norwegian illustrator and writer Thorbjørn Egner. In the zoo the "My Africa" exhibition allows you to move along a bridge observing native savanna animals such as giraffes and zebras. The park is 11 km (6 mi) east of town ✉*Kristiansand Dyreparken, Kardemomme By* ☎*38–04–97–00* ⊕*www. dyreparken.no* ✉*NKr 310, includes admission to all parks and rides; discounts offered off-season, reduced fee for children (up to 13)* ☉*June–Aug., daily 10–7; Sept.–May, weekdays 10–3, weekends 10–5.*

At the **Kristiansand Kanonmuseum** *(Cannon Museum)* you can see the cannon that the occupying Germans rigged up during World War II. With calibers of 15 inches, the cannon was said to be capable of shooting a projectile halfway to Denmark. In the bunkers, related military materials are on display. ✉*Møvik* ☎*38–08–50–90* ⊕*www.kanonmuseet.no* ✉*NKr 50* ☉*Mid-June–mid-Aug., daily 11–6; mid-May–mid-June and mid-Aug.–Sept., Mon.–Wed. 11–3, Thurs.–Sun. 11–5; rest of year Sun. noon–4. Prebooked tours available all year.*

⟲ **Vest-Agder Fylkesmuseum** *(County Museum)*, the region's largest cultural museum, has more than 40 old buildings on display. The structures, transported from other locations in the area, include two *tun*—farm buildings traditionally set in clusters around a common area—which suited the extended families. If you have children with you, check out the old-fashioned toys, which can still be played with. The museum is 4 km (2½ mi) east of Kristiansand on Route E18. ✉*Vigevn. 22B, Kongsgård* ☎*38–10–26–80* ⊕*www.museumsnett.no/vafymuseum* ✉*NKr 30* ☉*Mid-June–mid-Aug., Tues.–Fri. 10–6, Sat.–Mon. noon–6; mid-Aug.–mid-June, Sun. noon–5.*

WORTH NOTING

Christiansholm Festning (✉*Østre Strandgt.* ☎*38–07–51–50* ☉*Mid-May–Aug., daily 9–9*) is a fortress on a promontory opposite Festningsgata. Completed in 1674, the circular building with 16-foot-thick walls has played more a decorative role than a defensive one; it was used once, in 1807 during the Napoleonic Wars, to defend the city against British invasion. Now it contains art exhibits.

A wealthy merchant-shipowner built **Gimle Gård** *(Gimle Manor)* around 1800 in the Empire style. Inside are furnishings from that period, including paintings, silver, and hand-printed wallpaper. To get there from the city center, head north across the Otra River on Bus 22 or drive to Route E18 and cross the bridge over the Otra to Parkveien. Turn left onto Ryttergangen and drive to Gimleveien; take a right. ✉*Gimlevn. 23* ☎*38–10–26–80* ⊕*www.gimlegaard.no* ✉*NKr 45* ☉*Mid-June–mid-Aug., daily noon–6; May–mid-June and mid-Aug.–early Jan., Sun. noon–5.*

The Gothic Revival **Kristiansand Domkirke** *(Kristiansand Cathedral)* from 1885 is the third-largest church in Norway. It often hosts summer concerts in addition to the weeklong International Church Music Festival in August. Organ, chamber, and gospel music are on the bill. ✉*Kirkegt.* ☎*38–10–77–50, 38–12–09–40 music festival* ✉*Free* ☉*June–Aug., daily 9–2.*

The striking rune stone in the cemetery of **Oddernes Kirke** (*Oddernes Church*) tells that Øyvind, godson of Saint Olav, built this church in 1040 on property he inherited from his father. One of the oldest churches in Norway, it has a baroque pulpit from 1704 and is dedicated to Saint Ola. ✉*Jegersbergvn. 2* ☎*38–19–68–60* ☜*Free* ☉*May–Aug., Sun.–Fri. 9–2.*

Fodor'sChoice
★
A favorite with hikers and strolling nannies, **Ravnedalen** (*Raven Valley*) is a lush park that's filled with flowers in springtime. Wear comfortable shoes to hike the narrow, winding paths up the hills and climb the 200 steps up to a 304-foot lookout. There is a café on-site, and open-air concerts in summer. ✉*Northwest of Kristiansand.*

WHERE TO EAT

$$$–$$$$
SEAFOOD
✕**Bølgen & Moi.** Toralf Bølgen and Trond Moi, two of Norway's most celebrated restaurateurs, opened this southernmost addition to their chain of high-profile restaurants. Near the old fishing pier the scene is more chic than rustic, with artwork and even dinnerware designed by local artist Kjell Nupen. Norwegian game and fish are cooked in an international style; try the panfried king crab with orange and carrot soup, or chili-glazed confit of duck with ginger sauce. ✉*Sjølystvn. 1A* ☎*38–17–83–00* ⊕*www.bolgenogmoi.no* ☰*AE, DC, MC, V.*

$$$$
SEAFOOD
✕**Luihn.** In the center of town, Luihn is an elegant, intimate restaurant, perfect for a quiet dinner. Fish dishes are a specialty, and the menu varies according to season. Don't hesitate to call in advance if you have any special cravings—providing they can get hold of it, the chefs can prepare just about anything for you. The wine selection is impressive. ✉*Rådhusgt. 15* ☎*38–10–66–50* ☰*AE, DC, MC, V* ☉*Closed Sun. No lunch.*

$$$$
SEAFOOD
★
✕**Sjøhuset Restaurant.** Considered one of the city's best restaurants, Sjøhuset was built in 1892 as a salt warehouse—a white-trimmed red building. The specialty is seafood. Take a seat on the sunny patio and dine on fresh lobster, or try the baked fillet of monkfish with Parma ham and sundried tomato pesto, or the cod and beetroot risotto. ✉*Østre Strandgt. 12A* ☎*38–02–62–60* ⊕*www.sjohuset.no* ☰*AE, DC, MC, V.*

WHERE TO STAY

$$–$$$
🏨**Clarion Ernst Park Hotel.** This rather traditional city hotel, established over 150 years ago, has interesting architecture and atmosphere, but convenience is the main reason most people stay here. It is central, and close to the city beach and main shopping street, Markens. The staff at the reception desk will gladly tell you about local attractions and help you purchase tickets to Dyreparken. **Pros:** pretty inside courtyard; live piano music; 100% smoke-free environment. **Cons:** some rooms can be noisy during peak hours; parking in the center is often difficult. ✉*Rådhusgt. 2* ☎*38–12–86–00* ⊕*www.ernst.no* ⇆*135 rooms, 5 suites* ♿*In-room: no a/c (some), Internet. In-hotel: restaurant, bars* ☰*AE, DC, MC, V* ☉|*BP.*

$$–$$$
☺
🏨**Quality Hotel Kristiansand.** Nicknamed "the children's hotel," this chain hotel, completely renovated in 2007, is perfect for young families on the go. Inside, there are a huge playroom, activity leaders, child care, and a children's buffet. Even more toys are outdoors. Rooms

are comfortable, with cheerful pastel walls and wood furniture. **Pros:** friendly staff; Olympic-size swimming pool. **Cons:** tiny rooms. ✉ *Sørlandsparken* ☎ *38–17–77–77* ⊕ *www.quality-kristiansand.no* ⤴ *210 rooms* ♿ *In-room: no a/c (some). In-hotel: restaurant, pool, children's programs (ages 3–12), Internet terminal* ☰*AE, DC, MC, V* ⬡*BP.*

$$–$$$ ⛄ **Rica Dyreparken Hotel.** Built like Noah's Ark, this modern hotel is designed to appeal to children of all ages. Inspired by the Kristiansand Dyreparken, many of the rooms go a little wild, with tiger-stripe chairs and paw prints on walls. Children have their own playroom and cinema on board this ark. **Pros:** child-friendly hotel; fun design; right next to the zoo. **Cons:** children everywhere; young kids and carpets in the restaurant don't seem to be the best combination. ✉ *Dyreparken, Kardemomme By* ☎ *38–14–64–00* ⊕ *www.ricadyreparkenhotel.no* ⤴ *160 rooms* ♿ *In-hotel: 2 restaurants, bar, children's programs (ages 3–12)* ☰*AE, DC, MC, V* ⬡*BP.*

AFTER DARK
Markens gate, the city's main street, is the place for clubbing, pubbing, and live music.

Club Ernst (✉ *Rådhusgt. 2* ☎ *38–12–86–00*) at the Clarion Hotel Ernst is a popular place to dance the night away. Party types in their late twenties and thirties head to **Lobby Bar** (✉ *Vestre Strandgt. 7* ☎ *38–11–21–00*) at Radisson SAS Caledonien Hotel. A younger crowd flocks to **Havana Etcetera** (✉ *Vestre Strandgt. 22* ☎ *38–02–96–66* ⊕ *www.havana-etc. no*) for up-to-date beats.

SPORTS AND THE OUTDOORS
Troll Mountain (✉ *Setesdal Rafting og Aktivitetssenter, Rte. 9, Evje* ☎ *37–93–11–77* ⊕ *www.troll-mountain.no*), about one hour's drive from Kristiansand, organizes many activities. Be it mountain climbing, sailing, biking, rafting, paintball, or even beaver or deer safaris, this is the place for outdoorsy types.

BIKING
Kristiansand has 70 km (42 mi) of bike trails around the city. The tourist office can recommend routes and rentals. **Kristiansand Sykkelsenter** (✉ *Grim Torv 3* ☎ *38–02–68–35* ⊕ *www.sykkelsenter.no*) rents bicycles and off-road vehicles.

CLIMBING
Whether you're an experienced pro or just a gung-ho beginner, you can rent climbing equipment or learn more about the sport from **Samsen Kulturhus** (✉ *Vestervn. 2* ☎ *38–00–64–00* ⊕ *www.samsen.com*).

FISHING
Just north of Kristiansand there's excellent trout, perch, and eel fishing at Lillesand's **Vestre Grimevann** lake. You can get a permit at any sports store or at the **Lillesand Tourist Office** (☎ *37–40–19–10 or 93–01–17–81* ⊕ *www.lillesand.com*).

HIKING
In addition to the gardens and steep hills of Ravnedalen, the **Baneheia Skog** (*Baneheia Forest*) is full of evergreens, small lakes, and paths that

are ideal for a lazy walk or a challenging run. It's just a 15-minute walk north from the city center.

RIDING

If you're at home in the saddle, then head to **Islandshestsenteret** (*The Icelandic Horse Center* ⊠*Søgne* ☎*38–16–98–82* ⊕*www.islandshest senteret.no*). Specializing in the Icelandic horse breed, this center offers courses, trips, and camping for children and adults.

SHOPPING

There are many shops next to Dyreparken in Kristiansand.

Kvadraturen (☎*38–02–44–11*) has 300 stores and eating spots. **Sørlandssenteret** (☎*38–04–91–00* ⊕*www.sorlandssenteret.no*) is one of the region's larger shopping centers, with 100 stores, a pharmacy, and a post office.

STAVANGER

256 km (123 mi) northwest of Kristiansand, 171 km (106 mi) south of Bergen, 453 km (281 mi) west of Oslo.

Stavanger has always prospered from the riches of the sea. During the 19th century, huge harvests of brisling and herring helped put it on the map as the sardine capital of the world. Some people claim the locals are called Siddis, from S (tavanger) plus *iddis*, which means "sardine label," although some linguists argue it's actually a mispronunciation of the English word "citizen."

During the past three decades a different product from the sea has been Stavanger's lifeblood—oil. Since its discovery in the late 1960s, North Sea oil hasn't just transformed the economy; Stavanger has emerged as cosmopolitan and vibrant, more bustling than other cities with a population of only 110,000. Norway's most international city, it has attracted residents from more than 90 nations. Roam its cobblestone streets or wander the harbor front and you're likely to see many cafés, fine restaurants, and lively pubs. For many visitors, Stavanger is a place to be entertained—the city was chosen as European Capital of Culture for 2008, a testimony to its rich, dynamic art scene.

GETTING HERE AND AROUND

Stavanger's Sola Airport, 14 km (11 mi) south of downtown, is served by SAS, with nonstop flights from Oslo, Bergen, and Kristiansand, and London and Aberdeen in the United Kingdom, as well as Copenhagen and Stockholm. The low-cost airline Norwegian also has flights from Oslo to Stavanger, and some European destinations. Widerøe specializes in flights within Norway, but also fly to Newcastle from Stavanger. Note, however, that flights to and from Stavanger tend to change seasonally; before planning, check with the airlines to be sure the route you're eyeing is being flown when you're hoping to travel.

The Flybussen (airport bus) leaves the airport every 20 minutes. It stops at hotels and outside the railroad station in Stavanger. It then heads back to the airport.

Nor-Way Bussekspress runs regularly between Stavanger and Oslo (10 hours), Bergen (5 hours), and Kristiansand (1 hour).

The Sørlandsbanen leaves Oslo S Station four times daily for the 8½- to 9-hour journey to Stavanger. Trains travel the 3½-hour Kristiansand–Stavanger route throughout the day (five to seven trains daily). For information on trains from Stavanger, call Stavanger Jernbanestasjon.

Driving from Bergen to Stavanger along the jagged western coastline is difficult and requires a detour of 150 km (93 mi), or many ferry crossings. When reaching the greater Stavanger area, you'll find toll booths, typically charging NKr 15, dotted around the city. The area around the Kulturhus in the Stavanger city center is closed to car traffic, and one-way traffic is the norm in the rest of the downtown area. Stavanger taxis are connected with a central dispatching office; journeys within Stavanger are charged by the meter, elsewhere strictly by distance.

Public transport within Stavanger is operated by the bus company Kolumbus. It's more than adequate for getting you to the major sites and then some. There's reason to consider not bothering with the bus, though; the center of town is pedestrians-only in places, and if you're of average fitness you could easily rely on your own two feet all day.

For guided tours, though, some of the best are via bus. Two-hour bus tours leave for Lysefjord (and the popular Preikestolen) from Vågen daily at 1 between June and August. Rødne Clipper Fjord Sightseeing offers three different tours. FjordTours operates sightseeing and charter tours by boat. Tide Flaggruten links Bergen and Stavanger in four hours (passengers only). There are no ferries between the two cities.

FESTIVAL CITY

Stavanger has earned the title "Festivalbyen" (festival city) for its year-round celebrations. More than 20 official festivals are held throughout the year—comedy, garlic, chili, food, chamber music, jazz, literature, beach volleyball, wine, belly dancing, vintage boats, emigrants, immigrants. There are probably just as many unofficial events, since locals love any reason to have a party. Contact **Destination Stavanger** (☎ *51-97-55-55* ⊕ *www.visit stavanger.com*) for a listing.

ESSENTIALS

Air Contacts Flybussen (☎ *51–59–90–60* ⊕ *www.flybussen.no/stavanger*). **Norwegian** (☎ *815–21–815 in Norway, 21–49–00–15 from outside Norway* ⊕ *www. norwegian.no*). **SAS** (☎ *800/221–2350 in the USA, 91–50–54–00 in Norway* ⊕ *www. flysas.com*). **Widerøe** (☎ *810–01–200 in Norway* ⊕ *www.wideroe.no*).

Boat and Ferry Contact Tide Flaggruten (☎ *51–86–87–80* ⊕ *www.tide.no*).

Bus Contacts Kolumbus (☎ *177* ⊕ *www.kolumbus.no*). **Ruteservice Stavanger, Nor-Way Bussekspress** (☎ *815–44–444* ⊕ *www.nor-way.no*).

Taxis Norgestaxi Stavanger (☎ *08000*). **Rogaland Taxi AS** (☎ *51–90–90–50*). **Stavanger Taxisentral** (☎ *51–90–90–90*).

Train Contacts NSB (*Norwegian State Railways* ☎ *815–00–888* ⊕ *www.nsb.no*).

Stavanger Jernbanestasjon (*Stavanger Train Station* ☎51–56–96–10).

Visitor and Tour Info Destinasjon Stavanger (✉*Rosenkildetorget* ☎51–97–55–55 ⊕*www.regionstavanger.com*). FjordTours (☎815–68–222 ⊕*www.fjordtours.no*). Tide Flaggruten (☎05505 ⊕*www.tide.no*). Rødne Clipper Fjord Sightseeing (☎51–89–52–70 ⊕*www.rodne.no*).

EXPLORING
TOP ATTRACTIONS

★ The fascinating **Norsk Hermetikkmuseum** *(Norwegian Canning Museum)*, part of the Stavanger Museum, is in a former canning factory. From the 1890s to the 1960s, canning fish products like brisling, fish balls, and sardines was Stavanger's main industry. On special activity days the public can take part in the production process, sometimes tasting newly smoked brisling—on the first Sunday of every month and Tuesday and Thursday in summer, the ovens used for smoking fish are stoked up once again. ✉*Øvre Strandgt. 88A* ☎51–84–27–00 or 51–52–65–91 ⊕*www.stavanger.museum.no* ✑*NKr 60* ☉*Mid-June–mid-Aug., daily 11–6; early June and late Aug., Mon.–Thurs. 11–3, Sun. 11–4; Sept.– May, Sun. 11–4 or by appointment.*

☾ Resembling a shiny offshore oil platform, the dynamic **Norsk Oljemuseum**
Fodor'sChoice *(Norwegian Petroleum Museum)* is an absolute must-see. In 1969 oil
★ was discovered off the coast of Norway. The museum explains how oil forms, how it's found and produced, its many uses, and its impact on Norway. Interactive multimedia exhibits accompany original artifacts, models, and films. A reconstructed offshore platform includes oil work- ers' living quarters—as well as the sound of drilling and the smell of oil. The highly recommended museum café, by restaurateurs Bølgen & Moi, serves dinners as well as lighter fare. ✉*Kjeringholmen, Stavanger Havn* ☎51–93–93–00 ⊕*www.norskolje.museum.no* ✑*NKr 80* ☉*Sept.– May, Mon.–Sat. 10–4, Sun. 10–6; June–Aug., daily 10–7.*

Fodor'sChoice The charm of the city's past is on view in **Old Stavanger,** northern
★ Europe's largest and best-preserved wooden house settlement. The 150 houses here were built in the late 1700s and early 1800s. Wind down the narrow cobblestone streets past small white houses and craft shops with many-paned windows and terra-cotta roof tiles.

★ **Preikestolen** *(Pulpit Rock).* A huge cube with a vertical drop of 2,000 feet, the Pulpit Rock is not a good destination if you suffer from ver- tigo—it has a heart-stopping view. The clifflike rock sits on the banks of the finger-shape Lysefjord. You can join a boat tour from Stavanger to see the rock from below, or you can hike two hours to the top on a marked trail. The track goes from Preikestolen Hytta, where there is a big parking lot.

WORTH NOTING
Rogaland Kunstmuseum *(Rogaland Museum of Fine Arts)* has the coun- try's largest collection of works by Lars Hertervig (1830–1902), the greatest Romantic painter of Norwegian landscapes. With Norwegian paintings, drawings, and sculptures, the museum's permanent collec- tion covers the early 19th century to the present. The Halvdan Haftsten

Collection has paintings and drawings done between the world wars. There's also a collection of works by Kitty Kielland. The museum is near Mosvannet (Mos Lake), which is just off highway E18 at the northern end of downtown. ✉ *Henrik Ibsensgt. 55, Mosvannsparken* ☎ *51–53–09–00* ⊕ *www.rkm.no* 🌐 *NKr 50* ⊙ *Tues.–Sun. 11–4.*

Along Strandkaien, warehouses face the wharf; the shops, offices, and apartments face the street on the other side. Housed in the only two shipping merchants' houses that remain completely intact is the **Sjøfartsmuseet** *(Stavanger Maritime Museum),* now part of the Stavanger Museum. Built between 1770 and 1840, the restored buildings trace the past 200 years of trade, sea traffic, and shipbuilding. Visit a turn-of-the-20th-century general store, an early-1900s merchant's apartment, and a sailmaker's loft. A reconstruction of a shipowner's office and a memorial are here, as are two 19th-century ships, *Anna af Sand* and *Wyvern,* moored at the pier. ✉ *Nedre Strandgt. 17–19* ☎ *51–84–27–00 or 51–52–59–11* ⊕ *www.stavanger.museum.no* 🌐 *NKr 50* ⊙ *Early–mid-June and mid-late Aug., Mon.–Thurs. 11–3, Sun. 11–4; mid-June–mid-Aug., daily 11–4; Sept.–Nov. and Jan.–May, Sun. 11–4 or by appointment.*

Legend has it that Bishop Reinald of Winchester ordered the construction of **Stavanger Domkirke** *(Stavanger Cathedral)* in 1125, so that the king could marry his third wife there after his divorce from Queen Malmfrid. The church was built in Anglo-Norman style, probably with the aid of English craftsmen. Patron saint St. Svithun's arm is believed to be among the original relics. Largely destroyed by fire in 1272, the church was rebuilt to include a Gothic chancel. The result: its once elegant lines are now festooned with macabre death symbols and airborne putti. Next to the cathedral is **Kongsgård,** formerly a residence of bishops and kings but now a school and not open to visitors. ✉ *Near Torget* 🎫 *Free* ⊙ *Mid-May–mid-Sept., Mon. and Tues. 11–6, Wed.–Sat. 10–6, Sun. 11–6; mid-Sept.–mid-May, Wed.–Sat. 10–3.*

The site where Norway was founded has been memorialized by the **Sverd i fjell** *(Swords in the Mountain).* The three huge bronze swords were unveiled by King Olav in 1983 and done by artist Fritz Røed. The memorial is dedicated to King Harald Hårfagre (Harald the Fairhaired), who through an 872 battle at Hafrsfjord managed to unite Norway into one kingdom. The Viking swords' sheaths were modeled on ones found throughout the country; the crowns atop the swords represent the different Norwegian districts that took part in the battle. ✉ *Hafrsfjord, on Grannesveien to Sola, 6 km (4 mi) south of Stavanger.*

Utstein Kloster. Originally the palace of Norway's first king, Harald Hårfagre, and later the residence of King Magnus VI, Utstein was used as a monastery from 1265 until 1537, when it reverted to the royal family. Just one bus departs for Utstein from Stavanger weekdays at 9 AM, and it doesn't return from the monastery until 4:05 PM, so it's best to hire a car. By bus or car it's about a half-hour trip to the palace, north of Stavanger on coastal Highway 1, through the world's second-longest undersea car tunnel. If you rent a car to get to Utstein Kloster, you can also take in the medieval ruins nearby on **Åmøy Island** as well as the lighthouse, **Fjøløy Fyr**. Turn left after the tunnel and look for the tourist information sign before the bridge. ☏*51–72–47–05* ⊕*www. utstein-kloster.no.*

As Stavanger grew into an important town in the Middle Ages, watchmen were hired to look out for fires, crime, and anything else out of the ordinary. The **Vektermuseet i Valbergtårnet** *(Watchman's Museum in the Valberg Tower)* examines the role the watchmen played in keeping the town safe. The Valbergtårnet was built in the 1850s to give a panoramic view of the town below. With so many wooden houses, an early warning was essential. The view remains as incredible as ever. ✉*Valbergtårnet* ☏*51–89–55–01* ⌦*NKr 20* ☺*Mon.–Wed. and Fri. 10–4, Thurs. 10–6, Sat. 10–2.*

WHERE TO EAT

Stavanger has established a reputation for culinary excellence. In fact, the city has the distinction of having the most bars and restaurants per capita in Norway. Many restaurant menus burst with sumptuous international dishes. The city is home to the Culinary Institute of Norway and hosts many food and wine festivals every year, including the Gladmat Festival, Garlic Week, Stavanger Wine Festival, and Potato Festival.

\$\$\$\$
ECLECTIC
✕**Craigs Kjøkken & Bar.** Oklahoman Craig Whitson's café-restaurant is a great place for wining as well as dining. Stylish glass cabinets house the collection of more than 600 bottles of wine, with a focus on Italy and the Rhone and Alsace regions of France. The food is seasonal, experimental, and eclectic, its influences ranging from Mediterranean to Asian. Try the Hardanger trout with caviar and pumpkin foam, for example, to get a taste of what can be done with local ingredients. The café hosts annual events such as chili and wine festivals. Whitson's offbeat sense of humor comes through in the "12 disciples" that sit against one wall—a dozen smoked, salted, and dried pigs' heads. ✉*Breitorget* ☏*51–93–95–90* ⊕*www.craig.no* ⊟*AE, DC, MC, V* ☺*No lunch. Closed Sun.*

\$\$–\$\$\$
TEX-MEX
✕**Harry Pepper.** Norway's first Tex-Mex restaurant is still considered one of the country's best. Earth tones, cacti, and tacky souvenirs combine to make the joint lighthearted and playful. Try the sizzling fajitas or the lime-grilled fish kebab served with triple pesto. Have a tequila shot or two at the lively bar. ✉*Øvre Holmegt. 15* ☏*51–89–39–59* ⊕*www.harry-pepper.no* ⊟*AE, DC, V* ☺*No lunch Tues.–Fri. Closed Sun. and Mon.*

\$\$\$–\$\$\$\$
NORWEGIAN
Fodor's Choice
★
✕**N. B. Sørensen's Dampskibsexpedition.** Norwegian emigrants waited here before boarding steamships crossing the Atlantic to North America 150 years ago. Restored in 1990, the historic wharf house is now a popular waterfront restaurant and bar. Emigrants' tickets, weathered wood, nautical ropes, old maps, photographs, and gaslights set the scene. At street level is an informal brasserie where you can get barbecued spareribs. Upstairs is an elegant and more expensive dining room with prix-fixe menus that change weekly, and include such entrées as a delicious grilled entrecôte with garlic, or lamb with eggplant caviar and sherry jus. ✉*Skagen 26* ☏*51–84–38–20* ⊕*www.herlige-restauranter. com* ⊟*AE, DC, MC, V.*

$$$
NORWEGIAN
✕ Sjøhuset Skagen. A sort of museum, this 18th-century former boat-house is filled with wooden beams, ship models, lobster traps, and other sea relics. The Norwegian and international menu has things like baked lime and chili-marinated halibut, bacalao (salt cod), and veal and baked fennel. ⊠ *Skagenkaien 16* ☎ *51–89–51–80* ⊕ *www.sjohusetskagen.no* ⊟ *AE, DC, MC, V.*

$$$$
SEAFOOD
✕ Straen Fiskerestaurant. This esteemed quayside fish restaurant doesn't mince words: it calls itself "world famous throughout Norway." The nostalgic interior filled with memorabilia and the white-clothed tables make the restaurant comforting and homey. If you're traveling with a group, reserve the bookshelf-lined library dining room. Try the famous fish and shellfish soup or the confit of trout (served with pickled cucumber spaghetti and mascarpone sorbet) to start, followed by the grilled monkfish in Madeira sauce, or the turbot in champagne foam. The three-course meal of the day is always the best value. The aquavit bar carries more than 30 varieties. ⊠ *Nedre Strandgt. 15* ☎ *51–84–37–00* ⊕ *www.herlige-restauranter.com* ⊟ *AE, DC, MC, V.* ☺ *Dinner only. Closed Sun.*

$$$$
ECLECTIC
✕ Timbuktu Bar and Restaurant. This is one of the Stavanger's trendiest restaurants. Within its airy interior of blond wood and yellow and black accessories, enthusiastic chefs serve Asian-inspired cuisine with African ingredients such as tuna fish from Madagascar. Known for its sushi and tapas-style dishes, the restaurant often has visiting celebrity chefs and hosts special events such as salsa parties. ⊠ *Nedre Strandgt. 15* ☎ *51–84–37–40* ⊕ *www.herlige-restauranter.com* ⊟ *AE, DC, MC, V.* ☺ *Dinner only. Closed Sun.*

$$$
NORWEGIAN
✕ Vertshuset Mat & Vin. The style of this restaurant matches the traditional Norwegian dishes served up by the kitchen. Amid wood walls, white lace curtains, and traditional paintings, you can enjoy popular dishes such as *lutefisk* and *pinnekjøtt* (in season), monkfish with pepper, and *komler* (dumplings) with salted meats. Also worth a taste are the lasagna or omelets. ⊠ *Skagen 10* ☎ *51–89–51–12* ⊟ *AE, MC, V.*

WHERE TO STAY

$$$–$$$$
▦ Clarion Hotel Stavanger. This downtown business hotel has an up-to-the-minute design. Famed local artist Kjell Pahr Iversen's vibrant paintings hang on the hotel's walls. The light, simple interior is punctuated by the clean lines of Philippe Starck lamps and Erik Jørgensen chairs. The rooms are also bright and simply furnished. **Pros:** comfortable rooms; the Relax center on the top floor; 24-hour room service. **Cons:** left-luggage room not secure (although theft is rarely a problem in Norway); the hotel gets fully booked, so reserve a room well in advance. ⊠ *Ny Olavskleiv 8* ☎ *51–50–25–00* ⊕ *www.clarionstavanger.no* ⇌ *250 rooms, 23 suites* ♿ *In-room: Internet. In-hotel: 2 restaurants, bar, gym* ⊟ *AE, DC, MC, V* ⫶⊙⫶ *BP.*

$$$
▦ Radisson SAS Atlantic Hotel Stavanger. In the heart of downtown, the Atlantic—Stavanger's largest hotel—overlooks Breiavatnet pond. All rooms are elegantly decorated in understated yellows, beiges, and reds, with plush furniture. The King Oscar lobby bar, Alexander Pub, and Café Ajax are popular with Stavanger's residents. **Pros:** generous size rooms; the sauna with great views over the city; huge buffet breakfast. **Cons:**

the staff could do better. ⊠*Olav Vs gt. 3* 🕾*51–76–10–00* ⊕*www. atlantic.stavanger.radissonsas.com* ⟿*350 rooms, 6 suites* ⚹*In-room: Internet. In-hotel: restaurant, bars* ☰*AE, DC, MC, V* ⦿❘*BP.*

$$–$$$ 🔅**Skagen Brygge Hotell.** A symbol of Stavanger, this classic hotel's white
★ wooden wharf houses are common subjects for city postcards and photographs. It has a well-deserved reputation for superb service. The blue-
accented, wood-beam rooms tend to have somewhat irregular shapes,
and only half the rooms face the harbor (the other half face the street).
On weekends Hovmesteren Bar is a popular nightspot. **Pros:** central
location; good views of the harbor if you're in a harborside room; professional service; Turkish baths. **Cons:** old-fashioned "request" booking online; no restaurant. ⊠*Skagenkaien 30* 🕾*51–85–00–00* ⊕*www.
skagenbryggehotell.no* ⟿*110 rooms, 2 suites* ⚹*In-room: Internet.
In-hotel: bar* ☰*AE, DC, MC, V* ⦿❘*BP.*

$$$ 🔅**Victoria Hotel.** Stavanger's oldest hotel was built at the turn of the
20th century and retains a clubby Victorian style, with elegant carved
furniture and floral patterns. Ask for a room overlooking the harbor.
Stavanger's museums, Gamle Stavanger, and shopping hot spots are all
within short walking distances. **Pros:** great location; stylish restaurant;
good breakfast. **Cons:** single rooms are small and in need of refurbish-
ment. ⊠*Skansegt. 1* 🕾*51–86–70–00* ⊕*www.victoria-hotel.no* ⟿*107
rooms, 3 suites* ⚹*In-hotel: restaurant, bar* ☰*AE, DC, MC, V* ⦿❘*BP.*

AFTER DARK

CAFÉS

Stavanger has its share of cozy and hip locations to have a drink,
read the papers, listen to live music, or just hang out. **Amys Coffeebar**
(⊠*Salvågergt. 7* 🕾*51–86–07–65* ⊕*www.amys.no*) is a sweet little spot
for an afternoon coffee or takeaway lunch. At **Café Italia** (⊠*Skagen 8*
🕾*51–85–92–90*), there's an Italian coffee bar, a restaurant, and even
a boutique selling Italy's top fashion names. **Café Sting** (⊠*Valberget
3* 🕾*51–89–38–78* ⊕*www.cafe-sting.no*), a combination restaurant,
nightclub, art gallery, and performance venue, is an institution.

News junkies head to Norway's first news café, **Newsman** (⊠*Skagen 14*
🕾*51–84–38–80*), for CNN on the TV and for Norwegian and foreign
periodicals. For a quick snack or a glass of freshly squeezed fruit juice,
stop by **Sitrus Sandwichbar** (⊠*Bakkegt. 7, entrance from Salvågergt.*
🕾*51–89–15–90*); the smoothies are delicious.

CLUBS AND PUBS

Stavanger clubs and pubs can show you a good time year-round. Walk
along Skagenkaien and Strandkaien streets for a choice of pubs and
nightclubs. In summer, harborside places with patios don't usually close
until dawn. **Checkpoint Charlie** (⊠*Nedre Strandgt. 5* 🕾*51–53–22–45*
⊕*www.checkpoint.no*) is popular with the twentysomethings, and
sometimes doubles as a concert venue.

College kids hang out at **Folken** (⊠*Ny Olavskleiv 16* 🕾*51–56–44–44*
⊕*www.folken.no*), an independent student club that frequently
holds rock concerts. Sun-kissed **Hansen Hjørnet** (⊠*Skagenkaien 18*

☎*51–89–52–80* ☯*Mid-May–mid-Sept.*) is a bar and restaurant that always attracts a crowd.

With its open fireplace and stone walls, **Nåloyet** (✉*Nedre Strandgt. 13* ☎*51–84–37–60*) is Stavanger's answer to the London pub. Dance the night away to pulsating sounds at the lively **Taket Nattklubb** (✉*Nedre Strandgt. 15* ☎*51–84–37–20*), popular with those in their twenties and thirties.

SPORTS AND THE OUTDOORS
FISHING
Angling for saltwater fish doesn't require a license or a fee of any kind. The local tourist office can help you get the permits required for other types of fishing.

North of Stavanger is the longest salmon river in western Norway, the Suldalslågen, made popular 100 years ago by a Scottish aristocrat who built a fishing lodge there. **Lakseslottet Lindum** (✉*Suldalsosen* ☎*52–79–91–61* ⊕*www.lakseslottet.no*) still has rooms, cabins, and camping facilities, as well as an upscale restaurant. The main salmon season is July through September.

Wear diving gear and you can go on a **Salmon Safari** (✉*Mo Laksegard, Sand* ☎*52–79–76–90* ⊕*www.molaks.no*), floating in the river 2 km (1 mi) to study wild salmon in their natural environment. On the island of Kvitsøy, in the archipelago just west of Stavanger, you can rent a converted fisherman's cabin, *rorbu,* complete with fish-smoking and -freezing facilities, and arrange to use a small sailboat or motorboat. **Kvitsøy Kurs & Konferanse** (*Kvitsøy* ☎*51–73–51–88* ⊕*www.kvitsoy-maritim. no*) can help with arrangements.

HIKING
Specialized books and maps are available through **Stavanger Turistforening** (✑*Postboks 239, 4001* ☎*51–84–02–00* ⊕*www.stavanger-turistforening.no*). The office can help you plan a hike through the area, particularly in the rolling Setesdalsheiene and the thousands of islands and skerries of the Ryfylke Archipelago. The tourist board oversees 33 cabins for members (you can join on the spot) for overnighting along the way.

HORSEBACK RIDING
Fossanmoen (✉*Forsand* ☎*51–70–37–61* ⊕*www.fossanmoen.no*) organizes riding camps and trips on Iceland ponies that go through scenic surroundings. They can last anywhere from an hour to all day.

ICE-SKATING
From November through March you can skate outdoors at **Kunstisbanen** (✉*Sørmarkvn. 18, Sørmarka* ☎*51–58–06–44*). **Stavanger Ishall** (✉*Siddishallen, Madlavn. 180* ☎*51–53–74–50* ⊕*www.stavanger-ishall.no*) has ice-skating from mid-September to mid-April.

SKIING
Skiing in the Sirdal area, 2½ hours from Stavanger, is possible from January to April. Special ski buses leave Stavanger on weekends at 8:30 AM

during the season. Especially recommended is **Sinnes** (☎38–37–12–02) for its non-hair-raising cross-country terrain. Downhill skiing is available at **Ålsheia,** which is on the same bus route. Other places to ski include **Gullingen skisenter, Suldal** (☎52–79–99–01), **Sauda skisenter, Sauda** (☎52–78–56–56 ⊕*www.saudaskisenter.no*), and **Stavtjørn alpinsenter** (☎51–45–17–17). Contact **Kolumbus** (☎177 ⊕*www.kolumbus. no*) for transportation information.

WATER SPORTS

Diving is excellent all along the coast—although Norwegian law requires all foreigners to dive with a certified Norwegian diver as a way of ensuring that wrecks are left undisturbed. If you just want to take a swim, plan a trip to local beaches such as Møllebukta and Madia, which are both deep inside the Hafrsfjord. **Solastranden** in Sola, has 2 km (1½ mi) of sandy beach ideal for windsurfing and beach volleyball. Other prime beach spots are Vaulen badeplass, Godalen badeplass, Viste Stranden, and Sande Stranden. The World Tour Beach Volleyball tournament is held downtown on a temporary beach volleyball court at the end of June. The local swimming pool is **Stavanger Svømmehall** (✉*Lars Hertervigsgt. 4* ☎51–50–74–51). **Gamlingen Friluftsbad** (✉*Tjodolfsgt. 53* ☎51–52–74–49) is an outdoor heated swimming pool that's open year-round.

SHOPPING

Kvadrat (✉*Gamle Stokkavei 1, Forus between Stavanger and Sandnes off the E39* ☎51–96–00–00 ⊕*www.kvadrat.no*) is Norway's biggest shopping center, with 160 shops, restaurants, a pharmacy, a post office, a state wine store, a big playground and a tourist office. In town **Stavanger Storsenter Steen & Strøm** (✉*Klubbgt. 5* ☎51–93–80–00) is a centrally located shopping center.

The area north of the cathedral has several pedestrianized streets with all the usual high street names and a few independent shops. But for something different, head for hip Øvre Holmegate, Stavanger's most colorful street. It's full of small boutiques selling original items, from fashion to books. **Syvende Himmel** (✉*Øvre Holmegate 21* ☎51–01–29–61) specializes in retro and alternative clothes and accessories in bright colors and funky designs. **Sjokoladepiken** (✉*Øvre Holmegate 27*) has handmade chocolates from all over the world. **Bøker & Børst** (✉*Øvre Holmegate 32* ☎51–86–04–76) is an independent bookshop/café with funky artwork on the walls, and a cozy garden at the back.

In an early-17th-century wharf house, **Straen Handel** (✉*Strandkaien 31* ☎51–52–52–02) has an impressive collection of knitted items, rosemaling, Norwegian dolls, trolls, books, and postcards. If jewelry's your passion, head to the city's best shop: **Sølvsmeden på Sølvberget** (✉*Sølvberggt. 5* ☎51–89–42–24).

BERGEN

Many fall in love with Bergen, Norway's second-largest city, at first sight. Seven rounded lush mountains, pastel-color wooden houses, historic Bryggen, winding cobblestone streets, and Hanseatic relics all make it a place of enchantment. Its many epithets include "Trebyen" (Wooden City; it has many wooden houses), "Regnbyen" (Rainy City, due to its 200 days of rain a year), and "Fjordbyen" (gateway to the fjords). Surrounded by forested mountains and fjords, it's only natural that most Bergensers feel at home either on the mountains (skiing, hiking, walking, or at their cabins) or at sea (fishing and boating). As for the rainy weather, most visitors quickly learn the necessity of rain jackets and umbrellas. Bergen is even the site of the world's first umbrella vending machine.

Residents take legendary pride in their city and its luminaries. The composer Edvard Grieg, the violinist Ole Bull, and Ludvig Holberg, Scandinavia's answer to Molière, all made great contributions to Norwegian culture. Today their legacy lives on in nationally acclaimed theater, music, film, dance, and art. The singer Sondre Lerche, pianist Leif Ove Andsnes, choreographer Jo Strømgren, and author Gunnar Staalesen all live in Bergen. Every year a host of lively festivals attracts national and international artists.

This harbor city has played a vital role in the Norwegian economy. Before the discovery of North Sea oil and Bergen's subsequent role in the development of Norway's oil industry, the city was long a major center of fishing and shipping. In fact, Bergen was founded in 1070 by Olav Kyrre as a commercial center. In the 14th century, Hanseatic merchants settled in Bergen and made it one of their four major overseas trading centers. The surviving Hanseatic wooden buildings on Bryggen (the quay) are topped with triangular cookie-cutter roofs and painted in red, blue, yellow, and green. Monuments in themselves (they are on the UNESCO World Heritage List), the buildings tempt travelers and locals to the shops, restaurants, and museums inside. In the evening, when the Bryggen is illuminated, these modest buildings, together with the stocky Rosenkrantz Tower, the Fløyen, and the yachts lining the pier, are reflected in the waters of the harbor—and provide one of the loveliest cityscapes in northern Europe.

GETTING HERE AND AROUND

AIR TRAVEL SAS, Norwegian, Widerøe and Sterling are the major airlines flying into Bergen. Flesland Airport is a 30-minute bus ride south of the center of Bergen at off-peak hours. The Flybussen (Airport Bus) departs every 15 minutes (less frequently on weekends) from the SAS Royal Hotel, the Radisson SAS Hotel Norge, and the bus station; it will run you about NKr 80. A taxi stand is outside the Arrivals exit. The trip into the city costs about NKr 250–NKr 300. Driving from Flesland to Bergen is simple, and the road is well marked. Bergen has an electronic toll ring surrounding it, so any vehicle entering the city weekdays between 6 AM and 10 PM has to pay NKr 15. There is no toll in the other direction.

BOAT AND FERRY TRAVEL Boats have always been Bergen's lifeline to the world. Fjord Line serves North Norway, Stavanger and Haugesund, and Hardangerfjord and Sunnhordland. There's also service to Sognefjord, Nordfjord, and Sunnfjord. The Smyril Line also has service between Bergen and Scotland, and the Flaggruten, operated by Tide, links Bergen and Stavanger.

Hurtigruten (the Coastal Steamer) departs daily from Frielenes Quay, Dock H, for the 11-day round-trip to Kirkenes in the far north. HSD express boats (to Hardangerfjord, Sunnhordland, Stavanger, and Haugesund) and Fylkesbaatane express boats (to Sognefjord, Nordfjord, and Sunnfjord) depart from Strandkai Terminalen. International ferries depart from Skoltegrunnskaien.

BUS TRAVEL Nor-Way Bussekspress operates several services between Oslo and Bergen in each direction daily. The journey takes 10–11 hours. Buses also connect Bergen with Trondheim and Ålesund. Western Norway is served by several bus companies, which use the station at Strømgt. 8.

Tide is the main bus operator in Bergen, with buses throughout the day and at night on weekends (Friday and Saturday until 4 AM).

CAR TRAVEL Bergen is 478 km (290 mi) from Oslo. Route 7 is good most of the way, at least until the ferry crossing at Hardangerfjord. The ferry, from Brimnes to Bruravik, runs from 5 AM to midnight and takes 10 minutes. From Granvin, 12 km (7 mi) farther north, to Bergen, Route 7 hugs the fjord part of the way, making for spectacular scenery, but the quality of the road deteriorates considerably. A quicker but less scenic drive is to follow Route 13 from Granvin to Voss, and take E16, an alternative route to Oslo, from Voss to Bergen. Be aware that there are lots of tunnels on that road. In winter, several mountain passes are prone to closing at short notice. The Public Roads Administration's road information line can give you the status of most roads.

Driving from Stavanger to Bergen involves two to four ferries and a long journey packed with stunning scenery. The Stavanger tourist information office can help plan the trip and reserve ferry space.

Downtown Bergen is enclosed by an inner ring road. The area within is divided into three zones, which are separated by ONE WAY and DO NOT ENTER signs. To get from one zone to another, return to the ring road and drive to an entry point for the desired zone. It's best to leave your car at a parking garage (the cheapest and most accessible is the ByGarasjen near the train station) and walk. You pay a NKr 15 toll every time you drive into the city—but driving out is free.

TAXI TRAVEL Taxi stands are in strategic locations downtown. Taxis are dispatched by the Bergen Taxi central office and can be booked in advance. Bergen Taxi runs the largest and most reliable service.

TRAIN TRAVEL The Bergensbanen has several departures daily in both directions on the Oslo–Bergen route; it's widely acknowledged to be one of the most beautiful train rides in the world. Trains leave from Oslo S Station for the 7½- to 8½-hour journey.

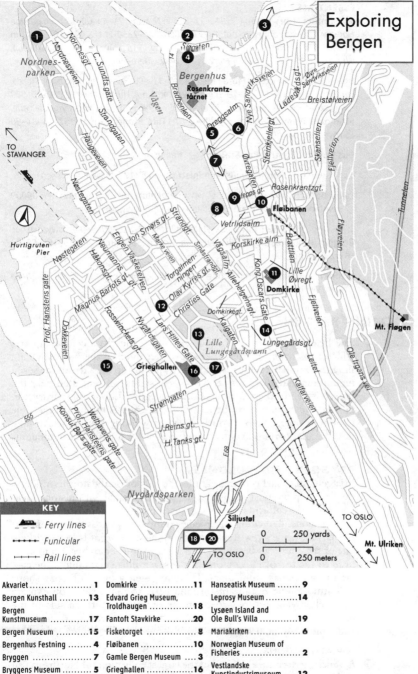

Exploring Bergen

KEY
- 🛥 *Ferry lines*
- •••• *Funicular*
- ┼┼┼ *Rail lines*

ESSENTIALS

Air Contacts Norwegian (☎ *815–21–815 in Norway, 21–49–00–15 from outside Norway* ⊕ *www.norwegian.no*). **SAS** (☎ *800/221–2350 in U.S., 91–50–54–00 in Norway* ⊕ *www.flysas.com*). **Sterling** (☎ *815–58–810* ⊕ *www.sterlingticket.com*). **Widerøe** (☎ *810–01–200 in Norway* ⊕ *www.wideroe.no*).

Boat and Ferry Contacts Fjord Line (☎ *815–33–500* ⊕ *www.fjordline.com*). **Fjord1 Fylkesbaatane** (☎ *57–75–70–00* ⊕ *www.fjord1.no*). *Hurtigruten* (☎ *810–30–000* ⊕ *www.hurtigruten.com*). **Smyril Line** (☎ *55–59–65–20* ⊕ *www.smyril-line.com*). **Strandkai Terminalen** (☎ *55–90–70–70*).**Tide Flaggruten** (☎ *51–86–87–80* ⊕ *www.tide.no*).

Bus Contact Central Bus Station (⊠ *Strømgt. 8* ☎ *177*).

Car Travel Info Public Roads Administration (☎ *175* ⊕ *www.vegvesen.no*).

Taxis Bergen Taxi (☎ *07000* ⊕ *www.bergentaxi.no*). **Norgestaxi** (☎ *08000* ⊕ *www.norgestaxi.no*). **Taxi1** (☎ *55–50–00–37* ⊕ *www.taxi1.no*).

Train Contacts NSB (*Norwegian State Railways* ☎ *815–00–888* ⊕ *www.nsb.no*). **Bergen Jernbanestasjon** (*Bergen Train Station* ⊠ *Strømgt. 4* ☎ *55–96–69–00* ⊕ *www.nsb.no*).

Visitor Info Bergen Tourist Office (⊠ *Vågsallmenningen 15014* ☎ *55–55–20–00* ⊕ *www.visitbergen.com*).

EXPLORING BERGEN

The heart of Bergen is Torgallmenningen, the city's central square, which runs from Ole Bulls plass to Fisketorget on the harbor, facing Bryggen. From here, the rest of Bergen spreads up the sides of the seven mountains that surround it, with some sights concentrated near the university and others near a small lake called Lille Lungegårdsvann. Fløyen, the mountain to the east of the harbor, is the most accessible for day-trippers. Before you begin your walking tour, you can take the funicular (cable car) up to the top of it for a particularly fabulous overview of the city.

BRYGGEN AND NORDNES

Bryggen, the wharf running right by the harbor on the northern side, is the first stop on most tourists' itinerary and loaded with history. Here you'll find the colorful wooden Hanseatic merchant houses that gave the area its name. Bergenhus, the medieval fortress, guards the entrance to the harbor, while a few steps back from the waterfront is Mariakirken, one of the country's best preserved Romanesque churches. From here, head to the top of Fløyen, one of the seven hills surrounding the city, via the Fløibanen (funicular). There are plenty of small, cozy shops and atmospheric restaurants around here, so make sure you explore the back streets too. Nordnes, on the opposite, southern side of the harbor, is mainly a residential area but features a great aquarium that's walkable from the fish market.

TOP ATTRACTIONS

 Akvariet. Here you will see one of the largest collections of North Sea fish and invertebrates in Europe, as well as tropical saltwater and freshwater fish. The aquarium has 60 tanks and two outdoor pools with seals, and penguins. Visit at feeding time, when the seals show off the skills they've learned both in and out of the water. Tanks inside are filled with schools of colorful tropical fish as well as Norwegian salmon and common eels, which tend to wrap around each other. There is also a section with alligators from different parts of the world on display. *The Aquarium: Bergen and the Local Coastline*—a 360-degree video directed by one of Norway's most beloved animators, the late Ivo Caprino—is shown every hour, as is *SOS Planet*, a 3-D film that you watch with special glasses. The aquarium is on Nordnes Peninsula, a 20-minute walk from the fish market. You can also get to it

THRIFTY SIGHTSEEING

The 24-hour **Bergen Card,** which costs NKr 190 (NKr 250 for 48 hours), gives free or discounted admission to most museums and attractions in Bergen; unlimited bus travel in central Bergen; parking at public meters and outdoor automatic ticket machines; unlimited funicular rides; and discounts in selected restaurants, and on car rentals, concerts, theater, and selected souvenirs. The card is available at the tourist office and in most hotels. The **Fjord Pass** (☎ *55-55-76-60* ⊕ *www.fjord pass.no*) gives considerable discounts on hotel rooms, and can be purchased at the railway station.

4

by taking Bus 11 or the ferry from the fish market. ⊠ *Nordnesbakken 4, Nordnes* ☎ *55-55-71-71* ⊕ *www.akvariet.com* ⬚ *NKr 150, NKr 100 in winter* ⊙ *May–Aug., daily 9–7; Sept.–Apr., daily 10–6. Feeding times: May–Aug., daily noon, 3, and 6; Sept.–Apr., daily noon and 3.*

❹ **Bergenhus Festning** *(Bergenhus Fortress).* The buildings here date from the mid-13th century. **Håkonshallen,** a royal ceremonial hall erected during the reign of Håkon Håkonsson between 1247 and 1261, was badly damaged by the explosion of a German ammunition ship in 1944, but was restored by 1961. Erected in the 1560s by the governor of Bergen Castle (Bergenhus), Erik Rosenkrantz, **Rosenkrantztårnet** *(Rosenkrantz Tower)* served as a combined residence and fortified tower. ⊠ *Bergenhus, Bryggen* ☎ *55-58-80-10* ⊕ *www.bymuseet.no* ⬚ *NKr 40 each* ⊙ *Mid-May–Aug., daily 10–4; Sept.–mid-May, Sun. noon–3. Closed during Bergen International Music Festival.*

❼ **Bryggen** *(The Wharf).* A trip to Bergen is incomplete without a trip to Bryggen. A row of mostly reconstructed 14th-century wooden buildings that face the harbor makes this one of the most charming walkways in Europe, especially on a sunny day. The originals were built by Hansa merchants, while the oldest reconstruction dates from 1702. Several fires, the latest in 1955, destroyed the original structures. Today the old merchant homes house various boutiques and restaurants. Bryggen has been a UNESCO World Heritage Site since 1979.

Fodor'sChoice ★

❽ **Fisketorget** *(Fish Market).* Turn-of-the-20th-century photographs of this pungent square show fishermen in Wellington boots and raincoats and women in long aprons. Now the fishmongers wear bright-orange rubber overalls as they look over the catches of the day. In summer the selection is mostly limited to shrimp, salmon, and monkfish. There is much greater variety and more locals shop here the rest of the year. There are also fruit, vegetable, and flower stalls, and some handicrafts and souvenir vendors at this lively market. You'll also find the world's first umbrella vending machine. Have a classic lunch of smoked shrimp or salmon on a baguette with mayonnaise and cucumber. ⊠ *Zacharias-bryggen, Bryggen* ☎ *55–31–56–17* ⊕ *www.torgetibergen.no* ☉ *June–Aug., daily 7–7; Sept.–May, Mon.–Sat. 7–4.*

🔟 **Fløibanen** *(Fløyen Funicular).* A magnificent view of Bergen and its sub-
★ urbs can be taken in from the top of **Mt. Fløyen,** the most popular of the city's seven mountains. The eight-minute ride on the funicular takes you to the top, 320 m (1,050 feet) above the sea. A car departs every half hour. Take a break at the restaurant and café (open daily in summer and weekends the rest of the year), the gift shop, or the children's play-ground. Stroll down the walking path back to downtown or explore the mountains that lead to Ulriken, the highest of the mountains surround-ing Bergen. ⊠ *Vetrlidsalmenning 21, Bryggen* ☎ *55–33–68–00* ⊕ *www.floibanen.no* ☉ *Sept.–Apr., Mon.–Sat. 8* AM*–11* PM*, Sun. 9* AM*–11* PM*; May–Aug., same start times, runs until midnight.*

WORTH NOTING

5️⃣ **Bryggens Museum.** This museum contains archaeological finds from the Middle Ages. An exhibit on Bergen circa 1300 shows the town at the zenith of its importance, and has reconstructed living quarters as well as artifacts such as old tools and shoes. Back then, Bergen was the largest town in Norway, a cosmopolitan trading center and the national capi-tal. ⊠ *Dreggsalmenning 3, Bryggen* ☎ *55–58–80–10* ⊕ *www.bymuseet.no* 🔳 *NKr 50* ☉ *Mid-May–Aug., daily 10–5; Sept.–mid-May, week-days 11–3, Sat. noon–3, Sun. noon–4.*

1️⃣1️⃣ **Domkirke** *(Bergen Cathedral).* The cathedral's long, turbulent history has shaped the eclectic architecture of the current structure. The Gothic-style choir and the lower towers are the oldest, dating from the 13th century. Note the cannonball lodged in the tower wall—it dates from a battle between English and Dutch ships in Bergen harbor in 1665. From June through August, a Sunday service is held in English at 9:30 AM in the Chapter House, an organ recital is held Thursday at noon, and there is a concert in the church every Sunday at 7:30 PM. September through May the Sunday concerts are held at 6 PM. ⊠ *Kong Oscars gt. and Domkirke gt., Bryggen* ☎ *55–59–32–70* ☉ *June–Aug., Mon.–Sat. 11–4; Sept.–May, Tues.–Fri. 11–12:30.*

9️⃣ **Hanseatisk Museum.** One of the best-preserved buildings in Bergen, the
★ Hanseatic Museum was the 16th-century office and home of an afflu-ent German merchant. The apprentices lived upstairs, in boxed-in beds with windows cut into the wall. Although claustrophobic, the snug rooms had the benefit of being relatively warm—a blessing in the unheated building. ⊠ *Finnegårdsgaten 1A, Bryggen* ☎ *55–54–46–90* ⊕ *www.museumvest.no* 🔳 *NKr 50, off-season NKr 30* ☉ *Mid-May–mid-Sept., daily 9–5; mid-Sept.–mid-May, Tues.–Sat. 11–2, Sun. 11–4, closed Mon.*

⑥ Mariakirken *(St. Mary's Church).*
Fodor's Choice Considered one of the most out-
★ standing Romanesque churches in
Norway, this is the oldest building
in Bergen used for its original pur-
pose. It began as a church in the
12th century but gained a Gothic
choir, richly decorated portals, and
a splendid baroque pulpit, much
of it added by the Hanseatic merchants who owned it from 1408 to
1766. See the gilded triptych at the
high altar that dates from the late Middle Ages. Organ recitals are held
every Tuesday at 7:30 PM from late June through August. ✉*Dreggen,
Bryggen* ☎*55–59–32–70* ✆*NKr 20, late June–Aug. only* ☉*Late June–
Aug., weekdays 9–11 and 1–4; Sept.–early June, Tues.–Fri. 11–12:30.*

**EN ROUTE TO THE
AQUARIUM**

If you're looking to spend a little
extra time in Nordenes, you can
stop at Nykirken (the new church)
on the way, or go for a swim at
the Nordnes open-air sea water
baths just behind the aquarium if
the weather permits.

4

② Norwegian Museum of Fisheries. The sea and its resources, territorial
waters, management and research, boats and equipment, whaling and
sealing, and fish farming are all covered in the exhibits here. There
are also substantial book, video, and photography collections. ✉*Bon-
telabo 2, Bryggen* ☎*55–32–27–10* ⊕*www.museumvest.no* ✆*NKr 30*
☉*June–Aug., weekdays 10–6, weekends noon–4; Sept.–May, weekdays
and Sun. 11–4. Closed Sat.*

DOWNTOWN: RASMUS MEYERS ALLÉ AND GRIEGHALLEN

This is the Downtown area, where most of the main museums, stores,
hotels and restaurants are concentrated. Peaceful Byparken is a popular place for a stroll in summer, or for a spot of sunbathing in between
two gallery visits. The Norwegian Theater is located at the end of Ole
Bulls plass, a tree-lined avenue with many cafés and restaurants—the
place to be in the evening.

TOP ATTRACTIONS

⑰ Bergen Kunstmuseum *(Bergen Art Museum).* An important Bergen insti-
Fodor's Choice tution and one of the largest museums in Norway, the Bergen Art
★ Museum is housed in buildings along the Lille Lungegårdsvann lake.
The museum divides into three separate collections, each housed in a
different building. The large, neoclassical **Lysverket** building, farthest
south, used to house the municipal power company, but was bought by
the city council and reopened as an art museum in 2003. The permanent
exhibit showcases both medieval icons and Dutch Renaissance masters.
The **Stenersen Collection,** found in the northernmost museum building,
is an extremely impressive collection of modern art for a town the size
of Bergen. Modern artists represented include Max Ernst, Paul Klee,
Vassily Kandinsky, Pablo Picasso, and Joan Miró, as well as Edvard
Munch. There's also a large focus here on Norwegian art since the
mid-18th century. The star of the complex, though, is undoubtedly the
middle building that houses the **Rasmus Meyer Collection.** When the businessman Rasmus Meyer (1858–1916) was assembling his superb collection of works by what would become world-famous artists, most of

them were unknowns. On display are the best Edvard Munch paintings outside Oslo, as well as major works by J. C. Dahl, Adolph Tidemand, Hans Gude, Harriet Backer, and Per Krogh. Head to the Blumenthal Room to see a fine 18th-century interior and some incredible frescoes. The NKR 50 ticket gets you into all three collections all day; feel free to break for a picnic lunch outside when you get peckish, then head back in for more. ⊠ *Bergen Art Museum, Rasmus Meyers Allé 3 and 7, Lars Hilles gt. 10, Downtown* ☎ *55–56–80–00* ⊕ *www.bergenartmuseum. no* ⊠ *NKr 50* ⊙ *Daily 11–5.*

WORTH NOTING

⓭ Bergen Kunsthall *(Bergen Contemporary Art Center).* Nestled snuggly between its more established cousins, this small museum focuses solely on contemporary art, usually Norwegian. It features two art galleries and a café, **Landmark,** which is popular among local art students and sometimes also doubles as an extra showroom, theater, or concert hall. ⊠ *Rasmus Meyers Allé 5, Downtown* ☎ *55–55–93–10* ⊕ *www. kunsthall.no* ⊠ *NKr 40, NKr 50 during special events* ⊙ *Tues.–Sun. noon–5.*

⓯ Bergen Museum. Part of the University of Bergen, this museum has two collections. The **Cultural History Department** has a fascinating collection of archaeological artifacts and furniture and folk art from western Norway. Some of the titles of the displays are "Viking Norway," "Roses and Legends in Norwegian Folk Art," and "Ibsen in Bergen"; the latter focuses on the famous playwright's six years in Bergen working with the local theater. The **Natural History Department** is perfect for lovers of the outdoors, since it includes botanical gardens. Exhibits with special focus on Norway include "The Ice Age," "Whales," (Northern Europe's largest collection) and "Hordaland" (Bergen's region) ⊠ *Haakon Sheteligs pl. 10 and Musépl. 3, Downtown* ☎ *55–58–31–40 or 55–58–29–49* ⊕ *www.bergenmuseum.uib.no* ⊠ *NKr 40, valid for both museums on same day* ⊙ *June–Aug., Tues.–Fri. 10–4, weekends 11–4; Sept.–May, Tues.–Fri. 10–3, weekends 11–4.*

⓷ Gamle Bergen Museum *(Old Bergen Museum).* This family-friendly open-air museum transports you to 18th- and 19th-century Bergen. Streets and narrow alleys with 40 period wooden houses show town life as it used to be. A baker, dentist, photographer, jeweler, shopkeeper, and sailor are represented. Local artists often hold exhibitions here. The grounds and park are open free of charge year-round. ⊠ *Nyhavnsveien 4, Sandviken* ☎ *55–39–43–00* ⊕ *www.bymuseet.no* ⊠ *NKr 50* ⊙ *Early May–Sept., daily 9–5; guided tours every hr 10–4.*

⓰ Grieghallen. Home of the Bergen Philharmonic Orchestra and stage for the annual International Festival, this music hall is a conspicuous slab of glass and concrete. The acoustics are marvelous. Built in 1978, the hall was named for the city's famous son, composer Edvard Grieg (1843–1907). From September to May, every Thursday and some Fridays and Saturdays at 7:30 PM, the orchestra gives concerts. Throughout the year, the hall is a popular venue for cultural events. ⊠ *Edvard Griegs pl. 1, Downtown* ☎ *55–21–61–00* ⊕ *www.grieghallen.no.*

⑭ Leprosy Museum. St. George's Hospital houses the Bergen Collection of the History of Medicine, which includes this museum. Although the current buildings date from the early 1700s, St. George's was a hospital for lepers for more than 500 years. This unusual museum profiles Norway's contribution to leprosy research. Many Norwegian doctors have been recognized for their efforts against leprosy, particularly Armauer Hansen, after whom "Hansen's disease" is named. ⊠ *St. George's Hospital, Kong Oscars gt. 59, Downtown* ☎ *55–96–11–55* ⊕ *www.bymuseet.no* ▧ *NKr 40* ⊙ *Mid-May–Aug., daily 11–4. Open Sun. in Sept.*

⑫ Vestlandske Kunstindustrimuseum *(West Norway Museum of Decorative Art).* This eclectic collection contains many exquisite art and design pieces. Its permanent "People and Possessions" exhibit spans 500 years and has everything from Bergen silverware to Ole Bull's violin, which was made in 1562 by the Italian master Saló. A fine collection traces the history of chair design. "The Art of China," the other permanent exhibition, presents one of Europe's largest collections of Buddhist marble sculptures alongside porcelain, jade, bronzes, textiles, and paintings. The silk robes embroidered with dragons and other ceremonial garments are stunning. Changing exhibitions focus on painting, decorative art, and design. ⊠ *Nordahl Bruns gt. 9, Downtown* ☎ *55–33–66–33* ⊕ *www.vk.museum.no* ▧ *NKr 50* ⊙ *Mid-May–mid-Sept., daily 11–5; mid-Sept.–mid-May, Tues.–Sun. noon–4.*

TROLDHAUGEN, FANTOFT, LYSØEN, AND ULRIKEN

Once you've gotten your fill of Bergen's city life, you can head out to the countryside to tour some of the area's lesser-known yet still interesting attractions. Music aficionados come from far and wide to see the homes of Edvard Grieg, Norway's foremost composer, and that of legendary violinist Ole Bull. The Fantoft Stave Church is also worth a visit if you're interested in architecture and/or the Middle Ages.

TOP ATTRACTIONS

⑱ Edvard Grieg Museum, Troldhaugen *(Hill of the Trolls).* Built in 1885, this was the home of Norway's most famous composer, Edvard Grieg. In the little garden hut by the shore of Lake Nordås, he composed many of his best-known works. In 1867 he married his cousin Nina, a Danish soprano. They lived in the white clapboard house with green gingerbread trim for 22 years beginning in about 1885. A salon and gathering place for many Scandinavian artists then, it now houses mementos—a piano, paintings, prints—of the composer's life. Its 1907 interior shows it the way that Grieg knew it. At Troldsalen, a concert hall seating 200, chamber music is performed. Summer concerts are held on Wednesday and weekends, and daily during the Bergen International Festival. Troldhaugen is located in Hop, 8 km (5 mi) south of Bergen. To get here, catch a bus from Platform 19, 20, or 21 at the bus station, and get off at Hopsbroen. Turn right, walk 200 yards, turn left on Troldhaugsveien, and follow the signs for roughly 2 km (1 mi). ⊠ *Troldhaugv. 65, Bergen Environs* ☎ *55–92–29–92* ⊕ *www.troldhaugen.com* ▧ *NKr 60* ⊙ *May–Sept., daily 9–6; Oct., Nov., and Apr., weekdays 10–2, weekends noon–6; mid-Jan.–Mar., weekdays 10–2.*

⑳ Fantoft Stavkirke *(Fantoft Stave Church).* During the Middle Ages, when
Fodor's Choice European cathedrals were built in stone, Norway used wood to cre-
★ ate unique stave churches. These cultural symbols stand out for their
dragon heads, carved doorways, and walls of staves (vertical planks).
Though as many as 750 stave churches may have once existed, only
30 remain standing. The original stave church here, built in Fortun in
Sogn in 1150 and moved to Fantoft in 1883, burned down in 1992.
Since then, the church has been reconstructed to resemble the original
structure. From the main bus station next to the railway station, take
any bus leaving from Platform 19, 20, or 21. ⊠*Fantoftvn. 38, Paradis*
☎*55–28–07–10* ⊠*NKr 30* ⊙*Mid-May–mid-Sept., daily 10:30–2 and
2:30–6. Closed on May 17 (Norway's national day).*

WORTH NOTING

⑲ Lysøen Island and Ole Bull's Villa. The beautiful villa of Norwegian violin virtuoso Ole Bull (1810–80) is on Lysøen, which means "island of
light." Bull was a musician and patron of great vision. In 1850, after
failing to establish a "New Norwegian Theater" in America, he founded
the National Theater in Norway. He then chose the young playwright
Henrik Ibsen to write full time for the theater, and later encouraged and
promoted another neophyte—15-year-old Edvard Grieg.

Built in 1873, this villa, with an onion dome, gingerbread gables, curved
staircase, and cutwork trim just about everywhere, has to be seen to be
believed. Stroll along the 13 km (8 mi) of pathways Bull created, picnic
or swim in secluded spots, or rent a rowboat. In summer (the only season that Bull lived here), concerts are performed in the villa.

To get here by bus (Monday–Saturday), take the Lysefjordruta bus (no.
566) from platform 19 or 20 at the main bus station to Buena Kai,
where the *Ole Bull* ferry will take you across the fjord to the island. By
car, it's a 25-km (15-mi) trip from Bergen to the ferry. Take road E39
south out of the city. Fork left onto Route 546, signposted FANA; continue straight over Fanafjell Mountain to Sørestraumen and follow signs
to Buena Kai from there. ⊠*Bergen Environs* ☎*56–30–90–77* ⊕*www.
lysoen.no* ⊠*NKr 30, includes guided tour; NKr 50 return ferry trip*
⊙*May 18–Aug., Mon.–Sat. noon–4, Sun. 11–5; Sept., Sun. noon–4.*

**OFF THE
BEATEN
PATH**

Siljustøl. Norway's most important composer of the 20th century, Harald Sæverud (1897–1992), called this unusual house home. He built it
in 1939 of wood and stone and followed old Norwegian construction
methods. Concerts are occasionally held here on Sunday at 3 PM (admission NKr 150). Take Bus 23 from the Bergen bus station, Platform
19. By car, drive 12 km (7 mi) from Bergen center to Route 580 heading toward the airport. ⊠*Siljustølsvegen 50* ☎*55–92–29–92* ⊕*www.
siljustol.no* ⊠*NKr 60* ⊙*Mid-June–mid-Sept., Sun. noon–4.*

WHERE TO EAT

"Bergen is the city with the ocean and sea completely in its stomach,"
someone once said. Bergensers love their seafood dishes: *Fiskepud-
ding* (fish pudding), *fiskekaker* (fish cakes), *fiskeboller* (fish balls), and

Bergensk fiskesuppe (Bergen fish soup). Delicious renditions of such classic dishes show up on local menus with great regularity.

Any Bergen dining experience should start at *Fisketorget*, the fish market. Rain or shine, fresh catches go on sale here in shiny, stainless-steel stalls. The fishmongers dole out shrimp, salmon, monkfish, and friendly advice. Usually, they have steamed *reker* (shrimp), or smoked *laks* (salmon), served on a baguette with mayonnaise and cucumber—a perfect quick lunch. As for desserts, *skillingsbolle*, a big cinnamon roll, or *sommerbolle*, the same with a custard center, are both popular.

> **FOLKLORE EXPERIENCE**
>
> The extensive **Fana Folklore** program is an evening of tradi-tional wedding food, dances, and folk music, plus a concert—at the 800-year-old Fana Church. Tickets are also available from the tourist office. ⊠ *FløΙο, Torgalmenning 9* ☎ *55-91-52-40* ⊕ *www.fanafolk lore.no* ⊠ *NKr 300, includes din-ner and return bus transportation* ⊙ *June-Sept., Thurs. and Fri. at 7* PM. *Catch the bus from Festplas-sen in the center of Bergen and return by 10:30* PM.

Lefse is a flat cake of oatmeal or barley that has a sugar or cream filling. Like other major Norwegian cities, Bergen has international cuisines from Tex-Mex, tapas, and Mediterranean to Japanese sushi restaurants. Some Oslo celebrity chefs—for example Bølgen & Moi—have also opened restaurants here.

BRYGGEN AND NORDNES

$$$
NORWEGIAN

✕ **Bryggeloftet & Stuene.** Dining here on lutefisk in fall and at Christ-mastime is a time-honored tradition for many Bergensers. Also con-sider the *pinnekjøtt* (lamb cooked on birch twigs) or the reindeer fillet in cream sauce. The hearty Norwegian country fare suits the somber, wooden dining room, with its fireplace and old oil paintings on the walls. ⊠ *Bryggen 11, Bryggen* ☎ *55-30-20-70* ⊕ *www.bryggeloftet. no* ⊟ *AE, DC, MC, V.*

$$$
NORWEGIAN
Fodor's Choice
★

✕ **Enhjørningen.** This restaurant is named after the unicorn that adorns the doorway of the old wooden building in which it is housed. Enhjørnin-gen has traditions dating back to the Middle Ages, but there's nothing medieval about the menu—it's contemporary Norwegian and it changes according to the day's catch. Try the famous fish soup to start, followed by herb-fried anglerfish with morel mushroom sauce, or the baked hali-but in saffron butter. Enhjørningen is in the running for best seafood restaurant in Bergen. ⊠ *Bryggen 29, Bryggen* ☎ *55-32-79-19* ⊕ *www. enhjorningen.no* ⊟ *AE, DC, MC, V* ⊙ *No lunch.*

$-$$
JAPANESE

✕ **Nama Sushi & Noodles.** The city's most popular sushi bar ("nama" means "fresh and raw" in Japanese) has garnered good reviews for its minimalist, aquatic-inspired interior, and half-sushi, half-noodles menu. Their fish comes fresh from the market nearby, and there are daily happy-hour sushi specials. The sashimi *moriawase* (assortment), the honey and lime pork fillet, and the chocolate fondant dessert are delicious. The cafe/bar is perfect for an afternoon coffee break. ⊠ *Lodin Lepps gt. 2 B, Bryggen* ☎ *55-32-20-10* ⊕ *www.namasushi.no* ⊙ *Open from 3* PM *Mon.–Sat., from 2* PM *on Sun.* ⊟ *AE, DC, MC, V.*

4

¢–$ **✕ Peppes.** This popular pizza chain has eight outlets in Bergen alone, but
PIZZA this branch is the best, and just a stone's throw from Bryggen wharf.
Thick crust pizzas come with a variety of toppings, from traditional
(a combo they've dubbed the American Way comes with meatballs,
peppers, and mushrooms) to exotic (the Thai Chicken is topped with
chicken, peanuts, pineapple, and fresh coriander). In summer there are
a few tables outside. ⊠ *Finnegården, Bryggen* 🕾 *22–22–55–55* 🖃 *AE,
DC, MC, V.*

$$$ **✕ To Kokker.** Ranked among Bergen's best restaurants by many, To Kok-
NORWEGIAN ker is on Bryggen wharf. The 300-year-old building has crooked floors
★ and slanted moldings (in that charming, rather than alarming, sort of
way) and the seafood and game are excellent. The menu changes with
the season, but if you get the chance try the Jerusalem artichoke soup
with smoked reindeer heart—a great starter that combines two tradi-
tional Norwegian staples—followed by the venison in chanterelle sauce.
⊠ *Enhjørningsgården, Bryggen 29, Bryggen* 🕾 *55–30–69–55* 🌐 *www.*
tokokker.no ⚖ *Reservations essential* 🖃 *AE, DC, MC, V* ☉ *Closed*
Sun. No lunch.

DOWNTOWN: RASMUS MEYERS
ALLÉ AND GRIEGHALLEN

$$ **✕ Boha.** This modern Italian-inspired restaurant is popular both for
CONTEMPORARY business dinners and romantic candlelight suppers. The chef does a
particularly good job with seafood. Try the fresh trout with confit mussels and Grand Marnier sauce, or the oven-baked cod. ⊠ *Vaskerelven*
6, Downtown 🕾 *55–31–31–60* 🌐 *www.boha.no* 🖃 *AE, DC, MC, V*
☉ *Dinner only. Closed Sun.*

$$$ **✕ Bølgen & Moi.** In the same building as the Bergen Art Museum, this
NORWEGIAN local outlet of Norway's Bølgen & Moi restaurant franchise is the per-
★ fect place for a break from the galleries. The lunch menu offers excel-
lent value for money, but the brasserie is well worth a visit later in
the evening. Try the turbot with asparagus and citrus hollandaise, a
modern take on a Norwegian classic. For a hearty lunch, try the fish
soup, or the crayfish sandwich. The well-stocked bar is a trendy meeting
place for local businesspeople. ⊠ *Rasmus Meyers Allé 9, Downtown*
🕾 *55–59–77–00* 🌐 *www.bolgenogmoi.no* 🖃 *AE, DC, MC, V.*

$$ **✕ Escalón.** Near the Fløibanen, this tiny tapas restaurant and bar is
SPANISH a trendy place to go for a bite or a drink. Taste the *gambas al ajillo*
(scampi in wine and garlic) or the *albódigas en salsa de tomate* (meatballs in tomato sauce). If you can't decide on what to go for, order
one of the *platos* and the kitchen will put a selection together for you.
⊠ *Vetrlidsalmenningen 21, Downtown* 🕾 *55–32–90–99* 🌐 *www.*
escalon.no 🖃 *AE, DC, MC, V.*

¢ **✕ Kroathai.** This small family-run Thai restaurant serves delicious,
THAI authentic Thai cuisine at very reasonable prices. There is a good selection of soups and rice and egg noodles, and all the usual favorites (pad
thai, green curries, and chicken satay) feature on the menu. If you're
feeling more adventurous, a few specialties from eastern Thailand—
such as the excellent beef salad—are also available. ⊠ *Nygårdsgaten*
29, Downtown 🕾 *55–32–58–50* 🖃 *AE, DC, MC, V.*

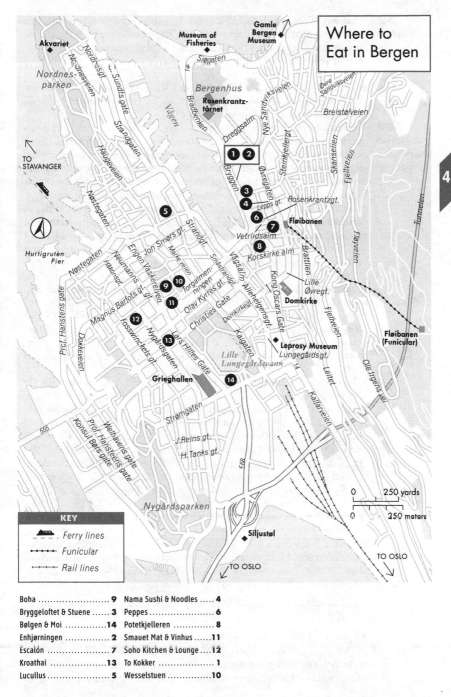

Where to Eat in Bergen

4

KEY

- Ferry lines
- Funicular
- Rail lines

$$$$
FRENCH

✕**Lucullus.** Although the eclectic interior—modern art matched with lace doilies and boardroom chairs—seems a bit out of kilter with the classic French menu here, don't be alarmed; the food is consistently good. The Hardanger trout with apple jelly and spinach is excellent. For a meatier treat, try the classic beef fillet, a house specialty. The five-course meal is particularly indulgent. ⊠ *Neptun Hotel, Walkendorfsgt. 8, Downtown* ☎ *55–30–68–20* ⊕ *www.neptunhotel.no Jacket and tie* ⊟ *AE, DC, MC, V* ⊗ *Closed Sun. No lunch.*

$$-$$$
CONTEMPORARY
Fodor'sChoice
★

✕**Potetkjelleren.** A popular contemporary restaurant in surroundings dating back to the Middle Ages, Potetkjelleren means "potato cellar," and the restaurant's two main dining rooms are indeed old brick-walled storage rooms in the basement. Everything but the menu seems slightly off-balance here: the chairs and tables have a rickety feel, mostly due to the uneven stone-tile floor. What the restaurant lacks in comfort it more than makes up for in quality and atmosphere: the cozy cellar is perfect for a romantic candlelight dinner, the service is friendly and efficient, and the kitchen turns out delicious dishes like panfried halibut with fennel polenta and organic pork with potato gnocchi and morel sauce. ⊠ *Kong Oscars gt. 1 A, Downtown* ☎ *55–32–00–70* ⊟ *AE, DC, MC, V* ⊗ *No lunch.*

$$
CONTEMPORARY

✕**Smauet Mat & Vinhus.** This is one of Bergen's least-expensive fine restaurants. Hidden away in a small alley near Ole Bulls plass, this cozy restaurant has a reputation for serving innovative Mediterranean and Norwegian cuisine. Try the baked lamb with braised fennel and foie gras glacé or one of the seafood dishes. ⊠ *Vaskerelvsmauet 1, Downtown* ☎ *55–21–07–10* ⊕ *www.smauet.no* ⚖ *Reservations essential* ⊟ *AE, DC, MC, V* ⊗ *No lunch.*

$$
ECLECTIC

✕**Soho Kitchen & Lounge.** Perhaps the owners of Soho couldn't decide whether to start a sushi bar or a modern Mediterranean-inspired place, as this restaurant has elements of both. It's an eclectic, interesting restaurant in a suitably schizoid environment that's either minimalist or excessive and flashy, depending on which way you're facing. The bento box is a pricey but tasty lunch deal with miso soup, sushi, and the dessert of the day. If you're hungry for more European flavors, try the slow-roasted duck breast with orange sauce. ⊠ *Håkonsgt. 27, Downtown* ☎ *55–90–19–60* ⊕ *www.sohokitchen.no* ⊟ *AE, DC, MC, V* ⊗ *No lunch. Closed Sun.*

$$
NORWEGIAN

⊡ **Wesselstuen.** Housed in a 18th-century wine cellar, this atmospheric restaurant is known for its convivial atmosphere and unpretentious, authentic Norwegian fare. This is a good place to try reindeer steak or *baccalao* (cod). Light meals and more international options are available. ⊠ *Øvre Ole Bulls pl. 6, Downtown* ☎ *55–55–49–49* ⊕ *www. wesselstuen.no* ⊟ *AE, DC, MC, V* ⊗ *Sun. lunch only.*

WHERE TO STAY

Bergen has a good selection of accommodation options for every traveler's budget and style. Most Bergen hotels are within walking distance of the city's shopping, restaurants, entertainment, and other attractions. Many hotels offer favorable summer and weekend rates depending on vacancies. Last-minute summer rates may be booked 48 hours prior to arrival June 16–August 31. Off-season (September–May) there are often weekend specials. Bergen Tourist Information Office will assist you in booking your accommodations for a fee.

BRYGGEN AND NORDNES

$$ **Best Western Hotell Hordaheimen.** Dating from 1913, one of the city's oldest and most distinctive hotels is on a quiet, central street. The lobby has a memorable collection of painted Norwegian furniture by Lars Kinsarvik. The hotel's café-restaurant, Kaffistova, is well known for its traditional fare, especially *klippfisk* (salted and sundried cod), fried mackerel, and smoked cod. Rooms are small but nicely decorated with simple Scandinavian-style furniture, much of it in beige and plum. **Pros:** newly refurbished rooms with flat-screen TVs; homemade breakfast; quiet location. **Cons:** the old rooms are not as nice as the new ones, and rather small. ✉ *C. Sundtsgt. 18, Nordnes* ☎ *55–33–50–00* ⊕ *www. hordaheimen.no* ⚲ *80 rooms, 8 suites* ♿ *In-hotel: restaurant* ⊟ *AE, DC, MC, V* ⦿ *BP.*

$$$ **Clarion Hotel Admiral.** Known as "the hotel with the sea on three sides," the Clarion has stunning views of the wharf, the fish market, and Mt. Fløyen. Book well in advance for the rooms with the best harbor views. Most rooms have upscale chain-hotel-style furnishings. Some of the suites, however, are decorated with hardwood antique reproductions. Sjøtonnen, the à la carte restaurant, specializes in seafood. After dinner, have a nightcap in the hotel's cognac-and-cigar lounge, which has burnished red-leather sofas. **Pros:** from harborside rooms with balconies, the view is nothing short of superior. **Cons:** some rooms look a bit tired. ✉ *C. Sundtsgt. 9–13, Nordnes* ☎ *55–23–64–00* ⊕ *www.admiral.no* ⚲ *211 rooms, 2 suites* ♿ *In-hotel: restaurant, bar, no-smoking rooms* ⊟ *AE, DC, MC, V* ⦿ *BP.*

$$$–$$$$ **Clarion Collection Hotel Havnekontoret.** Housed in a completely reno-
★ vated building that dates to the 1920s, this classy new hotel is conveniently located right on Bryggen. The comfortable rooms feature most modern conveniences and are tastefully decorated in shades of brown and purple. The common areas, which have retained many of the original features, are stylish yet welcoming. **Pros:** stylish design throughout; free waffles, coffee, and evening buffet; some rooms have panoramic views of the harbor. **Cons:** low ceiling in top-floor rooms; service can hit or miss; some rooms are quite small. ✉ *Slottsgt. 1, Bryggen* ☎ *55–60–11–00* ⊕ *www.choicehotels.no* ⚲ *116* ♿ *In room: DVD, Internet. In hotel: restaurant, gym* ⊟ *AE, DC, MC, V* ⦿ *BP.*

$$$–$$$$ **First Hotel Marin.** On the harborside near Bryggen, in an elegant brick
★ building that once housed one of Bergen's largest print shops, this business hotel is within walking distance of the city's buses, ferries, and trains. Every room has a bathtub and is decorated in yellows and blues, with oak furniture and hardwood floors. Some rooms feature original artwork from local artists. The penthouse suites have magnificent views of Bergen. If you play your cards right during winter (the off-peak season), you can find significantly lower rates at which to enjoy your time here. Definitely look into it if you're here in the winter months. **Pros:** stylish rooms; helpful staff; sauna; good deals in off-peak season.

4

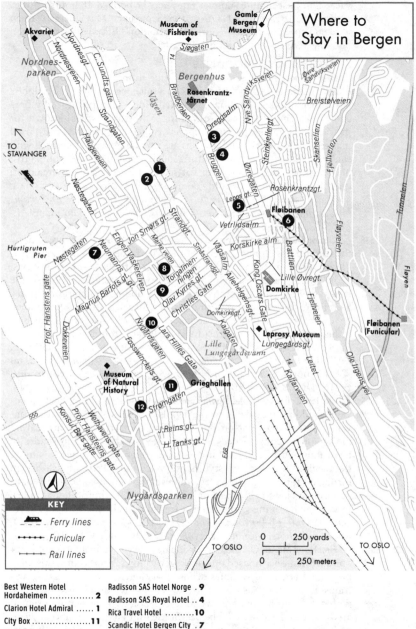

Where to Stay in Bergen

Cons: some rooms can be noisy in summer. ✉ *Rosenkrantzgt. 8, Bryggen* ☎ *53–05–15–00* ⊕ *www.firsthotels.com* ↪ *152 rooms, 25 suites* ♿ *In-hotel: restaurant, bar, gym, no-smoking rooms* ⊟ *AE, DC, MC, V* ⊺⊙⒧ *BP.*

$$$–$$$$ 🏨 **Radisson SAS Royal Hotel.** Behind Bryggen, this hotel stands where old warehouses used to be. Ravaged by nine fires since 1170, the warehouses were repeatedly rebuilt in the same style, which has been carried over into the Radisson's facade. The small but comfortable rooms have light gold walls and wood accents. Under a glass ceiling, the Almenningen Restaurant serves Scandinavian and international dishes as well as light snacks. The Madam Felle pub and bar on the waterfront is known for its live jazz and rock music, as well as its whiskeys. Engelen nightclub keeps people dancing until the early hours. **Pros:** excellent location; sauna; efficient service. **Cons:** smallish rooms ✉ *Ole Bulls Plass 4 Bryggen* ☎ *55–54–30–00* ⊕ *www.radissonsas.com* ↪ *273 rooms, 10 suites* ♿ *In-room: Internet. In-hotel: 2 restaurants, bar, pool, gym* ⊟ *AE, DC, MC, V* ⊺⊙⒧ *BP.*

¢   🏨 **Skansen Pensjonat.** This is a good budget option in an otherwise not-so-budget neighborhood for lodging. The small pension is welcoming and rooms are cozy and comfy, although facilities are limited. It's like a home away from home. **Pros:** warm and friendly atmosphere; the balcony room on the first floor has big windows and great views. **Cons:** shared baths; no lift. ✉ *Vetrlidsallmenningen 29, Bryggen* ☎ *55–31–90–80* ⊕ *www.skansen-pensjonat.no* ↪ *11 rooms, 2 apartments* ♿ *In-room: no TV (some). In-hotel: Internet terminal.* ⊟ *AE, DC, MC, V* ⊺⊙⒧ *BP.*

DOWNTOWN: RASMUS MEYERS ALLÉ AND GRIEGHALLEN

¢   🏨 **City Box.** If all you need is a bed to crash in at the end of the day, City Box might be just the place for you. This hotel, located near Grieghallen, has been providing basic but comfy rooms at hard-to-beat prices since 2006. Don't expect any freebies here, or staff to pamper you (reception is unmanned after hours), but at these prices, who cares? Five family rooms are available, and there is a small café on-site. **Pros:** low prices; clean, simple design. **Cons:** no phone or TV in the rooms; staff not always on hand; you can't pay by cash after hours. ✉ *Nygårdsgt. 31, Downtown* ☎ *55–31–25–00* ⊕ *www.citybox.no* ↪ *53 rooms* ♿ *In-room: no phone, no TV. In-hotel: café* ⊟ *AE, DC, MC, V* ⊺⊙⒧ *EP.*

$
★   🏨 **Hotel Park Pension.** Near the university, this intimate family-run hotel, one of Norway's historic hotels, is in a well-kept Victorian structure built in the 1890s. Both the public rooms and the guest rooms are furnished with antiques. It's a short distance to Grieghallen, downtown, and the bus and railway stations. **Pros:** small size; quiet residential area; free parking. **Cons:** the walk to the heart of downtown isn't far, but can feel like it since it's uphill; limited facilities. ✉ *Harald Hårfagres gt. 35, University District* ☎ *55–54–44–00* ⊕ *www.parkhotel.no* ↪ *33 rooms* ♿ *In-hotel. restaurant* ⊟ *AE, DC, MC, V* ⊺⊙⒧ *BP.*

$$$–$$$$ 🏨 **Radisson SAS Hotel Norge.** A Bergen classic, this hotel attracts VIPs, from prime ministers to musicians. The architecture is modern, with large salmon-color, dark-wood rooms that blend contemporary Scandinavian

comfort with traditional warmth. The restaurant T.G.I. Friday's has American-style fare, and the Contra Bar and Library Bar are popular with locals and visitors alike. The Metro nightclub is packed on weekends. The hotel's fresh smorgasbord breakfast is the perfect way to start your day. Ask for a room facing Lille Lungegårdsvann for a scenic view. **Pros:** friendly, helpful staff; sauna; central location; comfortable rooms. **Cons:** rooms facing Ole Bulls plass can be noisy at night. ✉ *Ole Bulls pl. 4, Downtown* ☎ *55–57–30–00* ⊕ *www.radissonsas.com* ⇆ *345 rooms, 12 suites* ♿ *In-room: Internet. In-hotel: restaurants, bars, pool, gym* ▤ *AE, DC, MC, V* ¶◎¶ *BP.*

$–$$　⬚ **Rica Travel Hotel.** Popular with business travelers, this hotel is steps away from Torgallmenningen. The rooms are stylish and the location is ideal, but there are few facilities. A public swimming pool and a popular fitness center are nearby. **Pros:** central location; well-appointed rooms. **Cons:** some rooms are small; can be noisy in summer. ✉ *Christiesgt. 5–7, Downtown* ☎ *55–36–29–00* ⊕ *www.rica.no* ⇆ *159 rooms* ♿ *In-room: Internet. In-hotel: restaurant, bar, parking (paid)* ▤ *AE, DC, MC, V* ¶◎¶ *BP.*

$$–$$$　⬚ **Scandic Hotel Bergen City.** This business hotel runs Bergen Congress Center, the city's largest convention center, and has warm, stylish, comfortable rooms. Take a seat in a plush armchair in the new City Bar and warm up in front of the open fire on a cold winter day. Staying here will put you right next to Bergen Kino (a cinema multiplex) and just a short walk from Den Nationale Scene theater, Grieghallen, and plenty of restaurants. **Pros:** modern rooms; kids' play area; open fire in City Bar in winter. **Cons:** some rooms are noisy; staff can't always cope at breakfast time; rooms in the older building aren't as nice as those in the newer one. ✉ *Håkonsgt. 2–7, Downtown* ☎ *55–30–90–80* ⊕ *www.scandichotels.com/bergencity* ⇆ *251 rooms, 3 suites* ♿ *In-room: Internet. In-hotel: restaurant, bar, meeting and conference facilities* ▤ *AE, DC, MC, V* ¶◎¶ *BP.*

$–$$
Fodor's Choice
★　⬚ **Thon Hotel Bristol.** The Bristol, built in the 1930s, is one of the most popular hotels in town and is within walking distance of the city's main sights. Rooms, which were all refurbished in 2008, are small but comfortable, and came stylishly-accented in white, black and maroon furnishings. This is excellent value for money. Several are wheelchair-accessible. **Pros:** good design throughout; the popular Egon restaurant is on-site. **Cons:** the rooms overlooking the street can be noisy; no a/c, so rooms get hot in summer. ✉ *Torgallmenningen 11, Downtown* ☎ *55–55–10–00* ⊕ *www.thonhotels.no/bristolbergen* ⇆ *134 rooms, 1 suite* ♿ *In-room: no a/c, Internet. In-hotel: restaurant* ▤ *AE, DC, MC, V* ¶◎¶ *BP.*

AFTER DARK

BARS AND CLUBS

Bergen is a university town, and the many thousand students who live and study here all year round contribute to making the city's nightlife livelier than you might expect for its size. Most nightspots center around Ole Bulls plass, the plaza at one end of Torgallmenningen. Within a stone's throw of the plaza you can find dozens of relaxing bars, lively pubs, dancing, live music, and trendy cafés.

For a quiet glass of wine in peaceful historic surroundings, try **Altona** (⊠*Strandgaten 81, Nordnes* ☎*55–30–40–72*), a bar in a 400-year-old wine cellar neighboring the Augustin Hotel. **Kamelon** (⊠ *Vågsalmenning 16, Downtown* ☎*91–87–07–23*), next door to the nightclub Mood, caters to a more lively crowd. Here you will often find live music, ranging from contemporary pop to folk, mostly by local artists.

If you prefer conversation over dancing, try **Logen Teater** (⊠*Øvre Ole Bulls pl. 6, Downtown* ☎*55–23–20–15*), a popular meeting place with live acoustic music every Sunday. **Metro,** in the Radisson SAS Norge (⊠*Nedre Ole Bulls pl. 4, Downtown* ☎*55–96–02–92*) is right in front of the Ole Bull statue, and is a nightclub popular among local twentysomethings. It features pulsating dance music, minimalist decor, and serious crowds on weekends. **Mood** (⊠ *Vågsalmenning 16, Downtown* ☎*55–55–96–55*) is one of Bergen's largest nightclubs, but is still usually packed weekends with local clubbers in their twenties and thirties.

CAFÉS

Café Opera (⊠*Engen 18, Downtown* ☎*55–23–03–15*) is a classic, both sumptuous and stylish. It's often crowded on Friday and Saturday nights, when they have DJs on. **Kafe Kippers** (⊠*Georgernes Verft 12, Nordnes* ☎*55–31–00–60*), Bergen's largest outdoor café, has cozy wool blankets and a spectacular view of the water at sunset.

Pygmalion (⊠*Nedre Korskirke Allmenning 4, Downtown* ☎*55–32–33–60*) serves tasty organic food and has contemporary art on the walls. Just up the road from Pygmalion is **Godt Brød** (⊠*Nedre Korskirke Allmenning 12, Downtown* ☎*55–32–80–00*), a popular organic bakery that makes scrumptious cinnamon rolls and delicious open-faced sandwiches and subs to order. A second location near the theater has more seating space and is often even busier.

GAY BARS

Bergen has an active gay community. Call Wednesday from 7 to 9 PM or check the Web site of **Landsforeningen for Lesbisk og Homofil Frigjøring** (☎*55–31–21–39*), the National Association for Lesbian and Gay Liberation, to ask about events in the city.

Bergen's most popular gay bar is **Fincken** (⊠*Nygårdsgt. 2A, Downtown* ☎*55–32–13–16* ⊕*www.fincken.no*), which is open daily until 1 AM.

LIVE MUSIC

Bergensers love jazz. The **Bergen Jazz Forum** (⊠*Sardinen USF, Georgernes Verft 12, Nordnes* ☎*55–30–72–50* ⊕*www.bergenjazzforum.no*) is *the* place to find it—there are concerts every Friday from September to May. The international **Nattjazz** festival (⊕*www.nattjazz.no*) offers more than 60 concerts in late May and early June.

Since the mid-'90s, Bergen has become a haven for up-and-coming pop and rock bands. A lot of them have their concert debut at **Garage** (⊠*Christies gt. 14, Downtown* ☎*55–32–19–80*), a hangout popular with local musicians. **Bergenfest** (☎55–21–50–60 ⊕*www.bergenfest. no*), runs from late April to early May and features several internationally known rock and blues artists.

Det Akademiske Kvarter (USF) (✉*Georgernes Verft 12, Nordnes* ☎55–58–99–10) is run by students from Bergen University, and there are pop, rock, and jazz concerts here on a weekly basis most of the year. During the university semester, the rock club **Hulen** (✉*Olaf Ryes vei 48, Møhlenpris* ☎55–33–38–30) attracts college students and other music enthusiasts to weekly rock concerts in a rebuilt air-raid shelter.

SPORTS AND THE OUTDOORS

Bergen is literally wedged between the mountains and the sea, and there are plenty of opportunities to enjoy the outdoors. Bergensers are quick to do so on sunny days. In summer, don't be surprised to see many Bergensers leaving work early to enjoy sports and activities outdoors, or just relax in the parks.

FISHING

With so much water around, it's no wonder sportfishing is a popular pastime in Bergen. Angling along the coast around Bergen is possible all year, although it is unquestionably more pleasant in summer. In late summer many move up the area rivers to catch spawning salmon and trout. Whether you prefer fishing in streams, fjords, or the open sea, there are several charter services and fishing tours available. Most can also provide all the fishing gear you need, but be sure to bring warm and waterproof clothes, even in summer.

The **Bergen Angling Association** (✉*Damsgårdsvn. 106, Downtown* ☎55–34–18–08 ⊕*www.sportsfiskere.no*) has information and fishing permits. A local fishing supply store, **Campelen** (✉*Strandgt. 17, Downtown* ☎93–41–29–58 ⊕*www.campelen.no*) also arranges fjord fishing, deep-sea fishing, and charter tours, all departing from central Bergen.

The **Weller** (☎55–19–13–03 or 40–82–58–28 ⊕*www.weller.no*) is a fishing boat often used by professional fishermen. They offer daily trips in summer, as well as chartered tours. **Sotra Rorbusenter** (✉*Spildepollen, Glesvær, Bergen Environs* ☎56–31–79–76 ⊕*www.rorbusenter. com*) offers boat rental, guided tours, and chartered tours from Sotra outside Bergen.

HIKING

Like most Norwegians, Bergensers love to go hiking, especially on one or more of the seven mountains that surround the city. **Bergen Turlag** (*Bergen Hiking Association* ✉*Tverrgt. 4–6, Downtown* ☎55–33–58–10 ⊕*www.bergen-turlag.no*) is a touring club that arranges hikes and maintains cabins for hikers. You can pick up maps of many self-guided walking tours around Bergen from the office, as well as from bookstores around Bergen.

Bergen Turlag stages the **7-fjellsturen**, or Seven-Mountain Hike, an event that attracts thousands of hikers for the one-day trek across seven nearby mountains in late May. Take the funicular up **Mt. Fløyen** (✉ *Vetrlidsallmenningen 21, Bryggen* ☎ *55–33 68 00* ⊕ *www.floibanen.no*), and minutes later you'll be in the midst of a forest. From the nearby gift shop and restaurant, well-marked paths fan out over the mountains. Follow Fløysvingene Road down for an easy stroll with great views of the city and harbor.

Mt. Ulriken (☎ *55–20–20–20* ⊕ *www.ulriken.no*) is popular with walkers and hikers of all levels. The easiest way to reach the summit is via the cable car from Haukeland University Hospital. (To get there, take the double-decker bus that leaves from Torget.) Once you get off the cable car, you'll find trails leading across the mountain plateau, **Vidden**, which is above the tree line. The plateau connects the Fløyen and Ulriken mountains, and you can hike between them in four to six hours. Views from the alpine trail are spectacular. Be advised that foggy and rainy weather, even in the summer months, can make hiking here dangerous. Consult the tourist information center or Bergen Turlag for maps and general advice.

FESTSPILLENE FESTIVAL

Bergen is known for its **Festspillene** (*International Festival*), held each year during the last week of May and the beginning of June. Famous names in classical music, jazz, ballet, the arts, and theater perform. Tickets are available at Grieghallen from the festival office (✉ *Lars Hilles gt. 3* ☎ *55–21–61–50* ⊕ *www.fib.no*). Tickets can also be ordered from **Billettservice** (☎ *815–33–133* ⊕ *www.billettservice.no*).

SHOPPING

SHOPPING CENTERS

Bergen has several cobblestoned pedestrian shopping streets, including Gamle Strandgaten, (Gågaten), Torgallmenningen, Hollendergaten, and Marken. Stores selling Norwegian handicrafts are concentrated along the Bryggen boardwalk. Near the cathedral, the tiny Skostredet has become popular with young shoppers. The small, independent speciality stores here sell everything from army surplus gear to tailored suits and designer trinkets. Most Bergen shops are open Monday–Wednesday and Friday from 9 to 5; Thursday from 9 to 7; and Saturday from 10 to 3. Bergen's shopping centers—Galleriet, Kløverhuset, and Bergen Storsenter—are open weekdays from 9 to 8 and Saturday from 9 to 6.

Sundt (✉ *Torgallmenningen 14, Downtown*) is the closest thing Norway has to a traditional department store, with everything from fashion to interior furnishings. But you can get better value for your kroner if you shop around for souvenirs and sweaters. **Kløverhuset** (✉ *Strandkaien 10, Downtown*), between Strandgaten and the fish market, has 40 shops under one roof, including outlets for the ever-so-popular Dale knitwear, souvenirs, leathers, and fur.

Galleriet, (✉ *Torgallmenningen 8, Downtown* ☎ *55–30–05–00* ⊕ *www.galleriet.com*) is the best of the downtown shopping malls, with over 70 shops. Here you will find **GlasMagasinet** and more exclusive small shops along with all the chains. **Bergen Storsenter** (✉ *Strømgt. 8, Downtown*

☎*55–21–24–60* ⊕*www.bergenstorsenter.no*), by the bus terminal near the train station, is a newer shopping center.

FOOD

Kjøttbasaren (✉*Vetrlidsalmenning 2, Downtown* ☎*55–55–22–23*) is in a restored 1877 meat market. The Meat Bazaar sells everything from venison to sweets. **Kvamme kolonial og fetevarer** (✉*Strandkaien 18, Downtown* ☎*55–23–14–25*) is a fine-foods store, selling rare Norwegian products like cured leg of indigenous wild mutton, as well as the usual dairy products and smoked and cured meats. Famous all over Norway, **Søstrene Hagelin** (✉*Olav Kyrres gt. 33, Downtown* ☎*55–32–69–49*) is a Bergen institution, a delicatessen that sells traditional fish balls, fish pudding, and other seafood products made following its secret recipes.

GLASS, CERAMICS, AND PEWTER

Hjertholm (✉*Galleriet Shopping Center, Torgallmenning 8, 5th fl., Downtown* ☎*55–31–70–27*) is the ideal shop for gifts; most everything is of Scandinavian design. The pottery and glassware are of the highest quality—much of it made by local artisans. **Tilbords, Bergens Glasmagasin,** in the same shopping center (☎*55–31–69–67*) claims to have the town's largest selection of glass and china, in both Scandinavian and European designs.

HANDICRAFTS

Berle Bryggen (✉*Bryggen 5, Bryggen* ☎*55–10–95–00* ⊕*www.sns.no*) has the complete Dale of Norway collection in stock and other traditional knitwear and souvenir items—don't miss the troll cave. **Husfliden** (✉*Vågsalmenning 3, Downtown* ☎*55–54–47–40*) caters to all your handicrafts needs, including a department for Norwegian national costumes. This is one of the best places to pick up handmade Norwegian goods, especially handwoven textiles and hand-carved wood items. **Oleana** (✉*Strandkaien 2A, Bryggen* ☎*55–31–05–20* ⊕*www.oleana. no*), the flagship store of the famous Norwegian designer by the same name, sells Norwegian wool sweaters, silk scarves from Tyrihans, and Norwegian silver.

Juhls' Silver Gallery (✉*Bryggen 39, Bryggen* ☎*55–32–47–40* ⊕*www. juhls.no*) has its own exclusive jewelry called "Tundra," which is inspired by the Norwegian north. **Theodor Olsens** (✉*Torgallmenningen 15, Downtown* ☎*55–55–14–80*) stocks silver jewelry of distinctive Norwegian and Scandinavian design.

TOYS

Take a stroll through **Troll** (✉*Bryggen, Bryggen* ☎*55–21–51–00*) for adorable, mean-looking trolls of all shapes and sizes. The same complex that holds Troll also has an all-year **Julehuset** (✉*Bryggen, Bryggen* ☎*55–21–51–00* ⊕*www.goshopnorway.com*), or Christmas House, full of cheery Norwegian *Nisser* (gnomes).

THE WEST COAST

The intricate outline of the fjords makes Norway's coastline of 21,347 km (13,264 mi) longer than the distance between the north and south poles. Among the world's most spectacular geological formations, a typical fjord consists of a long, narrow, deep inlet of the sea, with steep mountainsides stretching into mountain massifs. Fjords were created by glacier erosion during the ice ages. In spectacular inlets like Sognefjord, Geirangerfjord, and Hardangerfjord, walls of water shoot up the mountainsides, jagged snowcapped peaks blot out the sky, and water tumbles down the mountains in an endless variety of colors. Lush green farmlands edge up the rounded mountainsides and the chiseled, cragged, steep peaks of the Jotunheimen mountains, Norway's tallest, seem to touch the blue skies.

The farther north you travel, the more rugged and wild the landscape. The still, peaceful Sognefjord is the longest inlet, snaking 190 km (110 mi) inland. At the top of Sogn og Fjordane county is a group of fjords referred to as Nordfjord, with the massive Jostedalsbreen, mainland Europe's largest glacier, to the south. In the county of Møre og Romsdal, you'll see mountains that would seem more natural on the moon—all gray rock—as well as cliffs hanging over the water below. Geirangerfjord is Norway's best-known fjord. In the south, the Hardangerfjord, Norway's fruit basket, is best seen in early summer when it's in full blossom.

Boat cruises are the classic way of exploring this region, but there's much to be gained by more up-close-and-personal experiences. You can walk or climb on one of Norway's 1,630 glaciers, remnants of the 30 ice ages that carved the fjords. Head to Eid and ride one of the ponylike Fjord horses, originally bred for farm work.

ÅNDALSNES

495 km (307 mi) north of Bergen, 354 km (219 mi) south of Trondheim.

Åndalsnes is an industrial alpine village of 3,000 people that is best known for three things: its position as the last stop on the railway, making it a gateway to fjord country; the Trollstigveien (Troll Path); and the Trollveggen (Troll Wall). The tourist office has special maps and guides outlining the popular trails and paths. The tourist office can also make arrangements for you to join a fishing trip to the fjords. Trips last four hours, and leave three times a day; the cost is NKr 250. Six or seven species of mostly whitefish, such as cod, live in the waters.

GETTING HERE AND AROUND

The *Dovrebanen* and *Raumabanen* between Oslo S Station and Åndalsnes via Dombås run three times daily in each direction. It's a 6½-hour ride. At Åndalsnes, buses wait outside the station to pick up passengers heading to points not served by the train. The 124-km (76-mi) trip to Ålesund takes close to two hours.

ESSENTIALS

Train Contact NSB (*Norwegian state railways* ☎*815–00–888* ⊕*www.nsb.no*).

Visitor Info Åndalsnes & Romsdal Tourist Board (✉ *Jernbanegt. 1* ☎ *71–22–16–22* ⊕*www.visitandalsnes.com*).

EXPLORING

★ From **Horgheimseidet,** which used to have a hotel for elegant tourists— often European royalty—you can view **Trollveggen** *(Troll Wall)*, Europe's highest vertical rock face at 3,300 feet. The birthplace of mountain-climbing sports in Scandinavia, this rock face draws elite climbers from all over.

Fodor'sChoice **Trollstigveien,** Norway's most popular tourist road, starts in Åndalsnes.
★ The road took 100 men 20 summers (1916–36) to build, in a constant struggle against the forces of rock and water. Often described as a masterpiece of construction, the road snakes its way through 11 hairpin bends up the mountain to the peaks named **Bispen** (the Bishop), **Kongen** (the King), and **Dronningen** (the Queen), which are 2,800 feet above sea level. The roads Trollstigveien and Ørneveien (at the Geiranger end) zigzag over the mountains separating two fjords. Roads are open only in summer. Halfway up, the road crosses a bridge over the waterfall **Stigfossen** (Path Falls), which has a vertical fall of nearly 600 feet. Walk to the lookout point, Stigrøra, by taking the 15-minute return path to the plateau. Signs show the way.

One of Norway's most famous mountaineers, Arne Randers Heen (1905–91), and his wife, Bodil Roland, founded the **Norsk Tindemuseum** *(Norwegian Alpine Museum)*, which is dedicated to mountain climbing and Alpine history in Norway. The museum, which recently relocated to new premises, consists of a multimedia show and an exhibition featuring, among other things, equipment and images depicting Alpine history from the first ascent of Romsdalshorn in 1828 up until today. Activities like mountain climbing, big-wall climbing, ice climbing, free climbing, mountain skiing and BASE jumping are covered. ✉*Jernbanegt. 3* ☎*71–22–36–08* ✉*NKr 90* ⊙*June–Aug., Tues.–Sun. 1–6.*

WHERE TO STAY

$$ ⊞**Grand Hotel Bellevue.** Travelers often begin their exploration of the region at this hotel. All the rooms are done in bright yellow, with old prints of the fjord on the walls. The hotel's restaurant, Trollstua, has delicious seafood dishes, based on fresh, local catches. **Pros:** good facilities; ample parking. **Cons:**not right by the fjord—though it's only a short walk away; popular with groups. ✉*Åndalsgt. 5* ☎*71–22–75–00* ⊕*www.grandhotel.no* ⟿*77 rooms, 4 suites* ⟁*In-hotel: 2 restaurants, 2 bars* ⊟*AE, DC, MC, V* ⊙❙*BP.*

ÅLESUND

240 km (150 mi) west of Åndalsnes.

On three islands and between two bright-blue fjords is Ålesund, home to 45,000 inhabitants and one of Norway's largest harbors for exporting dried and fresh fish. About two-thirds of its 1,040 wooden houses were

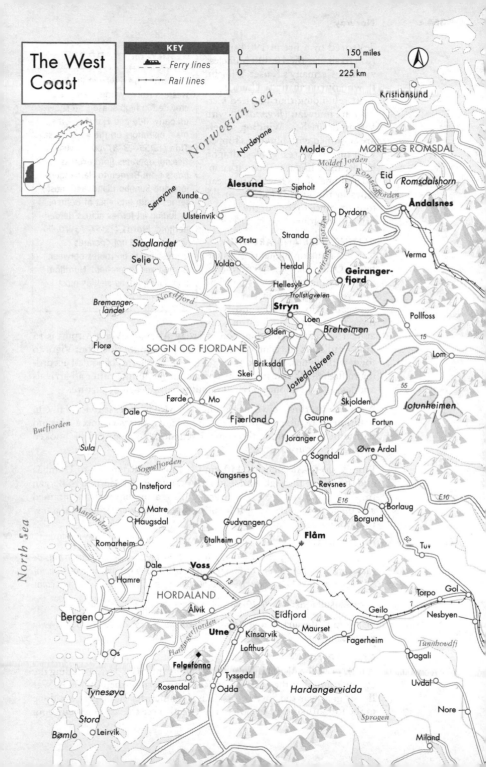

destroyed by a fire in 1904. In the rush to shelter the 10,000 homeless victims, Germany's Kaiser Wilhelm II, who often vacationed here, led a swift rebuilding that married German art nouveau (*Jugendstil*) with Viking flourishes. Winding streets are crammed with buildings topped with turrets, spires, gables, dragon heads, and curlicues. Today it's considered one of the few art-nouveau cities in the world. Inquire at the tourism office for one of the insightful walking tours.

GETTING HERE AND AROUND

SAS has nonstop flights to Ålesund from Oslo, Bergen, Trondheim, and Stavanger. Low-cost airline Norwegian has also started a route between Oslo and Ålesund, with three flights daily during the week

> ### FERRY TRANSPORT
>
> Car ferries are a way of life in western Norway. They can get crowded in high season, so show up early. Tide and Fjord1 are the main operators on the west coast. **Tide** (☎ 55-23-87-00 ⊕ www. tide.no) operates fjord express boats from Bergen to Hardangerfjord and Sunnhordland, and most ferries south and east of Bergen, including all ferries across Hardangerfjord. **Fjord1** (☎ 57-75-70-00 ⊕ www.fjord1.no) operates express boats on routes between Bergen and Sognefjord, Nordfjord and Sunnfjord, as well as most ferries north of Bergen.

and on Sunday, and one flight on Saturday. Ålesund's Vigra Airport is 15 km (9 mi) from the center of town. It's a 25-minute ride from Vigra to town with Flybussen. Tickets cost NKr 80. Buses are scheduled according to flights—they leave the airport about 10 minutes after all arrivals and leave town about 60 or 70 minutes before each departure.

A catamaran runs between Ålesund and Molde at least twice daily. In addition to regular ferries to nearby islands, boats connect Ålesund with other points along the coast. Excursions by boat can be booked through the tourist office.

From Oslo to Ålesund it's 450 km (295 mi) on Route E6 to Dombås and then E136 through Åndalsnes to Ålesund. From Ålesund to Bergen the E39 is a 381-km (237-mi) drive. It's reasonably well maintained and open most of the year. It involves several ferry crossings and a few tollbooths.

ESSENTIALS

Air Contacts Norwegian (☎ 815-21-815 in Norway, 21-49-00-15 from outside Norway ⊕ www.norwegian.no). **Flybussen** (☎ 815-00-535 ⊕ www.flybussen.no). **SAS** (☎ 800/221-2350 in the USA, 91-50-54-00 in Norway ⊕ www.flysas.com).

Taxis Ålesund Taxi (☎ 70-10-30-00).

Visitor Info Ålesund Tourist Board (✉ Skateflukaia ☎ 70-15-76-00 ⊕ www. visitalesund.com).

EXPLORING

Fodor's Choice ★ A little gem, the **Ålesunds Museum** highlights the city's past, including the escape route that the Norwegian Resistance established in World War II—its goal was the Shetland Islands. Handicrafts on display are done in the folk-art style of the area. You can also see the art nouveau room and learn more about the town's unique architecture. ⊠*Rasmus Røn-nebergsgt. 16* ☎*70–12–31–70* ⊕*www.aalesunds.museum.no* ⊠*NKr 40* ⊙*Mon.–Sat. 11–3, Sun. noon–3.*

You can drive or take a bus up nearby Aksla Mountain to a vantage point, **Kniven** *(the knife)*, for a splendid view of the city—which absolutely glitters at night. ☎*70–13–68–00 for bus information.*

Ⓒ **Ålesund Akvarium, Atlanterhavsparken** *(Atlantic Sea Park).* Teeming with aquatic life, this is one of Scandinavia's largest aquariums. Right on the ocean, 3 km (2 mi) west of town, the park emphasizes aquatic animals of the North Atlantic, including anglers, octopus, and lobster. See the daily diving show at which the fish are fed. The divers actually enter a feeding frenzy of huge, and sometimes aggressive, halibut and wolffish. One of the newest attractions, the Humbodt penguins, are also popular with children. After your visit, have a picnic, hike, or take a refreshing swim at the adjoining Tueneset Park. Bus 18, which leaves from St. Olavs Plass, makes the 15-minute journey to the park once every hour during the day, Monday through Saturday. ⊠*Tueneset* ☎*70–10–70–60* ⊕*www.atlanterhavsparken.no* ⊠*NKr 120* ⊙*June–Aug., Sun.–Fri. 10–7, Sat. 10–4; Sept.–May, Mon.–Sat. 11–4, Sun. 11–6.*

OFF THE
BEATEN
PATH
Runde. Norway's southernmost major bird rock—one of the largest in Europe—is the breeding ground for some 200 species, including puffins, gannets, and cormorants. The region's wildlife managers maintain many observation posts here. In summer, straying into the bird's nesting areas is strictly forbidden. A catamaran leaves from Skateflua quay in Ålesund for the 25-minute trip to Hareid, where it connects with a bus for the 50-km (31-mi) trip to Runde. A path leads from the bus stop to the nature reserve. Call Herøy Kommune for more information. (☎*70–08–13–00* ⊕*www.heroy.kommune.no*).

WHERE TO EAT AND STAY

$$
CONTEMPORARY
✕**Fjellstua.** This mountaintop restaurant has tremendous views over the surrounding peaks, islands, and fjords. There is also a terrace for when weather allows. On the menu, try the Norwegian bacalao, baked salmon, and homemade rissoles. ⊠*Top of Aksla Mountain* ☎*70–10–74–00* ⊕*www.fjellstua.no* ⊟*AE, DC, MC, V* ⊙*Closed Jan. Lunch only from Feb.–Apr.; lunch and early dinner from May to Sept.*

$$
★
Rica Hotel Scandinavie. Now part of the Rica chain, this hotel has impressive towers and arches and dates back to 1905. The modern rooms are beautifully decorated, especially those done in an art nouveau style. ⊠*Løvenvoldgt. 8* ☎*70–15–78–00* ⊕*www.choicehotels. no* ⊯*70 rooms* ⚅*In room: Internet. In-hotel: restaurant, bar* ⊟*AE, DC, MC, V* ⓧ*EP.*

GEIRANGERFJORD

85 km (52½ mi) southwest of Åndalsnes.

★ The Geirangerfjord made the UNESCO World Heritage List in 2005 and is Norway's most spectacular and perhaps best-known fjord. The 16-km-long (10-mi-long), 960-foot-deep Geirangerfjord's most stunning attractions are its roaring waterfalls—the Seven Sisters, the Bridal Veil, and the Suitor. Perched on mountain ledges along the fjord, deserted farms at Skageflå and Knivsflå are being restored and maintained by local enthusiasts.

The village of Geiranger, at the end of the fjord, is home to only 300 year-round residents, but in spring and summer its population swells to 5,000 due to visitors traveling from Hellesylt to the east. In winter, snow on the mountain roads means that the village is often isolated.

★ The most scenic route to Geiranger is the two-hour drive along Route 63 over **Trollstigveien** from Åndalsnes. Once you are here, the Ørneveien (Eagles' Road) road to Geiranger, which has 11 hairpin turns and was completed in 1952, leads directly to the fjord.

WHERE TO STAY

$$–$$$ Union Hotel. One of the biggest hotels in the vicinity of Geirangerfjord, the Union is famous for its location near the fjords. Decked out in rosemaling-decorated wood furniture, the lobby has a country feel, although the rooms are modern. Ask for one of the rooms with good fjord views. ☒ *Off Rte. 63, Geiranger* ☎ *70–26–83–00* ⊕ *www.union-hotel. no* ⤸ *151 rooms, 17 suites* ⌂ *In-hotel: 2 restaurants, bar, pools* ☐ *AE, DC, MC, V* ⊘ *Closed Jan. and Feb.*

HIKING

Trekking through fjord country can occupy a few hours or several days. Trails and paths are marked by signs or cairns with a red T on them. Area tourist offices and bookshops have maps, and of course you can always ask residents for directions or destinations.

STRYN

150 km (93 mi) south of Ålesund.

Stryn, Loen, and Olden, at the eastern end of Nordfjord, were among the first tourist destinations in the region. English salmon fishermen became the first tourists in the 1860s. By the end of the 19th century more hotels had been built, and cruise ships added the area to their routes. Tourism grew into an important industry. The most famous attraction in Stryn is the Briksdal Glacier, which lies between cascading waterfalls and high mountaintops. It's one arm of the Jostedal Glacier.

GETTING HERE AND AROUND

From Geiranger to Stryn, take the ferry across Geirangerfjord to Hellesylt, a 55-minute ride. It's about 50 km (30 mi) from Hellesylt to Stryn on Route 60. There is no train station in Stryn, but buses link Stryn with Ålesund, with at least two departures daily.

ESSENTIALS

Bus Contact Nor-Way Bussekspress (☎ *815–44–444* ⊕ *www.nor-way.no*).

Ferry Contact Fjord1 MRF (☎ *71–21–95–00* ⊕ *www.fjord1.no*).

Visitor Info Stryn & Nordfjord Tourist Board (☒ *Stryn* ☎ *57–87–40–40* ⊕ *www. nordfjord.no*).

EXPLORING

Covering the mountains between the Sognefjord and Nordfjord, **Jostedalsbreen Glacier** is the largest in Europe. There are about a hundred known routes for crossing Jostedal Glacier; if you want to hike it, you must have a qualified guide. Contact the Jostedalsbreen Glacier National Park Center or another tourist office. Such hikes should only be attempted in summer; mountain boots and windproof clothing are both essential.

Many of Jostedalsbreen's arms are tourist attractions in their own right. The best-known arm, **Briksdal Glacier,** lies at the end of Oldedal Valley, about 20 km (12 mi) south of Olden. It can be visited by bicycle, by car, or on foot from April to October.

Right outside Stryn, **Jostedalsbreen Nasjonalparksenter** (*Jostedalsbreen Glacier National Park Center* ☎57–87–72–00 ⊕*www.jostedalsbre.no*) covers the glacier and the surrounding region in detail. Landscape models, mineral and photograph collections, films, and dioramas describe the region's unique geography, flora, and fauna. The Geological Park, which opened in 2005, features a comprehensive collection of local rocks. There's also a garden of 325 types of wildflowers. ⊞*NKr 75* ⊗ *Mid-May–June 10–4; Aug.–mid-Sept. 10–4; rest of year, groups only by arrangement.*

WHERE TO EAT

$ ✕**Briksdalsbre Fjellstove** (*Briksdal Glacier Mountain Lodge*). The cafeteria at this lodge has a no-frills menu of fresh, hearty country fare. The
NORWEGIAN trout, the fillet of reindeer, and the deep-fried cod's jaws are all worth a try. Accommodation is also available, and as you'd expect from its location, a large gift shop is nearby. ⊠*Briksdalsbre* ☎57–87–68–00 ☰*AE, DC, MC, V.*

$$–$$$ ✕**Kjenndalstova Kafé and Restaurant.** Perhaps western Norway's best-kept
NORWEGIAN secret, this café and restaurant serves up delicious traditional dishes. Close to Kjendal's glacier, towering mountains, cascading waterfalls, and a pristine lake, the scenery from the restaurant alone is well worth a visit. Try the fried fresh trout, the fish stew, and the dessert cakes. ⊠*Prestestegen 15, Loen* ☎94–53–83–85 ☰*AE, DC, MC, V* ⊗*Closed Oct.–Apr.*

WHERE TO STAY

$$$ ⌂**Alexandra.** This hotel was built in 1884, but has been entirely refur-
★ bished with stone and oak in a modern style. It remains one of the most luxurious hotels in the region. The rooms are spacious and decorated in cheerful, light colors. Many offer a spectacular view of either the fjord or the entrance to Lodalen valley. The hotel also has a popular spa, and the friendly staff—some in traditional folk costumes—can assist in arranging various outdoor activities in the Nordfjord area. **Pros:** superb location; extensive leisure facilities. **Cons:** room design is not exactly modern. ⊠*N-6789 Loen* ☎57–87–50–00 ⊕*www.alexandra. no* ⌖*172 rooms, 17 suites* ⌂*In-hotel: 3 restaurants, 2 cafés, bars, tennis court, pool, gym* ☰*AE, DC, MC, V* ⏊*MAP.*

$$$ 🛏**Olden Fjordhotel.** Close to the fjord and cruise terminal, this modern hotel has simple, comfortable rooms with standard, chain hotel–style furniture and balconies overlooking the fjord. Glossy hardwood floors in most common areas and some rooms lend the hotel a degree of sophistication. An extremely helpful and friendly staff will ensure a pleasant stay. Allergen-free rooms and larger rooms for families are also available. **Pros:** balconies overlooking the fjord; great food; pedaloes and rowing boats available for guests. **Cons:** no Internet access in the rooms. ✉*N-6788, Olden* ☎*57–87–04–00* ⊕*www.olden-hotel.no* ⇆*60 rooms* ⌂*In-hotel: restaurant, bar* ▤*AE, DC, MC, V* ⍟*BP and AI.*

$$–$$$ 🛏**Visnes Hotel.** Dating from 1850, this small hotel has lovely individually decorated rooms filled with pretty antiques. The walls are lined with old-fashioned wallpaper, and most rooms have balconies overlooking the fjord. The hotel is five minutes from Stryn's center. Specialities in the restaurant include smoked salmon and venison. The nearby Villa Visnes, a restored 1898 home with classic Norwegian carved-wood dragons arching out from the eaves, now houses an apartment and conference center. **Pros:** well-kept period building; family-run; excellent food. **Cons:** not right in the center of Stryn. ✉*Prestestegen 1, Stryn* ☎*57–87–10–87* ⊕*www.visnes.no* ⇆*14 rooms, 1 suite* ⌂*In-hotel: restaurant* ▤*AE, DC, MC, V* ⍟*BP.*

SPORTS AND THE OUTDOORS

In addition to taking a guided walk on the glaciers, you can follow the many other trails in this area. Ask at the Stryn tourist office for a walking map and hiking suggestions.

SKIING

The **Stryn Sommerskisenter** *(Summer Ski Center)* has earned a reputation as northern Europe's best summer-skiing resort. Its seasons last from May through August, depending on the weather. The trails run over Tystig Glacier. The center has a ski school, a snowboard park, and cross-country trails. Skis, snowboards and snowshoes are available for rent. ✉*Rte. 258 (aka Old Strynefjell Mountain Route) near Videseter* ☎*57–87–54–74* ⊕*www.strynefjellet.com* ⊙*May–Aug., daily 10–4.*

FLÅM

66 km (41 mi) northeast of Voss.

One of the most scenic train routes in Europe zooms from Myrdal, high into the mountains and down to the town of Flåm. After the day-trippers have departed, it's a wonderful place to extend your tour and spend the night.

GETTING HERE AND AROUND

From Voss take the E16 heading northeast—it takes about an hour to get to Flåm. The road passes Naerøyfjord, Norway's narrowest fjord, and one of its most spectacular.

Flåm railway station is the starting point (or terminus) of the famous Flåmbana. Trains go to Myrdal, with connections to both Voss and Geilo.

Buses also link Flåm with Voss (1 hour 15 minutes) and Geilo (via Gol; 3 hours 30 minutes).

ESSENTIALS

Bus Contact Nor-Way Bussekspress (☎ *815–44–444* ⊕ *www.nor-way.no).*

Train Contact Flåmsbana (☎ *57–63–21–00* ⊕ *www.flaamsbana.no).*

Visitor Info Flåm Tourist Board (⊠ *Railroad station* ☎ *57–63–14–00* ⊕ *www. visitflam.com).*

EXPLORING

The **Flåmsbana** *(Flåm Railway)* is only 20 km (12 mi) long, but it takes 40 to 55 minutes (one-way) to travel the 2,850 feet up the steep mountain gorge. The line includes 20 tunnels. A masterpiece of Norwegian engineering, it took 20 years to complete, and is today one of Norway's prime tourist attractions, with more than 500,000 visiting each year. ⊠ *Flåm train station* ☎ *57–63–21–00* ⊕ *www.flaamsbana.no.*

If you have time to kill before the train departs, make sure you visit the **Flåmsbana Museet** *(Flåm Railway Museum).* Building the Flåm Railway was a remarkable feat in engineering, and this museum illustrates the challenges the builders faced in detail. You'll find it in the old station building, just 300 feet from the present one. ⊠ *Flåm train station* ☎ *57–63–23–10* ⊕ *www.flamsbana-museet.no/default.asp* ⌦ *Free* ⊙ *May–Sept., daily 9–5; Oct.–Apr., daily 1:30–3.*

WHERE TO STAY

$$–$$$ ⬚ **Fretheim Hotell.** One of western Norway's most beautiful hotels, the Fretheim has a classic, timeless look. Staying true to the Fretheim's 1866 roots, the rooms are furnished simply. Book in advance for a room with a fjord view. Rooms in the new northern wing of the hotel are slightly higher in standard than the older ones, although the price is exactly the same. If you can spring for a suite, you'll have more space and nicer furnishings. There's a spectacular view of the fjord from the restaurant and bar. **Pros:** superb location; excellent food. **Cons:** not all the rooms have a view of the fjord. ⊠ *Flåm Harbor, Flåm* ☎ *57–63–63–00* ⊕ *www. fretheim-hotel.no* ⇗ *104 rooms, 7 suites* ⌕ *In-hotel: restaurant, bar* ⊟ *AE, MC, V* ⎮⊚⎮*BP (FAP also available).*

SHOPPING

Saga Souvenirs (⊠ *Flåm train station* ☎ *57–11–00–11* ⊕ *www.sagasou venir.no)* is one of the largest gift shops in Norway. The selection of traditional items includes knitwear, wood and ceramic trolls, and jewelry.

VOSS

80 km (50 mi) north (1 hr by train) from Bergen.

Set between the Hardanger and Sogne fjords, Voss is in a handy place to begin an exploration of Fjord Norway. Once considered a stopover, Voss now attracts visitors drawn by its concerts, festivals, farms, and other attractions. Norwegians know Voss best for its skiing and famous jazz festival—Vossajazz—held annually in March. People come from all over Norway for the Sheep's Heads Festival, a celebration of the culinary delicacy of this area.

GETTING HERE AND AROUND

Voss is easily accessible from Bergen via the E16. The 102-km (63-mi) drive takes around 90 minutes. The E16 runs all the way to Oslo. In summer an alternate route is via Route 13 from Voss to Granvin, and from there pick up Route 7, across the Hardangervidda plateau to Oslo.

Buses run between Voss and Bergen several times daily. The journey takes 1 hour 45 minutes. Buses also link Voss and Oslo, and the journey takes between 7½ and 9 hours.

Voss is accessible via the *Bergensbanen* between Oslo and Bergen. Express trains run several times daily from Oslo and Bergen; all stop at both Voss station and Myrdal. There are also local trains from Bergen that run to Voss. The steep *Flåmsbanen* railway, featured in the "Norway in a Nutshell" tour, runs from Myrdal to Flåm.

ESSENTIALS

Train Contact **NSB** (*Norwegian state railways* ☎ 815-00-888 ⊕ www.nsb.no).

Bus Contact **Nor-Way Bussekspress** (☎ 815-44-444 ⊕ www.nor-way.no).

Visitor Info **Voss Tourist Board** (✉ Uttrågt. 9 ☎ 56-52-08-00 ⊕ www.visitvoss. no).

EXPLORING

Galleri Voss shows the works of Norwegian artists in a bright, airy space. ✉ Stallgt. 6–8 ☎ 56–51–90–18 ⊙ Tues., Wed., Fri., and Sat. 10–4, Thurs. 10–6, Sun. noon–3.

Dating from 1277, the enchanting **Voss Kyrkje–Vangskyrkja** *(Voss Church)* holds services every Sunday at 11 AM. Take a walk through to see the stained glass within. Concerts are occasionally held here. Guided tours are available. ✉ Vangsgt. 3 ☎ 56–52–38–80 ⊠ NKr 15 ⊙ June–Aug., Mon.–Sat. 10–4, Sun. 1–4.

Perched on the hillside overlooking Voss, **Mølstertunet** is an open-air museum. The 16 farm buildings here were built between 1600 and 1870. Along with handcrafted tools and other items, they reveal much about area farmers' lives and struggles. ✉ Mølstervn. 143 ☎ 56–51–15–11 ⊕ www.vossfolkemuseum.no ⊠ NKr 45 ⊙ Mid-May–mid-Sept., daily 10–5; mid-Sept.–mid-May, weekdays 10–3, Sun. noon–3.

WHERE TO STAY

$$$ 🖫 **Fleischer's Hotel.** One of Norway's historic wooden hotels, the beau-
★ tiful, gabled Fleischer looks like a manor from a fairy tale. Its carved wood dragons are fine examples of stave church-style architecture, developed in Hardanger in the late 19th century. First seen in churches, the style became fashionable and eventually was used all over southern Norway to decorate everything from silverware and furniture to prominent buildings like this luxurious hotel. Rooms in the old wing still have some flavor from that era. The restaurant Magdalene serves

traditional renditions of sheep's head, grilled venison, fresh mountain trout, and salmon dishes. The hotel is steps away from the railway tracks leading to Bergen. **Pros:** excellent location; plenty of period features; restaurant serves local, seasonal specialties. **Cons:** the rooms in the newer wing of the hotel and the apartments are not as atmospheric as those in the main building. ⊠ *Evangervegen 13* ☎ *56–52–05–00* ⊕ *www.fleischers.no* ⇆ *115 rooms* ♿ *In-hotel: restaurant, bar, pool* ☰ *AE, DC, MC, V* ❙◯❙ *BP.*

$$$ 🏨 **Stalheim Hotel.** Originally a coach station on the old postal route from
★ Oslo to Bergen, this hotel is perched high over the 13 hairpin turns of the dramatic Stalheimskleiva road, halfway between Voss and Flåm. The rooms are comfortable, and an interesting folk museum is on the premises, but it's the view that really makes the Stalheim Hotel worth a visit. To get there by car, follow Route E16. If you're on the Norway in a Nutshell tour, run by Fjord Tours AS, one of the regular stops is just outside the hotel. You can hop off the bus there and pick up the tour again the next day. **Pros:** stunning views; buffet lunch and dinner. **Cons:** the hotel is used by many tour operators, so big groups often stay here; there isn't much to do in the area in the evening. ⊠ *Stalheim* ✚ *32 km (22 mi) north of Voss* ☎ *56–52–01–22* ⊕ *www.stalheim.com* ⇆ *124 rooms* ♿ *In-room: no TV. In-hotel: restaurant, bar* ☰ *AE, DC, MC, V* ❙◯❙ *BP.*

SPORTS AND THE OUTDOORS

FISHING

The tourist information office in Voss sells fishing licenses and has a fishing guide to the nearly 500 lakes and rivers in the area where fishing's allowed. Fishing licenses (one day for NKr 50, three days for NKr 100, season permit NKr 300) are also sold at campsites and the post office.

HIKING

Walks and hikes are especially rewarding in this region, with spectacular mountain and water views everywhere. Be prepared for abrupt weather changes in spring and fall. Voss is a starting point for mountain hikes in Slølsheimen, Vikafjell, and the surrounding mountains. Contact the Voss Tourist Board for tips. **Hangursheisen** (☎ *56–53–02–20* ⊕ *www.vossresort.no*) is a cable car that runs from the center of Voss to Hanguren mountain. The summit is a good starting point for skiing in winter, and hiking and mountain biking in summer.

PARAGLIDING

One of the best places to paraglide in Norway, Voss has easily accessed starting points and constant thermals. The tandem season runs roughly from mid-April to mid-October. To take a tandem paraglider flight (in which an instructor goes with you), you must weigh between 70 and 240 pounds. The flight lasts an hour and costs NKr 1,500. Contact **Nordic Ventures** (☎ *56–51–00–17* ⊕ *www.nordicventures.com*).

RIVER SPORTS

Rivers around Voss are ideal for river paddling, kayaking, and other water sports. **Nordic Ventures** (☎ *56–51–00–17* ⊕ *www.nordicventures.*

com) runs guided sea-kayak tours past the waterfalls and mountains of Sognefjord from April to October; prices start at NKr 650. **Voss Rafting Senter** (☎ *56–51–05–25* ⊕ *www.vossrafting.no*) offers rafting, riverboarding, and canyoneering at prices beginning around NKr 500. **Voss Ski & Surf** (☎ *56–51–30–43*) offers one- to three-day courses in river kayaking for both beginners and experienced kayakers, as well as a half-day introduction course. Prices start at NKr 990 for a full day. They also book kayak trips with instructors.

SKIING
Voss and its varied mountain terrains are ideal for winter sports. An important alpine skiing center in Norway, **Voss Resort Fjellheisar** (☎ *56–53–02–20* ⊕ *www.vossresort.no*) has 40 km (25 mi) of alpine slopes, one cable car, 12 ski lifts, 20 km (12.5 mi) of marked crosscountry trails, a snowboard park, a ski school, and ski rental.

UTNE

65 km (41 mi) south of Voss.

In the very heart of Hardanger lies Utne, a tiny village that rests at the tip of the peninsula dividing the inlet of Hardangerfjord from the arm that stretches south towards Odda, the Sørfjord. It's an excellent starting point for exploring the area. Going south on both sides of the fjord, you can explore farming communities with traditions dating back to the Middle Ages, or go hiking in the steep mountainsides and the plateaus or glaciers beyond.

GETTING HERE AND AROUND
To get to Utne from Voss, take Route 13 to Granvin, and then Route 7 to Kvanndal where you catch the ferry to Utne. Buses are available from both Bergen and Voss to Kvanndal several times daily.

ESSENTIALS
Boat and Ferry Contact Tide (☎ *05505* ⊕ *www.tide.no*).

Bus Contact Skyss Hardangerlinja (☎ *55–55–90–70* ⊕ *www.skyss.no*).

Visitor Info Utne Tourist Board (☎ *53–66–18–22*). **Reisemål Hardangerfjord AS** (☎ *56–55–38–70* ⊕ *www.hardangerfjord.com*).

EXPLORING
Hardanger Folkemuseum is within walking distance of the ferry landing at Utne. Focusing primarily on local heritage, it's one of the largest and best museums of its kind in western Norway. The exhibit on folk costumes is particularly good, and several of the oldest surviving *Hardingfele* (Hardanger fiddles) are on display here. The ornate, usually eight-stringed fiddle was developed in Hardanger and produces a unique sound that inspired great Norwegian composers like Ole Bull and Edvard Grieg. ⊠ *Utne* ☎ *53–67–00–40* ⊕ *www.folkemuseum.hardanger. museum.no* ☑ *NKr 50* ☉ *May, daily 10–4; June–Aug., daily 10–5; Sept.–Apr., weekdays 10–3.*

Agatunet is an open-air museum composed of a cluster of old farm-houses—the oldest dating back to the 13th century. Serfdom was not practiced widely in western Norway. In some communities independent farmers clustered their houses together, and divided the pastures and orchards evenly. Although this led to some bizarre situations, like two farmers owning one half of the same apple tree, this semi-communal farming system was practiced until the 19th century. Very few clustered villages remain today, however, and even fewer are in as pristine condition as the Agatunet. The admission covers guided tours and indoor exhibits. Wandering the idyllic grounds is free. ⊠ *Aga, 17 km (11 mi) south of Utne* ☎ *53–66–22–14* ⊕ *www.agatunet.no* ✉ *NKr 50* ⊙ *Mid-May–mid-Aug., daily 11–5.*

On the eastern side of the Sørfjord is the village of **Lofthus,** one of the oldest fruit-farming communities in the area—and a spectacular sight in late spring and early summer when its 450,000 fruit trees are in bloom. The last week in July, **Morellfestivalen** (*the Morello Festival* ⊕ *www.morellfestivalen.no*) celebrates the sweet cherry of the same name, brought here in 1146 by traveling Yorkshire monks. The main event is the Norwegian Championship in Morello Pit Spitting. To get to Lofthus, take the ferry from Utne to Kinsarvik, and follow Route 13 toward Odda, approximately 10 km (6 mi).

The **Folgefonna** glacier straddles the mountain ridge between Rosendal and Sørfjorden. Folgefonna is actually a set of three glaciers, Nordfonna, Midtfonna, and Sørfonna. The latter is the third-largest glacier in Norway. Several hiking paths lead up to the glacier, but you should only attempt to hike on the glacier itself accompanied by a guide. Good footwear and wind- and waterproof clothing are essential, even on sunny days. The easiest way to get up close to the glacier is to drive up to the **Folgefonn Sommarskisenter** (*Folgefonna Summer Ski Center*) from Jondal, 31 km (19 mi) south of Utne. The drive from Jondal up to the glacier itself is spectacular though bumpy. *Ski center:* ⊠ *Jondal* ☎ *57–87–54–74 or 46–80–59–66* ⊕ *www.folgefonn.no* ⊙ *May–Aug., daily 9–4.*

OFF THE BEATEN PATH

Baroniet Rosendal. In 1658 a wealthy Norwegian heiress, Karen Mowat, wedded a Danish nobleman, Ludvig Rosenkrantz, and the two were given a farm at Hatteberg, tucked away in a valley west of Folgefonna, as their wedding present. They built a castle on the land, and a few years later the king of Denmark and Norway at the time, Christian V, gave the estate status as a barony, the only one of its kind in Norway. The estate was bequeathed to the University of Oslo in 1927, and today the barony is a combined museum, theater, and gallery with its own bed-and-breakfast on the premises. The castle is in fact a small-ish mansion, decorated in a variety of styles spanning the barony's history over 250 years and surrounded by a rose garden and stunning scenery. In summer there are concerts, lectures, and performances in the mansion or the courtyard. In mid-July the **Theatre Set-Up** company from London performs Shakespeare plays in English. ⊠ *Rosendal* ⊕ *From Utne, follow Rte. 550 south toward Odda, then take Folgefonn tunnel (toll) west and follow Rte. 48 to Rosendal* ☎ *53–48–29–99* ⊕ *www.baroniet.no*

📷 *NKr 75 off-season, NKr 100 in high season, concerts NKr 150–NKr 290* ⊘ *Late June–mid-Aug., daily 10–5, guided tours every 30 mins; May–late June and mid-Aug.–early Sept., daily 11–3; guided tours every hr; early Sept.–late Sept., guided tours at noon only.*

WHERE TO STAY

$$$–$$$$ 🏨 **Hotel Ullensvang.** This large hotel by the fjord in Lofthus offers comfortable, modern rooms. The restaurant, Zanoni, has a great view of both the fjord and the Folgefonna glacier. Rooms with a fjord and glacier view are about NKr 300 more expensive than those without the views. **Pros:** terrace by the fjord; great food and wine; superb location. **Cons:** many tour groups use the hotel. ⊠ *Lofthus* 🕿 *53–67–00–00* ⊕ *www.hotel-ullensvang.no* ⬦ *157 rooms, 16 suites* ⌂ *In-room: Internet. In-hotel: restaurant, bar, pool, gym* 🖃 *AE, DC, MC, V* 🍴 *BP; AI on weekend.*

$$$ 🏨 **Utne Hotel.** This small, cozy hotel has been in continuous operation
Fodor's Choice   since it was built in 1722, making it Norway's oldest. The white wooden
★   main building has a wood-paneled, hand-painted dining room decorated with copper pans, old china, and paintings. All 26 rooms have their own distinct design flavor, and several are furnished with unique antiques and artwork from the area. Utne Hotel fills up fast in high season, so book well in advance. **Pros:** charming period building; individually decorated rooms; friendly and attentive service. **Cons:** the rooms can be chilly in winter. ⊠ *Utne* 🕿 *53–66–64–00* ⊕ *www.utnehotel.no* ⬦ *26 rooms* ⌂ *In-hotel: restaurant, bar* 🖃 *AE, DC, MC, V* 🍴 *BP.*

SPORTS
HIKING
Steep paths lead from Lofthus up to the westernmost part of the Hardangervidda plateau—they're breathtaking in both senses of the word, so leave time for resting your legs and taking pictures. One of the most beautiful routes is the Monk Steps trail, from Lofthus to Nosi, which leads to a viewpoint 950 meters (3,117 feet) over the fjord. Allow four hours for the return trip. Contact the local tourist office for tips and further hiking suggestions. **Folgefonni Breførarlag** (🕿 *55–29–89–21 or 95–11–77–92* ⊕ *www.folgefonni-breforarlag.no*) offers guided tours on the Folgefonna glacier.

CENTRAL NORWAY

Central Norway is dominated by Hardangervidda, Europe's largest mountain plateau. Several mountain areas and valleys—Hallingdal, Numedal, and Hemsedal—surround the plateau. North of Oslo are the famous valleys of Gudbrandsdalen and Valdres, and the mountain regions of Rondane, Dovrefjell, and Jotunheimen. Route 7 crosses Hardangervidda, and the Oslo-to-Bergen railway serves many towns in the region, including some in remote mountain areas that are hard to reach, such as Finse. Traveling by car involves lots of mountain driving, and may be impeded by the occasional avalanche or bad winter weather.

HEMSEDAL

220 km (136 mi) northwest of Oslo and 275 km (170 mi) east of Bergen.

The mountains in the area are nicknamed the Scandinavian Alps, and Hemsedal has some of Norway's most stunning high-mountain scenery: you can see mountains and glaciers, numerous lakes, four rivers, as well as fjords and cascading waterfalls. It's the country's most popular skiing town, where Norway's top skiers and snowboarders live and train. The Maifestivalen (May Festival), which takes place on the first weekend of May, marks the end of the ski season; it's a well-attended event. In the summer months you can hike, play golf, and go fishing.

GETTING HERE AND AROUND
From Oslo take the E16 to Hønefoss, and then follow Route 7 to Gol. Change for Route 52 at Gol. The bus company Nor-Way Bussekspress serves Hemsedal—journey time 4½ hours. There is no train station at Hemsedal. The nearest station is in Gol, 30 km (18.5 mi) away. The local bus, route 360, connects with the railway station in Gol. It is operated by Sogn Billag, part of Fjord1.

ESSENTIALS
Bus Contacts Nor-Way Bussekspress (☎815-44-444 ⊕www.nor-way.no). **Fjord1 Sogn Billag** (☎32-05-99-54 ⊕www.fjord1.no/sognbillag).

Visitor Info Hemsedal Tourist Board (☎32-05-50-30 ⊕www.hemsedal.com).

WHERE TO EAT AND STAY
$ ✕**Hemsedal Café.** This hip café is a place to see and be seen, or you
CAFÉ can just come for the simple dishes like burgers, pasta, Thai chicken,
★ spareribs, or the filling skier's breakfast. There is also a children's menu.
⊠*Brustabygge* ☎*32-05-54-10* ☐*AE, DC, MC, V.*

$$-$$$ ☆**Harahorn.** On a mountaintop 3,280 feet above Hemsedal's center,
★ Harahorn is comprised of 12 mountain cabins clustered around the main house. Decorated in deep blues and earthy shades, the luxurious *bonderomantikk* (country romantic) pine cabins are filled with antiques and art. You can visit the hotel just to dine at the main house's restaurant, or opt to stay here. There are many outdoor sports and activities available, such as skiing, dogsledding, mountain climbing, and moose safaris. **Pros:** traditional-style bedrooms come complete with fireplace; extensive wine cellar; stunning location. **Cons:** steep rates in high season. ⊠*N-3560 Hemsedal* ☎*32-05-51-10* ⊕*www.harahorn. no* ➥*35 rooms and cabins* ♿*In-hotel: restaurant, bar* ☐*AE, DC, MC, V* ⦿*MAP.*

$$$$ ☆**Skarsnuten Hotell.** This mountainside hotel perches like an eagle's
Fodor'sChoice nest over the village of Skarsnuten Landsby. The modern, minimal-
★ ist interior is dominated by glass, steel and slate. Framed mountain-sports photographs line the white walls, and rooms have spectacular views and names like Little Matterhorn. Take the hotel's ski lift down to Hemsedal Skisenteret, the hotel's ski resort. The restaurant is well regarded for its European-inspired menu based on seasonal Norwegian ingredients. **Pros:** stunning views; bright, airy design; excellent

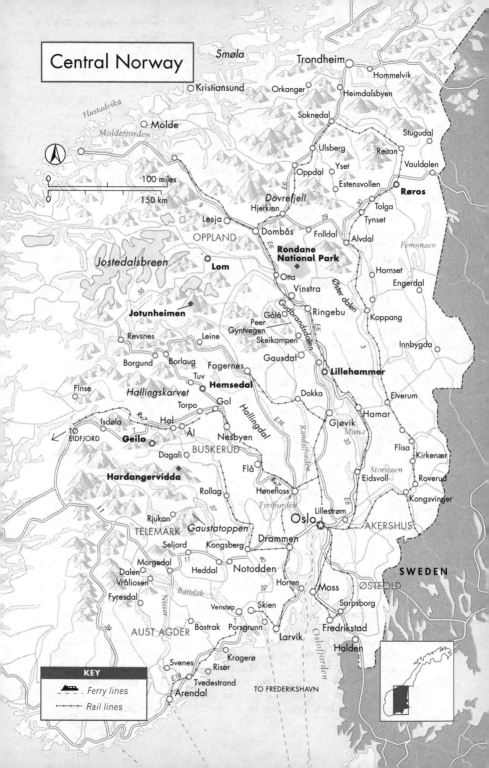

food. **Cons:** steep rates ⊠*Skarsnuten Landsby* ⏚*PB110, N 3561, Hemsedal* ☎*32–06–17–10* ⊕*www.skarsnutenhotell.no* ↩*35 rooms, 2 suites* ♿*In-hotel: restaurant, bar, laundry facilities, no-smoking rooms* ☰*AE, DC, MC, V* ◯|*FAP*.

SPORTS AND THE OUTDOORS
HIKING AND CLIMBING
Experienced guides at **Norske Opplevelser AS** (☎*32–06–00–03* ⊕*www. norskeopplevelser.no*) offer mountain touring and climbing courses year-round. **Hemsedal Fjellsport** (☎*41–12–63–21* ⊕*www.hemsedalfjell sport.no*) also has climbing courses.

HORSEBACK RIDING
Elvestad Fjellridning (☎*90–88–45–45*) offers day riding trips in the forest and mountains for all levels of riders, from late June through August, for about NKr 750 per person.

PARAGLIDING
Paraglide in tandem with an experienced instructor. **Oslo Paragliding Klubb** (☎*92–81–95–45* ⊕*www.opk.no*) has its main base in Hemsedal. Prices start at NKr 1,500 for a tandem flight.

SKIING
Hemsedal Skisenteret (☎*32–05–50–60* ⊕*www.hemsedal.com*) has 34 km (21 mi) of alpine slopes, 210 km (130 mi) of cross-country trails, 17 ski lifts, a terrain park, and Norway's largest ski arena for children. The Ski School has superbly run courses for novices from children to adults.

GEILO

43 km (26.5 mi) west of Hemsedal, 240 km (149 mi) northwest of Oslo and 279 km (173 mi) east of Bergen.

More than a million visitors a year head to the slopes and cross-country trails of this *alpeby* (Alpine town) halfway between Oslo and Bergen. Many people ski directly from their hotel or cabin doors. Plan ahead if you want to visit at Easter, since Norwegians flock here for a final ski weekend. The summer season, beginning in June, has such activities as guided mountain walks, horseback riding, and fishing.

GETTING HERE AND AROUND
From Oslo take the E16 to Hønefoss, and then follow Route 7 to Geilo.

Bus companies Nor-Way Bussekspress and Nettbuss both have services connecting most interior cities, including Geilo. Hallingdal Billag (now part of Fjord1) has service between Oslo and Geilo.

There are several train departures daily between Oslo and Geilo. The journey takes 3½ to 4 hours.

ESSENTIALS
Bus Contacts Fjord1 Hallingdal Billag (☎*32-08-60-60* ⊕ www.fjord1.no). **Nettbuss** (☎*815-00-184 or 177* ⊕ www.nettbuss.no). **Nor-Way Bussekspress** (☎*815-44-444* ⊕ www.nor-way.no).

Train Contact **NSB** (*Norwegian State Railways* ☎815–00–888 ⊕*www.nsb.no*).

Visitor Info **Geilo Tourist Board** (☎32–09–59–00 ⊕*www.geilo.no.en*).

EXPLORING

In the center of Geilo, the 17th-century farm of **Geilojordet** is a part of Hol Bygdemuseum. The cattle house, storage house, farmer's living quarters, and other buildings were brought here from the surrounding area and then restored. Cultural activities and events, such as rosemaling, wood carving, and folk-music performances, take place here. A café serves coffee, waffles, *rømmebrød* (sour-cream loaf), *lefse* (potato pancakes filled with sugar or cream), and other traditional sweets. ⊠ *Hagafoss* ☎*32–09–59–00 tourist office* ☞*Free* ☉*Late June–mid-Aug., daily 11–4.*

WHERE TO EAT AND STAY

Norway's most popular resort town has many hotels, mountain lodges, traditional cabins, apartments, and camping sites. Rooms are booked early for high season: you can contact **Geilo Booking** (☎*32–09–59–00* ⊕*www.geilo.no*), operated by the Geilo Tourist Board, for advice on accommodations.

$$$$
NORWEGIAN

✗ **Halling-stuene.** The region's best-known chef, Frode Aga, has become a celebrity through his cookbooks and television appearances. His downtown restaurant has an elegant, rustic *bonderomantikk* style. His modern Norwegian cuisine features fish and game with an international influence. Start off with some local cured meats and goat cheese, followed by classic Aga dishes like reindeer fillet with fresh vegetables and creamed game sauce, or the herb-baked mountain trout. ⊠ *Geilovn. 56* ☎*32–09–12–50* ⊕*www.hallingstuene.no* ☐*AE, DC, MC, V* ☉*Closed May, dinner only.*

$$$
★

☷ **Dr. Holms Hotel.** Built in 1909 as a sanitorium for asthma sufferers, the building is now a well-established resort hotel. Resembling a luxury mountain cabin, the hotel has elegantly decorated rooms and panoramic views of the surrounding mountains. Its Brasserie restaurant serves Continental-Norwegian dishes. Have drinks by the fire in the classy Ski bar, one of Norway's most popular après-ski bars. You can read in the peaceful (2,000 volume-strong) library, bowl a game at the hotel diner's bowling alley, or be pampered in the Japanese-style Dr. Holms Spa, the only Shiseido spa in Scandinavia. Make reservations well in advance. **Pros:** charming, atmosphereic hotel near the slopes; large rooms; good food. **Cons:** there is no adult-only time at the spa, so your time there might involve the pitter-patter of little feet, especially during the holidays; belongings have been known to disappear from the locker rooms. ⊠*Timrehaugvn. 2* ☎*32–09–57–00* ⊕*www.drholms. com* ⨑*124 rooms, 3 suites* ☖*In-hotel: restaurant, bars, pools, gym, spa, no-smoking rooms* ☐*AE, DC, MC, V* ☉❘*BP.*

SPORTS AND THE OUTDOORS
BIKING

Ask for bike maps at the Geilo tourist information office. Besides Rallarvegen, the Adventure Road, and Numedalsruta, there's excellent cycling in the countryside around Geilo on mountain roads. Bike rentals are available through **Intersport Geilo** (☎ *32–09–55–80* ⊕ *www. intersport-geilo.no*) for NKr 200 per bike per day.

FISHING

Geilo's 90 mountain lakes and river stretches are open to the public from June to September and most are well stocked with trout. Inquire about recreation maps for Geilo and Hallingskarvet at the tourist office. Fishing permits, which are mandatory, are available in local sport shops, campsites, and at the Geilo tourist office for NKr 50 per day. Fishing tackle and boat rentals can be organized through **Geilo Camping** (☎ *32–09–07–33*) for NKr 120 a day, while rowboats cost NKr 90 for three hours.

HORSEBACK RIDING

Many Geilo businesses offer horseback riding and riding lessons and lead mountain trips, which can last from several hours to a week. **Geilo Hestesenter** (☎ *32–09–01–81*) operates June through October and offers trips and courses for both beginners and experienced riders, with tours lasting from one hour to a weekend. **Stall Brusletto** (☎ *32–09–12–54 or 90–56–83–05*) has tours lasting from three hours to two days.

MOUNTAIN HIKES AND WALKS

For independent walking, **Den Norske Turistforening (DNT)** (*Norwegian Mountain Touring Association* ☎ *22–82–28–22* ⊕ *www.turistforeningen. no*) has marked trails across the Hardangervidda plain and in the countryside around Hallingskarvet. Inquire at the tourist office about DNT routes and the use of their cabins.

Experienced guide Turid Linseth of **Hardangervidda Fjellguiding** (☎ *97–54–18–60* ⊕ *www.fjellguiding.no*) offers designed guided mountain walks and ski trips for all levels and interests, as well as snowshoe and Nordic walking excursions.

SKIING

Geilo has 39 Alpine slopes, three snowboard parks, 20 lifts, and plenty of slopes for children on both sides of the valley. Kite-skiing is popular here, with some of the best conditions in the world. You can purchase a downhill ski pass that allows you to use all the lifts. A free shuttle bus goes between the five ski centers. For cross-country skiers, there are 220 km (137 mi) of groomed and marked cross-country trails through woodland, Hardangervidda's hills and moors, and around Hallingskarvet, which is 6,341 feet above sea level. Snow rafting is the latest winter thrill: participants slide down snowy slopes on rubber rafts. Contact **Geilo Skiheiser** (☎ *32–09–59–20* ⊕ *www.skigeilo.com*) for further information.

If you're looking for a younger crowd, be sure to spend some time near **Halstensgård** (☎ *32–09–10–20*) and **Havsdalsenteret** (☎ *32–09–17–77*), two Geilo-area ski hubs that attract younger crowds to their long Alpine slopes. **Vestlia** (☎ *32–09–55–10*), west of the Ustedalsfjord, has easier slopes so it's a good choice for families.

HARDANGERVIDDA

The Hardangervidda lies approximately 200 km (124 mi) west of Oslo, and 175 km (108 mi) east of Bergen. It is 90 km (56 mi) from Geilo to Eidfjord.

Norwegians take great pride in their largest national park, which is also Europe's largest mountain plateau at 10,000 square km (3,861 square mi). Hardangervidda is home to the largest wild reindeer herds in Europe and is the southernmost outpost of the arctic fox, snowy owl, and other arctic animals and plants. A plateau with a thousand lakes, it has gently rolling hills and wide stretches of level ground. In the west the mountains are more dramatic, the plant life richer, the climate wetter, and temperatures more moderate. In the east the small amount of snow means that it's an almost barren, windswept moorland.

Some 250 Stone Age sites have been found in Hardangervidda. The earliest date from 6,300 BC, which proves that man reached the plateau at the same time as the reindeer. When touring the plateau, either on horseback or on foot, you can find a trail for any level of ability. Den Norske Turistforening (DNT; The Norwegian Mountain Touring Association) has built cabins along the trails. The association organizes tours and activities. All plant and animal life is protected by law. Respect the area to make sure it remains a thing of beauty.

GETTING HERE AND AROUND
To drive from Oslo, take the E16 to Hønefoss, and then follow Route 7, the main road to cross the Hardangervidda. You can stop at a number of places; Geilo and Eidfjord are convenient towns along Route 7; Dagali, on Route 40 (a few kilometers south of Geilo), is another popular entry point.

Nor-Way buses connect most towns near the Hardangervidda.

Myrdal, Finse, and Geilo are the most convenient starting points for exploring the Hardangervidda if you're taking the Bergen Railway from Oslo (each has its own stop). There is no train station at Eidfjord.

ESSENTIALS
Bus Contact Nor-Way Bussekspress (☎ *815–44–444* ⊕ *www.nor-way.no*).

Train Contact NSB (*Norwegian State Railways* ☎ *815–00–888* ⊕ *www.nsb.no*).

Visitor Info Eidfjord Tourist Board (☎ *53–67–34–00* ⊕ *www.visiteidfjord.no*).

EXPLORING
At the foot of Vøringfossen waterfall and Måbødalen valley, the **Hardangervidda Natursenter Eidfjord** (*Hardangervidda Nature Center at Eidfjord*) focuses on the area's geology, biology, and archaeology. Over half a billion years ago Norway was south of the equator. Twenty-five million years ago glaciers began their descent over Norway. An interactive program explains how glaciers form, grow, and recede. ⊠ *Øvre Eidfjord* ☎ *53–66–59–00* ⊕ *www.hardangervidda.org* NKr 110 ☉ *Mid-June–mid-Aug., daily 9–8; mid-Aug., Sept., Oct., Apr., and May, daily 10–6; Nov.–Mar., by arrangement.*

SPORTS AND THE OUTDOORS
MOUNTAIN HIKES AND WALKS
About an hour's drive north of Geilo is Hardangervidda's highest peak, **Hardangerjøkulen** (*Hardanger Glacier*), at 6,200 feet. In summer you can join guided glacier walks led by **Jøklagutane** (☎ 99–33–12–22 ⊕ *www. joklagutane.no*). Near Hardangerjøkulen you can take a guided hike to the archaeological digs of 8,000-year-old Stone Age settlements.

For independent walking, **Den Norske Turistforening (DNT)** (*Norwegian Mountain Touring Association*) (☎ 22–82–28–22 ⊕ *www.turistforeningen. no*) has marked trails across the Hardangervidda and in the countryside around Hallingskarvet. Inquire at the tourist office about DNT routes and the use of their cabins.

Experienced guide Turid Linseth of **Hardangervidda Fjellguiding** (☎ 97–54–18–60 ⊕ *www.fjellguiding.no*) offers designed guided mountain walks and ski trips for all levels and interests, as well as snoeshoe and Nordic walking excursions.

BIKING
In summer, cycling enthusiasts flock to **Rallarvegen,** widely considered to be one of the best mountain-biking routes in the world. The ride is on a gentle incline from Haugastøl, at 2,950 feet about sea level, to Finse, at 4,008 feet above sea level. Bike rental is available through **Haugastøl Tourist Center** (☎ 32–08–75–64) or at the Finse 1222 Hotel.

RAFTING
Dagali Opplevelser (☎ 32–09–38–20 ⊕ *www.dagaliopplevelser.no*) lead white-water trips with international guides on the Numeral River.

LILLEHAMMER

40 km (25 mi) from Gjøvik, 180 km (111 mi) from Oslo.

Many Norwegians have great affection for Lillehammer, the winter-sports resort town that hosted the 1994 Winter Olympics. In preparation for the games, the small town built a ski-jumping arena, an ice-hockey arena, a cross-country skiing stadium, and a bobsled and luge track. Lillehammer is known for the slopes on the mountains Nordseter and Sjusjøen; Vinterspillene, its Winter Arts Festival, held in February; and its many old wooden buildings. Lillehammer is a cultural center as well. It hosts the Norwegian Literature Festival in May, and is home to one of the best collections of Norwegian art in the country. Sigrid Undset, who won the Nobel Prize in literature in 1928, lived in the town for 30 years.

GETTING HERE AND AROUND
The wide, two-lane Route E6 north from Oslo passes through Lillehammer. For a more scenic alternative, follow Route 33 on the western bank of Lake Mjøsa, via Gjøvik.

Nor-Way buses link Lillehammer and Oslo with four departures daily. The journey takes just under three hours. There are also regular train services between Lillehammer and Oslo throughout the day. The ride's about two hours and 15 minutes.

The nearest airport is Oslo's Gardermoen Airport; *Oslo Getting Here and Around, Above, for flight details.*

ESSENTIALS

Bus Contact Nor-Way Bussekspress (☎ *815-44-444* ⊕ *www.nor-way.no).*

Train Contact NSB *(Norwegian State Railways* ☎ *815-00-888* ⊕ *www.nsb.no).*

Visitor Info Lillehammer Tourist Board (✉ *Jernbanetorget 2* ☎ *61-28-98-00* ⊕ *www.lillehammerturist.no).*

EXPLORING

Fodor's Choice
★ One of the most important art collections in Norway is housed at the **Lillehammer Kunstmuseum** *(Lillehammer Museum of Art),* which opened in 1927. The 1,000 works include pieces by Edvard Munch, J. C. Dahl, Erik Werenskiold, Christian Krogh, and Adolph Tidemand. The original 1963 building has been remodeled and joined by a new building designed by Snøhetta, the firm behind the new Oslo Opera House. Sculptor Bård Breivik created a sculpture garden using stone and water between the two buildings. ✉ *Stortorgt. 2* ☎ *61-05-44-60* ⊕ *www. lillehammerartmuseum.com* ✑ *NKr 60* ☉ *July and Aug. daily 11-5; rest of year Tues.-Sun. 11-4.*

☾ Europe's largest open-air museum, **Maihaugen** was founded in 1887.
★ This massive collection of folk life artifacts comes from Anders Sandvig, an itinerant dentist who accepted odds and ends—and eventually entire buildings—from the people of Gudbrandsdalen in exchange for his services. Eventually Sandvig turned the collection over to the city of Lillehammer, which provided land for the museum. The exhibit "We Won the Land" is an inventive meander through Norway's history. It begins in 10,000 BC. After walking past life-size, blue-hued mannequins representing periods like the Black Death and the 400 years of Danish rule, you reach unsettling exhibits about the 20th century. ✉ *Maihaugvn. 1* ☎ *61-28-89-00* ⊕ *www.maihaugen.no* ✑ *NKr 100, includes guided tour (NKr 80 in off-peak season)* ☉ *Oct.-mid-May, Tues.-Sun. 11-4; mid-May-Sept., daily 10-5.*

The **Norges Olympiske Museum** *(Norwegian Olympic Museum)* covers the history of the games from their start in ancient Greece in 776 BC. Multimedia presentations and artifacts like sailboats and skis illustrate Norwegian sporting history in the **Gallery of Honor.** Some of the exhibition captions are in English. ✉ *Håkons Hall, Olympic Park* ☎ *61-25-21-00* ⊕ *www.ol.museum.no* ✑ *NKr 75* ☉ *Mid-May-Sept., daily 10-5; Oct.-mid-May, Tues.-Sun. 11-4.*

The **Olympiaparken** has a range of winter as well as summer activities. You can visit the ski-jump tower and take the chairlift to the top for some stunning views, or step inside the bobsled simulator at the **Lysgårdsbakkene Ski Jump Arena,** where the Winter Olympics' opening and closing ceremonies were held. Also in the park are **Håkons Hall,** the main hockey arena during the Olympic Games, which now holds sporting events and includes simulated, indoor golf-course holes. The **Birkebeineren Ski Stadium** holds cross-country and biathlon events. You can go tobogganing at the **Kanthaugen Freestyle Arena.** And at the **Olympic Bobsleigh and Luge Track** you can bobsled on ice. This involves a rubber bobsled with wooden runners that seats five passengers and can travel as fast as 80 kph (50 mph). ⊠*Lillehammer Olympiapark* ☎*61–05–42–00* ⊕*www.olympiaparken. no* ⊠*NKr 80 for entry to chairlift, ski jump, and simulator; fee varies for athletic events* ☉*Varies seasonally and by event.*

OFF THE BEATEN PATH

☾

Hunderfossen Park. The world's biggest troll sits atop a cave in this popular amusement park. The Eventyrslottet, or fairy-tale castle, rings in at 37 meters (121 feet) and is a must-see. There's a petting zoo for small children, plenty of rides, a mini waterpark with inflatable slides and water canons, a go-karting track, a rafting river, and a five-screen theater. The park is 13 km (8 mi) north of Lillehammer. ⊠*Fåberg* ☎*61–27–55–30* ⊕*www.hunderfossen.no* ⊠*NKr 300, discounted entrance fee in off-peak season* ☉*Late May–late June, daily 10–5; late June–early Aug., daily 10–7; early Aug.–early Sept., daily 10–5.*

WHERE TO EAT

$$–$$$
CONTEMPORARY

✕**Blåmann Restaurant & Bar.** This restaurant, named after a Norwegian folktale about a buck called Blueman, is popular with locals and tourists alike. The menu features a mix of Mexican staples, pasta, steaks, as well as Norwegian specialties and more international options. Try the tacos, or a reindeer or ostrich steak. There is a pleasant terrace, and a bar upstairs. ⊠*Lilletorget 1* ☎*61–26–22–03* ⊕*www.blaamann.com* ⚖*Reservations essential* ⊟*AE, DC, MC, V.*

$
ECLECTIC

✕**Nikkers, Svare & Berg.** Nikkers, in a distinctive yellow building just a few steps from Lillehammer's main pedestrian street, boasts a buzzing, modern bar on the first floor, and a relaxed patio at street level. Right next door, Svare & Berg has a roaring fireplace, turquoise chairs and banquettes, and colorful paintings by local artist Per Rosenberg hanging on the walls. These neightboring restaurant-bars share the same owner and international cuisine, ranging from nachos to pastas. ⊠*Elvegt. 18* ☎*61–24–74–30* ⊟*AE, DC, MC, V.*

WHERE TO STAY

¢–$

⊞**Birkebeineren Hotel/Motel & Apartments.** Ski trails and hiking terrain are steps away from this small complex, which offers accommodation in hotel and motel rooms, as well as in chalet-style apartments (note, though, that the apartments run a bit steeper than hotel and motel rooms). The cream-color rooms are understated and country-style. Black-and-white photographs of skiers decorate the walls. **Pros:** the apartments are very cozy; big outside area; lounges with fireplaces. **Cons:** not right in the town center; the motel rooms are plain. ⊠*Birkebeineren 24, Olympiaparken* ☎*61–05–00–80* ⊕*www.birkebeineren. no* ⊯*48 hotel rooms, 13 motel rooms, 40 apartments* ♿*In-room: Internet (some). In-hotel: restaurant, laundry room* ⊟*AE, DC, MC, V* ⫴*BP.*

$$–$$$
★

⊞**Mølla Hotell.** In this converted 1863 mill the small reception area gives the feeling of a private home. The yellow rooms in the former grain silo have rustic pine furniture. At the top of the silo, the Toppen Bar

4

gives you a panoramic view of the Olympic ski jump and Lake Mjøsa. The Egon Restaurant, with its thick stone walls, wooden beams, and many nooks and crannies, is the perfect setting for a romantic dinner by the Mesna River. **Pros:** flat-screen plasma TVs; view from the Toppen Bar is great; cozy restaurant. **Cons:** the yellow building's exterior can be off-putting. ☒*Elvegt. 12* ☎*61–05–70–80* ⊕*www.mollahotell. no* ⌁*58 rooms* ♿*In-room: Internet. In-hotel: restaurant, bar* ▤*AE, DC, MC, V* ⧖*BP.*

$$–$$$ ⊞ **Rica Victoria Hotel.** Red burnished leather chairs dot the library–style lobby at this central hotel. Guest rooms are furnished in styles ranging from pure rural romanticism to more classic. The hotel has eight "ladies rooms," each with bed alcove and rocking chair. Victoria Stuen and Dolly Dimple's, the hotel's two restaurants, face a pedestrian street. **Pros:** very central location; free parking; cozy fireplace in the lobby. **Cons:** some dated 1970s decor; it's a bit of a climb up a steep road from the train station. ☒*Storgt. 84B* ☎*61–25–00–49* ⊕*www.rica.no* ⌁*109 rooms, 17 suites* ♿*In-room: Internet. In-hotel: 2 restaurants, bar* ▤*AE, DC, MC, V* ⧖*BP.*

SPORTS AND THE OUTDOORS

A highlight of Lillehammer's ski year is the **Birkebeineren cross-country ski race.** The Birkebeiners were a faction in Norway's 13th-century civil war, who got their name because they wrapped their legs in birch bark (hence *birkebeiner*—birch legs). Birch bark was commonly used as footwear by people who couldn't afford wool or leather leggings. The 54-km (33-mi) ski race, held every year in March, commemorates the trek of two Birkebeiner warriors who carried the heir to the throne, Prince Haakon, to safety from the rival Bagler faction who were pursuing him. The backpack carried by participants during the race is meant to symbolize the young prince being brought to safety through harsh weather conditions.

FISHING

Within Troll Park, the **Gudbrandsdalåen** is touted as one of the best-stocked rivers in the country, and the size and weight of Mjøsa trout (locals claim it's 25 pounds) is legendary. Contact the local tourist board for information about fishing seasons, how to get the required national and local licenses, and other useful tips.

HIKING AND BICYCLING

The Nordseter and Sjusjøen tourist centers are good starting points for mountain-biking and -hiking excursions. From **Nordseter Aktivitetssenter** (☒*Off Rte. 6* ☎*61–26–40–37* ⊕*www.nordseter.no*), about 15 km (9 mi) from the city center, you can hike to Mt. Neverfjell, at 3,573 feet. There you can see the Jotunheimen and Rondane mountain ranges. The center rents mountain bikes, canoes, and boats, and organizes moose safaris. Mt. Lunkefjell (3,320 feet) is a popular hiking destination accessible from **Sjusjøen Sport & Aktiviteter** (☒*Sjøen* ☎*62–36–30–04* ⊕*sjusjoen-sport.no*). Regular bicycles and mountain bikes can be rented. The center also organizes walks, bicycle and fishing trips, and canoeing.

RAFTING AND CANOEING
The **Sjoa River,** close to Lillehammer, offers some of the most challenging rapids in the country. Contact **Heidal Rafting** (☎ 61–23–60–37 ⊕ *www. heidalrafting.no*).

SKIING
Lillehammer–Sjusjøen and Nordseter and the four other nearby skiing destinations—Hafjell, Skeikampen, Kvitfjell, and Gålå—are collectively called **Lillehammer Ski Resorts** (⊕ *www.lsr.no*). Together, they have 43 lifts, 88 pistes, 5 terrain parks, and more than 1,500 km (932 mi) of cross-country trails. Each destination has its particular charm. A Lillehammer Ski Resorts Pass admits you to all five. With both high-mountain and forest terrain, **Hafjell** (✉ *10 km [6 mi] north of Lillehammer* ☎ 61–27–47–00 ⊕ *www.hafjell.com*) is the largest Alpine facility. Snow conditions are generally stable here. The Hunderfossen Familiepark with snowboarding is popular. There's also a child-care center, a ski school, and several after-ski entertainment spots.

Gålå (✉ *Near Vinstra, 89 km [40 mi] north from Lillehammer via E6* ☎ 61–29–76–61 ⊕ *www.gala.no*) is an all-around ski facility, with spectacular high-mountain terrain and views of Jotunheimen and Rondane national parks. It has cross-country trails and organized activities that include ice fishing, snow rafting, sledding, winter riding, and sleigh riding.

SHOPPING
Most of Lillehammer's 250-odd shops are on or near Storgata Street, Lillehammer's main pedestrian street. From Lilletorget you can walk to the old industrial area of Mesna Brug, where there's the Mesnasenter (Mesna Center) group of clothing and craft shops. **Husfliden** (✉ *Sigrid Undset pl., Storgt. 47* ☎ 61–26–70–70 ⊕ *www.husfliden.no*), one of the biggest and oldest home crafts stores in Europe, specializes in hand-knit sweaters and traditional and handmade goods from the Gudbrandsdalen area.

RONDANE NATIONAL PARK

310 km (192 mi) north of Oslo, 520 km (323 mi) northeast of Bergen.

Rounded, harmonious mountains distinguish Rondane National Park, Norway's oldest, as you travel north from Vinstra on Route E6. A good point of entry to the park is the resort of Høvringen, off Route E6. For thousands of years the area has given hunters their livelihood, and they've left their mark in the form of reindeer traps and burial mounds. Today Rondane is a popular recreation area, attracting hikers and skiers. Ten of the peaks rise more than 6,500 feet. Norwegian artist Harald Sohlberg (1869–1935) immortalized the Rondane mountains in his painting *Vinternatt i Rondane,* which was declared Norway's national painting in 1995 and hangs in the National Gallery in Oslo.

GETTING HERE AND AROUND

Taking the E6 north from Oslo will eventually lead you through Vinstra and Otta, the park's closest towns. Nor-Way buses link these two towns with Oslo, with three departures daily. The journey takes just under four hours.

There are also several train services between Vinstra and Otta and Oslo daily. The journey takes 3½ hours.

ESSENTIALS

Bus Contact **Nor-Way Bussekspress** (☎815–44–444 ⊕ www.nor-way.no).

Train Contact **NSB** (*Norwegian State Railways* ☎815–00–888 ⊕ www.nsb.no).

Visitor Info **Rondane NP** (⊕ www.visitrondane.com).

WHERE TO STAY

$$$–$$$$ ⬚ **Rondablikk Hotell.** Nestled in the mountains, near Kvam, Rondablikk has spectacular views of Rondane National Park and several lakes. Rooms are simply furnished and comfortable. Many guests spend their days cross-country skiing or mountain hiking. Every August, Norway's best musicians play on the hotel's outdoor stage as part of the Peer Gynt Festival. **Pros:** great location; live music in the evening. **Cons:** not the most modern of hotels; minimum two-night stay. ⊠ *Rte. E6, Kvam* ☎ *61–29–49–40* ⊕ *www.rondablikk.no* ⤏ *72 rooms* ⅙ *In-hotel: restaurant, bar, pool* ⊟ *AE, DC, MC, V* ⅢⅠ *BP (MAP also available).*

SPORTS AND THE OUTDOORS

BOATING

Guided canoe safaris or independent trips are possible on four mountain lakes along the Peer Gynt Road. Contact **Gålå Sommer Arena** (☎ *61–29–76–30* ⊕ *www.gala.no*) and **Fefor Høifjellshotell** (☎ *61–29–00–99* ⊕ *www.fefor.no*).

HIKING

A network of marked trails and footpaths such as those kept by the **DNT (Norwegian Mountain Touring Association)** (☎ *40–00–18–68* ⊕ *www.turistforeningen.no*) the **Peer Gynt Trail,** and the **Pilgrims' Track** offer varied challenges. You can pick up maps at **Vinstra Skysstasjon** (*Vinstra Tourist and Transport Centre* ⊠ *Øvre Årdal* ☎ *61–29–47–70*).

HORSEBACK RIDING

Sulseter Rideleir (☎ *61–29–13–21* ⊕ *www.sulseter.no*) offers weeklong and weekend treks in Rondane National Park.

SKIING

Considered one of the best resorts for cross-country skiing (there are 630 km [391 mi] of trails), the **Peer Gynt Ski Region** (☎ *61–29–73–20*) includes Espedalen, Fefor, Gålå, Skei, and Kvitfjell. For downhill skiers there are pistes for all levels in Snowboard, Telemark, and Alpine.

LOM AND JOTUNHEIMEN

62 km (38 mi) west of Otta, via Rte. 15.

Jotunheimen, or "the Home of the Giants," is mainland Norway's major massif and a popular area with hikers and climbers in summer. Established in 1980, the national park covers a surface of 1,145 square km and stretches from the eastern inland to the west coast, offering a wonderfully varied landscape.

GETTING HERE AND AROUND

From Oslo take the E18 northwest to Fagernes, and then Route 51 to Beitostølen. From there you can follow the scenic Valdresflya, which has wonderful views over the eastern part of Jotunheimen and the Besseggen Ridge. From Beitostølen to Lom is 140 km (87 mi). Route 55 between Lom and Gaupa is known as Sognefjellet, and is a popular National Tourist Road. It crosses the Jotunheimen and again, offers breathtaking scenery through the massif. It can be closed in bad weather, though, particularly in winter, so check before traveling. The bus company JVB TUR serves Jotunheimen and Valdres. Nor-Way express buses link Oslo and Lom four times daily; the trip takes 6½ hours. There is no train station in Lom; head to nearby Otta instead. There are several departures daily from there to Oslo.

ESSENTIALS

Bus Contact JVB TUR (☎*61–36–59–00* ⊕ *www.jvb.no).*

Visitor Info Lom/Jotunheimen Reiseliv Tourist Board (☎*61–21–29–90* ⊕*www. visitjotunheimen.com).*

EXPLORING

One of the park's well-known landmarks is **Galdhøpiggen**, the country's highest mountain, at 8,098 feet. Established in 1980, the park covers an area of 1,150 square km (444 square mi), and contains 27 of Norway's highest peaks. The rural town of Lom is distinguished by its dark-brown painted log cabins and a stave church from 1170.

One of Norway's oldest and most beautiful stave churches, **Lom Stavkyrkje** *(Lom Stave Church),* dates to the 12th century and still is the principal church in Lom. Its oldest section is Romanesque; the church was enlarged in 1634. Wood-carver Jakop Sæterdalen created the choir stalls and the pulpit. The church's baroque painting collection is one of Norway's largest. ✉*2686* ☎*97–07–53–97* 🖮*NKr 40* ⊗*Mid-May– mid-June and mid-Aug.–mid-Sept., daily 10–4; mid-June–mid-Aug., daily 9–8.*

A woolly mammoth looms at the entrance to **Norsk Fjellmuseum** *(Norwegian Mountain Museum).* The museum focuses on people's relationship with the Norwegian mountain landscape, from the primitive hunters and gatherers who lived here to modern Norwegian society, with its belief in leisure time and outdoor recreational activities. One of the most interesting exhibits deals with early mountaineering and mountain road building. The National Park exhibit makes for an interesting introduction to the flora, fauna, and topography of Jotunheimen.

✉ *Town Center* ☎ *61–21–16–00* ⊕ *www.fjell.museum.no* 💷 *NKr 60* ⊙ *May–mid-June weekdays 9–4, weekends 11–5; mid-June–mid-Aug., weekdays 9–7, weekends 10–7; mid-Aug.–Sept., weekdays 9–4, weekends 11–5; Oct.–Apr., weekdays only 10–3.*

Torgeir Garmo shares his passion for geology in his geological museum and jewelry gallery in the **Fossheim Steinsenter** *(Fossheim Stone Center)*. His collection is the largest private exhibition of Norwegian minerals and precious stones in the country. In the sales galleries you can buy jewelry, minerals, and fossils. The Collector Mania museum shows rare objects that people have collected through the ages. ✉ *Lom* ☎ *61–21–14–60* ⊕ *www.fossheimsteinsenter.no* 💷 *Free* ⊙ *June–Aug., daily 10–7, otherwise by appointment.*

Glaciers, lakes, fertile valleys, and mountains make up **Jotunheimen National Park,** of which 90% lies in the municipality of Lom.

WHERE TO STAY

$$$
★
🏨 **Fossheim Turisthotell.** Svein Garmo and his family have run this mountain hotel since it began as a staging post in 1897. Solid-timber walls and antique furnishings give it a cozy look. Chef Kristoffer Hovland and his dishes based on local ingredients have made the restaurant popular. Among the best-known dishes is the succulent fillet of reindeer. In summer take a seat in the aromatic outdoor café Urtehagen, surrounded by herbs and flowers. **Pros:** great views; top-notch food; beautiful log huts. **Cons:** the annex isn't as nice as the main building. ✉ *Off Rte. E6, Lom* ☎ *61–21–95–00* ⊕ *www.fossheimhotel.no* ↪ *46 rooms, 3 apartments, 2 cabins* ♿ *In-hotel: restaurant, bar* ⊟ *AE, DC, MC, V* ⏻ *BP.*

$$$$
FodorsChoice
★
🏨 **Røisheim Hotel.** Formerly a farm and coaching inn, this beautiful property is made up of 12 well-preserved buildings, most from the 18th century and one dating back to the 16th century. Rooms with hardwood floors and antique furniture retain the traditional look and feel of the original interior. Some even have a fireplace. The restaurant is renowned for its excellent cuisine, which revolves around local and seasonal ingredients, and vast wine cellar. Walking trails in the area will leave you speechless at the beauty of the Jotunheimen range's peaks and glaciers. **Pros:** fantastic location in a high-mountain pass near the road to Sognefjell, about 12 km (7½ mi) outside Lom; superb food and wines; beautiful accommodation. **Cons:** steep prices; the hotel is only open in summer. ✉ *Bøverdalen* ☎ *61–21–20–31* ⊕ *www.roisheim.no* ↪ *24 rooms* ♿ *In-hotel: restaurant, bar* ⊟ *AE, DC, MC, V* ⏻ *AI* ⊙ *Closed Sept.–Apr.*

SPORTS AND THE OUTDOORS

FISHING

Lom Fiskeguiding DA (☎ *61–21–10–24* ⊕ *www.lomweb.com/fisk*) rents fishing boats and organizes fishing trips.

HIKING AND GLACIER WALKING

Juvasshytta (☎ *61–21–15–50*) organizes guided walks to Galdhøpiggen, Norway's highest peak, daily in summer. **Natur Opplevingar** (☎ *61–21–11–55* ⊕ *www.naturopplevingar.no*) offers glacier walks and guided hikes to a range of summits in Jotunheimen, as well as climbing courses in Lom.

HORSEBACK RIDING
Jotunheimen Hestesenter (*Jotunheimen Equestrian Center* ✉ *Ruubergstøl len* ☎ *61–21–18–00*) has mountain riding tours for all ages, beginner to advanced, on Icelandic horses.

RAFTING
Several local outfitters cater to your Sjoa River rafting needs, including **Lom Rafting** (☎ *90–04–62–61* ⊕ *www.lomrafting.no*) and **Skjåk Rafting** (☎ *99–77–50–88* ⊕ *www.skjak-rafting.no*).

SUMMER SKIING
You can go summer skiing at **Galdhøpiggen Sommerskisenter** (✉ *Lom* ☎ *61–21–17–50* ⊕ *www.gpss.no*) on a glacier 6,068 feet above sea level.

RØROS

157 km (97 mi) south of Trondheim.

At the northern end of the Østerdal, the long valley to the east of Gudbrandsdalen, lies Røros, one of Norway's great mining towns. It is famed for its well preserved wooden buildings (many with maintained turf roofs), wooden church, and mine (now a museum). For more than 300 years practically everyone who lived in this one-company town was connected with the copper mines. In 1980 Røros was named a UNESCO World Heritage Site. Norwegian artist Harald Sohlberg's paintings of Røros made the town famous. His statue now stands in Harald Sohlberg's plass, looking down the stretch of road that he immortalized.

GETTING HERE AND AROUND
Røros's tiny airport is used by local airline Widerøe (which offers regular flights to Oslo) and a handful of small private operators.

Nor-Way Express buses link Røros and Trondheim in just under three hours. There are several services a day. The journey to Oslo takes six hours, and there is only one departure daily.

Røros is on the Oslo–Trondheim train line, with several services a day in both directions.

ESSENTIALS
Air Contact Widerøe (☎ *810–01–200 in Norway* ⊕ *www.wideroe.no*).

Bus Contact Nor-Way Bussekspress (☎ *815–44–444* ⊕ *www.nor-way.no*).

Train Contact NSB (*Norwegian State Railways* ☎ *815–00–888* ⊕ *www.nsb.no*).

Visitor Info Røro Tourist Board (☎ *72–41–00–00* ⊕ *www.rorosinfo.com*).

EXPLORING
The **Bergstadens Ziir** *(Røros Church)* towers over the wooden houses of the town. The eight-sided stone structure dates from 1784. On the tower you can see the symbol of the mines. Called "the mountain's cathedral,"

it can seat 1,600, quite surprising in a town with a population of only about 3,500. The pulpit looms above the center of the altar, and seats encircle the top perimeter. At press time, the church was undergoing renovations and not due to open to the public until summer of 2010. If you're visiting before then, you can still arrange guided tours with the tourist office. ⊠*Peder Hiorts gt. 2* 🕿*72–41–00–50* 🖃*NKr 25.*

OFF THE BEATEN PATH

Olavsgruva mine. In 1977, Norway's copper works went bankrupt; this is the only Norwegian copper mine that was saved for posterity. Known as Olavsgruva, it consists of Nyberget (first operated in 1650) and Crown Prince Olav's Mine (dating from much more recent times: 1936). A museum has been built over the mine shafts. Visitors can walk 164 feet underground and approximately 1,640 feet into the Miners' Hall, complete with sound and light effects. Bring warm clothing and good shoes, as the temperature below ground is about 5°C (41°F). ⊠*Near Rte. 31* 🕿*72–40–61–70* 🖃*NKr 80* ⊘*Guided tours early June and late Aug.–early Sept., Mon.–Sat. at 1 and 3, Sun. at noon; late June–mid-Aug., daily at 10:30, noon, 1:30, 3, 4:30, and 6; early Sept.–May, Sat. at 3.*

★ Røros's main attraction is the **Old Town,** with its 250-year-old workers' cottages, slag dumps, and managers' houses, one of which is now City Hall. Descendants of the man who discovered copper ore in Røros live in the oldest of the nearly 100 protected heritage buildings. A 75-minute tour starts at the information office and ends at the church. ⊠*Peder Hiorts gt. 2* 🕿*72–41–00–50* 🖃*NKr 60* ⊘*Tours June and late Aug.–mid-Sept., Mon.–Sat. at 11; July–mid-Aug., Mon.–Sat. at 10, noon, 1, 2, and 3, Sun. at 1; mid-Sept.–May, Sat. at 11.*

Røros Museum *(Smelthytta)* is in an old smelting plant, opened in 1646. In 1953 a fire destroyed the smelting works in Røros; the plant was closed and the machines were moved to Sweden. "Smelthytta," the smelting house, has been reconstructed using drawings of the workshop from 1888. Exhibitions show models of waterwheels, lift mechanisms, horse-driven capstans, mine galleries, and 19th-century clothing. ⊠*Malmplassen* 🕿*72–40–61–70* ⊕*rorosmuseet.no* 🖃*NKr 60, NKr 100 for combined ticket with mine* ⊘*Late-June–mid-Aug., daily 10–6; mid-Aug.–early Sept. and early to late June, weekdays 11–4, weekends 11–3; early Sept.–May, weekdays 11–3, weekends 11–2.*

WHERE TO STAY

If you want to explore the green, pastured mountains just south of Røros, more than a dozen farmhouses take overnight visitors. Some are *hytter* (cabins), but others, such as the **Vingelsgaard Gjestgiveri** (🕿*62–49–48–20* ⊕*www.vingelsgaard.no*), have entire wings devoted to guest rooms. Rates at Vingelsgaard start at NKr 660 (breakfast extra). Contact **Vingelen Turistinformasjon** (🕿*62–49–46–65* ⊕*www.vingelen.com*) for information on farmhouse stays throughout the Røros area.

$$ 🛏**Bergstadens Hotel.** An elegant, country-style hotel, this Røros landmark blends original features with modern furniture and conveniences. The staff is warm and friendly, creating a personal and intimate mood.

The restaurant has a changing menu of traditional Norwegian fare. Note that on weekends, the rate increases substantially ($$$$) but includes all meals. **Pros:** central location; helpful staff; good breakfast. **Cons:** worn beds; hallways retain food smells. ☒ *Oslom 2* ☎ *72–40–60–80* ⊕ *www.bergstaden.no* ☞ *90 rooms, 4 suites* ⋏ *In-hotel: 2 restaurants, bars, pool* ⊟ *DC, MC, V* ⦿ *BP or MAP at weekends.*

SPORTS AND THE OUTDOORS
BOATING
Femunden and Hodal lakes make great starting points for day trips or longer tours. A canoeing trip on your own or accompanied by a guide can be memorable. **Hodalen Fjellstue** in Tolga (☎ *62–49–60–39*) has boat and fishnet rentals and fishing permits.

CYCLING
Easy terrain in the Røros region makes it ideal for cyclists. The Røros tourist office offers bicycling package tours, which include maps and accommodation.

DOGSLED TOURS
Contact **Heimly Huskies Adventure** (☎ *72–41–41–94* ⊕ *www.roroshusky. no*) for dogsled tours with authentic Siberian huskies lasting from one hour to one week.

FISHING
Fishing is possible in the Gaula, one of Norway's finest salmon rivers, or in the Glåma, Norway's longest river, recommended for grayling and trout. An angling guidebook and fishing licenses are sold at the tourist office, in shops and gas stations, and at the rangers' office in Holtålen. Skilled guides can show you the area and advise you on where and how to fish, preserving and cooking your catch. Contact **Ålen Fjellstyre** (☎ *72–41–55–77*).

TRONDHEIM TO THE NORTH CAPE

Wild and beautiful, northern Norway is known for its fast-changing weather and vast distances, and is famous as the land of the northern lights, midnight sun, and polar night. It's a land marked by high mountains, glaciers, fjords, islands, and rocky shores. The Gulf Stream warms the coast, making it the longest ice-free coast in the polar regions. Basking in the midnight sun is one of Norway's most popular attractions; every year, thousands of people flock to Nordkapp (the North Cape) for it. To cater to the large number of visitors, northern Norway has well-run tourist offices which stock excellent maps and travel literature on the area.

TRONDHEIM

494 km (307 mi) north of Oslo, 657 km (408 mi) northeast of Bergen.

One of Scandinavia's oldest cities, Trondheim is Norway's third largest, with a population of 150,000. Founded in 997 by Viking king Olav Tryggvason, it was first named Nidaros (still the name of the cathedral), a composite word referring to the city's location at the mouth of the Nid River. The city was also the first capital of Norway, from AD 997 to 1380. Today Trondheim is a university town as well as a center for maritime and medical research, but the wide streets of the historic city center are still lined with brightly painted wood houses and striking warehouses.

GETTING HERE AND AROUND

AIR TRAVEL   SAS, Norwegian, and Widerøe carriers offer extensive connections throughout northern Norway. Widerøe flies to 27 destinations in the region, including Honningsvåg, the country's northernmost airport and the one closest to the North Cape. Trondheim's Værnes Airport is 32 km (21 mi) northeast of the city.

BOAT AND   **Hurtigruten** (the coastal express boat, which goes to 35 ports from
FERRY TRAVEL   Bergen to Kirkenes) stops at Trondheim, southbound at St. Olav's Pier, Quay 16, northbound at Pier 1, Quay 7. Other stops between Trondheim and the North Cape include Bodø, Stamsund and Svolvær (Lofotens), Sortland (Vesterålen), Harstad, Tromsø, Hammerfest, and Honningsvåg.

For travel on the *Hurtigruten* boat between any points along the route, it is possible to buy tickets on board.

BUS TRAVEL   Bus 135 (Østerdalsekspress) runs overnight from Oslo to Trondheim via Røros. Buses also connect Bergen and Ålesund with Trondheim.

Nor-Way Bussekspress can help you put together a bus journey to destinations in the north. The Ekspress 2000 travels regularly between Oslo, Trondheim, Kautokeino, Alta, Nordkapp, and Hammerfest. Note that in the north, buses go virtually everywhere, but they don't go often. Get a comprehensive bus schedule from a tourist office or travel agent before making plans.

All local Trondheim buses stop at the Munkegata–Dronningens Gate intersection. Some routes end at the bus terminal at Trondheim Sentralstasjon.

CAR TRAVEL   Trondheim is about 494 km (308 mi) from Oslo: a seven- to eight-hour drive. Speed limits are 80 kph (50 mph) or 100 kph (60 mph) much of the way. The two alternatives are the E6 through Gudbrandsdalen or Route 3 through Østerdalen. It's 723 km (448 mi) from Trondheim to Bodø on Route E6, which goes all the way to Kirkenes. There's an NKr 30 toll on E6 just east of Trondheim. The highway toll also covers the NKr 11 toll (6 AM–10 PM) for cars entering the downtown area. Anyone who makes it to the North Cape sans tour bus will be congratulated with an NKr 150 toll.

Most roads in northern Norway are quite good, although there are always narrow and winding stretches, especially along fjords. Distances are formidable. Route 17—the Kystriksvegen (Coastal Highway) from Namsos to Bodø—is an excellent alternative to E6. Getting to Tromsø and the North Cape involves additional driving on narrower roads off E6. In winter, near-blizzard conditions and icy roads sometimes make it necessary to drive in a convoy. You must also drive with special studded winter tires.

TRAIN TRAVEL The Dovrebanen has frequent departures daily on the Oslo–Trondheim route. Trains leave from Oslo S Station for the seven- to eight-hour journey. Trondheim is the gateway to the north, and two trains run daily in each direction on the 11-hour Trondheim–Bodø route. The Nordlandsbanen has three departures daily in each direction on the Bodø–Trondheim route. The *Ofotbanen* has two departures daily in each direction on the Stockholm–Narvik route, a 21-hour journey.

ESSENTIALS
Air Contacts Norwegian (☎ *815-21-815* ⊕ *www.norwegian.no*). **SAS** (☎ *800/221-2350 in U.S., 91-50-54-00 in Norway* ⊕ *www.flysas.com*). **Widerøe** (☎ *810-01-200* ⊕ *www.wideroe.no*).

Boat and Ferry Contact Hurtigruten (☎ *810-30-000* ⊕ *www.hurtigruten.com*).

Bus Contacts Ekspress 2000 (☎ *78-44-40-90*). **Nor-Way Bussekspress** (☎ *815-44-444*). **Trondheim Sentralstasjon (Trafikanten Midt-Norge)** (☎ *73-88-39-00 or 177 if calling from within the local area*).

Taxis Trøndertaxi (✉ *Trondheim* ☎ *073-73in Norway, 93-00-73-73 from abroad* ⊕ *www.trondertaxi.no*).

Train Contact NSB (*Norwegian state railways* ☎ *815-00-888* ⊕ *www.nsb.no*).

Visitor Info Finnmark Tourist Board (☎ *78-44-90-60* ⊕ *www.finnmark.com* for information on Finnmark and North Cape). **Nordland Reiseliv** (☎ *75-54-52-00* ⊕ *www.visitnordland.no* for information on Tromsø and Lofoten Islands). **Trondheim Tourist Board** (✉ *Munkegt. 19, Torget* ☎ *73-80-76-60* ⊕ *www.trondheim.com*).

EXPLORING
Trondheim is home to some wonderful historical buildings and sites. Take in the cathedral where Norway's kings are crowned, visit some of the oldest buildings in the country, and marvel at the country's largest entirely-wooden palace. If that's not your thing, stop in at a museum, or just enjoy the relatively mild climate as you walk along the river Nid, admiring the view.

TOP ATTRACTIONS
King Olav formulated a Christian religious code for Norway in 1024, during his reign. It was on his grave that **Nidaros Domkirke** *(Nidaros Cathedral)* was built. The town became a pilgrimage site for the Christians of northern Europe, and Olav was canonized in 1164. Although construction began in 1070, the oldest existing parts of the cathedral date from around 1150. It has been ravaged on several occasions by fire and rebuilt each time, generally in a Gothic style. Since the Middle Ages, Norway's kings have been crowned and blessed in the cathedral.

The crown jewels are on display here. Forty-five-minute guided tours are offered in English from mid-June to mid-August, weekdays at 11 and 4. ✉ *Kongsgårdsgt. 2* ☎ *73–53–91–60* ⊕ *www.nidarosdomen.no* ◻ *NKr 50, free entry from mid Sept. to end of Apr. Ticket also permits entry to Erkebispegården* ◑ *May–early June and early Aug.–mid-Sept., weekdays 9–3, Sat. 9–2, Sun. 1–4; early June–early Aug., weekdays 9–6, Sat. 9–2, Sun. 1–4; mid-Sept.–Apr., weekdays noon–2:30, Sat. 11:30–2, Sun. 1–3.*

The **Erkebispegården** *(Archbishop's Palace)* is the oldest secular building in Scandinavia, dating from around 1160. It was the residence of the archbishop until the Reformation in 1537; after that it was a residence for Danish governors, and later a military headquarters. The oldest parts of the palace, which face the cathedral, are used for government functions. The **Archbishop's Palace Museum** has original sculptures from Nidaros Cathedral and archaeological pieces from throughout its history. Within the Erkebispegården's inner palace you will find the **Rustkammeret/Resistance Museum,** which traces the development of the army from Viking times to the present through displays of uniforms, swords, and daggers. The Resistance Museum deals with events in central Norway during World War II, and its memorial hall remembers those who lost their lives. ✉ *Kongsgårdsgt.* ☎ *73–53–91–60* ⊕ *www.nidarosdomen.no* ◻ *NKr 50. Ticket also permits entry to Nidaros Cathedral* ◑ *Archbishop's Palace Museum: May–mid-June and mid-Aug.–mid-Sept., Mon.–Sat. 9–3, Sun. 1–4; mid-June–mid-Aug., weekdays 9–5, Sat. 9–2, Sun. 1–4; mid-Sept.–Apr., Mon.–Sat. 11–3, Sun. noon–4. Resistance Museum: June–Aug., weekdays 9–3, weekends 11–4; Mar.–May, Sept., and Oct., weekends 11–4; guided tours by appointment.*

Ringve Museum Norway's national museum of music and musical instruments consists of two permanent exhibitions. The "Museum in the Manor House" has been preserved as it was when Ringve's founder, Victoria Bachke, opened the museum in 1952. The distinctive interiors, which date back to the 1860s and '70s, make a fitting setting for the collection of classical music instruments on display. The "Museum in the Barn," meanwhile, focuses on modern sound and light technology. There are musical demonstrations and guided tours in English daily in summer. ✉ *Lade Allé 60* ☎ *73–87–02–80* ⊕ *www.ringve.com* ◻ *NKr 75* ◑ *Opening times vary; call to check.*

Near the ruins of King Sverre's medieval castle is the **Sverresborg Trøndelag Folkemuseum,** which has re-creations of coastal, inland, and mountain-village buildings that depict life in Trøndelag during the 18th and 19th centuries. The Haltdalen stave church, built in the 1170s, is the northernmost preserved stave church in Norway. In the Old Town you can visit a 1900 dentist's office and an old-fashioned grocery that sells sweets. The audiovisual **Trønderbua** depicts traditional regional wedding ceremonies with artifacts and a 360-degree film. During the summer there are farm animals on-site, and a range of activities for children. ✉ *Sverresborg Allé 13* ☎ *73–89–01–10* ⊕ *www.sverresborg.no* ◻ *NKr 80* ◑ *June–Aug., daily 11–6; Oct.–May, weekdays 11–3, weekends noon–4.*

Fodor's Choice Scandinavia's largest wooden palace, **Stiftsgården,** was built between
★ 1774 and 1778 as the home of a prominent widow. Sold to the state in
1800, it's now the official royal residence in Trondheim. The architecture and interior are late baroque and highly representative of 18th-cen-
tury high society's taste. Tours offer insight into the festivities marking
the coronations of the kings in Nidaros Domkirke. ✉ *Munkegt. 23*
☎ *73–80–89–50* ☜ *NKr 60* ☉ *June–mid-Aug., Mon.–Sat. 10–5, Sun.
noon–5. Tours on the hr.*

WORTH NOTING

Built by J. C. Cicignon after the great fire of 1681, the **Kristiansten Festning** *(Kristiansten Fort)* saved the city from conquest by Sweden in 1718.
During Norway's occupation by Germany, from 1940 to 1945, members of the Norwegian Resistance were executed here; there's a plaque
in their honor. The fort has a spectacular view of the city, the fjord,
and the mountains. ☎ *73–99–52–80* ☜ *Free* ☉ *June–Aug., weekdays
10–3, weekends 11–4.*

★ The Tiffany windows are magnificent at the **Nordenfjeldske Kunstindustrimuseum** *(National Museum of Decorative Arts)* , which houses an
impressive collection of furniture, silver, and textiles. The Scandinavian
Design section features a room interior designed by the Danish architect
Finn Juhl in 1952. The 1690 bridal crown by Adrian Bogarth is also
memorable. "Three Women–Three Artists" features tapestries by Han-
nah Ryggen and Synnøve Anker Aurdal, and glass creations by Benny
Motzfeldt. ✉ *Munkegt. 5* ☎ *73–80–89–50* ⊕ *www.nkim.museum.no*
☜ *NKr 60* ☉ *June–late Aug., Mon.–Sat. 10–5, Sun. noon–5; late Aug.–
May, Tues., Wed., Fri., and Sat. 10–3, Thurs. 10–5, Sun. noon–4.*

Near Nidaros Cathedral, the **Trondheim Kunstmuseum** *(Trondheim Art
Gallery)* houses some 4,000 works of art dating from as early as 1800.
Regional artists represented include Håkon Bleken, Jakob Weidemann,
Adolph Tidemand, Christian Krohg, and Harald Solberg. ✉ *Bispegt.
7B* ☎ *73–53–81–80* ⊕ *www.tkm.museum.no* ☜ *NKr 50* ☉ *Mid-June–
mid-Aug., daily 10–5; mid-Aug.–mid-June, Tues.–Sun. 11–4.*

▌ **OFF THE
BEATEN
PATH**

Munkholmen *(Monks' Island).* Now a swimming and recreation area,
Monk's Island was Trondheim's execution grounds in ancient times. In
the 11th century, Benedictine monks built a monastery on the island,
likely one of the first monasteries in Scandinavia. In 1658 the monastery
was converted into a prison and fort and, later, a customs house. There
is a display of handicrafts in what was once the caretaker's house. Boats
to the island depart from the fish market. ☎ *73–80–63–00* ⊕ *www.
lilletorget.no* ☜ *NKr 55 (return)* ☉ *Mid-May–early Sept., boats depart
daily on the hr 10–6.*

Norway's oldest institution of science, the **NTNU Vitenskapsmuseet**
(NTNU Science Museum) covers flora and fauna, minerals and rocks,
church history, southern Sami culture, and archaeological finds. The
eclectic exhibits have relics from the Bronze Age as well as ecclesias-
tical articles from the 13th to 18th century. ✉ *Erling Skakkes gt. 47*
☎ *73–59–21–45* ⊕ *www.ntnu.no/vmuseet* ☜ *NKr 25* ☉ *May–mid-*

Sept., weekdays 9–4, weekends 11–4; mid-Sept.–Apr., Tues.–Fri. 9–2, weekends noon–4.

Off Munkegata, near the water, you can see an immense variety of seafood at **Ravnklohallen Fiskehall** (*Fish Market* ☎73–52–55–21 ⊕*www. ravnkloa.no*).

A former 1725 prison now houses the little **Trondhjems Sjøfartsmuseum** *(Maritime Museum).* Models of sailing ships, figureheads, marine instruments, and photographs of local ships make up the exhibits. Standouts include a harpoon gun from a whaler and recovered cargo from *The Pearl,* a frigate that was wrecked in 1781. ✉*Fjordgt. 6A* ☎73–89–01–10 ⊠*NKr 25* ☉*June–Aug., daily 10–4.*

WHERE TO EAT

Trondheim is known for the traditional dish *surlaks* (marinated salmon served with sour cream). A sweet specialty is *tekake* (tea cake), which looks like a thick-crust pizza topped with a lattice pattern of cinnamon and sugar. The city's restaurant scene is vibrant and evolving, with more and more international restaurants serving Continental food, and bars and cafés where the city's considerable student population gathers.

$$$$
INTERNATIONAL
★
✕**Credo.** This restaurant might not look like much from the outside, but it is one of Trondheim's best—with prices to match. The menu changes daily but you can expect consistently superb food, supported by a good wine list and expert service. They do everything well, but are particularly strong on fish and seafood, and often use fruit as vegetables. Although the menu changes regularly, typical dishes include tartar of plaice with grated, unripe mango; fried plaice with lime foam and avocado and melon salad; skate with soy-and-oyster-sauce honey and oranges. A winner with both critics and punters. There is a trendy bar upstairs. ✉*Orjaveita 4* ☎73–53–03–88 ⊕*www.restaurantcredo. no* ⌨*Reservations essential* ⊟*AE, DC, MC, V* ☉*Dinner only, closed Sun.*

$$$
TEX-MEX
✕**Grønn Pepper.** Tex-Mex is popular throughout Norway, and this Trondheim restaurant serves a good rendition. Striped, vibrant Mexican blankets brighten up the hardwood floors and dark-wood furniture. Mexican beer and tequila go well with the fiery food on offer, which includes some Cajun and creole dishes. ✉*Søndregt. 17 and Fjordgt. 7* ☎73–53–26–30 ⊕*www.gronnpepper.no* ⊟*AE, DC, MC, V.*

$$$
SEAFOOD
★
✕**Havfruen Fiskerestaurant.** "The Mermaid," which celebrated 20 years in business in 2007, is Trondheim's foremost and most stylish fish restaurant. Taking its cues from France, the restaurant excels at bouillabaisse as well as many other fish dishes, which change seasonally. The warm decor uses orange, greens, and reds accented by wood. The wine list includes a wide range of whites, highlighting dry French varieties. ✉*Kjøpmannsgt. 7* ☎73–87–40–70 ⊕*www.havfruen.no* ⊟*AE, DC, MC, V* ☉*Closed Sun. No lunch.*

$$$
NORWEGIAN
✕**Vertshuset Tavern.** Housed in what was once a 1739 tavern in downtown Trondheim, this restaurant is now part of the Trøndelag Folk Museum. The traditional menu includes homemade fish cakes and meatballs; *rømmegrøt* (sour-cream porridge); creamed fish soup and *spekemat*

LOFOTEN ISLANDS

The spectacular Lofoten Islands are considered by many to be the most beautiful part of Norway. In November 2007, National Geographic Traveler even rated them as the third most appealing islands in the world. The rugged peaks towering over quaint little fishermen's villages and the abundant birdlife have been drawing many a tourist, artist and wildlife lover for decades.

Here you can go on a whale safari (orcas, or killer whales, can be spotted from October to March), try your hand at deep-sea fishing, dive, hike, ski, cycle, climb, play golf, or just relax, with some of nature's most striking scenery as background.

For a truly authentic experience, stay in an old fashioned *rorbu* (a restored fisherman's cabin) right by the water's edge–but book early to avoid disappointment, as these cabins are extremely popular with both foreign and Norwegian tourists alike and get snatched up months in advance.

GETTING THERE

The Lofast link road opened in November 2007, and now connects the Lofoten Islands without the need for a ferry connection. There is no toll for the road. The drive from Evenes (Narvik's main airport) to Svolvaer now takes less than 2½ hours.

(cured meat). ✉*Sverresborg Allé 11* ☎*73–87–80–70* ⊕*www.tavern. no* ▤*AE, DC, MC, V.*

WHERE TO STAY

$$$–$$$$ 🏨**Britannia Hotel.** Opened in 1897, the Britannia was Trondheim's first great luxury hotel. The well-appointed rooms come in a variety of styles, including rooms specifically for women and rooms featuring works by artists who have stayed at the hotel over the years. The hardest part might be deciding which of its restaurants to eat in. The elegant Palmehaven Restaurant is popular for special occasions and serves breakfast, lunch, and dinner; on the weekend, you can dance to live orchestra music. The Jonathan Restaurant is more rustic and laid back, and the Hjørnet Bar & Brasserie is ideal for a quick bite in a relaxed atmosphere. 1897, meanwhile, caters to small functions and groups and serves gourmet food. If the decision making has you stressed, head to the spa, which opened in late 2008, and avail yourself of the swimming pool, floating pool, saunas, gym, and treatment rooms. **Pros:** oozes charm; lots of dining options. **Cons:** expensive; rooms vary in quality. ✉*Dronningensgt. 5* ☎*73–80–08–00* ⊕*www.britannia.no* ⬑*247 rooms, 11 suites* ⭑*In-room: Internet. In-hotel: 4 restaurants, bars* ▤*AE, DC, MC, V* ⦿*BP.*

$$$–$$$$ 🏨**Clarion Hotel Grand Olav.** This reasonably priced hotel is in the same building as Trondheim's large concert hall. The interior is decorated with vibrant paintings and rich, bold colors, and all the rooms were renovated in 2007. **Pros:** flat-screen TVs and DVD players in all the rooms; central location; rooms are spacious. **Cons:** seems like most of the bathrooms were left alone during the renovation; no restaurant. ✉*Kjøpmannsgt. 48* ☎*73–80–80–80* ⊕*www.choicehotels.no* ⬑*100*

rooms, 6 suites ⟁*In-room: Internet. In-hotel: bar* ⊟*AE, DC, MC, V* ⦿⎮*BP.*

$$$–$$$$ ⛭**Radisson SAS Royal Garden Hotel.** This extravaganza of glass on the
★ Nid River is Trondheim's largest hotel. The marble accented atrium
is full of thriving plants. Sun-kissed yellow rooms are subtly accented
with deep blues and reds. Prins Olav Grill is the hotel's main restau-
rant. The breakfast room Bakkus Mat & Vin is also ideal for lunch or
a casual dinner overlooking the river. The Galleriet Bar is a popular
meeting place for drinks. Musicians perform several nights a week in
the Blue Garden bar. **Pros:** stunning architecture and decor; good ser-
vice; huge buffet breakfast. **Cons:** single rooms are on the small side.
⊠*Kjøpmannsgt. 73* ☎*73–80–30–00* ⊕*www.radissonsas.com* ⌕*289
rooms, 9 suites* ⟁*In-room: Internet. In-hotel: restaurant, bar, pool, gym*
⊟*AE, DC, MC, V* ⦿⎮*BP.*

AFTER DARK

Olavskvartalet is the center of much of the city's nightlife, with dance
clubs, live music, bars, and cafés.

The bustling **Mojo** (⊠*Nordregt. 24,* ☎*73–60–06–40*) is a funky tapas
restaurant and bar with great cocktails and DJs. It is open until 3 AM on
weekends. Young people in search of cheap drinks, live music, and dancing
gravitate toward **Samfundet** (⊠*Elgesetergt. 1* ☎*73–89–95–00* ⊕*www.
samfundet.no/english*), the home of Trondheim's student society.

Metro (⊠*Kjøpmannsgt. 12* ☎*73–52–05–52*), formerly Café Remis,
is Trondheim's only gay bar/club, and has DJ music on the weekend.
Downtown, in the area known as Solsiden (the Sunny Side), are several
bars and clubs with outdoor terraces that make great summer spots.
Monkey Bar (⊠*TMV-Kaia 5, Nedre Elvehavn,* ☎*73–60–04–44*) is prob-
ably the most popular. **Choco Boco** (⊠*Verfts gt. 2E* ☎*73–80–79–90*
⊕*www.choco.no*) is a chocolate-obsessed café.

SPORTS AND THE OUTDOORS

CYCLING

Some 300 **Trondheim Bysykkel City Bikes** can be borrowed in the city cen-
ter. Parked in easy-to-see stands at central locations, the distinctive red
and white bikes have shopping baskets. In order to rent a bicycle, you
need to purchase a subscription card at the tourist office. The subscrip-
tion, valid for a year, costs NKr 70.

The Trampe elevator ascends the steep Brubakken Hill near Gamle
Bybro and takes cyclists nearly to Kristiansten Festning (Kristiansten
Fort). Contact the tourist office to get the card you need in order to
use the Trampe.

FISHING

The Nid River is one of Norway's best salmon and trout rivers, famous
for its large salmon (the record is 70 pounds). You can fish right in the
city, but you need a license. For further information and fishing licenses,
contact **TOFA (Trondheim og Omland Jakt-og Fiskeadministrasjon)** (⊠*Leir-
fossvn. 76* ☎*73–96–55–80* ⊕*www.tofa.org*).

HIKING AND WALKING

Bymarka, a wooded area on Trondheim's outskirts, has a varied and well-developed network of trails—60 km (37 mi) of gravel paths, 80 km (50 mi) of ordinary paths, 250 km (155 mi) of ski tracks. The **Ladestien** *(Lade Trail)* is a 14-km (9-mi) trail that goes along the edge of the Lade Peninsula and offers great views of Trondheimsfjord. The **Nidelvstien Trail** runs along the river from Tempe to the Leirfossene waterfalls.

SKIING

Bymarka and Estenstadmarka, wooded areas on the periphery of Trondheim, are popular with cross-country skiers. Bymarka's Skistua (ski lodge) also has downhill runs.

Vassfjellet Skisenter (☎72–83–02–00 ⊕*www.vassfjellet.com*), 8 km (5 mi) south of Trondheim's city limits, has 6 tow lifts and 10 runs. There are facilities for downhill and telemark skiing as well as snowboarding and tobogganing. In season (roughly mid-October through Easter), the center is open daily, and ski buses run every evening and weekend. Ski and snowboard hire is available, and there is a ski school on-site (as well as a cafeteria).

SHOPPING

Trondheim's **Mercur Centre** (⊠*Kongensgt. 8* ☎73–87–65–00 ⊕*www. mercursenteret.no*) and **Trondheim Torg** (⊠*Kongensgt. 11* ☎73–80–77–40 ⊕*www.trondheimtorg.no*) shopping centers have helpful staffs and interesting shops.

Arne Ronning (⊠*Nordregt. 10* ☎73–53–13–30) carries fine sweaters by Dale of Norway. Trondheim has a branch of the handicraft store **Husfliden** (⊠*Olav Tryggvasongt. 18* ☎73–83–32–30). For knitted sweaters by such makers as Oleana and Oda, try **Jens Hoff Garn & Ide** (⊠*Olav Tryggvasongt. 20* ☎73–53–15–27). Founded in 1770 and Norway's oldest extant goldsmith, **Møllers Gullsmedforretning** (⊠*Munkegt. 3* ☎73–52–04–39 ⊕*www.gullsmedmoller.no*) sells versions of the Trondheim Rose, the city symbol since the 1700s.

ARCTIC CIRCLE CENTER

80 km (50 mi) north of Mo i Rana.

★ A bleak stretch of treeless countryside marks the beginning of the Arctic Circle. Here you'll find the **Arctic Circle Center** *(Polarsirkelsenteret)* (⊠*Rte. E6, Rognan* ☎75–12–96–96 ⊕*www.polarsirkelsenteret.no* ⌨*NKr 50* ⊙*May and mid-Sept., daily 10–6; June–mid-July and mid-Aug.–late Aug., daily 9 AM–8; mid-July–mid-Aug., daily 8 AM–10 PM.*), right on the line in the Saltfjellet Mountains. Here you can build a small cairn as evidence you passed the circle. You can also get an Arctic Circle certificate to show the folks back home.

GETTING HERE AND AROUND

The Arctic Circle center is on the E6 (the main south-north road) in Nordland, 80 km (50 mi) north of Mo i Rana. If you're traveling without a car, any bus company travelling north from Mo i Rana can get you there.

TROMSØ

1,800 km (1,118 mi) north of Bergen and 250 km (155 mi) north of Narvik.

Tromsø surprised visitors in the 1800s: they thought it very sophisticated and cultured for being so close to the North Pole—hence its nickname, the Paris of the North. It looks the way a polar town should—with ice-capped mountain ridges and jagged architecture that is an echo of the peaks. The midnight sun shines from May 21 to July 21, and it is said that the northern lights decorate the night skies over Tromsø more than over any other city in Norway. Tromsø is home to only 58,000 people, although the city's total area—2,558 square km (987 square mi)—is actually the most expansive in Norway. The downtown area is on a small, hilly island connected to the mainland by a slender bridge. The 13,000 students at the world's northernmost university are one reason the nightlife here is uncommonly lively.

GETTING HERE AND AROUND

Tromsø is a crossroads for air traffic between northern and southern Norway and is served by SAS, Norwegian, and Widerøe. The airport is 3 km (2 mi) northwest of the town center. The *Hurtigruten* coastal express boat calls at Tromsø.

When coming from the south, follow the E6 (the main road north) pass Narvik before taking the E8 heading west at Nordkjosbotn. Nor-Way long distance busses serve Tromsø. Tromssbus (operated by Cominor) is the local operator in the Tromsø area. There is no train station in Tromsø.

ESSENTIALS

Air Contacts Norwegian (☎ 815–21–815 in Norway, 21–49–00–15 from outside Norway ⊕ www.norwegian.no). **SAS** (☎ 800/221-2350 in U.S., 91–50–54–00 in Norway ⊕ www.flysas.com). **Widerøe** (☎ 810–01–200 in Norway ⊕ www.wideroe.no).

Boat and Ferry Contact Hurtigruten (☎ 810–30–000 ⊕ www.hurtigruten.com).

Bus Contacts Nor-Way Bussekspress (☎ 815–44–444 ⊕ www.nor-way.no). **Tromsbuss (Cominor)** (☎ 40–55–40–55 ⊕ www.cominor.no).

Taxis Tromsø Taxi (☎ 03011 ⊕ www.tromso-taxi.no).

Visitor Info Tromsø Tourist Board (✉ Kirkegt. 2 ☎ 77–61–00–00 ⊕ www. destinasjontromso.no).

EXPLORING
TOP ATTRACTIONS

The **Ishavskatedralen** *(Arctic Cathedral)* is the city's signature structure. Designed by Jan Inge Hovig, it's meant to evoke the shape of a Sami tent as well as the iciness of a glacier. Opened in 1964, it represents northern Norwegian nature, culture, and faith. The immense stained-glass window depicts the Second Coming. There are concerts in summer. ✉ *Hans Nilsens v. 41, Tromsdalen* ☎ *77–75–34–40* ⊕ *www.ishavskatedralen. no* 🎫 *NKr 25* ⊙ *June–mid-Aug., Mon.–Sat. 9–7, Sun. 1–7; mid-Aug.– mid-Sept., daily 3–6; mid-Sept.–May, daily 4–6.*

4

☾ The **Tromsø Museum, Universitetsmuseet,** northern Norway's largest museum, is dedicated to the nature and culture of the region. Learn about the northern lights, wildlife, fossils and dinosaurs, minerals and rocks, and church art from 1300 to 1800. Outdoors you can visit a Sami *gamme* (turf hut), and a replica of a Viking longhouse. The pretty Arctic-Alpine botanical garden is the most northernly in the world, at roughly the same latitude as Alaska's north coast. ⊠ *Universitetet, Lars Thørings v. 10* ☏ *77–64–50–00* ⊕ *uit.no/tmu* ▤ *NKr 30* ⊙ *June–Aug., daily 9–6; Sept.–May, weekdays 9–3:30, Sat. noon–3, Sun. 11–4.*

In an 1830s former customs warehouse, the **Polarmuseet i Tromsø** *(Polar Museum)* documents the history of the polar region, focusing on Norway's explorers and hunters. ⊠ *Søndre Tollbugt. 11B* ☏ *77–60–66–30* ⊕ *www.polarmuseum.no* ▤ *NKr 50* ⊙ *Mar.–mid-June, daily 11–5; mid-June–mid-Aug., daily 10–7; mid-Aug.–Sept., daily 11–5; Oct.– Feb., daily 11–3.*

☾ Housed in a striking modern building by the harbor, the adventure center **Polaria** examines life in and around the polar and Barents regions. Explore the exhibits on polar travel and arctic research, then check out two panoramic films—one from Svalbard, one from Antarctica. The aquarium has sea mammals, including seals. ⊠ *Hjalmar Johansens gt. 12* ☏ *77–75–01–00* ⊕ *www.polaria.no* ▤ *NKr 95* ⊙ *Mid-May–mid-Aug., daily 10–7; mid-Aug.–mid-May, daily noon–5.*

☾ To get a sense of Tromsø's immensity and solitude, take the **Fjellheisen** *(cable car)* from behind the cathedral up to the mountains, just a few minutes out of the city center. **Storsteinen** (Big Rock), 1,386 feet above sea level, has a great city view. In summer a restaurant is open at the top of the lift. ⊠ *Sollivn. 12* ☏ *77–63–87–37* ⊕ *www.fjellheisen.no* ▤ *NKr 95* ⊙ *Mid-May–mid-Aug., daily 10–1 AM; mid-Aug.–mid-Sept., daily 10–10; mid-Sept.–end Sept., daily 10–5; Oct.–mid-May, weekends 10–5.*

WORTH NOTING

Ludvik Mack founded **Macks Ølbryggeri** *(Mack's Brewery)* in 1877 and it is still family owned. You can take a guided tour, at the end of which you're given a beer stein, pin, and a pint of your choice (might we suggest the Arctic Beer?) in the Ølhallen pub, Tromsø's eldest. Call ahead to reserve a place on the tour. ⊠ *Storgt. 4* ☏ *77–62–45–00* ⊕ *www.mack. no* ▤ *NKr 130* ⊙ *Guided tours mid-June–mid-Aug., Mon.–Thurs. at 1 and 3; rest of year, Mon.–Thurs. at 1.*

WHERE TO EAT

$$$
SEAFOOD
✕ **Vertshuset Skarven.** Whitewashing recalls the Greek Islands at this landmark restaurant known for its fish. Sample the seaweed and shellfish soup, fresh mussels, or seal lasagna. The lunch buffet is good value. The Skarvens Biffhus and Sjømatrestauranten Arctandria restaurants are in the same building. The pleasant terrace is usually packed in summer. ⊠ *Strandtorget 1* ☏ *77–60–07–20* ⊕ *www.skarven.no* ⌱ *Reservations essential* ▤ *AE, DC, MC, V.*

WHERE TO STAY

$$$ ⊞ **Clarion Collection Hotel With.** This comfortable hotel on the waterfront has a great location. Breakfast and dinner are included in the room price. The ever-popular top-floor lounge has skylights. **Pros:** complimentary coffee, waffles, and supper; sauna. **Cons:** no restaurant on-site. ⊠*Sjøgt. 35–37* ☎*77–66–42–00* ⊕*www.choice.no* ☎*76 rooms* ⚄*In-room: Internet. In-hotel: restaurant, bar* ⊟*AE, DC, MC, V* ⑩*MAP.*

$$–$$$ ⊞ **Quality Hotel Saga.** Centrally located on a pretty town square, this hotel has basic rooms that are loaded with blond wood and warm colors. The hotel serves a free buffet-style dinner for all guests. **Pros:** friendly staff; great views; 100% smoke-free hotel. **Cons:** problems with Internet connection; not the best breakfast in town. ⊠*Richard Withs pl. 2* ☎*77–60–70–00* ⊕*www.sagahotel.no* ☎*66 rooms, 1 suite* ⚄*In-room: Internet. In-hotel: restaurant, no-smoking rooms* ⊟*AE, DC, MC, V* ⑩*BP.*

$$$ ⊞ **Radisson SAS Hotel Tromsø.** You can see splendid views over the Tromsø shoreline at this modern hotel. Rooms are small but stylish, and the service is professional and efficient. **Pros:** newly refurbished with quality furnishings and stylish design; the relaxation center affords great views of the area; two popular restaurants on-site. **Cons:** no hotel parking; staff not always helpful. ⊠*Sjøgt. 7* ☎*77–60–00–00* ⊕*www. radissonsas.com* ☎*259 rooms, 10 suites* ⚄*In-room: Internet. In-hotel: restaurant, bars, gym* ⊟*AE, DC, MC, V* ⑩*BP.*

$$$–$$$$ ⊞ **Rica Ishavshotel.** Shaped like a ship, Tromsø's snazziest hotel is right
★ at the harbor and stretches over the sound toward Ishavskatedralen. Inside, polished wood furnishings with brass trim evoke the life of the sea. Guests represent a mixture of business executives, tourists, and participants at scientific conferences. **Pros:** breakfast buffet is excellent, and even includes vitamins; the Skibsbroen Bar on the top floor has stunning views; comfortable rooms. **Cons:** not that much storage room. ⊠*Fr. Langesgt. 2* ☎*77–66–64–00* ⊕*www.rica.no* ☎*180 rooms* ⚄*In-room: Internet. In-hotel: 2 restaurants, bars* ⊟*AE, DC, MC, V* ⑩*BP.*

AFTER DARK

Rock music and the city's largest selection of beer are at the **Blå Rock Café** (⊠*Strandgt. 14–16* ☎*77–61–00–20* ⊕*www.blarock.no*), which has a popular jukebox, live concerts and DJs on weekends. The university's café and cultural center **DRIV** (⊠*Søndre Tollbod gt. 3* ☎*77–60–07–76* ⊕*www.driv.no*) is in a 1902 quayside building. Concerts, theater, and other cultural events are staged here.

One of the city's largest cafés, **Meieriet Café & Storpub** (⊠*Grønnegt. 37/39* ☎*77–61–36–39*) has burgers, pasta, salads, and wok dishes, billiards, backgammon, newspapers, Internet, and DJs on weekends. Since 1928, polar explorers, arctic skippers, hunters, whalers, and sealers have been meeting at Mack Brewery's **Ølhallen** (⊠*Storgt. 5* ☎*77–62–45–80* ⊕*www.olhallen.no*).

At **Rica Ishavshotel** (⊠*Fr. Langesgt. 2* ☎*77–66–64–00*) you can see some of the best views in the city from the fifth-floor Skibsbroen Bar. **Victoria Fun Pub/Strut/Postboks 17** (⊠*Grønnegt. 81* ☎*77–68–49–06*), a lively evening entertainment complex, has something for everyone. Strut is a funky, retro nightclub playing 1970s and early '80s hits, while Postboks 17 is a chilled-out bar popular with students. A broader range of ages is found at the English-style Victoria.

SPORTS AND THE OUTDOORS

DOGSLEDDING

Some 20 km (12 mi) outside the city, **Tromsø Villmarkssenter** (☎77–69–60–02 ⊕*www.villmarkssenter.no*) organizes winter dogsledding trips, glacier walking, kayaking, summit tours, and Sami-style dinners, which take place around a campfire inside a *lavvu* (a Sami tent).

HIKING AND WALKING

Tromsø has more than 100 km (62 mi) of walking and hiking trails in the mountains above the city. They're reachable by funicular. Stay overnight in the middle of the Lyngen Alps, then set out for guided mountain and glacier walking with **Lyngsfjord Adventure** (☎77–71–55-88 ⊕*www. lyngsfjord.com*). **Svensby Tursenter** (☎77–71–22-25) offers accommodation in small, self-service huts at the foot of the Lyngen Alps and arranges dogsledding, northern lights–viewing safaris, and fishing tours. **Troms Turlag-DNT** (☎77–68–51–75 ⊕*www.turistforeningen.no/troms*) organizes tours and courses and has overnight cabins.

HORSEBACK RIDING

Holmeslet Gård in Tromsdalen (☎77–61–99–74 ⊕*www.holmesletgard. no*) has horseback riding, carriage tours, northern lights–viewing adventures, and sleigh rides.

NORDKAPP

34 km (21 mi) north of Honningsvåg.

Most of those who journey to Nordkapp (North Cape), the northernmost tip of Europe, are in it for a taste of this unique, otherworldly, rugged yet delicate landscape. You'll see an incredible treeless tundra, with crumbling mountains and sparse dwarf plants. The subarctic environment is very vulnerable, so don't disturb the plants. Walk only on marked trails and don't remove stones, leave car marks, or make campfires. Because the roads are closed in winter, the only access is from the tiny fishing village of Skarsvåg via Sno-Cat, a thump-and-bump ride that's as unforgettable as the desolate view.

GETTING HERE AND AROUND

Honningsvåg Airport, 30 km (18.6 mi) south of North Cape, has direct flights from Tromsø and Kirkenes, operated by Widerøe. Hurtigruten, the ship company, calls at Honningsvåg on its way to Kirkenes from Bergen, and then again on the way back. The company Connex FFR runs the daily bus departures from the airport to the North Cape, but all tickets are booked through the Nordkapp tourist office so you'll need to contact them directly.

The E69 goes all the way to the North Cape, with a 6.8-km (4-mi) long underwater tunnel linking the mainland with the island of Magerøya. There is a toll to go through the tunnel (NKr 140). The North Cape is

210 km (130 mi) north of Alta, and the journey from one to the other takes about three hours.

ESSENTIALS

Air Contact Widerøe (☎ 810-01-200 in Norway ⊕ www.wideroe.no)

Bus Contact Nordkapp Reiseliv (✉ Fiskerivn. 4 Honningsvåg ☎ 78-47-70-30 ⊕ www.nordkapp.no).

Cruise Contact Hurtigruten (☎ 810-30-000 in Narvik ⊕ www.hurtigruten.com).

Visitor Info Nordkapp Reiseliv (✉ Fiskerivn. 4, Honningsvåg ☎ 78-47-70-30 ⊕ www.nordkapp.no).

EXPLORING

The contrast between this near-barren territory and **Nordkapphallen** *(North Cape Hall)*, the tourist center, is striking. Blasted into the interior of the plateau, the building is housed in a cave and includes an ecumenical chapel, a souvenir shop, and a post office. Exhibits trace the history of the cape, from Richard Chancellor, an Englishman who drifted around it and named it in 1533, to Oscar II, king of Norway and Sweden, who climbed to the top of the plateau in 1873. Celebrate your pilgrimage to the Nordkapp at Café Kompasset, Restaurant Kompasset, or at the Grotten Bar coffee shop. ✉ Nordkapplatået ☎ 78-47-68-60 ☑ NKr 200 ☉ Call for hrs.

SPORTS AND THE OUTDOORS

BIRD SAFARIS

Gjesvær Turistsenter (☎ 78-47-57-73 ⊕ www.birdsafari.com) organizes bird safaris from May to August. **Nordkapp Reiseliv** (☎ 78-47-70-30 ⊕ www.nordkapp.no) books adventures and activities including bird safaris, deep-sea fishing, boat excursions, and winter expeditions.

DEEP-SEA FISHING

The waters around the North Cape are among the best fishing grounds in the world. Here you can catch large cod, halibut, catfish, and haddock, as well as the *kongekrabbe* or giant crab, a much-prized delicacy. Many operators offer deep-sea fishing tours. Contact **Nordkapp Reiseliv** (☎ 78-47-70-30 ⊕ www.nordkapp.no) or **Nordkapp Safari** (☎ 78-47-52-33 ⊕ www.nordkappsafari.no).

DIVING

Scuba dive at the top of Europe with **North Cape Adventures** (☎ 78-47-22-22 ⊕ www.nordkapp.com), which also provides deep-sea rafting, kayaking, ski and guided tours, and bike rentals.

RAFTING

Deep-sea rafting is as exhilarating as it is beautiful. Among the tours offered is a three-hour trip to the North Cape. Call **Nordkapp Safari** (☎ 78-47-52-33 ⊕ www.nordkappsafari.no). They also offer deep-sea fishing and diving trips.

Sweden

WORD OF MOUTH

"Interesting note: The people are very attractive. There is a youthful exuberance and vitality about them, no doubt owing to the free health care, free college, 6 weeks of vacation and the very relaxed lifestyle."

—trebex

"July is holiday month in Sweden, and some businesses/factories do close—but all usual holiday infrastructure such as shops/stores/entertainment/museums are open—often on extended hours. Just don't try to get a plumber or an electrician in July."

—FurryTiles

Updated by
Rob Hincks

SWEDEN REQUIRES THE VISITOR TO travel far, in both distance and attitude. Approximately the size of California, Sweden reaches as far north as the arctic fringes of Europe, where glacier-topped mountains and thousands of acres of forests are broken only by wild rivers, pristine lakes, and desolate moorland. In the more populous south, roads meander through miles of softly undulating countryside, skirting lakes and passing small villages with sharp-pointed church spires.

Once the dominant power of the region, Sweden has traditionally looked inward to find its own Nordic solutions. During the Cold War, its citizens were in effect subjected to a giant social experiment aimed at creating a perfectly just society, one that adopted the best aspects of both socialism and capitalism.

Recession in the late 1980s saw Sweden make adjustments that lessened the role of its all-embracing welfare state in the lives of its citizens. The adjustments continued through successive governments of both left- and right-wing persuasion. Today, the social safety net once so heavily relied upon by Swedes is somewhat less comprehensive, a reflection perhaps of modern economics rather than any temporary budgetary hiccup.

Sweden took off with the rest of the globe with the explosion of the Internet and new technology and watched with it as the bubble burst at the start of the new millennium. It continues to be one of the world's dominant players in the information-based economy, and new technology is widely used throughout Sweden

On the social front, an influx of immigrants is reshaping what was once a homogeneous society. Sweden continues to face political and social difficulties in the areas of immigration and integration, although the tension appears to be fading slightly as more artists, musicians, actors, directors, and writers with immigrant backgrounds receive national recognition for their work.

Sweden is an arresting mixture of ancient and modern. The countryside is dotted with runic stones and timbered farmhouses, recalling its Viking past and more recent agrarian culture. Venture to the country's cities, however, and you'll find them to be modern, their shop windows filled with the latest in consumer goods and fashions.

Swedes are reluctant urbanites: their hearts and souls are in the forests and the archipelagoes, and to there they faithfully retreat, when weather allows, to enjoy the silence. The country, frankly, is stunning, with natural assets in spades. Moose, deer, bears, and lynx roam the forests, coexisting with the whine of power saws and the rumble of logging machines. Logging remains the country's economic backbone.

ORIENTATION AND PLANNING

GETTING ORIENTED

The country's focal point is its capital, Stockholm, itself a jumping-off place for the remarkable beauty of the archipelago that lies to its east. On the west coast, Göteborg (Gothenburg) is Sweden's standout second city. To its north lies Bohuslän, to the south the Swedish Riviera: two coastal regions that buzz with life in the summer months. Sweden's southern tip is home to a lovely mix of farmland, forests, and châteaus, and includes the regions of Skåne, Småland ("The Kingdom of Glass"), and the island of Öland. Dalarna, the country's heartland, is centered on Lake Siljan and the town of Mora; this is where Swedish folklore and traditions are most visible.

Stockholm. Built on 14 small islands, the city is an intriguing mix of global commerce and local craft, modern design and ancient architecture, bustling metropolis and peaceful green space. In the summer months, life takes to the streets—and to the water. Summer is also a great time to take in what some say is Stockholm's best attraction: its mixed, modern, self-assured, beautiful population. People-watching has never been more fun.

Side Trips from Stockholm. On Stockholm's doorstep is one of the world's most beautiful archipelagoes; with more than 25,000 islands fringing the city, it's easy for everyone to find a space to call their own, even on the weekend when city dwellers flock here by the thousands. Farther afield is Gotland, whose Viking remains, unspoiled wilderness, and busy summer social life make for a holiday paradise. To the north of Stockholm is Uppsala, home to one of Europe's oldest seats of learning.

Göteborg (Gothenburg). Göteborg uses its position to its advantage. From as far back as Viking times the city has been a hub of international trade. Today Göteborg is a thriving, commercial, cosmopolitan place with a cultural and architectural status far beyond what you'd expect from its size. Its people remain down to earth, though, and have a reputation for being particularly funny and vibrant.

Bohuslän. Though this traditional nonadministrative province stretches directly north from civilized Göteborg, it couldn't feel farther away. The rugged, rocky coastline of Bohuslän is stunning in its wild natural beauty. Pastel-painted fishing villages, clinging for dear life to the exposed rocks, are a haven for summer sailors, tourists, and locals. Be sure to sample this region's extraordinary seafood out on one of its many boardwalks.

Swedish Riviera. Much like its more famous French and Italian namesakes, this is where Sweden's wealthy and beautiful come to rub shoulders and top up their tans. Unlike its namesakes, there's room for everyone on mile upon mile of glorious sandy beach. Inland, you'll find relics of a less genteel Swedish past; the region's medieval fortifications tell tales of centuries of bloody battles with neighboring Danes.

TOP REASONS TO GO

■ **Tickle your taste buds.** A new wave of Swedish chefs is hell-bent on putting Sweden on the culinary map—and succeeding. Industry investment, the finest raw ingredients, and a thirst for the exotic has seen new Swedish cuisine become competitive with the absolute best of Europe's kitchens. Dinner on the terrace at Stockholm's Oaxen might blow your entire holiday budget, but you'll remember it for the rest of your life.

■ **Get out there.** The right to roam freely is part of the Swedish constitution, and you'd be hard-pressed to find an outdoor space not worth exploring here, from the mountains of the north to the rolling fields in the south. But you don't have to roam far if a long journey isn't in the cards; a couple of days right in Stockholm's archipelago is hard to beat.

■ **Stay up late.** There's something remarkably life-affirming about a Swedish summer night. There are northerly places throughout the world that experience obscene amounts of daylight around the summer solstice, but there's just something special about the light here from mid-June to the end of July that's hard to describe. The farther north you go, the more pronounced the effect.

The South and the Kingdom of Glass. Dense beech forests and sun-dappled lakes are the lifeblood of Småland's isolated villages whose names are bywords for fine crystal glassware: Kosta, Orrefors, and Boda. Further south, the landscape opens up in Skåne where lush farmland, rolling coastal headlands, seemingly endless sandy beaches and the delightful city of Malmö are the main draw.

Dalarna: The Folklore District. Dalarna is Sweden's spiritual heartland and the focal point of most of the country's myth, symbolism and tradition. The region is centered on Lake Siljan, bordered by a road that takes you through beautiful forests and ancient villages with red painted farmhouses. Along the way, take in the places and landscapes that inspired Sweden's myths and legends—as well as Sweden's national symbol, the wooden Dala horse.

PLANNING

WHEN TO GO

The official tourist season—when hotel rates generally go down and museum and castle doors open—runs from mid-May through mid-September. The whole country goes mad for Midsummer Day, in the middle of June. Many attractions close in late August, when the schools reopen at the end of the Swedish vacation season. Although many of the more traditional attractions are closed for the winter, there is skiing, skating, ice fishing, and sleigh riding on offer throughout the country.

CLIMATE

Summer (mid-May through mid-September) is Sweden's balmiest time of year; days are sunny and warm, and nights refreshingly cool. Summer is also mosquito season, especially in the north, but also as far south as Stockholm. The colors of autumn fade out as early as September, when the rainy season begins. The weather can be bright and fresh in the spring and fall (although spring can bring lots of rain), and many visitors prefer sightseeing when there are fewer people around. Winter comes in November and stays through March, sometimes longer. In Sweden this season is an alpine affair, with subzero temperatures. The days can be magnificent when the snow is fresh and the sky a brilliant Nordic blue.

The following are average daily maximum and minimum temperatures for Stockholm.

Jan.	23°F	-5°C	May	48°F	6°C	Sept.	48°F	9°C
	30°F	-1°C		60°F	16°C		59°F	15°C
Feb.	22°F	-6°C	June	52°F	11°C	Oct.	41°F	5°C
	30°F	-1°C		69°F	21°C		49°F	9°C
Mar.	27°F	-3°C	July	56°F	13°C	Nov.	33°F	1°C
	37°F	3°C		71°F	22°C		40°F	4°C
Apr.	34°F	1°C	Aug.	54°F	12°C	Dec.	26°F	-3°C
	47°F	8°C		68°F	20°C		34°F	1°C

BUSINESS HOURS

Banks are open weekdays 9:30–3; larger branches until 5 and 6 on Thursday. The bank at Arlanda International Airport is open every day with extended hours, and the Forex and X-Change currency exchange offices also have extended hours. Take a queue-number ticket from near the door and wait your turn. It's not uncommon to come across cashless bank branches in some smaller towns so it's worth checking before traveling. Major holidays include: New Years Day, Epiphany, Good Friday, Easter Sunday and Monday, International Workers' Day (May 1), Ascension (40 days after Easter), Whitsun/Pentacost (Sunday and Monday 10 days after Ascension), National Day (June 6), Midsummer Eve and Day (late June), All Saints, Christmas Eve and Day, and Boxing Day (day after Christmas).

GETTING HERE AND AROUND

AIR TRAVEL

From North America to Stockholm Arlanda Airport, Continental has direct flights from Newark, New Jersey; Delta has direct flights from Atlanta, Georgia; Finnair has flights with connections through Helsinki; Icelandair has flights with connections through Reykjavík; Scandinavian Airlines System (SAS) has direct flights, as well as additional flights with connections through Copenhagen (United co-shares with SAS-operated flights); US Airways has direct flights from Philadelphia, Pennsylvania.

From the United Kingdom, British Airways has direct flights to Stockholm Arlanda; Ryan Air has direct flights to Stockholm Vasteras and Skavska airports as well as Göteborg City airport; Sterling has direct flights to Stockholm Arlanda, and Scandinavian Airlines System has direct flights to Stockholm Arlanda and Göteborg Landvetter.

Inside Sweden, Malmö Aviation, Norwegian Air Shuttle, SAS, and Skyways connect all major cities by regular flights.

Contacts British Airways (⊕ *www.ba.com*). **Continental** (⊕ *www.continental. com*). **Delta** (⊕ *www.delta.com*). **Finnair** (⊕ *www.finnair.com*). **Iceland Air** (⊕ *www. icelandair.com*). **Malmö Aviation** (⊕ *www.malmoaviation.se*). **Norwegian Air Shuttle** (⊕ *www.norwegian.se*). **Ryan Air** (⊕ *www.ryanair.com*). **SAS** (⊕ *www. flysas.com*). **Skyways** (⊕ *www.skyways.se*). **Sterling** (⊕ *www.sterling.dk*). **United** (⊕ *www.united.com*). **U.S. Airways** (⊕ *www.usairways.com*).

BIKE TRAVEL

Cycling is a very popular sport in Sweden, and the south of the country, with its low-lying, flat landscape, is perfect for the more genteel cyclist. All major towns and cities have cycle paths and designated cycle lanes. Bike-rental costs average around SKr 100 per day. Tourist offices and the Swedish Touring Association have information about cycling package holidays. The Swedish bicycling organization, Cykelfrämjandet (National Cycle Association), publishes a free English-language guide to cycling trips. Various companies, including Cycling Sweden, offer a variety of cycling tours around the country.

Contacts Cycling Sweden (⊠ *Tranmog. 10, Katrineholm* 🕾 *0150/55091* ⊕ *www. cyclingsweden.se*). **Cykelfrämjandet** (⊠ *Helsingborg* 🕾 *08/54591030* ⊕ *www2. cykelframjandet.se*). **Swedish Tourist Association** (*STF* 🗋 *Box 25, 101 20, Stockholm* 🕾 *08/4632100* ⊕ *www.svenskaturistforeningen.se*).

BOAT AND FERRY TRAVEL

Taking a ferry is not only fun, it is often necessary in Scandinavia. Many companies arrange package trips, some offering a rental car and hotel accommodations as part of the deal. The word *ferry* can be deceptive; generally, those vessels so named are more like small-scale cruise ships, with sleeping quarters, several dining rooms, shopping, pool and sauna, and entertainment.

Silja Line and Viking Line operate massive cruise ship–style ferries daily between Stockholm and Helsinki, either for single journeys or round-trip, two-day cruises. Unity Line operates a ferry service between Ystad and Świnoujście, Poland, where a minibus will be waiting to take you to the historic city of Szczecin, Poland. ScandLines operates a frequent ferry service between Helsingborg and Helsingør, Denmark.

Contacts Scandlines (🕾 *46/42186100* ⊕ *www.scandlines.se*). **Silja Line** (🕾 *46/8222140* ⊕ *www.tallinksilja.se*). **Unity Line** (🕾 *46/0411556900* ⊕ *www. unityline.se*). **Viking Line** (🕾 *46/84524000* ⊕ *www.vikingline.se*).

BUS TRAVEL

There is excellent bus service between all major towns and cities. Consult the *Yellow Pages* under "Bussresearrangörer" for the telephone numbers of the companies concerned. Recommended are the services offered to different parts of Sweden from Stockholm by Swebus. When buying a single ticket for local bus journeys, it is usual to pay the driver on boarding. Coupons or multiple tickets for longer journeys should be purchased before your journey from the relevant bus company.

Contacts **Svenska Buss** (☎0771/676767 ⊕ www.svenskabuss.se). **Swebus Express** (☎0771/218218 ⊕ www.swebus.se).

CAR TRAVEL

The Øresundsbron, the 8-km (5-mi) bridge between Malmö and Copenhagen, simplifies car travel and makes train connections possible between the two countries. Ferry service is cheaper but slower—it takes 45 minutes to make the crossing, compared to 15 minutes by car.

Sweden has an excellent highway network of more than 80,000 km (50,000 mi). The fastest routes are those with numbers prefixed with an *E* (for "European"), some of which are the equivalent of American highways or British motorways. The size of the country compared to its population means that most roads are relatively traffic free. Rush hour in major cities can bring frustrating traffic jams.

Also be aware that there are relatively low legal blood-alcohol limits and tough penalties for driving while intoxicated in Scandinavia; Sweden, Iceland, and Finland have zero-tolerance laws. Penalties include license suspension and fines or imprisonment, and the laws are sometimes enforced by random police roadblocks in urban areas on weekends. An accident involving a driver who has an illegal blood-alcohol level usually voids all insurance agreements, making the driver responsible for all medical and car-damage bills.

Major car-rental companies such as Avis, Budget, Europcar, and Hertz have facilities in all major towns and cities as well as at airports. Various service stations also offer car rentals, including Q8, Shell and Statoil. See the *Yellow Pages* under "Biluthyrning" for telephone numbers and addresses. Renting a car is a speedy business in Sweden, with none of the usual lengthy documentation and vehicle checks; show your passport, license, and credit card, pick up the key, and away you go.

Rates in Stockholm begin at $85 a day and $220 a week for a manual-drive economy car without air-conditioning and with unlimited mileage. This does not include tax on car rentals, which is 25% in Sweden. A service charge also is usually added, which ranges from $15 to $25.

If you plan on extensive road touring, consider buying the *Vägatlas övor Sverige,* a detailed road atlas published by the Mötormännens Riksförbund, available at bookstores for around SKr 300.

Drive on the right, and—no matter where you sit in a car—seat belts are mandatory. You must also have at least low-beam headlights on at all times. Cars rented or bought in Sweden will have automatic headlights, which are activated every time the engine is switched on. Signs indicate five basic speed limits, ranging from 30 kph (19 mph) in school or playground areas to 110 kph (68 mph) on long stretches of E roads.

GASOLINE Sweden has some of the highest gasoline rates in Europe, about SKr 13.50 per liter (about SKr 50 per gallon). Lead-free gasoline is readily available. Gas stations are self-service: pumps marked SEDEL are automatic and accept SKr 20, SKr 50 and SKr 100 bills; pumps marked KASSA are paid for at the cashier; the KONTO pumps are for customers with credit cards.

PARKING   Parking meters and, increasingly, timed ticket machines operate in larger towns, usually between 8 AM and 6 PM. The fee varies from about SKr 6 to SKr 40 per hour. Parking garages in urban areas are mostly automated, often with machines that accept credit cards; LEDIGT on a garage sign means space is available. Many streets in urban areas are cleaned weekly at a designated time on a designated day, during which time parking is not allowed, not even at meters. Times are marked on a yellow sign at each end of the street. Try to avoid getting a parking ticket, which can come with fines of SKr 300–SKr 800.

CRUISE TRAVEL

You can go on one of the highly popular cruises of the Göta Canal, which traverse rivers, lakes, and, on the last lap, the Baltic Sea. A lovely waterway, the Göta Canal with its 65 locks links Göteborg, on the west coast, with Stockholm, on the east. Cruise participants travel on fine old steamers, some of which date back almost to the canal's opening, in 1832. The oldest and most desirable is the *Juno*, built in 1874. Prices start at SKr 8975 for a bed in a double cabin. For more information contact the Göta Canal Steamship Company.

Contact **Göta Canal Steamship Company** (☎*03/1806315* ⊕*www.gotacanal.se*).

TRAIN TRAVEL

Sweden's SJ (*Statens Järnvägar* ⊕*www.sj.se*), is the state railway operator. SJ has a highly efficient network of comfortable electric trains. On nearly all long-distance routes there are buffet cars and, on overnight trips, sleeping cars and couchettes in both first- and second class. Seat reservations are advisable, and on some trains—indicated with *R, IN,* or *IC* on the timetable—they are compulsory. Reservations can be made right up to departure time. The high-speed X2000 train has been introduced on several routes; the Stockholm–Göteborg run takes just under three hours. Travelers younger than 25 years travel at a discounted fare. Up to two children younger than 15 years may travel for SKr 5 if accompanied by an adult.

RESTAURANTS

Sweden's major cities offer a full range of dining choices, from traditional to international restaurants. Outside the cities, restaurants are usually more local in influence. Investments in training and successes in international competitions have spurred restaurant quality to fantastic heights in Sweden. It is worth remembering, though, that for many years eating out was prohibitively expensive for many Swedes, giving rise to a home-socializing culture that still exists today. For this reason many smaller towns are bereft of anything approaching a varied restaurant scene.

HOTELS

Two things about Swedish hotels usually surprise travelers: the relatively limited dimensions of the beds and the generous size and variety of the breakfasts, usually included in the room price. Otherwise, hotel guests in Sweden can expect facilities and service comparable to what they'd expect elsewhere. Most major cities offer a full range of accommodations, from budget hostels to chic boutiques and five-star business hotels. Country inns and bed-and-breakfasts can be full of character and good value for money. During the summer months and at weekends, many Swedish hotels offer reduced room rates, some by as much as 50%. That said, July is the Swedish holiday month and hotels are notoriously busy. Make reservations wherever possible. Many older hotels, particularly the country inns and independently run smaller hotels in the cities, do not have private bathrooms. Inquire about this ahead of time if this is important to you. Whatever their size, almost all Swedish hotels provide scrupulously clean accommodations and courteous service.

An official annual guide, *Hotels in Sweden,* published by and available free from the Swedish Travel and Tourism Council, gives comprehensive information about hotel facilities and prices. The Sweden Hotels group has 25 independently owned hotels and its own classification scheme. Countryside Hotels includes 43 select resort hotels, some of them restored manor houses or centuries-old inns.

Contacts Countryside Hotels (☎ *031/131870* ⊕ *www.countrysidehotels.se).* **Sweden Hotels** (☎ *0771/777800* ⊕ *www.swedenhotels.se).*

CHALET RENTALS
With 250 high-standard chalet villages, Sweden's classic chalet accommodations—furnished vacation cabins that strive for a homey feel— are a sure bet and can often be arranged on the spot at tourist offices. Many are organized under the auspices of the Swedish Tourist Association (STF). DFDS Seaways in Göteborg arranges package deals that combine a ferry trip from Britain across the North Sea and a stay in a chalet village.

Contacts DFDS Seaways (☎ *042/266000 in Sweden, 0871/5229955 in U.K.).* **Swedish Tourist Association (STF)** (☎ *08/4632100* ⊕ *www.svenskaturist foreningen.se).*

CAMPING
There are 760 registered campsites nationwide, many close to uncrowded swimming places and with fishing, boating, or canoeing; they may also offer bicycle rentals. Prices range from SKr 75 to SKr 145 per 24-hour period. Many campsites also offer accommodations in log cabins at various prices, depending on the facilities offered. Most are open between June and September, but about 200 remain open in winter for skiing and skating enthusiasts. Sveriges Camping och Stugföretagares Riksorganisation (Swedish Campsite and cottage Owners' Association or SCR) publishes, in English, an abbreviated list of sites.

Contacts Sveriges Camping och Stugföretagares Riksorganisation (⌂ *Box 5079, 402 22 Göteborg* ☎ *031/3556000* ⊕ *www.camping.se).*

FARM AND COTTAGE HOLIDAYS

The old-fashioned farm or countryside holiday is becoming increasingly available to tourists. You can choose to stay on the farm itself and even participate in daily activities, or you can opt to rent a private housekeeping cottage. Contact the local tourist board or Stay on a Farm for details.

Contact Stay on a Farm (⌂ *Söndrumsv. 35, 302 39 Halmstad, Sweden* ☎ *035/127870* ⊕ *www.bopalantgard.org).*

WHAT IT COSTS IN SWEDISH KRONOR					
	¢	$	$$	$$$	$$$$
Restaurants	under 100	100–150	150–250	250–420	over 420
Hotels	under 1,000	1,000–1,500	1,500– 2,300	2,300–2,900	over 2,900

Restaurant prices are for a main course at dinner. Hotel prices are for two people in a standard double room in high season.

ESSENTIALS

EMERGENCIES The emergency number within the European Union is 112. The Larmtjänst organization, run by a confederation of Swedish insurance companies, provides a 24-hour breakdown service; its phone number is 41116270. The American embassy is in Stockholm.

Contacts General Emergency Number (☎ *112 EU*). **Larmtjänst** (☎ *41116270* ⊕ *www.larmtjanst.se*). **U.S. Embassy** (✉ *Strandv. 101, Dag Hammarskjölds väg 31, Stockholm* ☎ *08/7835300* ⊕ *stockholm.usembassy.gov*).

LANGUAGE Swedish is closely related to Danish and Norwegian. After *z*, the Swedish alphabet has three extra letters, *å, ä,* and *ö,* something to bear in mind when using the phone book. Another phone-book alphabetical oddity is that *v* and *w* are interchangeable; Wittström, for example, comes before Vittviks, not after. And after all that, you'll be glad to know that most Swedes are happy to speak English.

MONEY MATTERS **Currency and Exchange.** The unit of currency is the krona (plural kronor), which is divided into 100 öre and is written as SKr or SEK. Coins come in SKr 1, SKr 5, and SKr 10. Bank notes come in denominations of SKr 20, SKr 50, SKr 100, SKr 500, and SKr 1,000. At this writing the exchange rates for the krona were SKr 6.5 to the U.S. dollar, SKr 6.09 to the Canadian dollar, SKr 11.78 to the British pound sterling, SKr 9.4 to the euro, SKr 5.47 to the Australian dollar, SKr 4.43 to the New Zealand dollar, and SKr 0.82 to the South African rand.

Traveler's checks and foreign currency can be exchanged at banks all over Sweden and at post offices displaying the NB EXCHANGE sign. Be sure to have your passport with you when exchanging money at a bank.

Pricing. Sweden's economy is stable, and inflation remains reasonably low. On the other hand, the Swedish cost of living is quite high. In some areas prices are comparable to European capitals; prices for certain goods and services may be higher. As in all of Scandinavia,

CUTTING COSTS

Traveling in Sweden can be an expensive undertaking, but there's certainly no reason to assume you'll have to break the bank. Here are some ways to keep costs down while still living it up.

AIR TRAVEL

There are several Web sites offering discounted airline tickets for flying inside Sweden. The best are Super Saver Travel, Fly Billigt, and Seat 24.

Contacts Super Saver Travel (⊕ www.supersavertravel.se). **Fly Billigt** (⊕ www.flybilligt.com). **Seat 24** (⊕ www.seat24.se).

FOOD

Take full advantage of the large buffet breakfast often included in the cost of a hotel room. At lunch look for a "menu" that offers a set two- or three-course meal for a set price. At dinner pay careful attention to the price of wine and drinks, since the high tax on alcohol raises these costs considerably.

GROUND TRANSPORTATION

City Cards can save you transportation and entrance fees in many of the larger cities, including Stockholm, Göteborg, and Malmö.

The Eurail and InterRail passes are both valid in Sweden (but some trains, such as the long distance X2000, may require reservations and/or supplements). Passes are valid for 3 to 21 days of consecutive travel; further discounts are offered for those under 26 or over 60 years of age. Most passes entitle you to certain ferry crossings between Sweden and Denmark or Poland. Passes also access discounted tickets on Silja Line ferries to Finland and price reductions at some hotels. SJ offers

a ticket, called a Tågplusbiljett, that works on trains, buses, and subways; it also organizes package trips with local tourist offices. Details are available at any railway station or from SJ.

Contacts SJ (⊕ www.sj.se). **Silja Line** (⊕ www.tallinksilja.se). **Scan Rail** (⊕ www.europeanrail.com). **Rail Europe** (⊕ www.raileurope.com).

HOTELS

Ask a travel agent about discounts, including summer hotel checks for Best Western and Scandic and enormous year-round rebates at SAS hotels for travelers over 65. All business-class passengers can get discounts of at least 10% at SAS hotels when they book through SAS. Also, with a ScanRail pass, you can receive discounts at these chains: Best Western, Sokos Hotels, Choice Hotels, and VIP Backpackers Resorts. Many of Sweden's larger hotels offer discounted weekend rates. If they're available, last-minute (as in same-day) hotel rooms booked at a tourist office can save you 50% off the normal price.

SHOPPING

Be aware that sales taxes can be very high, but foreigners can get some refunds by shopping at tax-free stores (⇨ Taxes, below).

5

alcoholic beverages and tobacco products are very expensive due to heavy taxation.

Sample Prices. A cup of coffee, SKr 25–SKr 40; a beer, SKr 40–SKr 60; a mineral water, SKr 15–SKr 30; a cheese roll, SKr 30–SKr 50; pepper steak à la carte, SKr 120–SKr 210; a cheeseburger, SKr 60; and pizza, starting at SKr 40.

Taxes. All hotel, restaurant, and departure taxes and the value-added tax (VAT, called *moms* all over Scandinavia) are automatically included in prices. The VAT is 25%; non-EU residents can obtain a 15% refund on goods of SKr 200 or more. To receive your refund at any of the 15,000 stores that participate in the tax-free program, you'll be asked to fill out a form and show your passport. The form can then be turned in at any airport or ferry customs desk. Keep all your receipts and tags; occasionally, customs authorities ask to see your purchases, so pack them where they will be accessible.

Tipping. In addition to the 12% value-added tax, most hotels usually include a service charge of 15%; it is not necessary to tip unless you have received extra services. Similarly, a service charge of 13% is usually included in restaurant bills. It is a custom, however, to leave small change when buying drinks. Taxi drivers and hairdressers expect a tip of about 10%.

PHONES There are plenty of pay phones in Sweden. Long-distance calls can be made from special telegraph offices called Telebutik, marked TELE. Swedish phone numbers vary in their number of digits. When dialing a Sweden number from abroad, drop the initial "0" from the local area code. The country code for Sweden is 46.

For directory assistance when calling from Sweden, call 118118, or 118119 for international calls. For operator assistance, 90200 is for in-country information and 0018 for international. To make an international call, dial 00, followed by the country code and then your number.

A local call costs a minimum of SKr 2. For calls outside the locality, dial the area code (see telephone directory). Public phones take only credit cards or prepaid Telefonkort (telephone card). A Telefonkort, available at Telebutik, Pressbyrån (large blue-and-yellow newsstands), Statoil gas stations or ICA supermarkets, costs SKr 40, SKr 60, SKr 100, or SKr 200. If you're making numerous domestic calls, the card saves money.

Most North American cellular phones less than five years old will work in Sweden. Check with your nearest phone dealer to find out. You'll also need to look into international roaming, a service provided (and charged) by your local network provider. If the cost seems worth it, set this service up before travelling. If this isn't possible, you can buy a prepaid sim card in Sweden at all major cellular phone retailers as well as ICA supermarkets, major gas stations, and Pressbyrån newsstands. Check before buying whether or not these work with your model of phone.

VISITOR
INFORMATION **Contact Visit Sweden** (⊠ *Grand Central Station, New York, NY* ☏ *212/885–9700* ⊠ *Box 3030, Kungsg. 36, Stockholm* ☏*08/7255500 or 08/7891000*).

STOCKHOLM

Stockholm is a city in the flush of its second youth. In the last 15 years Sweden's capital has emerged from its cold, Nordic shadow to take the stage as a truly international city. What started with entry into the European Union in 1995, gained pace with the extraordinary IT boom of the late 1990s, strengthened with the Skype-led IT second-wave of 2003, and solidified with the hedge fund invasion of the mid-noughties is still happening today as Stockholm gains even more global confidence. And despite more recent economic turmoil, Stockholm's 1 million or so inhabitants have, almost as one, realized that their city is one to rival Paris, London, New York, or any other great metropolis.

With this realization comes change. Stockholm has become a city of design, fashion, innovation, technology, and world-class food, pairing homegrown talent with international standard. The streets are flowing with a young and confident population keen to drink in everything the city has to offer. The glittering feeling of optimism, success, and living in the "here and now" is rampant in Stockholm.

Of course, not everyone is looking to live so much in the present; for them, luckily, Stockholm also has plenty of history. Positioned where the waters of Lake Mälaren rush into the Baltic, Stockholm has been an important Baltic trading site and an international city of some wealth for centuries.

Built on 14 small islands joined by bridges crossing open bays and narrow channels, Stockholm boasts the story of its history in its glorious medieval old town, grand palaces, ancient churches, sturdy edifices, public parks, and 19th-century museums—its history is soaked into the very fabric of its airy boulevards, built as a public display of trading glory.

GETTING HERE AND AROUND

AIR TRAVEL Stockholm's Arlanda International Airport is 42 km (26 mi) from the city center; a freeway links the city and airport. Travel between Arlanda International Airport and Stockholm has been greatly improved with the completion of the Arlanda Express, a high-speed train service. The yellow-nose train leaves every 15 minutes (and every 10 minutes during peak hours), travels at a speed of 200 kph (125 mph), and completes the trip from the airport to Stockholm's central station in 20 minutes; single tickets cost SKr 220.

Flygbussarna (airport buses) leave both the international and domestic terminals every 10–15 minutes from 6:30 AM to 11 PM, and make a number of stops on the way to their final destination at the Cityterminalen at Klarabergsviadukten, next to the central railway station. The trip costs SKr 110 and takes about 40 minutes.

A bus-taxi combination package is available. The bus lets you off by the taxi stand at Haga Forum, Järva Krog, or Cityterminalen and you present your receipt to the taxi driver, who takes you to your final destination. A trip will cost between SKr 200 and SKr 300, depending on your destination.

GET AROUND FOR LESS

The cheapest way to travel around the city is on the Stockholm à la Carte discount card. In addition to unlimited transportation on city subway, bus, and rail services, it offers free admission to more than 60 museums and several sightseeing trips. The card costs SKr 220 for 24 hours, SKr 450 for two days, and SKr 640 for three days; you can purchase the card from the tourist center at Sweden House on Hamngatan, from the Hotellcentralen accommodations bureau at the central station, and from the tourist center at Kaknäs Tower. Alternatively, single ride tickets are available at station ticket counters and on buses (still cheaper: buy an SL Tourist Card from any Pressbyrån newsstand).

For taxis be sure to ask about a *fast pris* (fixed price) between Arlanda and the city. It should be between SKr 490 and SKr 510, depending on the final destination. The best bets for cabs are Taxi Stockholm, Taxi 020, and Taxi Kurir. All major taxi companies accept credit cards. Watch out for unregistered cabs, which charge high rates and won't provide the same service.

BIKE TRAVEL One of the best ways to explore Stockholm is by bike. There are bike paths and special bike lanes throughout the city, making it safe and enjoyable. Bike rentals will be about SKr 150 per day. One of the best places to ride is on Djurgården. Cykel & Mopeduthyrning service that area.

BOAT AND FERRY TRAVEL Waxholmsbolaget (Waxholm Ferries) offers the Båtluffarkortet (Inter Skerries Card), a discount pass for its extensive commuter network of archipelago boats; the price is SKr 380 for five days of unlimited travel. The Strömma Kanalbolaget operates a fleet of archipelago boats that provide excellent sightseeing tours and excursions.

Contacts Strömma Kanalbolaget (☎ *08/12004000* ⊕ *www.stromma.se*). **Waxholmsbolaget** (☎ *08/6795830* ⊕ *www.waxholmsbolaget.se*).

BUS TRAVEL All the major bus services, including Flygbussarna, Swebus Express, Svenska Buss, and Interbus, arrive at Cityterminalen (City Terminal), next to the central railway station. Reservations to destinations all over Sweden can be made by calling Swebus.

Stockholm has an excellent bus system, which is operated by SL (Stockholm Local Traffic). Tickets work interchangeably on buses and subways in the city. Late-night bus service connects certain stations when trains stop running. The comprehensive bus network serves the entire city, including out-of-town points of interest, such as Vaxholm and Gustavsberg.

CAR TRAVEL Rental cars are readily available in Sweden and are relatively inexpensive. Because of the availability and efficiency of public transport, there

TICKET FARES, DECODED

All downtown Stockholm trips will be SKr 40. As you travel farther afield, zones are added to the fare in increments of SKr 10. Each ticket is good for one hour on both the bus system and the subway. The Rabatt-kupong pass costs SKr 180 and is good for 10 trips downtown (fewer if you travel in more zones) via subway or bus; there's no expiration date. For the real pavement-pounder, purchase a 24-hour pass (includes ferries between Djurgården, Nybroplan, and Slussen) for SKr 100 or a 72-hour pass (includes Skansen, Gröna Lund Tivoli, and Kaknäs Tower admissions) for SKr 200. Ask about kid and senior discounts.

is little point in using a car within the city limits. If you are traveling elsewhere in Sweden, you'll find that roads are uncongested and well marked but that gasoline is expensive. All major car-rental firms are represented, including Avis, Hertz, and Sixt. Statoil gas stations also rent out cars, as do local Swedish companies such as Berras and Auto, which can sometimes have better prices than the major companies.

Approach the city by either the E20 or E18 highway from the west, or the E4 from the north or south. The roads are clearly marked and well sanded and plowed in winter. Signs for downtown read CENTRUM. Driving in Stockholm is often deliberately frustrated by city planners, who have imposed many restrictions to keep traffic down. Keep an eye out for bus lanes, marked with BUSS on the pavement. Driving in that lane can result in a ticket. Get a good city map, called a Trafikkarta, available at most service stations for around SKr 75.

SUBWAY TRAVEL   The subway system, known as T-banan (Tunnelbanan, with stations marked by a blue-on-white T), is the easiest and fastest way to get around. Servicing more than 100 stations and covering more than 96 km (60 mi) of track, trains run frequently between 5 AM and 3 AM. In 2000 the subway system was bought from SL by Connex, the same company that runs the subways in Paris and London. Tickets for Stockholm subways and buses are interchangeable. Maps and timetables for all city transportation networks are available from the SL information desks at Sergels Torg, the central station, Slussen, and online.

TAXI TRAVEL   Stockholm's taxi service is efficient but overpriced. If you call a cab, ask the dispatcher to quote you a *fast pris* (fixed price), which is usually lower than the metered fare. Reputable cab companies are Taxi 020, Taxi Stockholm, and Taxi Kurir. Taxi Stockholm has an immediate charge of SKr 36 whether you hail a cab or order one by telephone. A trip of 10 km (6 mi) should cost about SKr 110 between 6 AM and 7 PM, SKr 115 at night, and SKr 123 on weekends.

TRAIN TRAVEL Both long-distance and commuter trains arrive at the central station in Stockholm on Vasagatan, a main boulevard in the heart of the city. For train information and ticket reservations 6 AM–11 PM, call the SJ number below. There is a ticket and information office at the station where you can make reservations. Automated ticket-vending machines are also available.

ESSENTIALS

Emergency Services CityAkuten (*Emergency Medical Care* ✉ *Apelbergsg. 48, City* ☎ *020/150150*). **CityAkuten Tandvården** (*Emergency Dental Care* ✉ *Olof Palmesg. 13A, Norrmalm* ☎ *08/4122900*).

Hospitals Karolinska Sjukhuset (✉ *Solna (just north of Stockholm), Solna* ☎ *08/5177000*). **Södersjukhuset** (✉ *Ringv. 52, Södermalm* ☎ *08/6161000*).

Police Polisen (*Stockholm Police Headquarters* ✉ *Norra Agneg. 33-37, Kungsholmen* ☎ *11414 for non-emergency, 112 for emergency*).

24-Hour Pharmacy C. W. Scheele (✉ *Klarabergsg. 64, City* ☎ *0771/450450*).

Taxis Taxi 020 (☎ *020/202020*). **Taxi Kurir** (☎ *08/300000*). **Taxi Stockholm** (☎ *08/150000*).

Visitor Info Stockholm Information Service (*Sweden House* ✉ *Hamng. 27, Box 7542, Stockholm* ☎ *08/50828508*). **Swedish Travel and Tourism Council** (✉ *Box 3030, Kungsg. 36, Stockholm* ☎ *08/7891000* ⊕ *www.visit-sweden.com*).

EXPLORING STOCKHOLM

Stockholm can be mapped and interpreted by its archipelago landscape. For the inhabitants there's a tribal status to each of the islands. Residents of Södermalm are fiercely proud of their rather bohemian settlement, while those who call Gamla Stan home will tell you that there is nowhere else like it. But for the visitor, Stockholm's islands have a more practical, less-passionate meaning: they help to dissect the city, both in terms of history and in terms of Stockholm's different characteristics, conveniently packaging the capital into easily handled, ultimately digestible areas.

The central island of Gamla Stan wows visitors with its medieval beauty, winding, narrow lanes and small café-lined squares. To the south, Södermalm challenges with contemporary boutiques, hip hangouts, and left-of-center sensibilities. North of Gamla Stan is Norrmalm, the financial and business heart of the city. Travel west and you'll find Kungsholmen, site of the Stadshuset (City Hall), where you'll find the first signs of residential leafiness. Turn east from Norrmalm and Östermalm awaits, an old residential neighborhood with the most money, the most glamorous people, the most tantalizing shops, and the most expensive street on the Swedish Monopoly board. Finally, between Östermalm and Södermalm lies the island of Djurgården, once a royal game preserve, now the site of lovely parks and museums.

NORRMALM

The area bounded by Stadshuset, Hötorget, Stureplan, and the Hallwylska Museet is essentially Stockholm's downtown, where the city comes closest to feeling like a bustling metropolis. Shopping, nightlife, business, traffic, dining—all are at their most intense in this part of town. Much of this area was razed to the ground in the 1960s as part of a social experiment to move people to the new suburbs. What came in its place, a series of modernist buildings, concrete public spaces, and pedestrianized walkways, garners support and derision in equal measure.

TOP ATTRACTIONS

❾ Hallwylska Museet *(Hallwyl Museum)*. This private late-19th-century palace, one of the first in Stockholm to have electricity and a telephone installed, has imposing wood-panel rooms and a collection of furniture, paintings, and musical instruments that can be best described as eclectic. The palace is decked out in a bewildering mélange of styles assembled by the apparently spendaholic Countess von Hallwyl, who left it to the state on her death. ⊠*Hamng. 4, Norrmalm* 🕾*08/4023099* ⊕*http:// hwy.lsh.se* 🖾*SKr 70* ⊗*Guided tours only. Tours in English July and Aug., Tues.–Sun. at 1; Sept.–June, Sun. at 1.*

❸ **Kulturhuset** *(Culture House)*. Since it opened in 1974, architect Peter
ᘓ Celsing's cultural center, a glass-and-stone monolith on the south side of Sergels Torg, has become a symbol of modernism in Sweden. Stockholmers are divided on the aesthetics of this building—most either love it or hate it. Here there are exhibitions for children and adults, a library, a theater, a youth center, an exhibition center, and a restaurant. Head to Café Panorama, on the top floor, to savor traditional Swedish cuisine and a great view of Sergels Torg down below. ⊠*Sergels Torg 3, City* 🕾*08/50831508* ⊕*www.kulturhuset.stockholm.se.*

❽ **Kungsträdgården.** Once the Royal kitchen garden, this is now Stockholm's smallest but most central park. It is often used to host festivals and events, but is best seen in its everyday guise: as a pleasant sanctuary from the pulse of downtown. Diseased trees removed in 2004 have been replaced by neat little glass-cube cafés selling light lunches, coffee, and snacks. ⊠*Between Hamng. and Operan.*

❶ **Stadshuset** *(City Hall)*. The architect Ragnar Östberg, one of the found-
Fodor'sChoice ers of the National Romantic movement, completed Stockholm's city
★ hall in 1923. Headquarters of the city council, the building is functional but ornate: its immense **Blå Hallen** (Blue Hall) is the venue for the annual Nobel Prize dinner, Stockholm's principal social event. Take a trip to the top of the 348-foot tower, most of which can be achieved by elevator, to enjoy a breathtaking panorama of the city and Riddarfjärden. ⊠*Hantverkarg. 1, Kungsholmen* 🕾*08/50829058* ⊕*www. stockholm.se* 🖾*SKr 60, tower SKr 20* ⊗*Guided tours only. Tours in English, June–Aug., daily 10, 11, noon, 1, 2, and 3; Sept., daily 10, noon, and 2; Oct.–May, daily 10 and noon. Tower open May–Sept., daily 10–4:30.*

❺ **Stockholms Stadsbiblioteket** *(Stockholm City Library)*. Libraries aren't always a top sightseeing priority, but the Stockholm City Library is among the most captivating buildings in town. Designed by the famous Swedish architect E. G. Asplund and completed in 1928, the building's cylindrical, galleried main hall gives it the appearance of a large birthday cake. Inside is an excellent "information technology" center with free Internet access—and lots of books, too. ⌂ *Sveav. 73, Vasastan* ☎ *08/50831100* ⊕ *www.biblioteket.se* ⊙ *Mon.–Thurs. 9–9, Fri. 9–7, and weekends noon–4.*

WORTH NOTING

❹ **Hötorget** *(Hay Market).* Once the city's hay market, this is now a popular gathering place where you're more likely to find apples and pears. Crowds come here to meet, gossip, hang out, or pick up goodies from the excellent outdoor fruit-and-vegetable market. Also lining the square are the Konserthuset (Concert Hall), fronted by a magnificent statue by Swedish-American sculptor Carl Milles, the PUB department store, and a multiscreen cinema Filmstaden Sergel. ⌂ *On corner of Kungsgatan and Sveaväg, Norrmalm.*

NEED A BREAK? Take the stairs down to the food hall **Kungshallen** beneath the large cinema at the southern end of Hötorget. This is subterranean market is the perfect spot to put up your feet and pick up a coffee. Or try the impressive array of Turkish meze on offer at the many bustling stalls.

❷ **Sergels Torg.** Named after Johan Tobias Sergel (1740–1814), one of Sweden's greatest sculptors, this busy junction in Stockholm's center is dominated by modern, functional buildings and a sunken pedestrian square with subterranean connections to the rest of the neighborhood. Visitors are often put off by its darkened covered walkways and youths in hooded tops, but it is relatively safe and a great place to witness some real Stockholm street life.

❻ **Strindbergsmuseet Blå Tornet** *(Strindberg Museum, Blue Tower).* Hidden away over a grocery store, this museum is dedicated to Sweden's most important author and dramatist, August Strindberg (1849–1912), who resided here from 1908 until his death four years later. The interior has been expertly reconstructed with authentic furnishings and other objects, including one of his pens. The museum also houses a library, printing press, and picture archives, and it is the setting for literary, musical, and theatrical events. ⌂ *Drottningg. 85, Norrmalm* ☎ *08/4115354* ⊕ *www.strindbergsmuseet.se* ⌂ *SKr 40* ⊙ *Tues.–Sun. noon–4.*

GAMLA STAN AND SKEPPSHOLMEN

Gamla Stan (Old Town) sits between two of Stockholm's main islands, and is the site of the medieval city. Just east of Gamla Stan is the island of Skeppsholmen, whose twisting cobble streets are lined with superbly preserved old buildings. As the site of the original Stockholm, history, culture, and a dash of old Europe come thick and fast around here. Understandably, Gamla Stan is also a magnet for tourists. Consequently there are plenty of substandard shops and restaurants ready to take your money in return for shoddy goods and bad food. Because of this, locals often make a big show of dismissing the area as a tourist trap,

Exploring Stockholm

NORRMALM

Train Station

Kulturhuset

KUNGS-HOLMEN

Stadshusbron

Hantverkargatan

Stadshuset

Klara Mälarstrand

← Mälaren

Riddarfjärden

RIDDAR HOLMEN

HELGEANDS HOLMEN

Kungliga Slottet

Skeppsholms-bron

GAMLA STAN

Köpmang. Brunnsgr.

Strömmen

Kornhamns-torg

Slussen

Söderm. torg

Söder Mälarstrand

SÖDERMALM

Bastugatan

Tavastgatan

Brännkyrkagatan

Hornsgatan

Blecktornsgränd

Bellmansgatan

Södergatan

Stadsgården

Katarinavägen

Tegnér-lunden

Kammakargatan

Humlegården

Brunnsgatan

Kungsgatan

Sture Plan

Östermalms-torg

Olof Palmes Gata

Kungsgatan

Bryggargatan

Hötorget

Sveavägen

Master Samuelsgatan

Smålandsgatan

Norr Malms-torg

Nybro-plan

Riddargatan

Sergels Torg

Hamngatan

Kungs-träd-gården

Fleming-gatan

Klarastrandsleden

Klarabergsviadukten

Klarabergsgatan

Vattugatan

Herkulesgatan

Karl XII:s Torg

Södra Blasieholmsh.

Nybrokajen

Kungsholms Strand

Tegel-Backen

Jakobsgatan

Fredsgatan

Gustav Adolfs Torg

Strömbron

Norr Mälarstrand

Centralbron

Vasabron

Riddarholms Torget

Myntgatan

Storkyrkobrinken

Riddarhus Torget

Västerlänggatan

Stora Nygatan

Lilla Nygatan

Slottsbacken

Centralbron

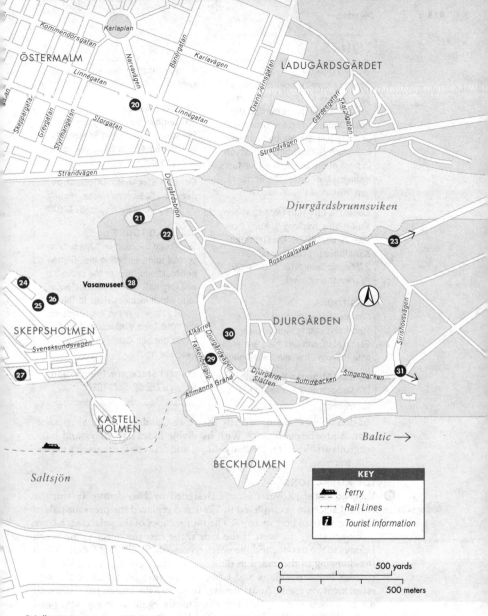

Östermalm

Kommendörsgatan
Karlaplan
Narvavägen
Banérgatan
Karlavägen
Östermalmsgatan

LADUGÅRDSGÄRDET

Linnégatan
Skeppargatan
Grevgatan
Styrmangatan
Storgatan
Linnégatan
Gärdesgatan
Skarpögatan

20

Strandvägen

Strandvägen

Djurgårdsbron

Djurgårdsbrunnsviken

21
22

23

Rosendalsvägen

24

Vasamuseet 28

25 26

Sirishovsvägen

SKEPPSHOLMEN

DJURGÅRDEN

Svensksundsvägen

Alkärret
Djurgårdsvägen
Falkenbergsg.

30

27

29

Allmänna Gränd

Djurgårds Slätten
Suntidsbacken
Singelbacken

31

KASTELL-HOLMEN

Baltic →

Saltsjön

BECKHOLMEN

KEY

🛥 Ferry

╟── Rail Lines

ℹ️ Tourist information

0   500 yards
0   500 meters

TOURS

BOAT TOURS

Strömma Kanalbolaget runs sightseeing tours of Stockholm. Boats leave from the quays outside the Royal Dramatic Theater, Grand Hotel, and City Hall. Stockholm Sightseeing, which leaves from Skeppsbron in front of the Grand, has four tours, including the "Under the Bridges" and "Historical Canal" tours.

Contacts **City Hall** (*late May–early Sept.* ✉ *Hantverkarg. 1, Kungsholmen* ☎ *08/50829000*). **Strömma Kanalbolaget** (✉ *Skeppsbron 22, Gamla Stan* ☎ *08/12004000* ⊕ *www.stromma.se*).

BUS TOURS

Comprehensive tours of much of Stockholm, taking in museums, Gamla Stan, and City Hall, are available through Strömma Kanalbolaget.

Contact **Strömma Kanalbolaget** (✉ *Skeppsbron 22, Gamla Stan*

☎ *08/12004000* ⊕ *www.stromma. se*).

PRIVATE GUIDES

You can hire your own guide from Stockholm Information Service. In summer be sure to book guides well in advance.

Contact **Stockholm Information Service** (✉ *Sweden House, Hamng. 27, Box 7542, City* ☎ *08/58714030*).

WALKING TOURS

Stockholm Information Serviceruns several tours, including the "Romantic Stockholm" tour of the cathedral and City Hall; the "Royal Stockholm" tour, which includes visits to the Royal Palace and the Treasury; and the "Old Town Walkabout," which strolls through Gamla Stan in just over one hour.

Contact **Stockholm Information Service** (☎ *08/58714030*).

but don't believe them. Secretly they love Gamla Stan and Skeppsholmen. And who wouldn't? With its divine hideaway alleys and bars, gorgeous architecture, specialty shops, and great restaurants, it's impossible to resist.

TOP ATTRACTIONS

⑮ Kungliga Slottet (*Royal Palace*). Designed by Nicodemus Tessin, the Royal Palace was completed in 1760 and replaced the previous palace that had burned here in 1697. The four facades of the palace each have a distinct style: the west is the king's, the east the queen's, the south belongs to the nation, and the north represents royalty in general. Watch the changing of the guard in the curved terrace entrance, and view the palace's fine furnishings and Gobelin tapestries on a tour of the **Representationsvän** (State Apartments). To survey the crown jewels, which are no longer used in this self-consciously egalitarian country, head to the **Skattkammaren** (Treasury). The **Livrustkammaren** (Royal Armory) has an outstanding collection of weaponry, coaches, and royal regalia. Entrances to the Treasury and Armory are on the Slottsbacken side of the palace. ✉ *Gamla Stan* ☎ *08/4026130* ⊕ *www.royalcourt.se* 🎟 *State Apartments SKr 90, Treasury SKr 90, Royal Armory SKr 90, combined ticket for all areas SKr 130* 🕐 *State Apartments and Trea-*

Fodor'sChoice
★

sury May–Aug., daily 10–4; Sept.–Apr., Tues.–Sun. noon–3. Armory May–Aug., daily 11–4; Sept.–Apr., Tues.–Sun. 11–4.

㉕ **Moderna Museet** *(Museum of Modern Art).* The museum's excellent col-
★ lection includes works by Picasso, Kandinsky, Dalí, Brancusi, and other international artists. You can also view examples of significant Swedish painters and sculptors and an extensive section on photography. The building itself is striking. Designed by the well-regarded Spanish architect Rafael Moneo, it has seemingly endless hallways of blond wood and walls of glass. ⊠*Skeppsholmen, City* ☏*08/51955200* ⊕*www.
modernamuseet.se* ⊠*SKr 80* ☉*Tues. 10–8, Wed.–Sun. 10–6.*

⑬ **Nationalmuseum.** The museum's collection of paintings and sculptures
Fodor'sChoice is made up of about 12,500 works, so allow at least an hour if you
★ want to see everything. The emphasis is on Swedish and Nordic art, but other areas are well represented. Look especially for some fine works by Rembrandt. The print and drawing department is also impressive, with a nearly complete collection of Edouard Manet prints. ⊠*Södra
Blasieholmshamnen, City* ☏*08/51954300* ⊕*www.nationalmuseum.
se* ⊠*SKr 100* ☉*Jan.–Aug., Tues. 11–8, Wed.–Sun. 11–5; Sept.–Dec.,
Tues. and Thurs. 11–8, Wed., Fri., and weekends 11–5.*

⑲ **Nobelmuseet.** The Swedish Academy meets at Börshuset (the Stock Exchange) every year to decide the winner of the Nobel Prize for literature. The building is also the home of the Nobel Museum. Along with exhibits on creativity's many forms, the museum displays scientific models, shows films, and has a full explanation of the process of choosing prizewinners. The museum does a good job covering the controversial selections made over the years. It's a must for Nobel Prize hopefuls and others. ⊠*Börshuset, Stortorget, Gamla Stan* ☏*08/534
81800* ⊕*www.nobelmuseum.se* ⊠*SKr 60* ☉*May.–Sept., Wed.–Mon.
10–5, Tues. 10–8; Oct.–Apr., Tues. 11–8, Wed.–Sun. 11–5.*

⑫ **Operan** *(Opera House).* Stockholm's baroque Opera House is almost more famous for its restaurants and bars than for its opera and ballet productions, but that doesn't mean an evening performance should be missed. There's not a bad seat in the house. For just SKr 35 you can even get a listening-only seat (with no view). Still, its food and drink status can't be denied. It has been one of Stockholm's artistic and literary watering holes since the first Operakällaren restaurant opened on the site in 1787. ⊠*Gustav Adolfs Torg, City* ☏*08/7914400* ⊕*www.
operan.se.*

⑱ **Stortorget** *(Great Square).* Here in 1520 the Danish king Christian II ordered a massacre of Swedish noblemen. The slaughter paved the way for a national revolt against foreign rule and the founding of Sweden as a sovereign state under King Gustav Vasa, who ruled from 1523 to 1560. One legend holds that if it rains heavily enough on the anniversary of the massacre, the old stones still run red. ⊠*Near Kungliga
Slottet, Gamla Stan.*

5

WORTH NOTING

㉖ Arkitekturmuseet. The Museum of Architecture uses models, photos, and drawings to tell the long and interesting story of Swedish architecture. Certain buildings shed light on specific periods, including the Stockholm Town Hall, Vadstena Castle, and the Helsingborg Concert House. The museum also hosts lectures, debates, and architectural tours of the city. ✉ *Skeppsholmen* ☎ *08/58727000* ⊕ *www.arkitekturmuseet.se* 💳 *SKr 50* ⊘ *Tues. 10–8, Wed.–Sun. 10–6.*

⑪ Medelhavsmuseet *(Mediterranean Museum)*. During the 1700s this building housed the Royal Courts. Then, in the early 1900s, the vast interior of the building was redesigned to resemble the Palazzo Bevilaqua in Bologna, Italy. The collection has a good selection of art from Asia as well as from ancient Egypt, Greece, and Rome. In the Gold Room you can see fine gold, silver, and bronze jewelry from the Far East, Greece, and Rome. ✉ *Fredsg. 2, City* ☎ *08/51955050* ⊕ *www.medelhavsmuseet.se* 💳 *SKr 60* ⊘ *Tues.–Thurs. noon–8, Fri.–Sun noon–5.*

㉔ Östasiatiska Museet *(Museum of Far Eastern Antiquities)*. If you have an affinity for Asian art and culture, don't miss this impressive collection of Chinese and Japanese Buddhist sculptures and artifacts. Although some exhibits are displayed with little creativity, the pieces themselves are always worthwhile. The more than 100,000 pieces that make up the holdings here include many from China's Neolithic and Bronze ages. ✉ *Skeppsholmen, City* ☎ *08/51955750* ⊕ *www.mfea.se* 💳 *SKr 60* ⊘ *Tues. 11–8, Wed.–Sun. 11–5.*

⑰ Riddarholmskyrkan *(Riddarholm Church)*. Dating from 1270, the Grey Friars monastery is the second-oldest structure in Stockholm, and has been the burial place for Swedish kings for more than 400 years. The redbrick structure, distinguished by its delicate iron-fretwork spire, is rarely used for services: it's more like a museum now. The most famous figures interred within are King Gustavus Adolphus, hero of the Thirty Years' War, and the warrior King Karl XII, renowned for his daring invasion of Russia, who died in Norway in 1718. The most recent of the 17 Swedish kings to be put to rest here was Gustav V, in 1950. The different rulers' sarcophagi, usually embellished with their monograms, are visible in the small chapels dedicated to the various dynasties. ✉ *Riddarholmen* ☎ *08/4026130* ⊕ *www.royalcourt.se* 💳 *SKr 30* ⊘ *June–Aug., daily 10–5; May and Sept., daily 10–4.*

⑭ Riksdagshuset *(Parliament Building)*. When in session, the Swedish Parliament meets in this 1904 building. Above the entrance, the architect placed sculptures of a peasant, a burgher, a clergyman, and a nobleman. Take a tour of the building not only to learn about Swedish government but also to see the art within. In the former First Chamber are murals by Otte Sköld illustrating different periods in the history of Stockholm, and in the current First Chamber a massive tapestry by Elisabet Hasselberg Olsson, *Memory of a Landscape*, hangs above the podium. ✉ *Riksg. 3A, Gamla Stan* ☎ *08/7864000* ⊕ *www.riksdagen.se* 💳 *Free* ⊘ *Tours in English late June–late Aug., weekdays 12:30 and 2; late Aug.–late June, weekends 1:30. Call ahead for reservations.*

⑯ **Svea Hovrätt** *(Swedish High Court).* The Swedish High Court commands a prime site on the island of Riddarholmen, on a quiet and restful quayside. Though it's closed to the public, you can sit on the water's edge nearby and watch the boats on Riddarfjärden (Bay of Knights) and, beyond it, Lake Mälaren. From here you can see the stately arches of Västerbron (West Bridge) in the distance, the southern heights, and above all, the imposing profile of City Hall, which appears almost to be floating on the water. At the quay you may see one of the Göta Canal ships.

㉗ **Svensk Form** *(Swedish Form).* This museum emphasizes the importance of Swedish form and design, although international works and trends are also covered. Exhibits include everything from chairs to light fixtures to cups, bowls, and silverware. Find out why Sweden is considered a world leader in industrial design. Every year the museum gives out a prestigious and highly coveted design award called Utmärkt Svenskt Form (Outstanding Swedish Design). The winning objects are then exhibited in fall. ✉*Holmamiralens väg 2, Skeppsholmen, City* ☎*08/4633130* ⊕*www.svenskform.se* 🎫*SKr 20* ⊙ *Wed. 5–8, Thurs. and Fri. noon–5, weekends noon–4.*

DJURGÅRDEN AND SKANSEN

Throughout history, Djurgården has been Stockholm's pleasure island. There was time when only the king could enjoy this enormous green space, and enjoy it he did. Today Stockholmers of all persuasions come here to breathe some fresh air, visit the island's many museums, stroll through the forests and glades, get their pulses racing at the Gröna Lund amusement park, or just relax by the water and watch the boats sail by. You can approach Djurgården from the water aboard the small ferries that leave from Slussen at the southern end of Gamla Stan. In summer, ferries also leave from Nybrokajen, or New Bridge Quay, in front of the Kungliga Dramatiska Teatern.

TOP ATTRACTIONS

㉙ **Gröna Lund Tivoli.** Smaller than Copenhagen's Tivoli or Göteborg's Lise-
☺ berg, this amusement park has managed to retain much of its historical charm, while making room for some modern, hair-raising rides among the pleasure gardens, amusement arcades, and restaurants. If you're feeling especially daring, try the Power Tower. At 350 feet, it's Europe's tallest free-fall amusement-park ride and one of the best ways to see Stockholm, albeit for about three seconds, before you plummet. There isn't an adult who grew up in Stockholm who can't remember the annual excitement of Gröna Lund's April opening. Go and you will see why. ✉*Allmänna Gränd 9, Djurgården* ☎*08/58750100* ⊕*www. tivoli.se* 🎫*SKr 70, not including tickets or passes for rides* ⊙*Late Apr.–mid-Sept., daily. Hrs vary but are generally noon–11 PM. Call ahead for specific information.*

㉓ **Rosendals Trädgården** *(Rosendal's Garden).* This gorgeous slice of green-
FodorŚChoice ery is a perfect place to spend a few hours on a late summer afternoon.
★ When the weather's nice, people flock to the garden café, which is in one of the greenhouses, to enjoy tasty pastries and salads made from

5

the locally grown vegetables. Pick your own flowers from the vast flower beds (paying by weight), stroll through the creative garden displays, or take away produce from the farm shop. ⊠ *Rosendalsterrassen 12, Djurgården* ☎ *08/54581270* ⊕ *www.rosendal stradgard.se* ⊠ *Free* ⊙ *May–Sept., weekdays 11–5, weekends 11–6; Oct.–Apr. call ahead for specific information.*

WORD OF MOUTH

"We took the ferry from the south end of Gamla Stan to Djurgarden. After landing at Tivoli [. . .] we walked to the Vasa Museum. In a short phrase—do not miss the Vasa Museum." —CraigT

③ **Skansen.** The world's first open-air museum, Skansen was founded in 1891 by philologist and ethnographer Artur Hazelius, who is buried here. He preserved examples of traditional Swedish architecture brought from all parts of the country, including farmhouses, windmills, barns, a working glassblower's hut, and churches. Not only is Skansen a delightful trip out of time in the center of a modern city, but it also provides insight into the life and culture of Sweden's various regions. In addition, the park has a zoo, carnival area, aquarium, theater, and cafés. ⊠ *Djurgårdsslätten 4951, Djurgården* ☎ *08/4428000* ⊕ *www. skansen.se* ⊠ *Park and zoo: Sept.–Apr. SKr 65; May–Aug. SKr 100. Aquarium SKr 75* ⊙ *Nov.–Feb., daily 10–3; Mar., Apr., and Oct., daily 10–4; May and Sept., daily 10–8; June–Aug., daily 10–10.*

㉘ **Vasamuseet** *(Vasa Museum).* The warship *Vasa* sank 10 minutes into its ★ maiden voyage in 1628, consigned to a watery grave until it was raised from the seabed in 1961. Its hull was preserved by the Baltic mud, free of the worms that can eat through ships' timbers. Now largely restored to her former glory (however short-lived it may have been), the man-of-war resides in a handsome museum. The sheer size of this cannon-laden hulk inspires awe and fear in equal measure. The political history of the world may have been different had she made it out of harbor. Daily tours are available year-round. ⊠ *Galärvarsv., Djurgården* ☎ *08/51954800* ⊕ *www.vasamuseet.se* ⊠ *SKr 95* ⊙ *June–Aug., daily 8.30–6; Sept.–May, Thurs.–Tues. 10–5, Wed. 10–8.*

WORTH NOTING

㉑ **Junibacken.** In this storybook house you travel in small carriages through the world of children's book writer Astrid Lindgren, creator of the irrepressible character Pippi Longstocking, among others. Lindgren's tales come alive as various scenes are revealed. Parents can enjoy a welcome moment of rest after the mini-train ride as the children lose themselves in the near-life-size model of Pippi Longstocking's house. It's perfect for children ages five and up. ⊠ *Galärvarsv., Djurgården* ☎ *08/58723000* ⊕ *www.junibacken.se* ⊠ *SKr 110* ⊙ *Jan.–May and Sept.–Dec., Tues.– Sun. 10–5; June and Aug., daily 10–5; July, daily 9–6.*

㉒ **Nordiska Museet** *(Nordic Museum).* An imposing late-Victorian structure housing peasant costumes from every region of the country and exhibits on the Sami (pronounced *sah*-mee)—Lapps, the formerly seminomadic reindeer herders who inhabit the far north—and many other aspects of

Swedish life. Families with children should visit the delightful "village life" play area on the ground floor. ⊠*Djurgårdsv. 6–16, Djurgården* ☎*08/51954600* ⊕*www.nordiskamuseet.se* ⊠*SKr 60* ⊙*Weekdays 10–1, weekends 11–5*

③① **Waldemarsudde.** This estate, Djurgården's gem, was bequeathed to the Swedish people by Prince Eugen upon his death, in 1947. It maintains an important collection of Nordic paintings from 1880 to 1940, in addition to the prince's own works. The rather grand stone terrace, situated above the entrance to Stockholm's harbor, is the perfect spot to perch and watch passing boats. ⊠*Prins Eugens väg 6, Djurgården* ☎*08/54583700* ⊕*www.waldemarsudde.com* ⊠*SKr 85* ⊙*Tues.–Sun. 11–5.*

ÖSTERMALM

Marked by waterfront rows of Renaissance buildings with palatial rooftops and ornamentation, Östermalm is a quietly regal residential section of central Stockholm. History and money are steeped into the very bricks and mortar of its elegant streets, which are lined with museums, fine shopping, and exclusive restaurants. On Strandvägen, or Beach Way, the boulevard that follows the harbor's edge from the busy downtown area to the staid diplomatic quarter, you can choose one of three routes. The waterside walk, with its splendid views of the city harbor, bustles with tour boats and sailboats. Parallel to the walk (away from the water) is a tree-shaded walking and bike path. Walk, rollerblade, or ride a bike down the middle, and you just might meet the occasional horseback rider, properly attired in helmet, jacket, and high polished boots. Take the route farthest from the water, and you will walk past upscale shops and expensive restaurants.

TOP ATTRACTIONS

OFF THE BEATEN PATH

Millesgården. This gallery and sculpture garden north of the city is dedicated to the property's former owner, American-Swedish sculptor Carl Milles (1875–1955) and is one of the most magical places in Stockholm. On display throughout the property are Milles's own unique works, and inside the main building, once his house, is his private collection. Millesgården can be easily reached via subway to Ropsten, where you catch the Lidingö train and get off at Herserud, the second stop. The trip takes about 30 minutes. ⊠*Carl Milles väg 2, Lidingö* ☎*08/4467590* ⊕*www.millesgarden.se* ⊠*SKr 80* ⊙*May–Sept., daily 11–5; Oct.–Apr., Tues.–Sun. noon–5.*

❼ **Östermalmstorg.** The market square and its neighboring streets represent old, established Stockholm. **Saluhall** is more a collection of boutiques than an indoor food market; the fish displays can be especially intriguing. At the other end of the square, **Hedvig Eleonora Kyrka,** a church with characteristically Swedish faux-marble painting throughout its wooden interior, is the site of frequent lunchtime concerts in spring and summer. ⊠*Nybrog. at Humlegårdsg., Östermalm.*

WORTH NOTING

②⓪ **Historiska Museet** *(Museum of National Antiquities).* Viking treasures and the Gold Room are the main draw, but well-presented temporary exhibitions also cover various periods of Swedish history. The gift shop here is excellent. ✉*Narvav. 13–17, Östermalm* ☎*08/51955600* ⊕*www.historiska.se* 🖃*SKr 60* ☉*May–Sept., daily 10–5; Oct.–Apr., Tues.–Sun. 11–5.*

🔟 Musik Museet. Inside what was the military's bread bakery from the 17th
Ⓒ century to the mid-1900s, the Music Museum has more than 6,000 instruments in its collection, with the focus on pieces from 1600 to 1850. Its 18th-century woodwind collection is internationally renowned. The museum also holds jazz, folk, and world-music concerts. Children are allowed to touch and play some of the instruments, and the motion-sensitive "Sound Room" lets you produce musical effects simply by gesturing and moving around. ✉*Sibylleg. 2, Östermalm* ☎*08/51955490* ⊕*www.musikmuseet.se* 🖃*SKr 40* ☉*Tues.–Sun. noon–5.*

WHERE TO EAT

The culinary whirlwind that swept through Stockholm's restaurant scene some 15 years ago continues to whip up innovation. What was once a dour landscape of overpriced, uninspiring eateries is now a creative hotbed of culinary achievement to rival any major European capital. Industry investment in training, receptivity to international influence and a flair for creativity all mean that Stockholm's best chefs have stayed way ahead of the game. Increasingly, this achievement is rubbing off on their mid-price colleagues and in terms of culinary experience per Krona, mid-range restaurants represent the best value for money in town. Two recent trends have seen many of the city's better restaurants pick up on this and offer more set-priced tasting menus and increasing numbers of wine by the glass—making even the most expensive restaurants relatively affordable. In terms of food, *New Swedish* remains the buzzword, with chefs looking no farther than their backyards for fine, seasonal, traditional ingredients, served with a modern twist. Of course, there are also many less-expensive restaurants with traditional Swedish cooking. Among Swedish dishes, the best bets are wild game and fish, particularly salmon, and the smorgasbord buffet, which usually offers a good variety at an inexpensive price. Reservations are often necessary.

NORRMALM

¢   ✗**Birkastans Restaurang & Pizzeria.** Sweden has made the pizza its own,
PIZZA with a shabby, but usually good takeaway pizza place on every street corner. This, though, is the best in town. It's diminutive size is inversely proportional to the owner's ambitions for offering choice and there are more than 80 different pizza combinations on the menu. You may have to wait a while for a table, but it's worth it. ✉*Vikingag. 16, Vasastan* ☎*08/321790* ⌲*Reservations not accepted* ▭*MC, V.*

$$$ ✗**Fredsgatan 12.** Without a doubt, this is one of the most creative res-
SCANDINAVIAN taurants in town. The showpieces are the two seven-course tasting
FodorsChoice menus: Tradition and Innovative, where dishes such as duck parfait
★ with cherry and pistachio (tradition) and chicken popcorn with truffle and curry (innovative) delight, confuse, and surprise in equal measure. The elegant, neutral-toned dining room oozes class and style; the

OUTSIDE THE CITY

There are a number of excellent sites only a short bus or subway ride from the city center, many of which can be combined. Stockholm's city environs very quickly become greener as you leave the bustling center. Trips to nearly all these places could be done in a morning or afternoon. Most are excellent ways to experience Sweden's delightful countryside.

Bergianska Trädgården. The beautiful Bergianska Botanical Gardens, on a peninsula extending out into the small bay of Brunnsvik, are a welcome respite from the city. They are only a short subway ride away. Paths weave along the water in the open park area. Visit Edvard Anderson's modern Växthus (Greenhouse) for its impressive Mediterranean and tropical environments. The century-old Victoriahuset (Victoria House) contains tropical plants as well, and has one of the best collections of water plants in the world. ⊠ *Frescativ. near university, Universitet* ☎ *08/54591700* ⊕ *www.bergianska. se* 🍽 *Park free, Greenhouse SKr 50, Victoria House SKr 20* ⊙ *Park daily yr-round; Victoria House May–Sept., daily 11–4, weekends 11–5; Greenhouse daily 11–5.*

Fjärilshuset *(Butterfly and Bird House)* After a short bus ride and a walk through the magnificent Haga Park, you could be in a room filled with hundreds of tropical butterflies. In the bird room, hundreds of birds of 40 species fly freely. The Haga Park itself is impressive and worth a lengthy stroll, but be sure to combine it with a trip to this oasis. ⊠ *Take Bus 515 from Odenplan subway stop, Haga* ☎ *08/7303981* ⊕ *www.fjarilshuset.se* 🍽 *SKr 00* ⊙ *Apr.–Sept., weekdays 10–5, weekends 11–6; Oct.–Mar., weekdays 10–4, weekends 11–5.*

Tyresö Slott *(Tyresö Castle)*. After a 20-minute bus ride from southern Stockholm, you'll find yourself in the gorgeous, romantic gardens that surround this castle, built in the 1660s. The Nordic Museum led the renovations that restored the grounds to their late-1800s glory. The main building is filled with elaborate salons, libraries, and studies, and the west wing has a nice café and restaurant. Be sure to leave time for both the castle and gardens. ⊠ *Take Bus 875 from Gullmarsplan to Tyresö Slott Tyresö* ☎ *08/51954550* ⊕ *www.nordiskamuseet.se* 🍽 *SKr 80* ⊙ *Sept. and Oct., daily 11–3; June 22–Aug. 19, Tues.–Sun. 11–4. Tours at noon, 1, and 2.*

5

refreshingly friendly, impressively knowledgable staff add a pleasant down-to-earth touch to the sky-high prices. This is haute cuisine at its very best. ⊠ *Fredsg. 12, City* ☎ *08/248052* ⋔ *Reservations essential* ⊟ *AE, DC, MC, V* ⊙ *Closed Sun. No lunch Sat.*

$$$
SCANDINAVIAN
★

✕ **Lux.** This former Electrolux household appliance factory, hence the name, is now an industrial-chic restaurant. Simple wood furniture and white-cloth tables contrast nicely with the exposed brick and wrought iron of the former work space. Light floods the restaurant through enormous windows during the day. At night the space is more subdued. Chefs Henrik Norström and Peter Johansson work the stoves here and also own the place. They use seasonal, local produce (revealing its source wherever possible), which they then prepare with creative, modern twists to produce outstanding dishes. ⊠*Primusg. 116, Lilla Essingen* ☎*08/6190190* ⌀*Reservations essential* ▤*AE, DC, MC, V* ⊘*Closed Mon. No lunch weekends.*

$$$
SCANDINAVIAN
★

✕**Prinsen.** Still in the same location as when it opened in 1897, the Prince serves both traditional and modern Swedish cuisine, but it is for the traditional that most people go. The interior is rich with mellow, warm lighting; dark-wood paneling; and leather chairs and booths. The restaurant is rightly known for its scampi salad and *Wallenbergare,* a classic dish of veal, cream, and peas. Downstairs you'll find a bar and a space for larger parties. ⊠*Mäster Samuelsg. 4, Norrmalm* ☎*08/6111331* ⌀*Reservations essential* ▤*AE, DC, MC, V* ⊘*No lunch weekends.*

$$$
ECLECTIC

✕**Restaurangen.** Flavor is the driving force behind this hip restaurant. It's also great fun to eat here. You build three-, five-, or seven-course meals from 20 flavors, 15 of which are salty and 5 of which are sweet. Each flavor has a letter next to it that corresponds to a list of wines by the glass that are recommended to best complement it. A large box of cutlery appears with enough in it to cover all your choices, and the wine is lined up with an identifying label on each glass. The food is a surprisingly successful mix of contemporary Asian, French, Spanish, Italian, and Swedish. The über-cool interior was created by three students from Stockholm's prestigious Beckman's School of Design. ⊠*Oxtorgsg. 14, Norrmalm* ☎*08/220952* ⌀*Reservations essential* ▤*AE, DC, MC, V* ⊘*No lunch Sat. Closed Sun.*

$$$
SCANDINAVIAN

✕**Rolfs Kök.** Small and modern, Rolfs is a casual restaurant serving excellent Swedish-French cuisine to a local and very loyal clientele. Try the perch with white asparagus, horseradish, and dill or the red wine–braised ox cheek with potato puree. ⊠*Tegnérg. 41* ☎*08/101696* ⌀*Reservations essential* ▤*AE, DC, MC, V* ⊘*No lunch weekends.*

$$
FRENCH

✕**Stockholms Matvarufabriken.** Although it's a bit hard to find, tucked away as it is on a side street, Stockholm's Food Factory is well worth seeking out. The popular bistro restaurant, serving French, Italian, and Swedish cuisine, is packed full on the weekends as young and old come to enjoy the exposed-brick, candlelight-infused dining room and the varied menu. Here omelets are taken to new levels with ingredients such as truffles and asparagus; the choices when it comes to fresh seafood are excellent. Brown-paper tablecloths and kitchen cloths used as napkins set the informal tone. ⊠*Idung. 12, Vasastan* ☎*08/320704* ⌀*Reservations essential* ▤*AE, DC, MC, V* ⊘*No lunch. Closed Sun.*

$
ECLECTIC

✕**Systrarna Lundberg.** A perfectly relaxed, down-to-earth, and friendly neighborhood restaurant. You are just as welcome here for a coffee as you are for one of their globally inspired main courses. Try the Japanese-style beef with jasmine rice, lamb with feta cheese, or the delicious Thai green curry. ⊠*Rörstrandsg. 12* ☎*08/305747* ⌀*Reservations not accepted* ▤*AE, DC, MC, V* ⊘*No lunch.*

¢
AMERICAN

✕**Texas Burger Co.** It may seem counterintuitive to be eating a meal in Stockholm at a restaurant with "Texas" in its name, but this no-frills eatery has great hamburgers at excellent prices and is popular with both visitors and locals. It's always busy, so be ready for atmosphere to boot. ⊠*Kungsg. 44* ☎*08/226040* ⚱*Reservations not accepted* ☰*AE, DC, MC, V.*

$$$

SEAFOOD

✕**Wedholms Fisk.** Noted for its fresh seafood dishes, Wedholms Fisk is appropriately set by a bay in Stockholm's center. High ceilings, large windows, and tasteful modern paintings from the owner's personal collection create a spacious, sophisticated space. The traditional Swedish cuisine, which consists almost exclusively of seafood, is simple but outstanding. The menu is divided by fish type, with a number of dish options for each type of fish. ⊠*Nybrokajen 17, City* ☎*08/6117874* ⚱*Reservations essential* ☰*AE, DC, MC, V* ⊘*Closed Sun. No lunch Sat. and July.*

GAMLA STAN, SKEPPSHOLMEN, AND DJURGÅRDEN

$$$

SCANDINAVIAN

✕**Den Gyldene Freden.** Sweden's most famous old tavern has been open for business since 1722. The haunt of bards and barristers, artists and ad people, Freden could probably serve sawdust and still be popular, but the food and staff are worthy of the restaurant's hallowed reputation. The cuisine has a Swedish orientation, but Continental influences spice up the menu. ⊠*Österlångg. 51, Gamla Stan* ☎*08/249760* ⚱*Reservations essential* ☰*AE, DC, MC, V* ⊘*Closed Sun.*

$$$

SCANDINAVIAN

✕**Eriks Bakficka.** A favorite among Östermalm locals, Eriks Bakficka is a block from the elegant waterside, a few steps down from street level. Inside, the black-and-white tile floor, white-painted stone walls, wood tables strewn with candles, and green-glass lamps give the place a relaxed and approachable ambience. Owned by the well-known Swedish chef Erik Lallerstedt, the restaurant serves Swedish dishes, including a delicious baked pike-perch with mussels and saffron. A lower-priced menu is served in the pub section. ⊠*Fredrikshovsg. 4, Östermalm* ☎*08/6601599* ⚱*Reservations essential* ☰*AE, DC, MC, V* ⊘*Closed Sun. No lunch Sat.*

$$$$

SCANDINAVIAN

★

✕**Frantzën Lindeberg.** Simple modernity reaches an art form at this tiny restaurant, which opened its doors on a cold January day in 2008. The interior marries warm-gray walls with oiled oak and crisp white linens to achieve understated elegance. Chefs Björn Frantzën and Daniel Lindeberg create exquisite dishes using imagination, passion and a little science. Dishes include mindblowing creations such as lightly seared hand-dived scallops with hay ashes and burned bread pudding, and knuckle of farm pork cooked in its own fat for three days. With only two set-priced menus to choose from (one 10 course, one 14-course) and no à la carte, eating here is not cheap—but it's also not to be missed. ⊠*Lilla Nyg. 21, Gamla Stan* ☎*08/208580* ⚱*Reservations essential* ☰*AE, DC, MC, V* ⊘*No lunch. Closed Sun. and Mon.*

$$$

STEAK

✕**Grill Ruby.** This American-style barbecue joint (at least as American as it is possible to be in Gamla Stan) is just a cobblestone's throw away from the statue of St. George slaying the dragon. Next door to its French cousin, Bistro Ruby, Grill Ruby skips the escargots and instead focuses on grilled meats and fish. The steak with french fries and béarnaise sauce is delicious. On Saturday an American-style brunch is served, where you can enjoy quesadillas and a big Bloody Mary while blues and country music drift from the speakers. ⊠*Österlångg. 14, Gamla Stan* ☎*08/206015* ⚱*Reservations essential* ☰*AE, DC, MC, V.*

5

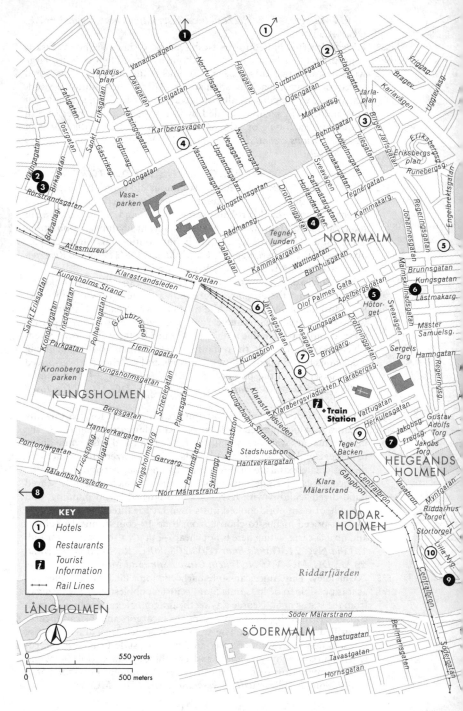

KEY

① Hotels

● Restaurants

ℹ Tourist Information

↔ Rail Lines

Where to Stay and Eat in Northern Stockholm

Restaurants ▼	
Birkastans Restaurang & Pizzeria	**2**
Basserie Godot	**10**
Cassi	**15**
Den Gyldene Freden	**22**
Eriks Bakfica	**16**
Frantzén Lindeberg	**9**
Fredsgatan 12	**7**
Grill Ruby	**20**
Källaren Movitz	**21**
Lisa På Udden	**19**
Lux	**8**
Matthias Dahlgren	**18**
Oscars	**14**
Prinsen	**13**
Restaurangen	**6**
Rolfs Kök	**4**
Stockholms Matvarufabriken	**1**
Sturehof	**12**
Systrarna Lundberg	**3**
Texas Burger Co.	**5**
Vapiano	**11**
Wedholms Fisk	**17**

Hotels ▼	
Berns Hotel	**20**
Best Western Time Hotel	**1**
Birger Jarl	**3**
Central Hotel	**7**
Claes på Hörnet	**2**
Clarion Sign	**6**
Diplomat	**19**
Grand Hotel	**22**
Hotel Esplanade	**18**
Hotel Gustav Wasa	**4**
Hotel Riddargatan	**13**
Hotel Stureplan	**11**
Lady Hamilton	**23**
Nordic Light Hotel	**8**
Örnsköld	**14**
Pärlan	**16**
Radisson SAS Strand Hotel	**21**
Reisen	**24**
Rica Hotel Gamla Stan	**25**
Scandic Anglais	**12**
Sheraton Hotel and Towers	**9**
Stockholm Plaza Hotel	**5**
Victory	**10**
Villa Källhagen	**17**
Wellington	**15**

5

$$ ✕ **Källaren Movitz.** At first glance Movitz looks like nothing more than
SCANDINAVIAN a typical European pub, which is exactly what it is upstairs. But down-
stairs it's a restaurant serving Swedish cuisine with French and Italian
influences. The refined table settings and abundant candlelight reflect-
ing off the curves of the light yellow walls of what used to be a potato
cellar in the 1600s make this an elegant place to dine. Dishes are simple
affairs with a real dinner-party-at-home feel; expect menu choices such
as game, pasta, salmon, and plenty of rich sauces. ⊠ *Tyska Brinken 34,
Gamla Stan* ☎ *08/209979* ⊟ *AE, DC, MC, V* ☉ *Closed Sun.*

$$ ✕ **Lisa På Udden.** Fish is the order of the day at this light and airy water-
SEAFOOD side restaurant on Stockholm's beautiful Djurgården island. The spa-
cious modern interior is decked out Scandinavian style: wood floors,
simple wood furniture, and primary colors. The main draw, though,
is the view across the water, through the restaurant's ample windows.
The tables fill up, especially on weekends, but if you don't have reservations you might get lucky if you turn up early or late. ⊠ *Biskopsv. 9,
Djurgården* ☎ *08/6609475* ⌔ *Reservations essential* ⊟ *MC, V.*

$$$ ✕ **Mathias Dahlgren.** It seemed like all of Stockholm was holding its
SCANDINAVIAN breath for Mattias Dahlgren to open his new eponymous restaurant at
Fodor's Choice the end of 2007 (his first since he shuttered the legendary Bon Lloc).
★ When the doors finally opened, a collective sigh of relief was audible:
success! From the elegant modern dining room to the food—simple,
artistically rendered local food which Dahlgren's dubbed "natural
cuisine"—this place doesn't disappoint. For his trouble he picked up
a Michelin star in his first six months. Don't miss this place. ⊠ *Grand
Hotel, S Blasieholmshamen 6103 27* ☎ *08/6793584* ⌔ *Reservations
essential* ⊟ *AE, DC, MC, V* ☉ *Lunch served weekdays in bar. No lunch
weekends. Closed Sun.*

ÖSTERMALM

$$ ✕ **Brasserie Godot.** This cool, sleek, minimal restaurant with friendly
FRENCH service and simple, delicious brasserie staples keeps its dining room
perpetually packed. The steak tatare is the best in town and the bar
is a great spot to hang with the locals before or after dinner. ⊠ *Grev-
tureg. 36* ☎ *08/6600614* ⌔ *Reservations essential* ⊟ *AE, DC, MC, V*
☉ *Closed Sun. No lunch.*

$$ ✕ **Cassi.** It doesn't get any better than this for authentic French-inspired
FRENCH cuisine. Think grilled cuts of meat with the finest french fries in town.
Fodor's Choice It's counter service here, so queue up, order, and watch while the chef
★ cooks your dinner. Don't expect any frills; save for a few French film
posters and shots of Paris, the interior design of this place isn't the
hippest. But that's not why you come: that would be the food. Dinner
service ends at eight so is not the best choice for night owls, but Cassi
is busiest and best at lunchtime anyway, when the daily set lunch can
reduce the price dramatically. And those guys in the corner—with the
cool suits, carafe of wine and copies of *Le Figaro*—they probably come
from the French Embassy right next door. Now that's a good sign.
⊠ *Naravägen 30* ☎ *08/6617461* ⌔ *Reservations not accepted* ⊟ *AE,
MC, V* ☉ *Closed Sat.*

¢ ✕ **Oscars.** A wonderful café from the 1940s where pretty much
CAFÉ everything—from the wood-paneled walls to the etched-glass

partitions—remains untouched. What *does* change, though, is the food: the Mediterranean-inspired lunch menu is revised daily. Oscars attracts a jovial crowd of local residents and nearby office workers. ☒*Naravägen 32.* ☏*08/6625226* ⌖*Reservations not accepted* ▭*AE, DC, MC, V* ◔*No dinner.*

$$$　✕**Sturehof.** This massive complex of a restaurant with two huge bars is a
SCANDINAVIAN　complete social, architectural, and dining experience amid wood paneling, leather chairs and sofas, and distinctive lighting fixtures. There's a bar directly facing Stureplan where you can sit on a summer night and watch Stockholmers gather at the nearby Svampen (the mushroomlike concrete structure that has been the city's meeting point for years). In the elegant dining room fine Swedish cuisine is offered. Upstairs is the O-Bar, a dimly-lit lounge filled well into the night with young people and loud music. ☒*Stureplan 2, City* ☏*08/4405730* ⌖*Reservations essential* ▭*AE, DC, MC, V.*

$　✕**Vapiano.** This 2007 addition to the international Italian restaurant
ITALIAN　chain continues to give fast food a good name. Queues are always long here, as locals can't seem to get enough of the build-your-own concept. Choose from around six different types of pasta, then watch the chefs as they blend the ingredients and sauces to your liking. There's pizza and salads on offer, too. Pick up a drink at the bar and grab a table in the wooden, yet still very sleek, dining room. And yes, you can pick the fresh herbs in the pots on your table if you want a little extra flavor. Everything you order is charged to a plastic card, which you swipe and pay off as you exit. ☒*Sturegatan 12* ☏*08/6622011* ⌖*Reservations not accepted* ▭*AE, DC, MC, V.*

SÖDERMALM

$　✕**Hermans.** Hermans is a haven for vegetarians out to get the most bang
VEGETARIAN　for their kronor. The glassed-in back deck and open garden both pro-
Fodor'sChoice　vide breathtaking vistas across the water of Stockholm harbor, Gamla
★　Stan, and the island of Djurgården. The food is always served buffet style and includes various vegetable and pasta salads, warm casseroles, and such entrées as Indonesian stew with peanut sauce and vegetarian lasagna. The fruit pies, chocolate cakes, and cookies are delicious. ☒*Fjällg. 23A, Södermalm* ☏*08/6439480* ▭*MC, V.*

$$　✕**Humlehof.** If you're feeling extra hungry and a bit tight on funds,
EASTERN　go straight to this Bavarian restaurant serving traditional Swedish
EUROPEAN　and eastern European dishes. Start by ordering an ice-cold Czech or Austrian draft beer, a bowl of what has to be the best goulash in Stockholm, and the *schweizer* (Swiss-style) schnitzel, which is as big as your face and served with salad and fried potatoes. If schnitzel's not your thing, try the panfried Haloumi cheese with sun-dried tomatoes, summer salad, and garlic bread. ☒*Folkungag. 128, Södermalm* ☏*08/6410302* ▭*MC, V.*

$　✕**Loopen Marin.** Come and chill under the coconut palms (plastic ones,
CAFÉ　of course) at this relaxed and friendly yacht club and restaurant. Non-
★　members are warmly welcomed, as are children. Cold beer, cocktails, snacks and simple dishes are the order of the day here, to be enjoyed from a deck chair as you take in the sunshine, lapping water, and pass-

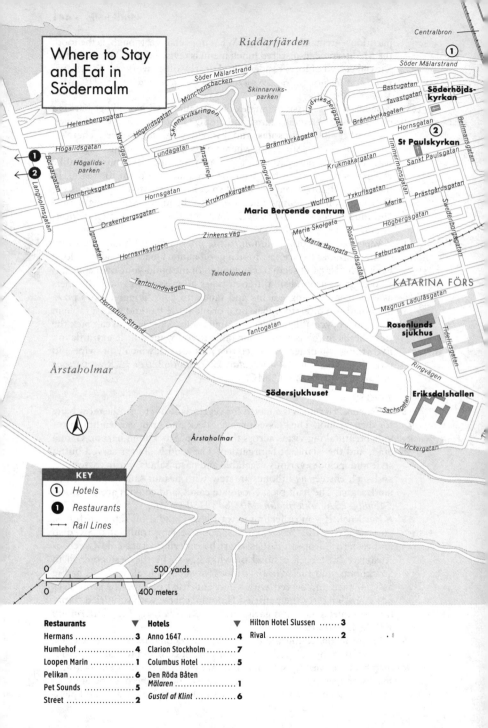

Where to Stay and Eat in Södermalm

Riddarfjärden

Centralbron

Söder Mälarstrand

Söderhöjds-kyrkan

St Paulskyrkan

Skinnarviks-parken

Heleneborgsgatan

Högalidsgatan

Skinnarviksringen

Ludviksbergsgatan

Brännkyrkagatan

Bastugatan

Tavastgatan

Brännkyrkagatan

Hornsgatan

Bellmansgatan

Sankt Paulsgatan

Högalidsgatan

Varvsgatan

Lundagatan

Ansgarieg.

Ringvägen

Krukmakargatan

Immenmansgatan

Prästgårdsgatan

Swedenborgsgatan

Högalids-parken

Borgargatan

Langholmsgatan

Hornbruksgatan

Hornsgatan

Krukmakargatan

Yxkullsgatan

Maria

Maria Beroende centrum

Wollmar

Maria Skolgata

Högbergsgatan

Drakenbergsgatan

Zinkens Väg

Maria Bangata

Rosenlundsgatan

Fatbursgatan

Lignagatan

Hornsviksstigen

KATARINA FÖRS

Tantolundsvägen

Tantolunden

Magnus Ladulåsgatan

Hornstulls Strand

Tantogatan

Rosenlunds sjukhus

Ringvägen

Hjelpsgatan

Årstaholmar

Södersjukhuset

Eriksdalshallen

Sachsgatan

Årstaholmar

Vickergatan

KEY

① Hotels

❶ Restaurants

↔ Rail Lines

0   500 yards

0   400 meters

ing boats. ⊠*Hornstulls Strand 6* ☎*08/844285* ⚓*Reservations not accepted* ⊟*No credit cards* ⊙*Closed Nov.–Apr.*

$$ ✕**Pelikan.** Beer, beer, and more beer is the order of the day at Pelikan, a
SCANDINAVIAN   traditional working-class drinking hall, a relic of the days when Söder-
Fodor's Choice   malm was the dwelling place of the city's blue-collar brigade. Today's
★   more bohemian residents find it just as enticing, with the unvarnished
wood-paneled walls, faded murals, and glass globe lights fulfilling all
their down-at-the-heel pretensions. The food here is some of the best
traditional Swedish fare in the city. The herring, meatballs, and salted
bacon with onion sauce are not to be missed. ⊠*Blekingeg. 40, Söder-
malm* ☎*08/55609090* ⚓*Reservations not accepted* ⊟*MC, V* ⊙*No
lunch Sun.–Thurs.*

$$ ✕**Pet Sounds.** This cool neighborhood restaurant is almost always filled
SCANDINAVIAN   with locals. Following in the fotsteps of Hannas Krog, this location's
previous incarnation, Pet Sounds remains a Södermalm hot spot. Chefs
expertly execute modern Swedish dishes like veal steak with onion compote and scallops with brown butter and roasted almods. The bar in
the basement is loud but pleasant. Local bands play there on occasion.
⊠*Skåneg. 80, Södermalm* ☎*08/6438225* ⊟*AE, DC, MC, V* ⊙*No
lunch Mon.–Wed. Closed Sun.*

$$$ ✕**Street.** This former garage has now been put to much better use as a
SCANDINAVIAN   light, spacious, and always-buzzing restaurant, café, and bar. It's part
of the deservedly hyped (and similarly named) Street, a waterside out-
door market, and there's always lots to see and buy in the area before
you take a load off. The food is modern, bistro-style Swedish, with
an emphasis on ecological, locally produced ingredients. ⊠*Hornstulls
Strand 4* ☎*08/6586350* ⚓*Reservations essential* ⊟*AE, DC, MC, V.*

WHERE TO STAY

Stockholm is—we'll say it—a relatively stagnant town when it comes
to hotel development, with few new openings each year. But, while the
hotel choices here are often not trendily brand-new, they're still plentiful
and include everything from grand five-star properties down to basic,
affordable hostel accommodation. Most Stockholm hotels have a dis-
tinctly Scandinavian design sensitivity. Who needs the latest designer
interior when there's plenty of fresh, nonfussy, reasonably elegant and
endlessly functional places to stay? Although Stockholm has a reputa-
tion for prohibitively expensive hotels, great deals can be found in sum-
mer, when prices are substantially lower and numerous discounts are
available. More than 50 hotels offer the "Stockholm Package," which
includes accommodations for one night, breakfast, and the Stockholm-
skortet, or Stockholm Card, which entitles the cardholder to free admis-
sion to museums and travel on public transport. Details are available
from travel agents, tourist bureaus, and the **Stockholm Information Service**
(✆*Box 7542, Stockholm 103 93* ☎*08/50828500*). Also try **Hotellcen-
tralen** (⊠*Centralstation, 111 20Stockholm* ☎*08/7892425*); the service
is free if you go in person, but a fee applies if you call.

All rooms in the hotels reviewed below are equipped with shower or
bath unless otherwise noted. Unless otherwise stated, hotels do not

have air-conditioning. Some hotels close during the winter holidays; call ahead if you expect to travel during that time.

NORRMALM

$$ ⚑**Best Western Time Hotel.** A pleasant, comfortable and somewhat stylish mid-price hotel can be hard to find in Stockholm. The Time Hotel is a particular standout in this category. The rooms are modern and thoughtfully put together, with nice touches like heated bathroom floors and fresh-cut flowers. Because the hotel is purpose built, all the rooms are of a good size. Many come with a French balcony; all have wood floors and working desks. **Pros:** very friendly service; large rooms. **Cons:** location isn't central; limited facilities. ⊠*Vanadisv. 12* ☎*08/854547300* ⊕*www.bestwestern.com* ⟿*144 rooms* &*In-room: Internet. In-hotel: room service, bar, Internet terminal, parking (paid), no-smoking rooms* ⊟*AE, DC, MC, V* ⦿*BP.*

$$$$ ⚑**Berns Hotel.** This ultramodern hotel was a hot spot when it opened its
★ doors in the late 19th century, and it retains that status today. Rooms here have hardwood floors, white walls, feather-stuffed white quilts and fabrics in cobalt blue, chocolate brown, moss green, and stone—a lesson in comfortable modernism. All feature a rotating wooden tower containing TV, CD player, and minibar. The restaurant/bar is a joint venture with restaurant entrepreneur and designer Terence Conran. Hotel rates include the use of a nearby fitness center with a pool. **Pros:** stylish rooms; fantastic restaurant; great bath products. **Cons:** some rooms are a little small; the bar gets rowdy weekend nights. ⊠*Näckströmsg. 8, City* ☎*08/56632000* ⊕*www.berns.se* ⟿*65 rooms, 3 suites* &*In-room: refrigerator, Internet. In-hotel: restaurant, room service, bar, Wi-Fi, no-smoking rooms* ⊟*AE, DC, MC, V* ⦿*BP.*

$$ ⚑**Birger Jarl.** At this high-design hotel the lobby doubles as a modern-art gallery, and exhibitions change frequently. Some rooms have been individually designed by several of the country's top designers (it costs extra to stay in these). Most rooms are not large, but all are well furnished and have nice touches, such as heated towel racks in the bathrooms. All double rooms have bathtubs. **Pros:** cool design; airy rooms; lively lobby. **Cons:** many rooms are small. ⊠*Tuleg. 8, Vasastan* ☎*08/6741800* ⊕*www.birgerjarl.se* ⟿*235 rooms* &*In-room: refrigerator (some), Internet. In-hotel: restaurant, room service, laundry service, Internet terminal, no-smoking rooms* ⊟*AE, DC, MC, V* ⦿*BP.*

$$ ⚑**Central Hotel.** Less than 300 yards from the central station, this practical hotel lives up to its name. The reception area is white, and its skylight gives the hotel a sense of freshness and simplicity. Rooms follow suit, with only the burgundy curtains and chairs interrupting the otherwise pleasing minimalism. Thanks to extra sound insulation, the chaos of Vasagatan remains outside the room. Bathrooms have showers, not bathtubs. **Pros:** good location; unfussy decor. **Cons:** sparse facilities; small bathrooms. ⊠*Vasag. 38, City* ☎*08/56620800* ⊕*www.profilhotels.se* ⟿*93 rooms, 1 suite* &*In-room: Wi-Fi. In-hotel: no-smoking rooms* ⊟*AE, DC, MC, V* ⦿*BP.*

$$ ⚑**Claes på Hörnet.** This may be the most exclusive—and smallest—hotel
★ in town, with only 10 rooms in a former 1739 inn. The rooms, comfortably furnished with period antiques, go quickly (book three or so months

in advance, especially around Christmas). The restaurant is worth visiting even if you don't spend the night: its old-fashioned dining room serves Swedish and Continental dishes such as outstanding *strömming* (Baltic herring) and cloudberry mousse cake. **Pros:** historical and charming; friendly service; wonderful restaurant. **Cons:** beds might be too soft for some; some rooms are very small. ⊠*Surbrunnsg. 20, Vasastan* ☎*08/165136* ⊕*www.claspahornet.se* ⬳*10 rooms* ⟐*In room: refrigerator, Internet. In-hotel: restaurant* ▭*AE, DC, MC, V* ⦿*BP.*

$$$ ⛰**Clarion Sign.** Big, brash, and right by Central Station, Clarion Sign burst onto the scene in 2008 with fanfare and promise. Part of the Choice Hotels chain, it's two main selling points seemed to be a roof terrace with year-round pool at the top (fantastic), and the first home-turf restaurant helmed by Swedish-born New York superstar chef Marcus Samuelsson at street level (passable). But what of in between? The rooms are big on Swedish design, generous in size and somewhere near middle on the luxury scale. Neither pure business behemoth nor dictionary-definition boutique, Clarion Sign is a well-balanced and very pleasant addition to Stockholm's hotel scene. **Pros:** big rooms; great roof terrace. **Cons:** drab location; impersonal service. ⊠*Östra Järnvägsg. 35* ☎*08/6769800* ⊕*www.clarionsign.se* ⬳*588 rooms* ⟐*In-room: safe, refrigerator, Internet. In-hotel: restaurant, room service, bar, pool, spa, laundry service, Internet terminal, no-smoking rooms* ▭*AE, DC, MC, V* ⦿*BP.*

$$ ⛰**Hotel Gustav Wasa.** The Gustav Wasa is in a 19th-century residential
Fodor's Choice   building and has fairly large, bright rooms with herringbone hard-
★   wood floors, original trim and details along the ceilings, and a funky blend of antiques and furniture that's more modern. Some rooms have wonderful original tiled fireplaces. Ask for a room with a window out to the street in order to get a direct view of the grand Gustav Wasa Church and the Odenplan. The other available view, of the inner courtyard, is much less exciting. The downtown location and lower prices make this an excellent place for budget travelers who prefer a friendly hotel. **Pros:** good location; very friendly staff; rooms are of ample size. **Cons:** basic facilities; small bathrooms. ⊠*Västmannag. 61, Vasastan* ☎*08/54544805* ⊕*www.gustavvasahotel.se* ⬳*41 rooms* *In-hotel: parking (paid)* ▭*AE, DC, MC, V* ⦿*BP.*

$$$ ⛰**Hotel Stureplan.** Following the demise of the Lydmar Hotel, the undis-
Fodor's Choice   puted best boutique to have ever graced Stockholm's sidewalks, the
★   city's hotel watchers were left wondering if they would ever recover. Then, along came Hotel Stureplan. Housed in a beautiful 18th-century mansion, Stureplan has pitched itself just right; the perfect mix between modern design, comfortable living, and functional hotel. Rooms come in small, medium, large, or extra large and are further categorized as classic (Gustavian furniture, stucco features, balconies, fireplaces) and loft (modern, minimal and light-filled). Whichever you choose, Stureplan has perfected the elusive art of making guests feel truly at home. **Pros:** to-die-for design; great service; perfect location. **Cons:** no restaurant; small rooms are very small. ⊠*Birger Jarlsg. 24* ☎*08/4406600* ⊕*www.hotelstureplan.se* ⬳*102 rooms* ⟐*In-room: safe, refrigerator,*

Internet. In-hotel: room service, bar, laundry service, Internet terminal, no-smoking rooms ☰*AE, DC, MC, V* ⦿|*BP.*

$$$–$$$$ ⊞**Nordic Light Hotel.** Next to Central Station, this modern center for the business traveler is the perfect choice for travelers with a predilection for cool design. The hotel focuses on simplicity, and, not surprisingly, light plays an important role, with responsive sound-and-movement systems in the lobby and multiple light settings, including light-therapy treatment, in the rooms. Rooms are a mix of dark wood, gray flannel, and black-and-white tile, with adjustable spotlights in the ceiling. **Pros:** great lobby scene; very comfortable rooms; fun. **Cons:** right by Central Station, a slightly sketchy area as areas here go; noisy rooms on the lower floors. ⊠*Vasaplan 7, City* ☎*08/50563000* ⊕*www.nordiclighthotel. se* ⇶*175 rooms* ⟐*In-room: refrigerator, Internet. In-hotel: restaurant, room service, bars, laundry service, Wi-Fi, parking (paid), no-smoking rooms* ☰*AE, DC, MC, V* ⦿|*BP.*

$$$ ⊞**Scandic Anglais.** Reopened and rejuvinated, the once drab hotel (part of the Scandic chain), is now a Stockholm hot spot (and still part of the Scandic chain). The rooms are a little plain, but have benefited from the refurbishment, leaving them with a very modern, fresh Scandinavian look (think white walls, dark wood floors and primary color bedspreads). The main draw here is the lobby bar, where locals and guests alike crowd the sofas on weekend evenings to sip champagne and cocktails and to mingle loudly. **Pros:** very cool lobby scene; great views. **Cons:** slightly boring rooms; small rooms. ⊠*Humlegårdsg. 23* ☎*08/51734000* ⊕*www.scandichotels.com* ⇶*230 rooms* ⟐*In-room: safe, refrigerator, Internet. In-hotel: restaurant, room service, bar, laundry service, Internet terminal, parking (paid), no-smoking rooms* ☰*AE, DC, MC, V* ⦿|*BP.*

$$$$ ⊞**Sheraton Hotel and Towers.** Popular with business executives, the Sheraton is also an ideal hotel for the tourist on a generous budget looking for comfort and luxury. The Sheraton unveiled a new look in 2008, shaking off its tired 1980s shroud to reveal a much cleaner, more stylish look. The rooms now feature natural tones, cool lighting, refinished bathrooms, and wood detail in all the places you'd expect it. English is the main language at the restaurant and bar, which fill up at night once the piano player arrives. The gift shop sells Swedish crystal and international newspapers. **Pros:** great location; big rooms; extremely comfortable beds. **Cons:** not popular with locals; terrible view from courtyard rooms. ⊠*Tegelbacken 6, City* ☎*08/4123400* ⊕*www.sheratonstockholm.com* ⇶*462 rooms, 30 suites* ⟐*In-room: safe, refrigerator, Internet, Wi-Fi. In-hotel: restaurant, room service, bar, gym, laundry service, Wi-Fi, parking (paid), no-smoking rooms* ☰*AE, DC, MC, V* ⦿|*BP.*

$$$ ⊞**Stockholm Plaza Hotel.** On one of Stockholm's foremost streets for shopping and entertainment, and only a short walk from the city's nightlife and business center, this hotel is ideal if you want to be in a central location. The building was built in 1884, and the Elite hotel chain took over in 1984. Rooms are furnished in an elegant, traditional manner, and many include the original stuccowork on the ceilings. **Pros:** very central location; amazing restaurant and bar; friendly staff. **Cons:**

5

small rooms; some rooms a little noisy. ⊠ *Birger Jarlsg. 29, Downtown* ☎ *08/56622000* ⊕ *www.elite.se* ⤺ *143 rooms, 4 suites* ⚤ *In-room: Internet, Wi-Fi. In-room: safe (some), refrigerator, Wi-Fi. In-hotel: restaurant, room service, bar, laundry service, parking (fee), no-smoking rooms* ☱ *AE, DC, MC, V* ⥮ *BP.*

GAMLA STAN AND SKEPPSHOLMEN

$$$$
Fodor'sChoice
★

🛏 **Grand Hotel.** At first glance the Grand seems like any other world-class international hotel, and in many ways it is. Its location is one of the best in the city, on the quayside just across the water from the Royal Palace. It boasts an impressive guest list. The service is slick, professional, and predicts your every need. The large rooms are sumptuous and decadent, with robes so fluffy, beds so soft, and antiques so lovely you may never want to leave. But the Grand offers something else: a touch of the uniquely Scandinavian. You can feel it in the relaxed atmosphere that pervades the hotel, you can smell it in the fresh, salt-tinged air that wafts through the open windows, and you can see it in the purity of the light that penetrates all corners of the hotel. If there is a more exquisite hotel anywhere in town, it is yet to be found. **Pros:** unadulterated luxury; world-class service; great bar. **Cons:** some rooms are small; faded in parts. ⊠ *Södra Blasieholmshamnen 8, Box 16424, City 10327* ☎ *08/6793500* ⊕ *www.grandhotel.se* ⤺ *386 rooms, 21 suites* ⚤ *In-room: safe, refrigerator, Wi-Fi. In-hotel: 2 restaurants, room service, bar, gym, spa, laundry service, Wi-Fi, no-smoking rooms* ☱ *AE, DC, MC, V* ⥮ *BP.*

$$$

🛏 **Lady Hamilton.** As charming as its namesake (hint: she was Lord Nelson's mistress), the Lady Hamilton is a modern hotel inside a typical Gamla Stan russet-red 15th-century building. Swedish antiques fill the guest rooms and common areas, including such obscure objects as old spirit cabinets, complete with original bottles. The breakfast room, furnished with captain's chairs, looks out onto the lively cobblestone street, and the subterranean sauna rooms, in whitewashed stone, provide a secluded fireplace and a chance to take a dip in the building's original, medieval well. **Pros:** veritably drips old-world charm; great location. **Cons:** rooms can be tiny; some views are restricted. ⊠ *Storkyrkobrinken 5, Gamla Stan* ☎ *08/50640100* ⊕ *www.ladyhamiltonhotel.se* ⤺ *34 rooms* ⚤ *In-room: refrigerator (some), Wi-Fi. In-hotel: restaurant, bar, no-smoking rooms* ☱ *AE, DC, MC, V* ⥮ *BP.*

$$$–$$$$

🛏 **Radisson SAS Strand Hotel.** An art-nouveau monolith, built in 1912 for the Stockholm Olympics, this hotel has been completely and tastefully modernized. It's on the water across from the Royal Dramatic Theater, only a short walk from the Old Town and the museums on Skeppsholmen. No two rooms are alike, but all are furnished with simple and elegant furniture, offset by white woodwork and hues of moss green and cocoa brown. The Strand restaurant has a sharp, urban feel, with a cool color scheme of stone, earth-brown, and natural greens. **Pros:** central location; elegant rooms; lively public areas. **Cons:** has a slight chain-hotel feel; beds too soft for some. ⊠ *Nybrokajen 9, Box 16396, City* ☎ *08/50664000* ⊕ *www.radissonsas.com* ⤺ *152 rooms* ⚤ *In-room: safe, refrigerator, Wi-Fi. In-hotel: restaurant, room service, bar, gym, laundry service, Wi-Fi, no-smoking rooms* ☱ *AE, DC, MC, V* ⥮ *BP.*

$$–$$$ ☷ **Reisen.** On the waterfront in Gamla Stan, this hotel opened in 1819. The rooms looking out over the water are fantastic, and for a small supplement you can get a room with a private sauna and Jacuzzi. A mix of nautical-inspired antiques and simple, modern furniture fill the rooms, many of which have original exposed brick and wood ceiling beams. There is a fine restaurant with a grill, tea and coffee service in the library, and what is reputed to be the best piano bar in town. Pros: very homely feel; great views from front rooms. Cons: a little busy in the public areas. ⊠*Skeppsbron 9, Gamla Stan* ☎*08/223260* ⊕*www. firsthotels.com* ⇆*144 rooms, 7 suites* &*In-room: refrigerator, Wi-Fi. In-hotel: restaurant, room service, bar, pool, spa, laundry service, Wi-Fi, no-smoking rooms* ⊟*AE, DC, MC, V.*

$$ ☷ **Rica Hotel Gamla Stan.** The feel of historical Stockholm living is rarely more prevalent than in this quiet hotel tucked away on a narrow street in one of the Gamla Stan's 17th-century houses. All rooms are decorated in the Gustavian style, with hardwood floors, Oriental rugs, and antique furniture. A short walk from the Gamla Stan metro stop, it's a perfect home base for later exploring. Pros: personal service; most rooms are comfortable. Cons: some rooms are small; basic facilities. ⊠*Lilla Nyg. 25, Gamla Stan* ☎*08/7237250* ⊕*www.rica.se* ⇆*51 rooms* &*In-room: refrigerator, Internet. In-hotel: no-smoking rooms.* ⊟*AE, DC, MC, V* ⎟⊙⎟*BP.*

$$$ ☷ **Victory.** Slightly larger than its brother and sister hotels, the Lord Nelson and Lady Hamilton, this extremely atmospheric Gamla Stan building dates from 1640. History defines the Victory: in the cellar you can see part of a medieval fortress wall, and, in the 1930s construction workers stumbled across Sweden's biggest silver treasure ever found, just beneath the hotel. The theme is nautical, with artifacts from the HMS *Victory*, as well as Swedish antiques. Each room is named after a 19th-century sea captain. Pros: great location; charming staff; superb restaurant. Cons: some very small rooms. ⊠*Lilla Nyg. 5, Gamla Stan* ☎*08/50640000* ⊕*www.victoryhotel.se* ⇆*45 rooms* &*In-room: refrigerator, Wi-Fi. In-hotel: restaurant, bar, no-smoking rooms* ⊟*AE, DC, MC, V* ⎟⊙⎟*BP.*

ÖSTERMALM

$$$–$$$$
Fodor's Choice
★
☷ **Diplomat.** Within easy walking distance of Djurgården, this elegant hotel is less flashy than most in its price range, but oozes a certain European chic, evident in its subtle, tasteful designs and efficient staff. The building is a turn-of-the-20th-century town house; rooms are all individual but have fresh colors, clean lines, and subtle hints of floral prints in common, and those in the front, facing the water, have magnificent views over Stockholm Harbor. The T-Bar, formerly a rather staid tearoom and restaurant, is now one of the trendiest bars among the city's upper crust. Pros: among the nicest rooms in the city; great service; fantastic views. Cons: rowdy breakfast room; limited public areas. ⊠*Strandv. 7C, Östermalm* ☎*08/4596800* ⊕*www.diplomathotel.com* ⇆*129 rooms* &*In-room: refrigerator, Internet. In-hotel: restaurant, room service, bars, gym, laundry service, Wi-Fi, no-smoking rooms* ⊟*AE, DC, MC, V* ⎟⊙⎟*BP.*

5

$$-$$$ ⊞**Hotel Esplanade.** Right on the water and only a few buildings down from Stockholm's Royal Dramatic Theater, Hotel Esplanade is a beautiful hotel with a real touch of old Stockholm. Somewhere between a family home, a guesthouse, and a hotel, Esplanade is a resplendent work of art nouveau. From the confection of external architecture to the oiled-wood floors and classic period furnishings, this is a real museum piece of a hotel. The rooms with a view of the water are worth the little extra money. Be sure to call well ahead to book a room, since many regulars return every year. **Pros:** homey; friendly; great location. **Cons:** a little pricey for such sparse facilities; beds might be too soft for some. ⊠*Strandv. 7A, Östermalm,* ☎*08/6630740* ⊕*www.hotelesplanade.se* ➽*34 rooms* ⌂*In-room: refrigerator, Ethernet. In-hotel: bar* ▤*AE, DC, MC, V* ⍟*BP.*

$$ ⊞**Hotel Riddargatan.** On its way to being a full-fledged design hotel, the Riddargatan may not be truly cutting-edge quite yet, but at these prices it's a great alternative for travelers who are conscious of style and budget in equal measure. The lobby pleases with its simplicity, the clean space broken only by the beech-wood wall panels and chocolate-brown leather sofas. The bedrooms are a calming blue, with splashes of color in the curtains and accessories. Furnishings are modern and simple, making for a restful space away from the city. **Pros:** good location; extremely comfortable beds; good-size rooms. **Cons:** slightly slow service; limited facilities. ⊠*Riddarg. 14, Östermalm* ☎*08/55573000* ⊕*www.profilhotels.se* ➽*58 rooms, 4 suites* ⌂*In-room: Wi-Fi. In-hotel: bar* ▤*AE, DC, MC, V* ⍟*BP.*

$-$$ ⊞**Örnsköld.** Right in the heart of the city, this hidden gem feels like an old private club, from its brass-and-leather lobby to the Victorian-style furniture in the moderately spacious, high-ceiling rooms. Rooms overlooking the courtyard are quieter, but those facing the street—not a particularly busy one—are sunnier. All the rooms are becoming a little faded, but somehow that seems to add to the charm. **Pros:** good price for location. **Cons:** small rooms. ⊠*Nybrog. 6, Östermalm* ☎*08/6670285* ⊕*www.hotelornskold.se* ➽*33 rooms* ⌂*In-room: safe, refrigerator, Wi-Fi. In-hotel: bar, parking (paid)* ▤*AE, MC, V* ⍟*BP.*

$
Fodor'sChoice
★
⊞**Pärlan.** The name of this hotel means the "Pearl" and that's exactly what it is. On the second floor of an early-19th-century building on a quiet street, the Pärlan is a friendly alternative to the city's bigger hotels. Furniture throughout is a mix of fine antiques and flea-market bargains, making it quirky and homey. A balcony looking out over the inner courtyard is a perfect spot for eating breakfast, which is served buffet style in the kitchen every morning. If you want to get a feel for what it's like to really live in this neighborhood, this is your best bet. Book far in advance because the rooms are almost always full. **Pros:** good location; homey feel. **Cons:** a little worn around the edges. ⊠*Skepparg. 27, Östermalm* ☎*08/6635070* ⊕*www.parlanhotell.com* ➽*9 rooms* ⌂*In-room: Wi-Fi* ▤*AE, MC, V.*

$$$
Fodor'sChoice
★
⊞**Villa Källhagen.** The changing seasons are on display in this beautiful country hotel, reflected through the huge windows, glass walls, and bedroom skylights. Rooms are spacious and furnished in light woods and beautifully colored fabrics. It's only a few minutes from the city

CAMPING IN STOCKHOLM

Yes, that's right: camping, right in and around a capital city, though it should come as no surprise once you remember that this is Sweden, after all. You can camp in the Stockholm area for SKr 90–SKr 150 per night. **Bredäng Camping** (⌧*127 31, Skärholmen* ☎*08/977071*) has camping and a youth hostel. Its facilities are excellent and include a restaurant and bar. At **Rösjöbaden Camping** (⌧*Sollentuna* ☎*08/962184*), a short drive north of town, you can fish, swim, and play minigolf and volleyball. Fifteen kilometers (9 mi) from Stockholm, in Huddinge, is **Stockholm SweCamp Flottsbro** (⌧*Huddinge* ☎*08/53532700*), where you can camp, play golf, rent canoes and bikes, and hang out on a beach.

5

center, but its woodland surroundings can make you feel a million miles away. The restaurant also relies heavily on the seasons, serving a delicious blend of fresh Swedish ingredients cooked with a French influence. **Pros:** country setting minutes from city; great restaurant. **Cons:** a little sleepy; difficult to get a table in the restaurant. ⌧*Djurgårdsbrunnsv. 10, N. Djurgården* ☎*08/6650300* ⊕*www.kallhagen.se* ⤶*36 rooms* ⌂*In-room: refrigerator, Internet. In-hotel: restaurant, bar, parking (free), no-smoking rooms* ☐*AE, DC, MC, V* ⏺❘*BP.*

$$$$ 🖼 **Wellington.** From the outside the building resembles the Industrihuset
★   (Industry House) across the street, but inside is a delightful hotel with polite, professional staff and quality service. In a quiet residential area in Östermalm near the Hedvig Eleonora Church and cemetery, the hotel is a calm home base from which to enjoy the city. Rooms have hardwood floors and a hint of Britishness about them in the tweeds, checks, and tartans used in chair covers, rugs, and bedspreads. Rooms facing the inner courtyard have balconies. Ask for a room on the top floor for a great view of the neighborhood's rooftops. **Pros:** large rooms; excellent service. **Cons:** though a great hotel, it's expensive for its category; many rooms have poor views. ⌧*Storg. 6, Östermalm* ☎*08/6670910* ⊕*www.wellington.se* ⤶*60 rooms* ⌂*In-room: refrigerator, DVD (some), Wi-Fi. In-hotel: restaurant, bar, laundry service, parking (paid)* ☐*AE, MC, V* ⏺❘*BP.*

SÖDERMALM

$$$ 🖼 **Anno 1647.** Named for the date the building was erected, this small,
★   pleasant hotel is a piece of Stockholm history. Rooms vary in shape, but all have original, well-worn pine floors with 17th-century-style furniture. There's no elevator in this four-story building. The bar and café are a popular local hangout. The menu is international. Guest DJs control the sound waves. **Pros:** unique historic atmosphere; efficient staff. **Cons:** a little creaky in places; rooms can feel a bit sparse. ⌧*Mariagränd 3, Södermalm* ☎*08/4421680* ⊕*www.anno1647.se* ⤶*42 rooms, 2 suites* ⌂*In-room: Wi-Fi. In-hotel: restaurant, bar* ☐*MC, V* ⏺❘*BP.*

$$$ ⊡**Clarion Stockholm.** A big business hotel with boutique aspirations, the Clarion suffers a little from this difficult mix but is nonetheless a good choice for those seeking big chain benefits (it's part of the huge Choice Hotels chain) with a little style thrown in. Rooms are extremely comfortable and outfitted in neutral, natural materials, dark woods, and white walls. Most have armchairs or a sofa. The public areas feature art exhibitions and live music events, and the bar is something of a local hot spot. **Pros:** public areas great for meeting locals; stylish rooms. **Cons:** location isn't central; a little impersonal. ⊠*Ringv.* 98 ☎*08/4621000* ⊕*www.clarionstockholm.com* ⤶*532 rooms* ⚹*In-room: safe, refrigerator, Internet. In-hotel: restaurant, room service, bar laundry service, Internet terminal, no-smoking rooms* ⊟*AE, DC, MC, V* ⍾*BP.*

$$ ⊡**Columbus Hotel.** Just a few blocks from busy Götgatan, the Colum-
Fodor's Choice bus is an oasis of calm in the busy urban streets of Södermalm. Built
★ in 1780, it was originally a brewery, then a jail, then a hospital, then a temporary housing area. Since 1976 the beautiful building, with its large, tranquil inner courtyard, has been a hotel. Rooms have wide beams, polished hardwood floors, antique furniture, and bright wallpaper and fabrics. Many look out over the courtyard, others on the nearby church. In summer breakfast is served outside. The peace and quiet this hotel provides, even though it's close to all the action, makes it ideal for a vacation. **Pros:** lovely setting, good-size rooms. **Cons:** basic facilities; a little outside the city center. ⊠*Tjärhovsg. 11, Södermalm* ☎*08/50311200* ⊕*www.columbus.se* ⤶*40 rooms* ⚹*In-hotel: restaurant, bar, parking (paid)* ⊟*AE, MC, V* ⍾*BP.*

¢–$ ⊡**Den Röda Båten Mälaren** *(The Red Boat).* Built in 1914, the *Mälaren* originally traveled the waters of the Göta Canal under the name of *Sätra.* Today she has to settle for sitting still in Stockholm as a youth hostel. The hostel cabins are small but clean and have bunk beds. Many have fantastic views of the town hall across the water. There are also four "hotel" rooms, which have private baths and nicer furniture and details. In summer the restaurant offers great views of Stockholm along with basic, traditional Swedish food. Breakfast costs an additional Skr 55, but sheets are included in your rate. **Pros:** great views; tranquil water sounds. **Cons:** tiny rooms; cramped public areas. ⊠*Södermälarstrand kajplats 6, Södermalm* ☎*08/6444385* ⊕*www.theredboat.com* ⤶*35 rooms, 4 with bath* ⊟*MC, V.*

¢–$ ⊡**Gustaf af Klint.** A "hotel ship" moored at Stadsgården quay, near the Slussen subway station, the **Gustaf af Klint** harbors 120 beds in its two sections: a hotel and a hostel. The hostel section has 18 four-bunk cabins and 10 two-bunk cabins; a 14-bunk dormitory is also available from May through mid-September. The hotel section has four single-bunk and three two-bunk cabins with bedsheets and breakfast included. The hostel rates are SKr 195 per person in a four-bunk room and SKr 220 per person in a two-bunk room; these prices do not include bedsheets or breakfast, which are available at an extra charge. All guests share common bathrooms and showers. There are a cafeteria and a restaurant, and you can dine on deck in summer with stunning views across to Gamla Stan. **Pros:** great views; waterside living. **Cons:** can get noisy at night; small rooms. ⊠*Stadsgårdskajen 153, Södermalm* ☎*08/6404077*

⊕*www.gustafafklint.se* ⇘*7 hotel cabins, 28 hostel cabins, 28 dormitory beds, all without bath* ௬*In-hotel: restaurant* ▤*AE, MC, V.*

$$$ 🖫**Hilton Hotel Slussen.** Working with what appears to be a dubious location (atop a tunnel above a six lane highway), the Hilton has pulled a rabbit out of a hat. Built on special noise- and shock-absorbing cushions, the hotel almost lets you forget about the highway. The intriguing labyrinth of levels, separate buildings, and corridors is filled with such unique details as a rounded stairway lighted from between the steps. The guest rooms are exquisitely designed and modern, with plenty of stainless steel and polished-wood inlay to accent the maroon color scheme. The hotel is at Slussen, easily accessible from downtown. Pros: killer views; great bar; big-chain benefits. Cons: feels slightly corporate; can be noisy in the public areas. ⊠*Guldgränd 8, Södermalm* 🕾*08/51735300* ⊕*www.hilton.com* ⇘*264 rooms, 28 suites* ௬*In-room: safe, refrigerator, Wi-Fi. In-hotel: 2 restaurants, room service, bar, pool, gym, laundry service, Wi-Fi, no-smoking rooms* ▤*AE, DC, MC, V* ⵏⵔ*BP.*

$$$ 🖫**Rival.** One of Stockholm's funkiest hotels burst onto the scene in
Fodor'sChoice 2003, causing as much of a stir among locals as its owner, pop group
★ ABBA's Benny Andersson, did when he broke into fame in the early 1970s. Rival is cool, but never to the point of being cold. Rooms here are full of delightful ideas—such as the glass bathroom walls that let you watch the bedroom television from the tub—and have a stylish comfort about them. Overstuffed duvets compete with plump armchairs for your attention, while modern art and photographs on the wall and stylish lamps and fixtures delight the eye. If you can tear yourself away from your room, downstairs you'll find a very cool bar, a restaurant, a bakery, and a cinema. Pros: thoughtfully designed rooms; great public areas. Cons: a little far from the center of town. ⊠*Mariatorget 3, Södermalm* 🕾*08/54578900* ⊕*www.rival.se* ⇘*99 rooms, 2 suites* ௬*In-room: safe, refrigerator, DVD, Wi-Fi. In-hotel: restaurant, room service, bar, laundry service, Wi-Fi, no-smoking rooms* ▤*AE, DC, MC, V* ⵏⵔ*BP.*

AFTER DARK

Stockholm's nightlife can be broken up into two general groups based on geography. First, there's Birger Jarlsgatan, Stureplan, and the city end of Kungsträdgården, which are more upscale and trendy, and thus more expensive. At the bars and clubs in this area it's not unusual to wait in line with people who look like they just stepped off the pages of a glossy magazine. To the south, in Södermalm, things are a bit looser and wilder, but that doesn't mean the bars are any less hip. At night Söder can get pretty crazy—it's louder and more bohemian, and partygoers often walk the streets.

Many establishments will post and enforce a minimum age requirement, which could be anywhere from 18 to 30, depending on the clientele they wish to serve, and they may frown on jeans and sneakers. Your safest bet is to wear black clothes, Stockholm's shade of choice. Most places are open until around 3 AM. Wherever you end up, a night of barhopping in Stockholm has fresher air now, served with a tinge of desperation: in the summer of 2005 smoking was banned in all bars, clubs, and restaurants in the country.

Stockholm's theater and opera season runs from September through May. Both Dramaten (the National Theater) and Operan (the Royal Opera) shut down in the summer months. When it comes to popular music, big-name acts such as Neil Young, U2, Eminem, and even the Backstreet Boys frequently come to Stockholm in summer while on their European tours. Artists of this type always play at Globen sports arena.

For a list of events pick up the free booklet *What's On* (⊕ *www.stock holmtown.com*), available from hotels, tourist centers, and some restaurants. It lists the month's events in both English and Swedish. For tickets to theaters and shows try **Biljettdirekt** (☏ *0771/707070*). The Thursday editions of the daily newspapers *Dagens Nyheter* (⊕ *www. dn.se*) and *Svenska Dagbladet* (⊕ *www.svd.se*) carry current listings of events, films, restaurants, and museums in Swedish. There's also a monthly guide called *Nöjesguiden* (the Entertainment Guide ⊕ *www. nojesguiden.se*), which has listings and reviews in Swedish.

BARS AND NIGHTCLUBS

Go to Stureplan (at one end of Birger Jarlsgatan) on any given weekend night, and you'll see crowds of people gathering around Svampen (the Mushroom), *the* meeting place for people getting ready to go out in this area.

★ **Berns Salonger** (✉ *Berns Hotel, Berzelii Park, City* ☏ *08/56632000*) has three bars—one in 19th-century style and two modern rooms—plus a huge veranda that's spectacular in summer. Music here gets so thumping you can hear it down the street. Don't let the name of **Hotellet** (✉ *Linneg. 18, Östermalm* ☏ *08/4428900*) fool you. Although originally designed as a hotel, it is now a very chic bar that has managed to retain that open lobby feel for its hot crowd. **Le Rouge** (✉ *Brunnsgränd 2, Gamla Stan* ☏ *08/50524430*) takes its cue from Le Moulin Rouge. Sit back in sumptuous surroundings of red velvet and heavy drapes and indulge in one of the most interesting cocktail menus in town. **Mosebacke Etablissement** (✉ *Mosebacke Torg 3, Södermalm* ☏ *08/6419020*) is a combined indoor theater, comedy club, and outdoor café with a spectacular view of the city. The crowd here leans toward over-thirty hipsters. The **O-bar** (✉ *Stureplan 2, Östermalm* ☏ *08/4405730*), located upstairs through the restaurant Sturehof, is where the downtown crowd gathers for late-night drinks and music ranging from bass-heavy hip-hop to hard rock. The **Sturehof** itself is a prime location for evening people-watching. The outdoor tables are smack-dab in the middle of Stureplan. Tucked away on a thriving bar and restaurant street **Paus** (✉ *Rörstrandsg. 18, Vasastan* ☏ *08/344405*), stands out for its great cocktails, relaxed atmosphere, and diminutive (read cozy, not claustrophobic) proportions. The clue to this place is in the name. **Riche** (✉ *Birger Jarlsgatan 2, Östermalm* ☏ *08/54503560*) is the hangout of choice for Stockholm's wealthy elite. Sit at the bar, sip champagne and wonder at the glamour of it all.

Spy Bar (✉ *Birger Jarlsg. 20, City* ☏ *08/6118408*) is one of Stockholm's most exclusive clubs. It's often filled with local celebrities and lots of glitz and glamour.

At Odenplan the basement bar of **Tranan** (✉ *Karlbergsv. 14, Vasastan* ☏ *08/52728100*) is a fun place to party in semidarkness to anything from ambient music to hard rock. Lots of candles, magazines, and art are inside. A trendy youngish crowd props up the long bar at **WC** (✉ *Skåneg. 51, Södermalm* ☏ *08/7022963*), with ladies' drink specials on Sunday. Luckily, the only things that'll remind you of the name (which stands for "water closet," or bathroom) are the holes in the middle of the bar stools.

Stockholm can also appease your need for pub-style intimacy. Guinness, ale, and cider enthusiasts rally in the tartan-clad **Bagpiper's Inn** (✉ *Rörstrandsg. 21, Vasastan* ☏ *08/311855*), where you can get a large selection of bar food.

★ **The Dubliner** (✉ *Smålandsg. 8, City* ☏ *08/6797707*), probably Stockholm's most popular Irish pub, serves up pub food, shows major sporting events on its big screen, and hosts live folk music on stage. It's not unusual to see people dancing on the tables. The very British **Tudor Arms** (✉ *Grevg. 31, Östermalm* ☏ *08/6602712*) is just as popular as when it opened in 1969. Brits who are missing home cooking will be relieved when they see the menu.

CLASSICAL MUSIC

International orchestras perform at **Konserthuset** (✉ *Hötorget 8, City* ☏ *08/102110*), the main concert hall. The **Music at the Palace series** (☏ *08/102247*) runs June through August. After Konserthuset, the best place for classical music is **Nybrokajen 11** (✉ *Nybrokajen 11, City* ☏ *08/4071700*), where top international musicians perform in relatively small halls. Off-season there are weekly concerts by Sweden's Radio Symphony Orchestra at **Berwaldhallen** (*Berwald Concert Hall* ✉ *Strandv. 69, Östermalm* ☏ *08/7845000*).

DANCE

When it comes to high-quality international dance in Stockholm, there's really only one place to go. **Dansenshus** (✉ *Barnhusg. 12–14, Vasastan* ☏ *08/50899090*) hosts the best Swedish and international acts, with shows ranging from traditional Japanese dance to street dance and modern ballet. You can also see ballet at the Royal Opera house.

DANCE CLUBS

Café Opera (✉ *Operahuset, City* ☏ *08/6765807*), at the waterfront end of Kungsträdgården, is a popular meeting place for young and old alike. It has the longest bar in town, fantastic 19th-century ceilings and details, plus dining and roulette, and major dancing after midnight. The kitchen offers a night menu until 2:30 AM. **Debaser** (✉ *Karl Johans torg 1, Södermalm* ☏ *08/4629860*) is the perfect place for those who like their dancing a bit wilder. The epicenter of Stockholm's rock music scene, this is where denim-clad legions come to shake their stuff. Down on Stureplan is **Sturecompagniet** (✉ *Stureg. 4, Östermalm*

☎08/6117800), a galleried, multifloor club where the crowd is young, the dance music is loud, and the lines are long.

FILM
Stockholm has an abundance of cinemas, all listed in the *Yellow Pages* under "Biografer." Current billings are listed in evening papers, normally with Swedish titles; call ahead if you're unsure. Foreign movies are subtitled, not dubbed. Most, if not all, movie theaters take reservations over the phone: popular showings can sell out ahead of time. Cinemas are either part of the **SF** chain or of **Sandrew Metronome.** Listings for each can be found on the wall at the theater or in the back of the culture pages of the daily newspapers. If you are interested in smaller theaters with character, try the **Grand** (✉*Sveav. 45, Norrmalm* ☎08/4112400), a nice little theater with two small screens and not a bad seat in the house. **Zita** (✉*Birger Jarlsg. 37, Norrmalm* ☎08/232020) is a one-screen theater that shows foreign films. A small restaurant is in the back.

GAY BARS
Hidden down behind the statue of St. George and the dragon on Gamla Stan, **Mandus Bar och Kök** (✉*Österlångg. 7, Gamla Stan* ☎08/206055) is a warm and friendly restaurant and bar perfect for drinking and talking late into the night. **Patricia** (✉*Stadsgården, Berth 25, Södermalm* ☎08/7430570) is a floating restaurant, disco, and bar right next to Slussen. And don't worry—the boat doesn't rock enough to make you sick. All are welcome at **TipTop** (✉*Sveav. 57, Norrmalm* ☎08/329800), but most of the clientele is gay. Men and women dance nightly to '70s disco and modern techno.

JAZZ CLUBS
The best and most popular jazz venue is **Fasching** (✉*Kungsg. 63, City* ☎08/53482964), where international and local bands play year-round. The classic club **Nalens** (✉*Regeringsg. 74, City* ☎08/50522200), which was popular back in the '50s and '60s, is back on the scene with major performances throughout the year; it has three stages.

OPERA
It is said that Queen Lovisa Ulrika began introducing opera to her subjects in 1755. Since then Sweden has become an opera center of standing, a launchpad for such names as Jenny Lind, Jussi Björling,
★ and Birgit Nilsson. **Operan** (*Royal Opera House* ✉*Jakobs torg 2, City* ☎08/7914300), dating from 1898, is now the de facto home of Sweden's operatic tradition. **Folkoperan** (✉*Hornsg. 72, Södermalm* ☎08/6160750) is a modern company with its headquarters in Södermalm. Casting traditional presentation and interpretation of the classics to the wind, the company stages productions that are refreshingly new.

ROCK CLUBS
Pub Anchor (✉*Sveav. 90, Norrmalm* ☎08/152000), on Sveavägen's main drag, is the city's downtown hard-rock bar. **Krogen Tre Backar** (✉*Tegnérg. 1214, Norrmalm* ☎08/6734400) is as popular among hard-rock fans as Pub Anchor is. It's just off Sveavägen. International rock acts often play at **Klubben** (✉*Hammarby Frabriksv. 13, Södermalm*

☎08/4622200), a small bar and club in the Fryshuset community center south of town.

THEATER

The exquisite **Drottningholms Slottsteater** (*Drottningholm Court Theater* ⊠*Drottningholm, Drottningholm* ☎08/6608225) presents opera, ballet, and orchestral music from May to early September; the original 18th-century stage machinery is still used in these productions. Drottningholm, the royal residence, is reached by subway and bus or by a special theater-bus (which leaves from the Grand Hotel or opposite the central train station). Boat tours run here in summer.

SPORTS AND THE OUTDOORS

Like all Swedes, Stockholmers love the outdoors and spend a great deal of time enjoying outdoor sports and activities. Because the city is spread out on a number of islands, you are almost always close to the water. The many large parks, including Djurgården and Haga Park, allow people to quickly escape the hustle and bustle of downtown.

The most popular summertime activities in Stockholm are golf, biking, rollerblading, tennis, and sailing. In winter people like to ski and ice-skate.

BEACHES

The best bathing places in central Stockholm are on the island of Långholmen and at Rålambshov, at the end of Norr Mälarstrand. Both are grassy or rocky lakeside hideaways. Topless sunbathing is virtually de rigueur.

BIKING AND ROLLERBLADING

Stockholm is laced with bike paths, and bicycles can be taken on the commuter trains (except during peak traveling times) for excursions to the suburbs. The bike paths are also ideal for rollerblading. You can rent a bike for between SKr 160 and SKr 260 per day. Rollerblades cost between Skr 90 and SKr 120. Most places require a deposit of a couple thousand kronor. **Cykelfrämjandet** (⊠*Thuleg. 43* ☎08/54591030 ⊕*www.cykelframjandet.a.se*), a local bicyclists' association, publishes an English-language guide to cycling trips. City and mountain bikes can be rented from **Cykel and Mopeduthyrning** (⊠*Strandv. at Kajplats 24, City* ☎08/6607959) for SKr 210.

BOATING

Boating in Stockholm's archipelago is an exquisite summertime activity. From May to September sailboats large and small and gorgeous restored wooden boats cruise from island to island. Both types of boats are available for rental. Walk along the water on Strandvägen, where many large power yachts and sailboats (available for charter) are docked. Sea kayaking has also become increasingly popular and is a delightful way to explore the islands.

Contact **Svenska Seglarförbundet** (*Swedish Sailing Association* ⊠*Af Pontins väg 6, Djurgården* ☎08/4590990 ⊕*www.ssf.se*) for information on sailing. **Svenska Kanotförbundet** (*Swedish Canoeing Association* ⊠*Rosvalla, Nyköping* ☎*0155/209080* ⊕*www.kanot.com*) has information on canoeing and kayaking. At the end of Strandvägen, before the bridge to Djurgården, is **Tvillingarnas Båtuthyrning** (⊠*Strandvägskajen 27, City* ☎*08/58815580*), which has large and small motorboats and small sailboats.

GOLF

There are numerous golf courses around Stockholm. Greens fees run from about SKr 450 to SKr 650, depending on the club. Contact **Sveriges Golfförbund** (⊠*Kevingestrand 20, Box 84, Danderyd* ☎*08/6221500* ⊕*www.golf.se*), which is just outside Stockholm, for information.

TENNIS

With stars such as Björn Borg, Stefan Edberg, and Joachim "Pim Pim" Johansson, it's impossible for tennis not to be huge in Stockholm. Contact **Svenska Tennisförbundet** (⊠*Lidingöv. 75, Box 27915, Stockholm* ☎*08/4504310* ⊕*www.tennis.se*) for information.

SHOPPING

If you like to shop till you drop, then charge on down to any one of the three main department stores in the central city area, all of which carry top-name brands from Sweden and abroad for both men and women. For souvenirs and crafts peruse the boutiques and galleries in Västerlånggatan, the main street of Gamla Stan. For jewelry, crafts, and fine art, hit the shops that line the raised sidewalk at the start of Hornsgatan on Södermalm. Drottninggatan, Birger Jarlsgatan, Biblioteksgatan, Götgatan, and Hamngatan also offer some of the city's best shopping.

DEPARTMENT STORES AND MALLS

FodorśChoice ★ Sweden's leading department store is the unmissable **NK** (⊠*Hamng. 18–20, across street from Kungsträdgården, City* ☎*08/7628000*); the initials, pronounced enn-*koh,* stand for Nordiska Kompaniet. You pay for the high quality here. **Åhléns City** (⊠*Klarabergsg. 50, City* ☎*08/6766000*) has a selection similar to NK, with slightly better prices. Before becoming a famous actress, Greta Garbo used to work at **PUB** (⊠*Drottningg. 63 and Hötorget, City* ☎*08/4021611*), which has 42 independent boutiques. Garbo fans will appreciate the small exhibit on level H2—a collection of photographs begins with her employee ID card.

★ **Bruno Galleria** (⊠*Götg. 36, Södermalm* ☎*08/6412751*) is a delightful glassed-in courtyard filled with cool clothing shops and interior-design stores; it's small, but perfectly appointed. **Gallerian** (⊠*Hamng. 37, City* ☎*08/7912445*), in the city center just down the road from Sergels Torg, is a large indoor mall closely resembling those found in the United States. It underwent a serious revamp in 2004, and is now the last word in designer-mall chic, with everything from toys to fashion, all in beautiful surroundings. **Sturegallerian** (⊠*Grev Tureg. 9, Östermalm* ☎*08/6114606*) is a midsize mall on super posh Stureplan that mostly carries exclusive clothes, bags, and accessories; it's mostly populated by rich, beautiful young shoppers.

MARKETS

Fodor'sChoice ★ For a good indoor market hit **Hötorgshallen** (✉ *Hötorget, City*), directly under Filmstaden. The market is filled with butcher shops, coffee and tea shops, and fresh-fish markets. It's also open daily and closes at 6 PM. **Street** (✉ *Hornstulls Strand 1, Södermalm*) is a waterside street market with stalls selling fashionable clothing, design, books, and other artsy and creative wares. If you're interested in high-quality Swedish food, try the classic European indoor market **Östermalms Saluhall** (✉ *Östermalmstorg, Östermalm*), where you can buy superb fish, game, bread, vegetables, and other foodstuffs—or just have a glass of wine at one of the bars and watch the world go by.

SPECIALTY STORES

AUCTION HOUSES

Perhaps the finest auction house in town is **Lilla Bukowski** (✉ *Strandv. 7, Östermalm* ☎ *08/6140800*), whose elegant quarters are on the waterfront. **Auktions Kompaniet** (✉ *Regeringsg. 47, City* ☎ *08/235700*) is downtown next to NK. **Stockholms Auktionsverk** (✉ *Jakobsg. 10, City* ☎ *08/4536700*) is under the Gallerian shopping center.

GLASS

Kosta Boda and Orrefors produce the most popular and well-regarded lines of glassware. The **Crystal Art Center** (✉ *Tegelbacken 4, City* ☎ *08/217169*), near the central station, has a great selection of smaller glass items. **Duka** (✉ *Sveav. 24–26, City* ☎ *08/104530*) specializes in crystal and porcelain at reasonable prices. **NK** carries a wide representative line of Swedish glasswork in its Swedish Shop, downstairs.

INTERIOR DESIGN

Sweden is recognized globally for its unique design sense and has contributed significantly to what is commonly referred to as Scandinavian design. All of this makes Stockholm one of the best cities in the world for shopping for furniture and home and office accessories.

On the corner of Östermalmstorg, in the same building as the marketplace, is **Bruka** (✉ *Humlegårdsg. 1, Östermalm* ☎ *08/6601480*), which has a wide selection of creative kitchen items as well as wicker baskets and chairs. Inside stylish mall Bruno Galleria, **David Design** (✉ *Gotg. 36, Södermalm* ☎ *08/6947575*) sells fine furniture, rugs, mirrors, and decorative items for the house. **DIS** (✉ *Humlegårdsg. 19, Östermalm* ☎ *08/6112907*) sells heavy dark-wood furniture that has an Asian flair. The rugs and pillowcases are also stunning.

★ For something little more classic, you can't do better than **Modernity** (✉ *Sibylleg. 6, Östermalm* ☎ *08/208025*). This is *the* place for ultimate 20th-century Scandinavian design, with names like Arne Jacobsen, Alvar Aalto, and Poul Henningsen represented in full force. Slightly out of the way, in the Fridhemsplan neighborhood in western Stockholm, **R.O.O.M.** (✉ *Alströmerg. 20, Kungsholmen* ☎ *08/6925000*) has an impressive assortment of Swedish and international tables, chairs, rugs, pillows, beds—the list goes on. It also has a great book selection, lots of nice ceramic bowls and plates, and many decorations and utensils for the kitchen and bathroom. Not just a clever play on words, **Stockhome** (⊠*Kungsg. 25, City* ☎*08/4111300*) has a great selection of things with which, well, to stock your home, including china, towels, glass, books, linen, even bicycles and patterned bandages. For elegant home furnishings, affluent Stockholmers tend to favor **Svenskt Tenn** (⊠*Strandv. 5A, Östermalm* ☎*08/6701600*), best known for its selection of designer Josef Franck's furniture and fabrics.

MEN'S CLOTHING

Men in search of a little "street cred" can head for **Beneath** (⊠*Kronobergsg. 37, Kungsholmen* ☎*08/6431250*), purveyor of ultrahip urban street wear and limited-edition labels. For suits and evening suits for both sale and rental, **Hans Allde** (⊠*Birger Jarlsg. 58, City* ☎*08/207191*) provides good old-fashioned service. **J. Lindeberg** (⊠*Grev Tureg. 9, Östermalm* ☎*08/6786165*) has brightly colored and highly fashionable clothes in many styles. The golf line has been made famous by Swedish golfer Jesper Parnevik. Top men's fashions can be found on the second floor of **NK** (⊠*Hamng. 18–20, City* ☎*08/7628000*), which stocks everything from outdoor gear and evening wear to swimsuits and workout clothes. The Swedish label **Tiger** (☎*08/7628772*), with a section inside NK, sells fine suits, shoes, and casual wear.

PAPER PRODUCTS

Fodor's Choice For unique Swedish stationery and office supplies in fun colors and styles,
★ go to **Ordning & Reda** (⊠*NK, Hamng. 18–20, City* ☎*08/7282060*).

WOMEN'S CLOTHING

★ Swedish designer **Anna Holtblad** (⊠*Grev Tureg. 13, Östermalm* ☎*08/54502220*) sells her elegant designs at her own boutique. She specializes in knitted clothes. **Filippa K** (⊠*Grev Tureg. 18, Östermalm* ☎*08/54588888*) has quickly become one of Sweden's hottest designers. Her stores are filled with young women grabbing the latest fashions. **Hennes & Mauritz** (*H&M* ⊠*Hamng. 22, City* ⊠*Drottningg. 53 and 56, City* ⊠*Sergelg. 1 and 22, City* ⊠*Sergels torg 12, City* ☎*08/7965500*) is one of the few Swedish-owned clothing stores to have achieved international success. Here you can find updated designs at rock-bottom prices. The clothes at **Indiska** (⊠*Drottningg. 53 and elsewhere, City* ☎*08/109193*) are inspired by the bright colors of India.

Kookai (⊠*Biblioteksg. 5, City* ☎*08/6119730*) carries trendy, colorful European designs for young women. **Neu** (⊠*Nytorgsg. 36, Södermalm* ☎*08/6422004*) is great for creations by up-and-coming designers that few have heard of, but, hopefully, many will know soon. One department store with almost every style and type of clothing and apparel is **NK** (⊠*Hamng. 18–20, City* ☎*08/7628000*). **Polarn & Pyret** (⊠*Hamng. 10, Gallerian, Drottningg. 29, City* ☎*08/6709500*) carries high-quality Swedish children's and women's clothing. For the modern rebel look, go to **Replay** (⊠*Kungsg. 6, City* ☎*08/231416*), where the collection covers everything from jeans to underwear. For lingerie and fashionable clothing at a decent price, go to **Twilfit** (⊠*Nybrog. 11, Östermalm*

☎*08/6637505* ✉*Sturegallerian 16, Östermalm* ☎*08/6110455*
✉*Gamla Brog. 3638, Norrmalm* ☎*08/201954*).

SIDE TRIPS FROM STOCKHOLM

Stockholm is a green, lively, and pleasant city—that cannot be denied. But travel a little farther from town and you will see why even Stockholmers make a regular and even hurried exit from their city on summer weekends. Immediately outside of Stockholm is the archipelago, meaning paradise on earth to a Swede with a boat and some time to kill. You can get lost among the many thousands of islands and skerries. As you'll see, pleasures here are simple: sunbathing on a rock, dipping in the chilly Baltic, enjoying a simple meal in a local bistro, and lazily watching the sun sink below the horizon.

Farther afield (south of Stockholm, in the Baltic) is the island of Gotland, a settlement whose medieval walls whisper of pirates and hidden treasure. For most people, though, it is the warm climate, stunning nature reserves, and legendary nightlife that bring them here year after year.

Uppsala, north of Stockholm, is one of Europe's oldest and most respected seats of learning. The town is full of medieval and Gothic buildings that are a testament to its long history and former position of power as capital of the country. But there's always the chance to let loose; this is a student town, after all.

DROTTNINGHOLM

★ *1 km (½ mi) west of Stockholm.*

Dating from the 17th century, Drottningholm castle is the permanent residence of Sweden's royal family. It's a huge palace, but with a modesty befitting a Scandinavian royal family they confine themselves to only a small corner of it, leaving the rest open to the public. The interior is a riot of European design history; the beautifully manicured gardens are even more impressive.

GETTING HERE AND AROUND
Boats bound for Drottningholms Slott leave from Klara Mälarstrand, a quay close to Stadshuset (City Hall). Call **Strömma Kanalbolaget** for schedules and fares. Alternatively, you can take the T-bana (subway) to Brommaplan, and any of Buses 177, 301–323, or 336 from there. Call **Stockholms Lokal Trafik** for details.

ESSENTIALS
Boat Contact Call **Strömma Kanalbolaget** (☎*08/12004000* ⊕ *www.strom makanalbolaget.com*).

Subway and Bus Contact Stockholms Lokal Trafik (☎*08/6001000* ⊕ *www. sl.se*).

EXPLORING DROTTNINGHOLM

Occupying an island in Mälaren (Sweden's third-largest lake) some 45 minutes from Stockholm's center, **Drottningholms Slott** *(Queen's Island Castle)* is a miniature Versailles dating from the 17th century. The royal family once used this property only as a summer residence, but, tiring of the Royal Palace back in town, they moved permanently to one wing of Drottningholm in the 1980s. Today it remains one of the most delightful of European palaces, reflecting the sense of style practiced by mid-18th-century royalty. The interiors, dating from the 17th, 18th, and 19th centuries, are a rococo riot of decoration with much gilding and trompe l'oeil. Most sections are open to the public. ☏08/4026280 ⊕*www.royalcourt.se* ⌨*SKr 70* ☉*May–Aug., daily 10–4:30; Sept., daily noon–3:30; Oct.–Apr., weekends noon–3:30; guided tours in summer only.*

The lakeside gardens of Drottningholms Slott are its most beautiful asset, containing **Drottningholms Slottsteater,** the only complete theater to survive from the 18th century anywhere in the world. Built by Queen Lovisa Ulrika in 1766 as a wedding present for her son Gustav III, the Court Theater fell into disuse after his assassination at a masked ball in 1792 (dramatized in Verdi's opera *Un Ballo in Maschera*). You can sign up for a backstage tour and see the original backdrops and stage machinery and some amazing 18th-century tools used to produce such special effects as wind and thunder. To get performance tickets, book well in advance at the box office; the season runs from late May to early September. A word of caution: the seats are extremely hard, so take a cushion. ☏08/7590406 ⊕*www.dtm.se* ⌨*SKr 60* ☉*May, daily noon–4:30; June–Aug., daily 11–4:30; Sept., daily 1–3:30. Guided tours in English at 12:30, 1:30, 2:30, 3:30, and 4:30.*

SIGTUNA

48 km (30 mi) northwest of Stockholm.

An idyllic town on a northern arm of Lake Mälaren, Sigtuna was the principal trading post of the Svea, the tribe that settled Sweden after the last Ice Age; its Viking history is still apparent in the many runic stones preserved all over town. Founded in 980, Sigtuna is Sweden's oldest town, and as such it's not surprising that it has Sweden's oldest street, Stora Gatan. After it was ransacked by Estonian pirates, its merchants went on to found Stockholm sometime in the 13th century. Little remains of Sigtuna's former glory, beyond parts of the principal church. The town hall dates from the 18th century, and the main part of the town dates from the early 1800s. There are two houses said to date from the 15th century.

GETTING HERE AND AROUND

Sigtuna can be reached by driving on E4 North to 263 or by taking a commuter train from Stockholm's central station to Märsta, where you change to Bus 570 or 575. It's a small enough town to stop into the Tourist office to ask the way to the ATM, post office, or nearest pharmacy should the need arise.

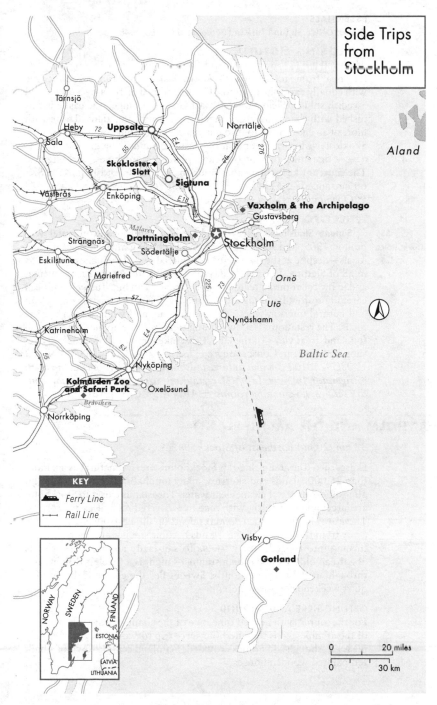

Side Trips from Stockholm

Tärnsjö

Heby 72 **Uppsala** Norrtälje

Sala 55 E4 276 *Aland*

Skokloster◆ Slott ○ **Sigtuna**

Västerås Enköping E18

Vaxholm & the Archipelago
Gustavsberg

Mälaren

Strängnäs **Drottningholm◆** ★ Stockholm
Södertälje ○

Eskilstuna

Mariefred E3 225 73 *Ornö*

57 *Utö*

Nynäshamn

Katrineholm E4 53

55 *Baltic Sea*

Nyköping

Kolmården Zoo and Safari Park◆ Oxelösund

Bråviken

Norrköping

KEY
🚢 *Ferry Line*
+—+ *Rail Line*

NORWAY SWEDEN FINLAND
ESTONIA
LATVIA
LITHUANIA

Visby ○

Gotland ◆

0   20 miles
0   30 km

ESSENTIALS
Tourist Office **Sigtuna Turism** (✉ *Storag. 33* ☎ *08/59480650).*

EXPLORING SIGTUNA

About 20 km (12 mi) northwest of Sigtuna and accessible by the same ferryboat from Stockholm is **Skokloster Slott,** an exquisite baroque castle with equally exquisite grounds. Commissioned in 1654 by a celebrated Swedish soldier, Field Marshal Carl Gustav Wrangel, the castle is furnished with the spoils of Wrangel's successful campaigns. Those with more of an enthusiasm for old machines than for old houses can visit the Skokloster Motormuseum on the castle grounds. The museum boasts a very fine collection of old cars, planes, motorbikes, and engines. The museum keeps the same hours as the castle and requires a SKr 60 entrance fee. ✉ *Bålsta* ☎ *018/4023070* ⊕ *www.lsh.se* 🎟 *SKr 75* ⊙ *Opening times vary so check ahead. Closed Mon.*

WHERE TO STAY

$$$
Fodor'sChoice
★

🏨 **Sigtuna Stadshotell.** Near the lakeshore, this beautiful hotel was built in 1909, and soon after became a central gathering place among locals—despite at the time being considered one of the ugliest buildings in all of Sigtuna. In its early days the hotel had Sigtuna's first cinema, and in the cellar the state liquor store operated an inn. Today it has been carefully restored and tastefully furnished. The emphasis is on a clean and natural interior, where oak, sandstone, and white cotton are the focus. The restaurant is a fine-dining treat, serving up modern Swedish food and great views of the lake. **Pros:** lake views; professional service; superb restaurant. **Cons:** rooms can feel a little spartan. ✉ *Stora Nyg. 3* ☎ *08/59250100* ⊕ *www.sigtunastadshotell.se* 🛏 *26 rooms* ⚐ *In-room: refrigerator, Internet. In-hotel: restaurant, room service, bar, spa, laundry service, no-smoking rooms* ▤ *AE, DC, MC, V* ⌘*BP.*

VAXHOLM AND THE ARCHIPELAGO

32 km (20 mi) northeast of Stockholm.

Skärgården (the archipelago) is Stockholm's greatest natural asset: more than 25,000 islands and skerries, many uninhabited, spread across an almost tideless sea of clean, clear water. The islands closer to Stockholm are larger and more lush, with pine tree–covered rock faces and forests. There are also more year-round residents on these islands. As you move away from the mainland, the islands become smaller and more remote, turning into rugged, rocky islets. To sail lazily among these islands aboard an old steamboat on a summer's night is a timeless delight, and throughout the warmer months Swedes flee the chaos of the city for quiet weekends on the waters.

GETTING HERE AND AROUND

For the tourist with limited time, one of the simplest ways to get a taste of the archipelago is the one-hour ferry trip to Vaxholm, an extremely pleasant, though sometimes crowded, mainland seaside town of small, red-painted wooden houses.

BOAT AND FERRY TRAVEL Regular ferry services to the archipelago depart from Strömkajen, the quayside in front of Stockholm's Grand Hotel. Boat cruises leave from the harbor in front of the Royal Palace or from Nybrokajen, across the street from the Royal Dramatic Theater. Ferries to the Feather Islands run almost constantly all day long in summer (April 29–September 17), from Slussen, Strömkajen, and Nybroplan. Contact Strömma Kanalbolaget, Waxholmsbolaget, or Fjäderholmarna.

An excellent way to see the archipelago is to purchase an **Inter Skerries Card,** which costs SKr 380 and allows unlimited boat travel throughout the islands for five days. Use the card for day trips from Stockholm, or go out for longer excursions and bounce around from island to island. The card is available at the Stockholm Tourist Center.

A great way to discover the remote, less-visited parts of the archipelago is to go out with **Sandhamnsguiderna,** a tour group that operates out of Sandhamn. Experienced guides will take you on tailor-made excursions, in small or large groups, to explore the outer reaches of the deserted archipelago. A tour price depends on how many people go and for how long.

TRAIN TRAVEL There are regular train services to Saltsjöbaden from Stockholm's Slussen station, on Södermalm and operated by SL (Stockholm Local Traffic). The journey takes about 20 minutes. To get to Trosa, take a one-hour train ride from Stockholm to Vagnhärad, where there is a bus waiting to take the 10-minute trip to Trosa.

ESSENTIALS

Boat and Ferry Contacts Fjäderholmarna (☎ *08/7180100*). **Stockholm Tourist Center** (✉ *Sweden House, Hamng. 27, Box 7542, Stockholm* ☎ *08/50828508*). **Strömma Kanalbolaget** (☎ *08/12004000* ⊕ *www.strommakanalbolaget.com*). **Waxholmsbolaget** (☎ *08/6795830* ⊕ *www.waxholmsbolaget.se*).

Tour Sandhamnsguiderna (☎ *08/6408040* ⊕ *www.sandhamnsguiderna.com*).

Train Contact SJ (☎ *0771/757575* ⊕ *www.sj.se*). **SL** (☎ *08/6001000* ⊕ *www.sl.se*).

Visitor Info Sweden House (✉ *Hamng. 27, Box 7542, Stockholm* ☎ *08/50828508*). **Trosa Turistbyrå** (☎ *0156/52222* ⊕ *www.trosa.com*). **Utö Turistbyrå** (☎ *08/50157410*). **Vaxholms Turistbyrå** (✉ *Söderhamnen, Vaxholm* ☎ *08/54131480* ⊕ *www.roslagen.se*).

EXPLORING VAXHOLM AND THE ARCHIPELAGO

For tips on exploring the area, head to the Vaxholms Turistbyrå (Vaxholm Tourist Office), in a large kiosk at the bus terminal adjacent to the marina and ferry landing. Hours are daily 10–5. There's also the Utö Turistbyrå (Utö Tourist Bureau) near the ferry landing. More information on Grinda is available from the Stockholm Tourist Center at Sweden House. If you are interested in a longer voyage out into the islands, there are several possibilities. Contact the Sweden House and ask for the "Destination Stockholm Archipelago" catalog, which lists more than 350 holiday homes for rent.

For booking accommodations, contact **Hotellcentralen** (☎*08/7892425*) in Stockholm's central station.

TOP ATTRACTIONS

One of the most popular excursions is to **Sandhamn**, the main town on the island of Sandön, which is home to about 100 permanent residents. The journey takes about three hours by steamship, but there are faster boats available. The Royal Swedish Yacht Club was founded here at the turn of the 20th century, and sailing continues to be a popular sport. Its fine-sand beaches also make it an ideal spot for swimming. Another option is to try scuba diving—introductory lessons are available; ask at the Sweden House for details. Explore the village of Sandhamn and its narrow alleys and wooden houses, or stroll out to the graveyard outside the village, where tombstones bear the names of sailors from around the world.

A little closer to Stockholm is the island of **Grinda**, long a popular recreation spot among Stockholmers. Rental cabins from the '40s have been restored to their original condition; there are about 30 of these available through **Grinda Stugby** (☎*08/54249072*).

The **Grinda Wärdshus** (☎*08/54249491*), a still-functioning inn from the turn of the 20th century, is one of the largest stone buildings in the archipelago. Since a number of walking paths cut through the woods and open fields, it takes just 15 minutes to walk from one end of Grinda to the other, and exploring is easy. The trip to the island takes about two hours.

At the far southern tip of Stockholm's archipelago lies **Trosa**, a town full of wooden houses that's right on the Baltic Sea. The tiny river that runs through the middle of the town is flanked by beautiful villas painted white, red, yellow, and mint green—a reflection of Trosa's heritage as a seaside retreat for stressed, wealthy Stockholmers. Around the small, cobbled town square are arts-and-crafts shops and market stalls selling fish, fruit, and vegetables.

Thirty kilometers (20 mi) northwest of Trosa, on the little island of **Fodor's**Choice Oaxen (accessible by bridge), is something of a culinary happening.
★ **Oaxen Skärgårdskrog** can be described, almost without argument, as the very best restaurant in Sweden. Set in an old wooden waterside manor house, Oaxen's interior is sleek and modern, with stunning Danish furniture, dark brown walls, crisp white linens, and oiled oak floors. The pricey-but-worth-it food is a breathtaking collection of modern-European-inspired culinary works of art. *⌖ Drive E4 south from Stockholm for about 40 minutes; take Hölö/Mörkö exit and follow signs to restaurant* ☎*08/55153105* ⊕*www.oaxenkrog.se.*

WORTH NOTING

An even quicker trip into the archipelago is the 20-minute ferry ride to **Fjäderholmarna** *(the Feather Islands)*, a group of four secluded islands. In the 19th-century the islands were the last chance for a refreshment stop for archipelago residents rowing into Stockholm to sell their produce. After 50 years as a military zone, the islands were opened to the public in the early 1980s. Today they are crammed with arts-and-crafts studios, shops, an aquarium, a small petting farm, a boat museum, a large cafeteria, an ingenious "shipwreck" playground, and even a smoked-fish shop.

If you'd prefer to stay on board a boat and simply cruise around the islands, seek out the *Blidösund*. A coal-fired steamboat built in 1911 that has remained in almost continuous service, the *Blidösund* is now run by a small group of enthusiasts who take parties of around 250 on evening music-and-dinner cruises. The cruises depart from a berth close to the Royal Palace in Stockholm. ⊠*Skeppsbron 11, Stockholm* ☎*08/243090* ☉*Departures early May–late Sept., Mon.–Thurs. 6:30* PM *(returns at 10:15* PM*)*.

WHERE TO EAT

$ ✕**Café Lena Linderholm.** Lena is the wife of folk singer and cookbook
CAFÉ writer Gösta Linderholm. She runs a very pleasant interior-design shop on the first floor of this old town house and a café on the second floor. Those with a passion for great coffee, overstuffed sandwiches, and delicious Swedish vanilla buns should make a beeline for this charming spot. ⊠*Rådhusg. 19, Vaxholm* ☎*08/54132165* ☐*No credit cards.*

$$ ✕**Dykarbaren.** The idea for this old wooden harborside restaurant came
SCANDINAVIAN from similar cafés in Brittany, France. Simple local dishes, mostly of fish, are served up in an informal wooden-table dining area. Originally just catering to local divers, Dykarbaren now serves everyone. ⊠*Strand-promenaden, Sandhamn* ☎*08/57153554* ☐*AE, DC, MC, V.*

$$ ✕**Finnhamns Krog.** This restaurant has a beautiful waterside setting on
SWEDISH the distant island of Finnhamn. Only accessible by a two-hour boat journey, it's well worth the trip; both for the scenic journey and especially for the food. Take a seat on the large terrace and tuck into modern Swedish food like sweet fried cured salmon with dill and marjoram, or Swedish classics like Baltic herring with mustard sauce. ⊠*Finnhamn* ☎*08/54246212* ☐*MC, V* ☉*Open Mon.–Thurs. Apr, May, Sept., and Oct. Closed Nov.–Mar.*

$$$ ✕**Fjäderholmarnas Krog.** A crackling fire on the hearth in the bar area
SWEDISH welcomes the sailors who frequent this laid-back restaurant. In case
★ you don't travel with your own sailboat, you can time your dinner to end before the last ferry returns to the mainland. The food here is self-consciously Swedish: fresh, light, and beautifully presented. The service is professional; it's a great choice for a special night out. ⊠*Fjäderhol-marna* ☎*08/7183355* ☐*AE, DC, MC, V* ☉*Closed Oct.–Apr. Open in Dec. for Christmas dinners.*

WHERE TO STAY

Lodging options in the archipelago vary from island to island. The larger, more inhabited islands often have at least one decent hotel, if not a few, whereas some of the smaller, more deserted islands have only an inn or two or camping facilities.

$$ ▥**Domans.** Right on the water and brimming with history, this family
★ run hotel dates from the early 20th century. The bedrooms are stuffed with floral patterns, iron bedsteads, feather quilts, lace, and linen. It's

worth splashing out extra on a large room or suite here. Their quirky names (Happy Accident, Princess and the Pea, La Dolce Vita, Madame Bomans Boudoir) are as charming as their sumptuous interiors. Downstairs there is a small bar. Lace tablecloths, chandeliers, and tangerine linens and fabrics help create a warm mood in the very good restaurant, where you can also dine outside in summer. The menu is unashamedly Swedish, with high-quality versions of classics like meatballs, salmon, and elk with lingonberries. **Pros:** most rooms are wonderful for the price; intimate atmosphere; great service. **Cons:** some rooms are very small. ⊠ *Hamnen, Trosa* ☎ *0156/52500* ⊕ *www.bomans.se* ⌨ *44 rooms* ♿ *In-room: refrigerator, Internet. In-hotel: restaurant, bar, spa, no-smoking rooms* ⊟ *AE, DC, MC, V* ⦿| *BP.*

$$
Fodor's Choice
★
FRENCH

⌨ **Grand Hotel Saltsjöbaden.** Many say that this is the only reason to come to the beautiful but quiet town of Saltsjöbaden. Next to the sea and the surrounding countryside, the hotel is one of the most breathtaking in the whole archipelago. Built in 1893, it's a castlelike concoction of white stone, arched windows, and towers. The huge rooms are filled with colorful period furniture and bold fabrics in deep blues and reds. The restaurant is perfect for summer dining, out on the terrace. **Pros:** huge rooms; fantastic views. **Cons:** not much to do near the hotel; busy bar and restaurant. ⊠ *Saltsjöbaden* ☎ *08/50617000* ⊕ *www.grandsaltsjobaden.se* ⌨ *140 rooms* ♿ *In-room: refrigerator, Internet. In-hotel: restaurant, room service, bar, tennis courts, pool, spa, laundry facilities, parking (free), no-smoking rooms* ⊟ *AE, DC, MC, V* ⦿| *BP.*

$$

⌨ **Grinda Wärdshus.** Housed in one of the archipelago's largest stone buildings, this 19th-century villa has homey rooms and bright, comfortable public areas. Since the hotel is right on the water, you may wish to take a refreshing dip in the sea before tackling the sumptuous breakfast buffet of Scandinavian classics. **Pros:** wonderful waterside location; great service; excellent food. **Cons:** basic facilities. ⊠ *Södra Bryggan, Grinda* ☎ *08/54249491* ⊕ *www.grindawardshus.se* ⌨ *28 rooms, 2 suites* ♿ *In-hotel: restaurant* ⊟ *AE, DC, MC, V* ⦿| *BP.*

$$

⌨ **Utö Värdshus.** The rooms are large and well laid out here, with traditional furniture resembling that found in a Swedish farmhouse—lots of old pine and comfy, plump cushioning. Choose between a room in the sprawling white main hotel or one of the 30 that are in a cabin on the grounds. The restaurant has a grand wooden ceiling lighted with chandeliers. The food is eclectic, ranging from salmon with dill to Cajun chicken. **Pros:** beautiful surroundings; lovely restaurant. **Cons:** limited facilities. ⊠ *Gruvbryggan, Utö* ☎ *08/50420300* ⊕ *www.uto-vardshus. se* ⌨ *34 rooms* ♿ *In-hotel: restaurant, bar, no-smoking rooms* ⊟ *AE, DC, MC, V* ⦿| *BP.*

GOTLAND

85 km (53 mi) south of Stockholm.

Gotland is Sweden's main holiday island, a place of ancient history, a relaxed summer-party vibe, wide sandy beaches, and wild cliff formations called *raukar*. Measuring 125 km (78 mi) long and 52 km (32 mi) at its widest point, Gotland is where Swedish sheep farming has its home. In its charming glades, 35 varieties of wild orchids thrive, attracting botanists from all over the world.

GETTING HERE AND AROUND

Regular and high-speed car ferries sail from Nynäshamn, a small port on the Baltic an hour by car or rail from Stockholm; commuter trains leave regularly from Stockholm's central station for Nynäshamn. Timetables change frequently, so it is best to consult the operating company, Gotland City Travel, before departure. The regular ferry takes about 5 hours; the fast ferry takes 2½ hours. Boats also leave from Oskarshamn, farther down the Swedish coast and closer to Gotland by about an hour. Call Gotland City Travel for more information.

Skyways flies from Stockholm's Bromma and Arlanda airports to Visby on Gotland. Flights are daily during summer.

The main tourist office is Gotlands Turistförening (Gotland Tourist Association) in Visby. You can also contact Gotland City Travel in Stockholm for lodging or ferry reservations.

5

ESSENTIALS

Boat and Ferry Info Gotland City Travel (✉ *Kungsg. 57* ☎ *08/4061500* ⊕ *www. destinationgotland.se*).

Flight Info Skyways (☎ *0771/959500* ⊕ *www.skyways.se*).

Car Rental Biltjänst (✉ *Endrev. 45, Visby* ☎ *0498/218790*). **MABI Rental Cars** (✉ *Visby* ☎ *0498/279396*).

Emergencies Visby Hospital (☎ *0498/269000*).

Visitor Info Gotland City Travel (☎ *08/4061500*). **Gotlands Turistförening & Visby Turistbyrå** (✉ *Hamng. 4, Visby* ☎ *0498/201700* ⊕ *www.gotland.info*).

EXPLORING GOTLAND

Gotland's capital, **Visby,** is a delightful hilly town of about 20,000 people. Medieval houses, ruined fortifications, churches, and cottage-lined cobbled lanes make Visby look like a fairy-tale place. Thanks to a very gentle climate, the roses that grow along many of the town's facades bloom even in November.

In its heyday Visby was protected by a wall, of which 3 km (2 mi) survive today, along with 44 towers and numerous gateways. It is considered the best-preserved medieval city wall in Europe after that of Carcassonne, in southern France. Take a stroll to the north gate for an unsurpassed view of the wall.

Visby's cathedral, **St. Maria Kyrka,** is the only one of the town's 13 medieval churches that is still intact and in use. Built between 1190 and 1225 as a place of worship for the town's German parishioners, the church has few of its original fittings because of the extensive and sometimes clumsy restoration work done over the years. That said, the sandstone font and the unusually ugly angels decorating the pulpit are both original features worth a look.

The **Länsmuseet på Gotland,** Gotland's county museum, contains examples of medieval artwork, prehistoric gravestones and skeletons, and silver hoards from Viking times. Be sure to also check out the ornate "picture stones" from AD 400–600, which depict ships, people, houses, and animals. ✉*Strandg. 14* ☎*0498/292700* 🌐*www.lansmuseetgotland.se* 🎫*SKr 75* ⏲*Mid-May–Sept., daily 11–5; Oct.–mid-May, Tues.–Sun. noon–4.*

The 4 km (2½ mi) of stalactite caves at **Lummelunda,** about 18 km (11 mi) north of Visby on the coastal road, are unique in this part of the world and are worth visiting. ✉*Lummelunds Bruk* ☎*0498/273050* 🌐*www.lummelundagrottan.se* 🎫*SKr 100* ⏲*May–Sept., daily 9–5.*

Curious rock formations dot the coasts of Gotland, remnants of reefs formed more than 400 million years ago, and two **bird sanctuaries, Stora** and **Lilla Karlsö,** stand off the coast south of Visby. The bird population consists mainly of guillemots, which look like penguins. Visits to these sanctuaries are permitted only in the company of a recognized guide. Contact each sanctuary for its tour times. ☎*0498/240450 for Stora, 0498/485248 for Lilla* 🎫*SKr 225 for Stora, SKr 200 for Lilla* ⏲*May–Aug., daily.*

WHERE TO EAT

$$$ FRENCH ★ ✕**Donners Brunn.** In a beautiful orange-brick house on a small square in Visby, the chef proprietor of this restaurant, Bo Nilsson, was once chef at the renowned Operakällaren in Stockholm. The menu uses excellent local ingredients to make French-influenced dishes that are reasonably priced, given their quality. The house specialty of Gotland lamb with fresh asparagus and hollandaise sauce is delicious. ✉*Donners Plats 3* ☎*0498/271090* ✍*Reservations essential* 💳*AE, DC, MC, V.*

$$ SCANDINAVIAN ✕**Konstnärsgården.** Hans and Birgitta Belin run a wonderful establishment in the tiny village of Ala. He is an artist, she a chef. As you eat your lovingly prepared food in this old manor-house restaurant, you can view and buy works by Hans and other artists. The venison that's often on the menu comes from deer raised on the premises, and in the summer months whole lambs are spit-roasted outdoors in the orchard gardens. ✉*30 km (19 mi) southeast of Visby, Ala* ☎*0498/55055* 💳*MC, V.*

$$ SWEDISH ✕**Krusmyntagården.** This marvelous little garden-café opened in the late '70s and has been passed down through several owners. The garden now has more than 200 organic herbs and plants, many of which are used in the evening barbecue feasts. ✉*Krusmyntav. 4* ☎*0498/296900* 💳 *MC, V.*

WHERE TO STAY

$$ 🏨**Strand Hotel.** An environmentally friendly hotel with efficient heating and cooling systems, the Strand may ease your conscience with its approach. In any case, the lap pool, sauna, and bright, comfortable rooms will ease your spirit. The clubby, relaxing bar has an adjoining library with large leather sofas. **Pros:** good location; easy on the environment. **Cons:** a little worn around the edges; limited facilities. ✉*Strandg. 34* ☎*0498/258800* 🌐*www.strandhotel.net* 🛏*110 rooms, 6 suites* 👍*In-room: refrigerator. In-hotel: restaurant, bar, pool, no-smoking rooms* 💳*AE, DC, MC, V* 🍽*BP.*

$ ⚌**Toftagården.** Near the Gotland coast about 20 km (12 mi) from Visby, the placid verdant grounds here are ideal for strolling, lazing about, and reading in the shade. The long sandy beach in Tofta is also nearby, as is the Kronholmen Golf Course. Most of the brightly furnished rooms, all on the ground floor, have their own terrace. There are also a number of cottages with kitchens—a two-night minimum stay is required for these. If the sea water at the beach is too cold, take a dip in the heated outdoor pool. The restaurant serves very good regional fare. **Pros:** beautiful location; perfect for families. **Cons:** limited facilities; rooms are a little tired. ⊠*Toftagården* ☎*0498/297000* ⊕*www.toftagarden.se* ⇥*70 rooms, 15 cottages* ⚐*In-room: kitchen (some). In-hotel: restaurant, pool* ⊟*AE, DC, MC, V* ⫢*BP.*

$ ⚌**Villa Alskog.** A short drive from the sandy beaches in the south of
★ Gotland, Villa Alskog is a delightful inn surrounded by beautiful open spaces, stone fences, and small groves of trees. The building dates from 1840 and was originally a residence for the local priest. Its 15 guest rooms are bright and simply furnished, with hardwood floors. Most have a private bath; when you reserve a room, verify that it's one that has its own bath. The location is ideal for swimming, hiking, and horseback riding. **Pros:** location great for outdoor activities; warm and friendly service. **Cons:** few facilities. ⊠*Alskog* ☎*0498/491188* ⇥*15 rooms* ⚐*In-hotel: restaurant* ⊟*MC, V* ⫢*BP.*

$$ ⚌**Wisby Hotell.** The tall, thin building that's now the Wisby dates from the 1200s and is at the junction of two narrow streets. A hotel since 1855, the ocher-color walls, light floral-patterned fabrics, dark wood, and vaulted ceilings give it old European grandeur. There are two excellent bars in the hotel, one a glassed-in courtyard that serves cocktails and the other a cozy pub with a good beer selection. **Pros:** kids love the cellar pool; a bargain for how luxe it is. **Cons:** some rooms feel faded; crowded bar and restaurant. ⊠*Strandg. 6* ☎*0498/257500* ⊕*www.wisbyhotell.se* ⇥*134 rooms* ⚐*In-room: refrigerator, Internet. In-hotel: restaurant, bars, room service, pool, spa, parking (paid), no-smoking rooms* ⊟*AE, DC, MC, V* ⫢*BP.*

5

NIGHTLIFE AND THE ARTS

Medeltidsveckan *(Medieval Week)*, celebrated in early August, is a citywide festival marking the invasion of the prosperous island by Danish king Valdemar on July 22, 1361. Celebrations begin with Valdemar's grand entrance parade and continue with jousts, an open-air market on Strandgatan, and street-theater performances re-creating the period.

In the ruins of **St. Nicolai,** the old dilapidated church in Visby, regular concerts are held throughout the summer months. Everything from folk to rock to classical is available. The tourist office has details.

There are many bars and drinking establishments on Gotland, but the best are in Visby. The town comes alive on summer nights; the best way to experience it is simply to wander the streets, follow the loudest noise, and go with the flow.

SPORTS AND THE OUTDOORS

Bicycles, tents, and camping equipment can be rented from **Gotlands Cykeluthyrning** (⊠*Skeppsbron 2* ☎*0498/214133* ⊕*www.gotland scykeluthyrning.com*). **Gotlandsleden** is a 200-km (120-mi) bicycle route around the island; contact the tourist office for details.

For an aquatic adventure, **Gotlands Upplevelser** (⊠ *Visby* ☎*0730/751678* ⊕*www.gotlandsupplevelser.se*) will rent you a canoe and a life jacket or windsurfing equipment. They also offer rock-climbing courses. Call for prices and locations.

UPPSALA

67 km (41 mi) north of Stockholm.

Uppsala is home to one of Europe's oldest universities, established in 1477. It is also a historic site where pagan (and extremely gory) Viking ceremonies persisted into the 11th century. As late as the 16th century, nationwide *tings* (early parliaments) were convened here. Today it is a quiet home for about 170,000 people. Built along the banks of the Fyris River, the town has a pleasant jumble of old buildings that is dominated by its cathedral, which dates from the early 13th century.

In recent years Uppsala has shaken off the shadow of nearby Stockholm and is emerging as a destination in its own right. The town has established itself as something of a center for medical research and pharmaceuticals. Add to the mix the student population, and Uppsala has become a thriving place, with housing and office developments springing up in equal numbers to restaurants, bars, cultural venues, and shops.

GETTING HERE AND AROUND

You can explore Uppsala easily on your own, but English-language guided group tours can be arranged through the Uppsala Guide Service. Trains between Stockholm and Uppsala run twice hourly throughout the day year-round. The cost of a one-way trip is SKr 75. For timetables and train information, contact SJ. The main tourist office run by the Uppsala Convention and Visitors Bureau is in the town center; in summer a small tourist information office is also open at Uppsala Castle.

ESSENTIALS

Tour Uppsala Guide Service (☎*018/7274818*).

Train Contact SJ (☎*0771/757575* ⊕*www.sj.se*).

Visitor Info Main Tourist Office (⊠*Fyris torg 8* ☎*018/7274800* ⊕*www.uppland. nu*).

EXPLORING UPPSALA

Uppsala's winding, ancient streets are made for exploring. The best way to see the town is to wander around and see what comes up. It's small enough that it is almost impossible to get lost. Around the university is the town's old center, rich with history and beauty. On the other side of the river is the commercial district, centered around the pedestrian street of Kungsängsgatan.

TOP ATTRACTIONS

Ideally you should start your visit with a trip to **Gamla Uppsala** *(Old Uppsala)*, 5 km (3 mi) north of the town. Here under three huge mounds lie the graves of the first Swedish kings—Aun, Egil, and Adils—of the 6th-century Ynglinga dynasty. Close by in pagan times was a sacred grove containing a legendary oak from whose branches animal and human sacrifices were hung. By the 10th century Christianity had eliminated such practices. A small church, which was the seat of Sweden's first archbishop, was built on the site of a former pagan temple.

The **Gamla Uppsala Museum** contains exhibits and archaeological findings from the Viking burial mounds that dominate the local area. The museum distinguishes between the myth and legends about the area and what is actually known about its history. ☎*018/239312* ✆*SKr 50* ⊙*May–Aug., daily 11–5; Sept.–Apr., Wed. and weekends noon–3.*

One of Uppsala's most famous sons, Carl von Linné, also known as Linnaeus, was a professor of botany at the university during the 1740s. He created the Latin nomenclature system for plants and animals. The botanical treasures of Linnaeus's old garden have been re-created and are now on view in **Linnéträdgården.** The garden's orangery houses a pleasant cafeteria and is used for concerts and cultural events. ✉*Svartbäcksg. 27* ☎*018/4712576* ⊕*www.linnaeus.uu.se* ✆*SKr 50* ⊙*May–Aug., daily 9–9; Sept.–Apr., daily 9–7.*

Completed in 1625, the **Gustavianum,** which served as the university's main building for two centuries, is easy to spot by its remarkable copper cupola, now green with age. The building houses the ancient anatomical theater—one of only seven in the world to function on natural light—where human anatomy lectures and public dissections took place. The Victoria Museum of Egyptian Antiquities is in the same building. ✉*Akademig. 3* ☎*018/4717571* ⊕*www.gustavianum.uu.se* ✆*SKr 40* ⊙*Tues.–Sun. 11–4.*

WORTH NOTING

★ The 362-foot twin towers of **Uppsala Domkyrka** *(Uppsala Cathedral)* —whose height equals the length of the nave—dominate the city skyline. Work on the cathedral began in the early 13th century, it was consecrated in 1435 and restored between 1885 and 1893. Still the seat of Sweden's archbishop, the cathedral is also the site of the tomb of Gustav Vasa, the king who established Sweden's independence in the 16th century. Inside is a silver casket containing the relics of St. Erik. ☎*018/187177* ⊕*www.uppsalacathedral.com* ✆*Free* ⊙*Daily 8–6.*

Gustav Vasa began work on **Uppsala Slott** *(Uppsala Castle)* in the 1540s. He intended the building to symbolize the dominance of the monarchy over the church. It was completed under Queen Christina nearly a century later. Students gather here every April 30 to celebrate the Feast of Valborg and optimistically greet the arrival of spring. Call the tourist center for more information. ✉*Ingång C, Uppsala* ✆*Castle SKr*

60 ⊗ *English guided tours of castle June–Aug., daily at 1 and 3.*

Uppsala Universitetet (*Uppsala University* ☎018/4710000 ⊕*www.uu.se*), founded in 1477, is known for the **Carolina Rediviva** university library, which contains a copy of every book published in Sweden, in addition to a large collection of foreign works. Two of its most interesting exhibits are the *Codex Argentus*, a Bible written in the 6th century, and Mozart's original manuscript for his 1791 opera *The Magic Flute*.

WHERE TO EAT

$$
ITALIAN
Fodor's Choice
★

✕**Il Forno Italiano.** From the outside, this place couldn't be more Swedish, housed as it is in a beautiful, centuries-old house opposite Uppsala's grand university building. Inside, though, a little bit of Italy takes over, with scrubbed-wood furniture, red check table cloths and exposed brick and whitewashed walls. The food wins no awards for surprises—it's mostly trusted Italian staples—but the service and the quality of what's on the plate is extremely good. There's no wine list; your knowledgeable waiter will talk you through the best options once you have ordered your food. All in all, this is one of the most pleasant dining experiences in Uppsala. ⊠*St. Olofsg. 8* ☎*018/103520* ⊟*AE, DC, MC, V.*

$$$
SCANDINAVIAN
★

✕**Guldkanten.** When Uppsala's grand old food hall burned down in 2002, Guldkanten burned with it. Now it's back with chef Anders Ericsson at the stoves, producing ambitious, modern, and delicious food inspired by Swedish ingredients and flavors from the Mediterranean and eastern Europe. Delightful dishes, such as tortellini of crab with fennel puree or pigeon with blinis, cabbage, and figs, are deftly presented and full of flavor. The restaurant is fronted by a sweeping semicircular window overlooking the river, and the interior is a subtle blend of dark wood and cream furnishings. ⊠*St. Eriks torg 8* ☎*018/150151* ⚑*Reservations essential* ⊟*AE, DC, MC, V.*

$
CAFÉ

✕**Günthers.** This classic old café has stood by the river for more than 100 years. On the wall as you enter is proof of royal appointment as cake makers to the king—still valid today. Inside, the dark-wood paneling, the thick carpet, and the solid wooden chairs and tables look as though they just might outlast the royal warrant. One side of the main room is taken up by huge glass cabinets containing exquisite cakes, delicate pastries, crusty well-filled sandwiches, and hot dishes like lasagna. Lunch here, ending with a few pieces of cake, should see you through until breakfast. ⊠*Östra Åg. 31* ☎*018/130757* ⊟*MC, V* ⊗*No dinner.*

THE FEAST OF VALBORG

The last day of April never fails to make the town become one big carnival—the Feast of Valborg. To celebrate the arrival of spring (and the end of the school year), students of the university don sailorlike hats and charge down the hill from the university library (try not to get in their way). The university chorus then sings traditional spring songs on the steps of the main building. And finally the whole town slips into mayhem. Thousands descend on the city as the streets are awash in champagne and celebrations. It's an age-old custom worth seeing, but it's not for the fainthearted.

$$ **✕Hyllan.** Suspended on a half floor above the rebuilt food hall, Hyllan
FRENCH is a dim, cozy place—some would even say it's romantic. Dark woods
and cream and red sofas and chairs set the mood in the bar; the dining
area follows suit. The food here consists of well-prepared bistro staples.
Think steaks, salads, mussels, cod with horseradish, and the like. It's a
busy, friendly place, especially at the bar, and makes for a great one-stop
night out. ⊠*St. Eriks torg 8* ☎*018/150150* ☐*AE, DC, MC, V.*

WHERE TO STAY

$$ **⊞Clarion Gillet.** First opened in 1971, Uppsala's largest hotel is now in
the hands of the Choice group of hotels. Rooms are bright and large,
with pleasant watercolors, soft furnishings, and hardwood floors. The
hotel is only a short walk from Uppsala's most famous buildings. The
public areas are a little bland and standardized, but very comfortable.
Pros: good-size rooms; excellent facilities; close to town center. **Cons:**
corporate-feeling public areas, some rooms can suffer from traffic noise.
⊠*Dragarbrunnsg. 23* ☎*018/681800* ⊕*www.choice.se* ⟿*160 rooms,
1 suite* ⚐*In-room: refrigerator, Internet. In-hotel: 2 restaurants, room
service, bar, pool, gym, laundry service, parking (paid), no-smoking
rooms* ☐*AE, DC, MC, V* ⧆*BP.*

$$ **⊞First Hotel Linné.** The namesake of this white-stone town-house hotel
with lush gardens is the botanist Linnaeus (Carl von Linné). The hotel's
interior is in harmony with the gardens outside: soft floral prints and
warm colors dominate. In winter, enjoy the huge open fireplace. Rooms
are done in a bright, modern Scandinavian design, with earth and red
tones and floral prints. **Pros:** very inviting public areas; very comfort-
able beds. **Cons:** some rooms are small. ⊠*Skolg. 45* ☎*018/102000*
⊕*www.firsthotels.com* ⟿*116 rooms, 6 suites* ⚐*In-room: refrigerator,
Wi-Fi. In-hotel: restaurant, room service, bar, laundry service, parking
(fee), no-smoking rooms* ☐*AE, DC, MC, V* ⧆*BP.*

$$ **⊞Grand Hotel Hörnan.** A mansionlike creation from 1906, the Hörnan's
city-center location means that it's near the train station and has views
of both the castle and the cathedral. The rooms are spacious and have
antique furnishings and soft lighting. Once the grandest hotel in town,
Hörnan has faded a bit these days, but still keeps its head up, retaining
a noble air of its former self. **Pros:** unrivaled location and views; history around every corner. **Cons:** almost no facilities; in need of a good
refurbishment. ⊠*Bandgårdsg. 1* ☎*018/139380* ⊕*www.grandhotell
hornan.com* ⟿*37 rooms* ⚐*In-room: Internet. In-hotel: bar* ☐*AE,
DC, MC, V* ⧆*BP.*

$$ **⊞Scandic Uplandia.** This branch of the giant Nordic chain has the usual
modern comforts and high-tech amenities expected of an international
business hotel. There's also the pleasing design that's found in the
best Scandinavian hotels. Blond wood accented with moss-green and
aquamarine fabrics gives the decor a sophisticated edge. Some rooms
are more recently refurbished and feature modern warm grey tones
and funky '70s-inspired wallpaper. **Pros:** good location; good facili-
ties. **Cons:** some rooms need refurbishing; some rooms are very small.
⊠*Dragarbrunnsg. 32* ☎*018/4952600* ⊕*www.scandichotels.com*
⟿*133 rooms, 2 suites* ⚐*In-room: refrigerator, Wi-Fi. In-hotel: res-*

5

taurant, room service, bar, gym, laundry service, Wi-Fi, parking (paid), no-smoking rooms ⊟*AE, DC, MC, V* ⊫❙*BP.*

NIGHTLIFE

Bowlaget (⊠*Skolg.* 6 ☎*018/553310*) is Uppsala's newest and coolest meeting spot. In this huge venue you can move between a modern bar and restaurant, a neon-blue bowling alley, a sports bar with plasma-screen TVs, and a very loud, very bumpin' nightclub. Enter for dinner, leave at dawn. For a relaxed evening, head to **Katalin** (⊠*Östra Station* ☎*018/140680*), a former goods shed behind the railway station, now a funky bar and restaurant. The emphasis here is on the music, with live jazz, rock, and Swedish pop making most people forget about dinner.

SHOPPING

Jaber (⊠*Fyris torg* 6 ☎*018/135050*) is something of a draw for the area's wealthy elite. It is a family-run clothes shop with a line of gorgeous international designs, matched only by the personal service it provides. **Öster om Ån** (⊠*Svartbäcksg. 18* ☎*018/711545*) is a handicraft cooperative that was formed many years ago. The co-op is still hugely popular today, offering a unique and beautiful range of ceramics, knitted goods, woodwork, and jewelry.

Trolltyg (⊠*Östra Åg. 25* ☎*018/146304*) has an exclusive selection of the sort of clean-line clothes and household furnishings for which Scandinavian design is known. The shop is wonderfully laid out and is a joy to explore, especially the fabrics section.

GÖTEBORG (GOTHENBURG)

Don't tell the residents of Göteborg that they live in Sweden's "second city," but not because they will get upset (people here are known for their amiability and good humor). They just may not understand what you are talking about. People who call Göteborg (pronounced YOO-teh-bor; most visitors stick with the simpler "Gothenburg") home seem to forget that the city is diminutive in size and status compared to Stockholm.

Spend a couple of days here and you'll forget, too. You'll find it's easier to ask what Göteborg hasn't got to offer rather than what it has. Culturally it is superb, boasting a fine opera house and theater, one of the country's best art museums, as well as a fantastic applied-arts museum. There's plenty of history to soak up, from the ancient port that gave the city its start to the 19th-century factory buildings and workers' houses that helped put it on the commercial map. For those looking for nature, the wild west coast and tame green fields are both within striking distance. And don't forget the food. Since it's inception in 1983, more than half of the "Swedish Chef of the Year" competition winners were cooking in Göteborg.

GETTING HERE AND AROUND

AIR TRAVEL Among the airlines operating to and from Göteborg are Air France, British Airways, Finnair, KLM, Malmö Aviation, Norwegian, and SAS. Landvetter Airport is approximately 26 km (16 mi) from the city.

Landvetter is linked to Göteborg by freeway. Buses leave Landvetter every 15–30 minutes and arrive 30 minutes later at Nils Ericsonsplatsen by the central train station, with stops at Lisebergsstationen, Korsvägen, the Elite Park Avenue, and Kungsportsplatsen; weekend schedules include some nonstop departures. The price of the trip is SKr 75. For more information, call Flygbussarna.

The taxi ride to the city center should cost no more than SKr 350.

BUS TRAVEL All buses arrive in the central city area, in the bus station next to the central train station. The principal bus company is Swebus, the national company based in Stockholm.

CAR TRAVEL Avis, Hertz, and Europcar have offices at the airport and the central railway station. Göteborg is reached by car either via the E20 or the E4 highway from Stockholm (495 km [307 mi]) from the east, or on the E6/E20 coastal highway from the south (Malmö is 290 km [180 mi] away). Markings are excellent, and roads are well sanded and plowed in winter.

TRAIN TRAVEL There is regular service from Stockholm to Göteborg, which takes a little over 4½ hours, as well as frequent high-speed (X2000) train service, which takes about 3 hours. All trains arrive at the central train station in Drottningtorget, downtown Göteborg. For schedules call SJ, the Swedish national rail company. Streetcars and buses leave from here for the suburbs, but the hub for all streetcar traffic is a block down Norra Hamngatan, at Brunnsparken.

PUBLIC TRANSPORT Stadstrafiken is the name of Göteborg's excellent transit service. Transit brochures, which are available in English, explain the various discount passes and procedures; you can pick one up at a TidPunkten office. The best bet for the tourist is the Göteborg Pass, which covers free use of public transport, various sightseeing trips, and admission to Liseberg and local museums, among other benefits. The card costs SKr 225 for one day and SKr 310 for two days; there are lower rates for children younger than 18. You can buy the Göteborg Pass as well as regular tram and bus passes at Pressbyrån shops, camping sites, and the tourist information offices.

TOURS For a view of the city from the water and an expert commentary on its sights and history in English and German, take one of the Paddan sightseeing boats. *Paddan* is Swedish for "toad," an apt commentary on the vessels' squat appearance. The boats pass under 20 bridges and take in both the canals and part of the Göta River.

A 90-minute bus tour and a two-hour combination boat-and-bus tour of the chief points of interest leave from outside the main tourist office at Kungsportsplatsen every day from mid-May through August and on Saturday in April, September, and October. Call the tourist office for schedules.

5

ESSENTIALS

Airlines Air France (☎ 08/51999990). **British Airways** (☎ 0770/110020). **Finnair** (☎ 0771/781100). **KLM** (☎ 08/58799757). **Malmö Aviation** (☎ 0771/550010). **Norwegian Air Shuttle** (☎ 0770/457700). **SAS** (☎ 0770/727727).

Airport and Transfers Landvetter Airport (☎ 031/941100 ⊕ www.lfv.se). **Flygbussarna** (☎ 0771/414300). **Scandinavian Limousine** (☎ 031/7942424). **Taxi Göteborg** (☎ 031/650000).

Bus Contact Swebus Express (☎ 0771/218218 ⊕ www.swebusexpress.se).

Car Rental Avis (☎ 031/946030 at airport, 031/805780 at central railway station). **Europcar** (☎ 031/947100). **Hertz** (☎ 031/946020).

Late-Night Pharmacy Vasen (✉ Götg. 12, in Nordstan shopping mall, Nordstan ☎ 0771/450450 ⊙ Mon.–Sun., 8 AM–10 PM).

Medical Services Folktandvården Dental-Service Emergencies (☎ 031/807800). **24-hour medical advice line** (☎ 031/7031500). **Östra Sjukhuset emergency room** (☎ 031/3420000).

Public Transport Info TidPunkten (✉ Drottningtorget, Brunnsparken, and Nils Ericsonsplatsen, Centrum ☎ 0771/414300).

Taxi Taxi Göteborg (☎ 031/650000).

Visitor and Tour Info Paddan (✉ Kungsportsplatsen, Centrum ☎ 031/609670 ⛟ SKr 125). **Göteborg's Turistbyrå** (✉ Kungsportsplatsen 2 ☎ 031/612500 ⊕ www.goteborg.com). **Nordstan shopping center** (✉ Nordstadstorget ☎ 031/612500).

EXPLORING GÖTEBORG

Göteborg begs to be explored by foot. A small, neat package of a city, it can be divided up into three main areas, all of which are closely interlinked. If your feet need a rest, though, there is an excellent streetcar network that runs to all parts of town. The main artery of Göteborg is Kungsportsavenyn (more commonly referred to as Avenyn, "the Avenue"), a 60-foot-wide tree-lined boulevard that bisects the city along a northwest–southeast axis. Avenyn starts at Göteborg's cultural heart, Götaplatsen, home to the city's oldest cultural institutions, where ornate carved-stone buildings keep watch over the shady boulevards of the Vasastan neighborhood lined with exclusive restaurants and bars. Follow Avenyn north and you'll find the main commercial area, now dominated by the modern Nordstan shopping center. Beyond is the waterfront, busy with all the traffic of the port, as well as some of Göteborg's newer cultural developments, in particular its magnificent opera house.

To the west of the city are the Haga and Linné districts. Once home to the city's dockyard, shipping, and factory workers, these areas are now chic, bohemian enclaves alive with arts-and-crafts galleries, antiques shops, boutiques selling clothes and household goods, and street cafés and restaurants.

The main tourist office is Göteborg's Turistbyrå in Kungsportsplatsen. There are also offices at the Nordstan shopping center and in front of the central train station at Drottningtorget.

A free English-language newspaper with listings called *Metro* is available in summer; you can pick it up at tourist offices, shopping centers, and some restaurants, as well as on streetcars.

Göteborg's Turistbyrå's Web site has a good events calendar.

The Göteborg Pass, available from the Göteborg tourist office, and on their Web site, offers discounts and savings for sights, restaurants, hotels, and other services around the city.

DOWNTOWN GÖTEBORG

A pleasant stroll will take you from Götaplatsen's 1930s architecture along Avenyn—the boulevard Kungsportsavenyn lined with elegant shops, cafés, and restaurants—to finish at Kungsportsplats. At the square the street becomes Östra Hamngatan and slopes gently up from the canal.

TOP ATTRACTIONS

 Götaplatsen *(Göta Place).* This square was built in 1923 in celebration Fodor's Choice of the city's 300th anniversary. In the center is the Swedish-American ★ sculptor Carl Milles's breathtaking fountain statue of Poseidon choking a codfish. Behind the statue stands the Konstmuseet, flanked by the **Konserthuset** (Concert Hall) and the **Stadsteatern** (Municipal Theater), contemporary buildings in which the city celebrates its important contribution to Swedish cultural life.

⑫ **Konstmuseet** *(Art Museum).* This impressive collection of the works of leading Scandinavian painters and sculptors encapsulates some of the moody introspection of the artistic community in this part of the world. The museum's Hasselblad Center devotes itself to showing the progress in the art of photography. The Konstmuseet's holdings include works by Swedes such as Carl Milles, Johan Tobias Sergel, impressionist Anders Zorn, Victorian idealist Carl Larsson, and Prince Eugen. The 19th- and 20th-century French art collection is the best in Sweden, and there's also a small collection of old masters. ⊠ *Götaplatsen* ☎ *031/3683500* ⊕ *www.konstmuseum.goteborg.se* ⊠ *SKr 40* ☉ *Tues. and Thurs. 11–6, Wed. 11–9, Fri.–Sun. 11–5.*

⑩ **Röhsska Museet** *(Museum of Arts and Crafts).* This museum's fine col-★ lections of furniture, books and manuscripts, tapestries, and pottery are on view. Artifacts date back as far as 1,000 years, but it's the 20th-century gallery, with its collection of many familiar household objects, that seems to provide the most enjoyment. ⊠ *Vasag. 37–39, Vasastan* ☎ *031/3683150* ⊕ *www.designmuseum.se* ⊠ *SKr 40* ☉ *Tues. noon–8, Wed.–Fri. noon–5, weekends 11–5.*

WORTH NOTING

 Domkyrkan *(Göteborg Cathedral).* The cathedral, in neoclassic yellow brick, dates from 1802, the two previous cathedrals on this spot having been destroyed by fire. Though disappointingly plain on the outside, the interior is impressive. Two glassed-in verandas originally used for the bishop's private conversations run the length of each side of the cathedral. The altar is impressively ornate and gilt. ⊠*Kyrkog. 28, Centrum* ☎*031/7316130* ⬛*Free* ☉*Weekdays 8–6, Sat. 9–4, Sun. 10–3.*

⑦ Feskekörkan *(Fish Church).* Built in 1872, this fish market gets its nickname from its Gothic-style architectural details. The beautiful arched and vaulted wooden ceiling covers rows and rows of stalls, each offering silvery, slippery goods to the shoppers who congregate in this vast hall. ⊠*Fisktorget, Rosenlundsg, Centrum.*

❸ Stadsmuseet *(City Museum).* Once the warehouse and auction rooms of the Swedish East India Company, a major trading firm founded in 1731, this palatial structure dates from 1750. Today it contains exhibits on the Swedish west coast, with a focus on Göteborg's nautical and trading past. One interesting exhibit deals with the East India Company and its ship the *Göteborg.* On its 1745 return from China, she sank just outside the city, while crowds there to greet the returning ship watched from shore in horror. ⊠*Norra Hamng. 12, Centrum* ☎*031/3683600* ⬛*SKr 40* ☉*Tues.–Sun. 10–5.*

COMMERCIAL GÖTEBORG

Take in Göteborg's port-side character, both historic and modern, at the waterfront development near the town center, where the markets and boutiques can keep you busy for hours.

TOP ATTRACTIONS

❶ Göteborgs Operan *(Gothenburg's Opera).* A statement in steel and glass, ★ the opera house opened in 1994, immediately dominating this section of the waterfront with its bold lines and shape. Set against a backdrop of the old docks, it makes for a striking image. The productions here are world-class and well worth seeing if you get the chance. ⊠*Christina Nilssonsg., Nordstan* ☎*031/131300 for bookings* ⊕*www.opera.se.*

❻ Trädgårdsföreningens Park *(Horticultural Society Park).* Beautiful open Fodor'sChoice green spaces, manicured gardens, and tree-lined paths are the perfect ★ place to escape for some peace and rest. Rose fanciers can head for the magnificent rose garden with 5,000 roses of 2,500 varieties. Also worth a visit is the Palm House, whose late-19th-century design echoes that of London's Crystal Palace. ⊠*Just off Kungsportsavenyn, Centrum* ☎*031/3655858* ⬛*SKr 100* ☉*Daily, 10–8.*

WORTH NOTING

❷ Maritima Centrum *(Marine Center).* In the world's largest floating maritime museum you'll find modern naval vessels, including a destroyer, submarines, lightship, cargo vessel, and various tugboats, providing insight into Göteborg's historic role as a major port. The main attraction is a huge naval destroyer, complete with a medical room in which a leg amputation operation is graphically re-created, with mannequins standing in for medical personnel. ⊠*Packhuskajen 8, Nordstan* ☎*031/105950* ⊕*www.goteborgsmaritimacentrum.com* ⬛*SKr 80* ☉*May–July, daily 10–6; Aug.–Apr., daily 10–4.*

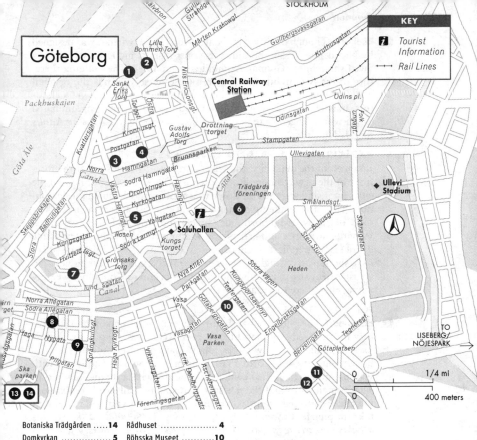

Göteborg

KEY

ℹ Tourist Information

←—→ Rail Lines

STOCKHOLM

Central Railway Station

Ullevi Stadium

Saluhallen

♦ Göteborgs Operan

Kungs torget

Heden

Vasa Parken

Götaplatsen

TO LISEBERG/ NÖJESPARK →

0   1/4 mi

0   400 meters

❹ Rådhuset. Though the town hall dates from 1672, when it was designed by Nicodemus Tessin the Elder, its controversial modern extension by Swedish architect Gunnar Asplund is from 1937. The building therefore offers two architectural extremes. One section has the original grand chandeliers and trompe l'oeil ceilings; the other has glass elevators, mussel-shape drinking fountains, and vast expanses of laminated aspen wood. Together they make a fascinating mix. ⊠ *Gustav Adolfs torg 1, Nordstan.*

EXPLORING HAGA AND LINNÉ DISTRICTS

Just west of the main city, the Haga and Linné districts are at the forefront of the new cosmopolitan Göteborg. These areas once housed the city's poor, and were so run-down that they were scheduled for demolition. They now make up some of the city's most attractive areas. The older of the two neighborhoods, the Haga district, is full of cozy cafés, secondhand stores, and artists' shops along cobbled streets. The Linné district is the trendiest neighborhood in Göteborg, and real-estate prices have shot up accordingly. Corner restaurants, expensive boutiques, and stylish cafés cater to neighborhood residents and to Göteborg's wealthy young elite, there to see and be seen.

TOP ATTRACTIONS

❽ Hagabadet. This stunning bathhouse was built at the end of the 19th century by the Swedish philanthropist Sven Renström. Originally used by local dock- and factory workers, it now plays host to Göteborg's leisure-hungry elite. It's well worth a visit. The pretty pool is art nouveau, with wall paintings, an arched ceiling, and lamps with a diving-lady motif. The Roman baths and the massage and spa area all exude relaxation, but the architecture alone is worth a visit, even if you don't intend to take the plunge. ⊠ *Södra Allég. 3, Haga* 🕾 *031/600600* 🖃 *SKr 360 for a 1-day pass to use facilities; otherwise free* ⊗ *Mon.–Thurs. 7 AM–9:30 PM, Fri. 7 AM–8:30 PM, Sat. 9–6, Sun. 10–6.*

Fodor's Choice
★

⓬ Haga Nygatan. The redbrick buildings that line this street were originally poorhouses donated by the Dickson family, the city's British industrialist forefathers. ROBERT DICKSON can still be seen carved into the facades of these buildings. Like most buildings in Haga, the buildings' ground floors were made of stone in order to prevent the spread of fire (the upper floors are wood). The Dickson family's impact on the architecture of the west of Sweden can also be seen in the impressive, fanciful mansion that belonged to Robert's grandson James, in Tjolöholm, to the south of Göteborg. ⊠ *Haga Nyg., Haga.*

WORTH NOTING

⓮ Botaniska Trädgården *(Botanical Gardens).* With 1,200 plant species, this is Sweden's largest botanical garden. Herb gardens, bamboo groves, a Japanese valley, forest plants, and tropical greenhouses are all on display. Once you've captured some inspiration, you can pick up all you need to create your own botanical garden from the on-site shop. ⊠ *Carl Skottsbergsg. 22A, Slottsskogen* 🕾 *031/7411101* 🖃 *Greenhouses SKr 20, park free* ⊗ *Park daily 9–sunset; greenhouses May–Aug., daily 10–5; Sept.–Apr., daily 10–4.*

⑬ Slottsskogen. Spend some time in this stunning area of parkland containing cafés, farm animals, a seal pond, Sweden's oldest children's zoo, and many birds—in summer even pink flamingos. Slottsskogen is one of the best parts of the city for relaxing. ✉ *South of Linnég., Slottsskogen* ⓣ *Daily dawn–dusk.*

WHERE TO EAT

Göteborg is filled with people who love to eat and cook, so you've come to the right place if you're interested in food. The fish and seafood here are some of the best in the world, owing to the clean, cold waters off Sweden's west coast. And Göteborg's chefs are some of the best in Sweden, as a glance at the list of recent "Swedish Chef of the Year" winners will confirm. Call ahead to be sure restaurants are open, as many close for a month in summer.

$
SCANDINAVIAN
Fodor'sChoice
★

✕ Amanda Boman. This little restaurant in one corner of the market hall at Kungsportsplats keeps early hours, so unless you eat an afternoon dinner, plan on lunch instead. The cuisine is primarily Swedish and is simply presented. A big white-china bowl of fish soup and a glass of white wine here is hard to beat, and you can watch the bustling market activity through the rising steam from your bowl. ✉ *Saluhallen, Centrum* ☎ *031/137676* ⊟ *AE, MC, V* ⓣ *Closed Sun. No dinner.*

$$$$
SCANDINAVIAN

✕ Basement. The delicious, locally produced, strictly seasonal food here is offered only as a fixed price full menu. Choose between four, six, or eight courses, with a glass of wine selected for each course as an extra cost. Chef Gustav Trädgårdh creates delicious small dishes for his daily changing menu, with the ambition that all guests leave having had a full range of culinary experiences. And that they do. The white walls and terra-cotta tile floor create an elegantly simple backdrop to the gourmet food. ✉ *Götaborgsg. 28, Vasastan* ☎ *031/282729* ⚠ *Reservations essential* ⊟ *AE, DC, MC, V* ⓣ *Closed Sun. No lunch.*

$$
MEDITERRANEAN

✕ Caleo. The name means *to be warmed* in Latin; certainly a suitable moniker for this place. The natural shades throughout the restaurant and the ever-smiling staff are enough to thaw even the most frozen of spirits. And the food, with all the warming, delicious flavors of the Mediterranean, is enough to make you want to get up and dance—something you won't be able to do in the slightly cramped dining room. ✉ *Engelbrektsg. 39, Vasastan* ☎ *031/7089340* ⊟ *AE, DC, MC, V* ⓣ *No lunch.*

$$$
SCANDINAVIAN
★

✕ Fond. Stefan Karlsson's fantastic restaurant can boast one of the best locations in Göteborg, right on the beautiful Götaplatsen. All the herbs and vegetables are grown by a farmer just 5 km (3 mi) from town. Karlsson loves to travel; the flavors he has picked up as a globe-trotter spice up his modern Swedish menu. From the semicircular dining room, diners looks out on the square. Almost-bare wooden tables and primary-color linens make an interesting informal contrast to the haute cuisine that emerges from the kitchen. ✉ *Götaplatsen, Vasastan* ☎ *031/812580* ⊟ *AE, DC, MC, V* ⓣ *Closed Sun. No lunch Sat.*

$
SEAFOOD

✕ Gabriel. A buffet of fresh shellfish and the fish dish of the day draw crowds to this restaurant on a balcony above the fish hall. You can watch

5

all the trading as you eat lunch. The butter-fried herring with mashed potatoes is highly recommended. ✉*Feskekörkan, Centrum* ☎*031/139051* ▭*AE, DC, MC, V* ⊘*Closed Sun. and Mon. No dinner.*

$$
SCANDINAVIAN
★
✕**Hemma Hos.** A relaxed, informal restaurant with a focus on simply enjoying good food. The menu is short and simple with classic flavors like lamb with root vegetables, veal fillet with herb-baked pumpkin, and salmon with a green herb ragout and red wine sauce. The crowd here is generally local, loud, and friendly; it's a real neighborhood joint. ✉*Haga Nygata 12, Haga* ☎*031/134090* ♟*Reservations essential* ▭*AE, DC, MC, V* ⊘*Closed Sun.*

$$$
SCANDINAVIAN
✕**Kock & Vin.** Unashamedly Swedish flavors dominate the short menu here. Steamed ling is partnered with horseradish and beets, venison with a cumin sauce, and monkfish with pickled leek and morel cream. The restaurant is small, intimate (elbow room can be a little tight), and perfectly dressed in cream, beige and brown—all bathed in soft candlelight. The staff are very relaxed, friendly and like nothing more than to discuss the ins and outs of the night's menu. ✉*Viktoriag. 12, Vasastan* ☎*031/7017979* ♟*Reservations essential* ▭*AE, DC, MC, V* ⊘*Closed Sun. No lunch.*

$$$
FRENCH
Fodor'sChoice
★
✕**Park Aveny Café.** This is a slick, modern and thoroughly cool French brasserie that could very well have you thinking you're in Paris or New York—until you hear the Swedish accents. Colors are monochrome, from the black-and-white-tile floor and zinc and black-laquer bar, to the white walls and coolly clad customers. The menu is purely classic (from steak tartar and butter fried sole to mountains of oysters) and the wine list is exceptional, with many of the 300 wines available by the glass. There is always a crowd here and it's always loud. ✉*Kungsportsavenyn 36, Centrum* ☎*031/7271076* ♟*Reservations essential* ▭*AE, DC, MC, V.*

$$$
SEAFOOD
Fodor'sChoice
★
✕**Sjömagasinet.** Since 1994 Leif Mannerström has headed up what is probably the best seafood restaurant in Sweden. Mannerström, a gray-bearded kitchen maestro, is something of a godfather on the Göteborg food scene and has for many years been the leading champion of west-coast fish. In the delightful oak-beamed dining room (a 200-year-old renovated shipping warehouse), you can eat carefully presented, delicious fish dishes with a classical French touch. An outdoor terrace opens up in summer, complete with authentic sea air. ✉*Klippans Kulturreservat, Kiel-terminalen* ☎*031/7755920* ♟*Reservations essential* ▭*AE, DC, MC, V.*

$$$
SCANDINAVIAN
★
✕**28+.** Step down from the street into this former wine-and-cheese cellar to find an elegant restaurant owned by two of the best chefs in Göteborg. Finely set tables, flickering candles, and country-style artwork evoke the mood of a rustic French bistro. Italian and Asian flavors blend their way into the impeccable Swedish dishes; choose a five- or seven-course meal, or take your pick à la carte. Note that one of the best wine cellars in Sweden is at your disposal. ✉*Götaborgsg. 28, Vasastan* ☎*031/202161* ♟*Reservations essential* ▭*AE, DC, MC, V* ⊘*Closed Sun.*

$$ ✗**Thörnströms Kök.** The steep climb up the street to Thörnströms is per-
SCANDINAVIAN fect for working up a thirst. Why not start then with a choice from the
★ excellent wine list, on which every wine is available by the glass. Take
your table in one of the three small and elegant dining rooms, and
enjoy a series of small dishes of modern European food using the finest
local ingredients. Staff here are friendly and very knowledgable about
the wines and the menu. ⊠*Teknologg. 3, Vasastan* ☎*031/162066*
⚐*Reservations essential* ▤*AE, DC, MC, V* ⊙*No lunch. Closed Sun.
and Mon.*

WHERE TO STAY

Some hotels close during the winter holidays; call ahead if you expect
to travel during that time. All rooms in the hotels reviewed below are
equipped with shower or bath unless otherwise noted. Göteborg also
has some fine camping sites if you want an alternative to staying in
a hotel.

$$ ⊡**Eggers.** Dating from 1859, Best Western's Eggers may have more
★ character and charm than any other hotel in the city. It is a minute's
walk from the train station and was probably the last port of call in
Sweden for many emigrants to the United States. Rooms vary in size,
and all are beautifully decorated, often with antiques. **Pros:** a real sense
of history; opulent rooms. **Cons:** noisy location; some rooms small and
oddly shaped. ⊠*Drottningtorget, Box 323, Centrum* ☎*031/806070*
⊕*www.hoteleggers.se* ⇌*65 rooms* ⚐*In-hotel: restaurant, bar, no-
smoking rooms* ▤*AE, DC, MC, V* ▯*BP.*

$$$ ⊡**Elite Park Avenue.** Now part of the ever-expanding Elite chain of
hotels, Elite Park Avenue, a Göteborg institution, has had a thorough
upgrade. It still has all the character of a hotel that has played host
to everyone from the Beatles and Michael Jackson to George H. W.
Bush (as confirmed by the brass plaque at reception), but now it has a
more up-to-date quality to brag about. The rooms have a pure, mod-
ern simplicity about them, with light fabrics and stylish Scandinavian
furniture. **Pros:** elegant; large rooms; excellent service; perfect location.
Cons: public areas are very public; some traffic noise on lower floors.
⊠*Kungsportsavenyn 36, Box 53233, Götaplatsen* ☎*031/7271000*
⊕*www.elite.se* ⇌*312 rooms* ⚐*In-room: safe, refrigerator, Internet,
Wi-Fi In-hotel: 2 restaurants, room service, bar, gym, laundry service,
no-smoking rooms* ▤*AE, DC, MC, V* ▯*BP.*

$$$ ⊡**Elite Plaza.** A five-minute walk from the central station, the Plaza is
Fodor's Choice one of the smartest hotels in the city. The palatial building, an archi-
★ tectural attraction itself, dates from 1889, and has been modernized
with care to give it an air of grandeur, quality, and restfulness. All
original features have been retained, from the stucco ceilings to the
English mosaic floors, and are tastefully matched with modern art and
up-to-date guest facilities. Rooms are comfortable and luxurious, with
earth tones, dark-wood furnishings, and beautiful marble-and-tile bathrooms. The only complaint is that they can be a little on the small side.
Pros: beautiful setting; excellent bar; great service. **Cons:** some small
rooms; really tiny bottles of shampoo. ⊠*Västra Hamng. 3, Box 110*

Where to Stay and Eat in Göteborg

KEY

① Hotels
❶ Restaurants
🛈 Tourist Information
←→ Rail Lines

6S, Centrum 40422 ☎*031/7204000* ⊕*www.elite.se* ⟿*124 rooms, 6 suites* ♿*In-room: safe, refrigerator, Internet, Wi-Fi. In-hotel: restaurant, room service, bar, gym, laundry facilities, Wi-Fi, no-smoking rooms* ☐*AE, DC, MC, V* |◎|*BP.*

$$ ⚏**First Hotel G.** Hotel G's arrival in 2007 added much needed spice to an ★ otherwise stagnant hotel scene in Sweden's second city. Like all properties in the innovative First chain, G offers quirky elegance, modern style, and great facilities at an excellent price. The lobby is spacious, bright and hung with pop-art murals. Rooms are the same, but add striking primary-color fabrics, dark woods and bold floral prints to the mix. It's hard to find such a modern, comfortable hotel at this price anywhere else in the city. The major drawback here is the location: it sits on top of the central station, so the area surrounding the hotel feels a little seedy. **Pros:** elegant; large rooms; lots of fun design. **Cons:** busy; noisy location. ✉*Nils Ericsonsplatsen 4, Centrum* ☎*031/637200* ⊕*www. firsthotels.com* ⟿*300 rooms* ♿*In-room: safe, refrigerator, Internet, Wi-Fi. In-hotel: restaurants, room service, bar, gym, laundry service, Wi-Fi, parking (paid), no-smoking room* ☐*AE, DC, MC, V* |◎|*BP.*

¢ ⚏**Göteborgs Vandrarhem.** This hostel is right next to the amusement park Liseeberg, so is perfect for families. Rooms are very basic, with pine furnishings and linoleum floors. Breakfast (SKr 60) is not included in the rates, which are per person in a shared apartment. **Pros:** great location; friendly staff. **Cons:** limited privacy; no facilities. ✉*Mölndalsv. 23, Liseberg* ☎*031/401050* ⊕*www.goteborgsvandrarhem.se* ⟿*200 beds, 2- to 6-bed apartments* ♿*In-room: no TV. In-hotel: Wi-Fi, no-smoking rooms* ☐*MC, V.*

$ ⚏**Lilton.** This unobtrusive bed-and-breakfast-style hotel is inside a small, ivy-covered brick building. Rooms are simple and comfortable, the service friendly and unfussy. **Pros:** very friendly atmosphere; good location **Cons:** small and basic rooms; no facilities. ✉*Föreningsg. 9, Vasastan* ☎*031/828808* ⊕*www.lilton.se* ⟿*14 rooms* ♿*In-room: no TV. In-hotel: no-smoking rooms* ☐*AE, MC, V* |◎|*CP.*

$$ ⚏**Quality Hotel 11.** On the water's edge in Eriksberg, Hotel 11 combines the warehouse style of the old waterfront with a modern interior of multitier terraces. Commonly used by large companies for business conferences, the hotel also welcomes families that want to stay across the harbor from downtown Göteborg. The rooms are clean, bright, and modern; some offer panoramic views of the harbor. **Pros:** good-size rooms; modern and stylish. **Cons:** big on conventions, not easily walkable from downtown. ✉*Masking. 11, Eriksberg* ⚓*From city follow signs to Norra Älvstranden* ☎*031/7791111* ⊕*www.hotel11.se* ⟿*260 rooms* ♿*In-room: Wi-Fi. In-hotel: restaurant, bar, no-smoking rooms* ☐*AE, DC, MC, V* |◎|*BP.*

$$$ ⚏**Radisson SAS Scandinavia.** Across Drottningtorget from the central train station, the Radisson SAS is a modern and spectacular international hotel. The attractive atrium lobby is home to a a bustling reastaurant and piano bar. Rooms are large and luxurious and decorated in pastel shades with the addition of rich and comfortable fabrics. Hotel guests receive a discount at the health club on the premises. **Pros:** good-sized rooms; easy access to transport links. **Cons:** rooms overlooking

5

atrium can be a little dark; feels corporate. ⊠*Södra Hamng. 5965, Centrum* ☎*031/7585000* ⊕*www.radissonsas.com* ⌁*349 rooms* ⅋*In-room: safe, refrigerator, Internet, Wi-Fi. In-hotel: restaurant, room service, bar, pool, gym, laundry service, no-smoking rooms* ⊟*AE, DC, MC, V* ♚|*BP.*

$ ⊡ **Royal.** Göteborg's oldest hotel, built in 1852, is small, family-owned,
★ and traditional. Make a stop in the entrance hall to admire the intricate, original ceiling paintings. Rooms, with parquet floors and their original stuccowork, are individually decorated with reproductions of elegant Swedish traditional furniture. The Royal is in the city center a few blocks from the central train station. **Pros:** charming; very comfortable beds. **Cons:** rooms can be small; limited facilities. ⊠*Drottningg. 67, Centrum* ☎*031/7001170* ⊕*www.hotel-royal.com* ⌁*84 rooms* ⅋*In-room: Wi-Fi. In-hotel: no-smoking rooms* ⊟*AE, DC, MC, V* ♚|*BP.*

AFTER DARK

BARS

Hipsters should head to **Barsiden** (⊠*Kungsportsavenyn 5, Centrum* ☎*031/7111541*), a painfully chic, minimalist bar where the city's beautiful ones pull up designer stools. As its name implies, **The Dubliner** (⊠*Östra Hamng. 50, Inom Vallgraven* ☎*031/139020*) is a brave attempt at re-creating what the locals imagine to be old Irish charm. It's the perfect place for a relaxed pint and a chat with the locals. If you're looking for an urbane bar, try **Nivå** (⊠*Kungsportsavenyn 9, Centrum* ☎*031/7018090*), a popular bar with a stylish tile interior and a crowd to match. **Uppåt Framåt** (⊠*Magasingatan 3, Centrum* ☎*031/138755*) has no pretensions to be anything other than a stylish, welcoming, superfriendly bar serving excellent cocktails in a cushion-filled lounge— something it achieves very well.

DANCE CLUBS AND CABARET

Deep (⊠*Kungsportsavenyn 15, Centrum* ☎*No phone*) is a hot and bustling club packed with thirtysomethings. The roof bar offers an often-welcome fresh-air break. At **Rondo** (⊠*Örgrytev. 5, Liseberg* ☎*031/400200*) you can dance the night away on Sweden's largest dance floor while surrounded by people of all ages. The crowd is always friendly, and there's a live band.

FILM

Like all Swedish cinemas, the ones in Göteborg show mostly English-language films. The films are subtitled, never dubbed. The strangest movie theater in town is **Bio Palatset** (⊠*Kungstorget, Centrum* ☎*031/174500*), a converted meat market turned into a 10-screen cinema. The walls are in various clashing fruit colors, and the floodlighted foyer has sections scooped out to reveal Göteborg's natural rock. **Hagabion** (⊠*Linnég. 13, Linnéstaden* ☎*031/422799*) is a good art-house cinema housed in an old ivy-covered school.

JAZZ CLUBS

Performers at **Jazzhuset** (⊠*Eric Dahlbergsg. 3, Vasastan* ☎*031/133544*) tend to play traditional, swing, and Dixieland jazz. Modern jazz enthusiasts usually head for **Nefertiti** (⊠*Hvitfeldtsplatsen 6, Centrum*

☎*031/7111533*), the trendy, shadowy club where the line to get in is always long.

MUSIC, OPERA, AND THEATER

Home of the highly acclaimed Göteborg Symphony Orchestra, **Konserthuset** (✉*Götaplatsen* ☎*031/7265300*) has a mural by Sweden's Prince Eugen in the lobby, original decor, and Swedish-designed furniture from 1935.

Operan (✉*Christina Nilssons gata, Packhuskajen* ☎*031/108000*), where Göteborg's opera company performs, incorporates a 1,250-seat auditorium with a glassed-in dining area overlooking the harbor.

SPORTS AND THE OUTDOORS

BEACHES

There are several excellent local beaches. The two most popular—though they're rarely crowded—are Askim and Näset. To reach Askim, take the Express Blå bus from the central station bus terminal. It's a 10-km (6-mi) journey south of the city center. For Näset, catch Bus 19 from Brunnsparken for the 11-km (7-mi) journey southwest of Göteborg.

FISHING

Mackerel fishing is popular here. The **MS** *Daisy* (☎*031/963018*), which leaves from Hjuvik on the Hisingen side of the Göta River, takes expeditions into the archipelago. If you are in town from the first Monday after the third Sunday in September through to May, you are there during lobster season. The *Daisy* also runs lobster fishing trips; this is your chance to catch the sweetest-tasting lobster in the world. With plenty of salmon, perch, and pike, the rivers and lakes in the area have much to offer. For details call Göteborg's **Sportfiskarnas Fishing Information Line** (☎*031/7730700*).

GOLF

Chalmers Golfklubb (✉*Härrydav. 50, Landvetter* ☎*031/918430*) was initially a golf club for Göteborg's Technical University, but is now open to the public. It has an 18-hole course, one of the area's best. All players are welcome, but as with all Swedish courses, you must have a handicap certificate to play. Among the many golf courses surrounding Göteborg, **Göteborgs Golfklubb** (✉*Golfbanev. 17, Hovås* ☎*031/282444*) is Sweden's oldest golf club. It has an 18-hole course.

INDOOR SWIMMING

Hagabadet (✉*Södra Allég. 3, Haga* ☎*031/600600*) is a calming sanctuary with a stunning art-nouveau pool, as well as a relaxing sauna and steam area. For something a little more lively, **Vatten Palatset** (✉*Häradsv. 3, Lerum* ☎*0302/17020*) is a decent indoor pool. As well as regular swimming, this huge complex offers indoor and outdoor adventure pools, waterslides, water jets, wave pools, bubble pools, and saunas.

SHOPPING

DEPARTMENT STORES

Åhléns (☎ 031/3334000), a national chain of mid-priced department stores, is in the Nordstan mall. For something much more upmarket (and more expensive), try the local branch of **NK** (✉ Östra Hamng. 42, Centrum ☎ 031/7101000) for men's and women's fashions and excellent household goods.

SPECIALTY STORES

ANTIQUES

Sweden's leading auction house, **Bukowskis** (✉ Kungsportsavenyn 43, Centrum ☎ 031/200360), is on Avenyn. For a memorable antiques-buying experience, check out **Göteborgs Auktionsverk** (✉ Tredje Långg. 9, Linnéstaden ☎ 031/7047700). There's a large amount of very good silver, porcelain, and jewelry hidden among the more trashy items. Viewings on Friday 10–2, Saturday 10–noon, and Sunday 11–noon precede the auctions on weekends starting at noon.

CRAFTS

If you are looking to buy Swedish arts and crafts and glassware, visit the various shops in **Kronhusbodarna** (✉ Kronhusg. 1D, Nordstan ☎ 031/7110832). They have been selling traditional, handcrafted quality goods, including silver and gold jewelry, watches, and handblown glass, since the 18th century.

MEN'S CLOTHING

Ströms (✉ Kungsg. 27, Centrum ☎ 031/177100) has occupied its street-corner location for two generations, offering clothing of high quality and good taste. **STUK** (✉ Södra Larmg. 16, Centrum ☎ 031/130842) sells what they describe as tailored denim, which means jeans, jackets, and trousers in denim and cotton for the semiformal but fashion-conscious shopper.

WOMEN'S CLOTHING

H & M (Hennes & Mauritz ✉ Kungsg. 55, Centrum ☎ 031/3399555) is perfect for something cheap and fashionable. **Moms** (✉ Vasag. 15, Vasastan ☎ 031/7113280) is a must for trendy street wear, with an excellent range of Nudie Jeans, the cool label born in Göteborg. **Ströms** (✉ Kungsg. 27–29, Centrum ☎ 031/177100) offers clothing of high quality and mildly conservative style.

FOOD MARKETS

There are several large food markets in the city area, but the most impressive is **Saluhallen** (✉ Kungsgtorget, Centrum ☎ 031/7117878). Built in 1889, the barrel-roof, wrought-iron, glass, and brick building stands like a monument to industrial architecture. Everything is available here, from fish, meat, and bakery products to deli foods, herbs and spices, coffee, cheese, and even just people-watching.

BOHUSLÄN

It was from the rocky, rugged shores of Bohuslän that the 9th- and 10th-century Vikings sailed southward on their epic voyages. This coastal region north of Göteborg provides a foretaste of Norway's fjords farther north. Small towns and lovely fishing villages nestle among the distinctively rounded granite rocks and the thousands of skerries (rocky isles or reefs) and larger islands that form Sweden's western archipelago. The ideal way to explore the area is by drifting slowly north of Göteborg, taking full advantage of the uncluttered beaches and small rustic fishing villages. Painters and sailors haunt the region in summer.

MARSTRAND

17 km (11 mi) west of Kungälv (via Rte. 168).

Unusually high stocks of herring used to swim in the waters around Marstrand, which is on an island of the same name. The fish made the town extremely rich. But after the money came greed and corruption: in the 16th century Marstrand became known as the most immoral town in Scandinavia, a reputation that reached its lowest point with the murder of a town cleric in 1586. Soon after this the town burned down and the fish disappeared. As Göteborg and Kungälv became major trade centers, in the early 19th century Marstrand turned to tourism. By 1820 all the town's wooden herring-salting houses had been turned into fashionable and lucrative bathhouses, and people still come to dip into the clear, blue waters and swim, sail, and fish.

GETTING HERE AND AROUND

The best way to explore Bohuslän is by car, and that holds for Marstrand. The E6 highway runs the length of the coast from Göteborg north to Strömstad, close to the Norwegian border, and for campers there are numerous well-equipped and uncluttered camping sites along the coast's entire length.

Buses to the region, including Marstrand, leave from behind the central train station in Göteborg; the main bus company is Västtrafik. The trip all the way through to Strömstad takes between two and three hours.

Regular train service along the coast connects all the major towns of Bohuslän. A train trip takes less time than the bus, but prices reflect this. Still, there's nothing quite like a train ride; for schedules call SJ.

ESSENTIALS

Bus Contact Västtrafik (☎ 0771/414300).

Tourist Info Göteborg Turistbyrå (✉ Kungsportsplatsen 2, Göteborg ☎ 031/612500 ⊕ www.goteborg.com). **Marstrand** (✉ Södra Strandg. 5 ☎ 0303/239940).

Train Contact SJ (✉ Göteborg ☎ 0771/757575 ⊕ www.sj.se).

EXPLORING MARSTRAND

Marstrand's main draw is **Carlstens Fästning,** the huge stone-wall castle that stands on the rock above the town. Tours of Carlstens Fortress are not completely in English, but most guides are more than willing to translate. The tours include a morbidly fascinating look at the castle's prison cells, where you can see drawings done in blood and hear tales of Carlstens's most famous prisoner, Lasse-Maja—he dressed up as a woman to seduce and then rob local farmers. ☎*0303/60265* ⊠*SKr 70* ☉*June–mid-Aug., daily 11–6; mid-Aug.–end of Aug., daily noon–4; Sept.–May, weekends 11–4.*

WHERE TO STAY

$$ 🏨 **Grand Hotell Marstrand.** History and luxury abound in this tile-roof hotel, which resembles a French château. Large balconies and verandas open onto a small park, beyond which lies the North Sea. Inside, the hotel is stylishly simple, with bold colors and clean Scandinavian furniture. The rooms are equally light and airy, and the bathrooms have white tiles and brass fittings. A windowed sauna in one of the towers looks out over the harbor. The traditional restaurant ($$) serves excellent local seafood specialties; the crayfish, simply boiled with dill, is a standout. **Pros:** wonderful historical building, great location. **Cons:** the grandeur here is faded in places. ⊠*Rådhusg. 2* ☎*0303/60322* ⊕*www. grandmarstrand.se* ⇄*22 rooms, 6 suites* ♿*In-room: Internet. In-hotel: restaurant, bar* ⊟*AE, DC, MC, V* ⊚❘*BP.*

$ 🏨 **Hotell Nautic.** This basic but good hotel is right on the harbor. The rooms are quite plain but functional, with wood floors and a small desk and chair. The building is a classic white-clapboard construction. **Pros:** perfect location, loads of nearby activities. **Cons:** rooms quite small. ⊠*Långg. 6* ☎*0303/61030* ⊕*www.hotellnautic.com* ⇄*29 rooms* ⊟*AE, DC, MC, V* ⊚❘*BP.*

SPORTS AND THE OUTDOORS

The coastline around Marstrand looks most beautiful from the water. **Franckes Marina** (⊠*Södra Strandg.* ☎*0303/61584* ⊕*www.franckes.se*) will rent you a boat, complete with captain, for cocktails, sightseeing, and fishing. It costs about SKr 2,00 for a two-hour excursion and SKr 650 for each additional hour. Fishing equipment is available for SKr 100 per person.

SHOPPING

The center of Marstrand is full of ancient cobbled streets, pastel-painted wooden houses, and arts-and-crafts shops selling locally inspired paintings, handicrafts, and ceramics. Else Langkilde of **Konstmärsateljé Langkilde** (⊠*Myren 71* ☎*0703/965131*) paints intriguingly with vivid colors.

LYSEKIL

30 km (19 mi) west of Uddevalla via E6 and Rte. 161.

Perched on a peninsula at the head of Gullmarn Fjord, Lysekil has been one of Sweden's most popular summer resorts since the 19th century, when the wealthiest citizens of Sweden would come to take the therapeutic waters. Back then, the small resort was made up mainly of fancy villas painted mustard and brown. Today you can still see the original houses, but among them now are amusement arcades and cotton-candy stalls.

GETTING HERE AND AROUND

Taking the E6 highway along the length of the coast from Göteborg north to road 162 for Lysekil is the most convenient way to travel here. You'll need to take the free ferry across Gullmarsfjord; it runs approximately every 20 minutes, and the crossing itself takes about 10 minutes. For campers there are numerous well-equipped and uncluttered camping sites along the E6.

Alternately, buses to the region leave from behind the central train station in Göteborg; the main bus company is Västtrafik.

Regular train service along the coast connects all the major towns of Bohuslän. The trip from Göteborg to Uddevalla is short and pleasant, but you'll need to transfer in Uddevalla for the shuttle bus to Lysekil. For schedules call SJ.

ESSENTIALS

Bus Contact Västtrafik (☎*0771/414300*).

Tourist Info Lysekil (✉*Södra Hamng. 6* ☎*0523/13050*). **Göteborg Turistbyrå** (✉*Kungsportsplatsen 2, Göteborg* ☎*031/612500* ⊕*www.goteborg.com*).

Train Contact SJ (✉*Göteborg* ☎*0771/757575* ⊕*www.sj.se*).

EXPLORING LYSEKIL

The surrounding coastline has great, rugged walking trails. These trails offer stunning views of the undulating skerries and islets that dot the water below. Guided botanical and marine walks can be organized by the **tourist office** (☎*0523/13050*).

Take any of the many flights of steps that start from Lysekil's main seafront road to get to **Lysekils Kyrka** *(Lysekil Church)*. Probably the town's most impressive landmark, Lysekil Church was carved from the pink granite of the area and has beaten-copper doors. Its windows were painted by Albert Eldh, the early-20th-century artist. ✉*Stora Kyrkog*.

Twenty minutes north of Lysekil on Route 162 is **Nordens Ark.** A cut above the usual safari parks, Nordens Ark is a sanctuary for endangered animals. This haven of tranquillity is home to red pandas, lynxes, snow leopards, and arctic foxes. The best way to see the elusive wild animals is to follow the small truck that delivers their food at feeding times. ✉*Åby Säteri, Hunnebostrand* ☎*0523/79590* ⊕*www.nordensark.se* 🎫*SKr 150* ☉*Mar.–mid-June, daily 10–5; mid-June–mid-Aug., daily 10–7; mid-Aug.–Oct., daily 10–5; Nov.–Feb., daily 10–4.*

OFF THE BEATEN PATH

Smögen. At the very tip of a westerly outcrop of land, Smögen is an ideal point for a quick stopover. To get here, head north on Route 162 and then west on Route 171 until it stops. The small village's red fishing huts, crystal-blue water, and pretty scrubbed boardwalks appear on many postcards of Bohuslän.

WHERE TO EAT AND STAY

$–$$
SEAFOOD
Fodor'sChoice
★

✕**Brygghuset.** A short boat ride and a walk through a breathtaking hilltop fishing village on the island of Fiskebäckskil will bring you to this lovely little restaurant. The interior is rustic, with wooden beams and plain wooden tables. Watch the chefs in the open kitchen as they prepare excellent local fish dishes. The ferry *Carl Wilhelmsson* leaves from outside the tourist office in Lysekil every half hour, bringing you to the restaurant 20 minutes later. ✉*Lyckans Slip, Fiskebäckskil* ☎*0523/22222* ⚓*Reservations essential* ⊟*AE, DC, MC, V.*

$$
SEAFOOD

✕**Prämen.** This modern-looking restaurant has large windows and is propped on legs that allow it to jut out over the water. The view is great; with the windows open you can smell the sea. You can feast on good portions of simply cooked local fish and wash it down with cold beer. ✉*Södra Hamng.* ☎*0523/13452* ⊟*AE, DC, MC, V.*

$

⌕**Lysekil Havshotell.** This tall, narrow hotel has great views from atop a cliff. Stripped-wood floors and a miscellany of furnishings and fabrics create relaxed surroundings. Many rooms have sofas and provide bathrobes. Only breakfast is served, and there's a stocked bar (done on the honor system) in each room. For the best view across the water, reserve Room 18, which costs SKr 200 extra. **Pros:** wonderful location; fantastic views. **Cons:** limited facilities; some rooms very small. ✉*Turistg. 13* ☎*0523/79750* ⊕*www.strandflickorna.se* ⟿*15 rooms, 2 suites* ⚲*In-room: Internet* ⊟*AE, MC, V* ⦿*BP.*

¢

⌕**Strand Vandrarhem.** This hostel on the seafront offers simple, friendly accommodations. Unless you stipulate otherwise and pay an additional fee, you may find yourself sharing the room with another guest (the rooms are outfitted with bunk beds). The welcome here is warm, and the breakfast (SKr 50 extra) is excellent. **Pros:** very friendly and welcoming; great location. **Cons:** no facilities; limited privacy. ✉*Strandv. 1* ☎*0523/79751* ⊕*www.strandflickorna.se* ⟿*20 rooms* ⊟*MC, V.* ⦿*EP.*

NIGHTLIFE AND THE ARTS

In July Lysekil comes alive to the sounds of the annual **Lysekil Jazz Festival.** Big-name Swedish, and some international, jazz musicians play in open-air concerts and in bars and restaurants. Contact **Lysekils Turistbyrå** (*Tourist office* ☎*0523/13050*) for details of events.

SPORTS AND THE OUTDOORS

For a taste of the sea air and a great look at some local nature, take one of the regular seal safaris. Boat trips to view these fascinating, wallowing, slippery mammals leave from the main harbor three times daily between June and August, cost SKr 130, and take about two hours. Details and times are available from **Lysekils Turistbyrå** (☎*0523/13050*).

STRÖMSTAD

90 km (56 mi) northwest of Uddevalla, 169 km (105 mi) north of Göteborg.

This popular Swedish resort claims to have more summer sunshine than any other town north of the Alps. Formerly Norwegian, it has been the site of many battles between warring Danes, Norwegians, and Swedes. A short trip over the Norwegian border takes you to Halden, where Sweden's warrior king, Karl XII, died in 1718.

GETTING HERE AND AROUND
The E6 highway runs all the way up to Strömstad from Göteborg, and the views can't be beat. Campsites dot the route; you can take three hours or three days to get here.

Buses to the Strömstad leave from behind the central train station in Göteborg; the main bus company is Västtrafik. The trip takes between two and three hours.

The train trip from Göteborg to Strömstad takes about two hours, and there are several trains each day. For schedules call SJ.

ESSENTIALS
Bus Contact Västtrafik (☎ *0771/414300).*

Tourist Info Göteborg Turistbyrå (✉ *Kungsportsplatsen 2, Göteborg* ☎ *031/612500* ⊕ *www.goteborg.com).* **Strömstad** (✉ *Torget, Norra Hamnen* ☎ *0526/62330* ⊕ *www.stromstadtourist.se).*

Train Contact SJ (✉ *Göteborg* ☎ *0771/757575* ⊕ *www.sj.se).*

EXPLORING STRÖMSTAD
Although it is of no particular historical importance, **Strömstads Kyrka** is well worth a visit just to marvel at its interior design. The Strömstad Church's seemingly free-form decoration policy throws together wonderfully detailed, crowded frescoes; overly ornate gilt chandeliers; brass lamps from the 1970s; and model ships hanging from the roof. ✉ *S. Kyrkog. 10* ☎ *0526/28500.*

WHERE TO EAT AND STAY

$$ ✕ **Göstases.** Somewhat resembling the interior of a wooden boat, this
SEAFOOD restaurant on the quayside specializes in locally caught fish and seafood. Knots, ropes, life preservers, stuffed fish, and similar paraphernalia abound. But it all pales when you see the low prices for fresh lobster, crab, prawns, and fish, all of which can be washed down with equally affordable cold beer. Sit outside in summer and watch the fishing boats bring in your catch and the pleasure boats float by. ✉ *Strandpromenaden* ☎ *0526/10812* ⊟ *MC, V.*

$$ 🛏 **Quality Spa and Resort Strömstad.** This newly opened spa hotel has proved a huge hit with relaxation seekers from all over Sweden. Rooms are large, light-filled and simply and tastefully furnished. Most have stunning views across the water; the larger rooms feature sitting areas and balconies, perfect for those long Swedish summer evenings. The spa is large and offers a comprehensive range of treatments from single treatments to weekend packages. Relaxation is guaranteed. **Pros:** great location; large rooms. **Cons:** can get very crowded during summer months. ✉ *Kebal 9* ☎ *0526/630300* ⊕ *www.stromstadspa.se* ⇘ *232 rooms, 116 suites* ⚭ *In-room: refrigerator, Wi-Fi. In-hotel: restaurant, bar, room service, spa, laundry service, parking (free), no-smoking rooms* ⊟ *AE, DC, MC, V* ⦿ *BP.*

SWEDISH RIVIERA

The coastal region south of Göteborg, Halland—locally dubbed the Swedish Riviera—is the closest that mainland Sweden comes to having a resort area. Fine beaches abound, and there are plenty of sporting activities. But Halland's history is dark, since it was the front line in the fighting between Swedes and Danes. Evidence of such conflicts can be found in its many medieval villages and fortifications. The region stretches down to Båstad, in the country's southernmost province, Skåne.

GETTING HERE AND AROUND

Buses to Falkenberg, Halmstad, and Båstad leave from behind Göteborg's central train station. By car, simply follow the E6/E20 highway south from Göteborg toward Malmö; the highway runs parallel to the coast. Regular train services connect Göteborg's central station with the region's towns, including all three discussed here.

ESSENTIALS

Bus Contacts Hallandstrafiken (☎ 0771/331030 ⊕ www.hlt.se). **Västtrafik** (☎ 0771/414300 ⊕ www.vasttrafik.se).

Car Rental Avis (☎ 031/946030 at Göteborg airport). **Europcar** (☎ 031/947100 in Göteborg, 035/188515 in Halmstad). **Hertz** (☎ 031/946020). **Statoil** (☎ 0431/70327 in Båstad).

Train Contact SJ (✉ Göteborg ☎ 0771/757575 ⊕ www.sj.se).

Visitor and Tour Info Båstad (✉ Köpmansg. 1 ☎ 0431/75045). **Falkenberg** (✉ Holgersg.11 ☎ 0346/886100). **Halmstad** (✉ Halmstad Slott ☎ 035/132320).

FALKENBERG

30 km (20 mi) south of Varberg, 100 km (60 mi) south of Göteborg.

With its attractive beaches and the plentiful salmon that swim in the Ätran River, Falkenberg is one of Sweden's most attractive resorts. Its Gamla Stan (Old Town) is full of narrow cobblestone streets and quaint old wooden houses.

EXPLORING FALKENBERG

Doktorspromenaden, on the south side of the river in the town center, is a beautiful walk set against a backdrop of heathland and shade trees. The walk was set up in 1861 by a local doctor in an effort to encourage the townsfolk to get more fresh air. ✉ Doktorspromenaden.

Although it does have the usual archaeological and historical artifacts depicting its town's growth and development, the **Falkenberg Museum** also has an unusual and refreshing obsession with the 1950s. The curator here thinks that is the most interesting period of history, and you can make up your own mind once you've learned about the local dance-band scene, visited the interior of a shoe-repair shop, and seen a collection of old jukeboxes. ✉ Skepparesträtet 2 ☎ 0346/886125 ▥ Free ⊙ June–Aug., Tues.–Sun. noon–4; Sept.–Oct., Tues.–Sat. noon–4.

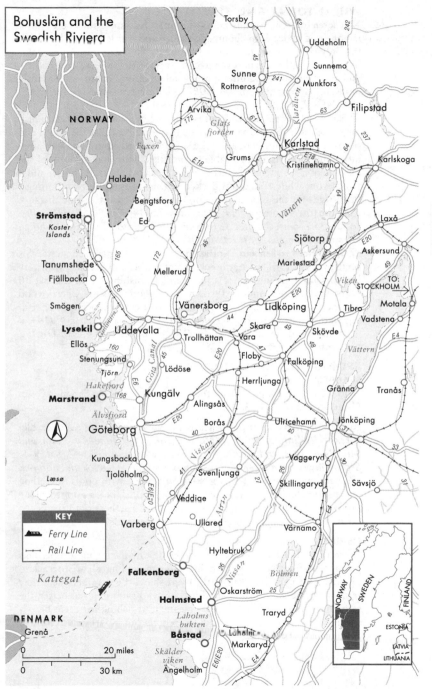

Bohuslän and the Swedish Riviera

NORWAY

Torsby

Uddeholm

Sunnemo

Sunne
Rottneros

Munkfors

Arvika

Filipstad

Glafs fjorden

Faxen

Grums

Karlstad

Kristinehamn

Karlskoga

Halden

Bengtsfors

Vänern

Strömstad
Koster
Islands

Ed

Sjötorp

Laxå

5

Tanumshede

Mariestad

Askersund

Fjällbacka

Mellerud

Viken
TO:
STOCKHOLM →

Smögen

Vänersborg

Lidköping

Tibro

Motala

Lysekil
Uddevalla

Skara

Skövde

Vadstena

Ellös

Trollhättan

Vara

Vättern

Stenungsund

Floby

Falköping

E4

Tjörn

Lödöse

Herrljunga

Hakefjord

Kungälv

Gränna

Tranås

Marstrand

Alingsås

Älvsfjord

Göteborg

Borås

Ulricehamn

Jönköping

Kungsbacka

Vaggeryd

Læsø

Tjolöholm

Svenljunga

Skillingaryd

Sävsjö

Veddige

Värnamo

KEY

Varberg

Ullared

Ferry Line

Rail Line

Hyltebruk

Kattegat

Falkenberg

Bolmen

Oskarström

Halmstad

Traryd

DENMARK

Laholms bukten

Grenå

Båstad

Laholm

Markaryd

0   20 miles

Skälder viken

0   30 km

Ängelholm

NORWAY   SWEDEN   FINLAND

ESTONIA

LATVIA
LITHUANIA

WHERE TO EAT AND STAY

$$ **✕ Källaren Lax.** The food is perhaps a little over ambitious here (think
SCANDINAVIAN lemon-fried plaice with champagne sauce and truffle butter), but that's
the only complaint you could throw at it. The menu uses (and cred-
its) local suppliers wherever it can, service is faultess, and helpful
and the refurbished, contemporary cellar dining room is pleasantly
modern. ✉ *Storg. 34* ☎ *0346/10874* � *Reservations essential* ▭ *AE,
DC, MC, V.*

$$ **▥ Elite Hotel Strandbaden.** A sprawling, white wood-and-glass building, Elite Hotel Strandbaden sits right on the beach at the south end
of town. The rooms here are quite small but well equipped, with amenities and modern, comfortable furnishings. Most have a view of the
sea. There is a state-of-the-art spa and health club in the hotel, and a
worth-your-while restaurant decked out in startling blue and orange.
Pros: right on the beach; very good restaurant. **Cons:** some distance
from the town center. ✉ *Havsbadsallén* ☎ *0346/714900* ⊕ *www.elite.
se* ↩ *135 rooms, 5 suites* ⚷ *In-room: refrigerator, Internet. In-hotel:
restaurant, bar, spa, gym* ▭ *AE, DC, MC, V* ⦿ *BP.*

$ **▥ Grand Hotel Falkenberg.** Not as imposing as the name suggests, this
pretty, yellow, 19th-century hotel is comfortable and friendly, with very
large rooms. The interior is a jumble of furnishings from the last 30
years, with the odd antique thrown in for good measure. Cherrywood
and rich fabrics are used throughout. **Pros:** central location; charming staff. **Cons:** noisy on the weekend. ✉ *Hotellg. 1* ☎ *0346/14450*
⊕ *www.grandhotelfalkenberg.se* ↩ *70 rooms, 3 suites* ⚷ *In-hotel: 2
restaurants, bars* ▭ *AE, DC, MC, V* ⦿ *BP.*

SPORTS AND THE OUTDOORS

BEACHES

A 15-minute walk south from the town center is **Skrea Strand,** a 3-km
(2-mi) stretch of sandy beach.

At the northern end of the beach is the huge swimming complex **Klit-
terbadet** (✉ *Klitterv.* ☎ *0346/886330* ▧ *SKr 35* ⊙ *June–Aug., Sun. and
Mon. 9–4, Tues. and Thurs. 6 AM–7 PM, Wed. and Fri. 9–7, Sat. 9–5;
Sept.–May, Mon. 4 PM–8 PM, Tues. and Thurs. 6 AM–8 AM and noon–8,
Wed. noon–8, Fri. noon–7, Sat. 9–5, Sun. 9–3*), with pools (including
one just for children), waterslides, a sauna, a whirlpool, a 50-meter-long
pool with heated seawater, and steam rooms. Farther south the beach
opens out onto some secluded coves and grasslands.

FISHING

In the 1800s Falkenberg had some of the best fly-fishing in Europe. This
prompted a frenzy of fishermen, including many English aristocrats, to
plunder its waters. But despite the overfishing, the Ätran is one of few
remaining rivers in Europe inhabited by wild salmon; even better, the
salmon are there in numbers that mean sport-fishing for them here is
sustainable. Fishing permits and rod rentals can be arranged through
the local **tourist office** (☎ *0346/886100*).

SHOPPING

Törngrens (⊠*Nyg. 32* ☎*0346/10354* ۞ *Weekdays 9–5*) is probably the oldest pottery shop in Scandinavia, and is now owned by the seventh generation of the founding family. Call ahead to make sure the shop is open.

HALMSTAD

40 km (25 mi) south of Falkenberg, 143 km (89 mi) south of Göteborg.

With a population of 55,000, Halmstad is the largest seaside resort on the west coast. The Norre Port town gate, all that remains of the town's original fortifications, dates from 1605. The modern town hall has interior decorations by the so-called Halmstad Group of painters, which formed here in 1929.

EXPLORING HALMSTAD

Most of Halmstad's architectural highlights are in and around **Stora Torget**, the large town square. In the middle is the fountain *Europa and the Bull*, by the sculptor Carl Milles. Around the square are many buildings and merchants' houses dating from Halmstad's more prosperous days in the last half of the 19th century.

★ The bizarre **Martin Luthers Kyrka** is unique among churches. Built entirely out of steel in the 1970s, its exterior resembles that of a shiny tin can. The interior is just as striking, as the gleaming outside gives way to rust-orange steel and art-deco furnishings that contrast with the outside. To some, Martin Luther Church may seem more like a temple to design, not deity. ⊠*Långg.* ☎*035/151961* ۞ *Weekdays 9–3, Sun. services at 10.*

In the 1930s the Halmstad Group, made up of six local artists, caused some consternation with their surrealist and cubist painting styles, influenced strongly by such artists as René Magritte and Salvador Dalí. The **Mjellby Konstmuseum** *(Mjellby Arts Museum)* contains some of the most important works created over the group's 50-year alliance. ⊠*Mjellby* ✚*4 km (2½ mi) from Halmstad* ☎*035/137195* ⊠*SKr 50* ۞ *Mar.–Oct., daily 1–5; July, daily 11–5.*

WHERE TO EAT AND STAY

$$

SCANDINAVIAN

✕ **Pio Matsal Bar.** Half informal bar and half bistro, this restaurant offers something for all. It's a bright and airy place with good service and excellent Swedish classics on the menu—the steak and mashed potatoes is wonderful. The list of drinks is extensive. ⊠*Storg. 37* ☎*035/210669* ⊟*AE, DC, MC, V.*

$

🏨 **Hotel Continental.** Built in 1903 in the national romantic style, the interior of this hotel has been nicely preserved. The sophisticated design includes exposed-brick walls, subtle spotlighting, and light wood fittings. The rooms are bright, modern, and spacious. Five rooms have whirlpool baths. **Pros:** exceptionally personal service; freshly baked bread for breakfast. **Cons:** no restaurant. ⊠*Kungsg. 5* ☎*035/176300* ⊕*www.continental-halmstad.se* ⟿*46 rooms, 3 suites* ⌂*In-room:*

Wi-Fi. In-hotel: bar, spa, Wi-Fi, parking (paid) ⊟*AE, DC, MC, V* ⏐○⏐*BP.*

$$ ⊞ **Scandic Hallandia.** A shiny white-tile floor, white ceiling tiles, and a circular podlike lobby create a strange first impression. But don't be alarmed. Rooms here come with all the space, comfort, modernity, and up-to-date technology you would expect from a Scandinavian hotel. **Pros:** very central; loans out free bikes to guests. **Cons:** lacks atmosphere. ⊠*Rådhusg. 4* ☎*035/2958600* ⊕*www.scandic-hotels.se* ⇘*155 rooms, 1 suite* ⚅*In-room: Internet. In-hotel: restaurant, bar, spa* ⊟*AE, DC, MC, V* ⏐○⏐*BP.*

SPORTS AND THE OUTDOORS

There are many good beaches around Halmstad. **Tjuvahålan,** extending west of Halmstad, has an interesting old smugglers' cove that provides pleasant walking. For details, contact the **tourist office** (☎*035/132320).*

BÅSTAD

35 km (22 mi) south of Halmstad, 178 km (111 mi) south of Göteborg.

In the southernmost province of Skåne, Båstad is regarded by locals as Sweden's most fashionable resort, where ambassadors and local captains of industry have their summerhouses. Aside from this, it is best known for its tennis. In addition to the **Båstad Open,** a grand prix tournament in late summer, there is the annual **Donald Duck Cup** in July, for children from ages 11 to 15; it was the very first trophy won by Björn Borg, who later took the Wimbledon men's singles title five times in a row.

EXPLORING BÅSTAD

Spurred on by Borg and other Swedish champions, such as Stefan Edberg and Mats Wilander, thousands of youngsters take part in the Donald Duck Cup each year. For details, contact the **Svenska Tennisförbundet** (*Swedish Tennis Association* ⊠*Kyrkog 6A* ☎*0431/78390).*

The low-rise shuttered buildings in the center of Båstad give it an almost French provincial feel. In the main square is **St. Maria Kyrka** *(St. Maria's Church)*, which looks much more solidly Swedish. Dating from the 15th century, the plain exterior hides a haven of tranquillity within the cool thick walls. The unusual altar painting depicts Christ on the cross with human skulls and bones strewn beneath him.

Norrviken Gardens, 3 km (2 mi) northwest of Båstad, are beautifully laid out in different styles, including a Japanese garden and a lovely walkway lined with rhododendrons. The creator of the gardens, Rudolf Abelin, is buried on the grounds. A restaurant, shop, and pottery studio are also on the premises. ☎*0431/369040* ⊕*www.norrvikenstradgardar.net* ⊠*SKr 60* ⊙*May–Sept., daily 10–6.*

WHERE TO EAT AND STAY

$$
SWEDISH
✕**Swenson's Krog.** Well worth the 3-km (2-mi) journey out of Båstad, this harbor-front restaurant was originally a fisherman's hut and has been converted into a magnificent dining room with cornflower-blue walls, wooden floors, and a glass roof. The menu is full of Swedish classics such as shrimp salad and delicious homemade meatballs. The service is friendly, with the family atmosphere really shining through. ⊠*Pål Romaresg. 2, Torekov* ☎*0431/364590* ⚭*Reservations essential* ☐*AE, DC, MC, V.*

¢'
SCANDINAVIAN
✕**Wooden Hut.** Actually, this restaurant has no name: it's just a wooden hut on the harbor side. It has no tables either. What this restaurant does have is simple and delicious smoked mackerel with potato salad, which will magically take you away from all the pomp and wealth that sometimes bogs Båstad down. Walk past all the hotels and restaurants, smell the fresh sea air, and get ready for a great meal. ⊠*Strandpromenaden* ☎*No phone* ⚭*Reservations not accepted* ☐*No credit cards.*

¢–$
🏨**Hjortens Pensionat.** A classic summer resort hotel, Hjortens Pensionat is Båstad's oldest inn. The antiques-filled rooms are light and the common areas are comfortably cluttered with ornaments and deep armchairs. Right in the center of Båstad, the hotel is close to shops, beaches, and tennis courts. **Pros:** lovely garden. **Cons:** basic facilities. ⊠*Roxmansv. 23* ☎*0431/70109* ⊕*www.hjorten.net* ⚑*42 rooms* ☾*In-hotel: restaurant, bar* ☐*DC, MC, V* ☻*BP.*

$$
🏨**Hotel Skansen.** Set in a century-old bathhouse, Skansen's interior reflects the best of modern design. Wonderfully simple earth, cream, and moss-green tones create a sense of comfort, simplicity, and relaxation. The lovely rooms, many with a glass roof or wall, are all decorated with furniture from Stockholm's cool interior shop R.O.O.M. Restaurant Sand ($–$$), with a sea view, serves stylish and well-prepared Swedish fare, with fish as a specialty. The bar is well stocked and they serve tapas in the lounge. **Pros:** very stylish; great location and food. **Cons:** service can feel a bit impersonal; long lines at checkout. ⊠*Kyrkog. 2* ☎*0431/558100* ⊕*www.hotelskansen.se* ⚑*173 rooms, 1 suite* ☾*In-room: Internet. In-hotel: restaurant, bar, spa* ☐*AE, DC, MC, V* ☻*BP.*

THE SOUTH AND THE KINGDOM OF GLASS

Southern Sweden is considered, even by many Swedes, to be a world of its own, clearly distinguished from the rest of the country by its geography, culture, and history. Skåne (pronounced *skoh*-neh), is one of Sweden's smallest provinces; here you'll find beautifully fertile plains, sand beaches, thriving farms, bustling historic towns and villages, medieval churches, and summer resorts. These gently rolling hills, extensive forests, and fields are broken every few miles by lovely castles, chronologically and architecturally diverse, that have given this part of Sweden the name Château Country.

The two other southern provinces, Blekinge and Halland, are also fertile and rolling and edged by seashores. Historically, these three provinces are distinct from the rest of Sweden: they were the last to be incorporated into the country, having been ruled by Denmark until 1658. They retain the influences of the Continental culture in their architecture, language, and cuisine, viewing the rest of Sweden—especially Stockholm—with some disdain.

Småland, to the north, is larger than the other provinces, with a harsh countryside of stone and woods. The area has many small glassblowing firms, and it is these glassworks, such as the world-renowned Kosta Boda and Orrefors, that have given the area the nickname the Kingdom of Glass.

Since it covers a fairly large area of the country, this region is best explored by car. The coastal road is a pleasure to travel on, with scenic views of long, sandy beaches and the welcoming blue sea. Inland, the hills, fertile plains, and thickly wooded forests are interconnected by winding country roads. The southern peninsula around the province of Skåne has the most urban settlements and, thanks to the spectacular Øresund Bridge, fast connections to Denmark and mainland Europe.

MÖLLE

★ *35 km (21 mi) northwest of Helsingborg, 220 km (132 mi) south of Göteborg, 235 km (141 mi) southwest of Växjö, 95 km (57 mi) northwest of Malmö.*

Mölle, in the far northwest of Skåne, is a small town set in spectacular isolation on the dramatic headland of the Kulla Peninsula. It is an old fishing village with a beautiful harbor that sweeps up to the Kullaberg Range. You will find beech forests, stupefying views, and rugged shores and beaches, surrounded on three sides by sea.

For those who love nature or want a break from cities and touring, Mölle is perfect. Not only is it a good base from which to explore, but the town itself has a charm that has never been tarnished by an overabundance of tourists or a relentless drive to modernize at all costs.

Today it is a relatively wealthy place, as the elaborate residences and the upmarket cars crowding the narrow streets show. Much of this wealth supposedly arrived when the more fortunate men of the sea returned to build mansions.

GETTING HERE AND AROUND

By car, take the E6 road south from Göteborg (or north from Malmö or E6's junction with the E4, which runs to Stockholm), then road 112 west in to Mölle. The closest places to rent a car are Helsingborg or Malmö, where the major companies have offices. To get here by rail, you need to first go to nearby Helsingborg, which has connections to most major towns and cities, then take one of the hourly buses into Mölle. Mölle itself is very compact and walkable; the tourist office for Mölle, though, is located in Höganäs, a few miles down the coast.

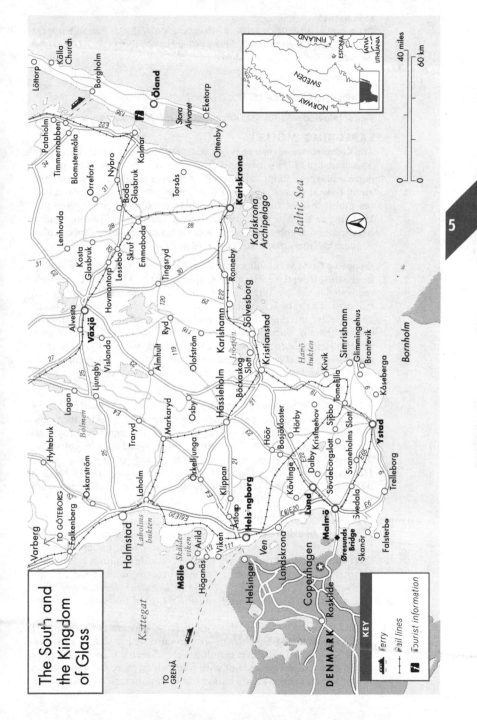

The South and the Kingdom of Glass

KEY

- ⛴ Ferry
- ┼┼┼ Rail lines
- 🛈 Tourist information

Baltic Sea

Bornholm

DENMARK

Copenhagen

Roskilde

Øresunds Bridge

Malmö

Lund

Helsingborg

Ystad

Kristianstad

Karlskrona

Karlskrona Archipelago

Växjö

Kalmar

Öland

Halmstad

Mölle

ESSENTIALS

Car Rental Avis (☎ *042/157080 in Helsingborg, 040/77830 in Malmö*). **Europcar** (☎ *042/170115 in Helsingborg, 040/71640 in Malmö*). **Hertz** (☎ *042/172540 in Helsingborg, 040/330770 in Malmö*).

Emergencies (☎ 112).

Train Travel SJ (☎ *0771/757575* ⊕ *www.sj.se*).

Visitor Info Höganäs Tourist Office (☎ *042/337774* ⊕ *www.hoganas.se*).

EXPLORING MÖLLE

The **Kullaberg nature reserve** is just outside Mölle and covers more than 35 square km (13½ square mi). You can walk, bike, or drive in. This natural playground includes excellent trails through beech forests and along coastal routes. There's a lighthouse here set in stark land that resembles that of the Scottish Highlands—it even has long-haired Highland cattle. The park contains cafés, a restaurant, safe swimming beaches, and a golf course that's one of Sweden's most spectacular. ⊕ *www.kullabergsnatur.se* ⊠ *SKr 40 per car.*

Krapperup Castle was built in 1570 over the ruins of a medieval stronghold dating from the 13th century. The present building was extensively renovated in the late 18th century, although remnants of the stronghold still exist. The garden is among Sweden's best-preserved parks. There's an art gallery and museum inside, and concerts and performance theater are held here in summer. It is 4 km (2½ mi) from Mölle on the main road to Helsingborg. ☎ *042/344190* ⊠ *Castle tours for groups of 10 minimum: SKr 80 gallery, museum SKr 40* ☉ *Call to book castle tour for group; gallery and museum May and Sept., weekends 1–6; June–Aug., daily 1–6.*

The haunting **Nimis and Arx** artworks are built of scrap wood and stone and stand on a rugged beach that can be reached only on foot. The artist Lars Vilks has been working on the weird, highly controversial structures since the 1970s. They are the most visited sight in Kullaberg. ⊠ *Head 2 km (1 mi) east out of Mölle to a road sign directing you to Himmelstorps Hembygdsgård. Following this sign you will reach a parking lot and an old farmhouse. From here it is a 1-km (½-mi) walk marked by small blue N symbols* ⊕ *www.turism.hoganas.se.*

WHERE TO EAT AND STAY

¢ 🔝 **Bed and Breakfast Solgården.** Run by an artistic woman who splits her year between here and a B&B in the South Pacific nation of Tonga, this quaint pension hosts poetry readings outside in summer. **Pros:** free Internet; bike hire available. **Cons:** small rooms; doesn't feel private. ⊠ *Byav. 102, Lerberget* ☎ *042/330430* ⊕ *www.solgarden-lerberget. se* ᐃ *In-room: Wi-Fi. In-hotel: Wi-Fi* ☉ *Closed mid-Sept.–mid-Apr.* ⦿ *BP.*

$$ 🔝 **Grand Hôtel.** The spectacular Grand Hôtel—a turreted building set high up on a hill above the town—has an unrivaled setting, great views, and a helpful staff. The best rooms are those with a sea view, but they are all pleasant and decked out with fresh white, blue, and aquamarine prints. For dining you have a choice of two restaurants: Maritime is the

hotel's main restaurant, serving excellent quality gourmet dishes. Seaside has a publike atmosphere and serves great food that's a little easier on the wallet than Maritime's; head out to the terrace for spectacular views. Pros: glorious views; spectacular setting Cons: some rooms are small and oddly shaped; it's a long climb to the hotel from down in the harbor. ⊠*Bökebolsv. 11* ☎*042/362230* ⊕*www.grand-molle.se* ⊐*42 rooms* ⚹*In-hotel: 2 restaurants, bar* ⊟*AE, D, MC, V* ⑩*BP.*

$$ 🚾 **Hotel Kullaberg.** At this luxurious hotel all the rooms are plush and decorated in themes. One room suggests *Out of Africa,* and another has a large biplane hanging from the ceiling. You may or may not love it, depending on your feelings about kitsch. Either way, there's no denying the Kullaberg is lush, and the views of the sea and the harbor are tough to beat. Take time to visit the ornate reading rooms and enjoy the personalized service. The main dining room here—with it's glassed-in veranda, white linen and fine silverware—is a throwback to gentler times. The more informal, marine-themed bar and brasserie looks like the sort of place Hemingway would have approved of. Pros: extremely personal service; best bar and restaurant in town. Cons: the busy interior design can be overwhelming. ⊠*Gyllenstiernas Allé 16* ☎*042/347000* ⊕*www.hotelkullaberg.se* ⊐*18 rooms* ⚹*In-room: Wi-Fi. In-hotel: 2 restaurants, bar, Wi-Fi* ⊟*AE, DC, MC, V* ⑩*BP.*

SPORTS

The **Skola Mölle Hamn** (⊠*Special Sports School, Södra Strandv. 6B* ☎*042/347705 or 070/3771210*) caters to most outdoor activities. It organizes trips and provides gear and training for mountaineers, scuba divers, and kayakers of all skill levels.

HELSINGBORG

221 km (137 mi) south of Göteborg, 186 km (116 mi) southwest of Växjö, 64 km (40 mi) north of Malmö.

Helsingborg, with a population of 120,000, may seem to the first-time visitor little more than a small town with a modern ferry terminal (there are about 125 daily ferry connections to Denmark and one a day to Norway). But the town has an illustrious history. Together with its twin town, Helsingør (Elsinore in William Shakespeare's *Hamlet*), across the Øresund, it controlled shipping traffic in and out of the Baltic for centuries—and there are even a few interesting sights, as well as a healthy selection dining and lodging options.

GETTING HERE AND AROUND

Helsingborg is easily accessible by car, directly from both the E4 and E6 motorways. There are direct rail connections from both Stockholm and Göteborg and long distance bus connections from several towns and cities. If you are traveling from Denmark, there are several regular direct links to Helsingør via ferry. Once in Helsingborg, there is a good local bus network for getting around.

ESSENTIALS

Boat and Ferry Contacts ACE Link (☎ *042/385880* ⊕ *www.acelink.se*). **HH-Ferries** (☎ *042/198000* ⊕ *www.hhferries.se*). **Scandlines** (☎ *0410/65000* ⊕ *www.scandlines.se*).

Bus Travel Skåne Trafik (⊕ *www.skanetrafiken.se*).

Car Rental Avis (☎ *042/157080*). **Europcar** (☎ *042/170115*). **Hertz** (☎ *042/172540*).

Emergencies (☎ *112*).

Train Contact SJ (☎ *0771/757575* ⊕ *www.sj.se*).

Visitor Info Helsingborg (✉ *Södra Storg. 1* ☎ *042/104350* ⊕ *www.helsing borgsguiden.com*).

EXPLORING HELSINGBORG

All that remains of Helsingborg's castle is **Kärnan** (the Keep), which was built in the late 14th century. It has walls 15 feet thick. This surviving center tower, built to provide living quarters and defend the medieval castle, is one of the most remarkable relics of its kind in the north. The interior is divided into several floors, which contain a chapel, an exhibition of kitchen implements, old castle fittings, and some weaponry. ✉ *Slottshagen* ☎ *042/105991* ☎ *SKr 20* ⊙ *Jan.–Mar., Tues.–Sun. 11–3; Apr. and May, Tues.–Fri. 9–4, weekends 11–4; June–Aug., daily 11–7; Sept., Tues.–Fri. 9–4, weekends 11–4; Oct.–Dec., Tues.–Sun. 11—3.*

Maria Kyrkan *(St. Mary's)*, begun in the early 14th century and finished 100 years later, is a fine example of Danish Gothic architecture. St. Mary's has several highlights: the 15th-century reredos, the silver treasure in the sacristy, and a memorial plaque to Dietrich Buxtehude (1637–1707), a prominent German composer as well as the church's organist. ✉ *Mariatorget, Södra Storg. 20* ☎ *042/372830* ⊙ *Aug.–June, daily 8–4; July, daily 8–6.*

Helsingborg's refurbished harborside area, **Norra Hamnen** *(Northern Harbor)*, has a pleasant marina with a string of architecturally impressive cafés and restaurants.

Fodor's Choice
★ In 1865 **Sofiero Slott** (Sofiero Palace) was built in Dutch Renaissance style by Prince Oscar and his wife, Sofia, as a summer home. Half a century later Oscar II gave the palace to his grandson, Gustav Adolf, and his wife, Margareta, as a wedding gift. Since the estate is now owned by the city of Helsingborg, you can gain access to Sofiero's park, a haven for more than 10,000 samples of 300 kinds of rhododendron, various statues donated by international artists, and a large English garden; nearby greenhouses have plant exhibits. A café and fine restaurant are on the grounds. ✉ *Sofierov., on road to Laröd* ☎ *042/137400* ☎ *SKr 80* ⊙ *Mid-Apr.–Sept., daily 11–5; guided tours only. Park, restaurant, and café open year-round.*

WHERE TO EAT

$$
★
SEAFOOD ✕ **Pålsjö Krog.** Beside the pier that leads out to the Pålsjö Bath House, this restaurant offers a beautiful view of the Øresund. The owners have partially restored the restaurant to its original 1930s style—note the

antique sofa in the lounge and the art on the walls. Seafood is the specialty in summer months, game in winter. Reservations are essential in summer. ⊠*Drottningg. 151* ☎*042/149730* ⊟*AE, DC, MC, V.*

$$ ✗**Restaurang La Petite.** If you are yearning for the delicacy of French cuisine and the genuine look and feel of a French restaurant, then look no further. La Petite has been here since 1975, suggesting success, and can also indulge the diner in Spanish and international meals. ⊠*Bruksg. 19* ☎*042/219727* ⊟*AE, DC, MC, V* ☉*Closed Sun.*

FRENCH

$$ ✗**SS Swea.** Those with a nautical bent or nostalgia for past traveling days will be well served at this restaurant ship modeled after cruise liners of old. The docked boat specializes in fresh seafood and international menus. Enjoy the wide-ranging menu but don't forget to disembark—there are no cabin bunks here. ⊠*Kungstorget* ☎*042/131516* ⊟*AE, DC, MC, V.*

SEAFOOD

WHERE TO STAY

$$ ⊞**Elite Hotel Mollberg.** Only a short walk from the central station, the Mollberg has spacious rooms with hardwood floors and large windows. Corner rooms have balconies that overlook a cobblestone square. The restaurant offers dining at reasonable prices. **Pros:** close to bus, train, and ferry terminals; classy service; good deals for early booking. **Cons:** narrow beds; some noise on lower floors. ⊠*Stortorget 18* ☎*042/373700* ⊕*www.elite.se* ↪*104 rooms, 7 suites* ⚲*In-room: refrigerator, Wi-Fi. In-hotel: restaurant, bar, room service, laundry service, parking (paid), no-smoking rooms* ⊟*AE, DC, MC, V* ⏺❙*BP.*

$$ ⊞**Radisson SAS Grand Hotel.** One of Sweden's oldest hotels has been completely renovated, maintaining its long-standing reputation for excellence. Public areas here are, as the name suggests, grand, with dark-wood paneling, chandeliers, and a mix of contemporary furniture and antiques. The smell of fresh flowers fills the hotel. Rooms are very well equipped to offer relaxed decadence; floors are rich, dark wood and fabrics, chairs, and cushions are lush brown and soft beige. Sleeping comfortably here is no problem. **Pros:** big rooms; luxury at a good price. **Cons:** can't open the shampoo without spilling it. ⊠*Stortorget 8–12* ☎*042/380400* ⊕*www.helsingborg.radissonsas.com* ↪*164 rooms, 8 suites* ⚲*In-room: refrigerator, Wi-Fi. In-hotel: restaurant, room service, bar, gym, Wi-Fi, no-smoking rooms* ⊟*AE, DC, MC, V* ⏺❙*BP.*

Fodor'sChoice
★

¢ ⊞**Villa Thalassa.** This youth hostel 3 km (2 mi) from the city center has fine views over Øresund. In the main building and in bungalow-style buildings, all with private patios, there are 172 bunks in two-, four-, and six-bunk rooms. The SKr 55 breakfast is not included. **Pros:** private patio, smoke-free. **Cons:** a little far from town; not all rooms have TV. ⊠*Dag Hammarskjölds väg* ☎*042/380660* ⊕*www.villathalassa. com* ↪*172 beds in 54 rooms* ⚲*In-room: no TV (some). In-hotel: no-smoking rooms* ⊟*No credit cards.*

NIGHTLIFE AND THE ARTS

The plush culture and art center, **Dunkers Kulturhus** (⊠*Kungsg. 11* ☎*042/ 107400*), stages an array of events in the fields of music, drama, visual arts, and cultural heritage.

5

Jazz in Helsingborg stages some of its events at a cozy club on Nedre Långvinkelsgatan and some in the culture and arts center Dunkers Kulturhus. If you strike on the right night, you may well find yourself in jazz heaven, since the organizers attract jazz musicians from all over. Admission varies depending on the performance. ✉ *Nedre Långvinkelsg. 22* ☎ *042/184900* ✉ *Dunkers Kulturhus, Kungsg. 11, Sundstorget* ☎ *042/107400.*

SPORTS AND THE OUTDOORS

If your bones are weary, visit **Øresundsmassage.** The professionally trained staff offers various massage services and can deal with problems such as cramping or poor blood circulation. ✉ *Roskildeg. 4* ☎ *042/127042* 🕓 *55 mins SKr 680* ☉ *Mon. and Wed. noon–7, Tues. and Thurs. 10–6.*

Consider taking a relaxing dip in the sound at the late 19th-century **Pålsjöbaden** (Pålsjö Bath House) just north of town. It's a Helsingborg tradition to sweat in a sauna and then jump into the cool waters of the channel—even in winter. After an evening sauna, nearby Pålsjö Krog is a good dinner option. ✉ *Drottningg. 151* ☎ *042/149707* 🕓 *Single visit SKr 30.*

LUND

34 km (21 mi) southeast of Landskrona via E6/E20 and Rte. 16, 25 km (15 mi) northeast of Malmö, 183 km (113 mi) southwest of Växjö.

One of the oldest towns in Europe, Lund was founded in 990. In 1103 Lund became the religious capital of Scandinavia, and at one time had 27 churches and eight monasteries—until King Christian III of Denmark ordered most of them razed to use their stones for the construction of Malmöhus Castle. Lund lost its importance until 1666, when its university was established—the second-oldest university in Sweden after Uppsala.

GETTING HERE AND AROUND

From the north, take the E4 and E6 motorways to Lund; there's lots of signage to guide you. There is a direct train from Stockholm twice a day (the trip takes four hours) and regular connections to Malmö, just 15 minutes by train. Once in Lund, make use of the easy and extensive bus network.

ESSENTIALS

Bus Travel Lund Bus (⊕ *www.stadstrafiken.lund.se*).

Car Rental Avis (☎ *046/145030*). **Europcar** (☎ *046/312897*). **Hertz** (☎ *046/306012*).

Emergencies (☎ 112).

Train Travel SJ (☎ *0771/757575* ⊕ *www.sj.se*).

Visitor Info Lund Tourist Office (✉ *Kykog. 11* ☎ *046/355040* ⊕ *www.lund.se*).

EXPLORING LUND

FodorśChoice
★

Lund's **Domkyrkan** *(Cathedral)*, consecrated in 1145, is a monumental gray-stone Romanesque cathedral, the oldest in Scandinavia. Since the Reformation it has been Lutheran. Its crypt has 23 finely carved pillars, but its main attraction is an astrological clock, Horologum Mirabile Lundense, dating from 1380 and restored in 1923. The "Miraculous Clock of Lund" depicts an amazing pageant of knights jousting on horseback, trumpets blowing a medieval fanfare, and the Magi walking in procession past the Virgin and Child as the organ plays *In Dulci Jubilo*. The clock plays at noon and at 3 Monday–Saturday and at 1 and 3 on Sunday. The oldest parts of the cathedral are considered the finest Romanesque constructions in Sweden. English and Swedish tours are available, and there are concerts at 10 AM on Sunday. ☎*046/358880* ⊠*Free* ⊗ *Weekdays 8–6, Sat. 9:30–5, Sun. 9:30–6.*

One block east of the cathedral is the **Botaniska Trädgården** *(Botanical Garden)*, which contains more than 7,000 specimens of plants from all over the world, including such exotics as the paper mulberry tree, from the islands of the South Pacific. ⊠ *Östra Vallg. 20* ☎*046/2227320* ⊠*Free* ⊗ *Daily 6 AM–8 PM, greenhouses daily noon–3.*

Right next to the Lund Art Gallery is **Krognoshuset**, Lund's best-preserved medieval residence, and a small but well-presented art gallery. The building itself is worth a look, but most days you will get the added bonus of a contemporary art exhibition showcasing anything from industrial design to video installations. ⊠ *Mårtenstorget* ☎*046/126248* ⊠*Free* ⊗ *Daily, year-round 11–5. Call ahead for exhibition details.*

The all-brick **Lund Konsthall** *(Lund Art Gallery)* may have a rather forbidding iron entrance and few windows, but skylights allow ample sunlight into the large exhibit room full of contemporary art by Swedish painters and sculptors, as well as some European artists. ⊠ *Mårtenstorget 3* ☎*046/355395* ⊠*Free* ⊗ *Mon.–Wed. and Fri. noon–5, Thurs. noon–8, Sat. 10–5, Sun. noon–6.*

WHERE TO EAT

$$
SCANDINAVIAN

✕**Bantorget 9.** The restaurant-bar inside this 19th-century building is true to the past, with restored woodwork and paintings on the ceilings, antique flowerpots and candleholders, and classical statues in the corners of the room. The menu offers traditional Swedish dishes plus some more intriguing entrées such as lamb with olives, pomegranate and rosemary. Bantorget 9 is a short walk from Lund's central train station. ⊠ *Bantorget 9* ☎*046/320200* ⊟*AE, DC, MC, V* ⊗ *Closed Sun.*

$$
SCANDINAVIAN

✕**Dalby Gästis.** This is one of Skåne's oldest inns and a gastronomic delight. The many red-meat dishes on the menu follow a tradition of history and quality, but innovative Swedish fare is served, too. Entrées such as the rich, somewhat gamey deer fillet with mushroom spring rolls and cranberry sauce are not for the faint of heart. Their Skånsk apple cake, a local delicacy, is not to be missed. Be sure to make reservations in summer. ⊠ *Tengsg. 6* ☎*046/200006* ⊟*AE, MC, V.*

$$ ✕**Godset.** Inside an old railroad warehouse right on the tracks near cen-
SCANDINAVIAN tral station, Godset's modern tables and chairs stand on rustic wooden
★ floors between brick walls. White Guide, the holy book of Swedish
food, named it best restaurant in Lund in 2007. On one wall hangs a
large 1950s clock taken from Mariakyrkan (Maria Church) in nearby
Ystad. The excellent menu is mostly seafood and meat dishes. Try the
reindeer fillet with spiced baked root vegetables, lingonberries, and shal-
lot jus. ⊠*Bang. 3* ☎*046/121610* ⊟*AE, DC, MC, V* ⊘*Closed Sun.*

$$ ✕**Restaurang Café Finn.** Connected to the Lund Konsthall, Café Finn is
SCANDINAVIAN an excellent option for lunch or dinner. The creamy lobster soup with
★ mussels is perfect if you're not overly hungry, but for a more substantial
meal go for the veal fillet with creamy red-onion sauce and grape jelly.
The walls have an extensive collection of museum exhibit posters from
the '60s, '70s, and '80s. Just outside is the Krognoshuset. ⊠*Mårtenstorget 3* ☎*046/130565* ⊟*AE, DC, MC, V.*

WHERE TO STAY

$$ 🏨**Grand Hotel.** This elegant red-stone hotel is in the heart of the city on a
★ pleasant square close to the railway station. All the rooms are furnished
differently, but most have a turn-of-the-20th-century decor and charm
in common. The fine restaurant serves an alternative vegetarian menu.
Pros: wide choice of rooms; fluffy bathrobes in every room. **Cons:** can
be noisy. ⊠*Bantorget 1* ☎*046/2806100* ⊕*www.grandilund.se* ⤶*84
rooms, 1 suite* ⚐*In-room: Wi-Fi. In-hotel: restaurant, parking (paid),
no-smoking rooms* ⊟*AE, DC, MC, V* ⲝ*BP.*

$$ 🏨**Hotel Lundia.** Only a few hundred feet from the train station, Hotel
Lundia is ideal for those who want to be near the city center. Built in
1968, the modern, four-story square building has transparent glass walls
on the ground floor. Rooms are decorated in a combination of Scandinavian and Japanese styles. **Pros:** stylish, thoughtfully designed rooms;
rooms for visitors with allergies available. **Cons:** limited choice in restaurant. ⊠*Knut den Stores torg 2* ☎*046/2806500* ⊕*www.lundia.se*
⤶*97 rooms, 1 suite* ⚐*In-room: Wi-Fi. In-hotel: restaurant, bar, no-
smoking rooms* ⊟*AE, DC, MC, V* ⲝ*BP.*

$ 🏨**Oskar.** A charming boutique-style hotel made up of two 19th-century
town houses, the hotel offers spacious, modern, and bright rooms with
white walls, colorful art, and oiled oak floors. All rooms are individually furnished with designer touches like chairs from Gunilla Allard
and lamps by the legendary Arne Jacobsen. Downstairs there's a café
and a beautiful garden where you can enjoy breakfast in the morning
and coffee throughout the day. **Pros:** excellent value for the rates; nicely
designed. **Cons:** no restaurant. ⊠*Bytareg. 3* ☎*046/188085* ⊕*www.
hotelloskar.se* ⤶*6 rooms* ⚐*In-room: DVD, Wi-Fi. In-hotel: no-smoking rooms* ⊟*AE, DC, MC, V* ⲝ*BP.*

NIGHTLIFE AND THE ARTS

★ **Basilika** (⊠*Stora Söderg. 13* ☎*046/2116660*) has a smallish dance floor
and also hosts live bands. On Friday and Saturday things don't get
going until 11 and rage on until 3. Expect young hipsters—a boon or
a burden depending on your taste.

The hot spot in town, **Stortorget** (✉ *Stortorget 1* ☎ *046/139290*), has live music as well as a DJ night and is popular with students. You won't get in here unless you are over 22.

SHOPPING

Saluhallen (✉ *Corner of Mårtenstorget and Botulfsg.*), known as Food-hall, is an adventure in itself, an excellent example of the traditional Swedish food house but also one that stocks delicacies from Italy, Japan, and beyond. Cheese, meats, fresh and pickled fish, and pastries are all in great supply. It is the perfect place to get some food for a picnic in one of Lund's many squares and parks.

Skånekraft (✉ *Östra Mårtensg. 5* ☎ *046/144777*) carries a wide range of ceramics, crafts, and designer goods.

MALMÖ

25 km (15 mi) southwest of Lund (via E22), 198 km (123 mi) southwest of Växjö.

Capital of the province of Skåne, with a population of about 265,000, Malmö is Sweden's third-largest city. It was founded at the end of the 13th century. The remarkable 8-km (5-mi) bridge and tunnel from Malmö to Copenhagen has transformed travel and trade in the area, cutting both time and costs, and replacing the ferries that used to shuttle between the two towns.

GETTING HERE AND AROUND

Malmö is served by the E6 motorway from Göteborg in the north and is close to the E4 motorway, which runs south from Stockholm. If you are coming from Copenhagen in Denmark, the OØresund Bridge carries car and train traffic into the heart of the city. It costs SKr 325 one-way.

Malmö's Sturup airport (MMX) is served with daily flights from three domestic carriers. It's approximately 30 km (19 mi) from Malmö itself and 25 km (15 mi) from Lund. Buses for Malmö and Lund meet all flights at Sturup Airport; the price of the trip is SKr 90 to either destination. A taxi from the airport to Malmö SKr 395.

Trains connect most towns in the south; contact SJ for details. There's regular service from Stockholm to Malmö, the trip takes about 6½ hours, and about 4½ hours by high-speed (X2000) train. The railway station is centrally located in Malmö. Trains between Malmö and Copenhagen take 35 minutes and run three times an hour during the day and once an hour at night. A one-way ticket is SKr 107.

Once in Malmö, the bus is the best way to get around town. If time is short and money less so, there are also plenty of taxis on hand any time of day.

ESSENTIALS

Airlines Direktflyg (☎ *0243/444700* ⊕ *www.direktflyg.se*). **Malmö Aviation** (☎ *0771/550010* ⊕ *www.malmoaviation.se*). **SAS** (☎ *0770/727727* ⊕ *www. flysas.com*).

Airport Transportation Sturup (☎ *040/6131000*). **Bus Information** (☎ *040/6696290*). **Taxi and Limousine Service** (☎ *040/70000*).

Bus Travel Malmö Bus (⊕ *www.malmo.com*).

Car Rental Avis (☎ *040/77830*). **Europcar** (☎ *040/71640*). **Hertz** (☎ *040/330770*).

Emergencies (☎ *112*).

Train Travel SJ (☎ *0771/757575* ⊕ *www.sj.se*).

Visitor Info Malmö Tourist Office (⊠ *Centralstationen [central train station]*) ☎ *040/341200* ⊕ *www.malmo.se*).

EXPLORING MALMÖ

The city's castle, **Malmöhus**, completed in 1542, was for many years used as a prison (James Bothwell, husband of Mary, Queen of Scots, was one of its notable inmates). Today Malmöhus houses a variety of **museums**, including the City Museum, the Museum of Natural History, and the Art Museum, which has a collection of Nordic art. Across the street are the Science and Technology Museum, the Maritime Museum, and a toy museum. ⊠ *Malmöhusv.* ☎ *040/344437* ⊠ *SKr 40 for all museums* ⊙ *June–Aug., daily 10–4; Sept.–May, daily noon–4.*

The houses and business buildings designed and erected for the 2001 **European Housing Expo** show 58 different types of housing. Wander around the development surrounding the Ribersborgsstranden waterfront, where the expo was held, in order to see the exteriors of more than 500 homes. They were sold as residences after the expo was over. (Look for Turning Torso, an architectural masterpiece that's still the talk of the town.) To get here, take bus number 2 from the central station to Västra Hamnen. ⊠ *Ribersborgsstranden waterfront.*

★ You can learn about Scandinavian art and design at the **Form/Design Center.** The center is run by SvenskForm, a nonprofit association that promotes top-quality design in Sweden; Swedish and other Scandinavian artworks are on display throughout the center. ⊠ *9 Lilla Torg* ☎ *040/6645150* ⊕ *www.formdesigncenter.com* ⊠ *Free admission* ⊙ *Tues.–Fri. 11–5, Thurs. 11–6, weekends 11–4.*

Lilla Torg is a cobblestone square with some of the city's oldest buildings, which date from the 17th and 18th centuries. It is clustered with cafés, restaurants, and bars and is a great place to wander or watch the world go by. Walk into the side streets and see the traditional buildings, which were originally used mainly to store grain and produce. Check out the Saluhallen (food hall), which contains Kryddboden, one of Sweden's best coffee purveyors.

The **Rådhuset** *(Town Hall)*, dating from 1546, dominates Stortorget, a huge, cobbled market square in Gamla Staden, and makes an impressive spectacle when illuminated at night.

Fodor's Choice One of Sweden's most outstanding art museums, **Rooseum,** is in a turn-
★ of-the-20th-century brick building that was once a power plant. It has exhibitions of contemporary art and a quality selection of Nordic

art. ⊠ *Gasverksg. 22* ☎ *040/121716* ⊕ *www.rooseum.se* 🏷 *SKr 40* ⊙ *Wed. 2–8, Thurs.–Sun. noon–6. Guided tours in Swedish and English weekends at 2, Thurs. and Fri. at 6:30, Wed. at 6.*

★ In Gamla Staden, the Old Town, look for the **St. Petri Church,** on Kalendegatan; dating from the 14th century, it is an impressive example of the Baltic Gothic style, with distinctive stepped gables. Inside there is a fine Renaissance altar.

WHERE TO EAT

$$$ ✕ **Årstiderna i Kockska Huset.** Formed by merging two discrete restaurants
SCANDINAVIAN that were in different locations, the combination is housed in a 16th-
★ century building with beautiful interiors. Several of the dining areas are in an underground cellar. Traditional Swedish dishes, often centered on beef, game, and seafood, are given a contemporary twist. Like the food, the wine list is excellent. ⊠ *Frans Suellsg. 3* ☎ *040/230910* ▤ *AE, DC, MC, V.*

$ ✕ **B & B.** It stands for *Butik och Bar* (Shop and Bar) and is named as
SWEDISH such because of its location in the food hall in central Malmö. There's always good home cooking, with dishes like grilled salmon and beef fillet with potatoes. Sometimes there's even entertainment at the piano. ⊠ *Saluhallen, Lilla Torg* ☎ *040/127120* ▤ *AE, DC, MC, V.*

$$$ ✕ **Johan P.** This extremely popular restaurant specializes in seafood and
SEAFOOD shellfish prepared in Swedish and Continental styles. White walls and crisp white tablecloths give it an elegant air, which contrasts with the generally casual dress of the customers. An outdoor section is open in summer. ⊠ *Saluhallen, Lilla Torg* ☎ *040/971818* ▤ *AE, DC, MC, V* ⊙ *Closed Sun.*

$$ ✕ **Salt & Brygga.** The traditional Swedish kitchen has found some inspi-
SCANDINAVIAN ration in the Mediterranean at this quayside restaurant. The restaurant
Fodor'sChoice not only uses only organic produce, but also uses ecologically friendly
★ alternatives for everything from the wall paint to the table linens and the staff's clothes. The restaurant's selection of organic wines and beers is unique for the region. ⊠ *Sundspromenaden 721116* ☎ *040/6115940* ▤ *AE, DC, MC, V.*

WHERE TO STAY

$$ 🏨 **Baltzar.** This turn-of-the-20th-century house in central Malmö makes a small, comfortable hotel. Rooms have the original hardwood floors and pleasing antique furniture, minichandeliers, and rich swathes of fabric hung at the tall windows. **Pros:** beautiful building; luxurious design. **Cons:** some rooms very small; limited choice in restaurant. ⊠ *Söderg. 20* ☎ *040/6655710* ⊕ *www.baltzarhotel.se* ⬋ *40 rooms* ⚃ *In-room: refrigerator. In-hotel: restaurant, room service, no-smoking rooms* ▤ *AE, DC, MC, V* ⏐◯⏐*BP.*

$$ 🏨 **Mäster Johan Hotel.** The plain exterior of this Best Western hotel
★ disguises a plush and meticulously crafted interior. A top-to-bottom redesign of a 19th-century building, with the focal point an Italianate atrium breakfast room, the Mäster Johan is unusually personal for a chain hotel. The rooms are impressive, with exposed plaster-and-stone walls, recessed lighting, luxurious beds, Bang & Olufsen televisions, marble bathrooms oak floors, Oriental carpets, and French cherrywood

furnishings. **Pros:** central location; large, bright rooms. **Cons:** close to noisy street; tiny gym. ✉ *Mäster Johansg. 13,* ☎*040/6646400* ⊕*www. masterjohan.se* ⇒*69 rooms* ⌂*In-room: Wi-Fi. In-hotel: restaurant, bar, room service, gym, laundry service, no-smoking rooms* ☰*AE, DC, MC, V* ❑*BP.*

$$–$$$ 🏨**Radisson SAS Hotel.** Only a five-minute walk from the train station, this modern luxury hotel has rooms decorated in several styles: Asian, maritime, and ecological—the latter being mostly furnished in recycled or biodegradable materials, although you would never know it. The restaurant serves Scandinavian and Continental cuisine, and there's a cafeteria. **Pros:** very large rooms; excellent bar. **Cons:** somewhat impersonal service. ✉ *Österg. 10* ☎*040/6984000* ⊕*www.radissonsas.com* ⇒*229 rooms, 4 suites* ⌂*In-room: refrigerator, Wi-Fi. In-hotel: restaurant, room service, bar gym, spa, laundry service, parking (paid), no-smoking rooms* ☰*AE, DC, MC, V* ❑*BP.*

NIGHTLIFE AND THE ARTS

Étage (✉*Stortorget 6* ☎*040/232060* ⌂*SKr 90 or more* ⊗*Mon., Thurs., Fri., and Sat.* 11 PM–5 AM) is a centrally located nightclub for hipsters, with two dance floors. It also has a piano bar for relaxing, as well as a restaurant. Dancing begins late under psychedelic lights Monday, Thursday, Friday, and Saturday. Karaoke, roulette, and blackjack tables are available.

The **Malmö Symfoni Orkester** (☎*040/343500* ⊕*www.mso.se*) is a symphony orchestra that has a reputation across Europe as a class act. Each concert is a finely tuned event. Performances are held at many venues, including outdoors; some are at the impressive Malmö Konserthus.

SHOPPING

Malmö has many quality housewares and design stores. **Cervera** (✉*Södra Förstadsg. 24* ☎*040/971230*) carries big-name glassware brands such as Kosta and Orrefors. There's an excellent selection of glass art as well as porcelain and china—and almost everything you might need in housewares. **Duka** (✉*Hansacompagniet Centre, Malmborgsg. 6* ☎*040/121141*) is a high-quality housewares shop specializing in glass, crockery, and glass art.

Formargruppen (✉*Engelbrektsg. 8* ☎*040/78060*) is an arts-and-crafts cooperative owned and operated by its 22 members. It sells high-quality woodwork, including cabinets. Quality ceramics, textiles, metalwork, and jewelry are also for sale. The **Form/Design Centre** (✉*Lilla Torg 9* ☎*040/6645150*) sells products related to its changing exhibitions on everything from ceramics to books. Also look here for the very latest in Scandinavian interior design.

At the summer market called **Möllevångstorget,** on the square of the same name, there is usually a wonderful array of flowers, fruit, and vegetables. It is an old working-class area and a nice place to stroll. The market is open Monday–Saturday.

YSTAD

64 km (40 mi) southeast of Malmö (via E65), 205 km (127 mi) southwest of Växjö

A smuggling center during the Napoleonic Wars, Ystad has preserved its medieval character with winding narrow streets and hundreds of half-timber houses built over a span of five centuries. A good place to begin exploring is the main square, Stortorget.

GETTING HERE AND AROUND

The best way to reach Ystad is by car. It's just a one-hour drive from Malmö, which has excellent transport links. In Malmö you should also take care of things like car rental and ATM visits.

The town center here is small enough to get around by foot (and pretty enough to want to do so).

ESSENTIALS

Emergencies (☎112).

Visitor Info Ystad (✉*St. Knuts Torg* ☎*0411/577681* ⊕*www.visitystad.com*).

EXPLORING YSTAD

The Franciscan monastery **Gråbrödraklostret** adjoins St. Peter's church and is one of the best-preserved cloisters in Sweden. The oldest parts date to 1267. Together, the church and monastery are considered the most important historical site in Ystad. ✉*Sankt Petri Kyrkoplan* ☎*0411/577286* 🎫*SKr 30* ☉ *Weekdays noon–5, weekends noon–4.*

The principal ancient monument, **St. Maria Kyrka** (*St. Mary's Church* ✉*Lilla Norregatan*) was built shortly after 1220 as a basilica in the Romanesque style, though there have been later additions. The watchman's copper horn sounds from the church tower beginning at 9:15 PM and repeating every 15 minutes until 1 AM. It's to proclaim that "all is well." The church lies behind Stortorget on Lilla Norregatan.

Sweden's best-preserved theater from the late 1800s, **Ystads Teater** (✉*Sjömansg. 13* ☎*0411/577199*) is a beautiful, ornate building. The dramatic interior adds a great deal to any performance seen here.

WHERE TO EAT AND STAY

$$ ✕**Bryggeriet.** A lovely cross-timbered inn, this restaurant brews its own
SCANDINAVIAN beer—there are two large copper boilers near the bar. It has a pleasant garden, and the brick vaulting of the dimly lighted interior gives it the appearance of an underground cavern. Juicy steaks are Bryggeriet's specialty. ✉*Långg. 20* ☎*0411/69999.*

$$ ✕**Lottas.** In an interesting two-story building on the main square in the
CONTEMPORARY heart of town, with lovely exposed red-brick interiors. Lottas offers several lighter fish dishes, including scallops in season. As is typical in Sweden, there are many red-meat options; the steaks are cooked and presented with care. 🏠*Stortorget 11* ☎*0411/78800.*

¢ 🏨**Anno 1793 Sekelgården Hotell.** Centered on a cobblestone courtyard, this small and comfortable family-owned hotel is in the heart of Ystad, a short walk from St. Maria's Church and the main square. The half-

5

timber buildings that make up the hotel date from the late 18th century, and in the summer breakfast is served in the courtyard. All the rooms are named and all are different. Most have a rural mix of scrubbed, flower-painted desks and chairs, typical of the Dalarna region. **Pros:** on-site microbrewery; romantic atmosphere. **Cons:** some rooms very small. ✉ *Långg. 18 271 23* ☎ *0411/73900* ⊕ *www.sekelgarden.se* ⤴ *18 rooms, 2 suites* ⟡ *In-hotel: restaurant, bar, Wi-Fi* ⊟ *AE, DC, MC, V* ⦿ *BP.*

$

Fodor'sChoice

★

⛭ **Hotel Continental.** The Continental opened in 1829, and is a truly stunning building, both inside and out. Take a good look at the lobby with its marble stairs, crystal chandelier, stained-glass windows, and marble pillars. No two guest rooms are alike, but are all presented in a style leaning towards Gustavian, with all its requisite carved wood and lace trim. The restaurant ($$) gives each dish its own flair and serves beautifully presented classic Skäne food. **Pros:** lots of character; great food. **Cons:** small rooms (some); reception closes at 10 PM ✉ *Hamng. 13* ☎ *0411/13700* ⊕ *www.hotelcontinental-ystad.se* ⤴ *52 rooms* ⟡ *In-room: Internet. In-hotel: restaurant, parking (paid), no-smoking rooms* ⊟ *AE, MC, V* ⦿ *BP.*

KARLSKRONA

111 km (69 mi) east of Kristianstad via E22, 201 km (125 mi) northeast of Malmö, 107 km (66 mi) southeast of Växjö.

A small city built on the mainland and on 33 nearby islands, Karlskrona achieved great notoriety in 1981, when a Soviet submarine ran aground a short distance from its naval base. The town dates from 1680, when it was laid out in baroque style on the orders of Karl XI. Because of the excellent state of preservation of the naval museum and other buildings in town, Karlskrona has been designated a World Heritage Site by UNESCO.

GETTING HERE AND AROUND

Karlskrona is best reached by car. There is a good local bus network, too, that connects the city to all other local towns and cities.

ESSENTIALS

Bus Travel Blekinge Bussar (⊕ *www.blekingetrafiken.se*).

Car Rental Avis (☎ *0455/311125*). **Europcar** (☎ *0455/388000*). **Hertz** (☎ *0455/ 14475*).

Emergencies (☎ *112*).

Visitor Info Karlskrona Tourist Office (✉ *Stortorget 2* ☎ *0455/303490* ⊕ *www. karlskrona.se*).

EXPLORING KARLSKRONA

Although the archipelago is not as large or as full of dramatic scenery as Stockholm's islands, Karlskrona is still worth the boat trip. One can be arranged through **Skärgårdstrafiken** (☎ *0455/78330*).

★ The **Admiralitetskyrkan** *(Admiralty Church)* is Sweden's oldest wooden church, built in 1685. It is an unusual variant of the Swedish church architecture. Although it was supposed to be temporary, the stone replacement was never built. The church is on Bastionsgatan on the naval island. Walk east a few minutes from Stortorget, the main square to get to the bridge.

★ The **Marinmuseum** *(Naval Museum)*, in a building dating from 1752, is one of the oldest museums in Sweden and has a superb collection perfect for those with a nautical bent. The shed for making rope is ancient (1692) and huge—nearly 1,000 feet long. The museum can also provide you with brochures of the port area, perfect for a pleasant walk. ✉*Stumholmen* ☎*0455/359302* 🖻*SKr 60* ⊙*June–Aug., daily 10–6; Sept.–May, daily noon–5.*

Stunning **Kungsholm Fort,** on the island of Kungsholmen, was built in 1680 to defend the town's important naval port. Perhaps the most impressive aspect of the fort is the round harbor, built into the fort itself with only a narrow exit to the sea. The fort is accessible only by a boat booked through the **tourist office** (✉*Stortorget* ☎*0455/303490*) on the main island of Trossö.

WHERE TO EAT AND STAY

$$ ✕**Lisas Sjökrog.** Floating on the sea, this docked ship is a great place to see a sunset and look out over the archipelago. The emphasis here is on seafood, including herring, halibut, and shellfish in season. You can also try well-prepared meat dishes and the popular summer salads. ✉*Fisktorget* ☎*0455/618383* 🖃*AE, MC, V* ⊙*Closed Sept.–Apr.*

SEAFOOD

$ ✕**Lokpalatset.** Formerly an art and design shop with a restaurant inside, the restaurant has taken over completely. The "Lok" part of the name refers to the building's even earlier life as a repair shop for railway locomotives. The restaurant's interior has a creative mix of Scandinavian and Japanese design. The menu is equally creative with Swedish, French, and Italian influences. ✉*Blekingeg. 3, Lokstallarna* ☎*0455/333331* 🖃*AE, DC, MC, V.*

SCANDINAVIAN

$ 🖬**First Hotel Statt.** The rooms are well appointed, the decor classic, and the style Swedish traditional. Built around 1900, this immaculate hotel with an ornate stairwell and candelabras in the lobby is in the heart of the city and is fully renovated. **Pros:** central location; free use of computer and printer. **Cons:** bar gets very rowdy on the weekend. ✉*Konnebyg. 37–39* ☎*0455/55550* ⊕*www.firsthotels.com* 🛏*107 rooms* &*In-room: refrigerator, Wi-Fi. In-hotel: restaurant, bar, no-smoking rooms* 🖃*AE, DC, MC, V* ⫶❏*BP.*

¢ 🖬**Hotel Conrad.** For simple but functional accommodations at a reasonable price, the Hotel Conrad is a good choice. Rooms are colored with very tasteful hues of chocolate brown and beige. It is a short walk from shopping, restaurants, and entertainment. **Pros:** free wireless Internet; free coffee and tea. **Cons:** room size and style varies widely. ✉*V. Köpmansg. 12* ☎*0455/363200* ⊕*www.hotelconrad.se* 🛏*58 rooms* &*In-room: Wi-Fi. In-hotel: parking (free), no-smoking* 🖃*AE, MC, V* ⫶❏*BP.*

5

ÖLAND

★ *99 km (62 mi) northeast of Karlskrona via E22, 300 km (161 mi)*
northeast of Malmö, 117 km (73 mi) southeast of Växjö.

The island of Öland is a magical and ancient place—and the smallest
province in Sweden. The area was first settled some 4,000 years ago
and is fringed with fine sandy beaches and dotted with old windmills,
churches, and archaeological remains.

The island also has spectacular birdlife—swallows, cranes, geese, and
birds of prey. Many migrate to Öland from Siberia. The southern part
of the island, known as Stora Alvaret, is a UNESCO World Heritage
Site due partly to its stark beauty and unique flora and fauna. After
you cross the bridge from Kalmar on the mainland, Be sure to pick up
a tourist information map (follow the signs as soon as you get on the
island); most of the scattered sights have no address.

Private car travel is allowed, but you can let the public bus shuttle you
around instead. Just be sure not to miss the Kalmar Slott just before
heading here over the bridge from Kalmar; this well-preserved castle is
a fascinating step back in time.

GETTING HERE AND AROUND
It's easiest to get to Öland by car. Other methods can be too time-con-
suming (bus) or too expensive (taxi). We also suggest hiring a car for
traveling around the island itself. The closest major car rental companies are in Karlskrona. To get onto the island take Route E22 through
the town of Kalmar and across the 6-km (4-mi) bridge.

ESSENTIALS
Car Rental Avis (☎ *0455/311125*). **Europcar** (☎ *0455/388000*). **Hertz** (☎ *0455/*
14475).

Emergencies (☎112).

Visitor Info Öland Tourist Office (✉ *Träffpunkt Öland, Färjestaden* ☎ *0485/560600*
⊕ *www.olandsturist.se*).

EXPLORING ÖLAND
Close to the bridge is the popular Historium, where slide shows, wax
figures, and constructed dioramas illustrate what Öland was like 10,000
years ago.

Head clockwise around the island. Borgholms Slott, the largest castle
ruin in northern Europe, is just outside the island's principal town,
Borgholm (25 km [15 mi] north of the bridge).

Heading farther north brings you to the town of Löttorp. From here,
drive west to Horns Kungsgård, a nature preserve on a lake that has a
bird-watching tower and walking trails.

Some 5 km (3 mi) north along the coast from Horns Kungsgård is
Byrum, a nature preserve with striking, wind-carved limestone cliffs.
Just a few more kilometers on is Skäftekärr, which has a culture museum,
a café, an Iron Age farm with an arboretum, and walking trails.

Turning back you will find Trollskogen, one of the island's three nature centers. On its trails are some majestic old oaks, prehistoric barrow graves, and pines. A little to the south is northern Europe's longest beach, a great swimming spot with sparkling white sand.

Pass back through Löttorp, heading south. Keep an eye out for the signs leading east off the main road for the intriguing Källa church ruins, some of the best on the island. Return to the main road and head south to Kappelludden, one of the island's best year-round bird sites. A medieval chapel's ruins and a lighthouse make this coastal spot very scenic.

Gråborg, a 6th-century fortress with massive stone walls 625 feet in diameter, is a must-see. To get here, head south from Långlöt and turn right at Norra Möckleby.

Return to Norra Möckleby and head south. About 2 km (1 mi) north of Seby are some strings of rune stones: engraved gravestones dating from 500 BC to AD 1050, stone circles, and cists and cairns. Continue south to come to the southeastern edge of Stora Alvaret, a stunning UNESCO World Heritage Site known for its stark beauty and unique flora and forna.

Just before you reach the 5th-century fortified village of Eketorp, you'll reach a turnoff for the Gräsgård, an important fishing village. Eketorp's castle is partially renovated; the area includes small tenants' fields from the Iron and Middle ages. Admission to the castle and its grounds is SKr 50.

Now drive north up the west coastal road. Shortly after Södra Möckleby you'll come across the impressive burial grounds of Gettlinge. The site was in use from the time of Christ into the Viking era, which lasted until 1050. Beginning in late spring, the land north of here blooms with many different wild orchids.

Farther on is Mysinge Tunukus, a Bronze Age site. A group of rune stones here is placed in a shape resembling a ship: it's beautiful at sunset. From here, continue on back the remaining 20 km (12 mi) to the bridge and mainland Sweden.

Fodor's Choice ★ The attractive coastal town of Kalmar, opposite the Baltic island of Öland, is dominated by the imposing **Kalmar Slott,** Sweden's best-preserved Renaissance castle. Part of it dates from the 12th century. The living rooms, chapel, and dungeon can be visited. This is definitely worth a stop on your way in or out of Öland. ⊠*Slottsv.* ☎*0480/451490* ⊕*www.kalmarslott.kalmar.se* ⊠*SKr 80* ⊗*Daily, May and June, 10–4; July 10–6; Aug. 10–5; Sept. 10–4. Other opening times vary, so check ahead.*

WHERE TO STAY

$ ▥**Guntorps Herrgård.** Spacious parkland surrounds this manor house, which is 2,500 feet from the center of Borgholm. Outside, there's a heated pool. The restaurant has hardwood floors, a grandfather clock on one wall, and copper pots hanging on another. **Pros:** personal service;

nice spa area. **Cons:** limited facilities; no food during the day. ✉387 *36 Borgholm* ☎*0485/13000* ⊕*www.guntorpsherrgard.se* ⇔*32 rooms* �*In-hotel: restaurant, spa, no-smoking rooms* ☰*AE, DC, MC, V.*

$ ⌯ **Halltorps Gästgiveri.** This 17th-century manor house has modernized duplex rooms decorated in Swedish landscape tones and an excellent restaurant. Driving north from Ölandsbron, it's on the left side of the road. **Pros:** wine tastings; patio; garden games. **Cons:** some small rooms. ✉*387 92 Borgholm* ☎*0485/85000* ⊕*www.halltorpsgastgiveri.se* ⇔*36 rooms* �*In-hotel: restaurant, parking (free), no-smoking rooms* ☰*AE, DC, MC, V.*

THE KINGDOM OF GLASS

Stretching roughly 109 km (68 mi) between Kalmar and Växjö.

Småland is home to the world-famous Swedish glass industry. Scattered among the rocky woodlands of Småland province are isolated villages whose names are synonymous with high-quality crystal glassware. This spectacular creative art was at its height in the late 19th century. The conditions were perfect: large quantities of wood to fuel the furnaces and plenty of water from the streams and rivers. At the time, demand was such that the furnaces burned 24 hours a day.

The region is still home to 16 major glassworks, many of them created through the merging of the smaller firms. You can still see glass being blown and crystal being etched by craftspeople. Most glassworks also have shops selling quality firsts and not-so-perfect seconds at a discount.

Though the glass factories generally prospered before and during the 1900s, this wealth didn't filter down to many of their workers or to Småland's other inhabitants. Poverty became so widespread that the area lost vast numbers of people to the United States from the late 19th through the 20th century. If you're an American with Swedish roots, chances are your ancestors are from this area. The Utvandrarnas Hus (Emigrants' House) in Växjö tells the story of this exodus.

GETTING HERE AND AROUND

There is no getting around it: to really explore this area properly you need a car. Head to Karlskrona to rent one, or to pick up things like cash or pharmacy supplies. The small town of Nybro (accessible from all the glassworks) has regular train links to Karlskrona if you're headed to town for a bit and want a break from driving.

ESSENTIALS

Car Rental Avis (☎*0455/311125*). **Europcar** (☎*0455/388000*). **Hertz** (☎*0455/ 14475*).

Train Travel SJ (☎*0771/757575* ⊕*www.sj.se*).

Visitor Info Kingdom of Glass tourist information (⊕*www.glasriket.se*).

EXPLORING THE KINGDOM OF GLASS

The Kingdom of Glass's oldest works is **Kosta Glasbruk**. Dating from 1742, it was named for the two former generals who founded it, Anders Koskull and Georg Bogislaus Stael von Holstein. Faced with a dearth of local talent, they initially imported glassblowers from Bohemia. The Kosta works pioneered the production of crystal (to qualify for that label, glass must contain at least 24% lead oxide). You can see glass-blowing off-season (mid-August–early June) between 9 and 3. To get to the village of Kosta from Kalmar, drive 49 km (30 mi) west on Route 25, then 14 km (9 mi) north on Route 28. ⊠ *Kosta* ☎ *0478/34529* ⊕ *www.kostaboda.se* ⊙ *Times vary; check ahead.*

Orrefors is one of the best-known glass companies in Sweden. Orrefors arrived on the scene late—in 1898—but set particularly high artistic standards. The skilled workers in Orrefors dance a slow, delicate minuet as they carry the pieces of red-hot glass back and forth, passing them on rods from hand to hand, blowing and shaping them. The basic procedures and tools are ancient, and the finished product is the result of unusual teamwork, from designer to craftsman to finisher. From early June to mid-August you can watch glass being blown. ⊠ *On Rte. 31, about 18 km (11 mi) east of Kosta Glasbruk* ☎ *0481/34000* ⊕ *www.orrefors.se* ⊙ *July, weekdays and Sat. 10–4, Sun. noon–4; Aug.–June, weekdays 9–3.*

Boda Glasbruk, part of the Kosta Boda Company, is the second-oldest glassworks, founded in 1864. The work here has an ethereal theme, with the designers drawing on cosmic bodies such as the sun and the moon. Much of the work has veils of violet and blue suspended in the crystal. ⊠ *Just off Rte. 25, 42 km (26 mi) west of Kalmar* ☎ *0481/42410* ⊙ *Times vary. Check ahead.*

Skruf Glasbruk began in 1896. Today it's a purveyor to the king of Sweden. The royal family, the ministry of foreign affairs, and the parliament have all commissioned work from Skruf. Local farmers encouraged the development of the glassworks because they wanted a market for their wood. The factory specializes in lead-free crystal, which has a unique iridescence and form. ⊠ *10 km (6 mi) south of Lessebo. Turn left at Åkerby* ☎ *0478/20133* ⊕ *www.skruf-bergdala.se* ⊙ *Weekdays 9–6, weekends 10–4. Glassblowing demonstrations weekdays 7–4.*

WHERE TO STAY

¢ 🏨 **Hotell Björkäng.** Set in a park that will give you plenty of opportunity to take evening strolls, the Björkäng has well-kept rooms. They have some rustic decorations, such as traditional ornaments, wood carved by nature, and glass pieces. You also have the opportunity to spend an evening in the glassblowing room. The dining room offers a range of good traditional Swedish food. **Pros:** family friendly; good local knowledge. **Cons:** basic facilities; no restaurant. ⊠ *Stora Vägen 2, Kosta* ☎ *0478/50000* ⇆ *26 rooms* ⚐ *In-hotel: parking (free)* ⊟ *MC, V* ⏱⊙ *BP.*

¢ 🏨 **Orrefors.** Simplicity and affordability are this small hotel's selling points. Set in a gray-color house from the 1930s, just a three-minute walk from the old Orrefors factory, rooms here are straightforward and very pleasant, with minimal furnishings. The staff is extremely friendly, the atmosphere is cozy, and the hotel is set in the authentic center of the Kingdom of Glass. The restaurant and bar are both pleasant. **Pros:** very friendly service; good restaurant. **Cons:** small rooms; basic facilities. ⊠*Kantav. 29, Orrefors* ☎*0481/30035* ⟿*10 rooms* ⟳*In-hotel: restaurant, bar, no-smoking rooms* ⊟*MC, V* ⟡*BP.*

VÄXJÖ

109 km (68 mi) northwest of Kalmar via Rte. 25, 198 km (123 mi) northeast of Malmö, 228 km (142 mi) southeast of Göteborg, 446 km (277 mi) southwest of Stockholm.

Some 10,000 Americans visit this town every year, for it was from this area that their Swedish ancestors departed in the 19th century. A large proportion of those emigrants went to Minnesota, attracted by the affordable farmland and a geography reminiscent of parts of Sweden. On the second Sunday of every August, Växjö celebrates Minnesota Day: Swedes and Swedish-Americans come together to commemorate their common heritage with American-style square dancing and other festivities. Beyond this, the city is really just a stopover.

GETTING HERE AND AROUND
Växjö is easily accessible by car. There are regular train services from Stockholm and all major towns on the west coast. Once here you can pick up a rental car or get around easily by bus.

ESSENTIALS
Bus Travel Länstrafiken Kronoberg (☎*0470/727550* ⊕*www.lanstrafikenkron. se/).*

Car Rental Avis (☎*0470/46610).* **Europcar** (☎*0470/753102).* **Hertz** (☎*0470/ 775712).*

Train Travel SJ (☎*0771/757575* ⊕*www.sj.se).*

Visitor Info Växjo Toourist officë (⊠*Norra Järbvägsg. 3* ☎*0470/41410).*

EXPLORING VÄXJÖ
The **Utvandrarnas Hus** (Emigrants' House), in the town center, tells the story of the migration, when more than a million Swedes—one quarter of the population—departed for the United States. The museum exhibits provide a vivid sense of the rigorous journey, and an archive room and a research center allow Americans with Swedish blood to trace their ancestry. The archives are open for genealogy research on weekdays. ⊠*Vilhelm Mobergsg. 4* ☎*0470/20120* ⊕*www.swemi.se* ⟐*SKr 40* ⊙*May–Aug., weekdays 9–5, Sat. 11–4; Sept.–Apr., weekdays 9–4, weekends 11–4.*

WHERE TO STAY
$ ⊞**Elite Hotel Statt.** Part of the ever-expanding Elite hotel chain, the Statt is popular with tourist groups. It has a convenient, central location. The building dates from 1853, but the rooms are up to modern standards,

with very pleasant cream and blue interiors. The hotel has a cozy pub, a restaurant and a nightclub. **Pros:** lovely fresh rooms; good location. **Cons:** very crowded and noisty public areas after dark. ✉*Kungsg. 6* ☏*0470/13400* ⊕*www.elite.se* ⇨*163 rooms* ⚷*In-room: Wi-Fi. In-hotel: restaurant, bar, gym, laundry service, parking (paid), no-smoking rooms* ▭*AE, DC, MC, V.*

DALARNA: THE FOLKLORE DISTRICT

A place of forests, mountains, and red-painted wooden farmhouses and cottages by pristine, sun-dappled lakes, Dalarna is considered the most traditional of all the country's 24 provinces. It is the favorite center for celebrations on Midsummer Day, when Swedes don folk costumes and dance to fiddle and accordion music around maypoles covered with wildflower garlands.

Dalarna played a key role in the history of the nation. It was from here that Gustav Vasa recruited the army that freed the country from Danish domination during the 16th century. The region is also important artistically, both for its tradition of naive religious decoration and for producing two of the nation's best-loved painters, Anders Zorn (1860–1920) and Carl Larsson (1853–1915), and one of its favorite poets, the melancholy, mystical Dan Andersson (1888–1920). He sought inspiration in the remote forest camps of the old charcoal burners.

Dalarna is a gloriously compact region, mostly consisting of a single road that rings Lake Siljan, the area's main attraction. A drive round the lake will take in most of the highlights, leaving you only to decide whether to travel clockwise or counterclockwise.

Dalarna is truly a region for all seasons. In June and July it is where every Swede wants to be, an idyllic reflection of everything that is good about Swedish summer. In the winter months, Dalarna offers some very fine skiing, skating, and winter sports. And spring and autumn bring changing colors and fine fishing in Lake Siljan.

GETTING HERE AND AROUND

AIR TRAVEL There are two flights daily from Stockholm to Dala Airport, which is 8 km (5 mi) south of Borlänge. Flights also arrive from Göteborg and Malmö. Bus 601 runs every half hour from Dala Airport to Borlänge; the trip costs SKr 20. From Borlänge there are connecting buses to Falun and other parts of the region. Mora Airport has one Skyways flight daily from Stockholm. The airport is 6 km (4 mi) from Mora; no buses serve the airport. A taxi from Dala Airport to Borlänge costs SKr 396, to Falun SKr 820. A taxi into Mora from Mora Airport costs SKr 355. Order taxis in advance through your travel agent or when you make an airline reservation. Book a cab by calling the Borlänge taxi service.

BUS TRAVEL Swebus runs tour buses to the area from Stockholm on weekends. The trip takes about four hours one-way.

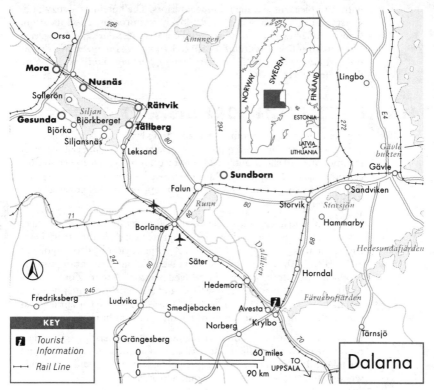

CAR TRAVEL Avis has offices in Borlänge and Mora. Europcar has an office in Borlänge. Hertz has offices in Borlänge Falun, and independent company Bilkompaniet—formerly a part of Hertz—rents cars in Mora.

From Stockholm take E18 to Enköping and follow Route 70 northwest. From Göteborg take E20 to Örebro and Route 60 north from there. Villages are well signposted.

TOUR Just next to the Mora train station, on the quay in the center of town, is the MS *Gustaf Wasa,* a beautiful old steamship that's used for sightseeing tours of Lake Siljan. Trips can take from two to four hours and range in price from SKr 80 to SKr 120. It's a good way to see the stunning countryside from another perspective.

TRAIN TRAVEL There is regular daily train service from Stockholm to both Mora and Falun.

ESSENTIALS
Airports Dala Airport (☎*0243/64500* ⊕*www.dalaflyget.se).* **Mora Airport** (☎*0250/ 30175* ⊕ *www.dalaflyget.se).*

Bus Contact Swebus Express (☎ *0200/218218* ⊕ *www.swebusexpress.se).*

Car Rental Avis (⊠ *Borlänge* ☎*0243/87080* ⊠ *Mora* ☎*0250/16711).* **Bilkompaniet** (⊠ *Mora* ☎*0250/28800).* **Europcar** (⊠ *Borlänge* ☎*0243/19050).* **Hertz**

(⊠ *Borlänge* ☎ *0243/257772* ⊠ *Falun* ☎ *023/58872*).

Emergencies Medical Resources Falun Hospital (☎ *023/492000*). **Mora Hospital** (☎ *0250/493000*). **24-hour medical advisory service** (☎ *023/492900*).

Taxis Borlänge Taxi (☎ *0243/13100*).

Tour and Visitor Info MS *Gustaf Wasa* (*Boat Tours*) (☎ *070/5421025*). **Leksand** (⊠ *Stationsg. 14* ☎ *0247/796130*).

DRIVING TO DALARNA
On the approach to the area from the south via Route 70, a 43-foot, bright orange-red Dala horse marks a rest stop just south of Avesta. It has a spacious cafeteria and a helpful tourist information center.

Ludvika (⊠ *Fredsg. 10* ☎ *0240/86050*). **Mora** (⊠ *Stationsv.* ☎ *0250/592020* ⊕ *www.siljan.se*). **Rättvik** (⊠ *Riksv. 40* ☎ *0248/797210*). **Sälen** (⊠ *Sälen Centrum* ☎ *0280/18700*).

Train Contact SJ (⊕ *www.sj.se*).

EN ROUTE

The town of Falun, 230 km (143 mi) northwest of Stockholm via E18 and Route 70, is famous for its copper mine. It began nearly 800 years ago in 1230, fueled Sweden's "Age of Greatness" in the 17th century, and generally held its own until a collapse in 1687; it eventually closed in 1992. Today the major part of the mine is an enormous hole in the ground that, in combination with the adjoining **Stora Museum,** has become Falun's principal tourist attraction. The one-hour tour through a network of old shafts and tunnels begins with a hair-raising 150-foot descent in an old elevator. Wear old shoes and warm clothing, since the copper-tinged mud can stain footwear and it's cold down there. ☎ *023/782030* ⊕ *www.falugruva.se* ▨ *Mine SKr 150, museum free with mine tour* ☉ *Mine May–Aug., daily 10–4; Sept.–mid-Nov., Mar., and Apr., weekdays 11–3, weekends 11–3. Museum May–Aug., daily 10–5; Sept.–Apr., weekdays 11–4, weekends 11–4.*

SUNDBORN

75 km (55 mi) southeast of Rättvik off Rte. 80.

★ In this small village you can visit **Carl Larsson Gården,** the lakeside home of the Swedish artist (1853–1915). Larsson was an excellent textile designer and draftsman who painted scenes from his family's busy domestic life. The house itself was creatively painted and decorated by Larsson's wife, Karin, also trained as an artist. Waits for guided tours in summer can take two hours. You'll receive a timed ticket and can visit the café or stroll around the garden or lake while you wait. ☎ *023/60053* ⊕ *www.sundborn.info* ▨ *Guided tours only, SKr 100* ☉ *May–Sept., daily 10–5; Jan.–Apr., 1 guided tour daily, weekdays at 11 in English.*

5

RÄTTVIK

48 km (30 mi) northwest of Falun via Rte. 80.

On the eastern tip of Lake Siljan, Rättvik is a pleasant town of timbered houses surrounded by wooded slopes. A center for local folklore, the town has several shops that sell handmade articles and local produce.

Every year in June, dozens of people wearing traditional costumes arrive in longboats to attend midsummer services at the town's 13th-century church, **Rättviks Kyrka,** which stands on a promontory stretching into the lake. Its interior contains some fine examples of local religious art.

Just to the west of Rättvik in the forest is **Vidablick.** The top of this tall wooden tower, more than 100 years old, will give you some of the most stunning views across Lake Siljan that you can find.

★ Once a lucrative open chalk mine, the huge multitier quarry left at **Dalhalla** (7 km [4½] mi north of Rättvik) has become one of the world's most beautiful outdoor stages. Opera, rock concerts, and amazing light shows are all presented here, where the sound is enhanced by the quarry's incredible acoustics. Guided tours of the more remote parts of the quarry can be booked year-round. ⊠*Stationshuset, Rättvik* ☎*0248/797950* ⊕*www.dalhalla.se* ⊠*SKr 50 for exhibition and tour* ⊙*Exhibition mid-May–Sept., daily 11–3 (July, daily 10–6).*

WHERE TO EAT AND STAY

$$
SCANDINAVIAN
★
✕**Sjövillan.** A spectacular modernist wooden house is home to this restaurant, whose interior design is in the less-is-more vein. The food is definitely more-is-more (especially the huge and delicious shrimp sandwich) and the view is quite possibly even more amazing than you could ever imagine. ⊠*Långbryggan* ☎*0248/13400* ▤*AE, MC, V.*

¢
▦**Hotell Vidablick.** Set on its own grounds, with a pleasant view of the lake from the veranda, this small hotel makes a welcome, relaxing stop. Rooms are modern and sparsely furnished, and there's a small private beach where you can take to the water, if it's warm enough. **Pros:** stunning lake views; close to a good handicraft center. **Cons:** very basic facilities. ⊠*Hantverksbyn* ☎*0248/30250* ⊕*www.hantverksbyn.se* ⇋*37 rooms* ⚭*In-hotel: bar, beachfront* ▤*AE, DC, MC, V* ⦿*BP.*

TÄLLBERG

9 km (5½ mi) south of Rättvik via Rte. 70, 57 km (35 mi) northwest of Falun via Rte. 80.

Tällberg is considered by many to be the real Dalarna. It was a sleepy town that few knew about, but an 1850 visit from Hans Christian Andersen put an end to all that. He extolled its virtues—tiny flower-strewn cottages, sweet-smelling grass meadows, stunning lake views—to such an extent that Tällberg quickly became a major tourist stop. This tiny village, one of the smallest in the region with only about 200 permanent residents, is packed with crowds in summer.

WHERE TO STAY

$ **Åkerblads.** A sprawling, low-built hotel, with parts dating from the
★ 1400s, Åkerblads is known primarily for its gourmet achievements.
The restaurant ($$) serves an interesting blend of Swedish and French
cuisine, including such dishes as pork roasted with eggplants and blue-
berries, and salmon with asparagus, truffle, and burgundy wine sauce.
The hotel rooms are comfortable, and most have very good views of
Lake Siljan. **Pros:** great views; very private; large gardens. **Cons:** not
wheelchair friendly. ⊠*Sjögattu 2* ☎*0247/50800* ⊕*www.akerblads.se*
↝*69 rooms, 3 suites* ⌂*In-room: Internet. In-hotel: restaurant, bar,
pool, spa, parking (free)* ⊟*AE, DC, MC, V* ⍥*BP.*

$$ **Hotel Dalecarlia.** There's a homey feel to this first-class hotel, which
Fodor'sChoice has exacting standards and good lake views. The lobby's comfy sofas
★ and darkened corners are welcoming spots to sink into. Rooms are large
and done in soft colors, and there is a spa and fitness center with pool,
sauna, and beauty treatments. The restaurant ($$) is candlelighted and
reminiscent of a farmhouse. It has oak beams, crisp white linen, and a
large open fireplace perfect for an after-dinner brandy. **Pros:** stunning
lake views; very good spa. **Cons:** often busy with conference trade; very
busy restaurant. ⊠*793 70 Tällberg* ☎*0247/89100* ⊕*www.dalecarlia.
se* ↝*80 rooms, 5 suites* ⌂*In-room: Wi-Fi. In-hotel: restaurant, bar,
pool, gym, spa, parking (free)* ⊟*AE, DC, MC, V* ⍥*BP.*

GESUNDA

38 km (24 mi) northwest of Leksand.

A chairlift from Gesunda, a pleasant little village, will take you to the
top of a mountain for unbeatable views over the lake.

The large island of **Sollerön** is connected to the mainland by a bridge at
Gesunda. The island has fine views of the mountains surrounding Siljan.
Several excellent beaches and an interesting Viking grave site are also
here. The church dates from 1775.

MORA

*50 km (31 mi) northwest of Leksand, 40 km (25 mi) northwest of Rät-
tvik via Rte. 70.*

To get to this relaxed lakeside town of 20,000, you can follow the
northern shore of Lake Siljan (there is a bridge at Färnäs), or follow
the lake's southern shore through Leksand and Gesunda to get a good
sense of Dalarna.

Mora is best known as the finishing point for the world's longest cross-
country ski race, the Vasalopp, which begins in March 90 km (56 mi)
away at Sälen, a ski resort close to the Norwegian border. The race
commemorates a fundamental piece of Swedish history: the successful
attempt by Gustav Vasa in 1521 to rally local peasants to the cause of
ridding Sweden of Danish occupation. The race attracts thousands of
competitors from all over the world, including the Swedish king. There

is a spectacular mass start at Sälen before the field thins out. The finish is eagerly awaited in Mora, though since the start of live television broadcasts, the number of spectators has fallen.

EXPLORING MORA

★ Mora is also known as the home of Anders Zorn (1860–1920), Sweden's leading impressionist painter, who lived in Stockholm and Paris before returning to his roots here and painting the local scenes for which he is now known. His former private residence—**Zorngården**—a large, sumptuous house designed with great originality and taste by the painter himself, has retained the same exquisite furnishings, paintings, and decor it had when he lived there with his wife. Next door, the **Zorn Museet** *(Zorn Museum)*, built 19 years after the painter's death, contains many of his best works. ⊠ *Vasag. 36* ☏ *0250/592310* ⊕ *www.zorn. se* ⛫ *Museum SKr 50, home SKr 60* ⊘ *Museum mid-May–mid-Sept., Mon.–Sat. 9–5, Sun. 11–5; mid-Sept.–mid-May, Mon.–Sat. noon–5, Sun. 1–5. Home (guided tours only) mid-May–mid-Sept., Mon.–Sat. 10–4, Sun. 11–4; mid-Sept.–mid-May, Mon.–Sat. noon–4, Sun. 1–4.*

If you're in Mora in July, head 15 km (9 mi) north on Route 45 to Orsa, a small, sleepy town that gets very noisy every Wednesday when the **Orsa Spelmän,** groups of traditional folklore music players, take part in what's called the Orsayran (Orsa Rush). The musicians take over the streets of the town, wandering and playing their instruments. It's great fun.

WHERE TO EAT AND STAY

$$ ✕ **Claras Restaurang.** This small restaurant has a very relaxed and inti-
SCANDINAVIAN   mate atmosphere. Chairs and tables are of stripped pine wood, and the white wooden bar has a New England feel to it. Bargain hunters will love the huge lunchtime salad buffet. Otherwise try the Moscowich, a beef dish with onion, garlic and caviar. ⊠ *Vasag. 38* ☏ *0250/15898* ⊟ *AE, DC, MC, V.*

$$ ⊡ **Best Western Mora.** Part of the Best Western Hotel consortium, this pleasant little hotel is in the town center, 5 km (3 mi) from the airport. Its comfortable rooms are brightly decorated. **Pros:** family rooms come complete with toys. **Cons:** small rooms. ⊠ *Strandg. 12* ☏ *0250/592650* ⊕ *www.bestwestern.com* ⇝ *141 rooms* ⌕ *In-room: Internet. In-hotel: restaurant, bar, pool, spa, parking (free), no-smoking rooms* ⊟ *AE, DC, MC, V* ⎢⎣*BP.*

$ ⊡ **Siljan.** Aside from the uninterrupted views over the lake, there's nothing to write home about here (unless the idea of having a radio is worthy of a postcard), but the small, modern hotel's central location is unbeatable. There is an excellent and lively pub, as well as a restaurant specializing in game. **Pros:** restaurant serves excellent game dishes. **Cons:** very basic rooms. ⊠ *Morag. 6* ☏ *0250/13000* ⊕ *www.hotellsiljan.se* ⇝ *46 rooms* ⌕ *In-room: Wi-Fi. In-hotel: restaurant, room service, bar, parking (free), no-smoking rooms* ⊟ *AE, DC, MC, V* ⎢⎣*BP.*

NORTH OF THE ARCTIC CIRCLE

The north of Sweden is a mysterious region of wide-open spaces where the silence is almost audible. Golden eagles soar above snowcapped crags; huge salmon fight their way up wild, tumbling rivers; rare orchids bloom in arctic heathland; and wild rhododendrons splash the land with color. The weather can change with bewildering speed: a June day can dawn sunny and bright; then the skies may darken and the temperature may drop to around zero as a snow squall blows in.

The once-nomadic Sami people carefully guard what remains of their identity while doing their best to inform the public of their culture. Many of the 17,000 Sami who live in Sweden still earn their living herding reindeer, but as open space shrinks the younger generation is turning in greater numbers toward the allure of the cities. Nowadays many Sami depend on the tourist industry for their living.

Hiking, climbing, canoeing, river rafting, and fishing are all popular in summer; skiing, ice-skating, and dogsledding are winter activities. A word of warning: in summer mosquitoes are a constant nuisance, so bring plenty of repellent—or better yet, consider rescheduling for fall, perhaps the best season to head north. Centrally located and well served with transport links, the city of Kiruna is the perfect base for exploring. There's little else to recommend it, unfortunately. **The Scandic Ferrum** ⊠ *Lars Janssonsg. 15* ☎ *0980/398600* ⊕ *www.scandichotels.com* is probably the best hotel in town. Rooms are modern, comfy, and well-equipped with fresh, natural tones and wooden floors; the hotel's bar, restaurant and sauna with a view will keep you entertained.

From here it is easy to rent a car and explore nearby Sarek, Abisko and Muddus national parks. You'll find a spectacular mix of bare glacial mountain peaks, lush forest, flower-strewn valleys, and marsh and bogland. Here you'll find Kebnekaise, Sweden's highest mountain at 7,000 feet above sea level.

Whatever you do in these wild and remote parts of northern Sweden, a trip to the rightly famous **Ice Hotel** (⊠ *Jukkasjärvi* ☎ *0980/66800* ⊕ *www.icehotel.com*) should not be overlooked. Built entirely of crystal clear local ice, the hotel stands from December to April every year before slowly melting away in the spring thaw. The hotel offers scooter safaris, wilderness cookery courses, and other activities.

GETTING HERE AND AROUND

Kiruna is best accessed by air or by train. SAS have two to three daily flights from Stockholm Arlanda, depending on the day and season. Once at Kiruna airport, it is a short bus or taxi journey into town. SJ, the national rail company, runs a night train from Stockholm every day, which arrives in Kiruna the following morning. Once you're here, rent a car.

ESSENTIALS

Taxi·Taxi Kiruna (☎ *0980/12020*).

Tourist Info Kiruna Tourist Office (⊠ *Lars Janssonsg. 17* ☎ *0980/18880*).

5

SPORTS AND THE OUTDOORS
SKIING
Dalarna's principal ski resort is **Sälen,** starting point for the Vasalopp, about 90 km (56 mi) west of Mora. Snow here is pretty much guaranteed from November to May, and there are more than 100 pistes to choose from, from simple slopes for the beginner to challenging black runs that weave through tightly forested slopes. For more information contact any of the tourist offices in Dalarna.

WALKING
For the energetic traveler it's possible to walk the 90-km (56-mi) **track from Sälen to Mora** that's used for the Vasalopp ski race in March. Along the way you may very well see some elk wandering through the forest. Day shelters, basic night shelters, fireplaces, tables, signposts, and restrooms are set up along the trail. Facilities are free, but a small donation of your choosing is suggested for the night shelters. Maps and other details can be obtained from the **Mora tourist office** (⊠ *Stationsv.* ☎ *0250/592020).*

NUSNÄS

6 km (4 mi) southeast of Mora via Rte. 70, 28 km (17 mi) northwest of Falun.

The lakeside village of Nusnäs is where the small, bright red–painted, wooden Dala horses are made. These were originally carved by the peasants of Dalarna as toys for their children, but their popularity rapidly spread in the 20th century. In 1939 they achieved international popularity after being shown at the New York World's Fair, and since then they have become a Swedish symbol.

Shops in the area are generally open every day except Sunday. The best place to buy painted horses is **Nils Olsson** (⊠ *Edåkersv. 17* ☎ *0250/37200).*

UNDERSTANDING SCANDINAVIA

Vocabulary

DANISH VOCABULARY

	ENGLISH	DANISH	PRONUNCIATION
BASICS			
	Yes/no	Ja/nej	yah/nie
	Thank you	Tak	tak
	You're welcome	Selv tak	**sell** tak
	Excuse me (to apologize)	Undskyld	**unsk**-ul
	Hello	Hej	hi
	Good-bye	Farvel	fa-**vel**
	Today	I dag	ee **day**
	Tomorrow	I morgen	ee **morn**
	Yesterday	I går	ee **gore**
	Morning	Morgen	**more**-n
	Afternoon	Eftermiddag	**ef-tah**-mid-day
	Night	Nat	nat
NUMBERS			
	1	en/et	een/eet
	2	to	toe
	3	tre	treh
	4	fire	fear
	5	fem	fem
	6	seks	sex
	7	syv	syoo
	8	otte	**oh**-te
	9	ni	nee
	10	ti	tee
DAYS OF THE WEEK			
	Monday	mandag	**man**-day
	Tuesday	tirsdag	**tears**-day
	Wednesday	onsdag	**ons**-day
	Thursday	torsdag	**trs**-day

ENGLISH	DANISH	PRONUNCIATION
Friday	fredag	**free**-day
Saturday	lørdag	**lore**-day
Sunday	søndag	**soo**(n)-day

USEFUL PHRASES

Do you speak English?	Taler du engelsk?	te-ler doo in-galsk
I don't speak Danish.	Jeg taler ikke dansk.	yi tal-ler **ick** Dansk
I don't understand.	Jeg forstår ikke.	yi fahr-store **ick**
I don't know.	Det ved jeg ikke.	deh **ved** yi ick
I am American/British.	Jeg er amerikansk/britisk.	yi ehr a-mehr-i-**kansk**/bri-**tisk**
I am sick.	Jeg er syg.	yi ehr **syoo**
Please call a doctor.	Kan du ringe til en læge?	can **doo** rin-geh til en lay-eh
Do you have a vacant room?	Har du et værelse?	har **doo** eet va(l)r-sa
How much does it cost?	Hvad koster det?	va cos-ta **deh**
It's too expensive.	Det er for dyrt.	deh ehr **fohr** dyrt
Beautiful	Smukt	smukt
Help!	Hjælp	yelp
Stop!	Stop	stop
How do I get to . . .	Hvordan kommer jeg til...	vorc-**dan** kom-mer yi til
. . . the train station?	banegården	**ban** eh-gore-en
. . . the post office?	postkontoret	**post**-kon-toh-raht
. . . the tourist office?	turistkontoret	too-**reest**-kon-tor-et
. . . the hospital?	hospitalet	hos-peet-tal-et
Does this bus go to . . .?	Går denne bus til . . .?	**goh** den-na boos til
Where is the bathroom ?	Hvor er toilettet?	vor **ehr** toi-le(tt)-et
On the left	Til venstre	til **ven**-strah
On the right	Til højre	til **hoy**-ah

ENGLISH	DANISH	PRONUNCIATION
Straight ahead	Lige ud	**lee** u(l)

DINING OUT

Please bring me . . .	Må jeg få . . .	mo yi foh
menu	menu	me-**nu**
fork	gaffel	gaf-**fel**
knife	kniv	kan-**ew**
spoon	ske	skee
napkin	serviet	serv-**eet**
bread	brød	brood
butter	smør	smoor
milk	mælk	malk
pepper	peber	**pee**-wer
salt	salt	selt
sugar	sukker	**su**-kar
water/bottled water	vand/dansk vand	van/dansk van
The check, please.	Må jeg bede om regningen.	mo yi bi(d) om **ri**-ning

FINNISH VOCABULARY

	ENGLISH	FINNISH	PRONUNCIATION
BASICS			
	Yes/no	Kyllä/ei	kue-leh/ay
	Please	Olkaa hyvä	ol-kah hue-veh
	Thank you very much.	Kiitoksia paljon.	kee-tohk-seeah pahl-yon
	You're welcome.	Olkaa hyvä.	ol-kah hue-veh
	Excuse me. (to get by someone)	Anteeksi suokaa	ahn-teek-see soo-oh-kah
	(to apologize)	Anteeksi	ahn-tehk-see
	Sorry.	Sori.	sor-ee
	Hello	Hyvää päivää terve	hue-veh paee-veh tehr-veh
	Hi	Hei	hay
	Good-bye	Näkemiin	neh-keh-meen
	Today	Tänään	teh-nehn
	Tomorrow	Huomenna	who-oh-men-nah
	Yesterday	Eilen	ay-len
	Morning	Aamu	ah-moo
	Afternoon	Iltapäivä	ill-tah-pay-va
	Night	Yö	ue-uh
NUMBERS			
	1	yksi	uek-see
	2	kaksi	kahk-see
	3	kolme	kohl-meh
	4	neljä	nel-yeh
	5	viisi	vee-see
	6	kuusi	koo-see
	7	seitsemän	sate-seh-men
	8	kahdeksan	kah-dek-sahn
	9	yhdeksän	ueh-dek-sen
	10	kymmenen	kue-meh-nen

ENGLISH	FINNISH	PRONUNCIATION

DAYS OF THE WEEK

Monday	maanantai	**mah**-nahn-tie
Tuesday	tiistai	**tees**-tie
Wednesday	keskiviikko	**kes**-kee-veek-koh
Thursday	torstai	**tohrs**-tie
Friday	perjantai	**pehr**-yahn-tie
Saturday	lauantai	**lou**-ahn-tie
Sunday	sunnuntai	**soon**-noon-tie

USEFUL PHRASES

Do you speak English?	Puhutteko englantia?	poo-hoot-teh-koh ehng-lahn-tee-ah
I don't speak Finnish.	En puhu suomea.	ehn **poo**-hoo **soo**-oh-may-ah
I don't understand.	En ymmärrä.	ehn **eum**-mehr-reh
I don't know.	En tiedä.	ehn **tee**-eh-deh
I am American/ British.	Minä olen amerikka-lainen/ englantilainen.	**mee**-neh **oh**-len **ah**-mehr-ee-kah-lie-nehn/ **ehn**-glahn-tee-lie-nehn
I am sick.	Olen sairas.	**oh**-len **sigh**-rahs
I need a doctor.	Tarvitsen lääkäri.	tar-vitt-sen leh-keh-rieh
Do you have a vacant room?	Onko teillä vapaata huonetta?	**ohn**-koh **tay**-leh **vah**-pah-tah **who**-oh-neht-tah?
How much does it cost?	Paljonko tämä maksaa?	**pahl**-yohn-koh **teh**-tmeh **mahk**-sah
It's too expensive.	Se on liian kallis.	**say** ohn **lee**-ahn **kahl**-lees
Beautiful	Kaunis	**kow**-nees
Help!	Auttakaa!	**ow**-tah-kah
Stop!	Seis!/Pysähtykää!	say(s)/**peu**-seh-teu-keh
How do I get to . . .	Voitteko sanoa miten pääsen . . .	**voy**-teh-koh **sah**-noh-ah **mit**-ten **peh**-sen
. . . the train station?	. . . asema (pääsen asemalle?)	**ah**-seh-mah (peh-sen ah-say-mah-leh)

ENGLISH	FINNISH	PRONUNCIATION
the post office?	posti (. . . paasen- póstiln?)	**pohs**-tee (**peh**-sen **pohs**-teen)
. . . the tourist office?	matkatoim-isto (. . . pääsen matkatoimistoon?)	**maht**-kah-**toy**- mees-toh (**peh**-sen **maht**-kah-**toy**-mees-tohn)
. . . the hospital?	sairaala (. . . pääsen sairaalaan?)	**sigh**-rah-lah (peh-sen sigh-rah-lahn)
Does this bus go to . . .?	Kulkeeko tämä bussi-n . . .?	**kool**-kay-koh **teh**-meh **boo**-see-n
Where is the bathroom?	Missä on W.C.?	**mihs**-seh ohn **ves**-sah
On the left	Vasemmalle	**vah**-say-**mahl**-leh
On the right	Oikealle	**ohy**-kay-ah-leh
Straight ahead	Suoraan eteenpäin	**soo**-oh-rahn **eh**-tayn-pa-een

DINING OUT

Please bring me . . .	Tuokaa minulle . . .	**too**-oh-kah mee-me- new-leh
menu	ruokalista	**roo**-oh-kah-lees-tah
fork	haarukka	**hahr**-oo-kah
knife	veitsi	**vayt**-see
spoon	lusikka	**loo**-see-kah
napkin	lautasliina	**lou**-tahs-lee-nah
bread	leipä	**lay**-pa
butter	voi	**voh**(ee)
milk	maito	**my**-toh
pepper	pippuri	**peep**-poor-ee
salt	suola	**soo**-oh-lah
sugar	sokeri	**soh**-ker-ee
water/bottled water	vesi/ kivennäisvesi	**veh**-see/**kee**-ven-eyes-veh-see
mineral water	Vichy	**vis**-soo
The check, please.	Lasku, olkaa hyvä/ Haluan maksaa.	**lahs**-kew, **ohl** kah **heu**-va/**hah**-lu-ahn **mahk**-sah

SWEDISH VOCABULARY

	ENGLISH	NORWEGIAN	PRONUNCIATION
BASICS			
	Yes/no	Ja/nei	yah/nay
	Please	Vær så snill	**vehr** soh snihl
	Thank you very much.	Tusen takk.	**tews**-sehn tahk
	You're welcome.	Vær så god.	**vehr** soh goo
	Excuse me.	Unnskyld.	**ewn**-shewl
	Hello	God dag	goo **dahg**
	Good-bye	Ha det	**ha** day
	Today	I dag	ee **dahg**
	Tomorrow	I morgen	ee **moh**-ern
	Yesterday	I går	ee **gohr**
	Morning	Morgen	**moh**-ern
	Afternoon	Ettermiddag	**eh-terr**-mid-dahg
	Night	Natt	naht
NUMBERS			
	1	en	ehn
	2	to	too
	3	tre	treh
	4	fire	**feer**-eh
	5	fem	fehm
	6	seks	sehks
	7	syv, sju	shew
	8	åtte	**oh**-teh
	9	ni	nee
	10	ti	tee
DAYS OF THE WEEK			
	Monday	mandag	**mahn**-dahg
	Tuesday	tirsdag	**teesh**-dahg
	Wednesday	onsdag	**oonss**-dahg

ENGLISH	NORWEGIAN	PRONUNCIATION
Thursday	torsdag	**tohsh**-dahg
Friday	fredag	**fray**-dahg
Saturday	lørdag	**loor**-dahg
Sunday	søndag	**suhn**-dahg

USEFUL PHRASES

Do you speak English?	Snakker De engelsk?	**snahk**-kerr dee **ehng**-ehlsk
I don't speak Norwegian.	Jeg snakker ikke norsk.	yay **snahk**-kerr **ik**-keh nohrshk
I don't understand.	Jeg forstår ikke.	yay fosh-**tawr ik**-keh
I don't know.	Jeg vet ikke.	yay veht **ik**-keh
I am American/ British.	Jeg er amerikansk/ engelsk.	yay ehr ah-mehr-ee-kahnsk/ehng-ehlsk
I am sick.	Jeg er dårlig.	yay ehr **dohr**-lee
Please call a doctor.	Vær så snill og ring etter en lege.	vehr soh snihl oh ring **eht**-ehrehn **lay**-geh
Do you have a vacant room?	Har du et rom som er ledig?	yay vil **yehr**-neh hah eht room
How much does it cost?	Hva koster det?	vah **koss**-terr deh
It's too expensive.	Det er for dyrt.	deh ehr for **deert**
Beautiful	Vakker	**vah**-kehr
Help!	Hjelp!	yehlp
Stop!	Stopp!	stop
How do I get to . . .	Hvor er . . .	voor ehr
. . . the train station?	jernbanestasjonen	yehrn-bahn-eh sta-**shoon**-ern
. . . the post office?	posthuset	**pohsst**-hewss
. . . the tourist office?	turistkontoret	tew-**reest**-koon-toor-er
. . . the hospital?	sykehuset	**see**-keh-hoo-seh
Does this bus go to . . .?	Går denne bussen til . . .?	gohr **den**-nah boos teel
Where is the bathroom?	Hvor er toalettene?	voor ehr too-ah-**leht**-te-ne

ENGLISH	NORWEGIAN	PRONUNCIATION
On the left	Til venstre	teel **vehn**-streh
On the right	Til høyre	teel **hooy**-reh
Straight ahead	Rett fram	reht **frahm**

DINING OUT

menu	meny	meh-new
fork	gaffel	gahff-erl
knife	kniv	kneev
spoon	skje	shay
napkin	serviett	ssehr-vyeht
bread	brød	brur
butter	smør	smurr
milk	melk	mehlk
pepper	pepper	pehp-per
salt	salt	sahlt
sugar	sukker	sook-kerr
water	vann	vahn
The check, please.	Jeg vil gjerne betale.	yay vil **yehr**-neh beh-**tah**-leh

NORWEGIAN VOCABULARY

	ENGLISH	SWEDISH	PRONUNCIATION
BASICS			
	Yes/no	Ja/nej	yah/nay
	Please	Var snäll; Var vänlig	vahr snehll; vahr vehn-leeg
	Thank you very much.	Tack så mycket.	tahk soh **mee**-keh
	You're welcome.	Var så god.	vahr shoh **goo**
	Excuse me. (to get by someone)	Ursäkta.	oor-**shehk**-tah
	(to apologize)	Förlåt.	fur-**loht**
	Hello	God dag	goo **dahg**
	Good-bye	Hej dä	ah-**yoo**
	Today	I dag	ee **dahg**
	Tomorrow	I morgon	ee **mor**-ron
	Yesterday	I går	ee **gohr**
	Morning	Morgon	**mohr**-on
	Afternoon	Eftermiddag	**ehf**-ter-meed-dahg
	Night	Natt	naht
NUMBERS			
	1	ett	eht
	2	två	tvoh
	3	tre	tree
	4	fyra	fee-rah
	5	fem	fem
	6	sex	sex
	7	sju	shoo
	8	åtta	oht-tah
	9	nio	nee-ah
	10	tio	tee-ah
DAYS OF THE WEEK			
	Monday	måndag	**mohn**-dahg

ENGLISH	SWEDISH	PRONUNCIATION
Tuesday	tisdag	**tees**-dahg
Wednesday	onsdag	**ohns**-dahg
Thursday	torsdag	**tohrs**-dahg
Friday	fredag	**freh**-dahg
Saturday	lördag	**luhr**-dahg
Sunday	söndag	**suhn**-dahg

USEFUL PHRASES

Do you speak English?	Talar du engelska?	tah-lahr doo ehng-ehl-skah
I don't speak Swedish.	Jag talar inte svenska.	yah tah-lahr **een**-teh **sven**-skah
I don't understand.	Jag förstår inte.	yah fuhr-**stohr een**-teh
I don't know.	Jag vet inte.	yah **veht een**-teh
I am American/ British.	Jag är amerikan/ engelsman.	yah air ah-mehr-ee-**kahn ehng**-ehls-mahn
I am sick.	Jag är sjuk.	yah air **shyook**
Please call a doctor.	Jag vill skicka efter en läkare.	yah veel **shee**-kah **ehf**-tehr ehn **lay**-kah-reh
Do you have a vacant room?	Har Ni något rum ledigt?	hahr nee noh-goht **room leh**-deekt
How much does it cost?	Vad kostar det?/ Hur mycketdeh kostar det?	vah **kohs**-tahr deh /hor **mee**-keh kohs-tahr deh
It's too expensive.	Den är för dyr.	dehn ay foor deer
Beautiful	Vacker	**vah**-kehr
Help!	Hjälp	yehlp
Stop!	Stopp!/Stanna!	stop/**stahn**-nah
How do I get to . . .	Kan Ni visa mig vägen till	kahn nee **vee**-sah may **vay**-gehn teel
. . . the train station?	stationen	stah-**shoh**-nehn
. . . the post office?	posten	**pohs**-tehn
. . . the tourist office?	en resebyrå	ehn-**reh**-seh-**bee**-roh
. . . the hospital?	sjukhuset	**shyook**-hoo-seht

ENGLISH	SWEDISH	PRONUNCIATION
Does this bus go to . . .?	Går den bussen här till . . .?	gohr dehn **boo**-sehn hehr teel
Where is the bathroom?	Var är toalett?/ toaletten?	vahr ay twah-**leht**/ twah-**leht**-en
On the left	Till vänster	teel **vehn**-stur
On the right	Till höger	teel **huh**-gur
Straight ahead	Rakt fram	rahkt **frahm**

DINING OUT

Please bring me . . .	Var snäll och hämta åt mig . . .	vahr snehl oh hehm-tah oht may
menu	matsedeln	maht-seh-dehln
fork	en gaffel	ehn gahf-fehl
k nife	en kniv	ehn kneev
spoon	en sked	ehn shehd
napkin	en servett	ehn sehr-veht
bread	bröd	bruh(d)
butter	smör	smuhr
milk	mjölk	myoolk
pepper	peppar	pehp-pahr
salt	salt	sahlt
sugar	socker	soh-kehr
water	vatten	vaht-n
The check, please.	Får jag be om notan.	fohr yah beh ohm **noh**-tahn

INDEX

Photo Credits: 6 (top), *Peeter Vissak/age fotostock.* 6 (bottom), *Wojtek Buss/age fotostock.* 8, *Henrik Trygg/Swedish Travel & Tourism Council.* 9, D. *Guilloux/viestiphoto.com.* 10, *J.D. Heaton/Picture Finders/age fotostock.* 14, *Atlantide S.N.C./age fotostock.* 16, *Chad Ehlers/age fotostock.* 18, *Walter Bibikow/viestiphoto.com.* 19 (left), *Sylvain Grandadam/age fotostock.* 19 (right), *Joe Viesti/viestiphoto.com.* 20, *Nils-Johan Norenlind/age fotostock.*

NOTES

NOTES

NOTES

NOTES

NOTES